ASIAN DEVELOPMENT
OUTLOOK 2016
ASIA'S POTENTIAL GROWTH

ASIAN DEVELOPMENT BANK

© 2016 Asian Development Bank
6 ADB Avenue, Mandaluyong City, 1550 Metro Manila, Philippines
Tel +63 2 632 4444; Fax +63 2 636 2444
www.adb.org

Some rights reserved. Published in 2016.
Printed in the Philippines.

ISBN 978-92-9257-385-0 (Print), 978-92-9257-386-7 (e-ISBN)
ISSN 0117-0481
Publication Stock No. FLS157678-3

Cataloging-In-Publication Data

Asian Development Bank.
        Asian development outlook 2016. Asia's potential growth.
Mandaluyong City, Philippines: Asian Development Bank, 2016.

1. Economics.   2. Finance.   3. Asia.   I. Asian Development Bank.

Contents

Foreword

Global headwinds notwithstanding, developing Asia will continue to contribute 60% of world growth. Weighing sluggish growth in the United States and the euro area, the transition of the People's Republic of China (PRC) to an economy led by consumption and services, and India's ongoing structural reform, *Asian Development Outlook 2016* forecasts 5.7% growth for developing Asia in 2016 and 2017.

Most subregions of developing Asia will see growth slow in 2016 before rebounding in 2017. Growth in South Asia, whose expansion was the highest of any subregion in 2015, is expected at 6.9% in 2016, accelerating to 7.3% in 2017 as reforms are implemented in India's financial sector. East Asia will see growth moderate in both years in tandem with the PRC, whose growth is expected to slow to 6.5% this year and 6.3% in 2017 as it contends with reduced investment among other factors.

Economic performance is poised to improve in Southeast Asia as the large economies of Indonesia and the Philippines ramp up investment, Viet Nam sustains its expansion, and Thailand gathers momentum, though Malaysia will slow further with weak oil prices. Meanwhile, low commodity prices will curb growth prospects in Central Asia and the Pacific, in part by constraining fiscal spending.

Regional inflation has been favorable to Asian economies, as low international food and fuel prices helped cut average inflation to 2.2% in 2015 from 3.0% in 2014. Inflation is likely to pick up to 2.5% in 2016 as domestic demand strengthens and to 2.7% in 2017 as global commodity prices recover slightly.

Uncertainties abound in the global economic environment, and risks to developing Asia's growth are mostly on the downside. This publication examines the implications of an unexpectedly sharp slowdown in the PRC, which could cut both global and regional growth by nearly 1.8 percentage points. The impact in the region would be mainly on trade volumes and commodity prices, the severity felt by each neighbor economy depending on its ability to accommodate and adapt to the changes.

Producer price deflation is associated with lower investment and lower economic growth and has become an emerging concern for many Asian economies. Thus, policy makers are advised to pay attention to falling producer prices because they compound producers' debt burdens and weigh on their investment decisions.

Asian Development Outlook 2016 examines in detail how the growth slowdown in Asia since the global financial crisis of 2008–2009 has affected the region's potential growth. Defined as the maximum growth rate associated with the full employment of productive resources, potential growth is determined by changing demographics and labor productivity.

Potential growth in the region has fallen by 2 percentage points since the global financial crisis. Absent structural reform, many economies in the region will see a further decrease because of unfavorable demographics, convergence with advanced economies, and spillover from growth moderation in the PRC.

To invigorate potential growth, policy reforms are needed. On top of promoting sound macroeconomic management, reform should offset the impact of less-favorable demographics by increasing female participation in the workforce, extending the working age, and raising labor productivity through capital investment and measures to reduce factor misallocation. Policies such as these can help sustain growth, thereby raising living standards and further reducing poverty in Asia.

TAKEHIKO NAKAO
President
Asian Development Bank

Acknowledgments

Asian Development Outlook 2016 was prepared by staff of the Asian Development Bank (ADB) in the Central and West Asia Department, East Asia Department, Pacific Department, South Asia Department, Southeast Asia Department, and Economic Research and Regional Cooperation Department, as well as in ADB resident missions. Representatives of these departments constituted the Regional Economic Outlook Task Force, which met regularly to coordinate and develop consistent forecasts for the region.

The authors who contributed the sections are bylined in each chapter. The subregional coordinators were Lyaziza Sabyrova, Dominik Peschel, and Christopher Hnanguie for Central Asia, Yolanda Fernandez Lommen for East Asia, Masato Nakane for South Asia, Sona Shrestha for Southeast Asia, and Christopher Edmonds and Rommel Rabanal for the Pacific.

A team of economists in the Economic Research and Regional Cooperation Department, led by Joseph E. Zveglich, Jr., director of the Macroeconomics Research Division, coordinated the production of the publication, assisted by Edith Laviña. Technical and research support was provided by Shiela Camingue-Romance, Cindy Castillejos-Petalcorin, Gemma Esther Estrada, Marthe Hinojales, Mary Ann Magadia, Nedelyn Magtibay-Ramos, Pilipinas Quising, Aleli Rosario, Dennis Sorino, Lea Sumulong, and Mai Lin Villaruel. Additional research support was provided by Emmanuel Alano, Zemma Ardaniel, Ruben Carlo Asuncion, and Michael Angelo Cokee. The economic editorial advisors Robert Boumphrey, Joshua Greene, Richard Niebuhr, Anthony Patrick, and Reza Vaez-Zadeh made substantive contributions to the country chapters and regional outlook. Background papers for the theme chapter benefited from comments from participants in a workshop in Seoul on 19–20 November 2015. Josef Yap provided editorial advice on the theme chapter.

Peter Fredenburg advised on ADB style and English usage. Alvin Tubio handled typesetting and graphics generation, in which he was assisted by Elenita Pura. Art direction for the cover design was by Anthony Victoria, with artwork from Design Muscle. Critical support for the printing and publishing of the report was provided by the Printing Services Unit of the ADB Office of Administrative Services and by the Publishing and Dissemination Unit of the ADB Department of External Relations. Heili Ann Bravo, Fermirelyn Cruz, Rhia Bautista-Piamonte, and Azaleah Tiongson provided administrative and secretarial support.

The Department of External Relations, led by Satinder Bindra, Omana Nair, and Erik Churchill, planned and coordinated the dissemination of *Asian Development Outlook 2016*.

Definitions

The economies discussed in *Asian Development Outlook 2016* (*ADO 2016*) are classified by major analytic or geographic group. For the purposes of this publication, the following apply:

- **Association of Southeast Asian Nations (ASEAN)** comprises Brunei Darussalam, Cambodia, Indonesia, the Lao People's Democratic Republic, Malaysia, Myanmar, the Philippines, Singapore, Thailand, and Viet Nam.
- **Developing Asia** comprises the 45 members of the Asian Development Bank listed below.
- **Central Asia** comprises Armenia, Azerbaijan, Georgia, Kazakhstan, the Kyrgyz Republic, Tajikistan, Turkmenistan, and Uzbekistan.
- **East Asia** comprises the People's Republic of China; Hong Kong, China; the Republic of Korea; Mongolia; and Taipei,China.
- **South Asia** comprises Afghanistan, Bangladesh, Bhutan, India, the Maldives, Nepal, Pakistan, and Sri Lanka.
- **Southeast Asia** comprises Brunei Darussalam, Cambodia, Indonesia, the Lao People's Democratic Republic, Malaysia, Myanmar, the Philippines, Singapore, Thailand, and Viet Nam.
- **The Pacific** comprises the Cook Islands, Fiji, Kiribati, the Marshall Islands, the Federated States of Micronesia, Nauru, Papua New Guinea, Palau, Samoa, Solomon Islands, Timor-Leste, Tonga, Tuvalu, and Vanuatu.

Unless otherwise specified, the symbol "$" and the word "dollar" refer to US dollars. *ADO 2016* is generally based on data available up to **9 March 2016**.

Abbreviations

ADB	Asian Development Bank
ADO	Asian Development Outlook
ASEAN	Association of Southeast Asian Nations
CPI	consumer price index
FDI	foreign direct investment
FSM	Federated States of Micronesia
FY	fiscal year
GDP	gross domestic product
GFC	global financial crisis
GVC	global value chain
ICT	information and communication technology
IMF	International Monetary Fund
Lao PDR	Lao People's Democratic Republic
M1	money that includes cash and checking accounts
M2	broad money that adds highly liquid accounts to M1
M3	broad money that adds time accounts to M2
NPL	nonperforming loan
OECD	Organisation for Economic Co-operation and Development
OPEC	Organization of the Petroleum Exporting Countries
PNG	Papua New Guinea
PPI	producer price index
PRC	People's Republic of China
RMI	Republic of the Marshall Islands
saar	seasonally adjusted annualized rate
SMEs	small and medium-sized enterprises
SOE	state-owned enterprise
US	United States of America
VAT	value-added tax

ADO 2016—Highlights

Developing Asia is projected to grow at 5.7% in both 2016 and 2017, down slightly from 5.9% in 2015, due chiefly to considerable global headwinds and moderating growth in the People's Republic of China.

Commodity price declines dragged inflation down to 2.2% in 2015. Regional inflation will revive to 2.5% in 2016 as domestic demand strengthens, and rise further to 2.7% in 2017 as global commodity prices recover.

Risks are tilted to the downside as tightening US monetary policy may heighten financial volatility, further moderation in the People's Republic of China could spill over into its neighbors, and producer price deflation may undermine growth in some economies.

Reform to raise labor productivity can invigorate developing Asia's potential growth.

Shang-Jin Wei
Chief Economist
Asian Development Bank

Rescuing growth in uncertain times

Slow going in a tough global environment

■ **Growth in developing Asia is forecast to dip slightly.** Gross domestic product (GDP) in the region will expand by 5.7% in 2016 and 2017, decelerating from 5.9% in 2015 in a difficult and uncertain global environment. Solid growth in India and a pickup in aggregate growth in the Association of Southeast Asian Nations (ASEAN) will help balance continued growth moderation in the People's Republic of China (PRC). Despite the slight dip, the region will contribute around 60% of global growth in the next 2 years, close to its contribution in the past 5 years.

» **Growth in the industrial economies is unlikely to pick up this year.** Aggregate growth in the major industrial economies—the United States (US), the euro area, and Japan—will stay at 1.8% in 2016 before inching up to 1.9% in 2017. In the US, expanding private consumption and investment will be tempered by weak external demand. While recovery in the euro area is gradually gaining ground, domestic and external risks abound, keeping growth from breaking out of its slow 2015 pace. Japan's growth will improve slightly, helped by a pickup in private consumption this year in anticipation of a value-added tax increase next year.

» **The PRC continues to shift away from its reliance on investment and exports.** Growth slowed further last year as exports faltered, labor shortages began to bite, and the short-term adverse impact of supply-side reform took its toll. Reduced investment in industries with excess capacity will be another factor moderating growth still further to 6.5% (within the government's target range of 6.5%–7.0%) and to 6.3% next year.

» **Strong public investment boosted growth in India despite weak exports.** Reform geared to attract more foreign direct investment progressed, and the authorities worked to repair corporate and bank balance sheets. While macroeconomic fundamentals are strong, progress on major structural reform is expected to be gradual. Growth momentum will be sustained at 7.4% in 2016 before picking up to 7.8% in 2017 with measures to fund stalled projects and an uptick in bank credit.

» **Stronger growth is seen for ASEAN.** Aggregate growth in the 10 ASEAN economies is forecast to accelerate steadily from 4.4% in 2015 to 4.5% in 2016 and 4.8% in 2017. Growth will be led by Indonesia as it ramps up investment in infrastructure and implements policy reform that spurs private investment. Solid consumption and investment will provide a lift to the Philippine economy. Thailand's recovery is expected to gather momentum, and Viet Nam will sustain vigorous expansion. In contrast, Malaysian growth will slip further with low oil prices and weak external demand.

» **Low commodity prices weigh on growth prospects in Central Asia and the Pacific.** Continued low oil prices are exerting pressure on fiscal spending in Azerbaijan, Kazakhstan, Papua New Guinea, and Timor-Leste, slowing subregional growth in Central Asia and the Pacific. While the expected pickup in oil prices will bring some relief in 2017, growth is expected to remain below the 5-year average pace to the forecast horizon.

■ **Most Asian economies benefit from low international food and fuel prices.** The large fall in oil and food prices tempered inflation. The regional rate eased from 3.0% in 2014 to 2.2% in 2015 as global oil prices fell by 47% and average food prices by 15%. Regional inflation will revive to 2.5% in 2016 as domestic demand strengthens and rise further to 2.7% in 2017 as global commodity prices recover.

■ **The regional current account surplus will narrow this year and next.** Subdued demand for manufacturing exports and continued low commodity prices will trim developing Asia's current account surplus from the equivalent of 2.9% of regional GDP in 2015 to 2.6% in 2016 and further to 2.4% in 2017. Yet the region's increasing global economic weight means its surplus will widen slightly to 0.7% of world GDP in 2016, up 0.1 percentage points from last year.

■ **Risks to the regional growth forecast remain tilted to the downside.** Future interest rate hikes by the US Federal Reserve may tighten global financing conditions. This, combined with broader weakness in emerging markets, could heighten investors' risk aversion and intensify global financial market volatility. A sharper-than-forecast growth slowdown in the PRC would further dim the global outlook and directly hurt regional exports and growth. Tepid prices for oil and other commodities cast a shadow over the prospects of Asia's commodity-dependent economies. Finally, El Niño looms as a major weather risk for economies that rely on agriculture. While consumer price inflation is generally low but positive, producer price deflation has emerged as a new spoiler in the PRC and other Asian economies.

Spillover from the People's Republic of China

■ **Growth moderation in the PRC weighs on regional growth.** Simulations estimate that the drop in PRC growth may have shaved as much as 0.3 percentage points from developing Asia's outlook. The PRC effect is largely centered on Asia, reflecting strong regional trade and production links. In contrast, the impact on the US and the euro area through trade is largely offset by the benefit of lower commodity prices. The unlikely event of a sharp growth decline in the PRC triggered by some type of financial shock would be significant, however, lopping nearly 1.8 percentage points off global growth. Simulations of such a scenario show oil prices down by 10%–25% relative to the baseline, while growth in Japan would lose 1.5 percentage points and in developing Asia 1.8 points.

■ **Ongoing structural change in the PRC is affecting its import structure.** Contributing to its growth moderation, the PRC is currently undergoing a structural transformation from growth led by exports and investment to growth grounded on domestic consumption. As a result, while investment has been the main growth driver since 2001—peaking at an 86% contribution to growth in 2009—consumption now contributes more than half. The PRC role in global value chains is also changing as rising wages shunt some activities to lower-cost economies and technological upgrades shift the PRC into activities that add more value. These structural changes are reflected in the sharp drop in the share of parts and components in PRC imports since the mid-2000s and a slight rise in the share of consumer goods.

■ **How PRC structural change affects an economy depends on the relationship.** Spillover from PRC restructuring into particular economies will differ depending on whether they are exporters of consumer goods, parts of the same production chain, or competitors, either current or potential. For example, the Republic of Korea has lost market share as the PRC increasingly mastered high technology, but Viet Nam has increased its share of parts and components in PRC imports as it has taken over from the PRC lower-skilled tasks within production chains. Other Asian economies may benefit too as the PRC withdraws from labor-intensive pursuits. Bangladesh, for one, has taken up garment manufacturing to become the world's second-largest garment exporter.

Emergent producer price deflation

- **The PRC and some other Asian economies recently experienced producer price deflation.** Slowing economic growth has combined with sharply lower oil prices to push producer price inflation into negative territory, though consumer price inflation remains mostly positive. In 2015, the PRC saw producer prices contract by 5.2% and, by February 2016, it had endured 48 consecutive months of producer price deflation. Deflation in the PRC may be transmitted to its neighbors through lower export prices, especially if the renminbi depreciates. In fact, producer prices fell in 2015 by 9.1% in Singapore, 6.7% in the Philippines, and 4.8% in Malaysia—and by smaller margins in India, the Republic of Korea, Thailand, and Hong Kong, China.

- **Commodity price shocks get diluted along distribution chains before affecting consumers.** The pass-through of oil and food prices thus tends to be lower for consumer prices than for producer prices. In the PRC, for example, the cumulative pass-through of a 1% drop in global oil prices after 4 quarters reached 14 basis points for producer prices but only 3 basis points for consumer prices. In Thailand, the cumulative pass-through of a 1% drop in global food prices reached 21 basis points for producer prices but only 7 basis points for consumer prices. The lower rate of consumer price pass-through may explain why episodes of producer price deflation are less rare.

- **Historically, falling producer prices are more common than declines in consumer prices.** An empirical study of 38 economies found 389 episodes of producer price deflation from 1947 to 2014 but only 145 episodes of consumer price deflation. In theory, deflation can spark a vicious cycle of weakening demand and falling prices, but evidence from episodes of declining consumer prices is mixed. Deflation in the postwar era cannot be accurately assessed by looking only at consumer prices because they may not adequately capture the pressures on firms.

- **Producer price deflation is associated with lower economic growth.** Average GDP growth per capita was lower in an 1870–2014 study sample during deflationary episodes than during inflationary ones. This held whether producer or consumer prices were considered, but regression analysis found stronger evidence of an inverse association for producer prices than for consumer prices. While the correlation of growth with consumer price deflation held only during the Great Depression, significant growth associations with producer price deflation held up for the full sample period, including the postwar subperiod 1947–2014. Income grew 1.4 percentage points faster during moderate producer price inflation than during producer price deflation in 1870–2014.

- **Restrained investment is one channel by which producer price deflation hampers growth.** The producer price index measures price changes from the viewpoint of producers and thus affects producer decisions such as on investment. In fact, producer price deflation tended to be followed by investment contractions, as 71% of economies that experienced significant deflation suffered investment decline.

Deflation can compound producers' debt burdens and thus discourage investment. A mix of higher debt and lower prices reduced investment in 45% of economies that experienced both.

■ **Policy makers should be aware of deflation's potential to harm economic growth.** Long-run historical comparisons do not rule out the possibility that deflation, especially producer price deflation, is negatively associated with growth. The data clearly show that high inflation as well as deflation can adversely affect growth. Because producer prices tend to be more volatile than consumer prices, and producer price deflation may therefore inflict greater damage on the economy, policy makers should monitor not only the consumer price index but also the producer price index.

Outlook by subregion

■ **Slowing growth is widespread across developing Asia.** Weak recovery in the major industrial economies, moderating growth in the PRC, and recession in the Russian Federation are hampering growth in other economies with strong ties to them through trade, investment, and remittances. Meanwhile, sharply lower global commodity prices are undermining growth in the region's oil producers, even as a presumed reciprocal boost to growth in oil importers remains elusive. Only Southeast Asia is forecast to see growth pick up in 2016, however modestly. The expected easing of these impediments to growth within the forecast horizon points to general improvement in 2017.

■ **East Asia will see growth drift lower as growth in the PRC moderates further.** Subregional growth slowed to 6.0% in 2015—a 0.6 percentage point drop from the previous year—as all economies slowed. The rate is expected to decline further to 5.7% in 2016. In the PRC, efforts to rein in debt accumulation, adverse short-term effects from supply-side reform, and emerging labor shortages will tamp down growth from 6.9% in 2015 to 6.5% this year and 6.3% in 2017. The Republic of Korea will have stable growth this year, and Taipei,China will accelerate on higher government investment. Meanwhile, declines in mining output will push growth in Mongolia below 1%, and lower tourism flows will slow growth in Hong Kong, China. Although rising domestic demand and an improving global economy will lift growth rates slightly higher in 2017 across most of the subregion, continued moderation in the PRC will weigh down the subregional average to 5.6% in 2017. Inflation fell to 1.3% last year with lower prices for oil and other commodities but will rise moderately to 1.6% this year and 2.0% in 2017 as domestic demand rebounds and commodity prices recover.

■ **South Asia is forecast to post the most rapid growth in developing Asia.** Growth in the subregion accelerated to 7.0% in 2015 and will accelerate further to 7.3% in 2017 after a hesitation at 6.9% this year. The subregion's prospects reflect heavy weighting for India, where growth is expected to dip marginally to 7.4% in 2016 as exports decline and both public and private investment slows, and then pick up to 7.8% in 2017 as investment revives. Apart from weakness in export demand, other economies in the subregion face unique challenges to growth: a devastating earthquake and a political standoff in Nepal, a drop in high-end tourism in the Maldives, and much-needed fiscal reform to deal with a buildup of excessive debt in Sri Lanka. Both Bangladesh and Pakistan see continued moderate growth benefitting from sustained progress toward macroeconomic and structural reform. Subregional inflation fell to 5.0% in 2015, benefitting from low oil and commodity prices, but is projected to revive to 5.2% in 2016 and 5.7% in 2017.

■ **Southeast Asia is seen reversing its growth slowdown in the next 2 years.**
Growth slowed in 7 of the 10 ASEAN economies, edging down the subregional average
to 4.4% in 2015. In Indonesia, growth moderated for a fourth year in a row. In Malaysia,
soft global demand and low oil prices cut growth by a full percentage point. Thailand's
recovery from a slump in 2014 was sluggish, while bad weather hurt agriculture in
many economies. In contrast, foreign direct investment in manufacturing and robust
construction propelled Viet Nam to its strongest expansion in 7 years. Aggregate growth
is forecast to pick up to 4.5% in 2016 and 4.8% in 2017. Infrastructure investment is seen
boosting growth in Indonesia, while Myanmar rebounds from devastating floods in 2015.
Malaysia, on the other hand, faces another year of decelerating growth. Southeast Asia's
aggregate inflation rate eased to 2.7% in 2015 in line with lower food and fuel prices.
Inflation is forecast to edge higher in most economies this year and next, but decelerating
inflation in Indonesia will hold the ASEAN average to 2.6% in 2016 and 2.9% in 2017.

■ **Central Asia's growth slowdown is forecast to deepen this year.** Plunging petroleum
prices, recession in the Russian Federation, and weakness in other trading partners took
their toll on Central Asia, where average growth plummeted to 2.9% in 2015 from 5.3%
a year earlier. Forecasts of even lower petroleum prices and continued recession in the
Russian Federation prompt a projection that average growth in the subregion will slow
further in 2016 to 2.1%, with contraction forecast for Azerbaijan and growth at only
0.7% for Kazakhstan. Growth is projected to recover somewhat to 2.8% in 2017 on
the strength of an improved external outlook and somewhat higher petroleum prices.
Steep currency depreciation in several economies helped push average inflation to
6.2% in 2015 from 5.7% last year. The lagged inflation effects of depreciation in 2015
and possible further currency weakness in some economies are projected to propel
average inflation to 10.8% in 2016 as acceleration occurs in all economies, with inflation
reaching double digits in Azerbaijan, Kazakhstan, the Kyrgyz Republic, and Uzbekistan.
Expected exchange rate stabilization should help rein in average inflation in the subregion
to 5.9% in 2017.

■ **The Pacific is poised for lower growth as the economy slows in Papua New Guinea.**
Growth in the Pacific held strong at 7.0% in 2015. This was largely attributable to
developments in Papua New Guinea, the predominant economy in the subregion,
where new liquefied natural gas production and exports powered high growth. The only
other economy to achieve high growth was Palau, where tourism drove expansion.
GDP contracted in Nauru because of damage to port facilities and in Vanuatu because
of a severe cyclone early in the year, while in energy-exporting Timor-Leste growth
plunged as oil and gas prices fell. Average growth across the subregion is expected to
fall to 3.8% in 2016 and further to 3.1% in 2017. In Fiji, cyclone damage is dragging
growth down to 2.7% in 2016, but the economy should rebound to 4.5% growth in 2017.
Inflation remained steady in 2015 at 3.4%, though Nauru experienced high inflation as
problems at the port affected trade. Inflation is expected to rise slightly to 4.5% in 2016
and 4.7% in 2017.

Asia's potential growth

Understanding the growth slowdown

- **Growth momentum has flagged in developing Asia since the global financial crisis.** From an average of 8.3% during 2006–2010, GDP growth in the region fell to 5.9% in 2015. This decline is likely to have repercussions for the region and the rest of the world. Developing Asia's success in lifting 1 billion individuals out of poverty during 1990–2012 hinged on its ability to sustain high rates of economic growth. Moreover, since the region currently accounts for more than a quarter of world GDP as valued at market exchange rates, a persistent slowdown in developing Asia threatens to undermine the fragile global recovery.

- **The right policy response depends on the nature of the region's slowdown.** Is it a temporary—albeit prolonged—effect of the business cycle? Or are more persistent changes under way? If weaker growth reflects slack demand such as softening export orders or a downturn in private investment, then fiscal or monetary stimulus may be needed for temporary support. But if supply-side factors are at play, and the growth moderation stems from slowing expansion of the region's productive capacity, then any revival of growth prospects may depend on structural policy reform.

- **Distinguishing temporary from persistent effects depends on gauging "potential growth."** Potential growth is the pace at which an economy is deemed able to expand with full employment and stable inflation—that is, when it is operating at its productive capacity. The idea of potential growth is not immutable, as it is influenced by the policies and institutions that characterize the particular economy.

  » **Deviations from potential come at the cost of macroeconomic stability.** Operating above potential stokes inflation, while producing below potential generates unemployment. Economies tend toward their potential in the long run, making potential growth essentially a speed limit on the pace of long-term poverty reduction.

  » **Structural reform can yield higher potential growth from given resources.** "Frontier potential growth" is the rate above potential growth that an economy could achieve if global best-practice policies and institutions prevailed. By lowering barriers to efficient labor and capital allocation, an economy can move closer to this conceptual maximum while maintaining macroeconomic stability.

- **Falling potential growth explains much of the region's post-crisis growth slowdown.** Estimated average potential growth for a sample of 22 Asian economies, which accounted for 98% of GDP in developing Asia in 2014, fell by almost 2.0 percentage points from its 2007 peak of 8.4%. Falling potential growth accounts for about 40% of the moderation in actual growth since the global financial crisis.

  » **Falling potential growth is widespread in the region.** When compared with average potential growth in 2000–2007, the post-crisis period 2008–2014 saw declines in 14 of the economies sampled, down by 1.1 percentage points in the PRC and by 2.1 points in the Republic of Korea.

» **Yet some economies sustained or improved their potential growth.** From the 2000–2007 average, potential growth in 2008–2014 picked up in economies as diverse as Indonesia (by 0.9 percentage points), Pakistan (0.9), the Philippines (0.5), and Uzbekistan (2.2). Bangladesh, Fiji, and India have maintained pre-crisis potential growth into the post-crisis period.

■ **Future gains in living standards and poverty elimination rest on a grasp of potential growth.** Identifying the institutional and policy constraints that keep an economy from achieving its frontier potential growth will be critical to counteract the current slowdown. Knowing which factors have driven potential growth in the past can guide policy makers' efforts to meet today's growth challenge.

Determinants of potential growth

■ **Shifting demographics and labor productivity growth determine potential growth.** Potential growth is the sum of growth in the labor force plus growth in potential labor productivity, or output per worker. Of these two factors, labor productivity growth accounted for about 80% of average potential growth from 2000 to 2014 in the 22 Asian economies studied. However, demographic changes have had significant effects in some economies. For example, working-age population growth explains about 50% of potential growth in Malaysia, 64% in Pakistan, and 47% in Singapore. Empirical estimates show that taking 1 percentage point off working-age population growth shaves 1 percentage point from potential growth. With demographic changes turning less favorable in most Asian economies, understanding what determines labor productivity growth is paramount to boosting future potential growth.

■ **Capital accumulation affects potential growth by lifting labor productivity.** Low-income economies can grow faster during the transition to their long-run potential growth rate by upgrading their equipment and infrastructure and by adopting existing technologies. However, this "advantage of backwardness" fades over the course of development as economies gain on their more advanced peers and eventually converge. Estimates indicate that an additional $1,000 dollars of initial income per capita lowers potential growth by 0.3 percentage points.

■ **A range of productivity-enhancing factors are amenable to policy interventions.** Estimates show that gains in tertiary education enrollment and trade openness can boost potential growth—especially in economies with the most room for improvement. Integrating into international financial markets can be beneficial, but the relationship depends on the economy's regulatory quality. Improvements to a range of institutional variables, which proxy for such things as government effectiveness and labor market flexibility, can also lift potential growth.

■ **Potential growth depends on a stable macro economy.** A volatile gap between actual growth and potential growth has, with consequent bouts of rising inflation or deepening unemployment, a significantly negative effect on potential growth. Reducing this volatility by 1.0 percentage point is estimated to pay a potential growth dividend of nearly 0.2 percentage points. Policies to push actual growth persistently above its potential have only a temporary effect on the economy's productive capacity.

■ **Removing obstacles to efficient factor allocation supports economic dynamism.**
An economy's frontier potential growth can be realized only when capital and labor are allocated to the most productive firms. Analysis of over 10,000 firms in 13 developing economies in Asia confirms that obstacles like judicial bias, unequal access to finance, excessive labor regulation, poor electricity supply, and corruption impede the efficient allocation of factors across firms, which makes them too large or too small, or too labor or capital intensive. Reform to remove these obstacles can enhance firms' efficiency, thus moving economies toward their frontier potential growth.

A "new normal" for potential growth?

■ **Potential growth since the global financial crisis differs sharply from before it.**
After accounting for changes in the determinants of potential growth, developing Asia's average potential growth still declined by 2.2 percentage points in 2008–2014 from its historical trend. Is this a new normal for Asia? It is true that the decline is slightly smaller than the 2.7 percentage point drop in global potential growth. However, without structural reform, potential growth in many countries in the region will slide further due to unfavorable demographics, convergence with advanced economies, and spillover from growth moderation in the PRC.

■ **The demographic drag on developing Asia's potential growth will intensify.**
The region previously benefited from a favorable age structure—the so-called demographic dividend—but slowing population growth and aging populations are turning this dividend into a burden. The United Nations projects that growth in the region's working-age population will be lower in 2015–2020 than in 2008–2014; this demographic effect alone could depress developing Asia's potential growth by 0.4 percentage points. Less favorable demographics span the region, with working-age population growth forecast higher among the sample economies only in Sri Lanka.

■ **Developing Asia's past success has narrowed the gap with the advanced economies.**
The advantage of backwardness, which allowed developing economies in Asia to grow by adopting existing technologies, is fading as they converge in sophistication with the advanced economies. Less scope for playing catch-up with the advanced economies will make some other determinants of potential growth, such as tertiary education and trade, more important to future growth. On the other hand, low- and middle-income economies still have scope to benefit from the convergence effect.

■ **Moderating growth in the PRC is spilling over to other economies.** Ripples from slower growth in the PRC, one of the largest economies in the world, are spreading globally, and strong trade and investment ties with close neighbors make the regional impact much more pronounced. Empirical analysis controlling for other determinants of potential growth shows a 1.0 percentage point decline in the actual growth rate in the PRC associated with a 0.2 percentage point reduction in potential growth worldwide and a 0.5 point decline in other Asian economies. As the PRC rebalances toward a more sustainable, consumption-driven growth model, its pace of expansion is forecast to ease further. However, if other economies can lift their potential growth, they can counteract some of the effect of PRC growth moderation.

Policies to invigorate potential growth

- **Policy changes can partly offset the labor squeeze.** Measures to increase female participation rates and extend the working age can boost the share of workers in the population. Especially for economies facing the most severe demographic changes, more flexible immigration policies may help firms that struggle to attract skilled labor.

- **The recipe for higher labor productivity has three ingredients.** They are a mix of public and private investment, policy and institutional reform, and sound macroeconomic management.

  - » **Capital investment is crucial to catch up with the advanced economies.** High on the list is government investment in infrastructure, an important public good. As the needs are large, governments must find creative financing solutions such as public–private partnership. To facilitate private investment, policy can incentivize companies to purchase new assets by, for example, accelerating depreciation.

  - » **Reform can move current potential toward the frontier.** Effective policy and higher-quality institutions can shore up Asia's long-term growth. If, over the next decade, the 22 sampled economies lifted their current scores on productivity-enhancing factors enough to close half of the gap to the best possible scores, their average annual potential growth could increase by almost 1.0 percentage point. Reforms that, for example, rationalize financial and labor markets, render rules that govern access to land more transparent, and improve governance and the business environment can boost potential growth by making firms more dynamic over time.

  - » **Sound macroeconomic management is the foundation for growth.** Implementing policies that lower the volatility of actual growth with respect to potential growth by 25% can add 0.1 percentage points to the region's potential growth.

- **The new normal today need not be developing Asia's future normal.** To ensure a healthy future for potential growth, Asia must employ the full range of policy responses to augment labor supply, improve labor productivity, enhance institutional quality, and maintain macroeconomic stability.

GDP growth rate and inflation, % per year

	Growth rate of GDP					Inflation				
	2013	2014	2015	2016	2017	2013	2014	2015	2016	2017
Central Asia	6.6	5.3	2.9	2.1	2.8	5.8	5.7	6.2	10.8	5.9
Armenia	3.3	3.5	3.0	2.0	2.3	5.8	3.0	3.7	3.8	4.0
Azerbaijan	5.8	2.8	1.1	−1.0	1.0	−0.5	1.4	4.0	12.0	5.2
Georgia	3.3	4.6	2.8	2.5	3.5	−0.5	3.1	4.0	5.0	4.0
Kazakhstan	6.0	4.3	1.0	0.7	1.0	5.8	6.7	6.6	12.6	4.6
Kyrgyz Republic	10.9	4.0	3.5	1.0	2.0	6.6	7.5	6.5	10.0	8.0
Tajikistan	7.4	6.7	6.0	3.8	4.0	5.0	6.1	5.1	8.5	7.5
Turkmenistan	10.2	10.3	6.5	6.5	7.0	6.8	6.0	6.0	6.6	6.0
Uzbekistan	8.0	8.1	8.0	6.9	7.3	11.2	8.4	9.0	10.0	11.0
East Asia	6.8	6.6	6.0	5.7	5.6	2.4	1.9	1.3	1.6	2.0
China, People's Rep. of	7.7	7.3	6.9	6.5	6.3	2.6	2.0	1.4	1.7	2.0
Hong Kong, China	3.1	2.6	2.4	2.1	2.2	4.4	4.4	3.0	2.5	2.7
Korea, Rep. of	2.9	3.3	2.6	2.6	2.8	1.3	1.3	0.7	1.4	2.0
Mongolia	11.6	7.9	2.3	0.1	0.5	9.9	12.8	6.6	3.0	7.0
Taipei,China	2.2	3.9	0.7	1.6	1.8	0.8	1.2	−0.3	0.7	1.2
South Asia	6.2	6.7	7.0	6.9	7.3	9.3	6.8	5.0	5.2	5.7
Afghanistan	3.7	1.3	1.5	2.0	3.0	7.4	4.6	−1.5	3.0	3.5
Bangladesh	6.0	6.1	6.6	6.7	6.9	6.8	7.3	6.4	6.2	6.5
Bhutan	3.6	3.8	5.9	6.4	6.1	8.8	9.6	6.6	4.0	5.0
India	6.6	7.2	7.6	7.4	7.8	9.8	6.7	5.0	5.4	5.8
Maldives	4.7	6.5	1.5	3.5	3.9	2.3	2.1	1.0	1.2	1.4
Nepal	3.8	5.1	3.0	1.5	4.8	9.8	9.1	7.2	10.5	8.2
Pakistan	3.7	4.0	4.2	4.5	4.8	7.4	8.6	4.5	3.2	4.5
Sri Lanka	3.4	4.9	4.8	5.3	5.8	6.9	3.2	3.8	4.5	5.0
Southeast Asia	5.0	4.5	4.4	4.5	4.8	4.2	4.1	2.7	2.6	2.9
Brunei Darussalam	−2.1	−2.3	−1.1	1.0	2.5	0.4	−0.2	−0.4	0.2	0.4
Cambodia	7.4	7.1	7.0	7.0	7.1	3.0	3.9	1.2	2.5	3.0
Indonesia	5.6	5.0	4.8	5.2	5.5	6.4	6.4	6.4	4.5	4.2
Lao People's Dem. Rep.	7.8	7.5	6.7	6.8	7.0	6.4	4.2	1.3	1.8	2.5
Malaysia	4.7	6.0	5.0	4.2	4.4	2.1	3.1	2.1	2.7	2.5
Myanmar	8.4	8.7	7.2	8.4	8.3	5.7	5.9	11.0	9.5	8.5
Philippines	7.1	6.1	5.8	6.0	6.1	3.0	4.1	1.4	2.3	2.7
Singapore	4.7	3.3	2.0	2.0	2.2	2.4	1.0	−0.5	−0.6	0.4
Thailand	2.7	0.8	2.8	3.0	3.5	2.2	1.9	−0.9	0.6	2.0
Viet Nam	5.4	6.0	6.7	6.7	6.5	6.6	4.1	0.6	3.0	4.0
The Pacific	3.8	9.4	7.0	3.8	3.1	4.9	3.5	3.4	4.5	4.7
Cook Islands	−1.7	−1.2	−0.5	0.0	0.2	2.6	1.6	3.0	1.8	2.0
Fiji	4.7	5.3	4.0	2.7	4.5	2.9	0.6	1.4	3.0	3.0
Kiribati	2.4	3.8	3.0	1.8	2.0	−1.5	2.1	1.4	0.3	0.8
Marshall Islands	1.9	−1.0	−0.5	1.5	2.0	1.9	1.1	0.5	2.0	2.5
Micronesia, Fed. States of	−3.6	−3.4	−1.5	2.5	3.5	2.2	0.7	−1.1	−0.3	0.3
Nauru	15.4	17.5	−10.0	3.0	15.0	0.5	3.0	11.4	6.6	1.7
Palau	−1.7	4.7	6.7	3.0	7.0	2.8	4.0	2.2	1.5	2.5
Papua New Guinea	5.0	13.3	9.9	4.3	2.4	5.0	5.2	5.1	6.0	6.0
Samoa	−1.9	1.2	1.4	2.0	0.5	−0.2	−1.2	1.9	2.0	2.0
Solomon Islands	2.8	2.0	3.2	3.0	2.8	5.4	5.2	−0.3	4.4	5.7
Timor-Leste	2.8	6.0	4.1	4.5	5.5	9.5	0.7	0.6	2.0	3.0
Tonga	−3.1	2.0	3.4	2.8	2.7	0.8	2.1	−0.7	−0.3	0.5
Tuvalu	1.3	2.0	2.0	3.5	3.0	2.0	1.1	2.0	3.5	2.0
Vanuatu	2.0	2.3	−1.0	2.5	3.8	1.4	1.0	2.5	1.9	2.4
Developing Asia	6.4	6.3	5.9	5.7	5.7	3.8	3.0	2.2	2.5	2.7

1

RESCUING GROWTH IN UNCERTAIN TIMES

Rescuing growth in uncertain times

Developing Asia faces a challenging global environment. Since the global financial crisis of 2008–2009, global economic expansion has consistently underperformed expectations (Figure 1.0.1). Lower international prices for oil and other commodities were supposed to be a boon to most economies, but the benefits have been slow to come even as the shock to commodity-dependent emerging economies has been immediate. Less-than-robust recovery in the industrial economies and slowing growth in emerging markets weigh on growth prospects everywhere. Volatility in global financial markets that stems from weakness in emerging markets and monetary tightening in the United States (US) is deepening the uncertainty stirred by the global slowdown.

Growth in developing Asia is thus expected to decelerate marginally from 5.9% in 2015 to 5.7% in both 2016 and 2017. The People's Republic of China (PRC) and India, the two largest economies, will strongly influence the region's growth outcome. Growth in the PRC will continue to decelerate during that economy's deliberate transition to a more balanced and sustainable growth paradigm. Somewhat stronger growth in India and the Association of Southeast Asian Nations (ASEAN) will help deflect the resulting headwinds.

Persistent sluggishness in the world economy underlines the importance of structural reform in developing Asia. The authorities must redouble their efforts to reform their domestic economies to boost potential growth. Broad diversity in the region means that reform objectives and priorities differ from country to country. Whether reform aims to make labor markets more flexible in the PRC, streamline procedures to accelerate public infrastructure investment in India, or improve the business environment to facilitate diversification away from oil dependence in Azerbaijan, it needs to be tailored to country circumstances.

Even as policy makers seek to improve productivity over the long run, they must remain vigilant against short-term risks posed by future US interest rate hikes that could worsen global financial market volatility, sharper-than-forecast growth moderation in the PRC, tepid commodity prices undermining growth in producer countries, and severe weather dampening agricultural production. The authorities may also be challenged by heretofore unfamiliar risks such as producer price deflation, which has recently emerged in some economies in the region.

1.0.1 World growth and forecasts

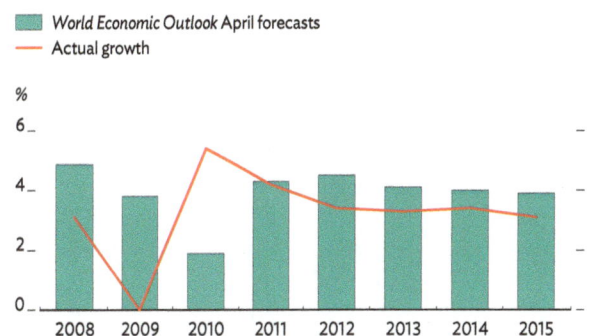

Note: Data for 2015 growth is an estimate as of January 2016. The forecasts are from the previous year's April issue of the *World Economic Outlook*.
Source: International Monetary Fund, *World Economic Outlook*, April 2007–2014, October 2015, and January 2016.
Click here for figure data

This chapter was written by Donghyun Park, Gemma Esther Estrada, Arief Ramayandi, Akiko Terada-Hagiwara, Xuehui Han, Madhavi Pundit, Cindy Castillejos-Petalcorin, Nedelyn Magtibay-Ramos, Pilipinas Quising, Dennis Sorino, and Joseph E. Zveglich, Jr., of the Economic Research and Regional Cooperation Department, ADB, Manila.

Slow going in a tough global environment

Growth in developing Asia is forecast to dip as the region faces difficult and uncertain times. Aggregate gross domestic product (GDP) in the region will expand by 5.7% in 2016, decelerating from 5.9% in 2015 (Figure 1.1.1). This slower expansion mirrors moderating growth in the PRC as it continues its shift toward a new normal with less dependence on investment and manufacturing for export. In 2017, growth in the region will remain steady, as continued growth moderation in the PRC will be counterbalanced by solid growth in India and a pickup in other larger economies, notably members of ASEAN. Average inflation in the region will rise from 2.2% in 2015 to 2.5% in 2016 on strengthening domestic demand and further to 2.7% in 2017, following an expected recovery in global commodity prices (Figure 1.1.2). The region's aggregate current account surplus will narrow from 2.9% in 2015 to 2.6% in 2016 and further to 2.4% in 2017, as exports are unlikely to rebound strongly for lack of external demand (Figure 1.1.3). Further, recovery in the industrial economies has been slow (Box 1.1.1).

1.1.1 GDP growth outlook in developing Asia

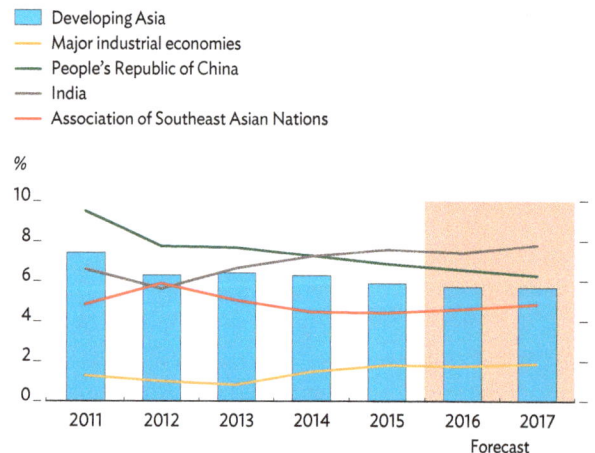

Note: The major industrial economies consist of the United States, the euro area, and Japan.
Sources: US Department of Commerce, Bureau of Economic Analysis, http://www.bea.gov; Eurostat, http://ec.europa.eu/eurostat; Economic and Social Research Institute of Japan, http://www.esri.cao.go.jp; Haver Analytics; Asian Development Outlook database; ADB estimates.
Click here for figure data

Growth stymied in 2015

The growth slowdown in developing Asia in 2015 was widespread, affecting most economies in the region, including all of East Asia and Central Asia and most of Southeast Asia. The region's deceleration mirrors continued growth moderation in the PRC. The average pace slipped from 6.3% in 2014 to 5.9% in 2015.

Growth in East Asia decelerated to 6.0% in 2015 from 6.6% in 2014 as exports withered. A large drag on growth across East Asia was growth moderation in the PRC. In Mongolia, growth dipped by 5.6 percentage points, and in Taipei,China by 3.2 points. Growth slipped by less than a percentage point in the subregion's two other economies, the Republic of Korea and Hong Kong, China, where strong domestic demand countered feeble exports.

In Central Asia, growth weakened to 2.9% in 2015 from 5.3% in 2014 as all eight economies posted slower growth on account of the huge drop in global oil prices and recession in the Russian Federation, a key trade partner and source of remittances. Growth in oil-dependent Kazakhstan and Turkmenistan decelerated the most, by over 3 percentage points. In Tajikistan and Uzbekistan, growth slowed less despite large falls in remittances and the return of migrant workers, thanks to timely and robust expansion in public investment.

1.1.2 Inflation in developing Asia

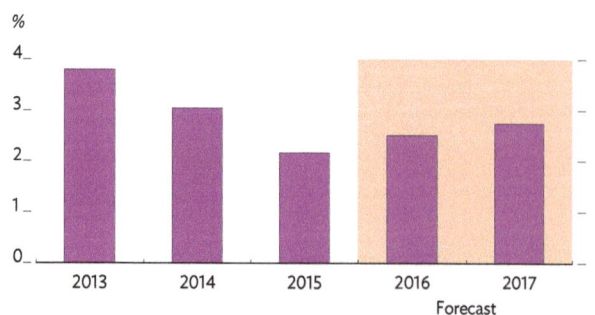

Source: Asian Development Outlook database.
Click here for figure data

1.1.1 Meager progress in the industrial economies

Lower prices for oil and other commodities are expected to persist during the forecast period, but they will not provide uplift in the major industrial economies: the US, the euro area, and Japan. While the negative output gap will gradually narrow, hardly any growth acceleration is expected in the major industrial economies as their combined economies grow by 1.8% in 2016 (as in 2015) and 1.9% in 2017 (box table).

GDP growth in the major industrial economies (%)

Area	2014	2015	2016	2017
	Actual		ADO projection	
Major industrial economies	1.5	1.8	1.8	1.9
United States	2.4	2.4	2.3	2.5
Euro area	0.9	1.6	1.5	1.6
Japan	0.0	0.5	0.6	0.5

ADO = Asian Development Outlook.

Notes: Average growth rates are weighted by gross national income, Atlas method. More details in Table A1.1 on page 29.

Sources: US Department of Commerce, Bureau of Economic Analysis, http://www.bea.gov; Eurostat, http://ec.europa.eu/eurostat; Economic and Social Research Institute of Japan, http://www.esri.cao.go.jp; Consensus Forecasts; Bloomberg; CEIC Data Company; Haver; World Bank, Global Commodity Markets, http://www.worldbank.org; ADB estimates.

The US economy expanded by 2.4% in 2015 with private consumption as a main source of growth, contributing 2.1 percentage points. Government investment added to private investment, and collectively they contributed roughly 0.9 percentage points to growth last year. The stronger US dollar has again worked against recovery momentum by slashing the contribution of net foreign trade and services by 0.6 percentage points. Inflation, both headline and core, remained muted as US dollar appreciation and low energy prices kept price pressures in check.

In December 2015, the Federal Reserve raised the federal funds rate for the first time since the global financial crisis began in 2008. The target range has been maintained since then on the expectation of low inflation and a slow pickup in economic activity in the near term. The US policy rate is forecast to average 0.6% in 2016 before increasing to around 1.8% by the end of 2017. While overall liquidity should remain loose in 2016, the strong dollar is still expected to drag on GDP growth by restraining net external demand throughout the year. As the private sector spends more on both consumption and investment, GDP in the US is projected to grow by 2.3% in 2016, modestly picking up to 2.5% next year.

Recovery in the euro area that began in 2014 failed to pick up momentum as growth leveled off toward the end of 2015. Business and consumer confidence dropped to a 1 year low as the region dove back into deflation at the turn of 2016. Labor markets improved throughout 2015, but demand was insufficient to generate inflation. A breakdown of regional GDP growth by component showed that private consumption contributed a relatively strong 0.9 percentage points in 2015, followed by fixed investment at 0.5 percentage points. Government consumption added 0.3 percentage points, but net exports dragged down growth as imports outpaced exports.

The European Central Bank announced further steps in March of this year toward expansive monetary policy to ease the cost of finance, spur growth, and counter deflation. It cut all the main interest rates and increased its monthly asset purchases by €20 billion. The composite purchasing managers' index is still above 50, indicating expansion, but it has steadily declined since December, which does not bode well for the strength of recovery hinted at the start of 2016. Consumption demand, which was the main driver of growth in 2015, lost steam toward the end of 2015. Weak global demand exacerbated by slower growth prospects in emerging economies may continue to dampen the external sector. In the absence of a strong catalyst, the euro area is expected to just about maintain the pace, expanding by 1.5% in 2016 and 1.6% in 2017.

Japan grew by a mere 0.5% in 2015, which nevertheless improved on zero growth in 2014 despite the lack of a strong growth engine. Private consumption dropped by 1.3% in the whole year as an unseasonably cool summer in the second quarter and an unseasonably warm winter in the fourth quarter dampened demand for indoor climate control and new apparel. Public works orders steadily declined last year as the government continued its fiscal consolidation. Trade activity, both exports and imports, shrank in 2015, but imports dropped much more than exports. Meanwhile, the labor market has become tighter with the unemployment rate falling to 3.2% in January 2016. While real wages are rising as the baby boom cohort reaches retirement, the slow pace of improvement is insufficient to stave off the threat of a return to deflation.

In response to sharper-than-expected drops in industrial production and soft inflation in December 2015, the Bank of Japan adopted negative interest rates in January 2016. Assuming that the value-added tax rate increase from 8% to 10% goes ahead as scheduled in April 2017, private consumption of durable goods and housing investment are expected to pick up in late 2016. However, there is some discussion that the tax increase should be further delayed if the economy continues to be weak. Growth will have to rely on domestic demand while demand for imported capital goods wanes in Japan's main trading partners, particularly the PRC. The purchasing managers' index is slightly above 50 but has dipped since December 2015, suggesting no strong recovery on the horizon. Japan's GDP is expected to grow by 0.6% in 2016 and, because of drag from the tax increase, by a slightly weaker 0.5% in 2017.

In Southeast Asia, growth slipped in aggregate only from 4.5% in 2014 to 4.4% in 2015 but declined in 7 of the 10 economies. In Indonesia, the largest ASEAN economy, growth decelerated for a fourth year in a row. In Malaysia, growth dipped as global demand weakened and hydrocarbon prices fell. In Thailand, growth picked up from a slump in 2014 but remained weak. Viet Nam was the only other economy with accelerating growth, driven by robust expansion in manufacturing and construction. The impact on agriculture of El Niño, a periodic weather event caused by temperature changes in the Pacific Ocean, partly accounted for growth slipping in the Philippines and other economies.

In contrast with slower growth elsewhere, growth in South Asia edged up from 6.7% in 2014 to 7.0% in 2015 as five of the eight economies posted higher growth. The improvement was led by India, where growth quickened to 7.6% in 2015 from 7.2% in 2014 on account of healthy expansion in private consumption and fixed investment, as well as robust growth in manufacturing. Steady growth in the rest of the South Asian economies, except Nepal and the Maldives, was buoyed by higher consumption and remittances, and by continued high growth in the region's biggest economy, India, which sustained subregional trade. Meanwhile, growth in Nepal was scaled down by an earthquake in April and a political standoff, and in the Maldives by a decline in high-end tourism.

In the Pacific, aggregate growth eased to 7.0% in 2015 from 9.4% in 2014 as growth slowed in the larger island economies. In the past, strong global commodity prices and large private investments in the mineral sector boosted growth in Papua New Guinea (PNG), but recent headwinds from low commodity prices and soft global demand have caused growth to falter. In Fiji, growth eased as activity slowed in sugar, fisheries, and timber, partly from unfavorable weather under El Niño, while in Timor-Leste contraction in public spending contributed to slower expansion of GDP measured without reference to the large offshore petroleum sector.

External demand dragged down growth in several large economies. In 6 of the 10 regional economies with data on contributions to growth, net exports subtracted from growth in 2015 (Figure 1.1.4). Domestic demand from private and government consumption was the dominant source of growth. Private consumption alone accounted for over half of growth in most of these economies.

In the first half of 2015, consumer confidence was bleak across most large economies (Figure 1.1.5). Confidence gradually picked up in the second half in Indonesia, the Republic of Korea, the Philippines, and Thailand. In the Philippines, a better outlook for business activity, jobs, and incomes has improved consumer sentiment. In the PRC, consumer sentiment fell on waning prospects for income growth against a backdrop of slower GDP growth overall. In Taipei,China, consumer confidence steadily weakened

1.1.3 Current account balance in developing Asia

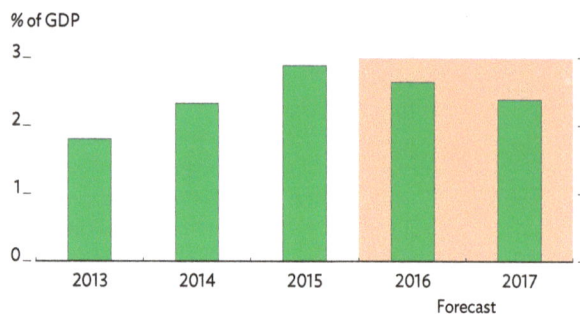

% of GDP

Source: Asian Development Outlook database.
Click here for figure data

1.1.4 Demand-side contributions to growth, selected economies

- Private consumption
- Government consumption
- Total investments
- Net exports
- Statistical discrepancy
- GDP growth

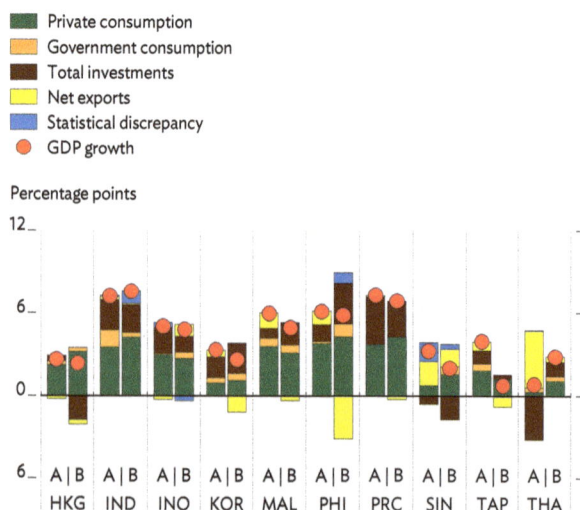

Percentage points

A = 2014, B = 2015, HKG = Hong Kong, China, IND = India, INO = Indonesia, KOR = Republic of Korea, MAL = Malaysia, PHI = Philippines, PRC = People's Republic of China, SIN = Singapore, TAP = Taipei,China, THA = Thailand.
Note: For the PRC, data on private consumption also cover government consumption.
Sources: Haver Analytics; CEIC Data Company (both accessed 5 March 2016).
Click here for figure data

from May to December in line with fragile growth in the first half that sank into contraction in the second half, further dimming prospects for employment and income. In Hong Kong, China, consumer confidence fluctuated, rising in the first half along with modest economic growth but slipping in the second half as declines hit tourist arrivals, particularly from the PRC, which accounted for over 70% of the total. Faced with sluggish economic growth and downbeat consumer sentiment, the authorities in Indonesia, the Republic of Korea, Malaysia, and Thailand announced stimulus measures in the second half to bolster economic growth. However, consumer confidence in Malaysia continued to deteriorate until the fourth quarter of 2015, hitting a record low 63.8. Consumer confidence also weakened in the Republic of Korea, Indonesia, and Thailand at the start of this year. In Taipei,China, confidence deteriorated once again in January but picked up in February.

The drop in consumer sentiment took its toll on retailing. In Taipei,China, retail sales tumbled in the second half of last year but began to recover gradually in the last quarter (Figure 1.1.6). Retail sales in Hong Kong, China likewise dropped in most months of 2015, reflecting lower tourism spending and, to some extent, volatility in the equity market. In Thailand, retail sales continued to contract in most months of 2015 but recovered toward the end. In Indonesia, they expanded in August at the weakest rate in 8 months, then picked up as a series of stimulus measures boosted consumer sentiment. In contrast with softness in most large economies, retail sales in the PRC held up well last year, thus advancing the country's structural shift toward consumption despite slipping consumer sentiment. Viet Nam continued to post high growth in retail sales that held steady, sustained by rising incomes.

1.1.5 Consumer confidence and expectations, selected developing Asia

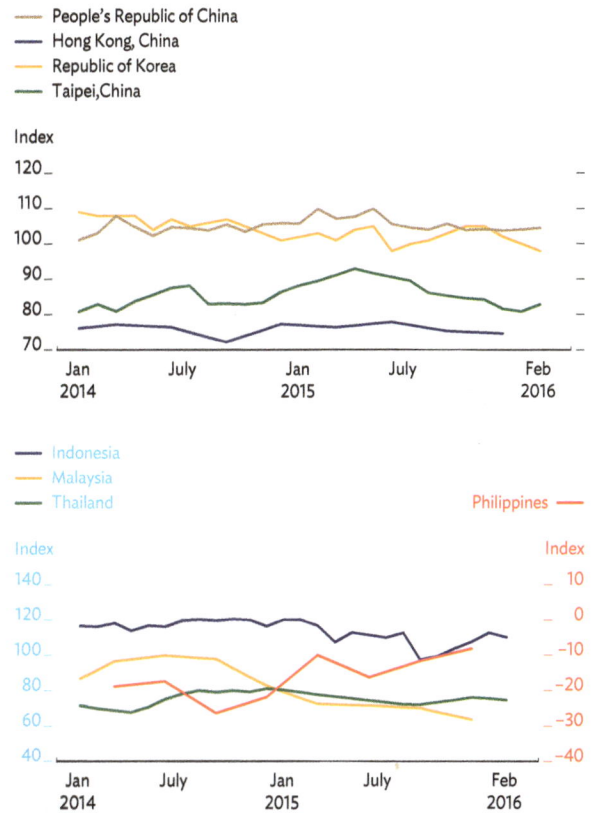

Note: Data for Malaysia, the Philippines, and Hong Kong, China are quarterly. For the People's Republic of China, Indonesia, the Republic of Korea, Malaysia, Thailand, and Taipei,China, a rating above 100 indicates rising optimism, while a score below it means deepening pessimism. For Hong Kong, China, January 2000 is the base year. Data for the Philippines refer to the percentage of households that were optimistic less the percentage that were pessimistic. A positive percentage point change indicates a favorable view, negative unfavorable.

Sources: Haver Analytics; CEIC Data Company (both accessed 17 March 2016).
Click here for figure data

1.1.6 Retail sales, selected developing Asia

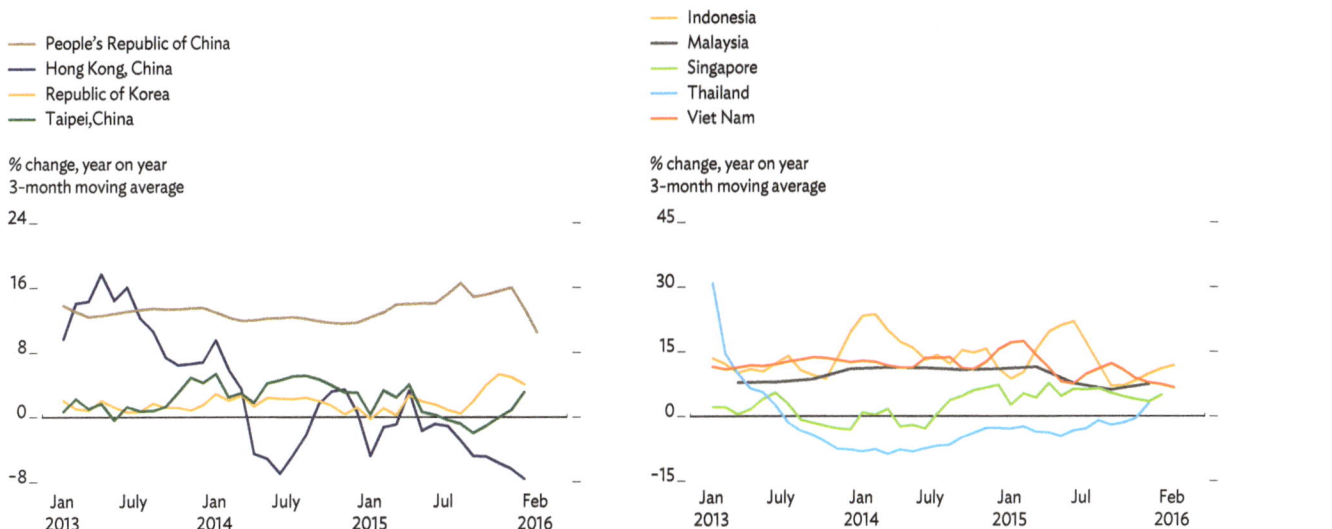

Note: Data for Malaysia refer to year-on-year quarterly percent change.
Source: Haver Analytics (accessed 16 March 2016).
Click here for figure data

1.1.7 Industrial production index

— Hong Kong, China
— Republic of Korea
— Singapore
— Taipei,China

— Indonesia
— Malaysia
— Philippines
Thailand —

% change, year on year
3-month moving average

% change, year on year
3-month moving average

% change, year on year
3-month moving average

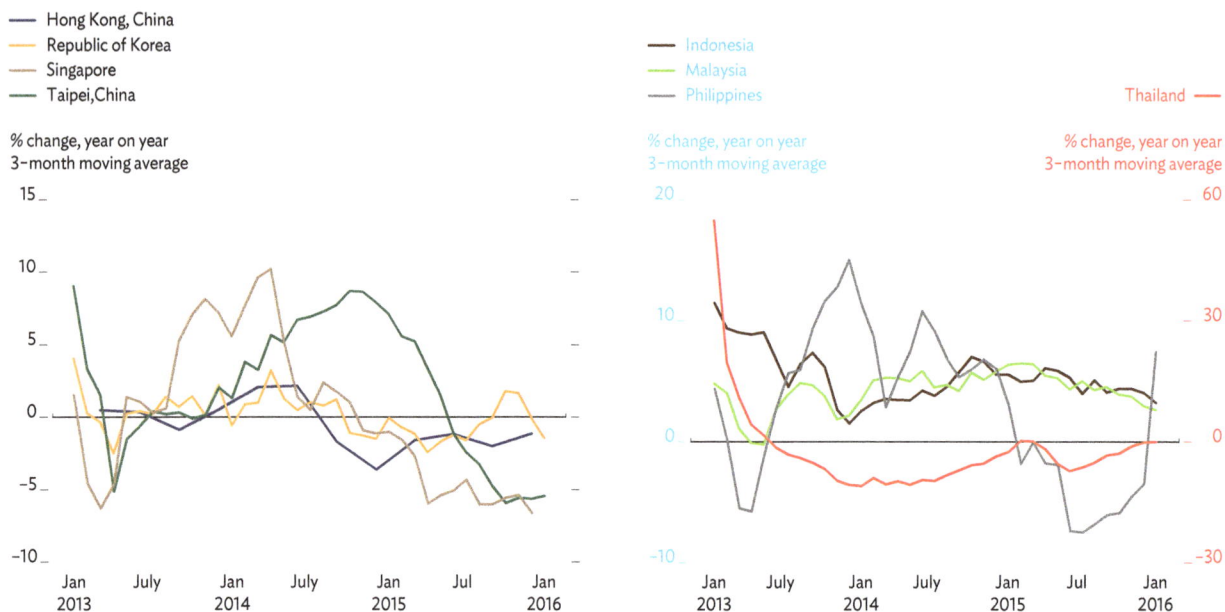

Note: Data for Hong Kong, China refer to year-on-year quarterly percent change.
Sources: Haver Analytics; CEIC Data Company (both accessed 17 March 2016).
Click here for figure data

Trends in industrial production reflect tepid economic expansion in export-oriented economies. In East Asia, industrial production contracted by 1.0% in the Republic of Korea, 1.7% in Taipei,China, and 1.5% in Hong Kong, China (Figure 1.1.7). Industrial production fell in Taipei,China as a wide array of manufacturing industries such as computers, telephones and mobile phones, audio and video products, and iron and steel registered declines. In Southeast Asia, industrial production expanded at a steady pace in Indonesia and Malaysia; in Thailand, it mildly recovered after a 5.2% plunge in the previous year. After posting modest gains in the past year, the Philippines and Singapore saw declines in industrial production for the first time since 2009. Singapore suffered a steep drop, by 5.1%, as production fell across several industries including machinery and equipment, metals, computers and electronic products, and pharmaceutical and related products.

Uncertainty in both the domestic and the external environment weakened investment. Singapore and Hong Kong, China suffered declines in gross investment, while the PRC, Indonesia, and Taipei,China saw investment expand at a slower pace (Figure 1.1.8). The slowdown in investment in the PRC continued in 2015 as real estate suffered a large housing overhang and manufacturing faced an uncertain business outlook and high corporate debt. In contrast, investment expanded at a faster pace in the Republic of Korea and the Philippines with good performances in both construction and investment in durable equipment. In Thailand, investment surged from contraction in the previous year, supporting recovery in the broader economy.

1.1.8 Contributions to investment growth in developing Asia

■ Gross fixed capital formation
■ Private gross fixed capital formation
■ Public gross fixed capital formation
■ Change in stocks
● Total investment

Percentage points

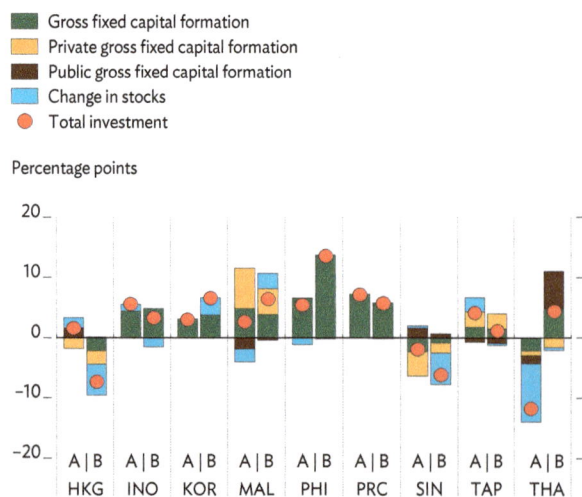

A = 2014, B = 2015, HKG = Hong Kong, China, INO = Indonesia, KOR = Republic of Korea, MAL = Malaysia, PHI = Philippines, PRC = People's Republic of China, SIN = Singapore, TAP = Taipei,China, THA = Thailand.
Sources: CEIC Data Company (accessed 16 March 2016); ADB estimates.
Click here for figure data

Diverging paths for India and the PRC

The region's two giants are headed in opposing directions, with the PRC slowing down as growth in India picks up. The PRC is in the midst of a structural shift toward more sustainable growth, while India, where income remains at a modest level long since vacated by the PRC, has more scope for rapid growth. As PRC policy makers pursue a smooth transition to more moderate growth, their Indian counterparts strive to maximize growth.

In the PRC, policy makers continued last year to focus more on growth quality than growth quantity, and on rebalancing the economy and eliminating excess capacity to target growth at about 7% (emphatically not a more precise figure) through fiscal stimulus and monetary easing. Growth in the PRC decelerated from 7.3% in 2014 to 6.9% in 2015, but it continued to account for about a third of global growth. In India, structural reform intended to attract more foreign direct investment is gradually moving forward, but further reform is needed to raise private investment and lift potential growth. Strong public investment helped India's economy accelerate growth from 7.2% in 2014 to an estimated 7.6% in 2015, the fastest rate among the region's larger economies. However, a challenging external environment is likely to moderate growth in both India and the PRC this year.

The difficulty of sustaining high growth in industrial production is manifest as the efforts of the PRC to rein in excess capacity are bedeviled by soft global demand. Further, production has been kept in check by an uncertain business outlook, especially for heavy industry. Growth in industrial production slowed to 6.1% in 2015 from 8.3% in 2014 (Figure 1.1.9). Production was held down by less upbeat business sentiment as, from August to December last year, the purchasing managers' index (PMI) languished below 50 (Figure 1.1.10). Meanwhile, growth in industrial production decelerated in most months in tandem with declining manufacturing exports. The continuing slowdown in industrial production reflects deep corrections in traditional heavy industries. In January and February this year, the PMI continued to linger below 50 as growth in industrial production further weakened to 5.4%. The expected slackening of manufacturing growth will be pronounced in heavy industry, while growth in consumer-oriented manufacturing is likely to hold up better. The government will continue to eliminate excess capacity in manufacturing as part of its structural reform. The likely moderating impact of reform and the weakening of growth momentum overall are forecast to bring gradual deceleration over the next 2 years.

In India, growth in industrial production accelerated in 2015, boosted by robust domestic demand. Industrial production expanded by 3.2%, up from 1.9% in 2014. The PMI registered a solid reading in most months, but business sentiment waned by year-end, when a PMI drop to 49.1 marked the first time since October 2013 that it fell

1.1.9 Production indicators

- Industrial production, India
- Electricity production, India
- Industrial production, People's Republic of China
- Electricity production, People's Republic of China

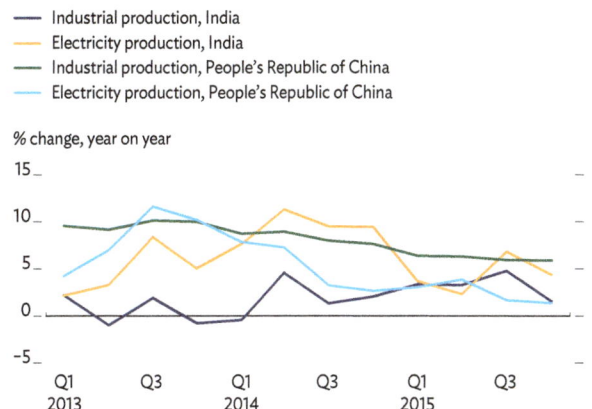

Q = quarter.
Sources: Haver Analytics; CEIC Data Company (both accessed 17 March 2016).
Click here for figure data

1.1.10 Merchandise exports and purchasing managers' index

- Purchasing managers' index, PRC   Export growth, PRC ——
- Purchasing managers' index, India   Export growth, India ——

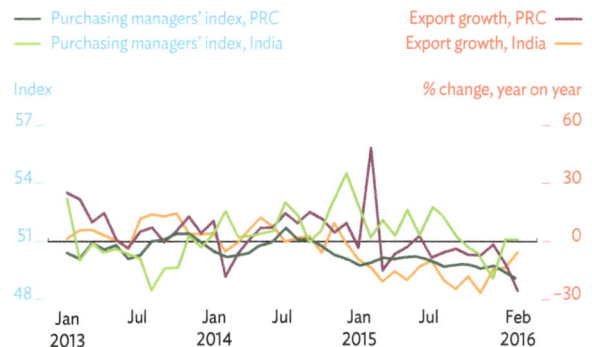

PRC = People's Republic of China.
Sources: Haver Analytics; CEIC Data Company (both accessed 17 March 2016).
Click here for figure data

below 50. A slide in the manufacturing PMI in December reflected a less favorable outlook on domestic demand exacerbated by floods in the southern part of the country, which affected a major automobile manufacturing hub. A decline in merchandise exports also worsened during the final quarter of 2015, further undermining business sentiment. The PMI recovered to 51.1 in January and February this year, along with expectations of an improvement in domestic demand. However, data on industrial production produced a contrasting picture, as it showed contraction in January for the third consecutive month. In sum, GDP growth in India is expected to dip marginally this year as expansion in public investment weakens under fiscal constraints, private corporations continue to deleverage, and external demand remains anemic.

Inflation broadly in retreat

Inflation was further subdued in developing Asia in 2015, falling to 2.2% from 3.0% in 2014. The deceleration partly tracked slowing economic growth across the region and the consequent weakening of demand-side inflationary pressures. Supply-side factors, in particular feeble global oil and food prices, also helped to tame inflation. Average Brent crude prices fell to $52/barrel in 2015 from $99/barrel in 2014, a 47% drop that was fivefold the 9% fall in average prices in 2014. Agricultural commodity prices also continued to decline, with the overall index falling by 13.1% and food prices by 15.4%, mainly from favorable supply conditions and soft energy prices. While the drop in prices has been largely due to supply factors, subdued demand has contributed.

The decline in developing Asia is part of the global trend toward lower inflation, which mirrors the global commodity slump and the fragility that besets the global economic outlook. For the major industrial economies—the US, the euro area, and Japan—aggregate inflation fell from 1.3% in 2014 to 0.2% in 2015, barely clinging to positive territory. Low inflation gave policy makers in many Asian economies the option to keep interest rates low to support demand and growth. While consumer prices rose in most economies, some of them, including the PRC and India, saw producer prices fall in 2015 (Figure 1.1.11). Asia has long been preoccupied with inflation, but deflation can present problems of its own by, for example, raising the real value of debt.

While inflation remained subdued in developing Asia as a whole, there were substantial differences across subregions (Figure 1.1.12). Inflation was lowest in East Asia, easing in aggregate to 1.3% in 2015 from 1.9% in 2014 as inflation in the PRC and the Republic of Korea hovered at only around 1% and Taipei,China experienced deflation. The PRC is of particular interest in light of substantial moderation in its growth momentum over the past few years. In tandem with its slowing economy, inflation fell from 5.4% in 2011 to 2.6%

1.1.11 Consumer and producer prices, 2015

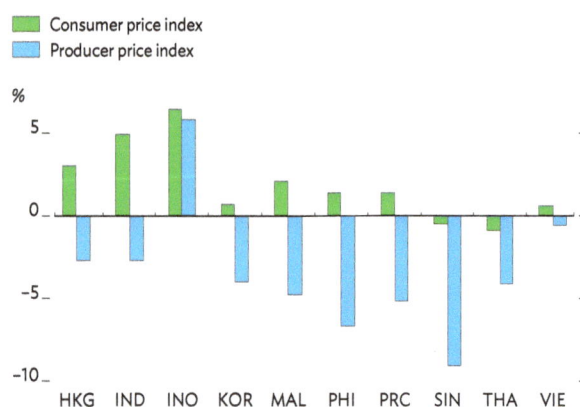

HKG = Hong Kong, China, IND = India, INO = Indonesia, KOR = Republic of Korea, MAL = Malaysia, PHI = Philippines, PRC = People's Republic of China, SIN = Singapore, THA = Thailand, VIE = Viet Nam.
Note: India shows the wholesale price index, not the producer price index.
Source: CEIC Data Company (accessed 15 March 2016).
Click here for figure data

1.1.12 Subregional inflation

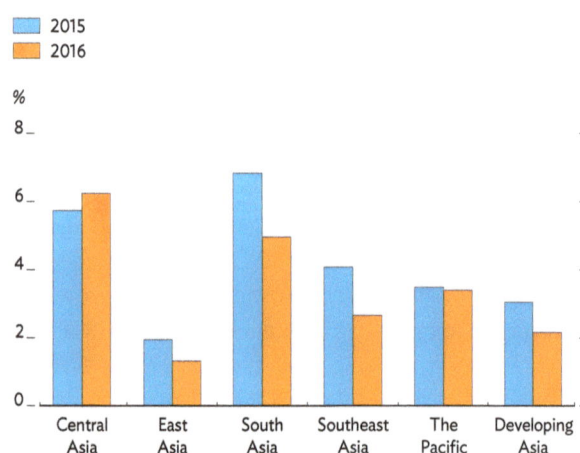

Source: Asian Development Outlook database.
Click here for figure data

in 2012 and 2013, and further to 1.4% in 2015 (Figure 1.1.13). In South Asia, inflation dipped to 5.0% from 6.8% in 2014 as all subregional economies except Sri Lanka saw lower inflation. Inflation eased to 2.7% from 4.1% in Southeast Asia, as Cambodia, the Lao People's Democratic Republic, the Philippines, Thailand, and Viet Nam all saw inflation drop by around 3 percentage points. In the Pacific, inflation slid only marginally to 3.4% from 3.5%. Central Asia was the only subregion where inflation nudged up. Widespread currency depreciation in this subregion helped push average inflation to 6.2% from 5.7% in 2014; accelerating inflation in Armenia, Azerbaijan, Georgia, and Uzbekistan outweighed deceleration in Kazakhstan, the Kyrgyz Republic, and Tajikistan.

Trade vitality tested

Merchandise exports from developing Asia declined by 8.1% in 2015, the first drop since 2009, as shipments from Central Asia, South Asia, and Southeast Asia fell by double digits in aggregate (Figure 1.1.14). Modest recovery in the industrial economies has not boosted export momentum. Instead, exports fell sharply owing to a combination of lower commodity prices and subdued global demand. The exports of oil-producing Kazakhstan and Turkmenistan fell by more than a third, dragging down aggregate Central Asian exports to about the same rate. Every East Asian economy saw its merchandise exports decline. PRC exports fell by 4.4%, largely because of smaller shipments to Japan, the Russian Federation, and Hong Kong, China. In Southeast Asia, exports fell in aggregate mainly because of steep declines in shipments from Indonesia, Malaysia, the Philippines, and Singapore. In the Pacific, aggregate exports increased by 34.4% on a surge recorded by PNG and Timor-Leste. Across the region, only 11 of 45 economies diverged from the trend and saw exports rise in 2015.

Growth moderation and structural shift in the PRC had a substantial impact on other economies' exports, considering the high portion of total exports that go to the PRC. In 2015, half of exports from Hong Kong, China went to the PRC, while in the Republic of Korea and Taipei,China the figure was about one-fourth. All economies in Figure 1.1.15 experienced a drop in total exports, with the decline in exports to the PRC greater than 10% for Indonesia, the Philippines, and Taipei,China. The fall in exports to the PRC was greater than the decline in exports to other markets in the case of the Philippines and Hong Kong, China.

Merchandise imports fell by 13.4%, nearly twice as much as exports (Figure 1.1.16). The trend was led by the heavily weighted PRC, which saw imports fall by 13.4%, an outcome from lower commodity prices and demand for

1.1.13 Growth and inflation, the People's Republic of China

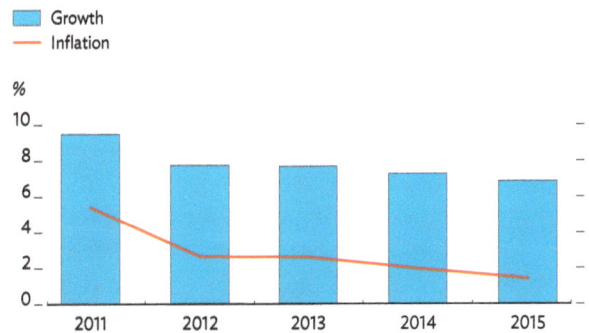

Source: *Asian Development Outlook* database.
Click here for figure data

1.1.14 Export growth by subregion

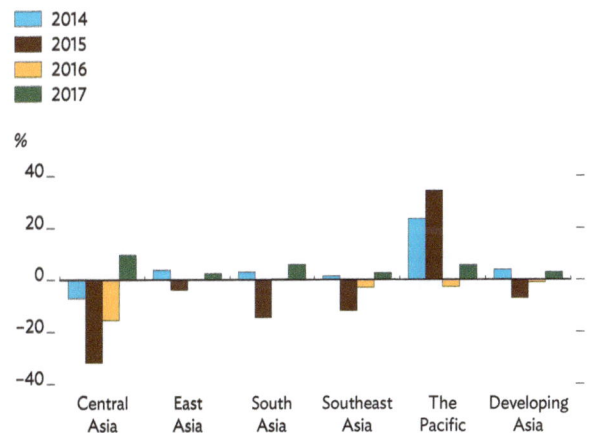

Source: *Asian Development Outlook* database.
Click here for figure data

1.1.15 Change in exports to the People's Republic of China and others, 2015

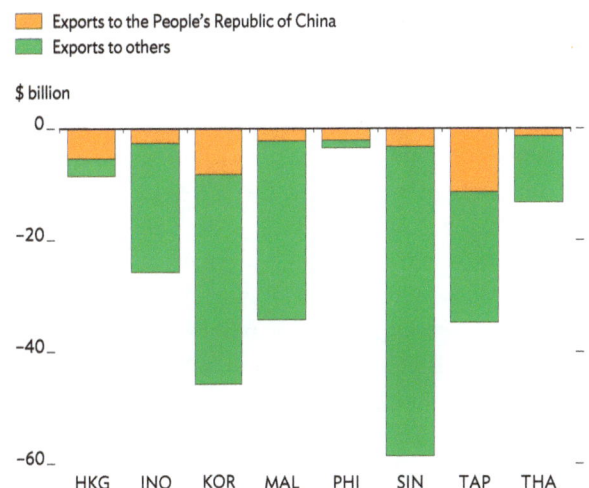

HKG = Hong Kong, China, INO = Indonesia, KOR = Republic of Korea, MAL = Malaysia, PHI = Philippines, SIN = Singapore, TAP = Taipei,China, THA = Thailand.
Source: CEIC Data Company (accessed 15 March 2016).
Click here for figure data

construction materials and energy, as well as from rising import substitution using local manufactures. The drop in imports occurred across all subregions but was particularly pronounced—and larger than the dive in exports—in East Asia and Southeast Asia. In Central Asia, the uniquely steep drop in imports, by one-fifth, was still less than the plunge in exports. Twelve economies across the region posted increases in imports, four of them in South Asia.

Feeble merchandise exports are expected to continue. Export growth is forecast to be flat this year as uncertainty persists. The decline in exports continued into the first 2 months of this year, dimming export prospects for the year. Only around 40% of regional economies are likely to see exports increase this year. This portion is projected to rise to over half next year as export growth accelerates to 2.8% on recovery in shipments from Central Asia and higher commodity prices, and as the region as a whole benefits from strengthening in global demand.

Imports are forecast to contract this year by 2.4%, and investment is expected to be less robust. Imports of intermediate goods and machinery are not likely to grow, as the PRC is seen reducing its total imports and other economies face lackluster external demand, and business sentiment has yet to pick up. Growth in imports to South Asia, projected at 4.3% in aggregate, will reflect import growth in more than half of the subregion's economies.

The regional current account surplus widened to equal 2.9% of combined GDP in 2015 from 2.3% in 2014 as imports shrank more sharply than exports (Figure 1.1.17). This year, the regional current account surplus will shrink to 2.6% of GDP with continuing declines in global oil prices, tight external demand, worsening current account deficits in oil-exporting countries, and narrowing surpluses in the larger Asian economies on account of weak manufacturing exports. Next year, the expected rebound in global commodity prices will narrow the aggregate deficit in Central Asia, but the larger East and Southeast Asian subregions are likely to post lower surpluses, thus further narrowing the region-wide aggregate current account surplus to 2.4% of GDP.

The declining trend in developing Asia's current account surplus parallels the global picture. The global current account surplus narrowed marginally from 1.1% of world GDP in 2014 to 1.0% in 2015 (Figure 1.1.18). Despite this, developing Asia's surplus relative to world GDP rose to 0.7% from 0.6% in the same period (as the PRC surplus rose to 0.4% from 0.3%), carrying forward a trend since 2011 and illustrating the region's mounting economic importance.

1.1.16 Import growth by subregion

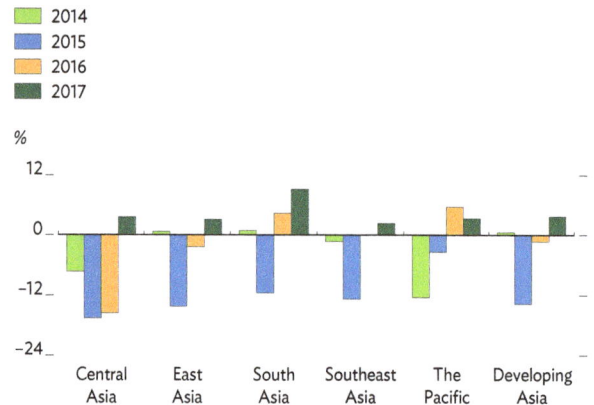

Source: Asian Development Outlook database.
Click here for figure data

1.1.17 Current account balance by subregion

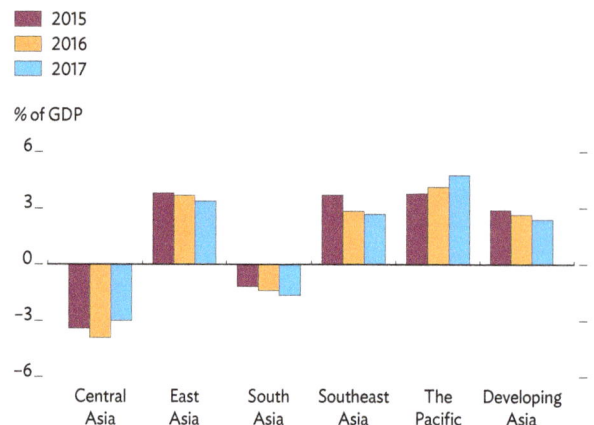

Source: Asian Development Outlook database.
Click here for figure data

1.1.18 World current account balance

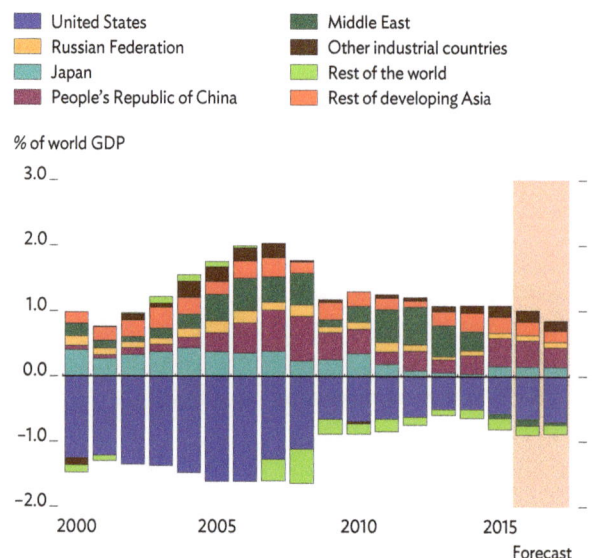

Sources: International Monetary Fund. 2015. World Economic Outlook database. October. www.imf.org; Haver Analytics (both accessed 14 March 2016).
Click here for figure data

Growth prospects tempered

GDP growth in developing Asia will slip to 5.7% in 2016 from 5.9% in 2015 as growth slows in 19 of the region's 45 economies and in four of its five subregions (Figure 1.1.19). Only Southeast Asia will post higher growth this year. Next year, growth will remain steady at 5.7% as further moderation in East Asia and the Pacific is offset by improved prospects in Central Asia, South Asia, and Southeast Asia. In 2017, 80% of regional economies are expected to post higher growth on the back of a recovery in external demand and further pickup in domestic demand. Despite growth slippage and stagnation over the next 2 years, the region will continue to account for a huge share of global growth, at 60%, close to its average share over the past 5 years.

Soft global demand and restructuring in the PRC will temper growth in East Asia from 6.0% in 2015 to 5.7% in 2016. The Republic of Korea will record steady growth this year, accelerating next year in tandem with improving global demand. Growth in Taipei,China will edge up this year and next, supported by rising government investment. Both Mongolia and Hong Kong, China will see growth slow this year and pick up only mildly next year, as deceleration in the PRC weighs heavily on their prospects.

Growth in Southeast Asia will accelerate to 4.5% this year and 4.8% next. The trend will be led by Indonesia as it raises investment and undertakes policy reform. Economic recovery in Thailand will gradually move forward over the next 2 years, bolstered by public investment. In the Philippines, solid growth will come from both private consumption and investment. As growth strengthens in the subregion, half of its economies are forecast to expand by at least 6.0% over the next 2 years.

South Asia will continue to see robust growth this year and next. As in the past year, this subregion will be the fastest-growing in Asia in the next 2 years. Despite the unfavorable external environment, growth will slip only mildly to 6.9% in 2016 as India enjoys solid though moderating growth and as expansion gains speed in six other subregional economies. Next year, growth in the subregion will surge to 7.3% as it quickens to 7.8% in India and accelerates in all other subregional economies except Bhutan.

The expected further drop in oil and gas prices will, along with lower remittances from a Russian Federation still mired in recession, drag down growth in Central Asia to 2.1% this year from 2.9% last year. Growth will slow in all economies except Turkmenistan, where it is expected to hold steady. Subregional growth will bounce back next year to 2.8% along with a recovery in global commodity prices.

In the Pacific, growth will plunge by almost half this year, dragged down by abrupt deceleration in the heavily weighted PNG from 9.9% in 2015 to 4.3% as prospects are further dampened by falling commodity prices. Growth in Fiji is poised to be lower this year following the devastating Tropical Cyclone Winston this February. By contrast, eight other subregional economies are expected to have faster growth this year.

1.1.19 GDP growth by subregion

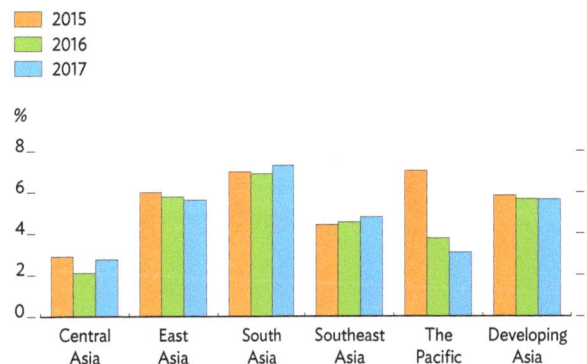

Source: *Asian Development Outlook* database.
Click here for figure data

Regional inflation is forecast to step up from 2.2% in 2015 to 2.5% in 2016 and 2.7% in 2017 (Figure 1.1.20). Inflation will rise this year on account of strengthening domestic demand and next year on recovery for global commodity prices. In the PRC, further price deregulation will help drive inflation higher to the forecast horizon. Aggregate inflation in East Asia will rise steadily in both years but remain benign. In South and Southeast Asia, inflation will hold somewhat steady in 2016 but accelerate in 2017. In Central Asia, elevated inflation this year will come partly from higher prices for imported goods following widespread currency depreciation, but inflationary pressures will ease in 2017. Higher inflation in the Pacific is forecast in light of the risk of currency depreciation in PNG and the expectation of strong domestic demand in the other economies.

1.1.20 Inflation by subregion

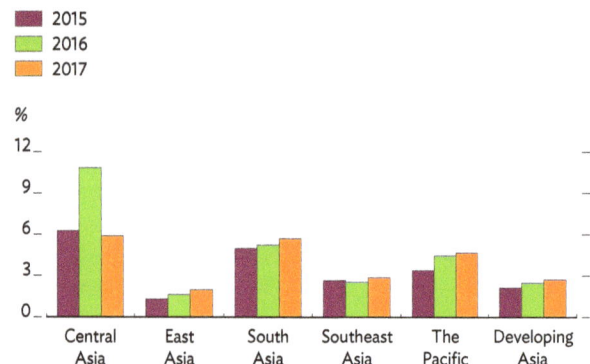

Source: Asian Development Outlook database.
Click here for figure data

Risks to the outlook

Against the backdrop of a difficult and uncertain global environment, risks to the outlook for this year clearly tilt toward the downside. While growth may still pleasantly surprise, upside risks to the forecast are few. On the other hand, the downside risks are formidable: slower PRC growth, higher US interest rates, volatile global financial markets, sharp slowdowns in commodity-producing economies, and general sluggishness in emerging markets.

Further US interest rate hikes may heighten global risk aversion, especially when viewing emerging markets in light of their slower growth. Heightened risk aversion may trigger in turn large and volatile capital flow reversals from emerging markets. Global financial markets have shown a great deal of volatility since the beginning of the year. Although the US Federal Reserve has refrained from further interest rate hikes since December 2015, chances are that further rate hikes will come this year. Tightening global liquidity could conspire with a broader emerging market slowdown to produce febrile and tense conditions in global financial markets. Further, higher US rates may cause an already strong US dollar to appreciate even more. This would raise the value of foreign debt in local currency terms, posing risks to economies with large debts.

An unexpectedly sharp growth slowdown in the PRC could have major implications for the regional outlook. The PRC is now the world's second largest economy, which means that its growth rate matters not only to the region—especially to the East and Southeast Asian economies that have close economic links with the PRC—but also to the world. Indeed, before the current slowdown, robust growth in the PRC had been a major positive factor in the global economy. The slowdown is not a major concern in and of itself, as it derives partly from a natural, healthy, and welcome transition to more sustainable and balanced growth rates. However, if the transition is poorly managed and deceleration starts to spiral, the adverse impact will be substantial.

As developing Asia as a whole is a major net importer of oil and other commodities, it should benefit from current weakness in global commodity prices. However, oil- and commodity-dependent economies in the region, especially in Central Asia and the Pacific, are hurt by the global commodity slump. In addition, Asian economies that export a lot to commodity-dependent countries such as oil-exporters in the Middle East, or depend on them for workers' remittances, will suffer losses. So the slump is not confined to commodity producers. The broad slowdown of emerging markets may harm the region's export and growth prospects (Figure 1.1.21).

The economic effects of El Niño are unpredictable. While they vary by country, and with each occurrence of El Niño, they may be substantially negative for some Asian economies. El Niño often significantly lowers rainfall in Asia and sometimes causes severe drought. As such, it poses greater risks to economies with relatively large primary sectors—agriculture, fishing, and mining—and to economies that are less diversified.

Producer price deflation is emerging as a new threat in some Asian economies. Developing Asia's growth slowdown since the global financial crisis has subdued inflationary pressures, which are even weaker with the recent slide in global prices for oil and other commodities. While low inflation gives Asian central banks greater scope for countercyclical monetary expansion designed to boost growth, it raises concerns about crossing the line into deflation. In fact, while consumer prices are still rising, albeit more slowly, producer prices are actually falling in some Asian economies. As of February 2016, producer prices had declined for 48 consecutive months in the PRC. Empirical analysis suggests that a negative relationship may hold between producer price deflation and economic growth. To avoid sliding into a low-growth trap, Asian policy makers would do well to monitor not only consumer prices but also producer prices.

1.1.21 GDP growth, developing economies

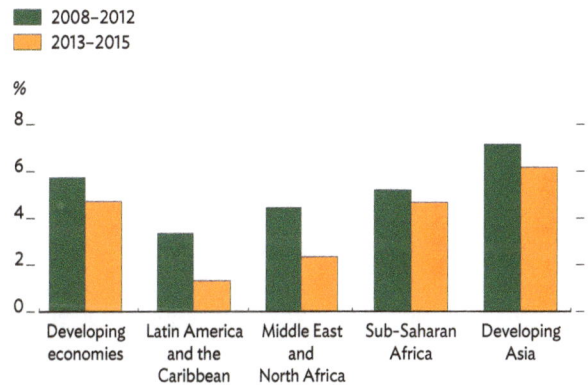

Note: Latin America and the Caribbean, Middle East and North Africa, and Sub-Saharan Africa are classifications in the International Monetary Fund's *World Economic Outlook* database. "Developing economies" combine these regions with developing Asia.

Sources: International Monetary Fund, *World Economic Outlook* database, October 2015; *Asian Development Outlook* database; ADB estimates.

Click here for figure data

Spillover from the People's Republic of China

The analysis above identifies economic slowdown in the PRC as a major downside risk to developing Asia's outlook. The magnitude of the risk depends critically on how much growth moderates, as the analysis below shows. In addition to slowing down, the PRC is undergoing a structural transformation with significant external effects. While the effect on other economies is likely negative in the immediate future, economies that adapt quickly to the new circumstances can reap future growth dividends.

Effects of growth moderation in the PRC

Growth in the PRC has been slowing and is expected to continue to slow over the medium term. The PRC growth rate was only 6.9% in 2015, almost half a percentage point below 2014 and, for the first time in a quarter of a century, lower than 7.0% on an annual basis. Moderation has been a continuous downward drift by a total of 2.6 percentage points since 2011. A slowdown was expected, but its extent keeps surprising, as seen in repeated downward revisions to growth forecasts (Figure 1.2.1).

A recent study examines the external impact of slowdown in the PRC (Abiad et al. 2016). It reflects several fluid structural factors. First, the PRC working-age population aged 15–59 started to shrink in 2012, and this demographic shift will drag on growth increasingly in the years to come. Second, the PRC economy is shifting away from industry and toward services on the supply side, and away from investment and toward consumption on the demand side. The decline in the contributions to growth from industry and investment is under way, but the rise in contributions from services and consumption growth has not yet fully offset the decline. Third, a natural process of convergence predicts that growth will slow as per capita income rises and as return on investment diminishes. The PRC has converged quickly in the past quarter century, with real GDP per capita rising ninefold since 1990. As labor costs have soared, the PRC has lost some of its attraction as a base for low-cost manufacturing. Wage costs are now almost four times higher than in Bangladesh, Cambodia, the Lao People's Democratic Republic, and Myanmar.

Cyclical factors play a role in growth moderation. External demand has been weaker than expected because recovery in the advanced economies has been lackluster following the global financial crisis of 2008–2009, and more recently emerging markets have faltered. These developments have dragged on PRC exports.

1.2.1 PRC growth and consensus forecasts

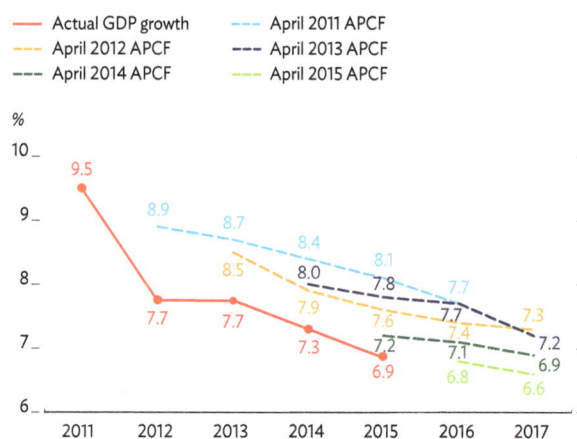

APCF = Asia Pacific Consensus Forecast, PRC = People's Republic of China.
Sources: International Monetary Fund, *World Economic Outlook* database, October 2015; Consensus Economics, Asia Pacific Consensus Forecast, various issues.
Click here for figure data

Efforts to maintain high growth after the global financial crisis exacerbated imbalances. PRC expansionary policy after 2010 increased investment and spending on infrastructure and substantially eased credit conditions to support growth. Partly because of this, debt has risen substantially since 2008, much of it channeled through unregulated shadow banks. This debt helped fuel overinvestment and excess capacity in certain sectors such as steel, as well as sharp increases in asset values. To contain these vulnerabilities, PRC authorities began paring back investment and tightening credit in mid-2013, which contributed to the slowdown. They reversed course in mid-2015, however, when growth seemed to be slowing more sharply than anticipated or desired.

Growth moderation has real effects on the rest of Asia but only modest impact on the US and Europe. Using the Global Projection Model, which models multiple blocks of economies to comprehensively and coherently generate global forecasts, Abiad et al. (2016) assessed the effects of the current PRC slowdown using "no slowdown" as the counterfactual scenario for comparison. Weaker PRC growth shaved almost a third of a percentage point off developing Asia's growth each year and a fifth of a percentage point off Japan's (Figure 1.2.2). This reflected strong intraregional trade and production linkages involving the PRC. In contrast, the impact on the US and Europe was modest, as their relatively small trade exposure to the PRC was offset by a boost from lower commodity prices. Global growth was almost a third of a percentage point lower than it would have been had the PRC economy not slowed.

Current worries that a sharp slowdown could strike in the near term are exaggerated, as the PRC has substantial policy buffers to respond to adverse shocks. Unlikely as such a scenario is even in the medium term, it is nevertheless useful to look at how it might affect Asia and the rest of the world. A sharp growth slowdown could materialize after one of the following events or, more likely, a combination of them: an unwinding of the credit boom, the bursting of asset market bubbles in real estate or financial markets, a sharp and sustained drop in investment, and worsening financial fragilities snowballing into a full-blown financial crisis.

Records of historical events from around the world show disorderly slowdowns from credit booms going bust, housing downturns, and financial crises slashing investment by about 10 percentage points as imbalances unwind (Table 1.2.1). Private and public consumption growth tends to decelerate as well, private by about 2 percentage points and public by 1 point. The typical decline in GDP growth during such disorderly slowdowns is by about 2–3 percentage points. However, because investment is a much larger share of GDP in the PRC than in most other economies, a decline in investment and consumption growth similar in size to past episodes in other economies would have larger effects in the PRC, taking about 4.5 percentage points off growth. The sheer size of the PRC and its contribution to global growth

1.2.2 Effects of the PRC growth moderation

- Commodity prices
- Trade and policies
- Total effect

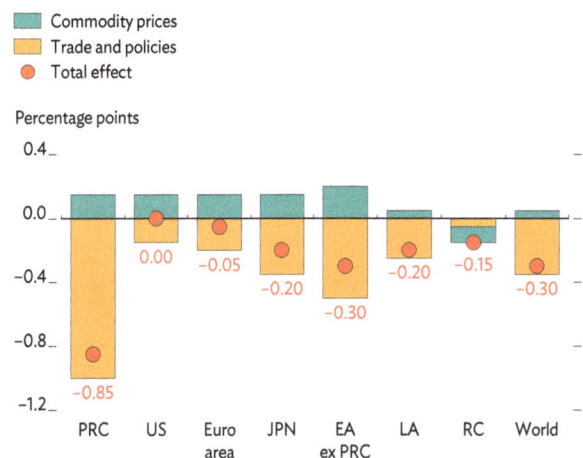

EA = emerging Asia (India, Indonesia, the Republic of Korea, Malaysia, the Philippines, Singapore, Thailand, Taipei,China, and Hong Kong, China), JPN = Japan, LA = Latin America (Brazil, Chile, Colombia, Mexico, and Peru), PRC = People's Republic of China, RC = remaining countries (Argentina, Australia, Bulgaria, Canada, the Czech Republic, Denmark, Estonia, Israel, New Zealand, Norway, the Russian Federation, South Africa, Sweden, Switzerland, Turkey, the United Kingdom, and Venezuela), US = United States.

Note: The effect is shown as deviation of GDP growth from the "no slowdown" scenario in the first 2 years.

Source: Abiad et al. 2016.

Click here for figure data

1.2.1 Magnitude of growth deceleration during disorderly slowdowns (percentage points)

	Real GDP	Government consumption	Investment	Private consumption	Imports	Exports
Credit boom to bust	–3.4	–1.0	–11.7	–2.8	–7.9	–3.1
Banking crisis	–2.0	–1.0	–8.0	–2.0	–6.3	–1.5
Housing downturn	–2.1	–0.2	–7.8	–2.2	–6.4	–3.0

Note: The growth deceleration is in the first 2 years after the event, relative to growth in the previous 5 years.
Source: Abiad et al. 2016.

suggest a disorderly slowdown would, combined with the current fragile recovery in the advanced economies, cause a substantial tightening of global financial conditions.

A sharp PRC slowdown would have significant adverse effects in all regions and on global growth (Figure 1.2.3). The sharper the slowdown in PRC demand, the larger the effects on trade and commodity prices, with oil prices falling by 10%–25% relative to the baseline. These two forces—the PRC slowdown and the resulting lower commodity prices—would tend to offset each other in both the US and Europe. But the additional negative shock from tightening global financial conditions would slow growth in these two regions by 0.60–0.65 percentage points relative to the baseline. The effects on Asia would be larger, with Japan's growth dropping by 1.50 percentage points and emerging Asia's by 1.80 percentage points. On the whole, global growth would be 1.75 percentage points lower.

Effects of structural change in the PRC

Attention has been duly paid to potential spillover into other economies from PRC growth moderation, but the cross-border implications of PRC structural transformation are often overlooked. As a result of its shift from investment-led growth to consumption-led growth, the PRC may import more consumption goods such as cosmetics, for example, and fewer investment goods such as machinery. Moreover, the PRC role in global value chains is changing. Rising wages have shifted some activities to lower-cost economies, and technological upgrades have and will move the PRC into activities that add more value. This transformation affects the types of intermediate goods imported into the PRC for further processing. And, as the PRC shifts growth away from exports to domestic demand, its role as an importer and assembler will decline and, with it, its imports of parts and components.

The rapid integration of the PRC into global value chains (GVCs) linking it to other East and Southeast Asian economies has bolstered its export success. The economy has positioned itself at the downstream end of the value chain, importing intermediate goods to assemble final products specifically for export to the US and elsewhere. Traditionally,

1.2.3 Effects of a sharp PRC slowdown

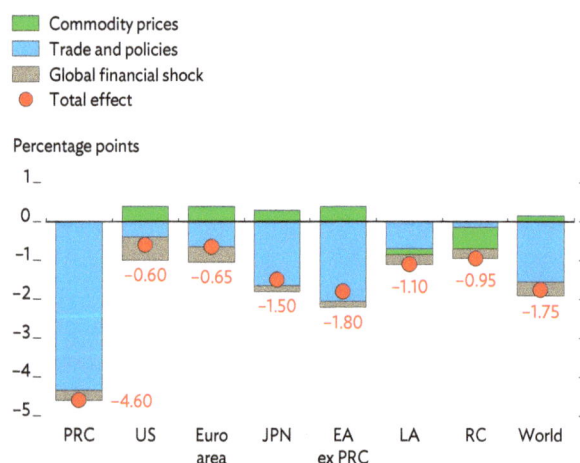

EA = emerging Asia (India, Indonesia, the Republic of Korea, Malaysia, the Philippines, Singapore, Thailand, Taipei,China, and Hong Kong, China), JPN = Japan, LA = Latin America (Brazil, Chile, Colombia, Mexico, and Peru), PRC = People's Republic of China, RC = remaining countries (Argentina, Australia, Bulgaria, Canada, the Czech Republic, Denmark, Estonia, Israel, New Zealand, Norway, South Africa, the Russian Federation, Sweden, Switzerland, Turkey, the United Kingdom, and Venezuela), US = United States.
Note: The effect is shown as deviation of GDP growth from the baseline in the first 2 years.
Source: Abiad et al. 2016.
Click here for figure data

economies that are technologically more advanced, such as Japan and the Republic of Korea, design the final goods and produce the more exacting parts and components that less advanced economies like the PRC then assemble into final goods for export. But the role of the PRC in GVCs is changing, as its growing technological capacity increasingly enables it to produce more parts and components itself, reducing its dependence on imports from neighboring countries.

At the same time, the PRC is rebalancing from investment toward consumption. The contributions of consumption, investment, government spending, and net exports to economic growth are considered here toward determining if the contribution of investment has been declining while the contributions of other components such as consumption have been rising. Figure 1.2.4 presents the contributions of consumption, investment, and net exports to GDP growth. Investment made the biggest contribution in most years from 2001, until it peaked at 86% in 2009. The contribution of total consumption, both public and private, has been rising since a dip in 2006 and has overtaken investment to contribute more than half of GDP growth. This supports the notion of a structural transformation in the PRC from an economy led by investment to one led by consumption.

Structural change has altered the position of the PRC in GVCs, as quantified by its GVC participation rate. This measure has two parts: the backward participation rate, which gauges the extent of foreign value added in a particular economy's exports, and the forward participation rate, which measures how much of the economy's domestic value added is included in the exports of other economies. As shown in Table 1.2.2, the share of foreign value added in PRC exports was 33.3% in 1995, increasing to 37.4% in 2005, but then falling back to 32.1% in 2011 as the share of imported intermediate goods in PRC exports declined. Meanwhile, PRC value added embodied in foreign exports has steadily risen from 9.5% in 1995 to 15.6% in 2011 as the PRC increasingly supplied intermediate products.

Structural transformation is reflected in the types of goods the PRC imports. Figure 1.2.5 plots the share of consumption goods versus parts and components in total imports of the PRC from 1995 to 2014. The share of parts and components in total imports shows an inverted U pattern with its peak at 39% in 2006 before falling off to 29% in 2014. This pattern is consistent with the timing of the rise and fall of GVC backward linkages detailed in Table 1.2.2. In contrast, the share of consumption goods in imports has stayed relatively flat, though there has been a slight uptick from its 3.2% trough in 2004 to 4.9% in 2014.

Spillover from structural transformation in the PRC into particular economies depends on whether they are exporters

1.2.4 Contributions to GDP growth in the People's Republic of China

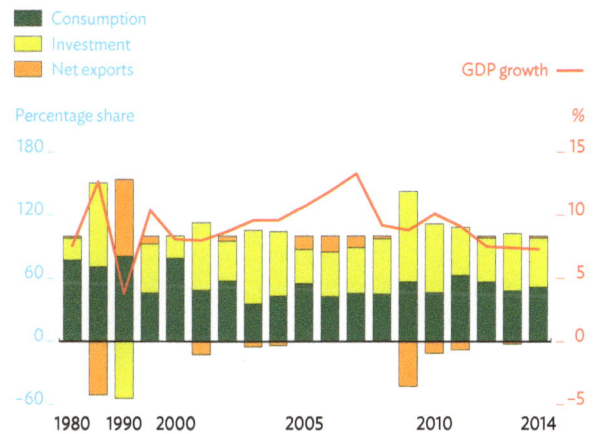

Notes: The contribution to GDP growth is based on real values. The data are collected from the National Bureau of Statistics' annual statistical yearbook for 2015, Tables 3–19. The real GDP growth rate in 2014 is collected from the *World Economic Outlook* database, October 2015.
Source: Lee, Park, and Shin, forthcoming.
Click here for figure data

1.2.2 PRC trade in value added in all industries

Year	Backward linkages (%)	Forward linkages (%)
1995	33.3	9.5
2000	37.2	10.8
2005	37.4	13.3
2011	32.1	15.6

PRC = People's Republic of China.
Note: Backward linkages are foreign value added as a percentage of PRC total exports. Forward linkages are the share of PRC domestic value added embodied in the exports of other economies.
Source: Trade in Value Added Database of the Organisation for Economic Co-operation and Development and the World Trade Organization.

1.2.5 Share of consumption goods versus parts and components in PRC imports

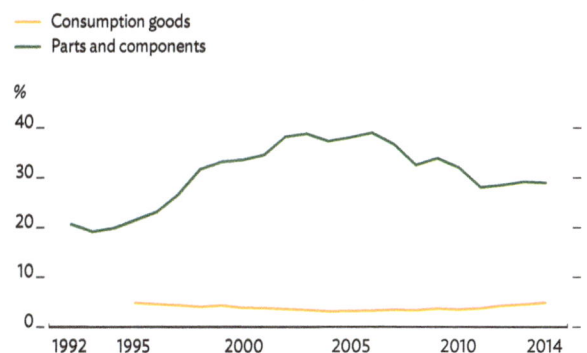

PRC = People's Republic of China.
Note: Data source is UN Comtrade database. Consumption goods refer to broad economic categories 112, 122, 522, 61, 62, and 63. The definition of parts and components is based on Athukorala (2010), with some adjustments to accommodate reporting changes in later years.
Source: Lee, Park, and Shin, forthcoming.
Click here for figure data

of consumer goods, part of the same production chain, or competitors, either current or potential. At this stage, the shift to a larger contribution to growth from consumption has not translated into a marked increase in the import of consumption goods. While domestic producers can still largely meet demand from PRC consumers, there may be opportunities for lower-cost producers to make inroads into the PRC, likely initially in the market for lower-end goods where there is more price sensitivity.

The share of parts and components in PRC imports began decline in 2006. Figure 1.2.6 plots the change in import share against the change in parts and components share from 2006 to 2014 for eight major economies in East and Southeast Asia. Each selected economy provided more than 1% of PRC imports in 2014. Viet Nam appears to be gaining market share as a GVC partner. This may be related to PRC firms moving offshore in line with the structural changes at home, as the execution of lower-skill production activities is increasingly moving to sites with lower labor costs. At the other end of the scale, advanced economies like the Republic of Korea and Hong Kong, China have seen their market shares eroded. This is consistent with the PRC shifting toward the high end of the GVC and its burgeoning role as a producer of parts and components.

A major catalyst of structural change in the PRC is a labor force that is shrinking and becoming more costly. The loss of the economy's competitive advantage in labor-intensive industries presents opportunities for economies that compete with the PRC primarily in third markets (Figure 1.2.7). These competitors can increase market share as the PRC withdraws. Bangladesh is already gaining market share as the PRC withdraws from low-end garment manufacturing, for example, and is now the world's second-largest garment exporter, after the PRC.

Concluding observations on PRC effects

Structural adjustment in the PRC has a short-term impact on the region that is negative. Simulations show that growth moderation in the PRC is expected to shave 0.3 percentage points from developing Asia's growth. Structural change will magnify the short-term impacts that growth moderation has on the exports of neighboring economies. However, in the medium term, structural transformation in the PRC may open up new export opportunities for economies in Asia and around the world. The economies that are better at catering to growing consumption and domestic demand in the PRC will enjoy more success in exporting to that market.

1.2.6 Change in parts and components share versus change in import share, 2006–2014

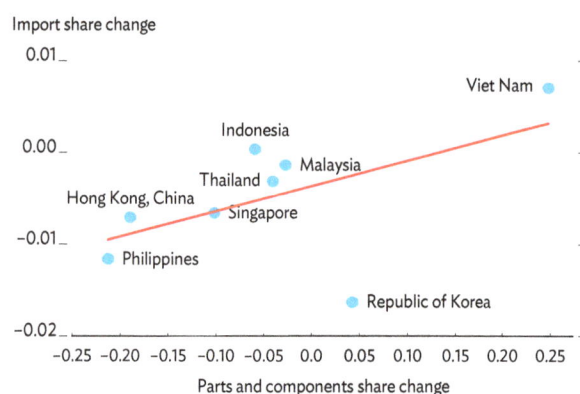

Note: The figure includes a sample of economies in developing Asia that accounted for at least 1% of PRC imports in 2014. The horizontal axis is the change in the share of parts and components in an economy's exports to the PRC from 2006 to 2014. The vertical axis is the change in the economy's share of total imports to the PRC in the same period.
Source: Lee, Park, and Shin, forthcoming.
Click here for figure data

1.2.7 Developing Asia index of competition with the PRC, 2014

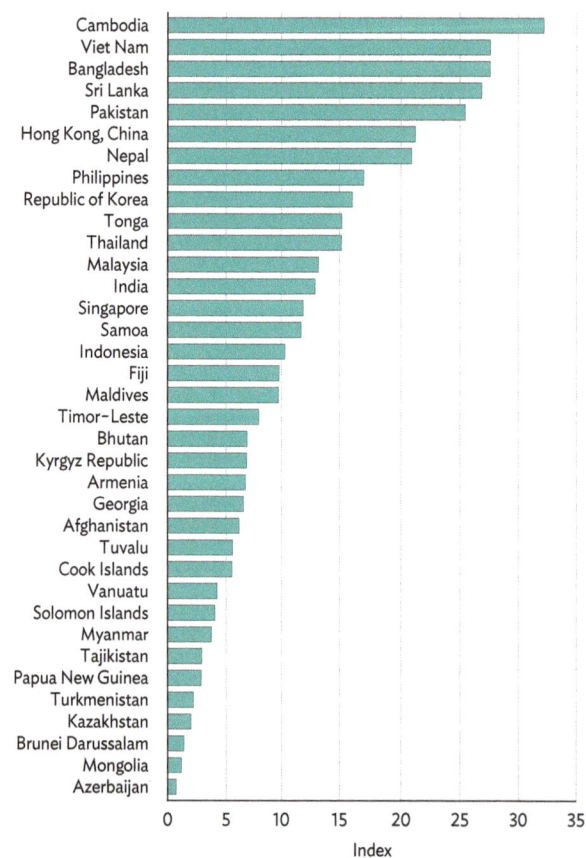

PRC = People's Republic of China.
Note: The index of competition measures the importance of the PRC in an economy's export markets, weighted by product, with 100 indicating total dominance and 0 indicating complete absence. Where the latest available data are not 2014, they are as follows: Tajikistan and Turkmenistan 2000, Tuvalu 2005, Myanmar 2010, Cook Islands and Vanuatu 2011, Bhutan and Papua New Guinea 2012, Cambodia, the Kyrgyz Republic, and Timor-Leste 2013.
Source: Abiad et al. 2016.
Click here for figure data

Emergent producer price deflation

Deflation has emerged as a relatively new macroeconomic risk in developing Asia. Once confined in Asia to Japan, deflation has spread to other East and Southeast Asian economies, as well as to India. The recent decline in global oil prices and slower economic growth have subdued inflationary pressures to the point that producer prices began to fall in some economies. As of February 2016, the PRC had experienced 48 consecutive months of producer price deflation. Fears are growing that deflation in PRC will be transmitted to its neighbors through lower prices for PRC exports. Already in 2015, producer price deflation was evident in the region, even though consumer price inflation remained largely positive (Table 1.3.1). Further, external demand for the region's products remains subdued, exerting further downward pressure on prices. All this raises the possibility that additional deflation could be in the pipeline.

1.3.1 CPI and PPI inflation rates, selected Asian economies

Economy	CPI inflation (%)		PPI inflation (%)	
	2015	December 2015	2015	December 2015
People's Republic of China	1.4	1.6	–5.2	–5.9
Hong Kong, China	3.0	2.5	–2.7	–3.2
India	5.0	5.6	–2.7	–0.7
Indonesia	6.4	3.4	5.8	5.2
Republic of Korea	0.7	1.3	–4.0	–4.0
Malaysia	2.1	2.7	–4.8	–1.6
Philippines	1.4	1.5	–6.7	–7.2
Singapore	–0.5	–0.6	–9.1	–7.7
Thailand	–0.9	–0.9	–4.1	–2.7
Viet Nam	0.6	0.6	–0.6	–1.3

CPI = consumer price index, PPI = producer price index.

Notes: The latest PPI inflation rate for Hong Kong, China is the fourth quarter of 2015, instead of December, for lack of published monthly data. For India, PPI refers to the wholesale price index.

Sources: CEIC Data Company (accessed 15 March 2016); *Asian Development Outlook* database.

Is deflation bad? Theory and evidence

The traditional view is that deflation is a danger to be avoided at all costs (e.g., Fisher 1933, Friedman and Schwartz 1963). Deflation makes domestic currency debts that are not indexed to prices, which in practice means most domestic currency debts, more difficult to service and repay. These difficulties create in turn balance sheet problems and losses for creditors, especially banks and other institutional investors. As debtors tighten their belts to avoid costly default, firms curtail investment projects, and households limit their spending. The expectation of falling prices tempts even financially healthy firms and households to delay investment and consumption in anticipation of still lower prices in the future. For all these reasons, deflation threatens to persist and gather momentum from the moment it emerges.

However, prices can decline not just because of negative demand shocks but also because of positive supply shocks. Indeed, benign positive supply shock was the dominant explanation for producer price deflation in the PRC for as long as that economy was growing strongly.

Empirical estimates in Borio et al. (2015) support the benign view. Looking at the association between the consumer price index (CPI) and the rate of GDP growth per capita since 1870 in a wide range of economies, the study found few significant differences in the rate of GDP growth between periods of inflation and deflation, the notable exception being the decade of the Great Depression starting in 1929, when both output and prices collapsed. The implication is that researchers have inappropriately generalized the experience of an exceptional period when deflation was extremely rapid and persistent to other circumstances where it is not applicable.

But the CPI may be less relevant to the decision making and behavior of producers than is the producer price index (PPI). By definition, the CPI measures price changes from the vantage of the buyer, while the PPI measures them from the vantage of the seller. This distinction may cause the two price indexes to behave differently. Seller and purchaser prices will differ because of government subsidies, sales and excise taxes, and distribution costs. Insofar as taxes, subsidies, and perhaps also distribution costs are slow to change, consumer prices may exhibit less volatility and more persistence than producer prices. Changes in international commodity prices also seem to affect producer prices and consumer prices differently, with a greater rate of pass-through to producers (Box 1.3.1).

If one is interested in the impact of deflation on production decisions, it makes sense to focus on producer prices. If one is interested in spending decisions, it makes sense to consider consumer prices and producer prices in combination, because, while consumer prices are the most relevant to the spending decisions of households, both are relevant to the spending decisions of firms. It is therefore worthwhile to revisit the association between deflation and economic growth using producer prices rather than consumer prices to see if the benign supply-shock view still holds.

1.3.1 Higher commodity price pass-through for producer prices

It is widely believed that the recent weakness in global oil and food prices helped contain inflationary pressures in Asian countries. Yet the effect of global commodity prices may differ for domestic producer prices, which are more relevant for producers, and consumer prices, which are more relevant for consumers. For both kinds of prices, the effect is determined by the extent of pass-through, or what portion of a rise or fall in global prices is eventually reflected in domestic prices.

Jongwanich, Wongcharoen, and Park (forthcoming) empirically analyzed the relationship between global oil and food prices and domestic producer and consumer prices in a sample of developing economies in Asia. The analysis is based on quarterly data, and it yields some interesting insights into the pass-through of global oil and food prices in the region.

The impact of global oil price changes on domestic prices is diluted along the distribution chain. The pass-through tends to be smaller for consumer prices than for producer prices. For example, in the PRC, the cumulative pass-through

of a 1% drop in global oil prices after 4 quarters reached 14 basis points for producer prices but only 3 basis points for consumer prices (box figure).

Part of the difference in the reaction between consumer and producer prices could arise from the different weight each index places on oil-derived products. The share of fuel and related petroleum products is generally more than 50% in producer prices but only around 30% in consumer prices. More generally, the share of tradable products is noticeably higher in producer prices. The gap between these two price indexes in each economy depends on the ability of firms to pass higher costs on to consumers. For example, private producers facing intense market competition may decide to cut their profit margins rather than try to charge consumers higher prices in the short term. Government policy measures such as fuel subsidies designed to help consumer pocketbooks may reduce or delay the pass-through of oil price changes to consumer price inflation, thereby widening the gap between producer and consumer prices.

Oil and food price pass-through

■ Producer price index
■ Consumer price index

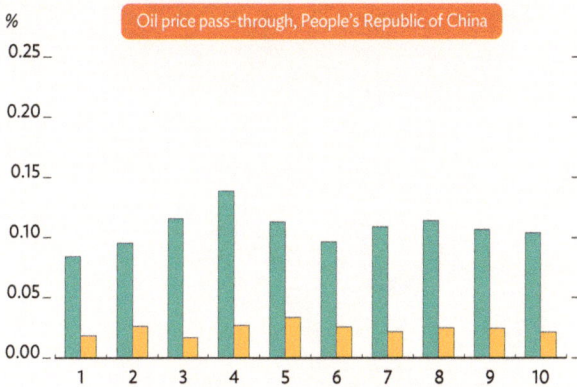

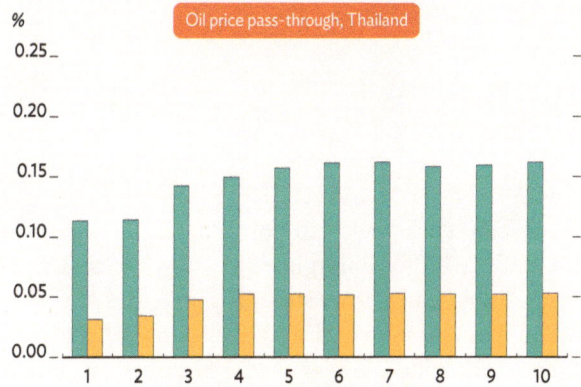

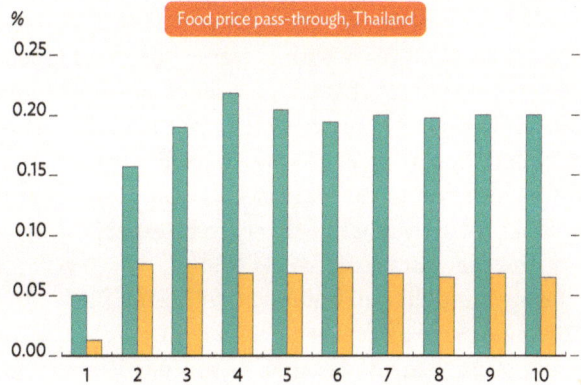

Note: The horizontal axes refer to quarterly periods.

Source: Jongwanich, Wongcharoen, and Park, forthcoming.

Click here for figure data

continued on the next page

1.3.1 *Continued*

The pass-through of oil prices to producer prices tends to be higher in oil-exporting economies than in oil importers. In Malaysia, an oil exporter, the pass-through of a 1% change in global oil prices to producers gradually increases from 12 basis points in the first quarter to reach a cumulative total of 21 basis points in the fourth quarter. For oil-importing economies, the cumulative annual pass-through of oil prices to producer prices is somewhat smaller. Singapore is an exceptional case in which the pass-through to producer prices is high because of the high intensity of oil use in total energy consumption, and possibly because Singapore re-exports a lot of refined oil products. Although Indonesia, the PRC, and Thailand import less than the Republic of Korea or Hong Kong, China, their pass-through of world oil prices to producer prices tends to be higher. This could reflect superior energy efficiency in the Republic of Korea, where the ratio of total energy consumption to GDP in 2011 was 10.7%, and in Hong Kong, China, where the ratio was 5.7%.

As in the case of world oil prices, the impact of world food price changes on domestic prices is diluted along the distribution chain. The pass-through tends to be lower for consumer prices than for producer prices. Significantly, the gap between the two price indexes tends to be higher for food prices than for oil prices. That is, the relatively larger impact of global prices on domestic producer prices is more pronounced for food than for oil. For example, in Thailand, the cumulative pass-through in 4 quarters of a 1% increase in global food prices is 21 basis points for producer prices but only 7 basis points for consumer prices. Many Asian governments still impose price controls and provide subsidies for households, which constrain the ability of producers to pass costs on to consumers.

In sum, the analysis indicates that the pass-through of global oil and food prices is higher for producer prices than for consumer prices. This supports the notion that the two prices behave differently and are determined by different factors. In addition, the higher pass-through for producer prices in developing Asia raises the possibility that the recent decline in global oil and food prices has a bigger effect on producer prices than on consumer prices, which is consistent with the higher incidence of producer price deflation than consumer price deflation currently besetting the region.

Reference
Jongwanich, J., P. Wongcharoen, and D. Park. Forthcoming. *Determinants of Consumer Price Inflation versus Producer Price Inflation in Asia*. Asian Development Bank.

Empirical findings on deflation

Eichengreen, Park, and Shin (forthcoming) updates the analysis of Borio et al. (2015) by enlarging the dataset with data on producer price indexes. Table 1.3.2 shows summary statistics for both CPI and PPI inflation and deflation in different eras and under different monetary regimes. Following Borio et al., the more recent study excludes observations from the war years 1914–1918 and 1939–1945 and, in the case of Spain, observations from the civil war years 1936–1939. It also excludes observations from years with extreme inflation higher than 100%.

The correlation between the change in the PPI and the CPI, at 0.88, is relatively high. There are well more than twice as many years of PPI as CPI deflation after World War II, while the number of years of PPI and CPI inflation in earlier periods is much more similar. This suggests that looking solely at CPI is likely to be especially problematic when analyzing the years since World War II.

Persistent deflation is defined, following Borio et al., as a period following a price peak when prices fail to recover to the peak for at least 5 years. More years of deflation of this persistent type were identified using the PPI rather than the CPI. In the postwar period, there are only 5 instances of persistent CPI deflation in the 38 economies in the sample but 29 instances of PPI deflation. Again, this encourages looking at both the PPI and the CPI, especially in the period following World War II.

1.3.2 Overview of periods of consumer and producer price index deflation

			Full sample (1870–2014)	Postwar (1947–2014)
All deflation	Consumer	Number of inflation years	2,940	2,332
		Number of deflation years	658	145
	Producer	Number of inflation years	2,443	1,914
		Number of deflation years	921	389
Persistent deflation	Consumer	Number of episodes	76	5
	Producer	Number of episodes	92	29
Correlation		All	0.88	0.92

Note: The 38 economies in the sample are Argentina, Australia, Austria, Belgium, Brazil, Canada, Chile, the People's Republic of China, Colombia, Denmark, Finland, France, Germany, Greece, Ireland, Italy, Japan, the Republic of Korea, Malaysia, Mexico, the Netherlands, New Zealand, Norway, Peru, the Philippines, Portugal, Singapore, South Africa, Spain, Sweden, Switzerland, Thailand, Turkey, the United Kingdom, the United States, Uruguay, Venezuela, and Hong Kong, China. The full sample excludes observations from the war years 1914–1918 and 1939–1945 and, in the case of Spain, observations from the civil war in 1936–1939. Also excluded are observations from years with inflation higher than 100%. Persistent deflation is defined as a period following a price peak when prices fail to recover to the peak for at least 5 years. The duration of persistent deflation is calculated from peak to trough. Eichengreen, Park, and Shin (forthcoming) has figures for other periods.

Source: Eichengreen, Park, and Shin (forthcoming) based on consumer and producer price indexes from Global Financial Database, International Historical Statistics 1750–2010 and International Financial Statistics, and per capita real GDP, from the Maddison Project and World Development Indicators.

Table 1.3.3 tabulates the GDP growth rate per capita in inflationary and deflationary years using both the CPI and the PPI. The inflationary years are divided into years of high and low inflation, greater or less than 10%, on the grounds that the disruptive effects of inflation are likely to be more pronounced when price increases are relatively rapid.

1.3.3 Consumer and producer price index deflation and per capita real GDP growth

		Average per capita real GDP growth		
		Full sample (1870–2014)	Great Depression (1930–1933)	Postwar (1947–2014)
Consumer price index	High inflation	2.31	−2.90	2.28
	Low inflation	2.74	2.46	2.83
	Deflation	1.17	−3.03	2.55
Producer price index	High inflation	2.42	3.47	2.28
	Low inflation	2.75	−1.82	2.84
	Deflation	1.40	−3.36	2.10

Note: The 38 economies in the sample are Argentina, Australia, Austria, Belgium, Brazil, Canada, Chile, the People's Republic of China, Colombia, Denmark, Finland, France, Germany, Greece, Ireland, Italy, Japan, the Republic of Korea, Malaysia, Mexico, the Netherlands, New Zealand, Norway, Peru, the Philippines, Portugal, Singapore, South Africa, Spain, Sweden, Switzerland, Thailand, Turkey, the United Kingdom, the United States, Uruguay, Venezuela, and Hong Kong, China. High inflation is higher than 10% and low inflation less than 10%. Persistent deflation is defined as a period following a price peak when prices fail to recover to the peak for at least 5 years. Eichengreen, Park, and Shin (forthcoming) has figures for other periods.

Source: Eichengreen, Park, and Shin (forthcoming) based on consumer and producer price indexes from Global Financial Database, International Historical Statistics 1750–2010 and International Financial Statistics, and per capita real GDP, from the Maddison Project and World Development Indicators.

1.3.4 Output growth and consumer and producer price index deflation: regression correlations, with equity prices

	Full sample (1870–2014)				Postwar (1947–2014)			
	(1)	(2)	(3)	(4)	(5)	(6)	(7)	(8)
Δ CPI	0.10***	0.10***			0.03	0.04		
	[0.024]	[0.023]			[0.029]	[0.028]		
Δ PPI			0.10***	0.10***			0.05**	0.06**
			[0.017]	[0.017]			[0.022]	[0.021]
Δ EP	0.01***	–0.00	0.01***	–0.01	0.00	–0.01	0.00	–0.01
	[0.004]	[0.006]	[0.004]	[0.006]	[0.003]	[0.006]	[0.003]	[0.006]
Δ EP^{def}		0.04***		0.04***		0.03**		0.03**
		[0.012]		[0.012]		[0.012]		[0.012]
Observations	2,311	2,311	2,217	2,217	1,645	1,645	1,592	1,592
R^2	0.044	0.053	0.069	0.078	0.005	0.013	0.017	0.025
Number of countries in sample	35	35	35	35	35	35	35	35

Note: The dependent variable is the log change of real GDP per capita. Δ CPI, Δ PPI, and Δ EP are, respectively, the log change in the consumer price index, the producer price index, and stock prices. Δ EP^{def} is the log change interacted with a dummy variable that is equal to one when the price index declines and zero otherwise. Country fixed effects allow differences across economies. Numbers in brackets are cluster-robust standard errors, and ** denotes significance at the 5% level and *** at the 1% level. Eichengreen, Park, and Shin (forthcoming) has results for other periods.

Source: Eichengreen, Park, and Shin (forthcoming) based on consumer and producer price indexes from Global Financial Database, International Historical Statistics 1750–2010 and International Financial Statistics, and per capita real GDP, from the Maddison Project and World Development Indicators. The stock price data are from the Global Financial Database, Bloomberg, and Schularick and Taylor (2012).

Growth is slower on average in years of high inflation than in years of low inflation. Over the full sample, growth is significantly slower in periods of deflation than in periods of either high or low inflation, whether inflation is measured using the PPI or the CPI.

Table 1.3.4 uses regression analysis to relate inflation and deflation to economic growth. Following Borio et al. (2015), panel regressions are estimated with country fixed effects to allow differences across economies. Changes in equity prices are included, as in Borio et al., to capture and control for the separate effects of asset price deflation. In the full sample, the coefficients on the change in both the CPI and the PPI are positive and highly significant, which is consistent with the idea that deflation is bad for economic growth. But for the CPI, all the explanatory power derives from the association of deflation with recession in the interwar period. This suggests that CPI deflation depressed growth only during the Great Depression. This is consistent with the findings of Borio et al.

The picture is different, however, for the PPI. Changes in the PPI are significantly related to growth, not just in the interwar period but also under the classical gold standard and since World War II. This result suggests that the harmful effect of deflation on growth was not confined to the Great Depression.

Restricting the sample to include only years with low inflation at less than 1% does not change the results materially. Why is producer price deflation potentially harmful? One possibility is that it compounds the debt burden on producers and thus discourages investment.

One of the most important decisions facing producers is investment. One can expect producer prices to affect producers' decision making and behavior, including those pertaining to investment. Han and Wei (forthcoming) explored the relationship between producer price deflation and investment. Figure 1.3.1 plots the quarterly changes in the PPI against changes in investment in the following quarter. In deflationary periods when the PPI fell, there is a clear positive relationship between changes in the PPI and changes in investment. That is, contraction in investment followed PPI deflation.

Han and Wei (forthcoming) examined whether PPI deflation causes investment contraction, using an autoregressive model (the change in investment being the dependent variable, and lagged changes in investment and the PPI the independent variables) with quarterly panel data from 1966 to 2014. PPI deflation was found to cause significant changes in investment. Among economies in which the PPI significantly affected investment, 71% experienced investment declines following PPI deflation. During inflationary periods, the impact of inflation on investment was much weaker. Only 42% of economies showing significant effects experienced investment expansion during PPI inflation. When considering persistence—defined as the PPI declining for at least 4 consecutive quarters—an additional 5% of countries were significantly affected. Persistent deflation was thus more damaging for investment.

Debts are an additional concern. Fisher (1933) pioneered the argument that debt and deflation were the major causes of economic depressions. Deflation raises the real value of debt, forcing debt liquidation that generates pessimism that feeds back into more deflation. The vicious spiral of deflation and debt liquidation may suppress investment, output, trade, and employment.

Introducing changes in the ratio of debt to GDP into the analysis, Han and Wei (forthcoming) found that investments were significantly affected by the joint effect of deflation and debt. The mix of higher debt and deflation reduced investment in 45% of the economies. The current wave of PPI deflation may depress or postpone investment, all the more so if debts also rise. Therefore, some grounds exist for concern over economies facing deflation and rising debt.

Concluding observations on deflation

The analysis suggests that policy makers in developing Asia should be aware of the potential harm to economic growth from deflation. Long-run historical data show deflation being negatively associated with economic growth. More in-depth regression analysis confirms the association between deflation and growth, which is stronger for producer price deflation than for consumer price deflation.

Changes in the CPI are more relevant to consumers, but changes in the PPI are more relevant to producers, so it is best to consider both when assessing the effect of deflation on growth. Interestingly, there are more episodes of persistent deflation, including since the middle of the 20th century, when viewed using the PPI rather than the CPI.

1.3.1 Relationship between changes in the PPI and changes in investment

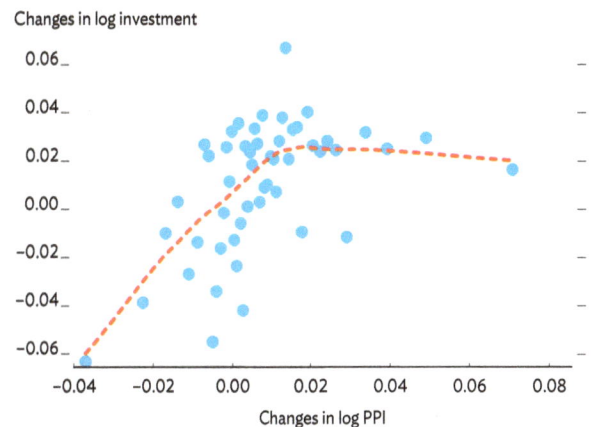

PPI = producer price index.

Notes: For economies without a PPI, the wholesale price index is used. The country quarter data is grouped into 50 groups of equal size along the x-axis. For each group, the group mean of changes of log PPI and changes of log investment are used to do the plotting.

Source: Han and Wei, forthcoming.

Click here for figure data

Further, producer prices tend to be more volatile than consumer prices. The present analysis shows that changes in the PPI are significantly and inversely related to growth, in both the full sample period 1870–2014 and the postwar period 1947–2014. Controlling for asset price booms and busts does not alter the conclusions about the potential dangers of deflation.

Finally, it is important to acknowledge that high inflation as well as deflation can have negative impact on economic growth, as this result comes through clearly in the data. In fact, inflation was the much larger concern in developing Asia until the recent emergence of deflation, mostly producer price deflation, in some regional economies. The evidence, while far from definitive, suggests that it would be prudent for the region's monetary authorities to keep an eye on deflation as well as inflation, and on producer prices as well as consumer prices. Empirical analysis of the deflation–growth nexus is a relatively new line of inquiry. The preliminary nature of the analysis calls for caution in interpreting the findings, but the findings suggest fertile ground for further research.

References

Abiad, A., M. Lee, M. Pundit, and A. Ramayandi. 2016. Moderating Growth and Structural Change in the People's Republic of China: Implications for Developing Asia and Beyond. *ADB Briefs* No. 53. Asian Development Bank.

Athukorala, P. 2010. Production Networks and Trade Patterns in East Asia: Regionalization or Globalization? *ADB Economics Working Paper Series* No. 56. Asian Development Bank.

Borio, C., M. Erdem, A. Filardo, and B. Hofmann. 2015. The Cost of Deflations: A Historical Perspective. *BIS Quarterly Review*. March.

Eichengreen, B., D. Park, and K. Shin. Forthcoming. *Deflation in Asia: Can the Dangers Be Dismissed?* Asian Development Bank.

Fisher, I. 1933. The Debt–Deflation Theory of Great Depressions. *Econometrica* 1(4).

Friedman, M. and A. Schwartz. 1963. *A Monetary History of the United States, 1867–1960*. Princeton University Press for the National Bureau of Economic Research.

Han, X. and S-J. Wei. Forthcoming. *PPI Deflation: How Prevalent and Damaging for Investment?* Asian Development Bank.

Jongwanich, J., P. Wongcharoen, and D. Park. Forthcoming. *Determinants of Consumer Price Inflation versus Producer Price Inflation in Asia*. Asian Development Bank.

Lee, H-H., D. Park, and K. Shin. Forthcoming. *Effects of the People's Republic of China's Structural Change on the Exports of East and Southeast Asian Economies*. Asian Development Bank.

Schularick, M. and A. Taylor. 2012. Credit Booms Gone Bust: Monetary Policy, Leverage Cycles and Financial Crises, 1870–2008. *American Economic Review* 102(2).

Annex: A challenging and uncertain global outlook

Growth in the major industrial economies of the United States (US), the euro area, and Japan is not likely to pick up this year. These economies are forecast to expand in aggregate by 1.8% in 2016, the same rate as in 2015, before inching up to 1.9% in 2017. Despite continued private sector expansion in the US, feeble global prospects point to US growth mildly slowing this year. While recovery in the euro area is gradually gaining ground, domestic and external risks abound and therefore argue for a growth forecast unchanged from last year. Japanese growth will improve slightly, helped by a pickup in private consumption this year in anticipation of a value-added tax (VAT) increase next year. Further declines in food and fuel prices in 2016 and a mild rebound in 2017 will keep inflationary pressures low and challenge central bankers in the euro area and Japan to avoid deflation (Table A1.1).

A1.1 Baseline assumptions on the international economy

	2014	2015	2016	2017
			ADO 2016	
	Actual	Estimate	Projection	
GDP growth (%)				
Major industrial economies[a]	1.5	1.8	1.8	1.9
United States	2.4	2.4	2.3	2.5
Euro area	0.9	1.6	1.5	1.6
Japan	0.0	0.5	0.6	0.5
Prices and inflation				
Brent crude spot prices (average, $ per barrel)	98.9	52.3	38.0	45.0
Food index (2010 = 100, % change)	–7.2	–15.4	–1.0	1.0
Consumer price index inflation (major industrial economies' average, %)	1.3	0.2	1.1	2.0
Interest rates				
United States federal funds rate (average, %)	0.1	0.1	0.6	1.4
European Central Bank refinancing rate (average, %)	0.2	0.1	0.0	0.0
Bank of Japan overnight call rate (average, %)	0.1	0.1	0.0	0.0
$ Libor[b] (%)	0.2	0.2	0.6	1.4

ADO = Asian Development Outlook, GDP = gross domestic product.

[a] Average growth rates are weighted by gross national income, Atlas method.

[b] Average London interbank offered rate quotations on 1-month loans.

Sources: US Department of Commerce, Bureau of Economic Analysis, http://www.bea.gov; Eurostat, http://ec.europa.eu/eurostat; Economic and Social Research Institute of Japan, http://www.esri.cao.go.jp; Consensus Forecasts; Bloomberg; CEIC Data Company; Haver Analytics; and the World Bank, Global Commodity Markets, http://www.worldbank.org; ADB estimates.

Recent developments in the major industrial economies

United States

The US economy expanded by 2.4% in 2015. Private consumption remains the main source of growth, contributing 2.1 percentage points to the annual gross domestic product (GDP) growth rate. Private investment provided 0.8 points to growth last year, slightly less than its contribution of 0.9 points in 2014. The government sector contributed 0.1 points, after having acted as a drag since 2011. The stronger US dollar again hurt export momentum, causing net foreign trade to subtract 0.6 percentage points from growth.

US economic activity in 2015 had a weak start, with growth at a seasonally adjusted annualized rate (saar) of 0.6% in the first quarter due to the harsh winter and a West Coast ports dispute. While GDP growth recovered strongly to 3.9% in the second quarter, growth in the remainder of the year was tepid, with all demand components soft in the fourth quarter (Figure A1.1).

After revival in the second quarter, growth in private consumption slowed for the rest of 2015 from a saar of 3.6% in the second quarter to 3.0% in the third and 2.0% in the fourth. The slowdown in the final quarter disappointed in light of an improvement in wages, albeit slight, and a further decline in gasoline prices. Retail sales remained flat in the second half of the year, and consumer confidence slipped below the pre-recession level from February 2015 onward, despite rising toward the end of the year (Figure A1.2). These trends suggest that private consumption, while not providing strong support for growth, will continue to be an important driver and likely remain relatively stable.

Investment increased in the first half of 2015 but receded in the second, constrained by inventory accumulation and slowing fixed investment outside of housing. The purchasing managers' index declined during the second half of the year to end at 54.9, which was still high enough to suggest further expansion in manufacturing. The industrial production index remained above the pre-crisis level throughout 2015 despite ending somewhat lower at 101.4 in December (2007 = 100). Trends in manufacturing and industrial production indicated continuing but slow gains in investment.

The labor market strengthened steadily during 2015. The unemployment rate improved rapidly, falling from 5.7% in January 2015 to 5.0% in December and 4.9% at the beginning of 2016. The average duration of unemployment also shortened, from 32 weeks at the beginning of the year to 28 weeks by the end of the year, though it edged up to 29 weeks at the beginning of 2016 (Figure A1.3). However, the improved employment situation did not bring much increase in average earnings, as weekly earnings

A1.1 Demand-side contributions to growth, United States

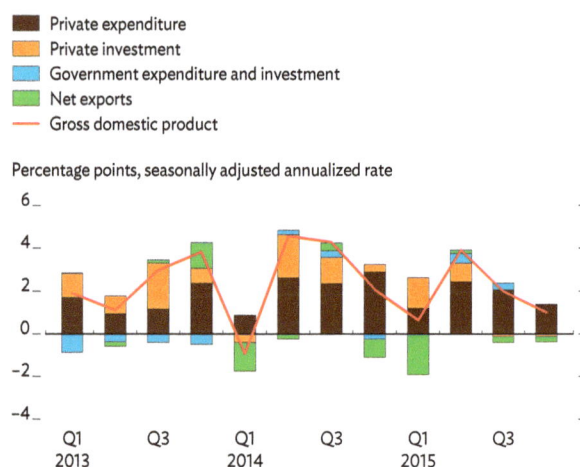

- Private expenditure
- Private investment
- Government expenditure and investment
- Net exports
- Gross domestic product

Percentage points, seasonally adjusted annualized rate

Q = quarter.
Sources: US Department of Commerce. Bureau of Economic Analysis. http://www.bea.gov; Haver Analytics (both accessed 9 March 2016).
Click here for figure data

A1.2 Business activity and consumer confidence indicators, United States

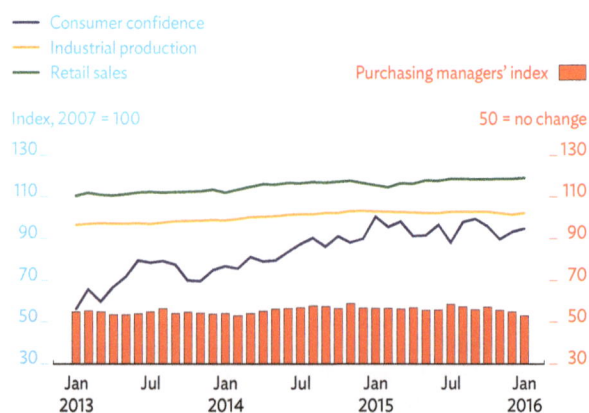

- Consumer confidence
- Industrial production
- Retail sales
- Purchasing managers' index

Index, 2007 = 100   50 = no change

Note: For the purchasing managers' index, a reading below 50 signals deterioration of activity, above 50 improvement. The index is compiled by the Institute for Supply Management.
Source: Haver Analytics (accessed 9 March 2016).
Click here for figure data

increased by only 2.4% annually. This mixed picture was broadly consistent with the slow improvement observed in manufacturing, which remained sluggish but continued to add jobs.

Inflation was muted, as both headline and core inflation were contained by US dollar appreciation and low energy prices. The fall in energy prices substantially reduced headline inflation early in 2015 and kept it low for almost the entire year (Figure A1.4). Headline inflation started to rise only toward the end of the year as the decline in energy prices slowed. Core inflation rose slowly but steadily throughout the year, consistent with a steady rise in consumption. The same trend continued through the beginning of 2016, when the combination of steady core inflation and slower declines in the energy prices raised headline inflation to an annual rate of 1.4%.

In December 2015, the Federal Reserve Board raised the target range of the federal funds rate for the first time since the beginning of the global financial crisis. The rate remained constant in January 2016, however, to keep monetary policy accommodative, with inflation projected to stay low in the near term and economic activity progressing only moderately. The board is monitoring global economic and financial developments closely to inform its future monetary policy. Conditions suggest that, unless US economic performance shows indisputable improvement, the policy rate is likely to remain unchanged for at least the first half of 2016. The policy rate is projected to average 0.6% in 2016 before rising to about 1.8% by the end of 2017. Thus, liquidity should remain loose in 2016.

The decision to maintain the policy rate and the resulting change in market expectations seem to have eased some of the pressure for the US dollar to appreciate. However, the strong dollar is still expected to drag on GDP growth by curbing net external demand throughout the year. The private sector is expected to continue expanding but not strongly enough to substantially raise the economy's growth rate. The US economy is therefore projected to grow moderately, by 2.3% in 2016 and 2.5% in 2017.

Euro area

Recovery in the euro area, which began in 2014, failed to gain momentum as growth leveled off toward the end of 2015. Business and consumer confidence dropped to a 1 year low even as deflation reappeared, signaling a slow start to 2016. Labor markets have improved, but demand is insufficient to generate inflation. The region faces a number of downside risks, both domestic and external, that could derail recovery, thus introducing an element of caution to the growth outlook.

GDP in the fourth quarter of 2015 grew by a saar of 1.3%, bringing annual growth for the year to 1.6%, the highest since 2011 (Figure A1.5).

A1.3 Unemployment rate and average duration, United States

— Unemployment, seasonally adjusted

Average duration — of unemployment

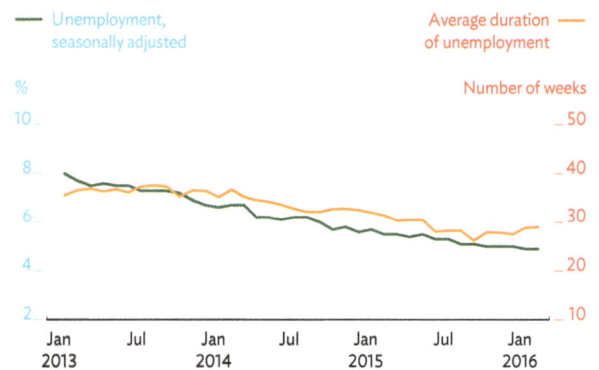

Source: Haver Analytics (accessed 9 March 2016).
Click here for figure data

A1.4 Inflation, United States

— Headline
— Core

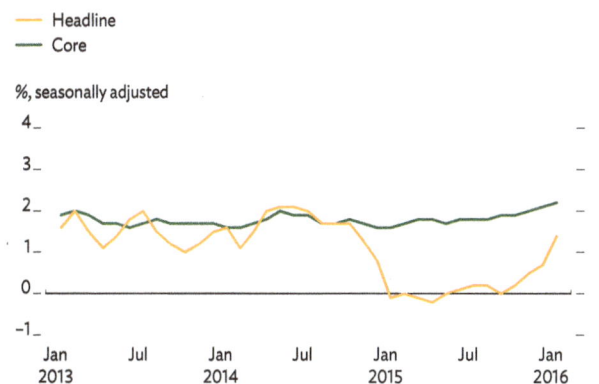

Source: Haver Analytics (accessed 9 March 2016).
Click here for figure data

Quarter over quarter, growth in the fourth quarter remained at 1.1% in Germany, and France recorded a slight rise by 0.1%, while economic activity slowed by 0.4% in Italy and 0.1% in Spain.

An examination of components showed that in the last quarter of 2015 fixed investment growth contributed a relatively strong 1.1 percentage points, while private consumption added only 0.5 points. Government consumption also contributed 0.5 points, an improvement over the previous quarter that probably reflected aid to immigrants. While domestic demand supported growth, net exports subtracted 1.2 percentage points from growth, as imports outpaced exports. The negative contribution from the external sector during 2 consecutive quarters suggests that the boost from a weaker euro may be fading.

Although investment rose, industry remained weak as the production index declined by 0.2% in the last quarter of 2015, after a minimal rise of 0.1% in the third (Figure A1.6). The composite purchasing managers' index exceeded 50, showing expanded activity, but the decline from 54.3 in December to 53.6 in January, and to a 13-month low of 53.0 in February, did not signal a strong recovery at the start of 2016. The European Commission's economic sentiment indicator also declined during the first 2 months of 2016.

Economic sentiment declined partly because of lower consumer confidence, which fell in February to its lowest since December 2014. It appears that consumption, the main driver of growth in 2015, lost steam toward the end of the year, as reflected in average growth of only 0.1% in retail sales in the last quarter of 2015. However, a pickup to 0.4% in January provided some cause for optimism. Going forward, growth in private consumption may benefit somewhat from low oil prices, easier credit, and falling unemployment.

The labor market has improved in the euro area, with the seasonally adjusted monthly unemployment rate declining steadily to 10.3% in January, the lowest since August 2011. However, the rate remains historically high and masks wide variation in joblessness across countries. Germany, which has the lowest unemployment rate in the region, saw a further drop from 4.4% in December to 4.3% in January. Spain and Italy, which have relatively high rates, also recorded declines, from 20.7% to 20.5% in Spain and from 11.6% to 11.5% in Italy. France, by contrast, saw an increase from 10.1% to 10.2% over the month. A number of other countries still face double-digit unemployment rates, including Croatia, Cyprus, Greece, Latvia, Portugal, and Slovakia, suggesting that there is plenty of excess capacity to restrain inflation.

The threat of deflation resurfaced, with the harmonized index of consumer prices dipping from 0.3% in January to −0.2% in February, dragged down partly by low energy prices (Figure A1.7). Core inflation, which excludes more volatile

A1.5 Demand-side contributions to growth, euro area

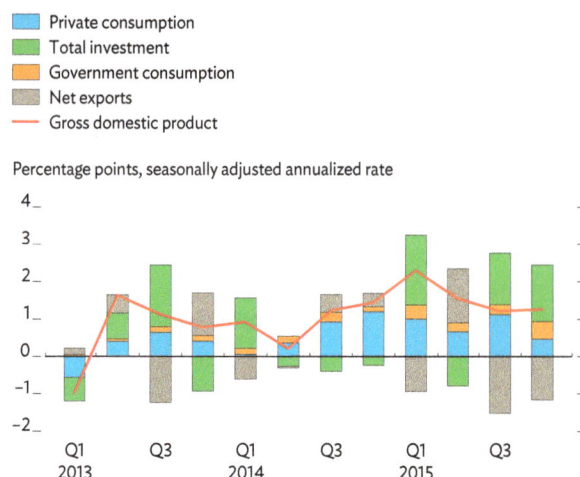

- Private consumption
- Total investment
- Government consumption
- Net exports
- Gross domestic product

Percentage points, seasonally adjusted annualized rate

Q = quarter.
Source: Haver Analytics (accessed 9 March 2016).
Click here for figure data

A1.6 Selected economic indicators, euro area

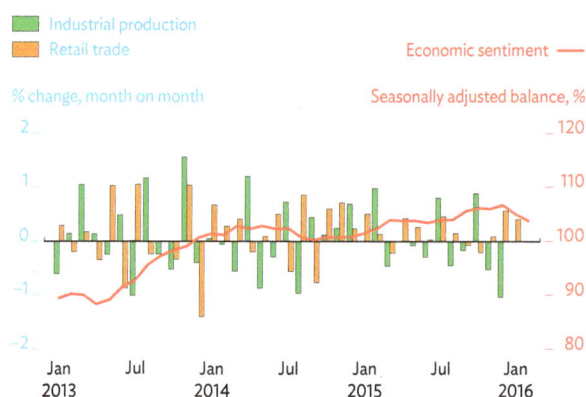

- Industrial production
- Retail trade
- Economic sentiment

% change, month on month   Seasonally adjusted balance, %

Source: Haver Analytics (accessed 9 March 2016).
Click here for figure data

A1.7 Inflation, euro area

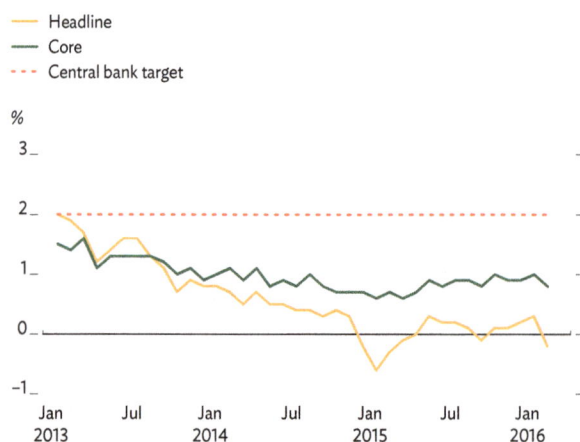

- Headline
- Core
- Central bank target

%

Source: Haver Analytics (accessed 9 March 2016).
Click here for figure data

components such as energy and food, fell from 1.0% to a 10-month low of 0.8%. This has worried the European Central Bank, which has a target rate of close to 2% for headline inflation over the medium term. In March 2016, the bank announced an expansion of its monetary easing policy package. Accordingly, all its main interest rates were cut: the refinancing rate from 0.05% to zero, the bank deposit rate from –0.30% to –0.40%, and the marginal lending facility rate from 0.30% to 0.25%. Monthly purchases under the asset purchase program will be increased from €60 billion currently to €80 billion every month, continuing at least until March 2017. Other expansionary measures include adding investment-grade bonds issued by nonbank corporations to the assets eligible for purchase and launching a new series of targeted refinancing operations for the longer term.

Recovery in the euro area lacks vigor, and recent survey data show signs of a drop in domestic economic activity at the beginning of the year. Weak global demand that is further compounded by slower growth prospects in emerging economies, particularly the People's Republic of China (PRC), may continue to constrain the external sector as well. Other risks to the outlook are global and regional financial volatility, fiscal pressures in some countries, the uncertain effects of immigration, and geopolitical tensions. A cautious outlook guides a forecast for moderate growth in 2016 at 1.5% and, in the absence of a strong catalyst, growth edging up to 1.6% in 2017.

Japan

The economy grew by only 0.5% in 2015. While this improved zero growth in 2014, Japan still lacked real growth momentum. Relatively strong growth in the first quarter was followed by contraction in the second and fourth. A fall in public investment and private consumption contributed to the weakness (Figure A1.8). As a result, the economy is operating below potential, with the cabinet office estimating the shortfall at the end of 2015 at 1.6% of GDP. Meanwhile, the labor market has tightened, with the unemployment rate declining by 0.3 percentage points from the start of 2015 to 3.2% by February 2016, while real wages rose. This probably reflects a labor shortage as the baby boom generation reaches age 65 and retires—a shortage exacerbated by economic recovery since 2013 being driven by labor-intensive sectors outside of manufacturing.

Weak private consumption and public investment were the major drags on growth in 2015. An unusually cold summer in the second quarter and warm winter in the fourth contributed to the 1.3% decline in private consumption. Orders for public works steadily decreased over the year as the government continued its fiscal consolidation. Industrial production has been adjusted downward in line with disappointing demand, and sales have risen too slowly to take up inventories. Private investment contributed 0.7 percentage points to growth despite continued sluggishness. Building starts and housing construction both started to slow toward the end of 2015, to reach

A1.8 Demand-side contributions to growth, Japan

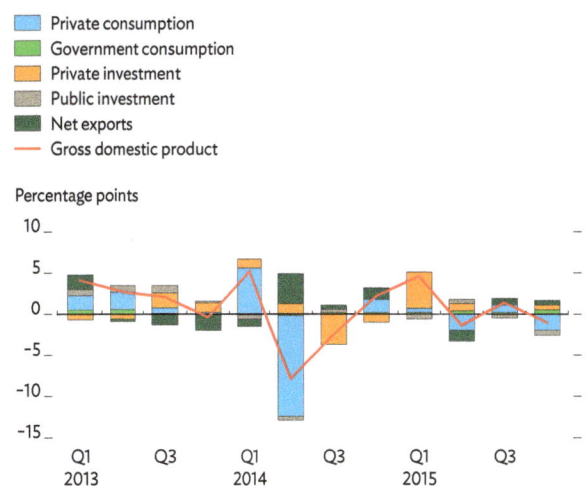

- Private consumption
- Government consumption
- Private investment
- Public investment
- Net exports
- Gross domestic product

Percentage points

Q = quarter.
Source: Haver Analytics (accessed 9 March 2016).
Click here for figure data

only 204 million square meters for the year as a whole. This was the second consecutive year of decline since 2013, when construction was strong before the VAT hike in 2014.

With growth in the fourth quarter weaker than expected, US expansion slowing down, and global risk aversion rising, the Japanese yen reversed course and began appreciating last year, rising by 9% in both nominal and real terms from July 2015 to the end of February 2016. Exports shrank in 2015, but imports shrank much more (Figure A1.9), causing the trade deficit in goods and services to narrow substantially from $128.6 billion in 2014 to $18.4 billion last year. While exports of consumer goods held up well, those of capital goods fell sharply by 10.3%, mainly due to weaker demand in the PRC. Overall, the external sector contributed 0.4 percentage points to growth in 2015. Primary income from foreign financial assets offset the trade deficit, and the current account registered a surplus equal to 3.3% GDP.

After the effects of the VAT increase in April 2014 faded, consumer inflation dropped from 2.3% in the first quarter of 2015 to 0.4% in the second. With continued weakening in oil prices in the second half of last year, inflation slowed steadily to average 0.8% in all of 2015, before turning negative in January 2016 (Figure A1.10). The Bank of Japan estimated that energy prices subtracted about 0.9 percentage points from core consumer inflation during the fiscal year (ending 31 March 2016), and this trend is expected to continue in 2016, although to a lesser degree if global oil prices recover somewhat. The rise in the GDP deflator remained positive at an average of 2.0% in 2015, up slightly from 1.7% in 2014.

Japan's economy will have to rely on domestic demand for growth as its main trading partners, particularly the PRC, demand fewer capital goods imports. Forward-looking indicators suggest that the real sector will also remain weak in the near term. The purchasing managers' index is above 50, indicating expansion, but it moderated slightly to 52.3 in January 2016 from 52.6 in December 2015. The Tankan survey of business conditions slowed in the fourth quarter of 2015 after picking up in the third quarter. Consumer confidence improved somewhat in 2015, but weakness emerged this year as the consumer confidence index fell for a second straight month in February to 40.1, the lowest since February 2015.

The Bank of Japan adopted negative interest rates in January 2016 in response to a sharper-than-expected drop in industrial production and weak inflation in December 2015. Delaying the VAT hike is on the table given the weakness in the economy, but this baseline assumes the VAT increase as scheduled with some fiscal stimulus. Private consumption of durable goods and housing investment are expected to pick up in 2016 in anticipation of a scheduled VAT hike in April 2017 from 8% to 10% in 2017 (Figure A1.11). In 2016, external demand is expected to improve but only gradually. GDP is expected to grow by 0.6%. In 2017, growth is expected to slow marginally to 0.5% with the VAT hike.

A1.9 Merchandise exports and imports, Japan

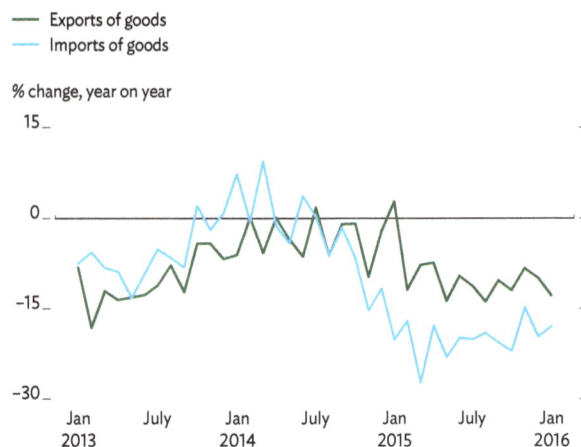

Source: Haver Analytics (accessed 9 March 2016).
Click here for figure data

A1.10 Inflation, GDP deflator, and real effective exchange rate, Japan

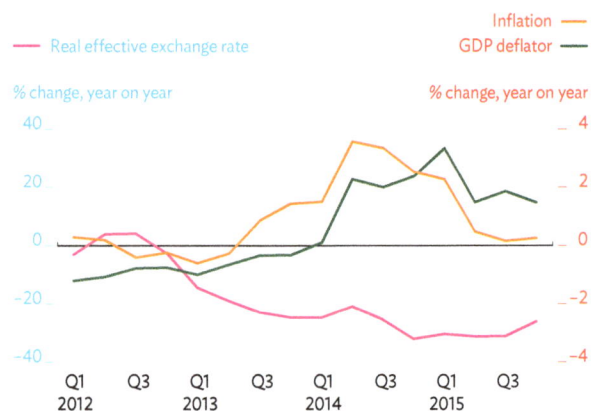

Q = quarter.
Source: Haver Analytics (accessed 9 March 2016).
Click here for figure data

Assuming that global oil prices rise only gradually in 2017 and output remains below potential, consumer inflation is likely to remain below 1.0% in 2016 before the VAT lifts it to 2.7% in 2017.

Australia and New Zealand

Australia is expected to grow moderately in 2016 and 2017. In the fourth quarter of 2015, its economy expanded by a saar of 2.6%, slower than growth at 4.4% in the previous quarter. Consumption remained the principal driver of growth, contributing 2.2 percentage points, with fixed capital subtracting 0.6 percentage points, and net exports of goods and services contributing almost nothing (Figure A1.12). Seasonally adjusted retail sales grew by 0.3% in January 2016, better than 0.02% growth in December. Consumer sentiment returned to positive territory in February 2016, rising to 101.3 points from January's 97.3 points. The seasonally adjusted unemployment rate rose marginally to 6.0% in January from 5.8% in the previous month. The Australian Industry Group's performance of manufacturing index, for which 50 is the threshold for growth, rose to 53.5 in February from 51.5 in January, better than the 49.5 average in 2015 and indicating expansion in manufacturing. Inflation was a seasonally adjusted 1.7% in the fourth quarter, slightly above the previous quarter's 1.5% and less than the Reserve Bank of Australia target of 2.0%–3.0%. Australia's economy is affected by moderating growth in the PRC, its largest trading partner, with mining particularly hard hit. Panelists for the FocusEconomics Consensus Forecast predict GDP to grow by 2.6% in 2016 and 2.9% in 2017, above the estimated 2.4% in 2015.

New Zealand's GDP growth accelerated from a saar of 2.9% in the second quarter of 2015 to 5.0% in the third, propelled by expanding net exports that contributed 6.2 percentage points. While fixed capital and private consumption also bolstered growth, adding 2.7 and 1.5 percentage points respectively, their contribution was more than offset by a decline in inventories (Figure A1.13). In the third quarter, seasonally adjusted retail sales rose by 1.4%, better than the previous quarter's 0.3%. The index of manufacturing performance increased to 57.9 in January from 57.0 in December 2015, indicating expansion as the index remained above the threshold of 50. The business confidence index plunged to 7.1 in February from 23.0 in December. However, consumer confidence remained upbeat, staying above 100 and increasing by 4.7 points to 110.7 in December. Inflation stayed far below the central bank's target range of 1.0%–3.0%, dropping to 0.1% in the last quarter of 2015 from 0.4% in the previous quarter. The seasonally adjusted unemployment rate improved marginally to 5.3% in the

A1.11 Housing and building starts in Japan, by floor area

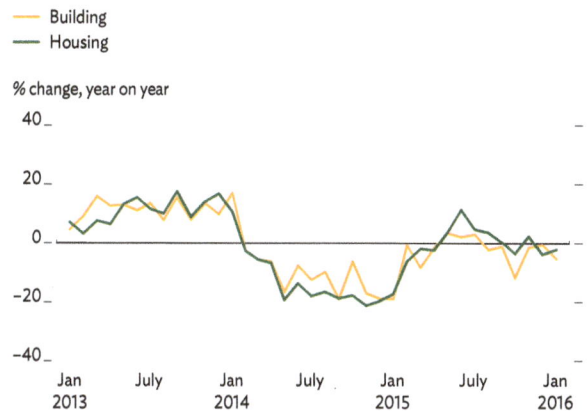

Building
Housing

% change, year on year

Source: Haver Analytics (accessed 9 March 2016).
Click here for figure data

A1.12 Demand-side contributions to growth, Australia

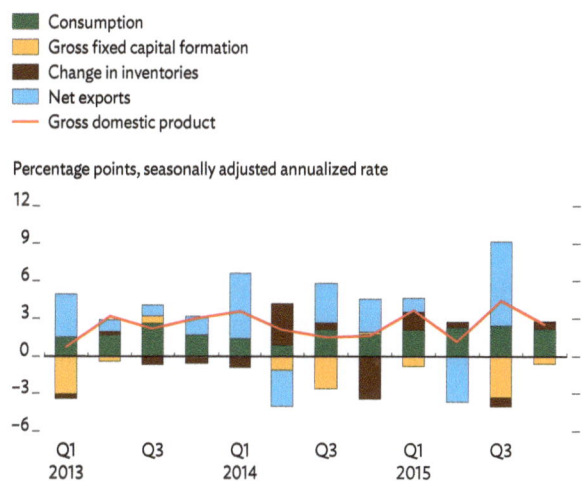

Consumption
Gross fixed capital formation
Change in inventories
Net exports
Gross domestic product

Percentage points, seasonally adjusted annualized rate

Q = quarter.
Source: Haver Analytics (accessed 9 March 2016).
Click here for figure data

A1.13 Demand-side contributions to growth, New Zealand

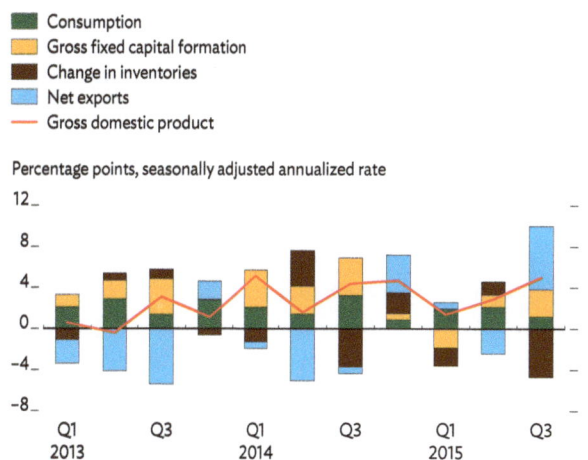

Consumption
Gross fixed capital formation
Change in inventories
Net exports
Gross domestic product

Percentage points, seasonally adjusted annualized rate

Q = quarter.
Source: Haver Analytics (accessed 9 March 2016).
Click here for figure data

fourth quarter from 6.0% of the previous quarter. With anticipated recovery in the global market for dairy products and a dynamic labor market—but with the PRC slowdown as a downside risk—FocusEconomics Consensus Forecast panelists project GDP growth in 2016 that matches the estimate for 2015 at 2.4%, increasing slightly to 2.6% in 2017.

Commodity prices

Commodity prices have declined over the past 4 years. While supply factors have largely explained the drop in prices, subdued demand has also played a role. Oil prices are expected to fall slightly in 2016 but will gradually recover during the year as supply from producers outside the Organization of the Petroleum Exporting Countries (OPEC) declines and global demand strengthens. With oil prices remaining low and food commodity markets well supplied, food prices should stabilize during the forecast period.

Oil price movements

Compared with the decline by more than 50% in the price of the international benchmark Brent crude in the second half of 2014—from a peak of $115/barrel on 19 June to $56/barrel at the end of the year—the drop in 2015 was more moderate. Brent crude finished 2015 at $36/barrel, down by 36%. The average price of oil, however, reveals a different story: While a barrel of oil averaged $99/barrel in 2014, or 9% below the 2013 average, the average price in 2015 was $52/barrel, or 47% below the 2014 average and almost half the average price in the period 2010–2014 (Figure A1.14). The last time Brent crude prices stayed in the $40–$50 range was from late 2008 to early 2009. Hopes of a price recovery during 2015 supported a rally from about $40 in the early months of 2015 to about $60 in April. But the rally proved short-lived, and prices remained below $50/barrel in the last quarter of the year, languishing in the $30s in December.

Low crude prices in 2015 reflected a confluence of factors, including continued abundant supply from non-OPEC producers, unrelenting resolve within OPEC to defend market share, receding concerns over supply disruptions, subdued global growth prospects, and the strengthening US dollar. After increasing by 2.4 million barrels per day (mbd) in 2014, the global oil supply grew in 2015 by 2.8%, or an additional 2.6 mbd, with non-OPEC producers contributing 1.4 mbd of the increase, or 53% (Figure A1.15). The US led non-OPEC oil production. US output of crude oil rose by more than 8% in 2015, with the production of light tight oil contributing the most. Although on a declining trend since the middle of 2015, light tight oil accounted for more than 40% of growth in non-OPEC supply.

OPEC, on the other hand, maintained its strategy to protect market share and raised crude oil production to 31.3 mbd. Most of the increase

A1.14 Price of Brent crude

Sources: Bloomberg; World Bank. Commodity Price Data (Pink Sheet). http://www.worldbank.org (both accessed 7 March 2016).
Click here for figure data

A1.15 Change in global oil demand and supply

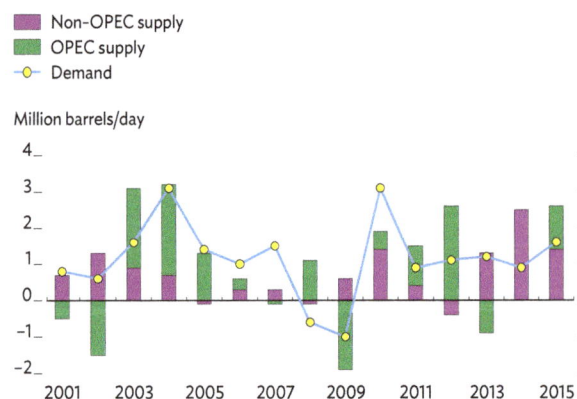

OPEC = Organization of the Petroleum Exporting Countries.
Source: International Energy Agency. Oil Market Report. Various issues.
Click here for figure data

came from Iraq and Saudi Arabia, whose combined additional output accounted for 87% of the rise in OPEC production. Outside the Gulf, OPEC production was fairly steady at around 8.0 mbd. Although volatility did ensue due to supply disruptions arising from geopolitical tensions, internal conflicts, and unplanned production outages—the US Energy Information Administration estimates that disruptions in 2015 removed an average of 2.8 mbd from global markets—the supply glut tempered the upward pressures, and oil prices remained low.

With global GDP growth remaining low and dollar appreciation tamping down any demand boost from low oil prices, growth in the world oil supply again outpaced demand growth. World oil demand increased by 1.6 mbd in 2015, or 1.7%. Although this was the highest in 5 years, it was not enough to keep oil prices from falling. Consequently, global oil inventories increased for the second consecutive year, by about 2 mbd in 2015, or more than twice the inventory buildup in 2014.

Price weakening has persisted in 2016. With the market oversupplied, market sentiment has played a key role in price determination. Following failure in OPEC to reach an official decision about oil production on 4 December 2015, Brent crude oil prices tumbled from $42/barrel to as low as $26/barrel by the third week of January 2016. News of OPEC members coordinating output cuts set off a price rally, but it was short-lived as the market sensed that a cut in production was unlikely. Lately, oil prices have been rising because of renewed talks in which a larger group of oil producers aim to freeze production, as well as because of a continuing decline in the number of active drilling rigs in the US, production outages in Nigeria and Kurdistan, and increased demand from the PRC. As of mid-March, Brent crude was trading in the range of $36–$40/barrel.

Oil price prospects

In its *Medium-Term Oil Market Report 2015*, the International Energy Agency concluded that oil supply will again exceed demand. However, the agency maintained that the 2015 volume increase, one of the highest in recent history, cannot be repeated in 2016. Low oil prices have prompted oil companies to scale back investment and production spending, and to defer exploration, restricting potential growth in oil supply. Supply from outside OPEC is forecast to decline by 0.6 mbd in 2016 and by 0.02 mbd in 2017. Most of the forecast decline is expected to be in the US, which largely reflects changes in light tight oil production, which is forecast to decline by nearly 0.6 mbd in 2016 and 0.2 mbd in 2017. Although non-OPEC supply is forecast to fall, this will be offset by higher production within OPEC, primarily from Iran, Iraq, and the United Arab Emirates. Although production freezes have been discussed, there has been no sign that OPEC will change its current stance, as some key members continue to offer price discounts to defend market share (Figure A1.16).

Supply disruptions will still affect oil prices, but oversupply has increased the market's tolerance for disruption. The Energy Information

A1.16 Price discounts to Asia

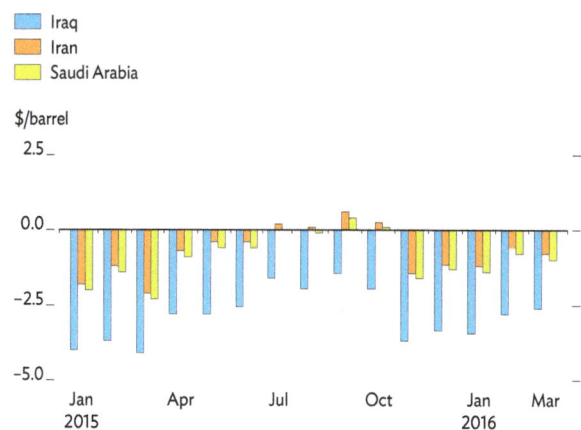

Note: Data refer to light crude price differential to the Oman/Dubai Benchmark.
Source: Bloomberg (accessed 7 March 2016).
Click here for figure data

Administration estimates that 2.7 mbd were removed from oil markets in February 2015. Conflicts in Iraq, Libya, Nigeria, South Sudan, Sudan, Syria, and Yemen continue to pose downside risks to supply.

Price recovery during the forecast period will be smaller than previously expected, owing to substantial inventory overhang, the prospect of additional supply from OPEC, the continuing strength of the US dollar, and weak demand. Growth in global oil demand is projected to be lower than in 2015, rising by 1.2 mbd in 2016 and 1.3 mbd in 2017. Factors holding down demand growth include lukewarm global industrial activity, slower growth in the PRC, and the waning boost to demand from low oil prices. In addition, weaker prices have spurred improved operating efficiency in the US shale oil industry, whose production declines have been smaller than earlier anticipated. Although a number of shale oil producers have scaled down operations, higher oil prices will encourage them to reenter the market, thereby exerting downward pressure on prices. Moreover, futures markets still signal a modest recovery in prices over the next 2 years (Figure A1.17). Barring large and sharp changes in global oil supply and demand, Brent crude prices are forecast to average $38 in 2016 and $45 in 2017.

Food price movements and prospects

Agricultural prices continued their decline for the fourth consecutive year, with the overall index falling by 13.1% in 2015. All sub-indexes decreased, with food prices showing the largest drop of 15.4%. The decline in prices came mainly from favorable supply conditions and low energy prices.

All food sub-indexes declined, with edible oils falling by 22% and grains by 15% (Figure A1.18). Every component of the price index for edible oils and meals declined in 2015. In particular, prices for three key components—palm oil, soybean meal, and soybeans—fell by more than 20%. Large soybean yields and stockpiles of soybean meal exerted downward pressure on prices. At the same time, the continued slump in oil prices depressed demand for palm oil and soybeans to make biodiesel fuel. Prices for wheat, maize, and rice also declined in 2015, reflecting ample supply from good crop yields. After rising in 2014, the "other food" index fell by 7.5% in 2015. Lower beef prices offset higher prices for chicken, and sugar prices continued to fall because of large accumulated stocks.

The decline in food prices has continued in 2016, with the index down by 12.7% in the first 2 months of the year. Global prices for wheat and maize declined as abundant wheat supplies and subdued international demand exerted downward pressure. However, prices for rice rose in February, owing to production pressures and increased demand from key importers such as Indonesia and the Philippines.

The Agricultural Market Information System of the Food and Agriculture Organization reported in March 2016 that the current

A1.17 Brent crude futures and spot price

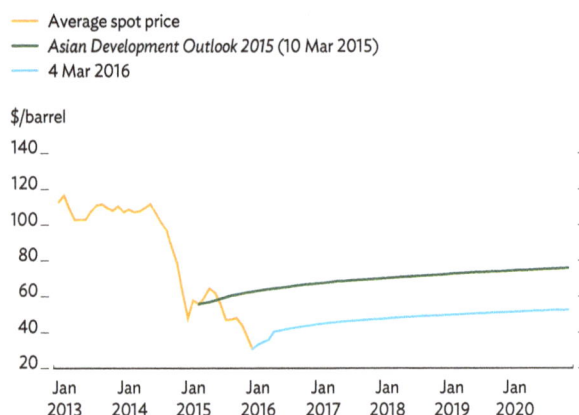

Source: Bloomberg (accessed 7 March 2016).
Click here for figure data

A1.18 Food commodity price indexes

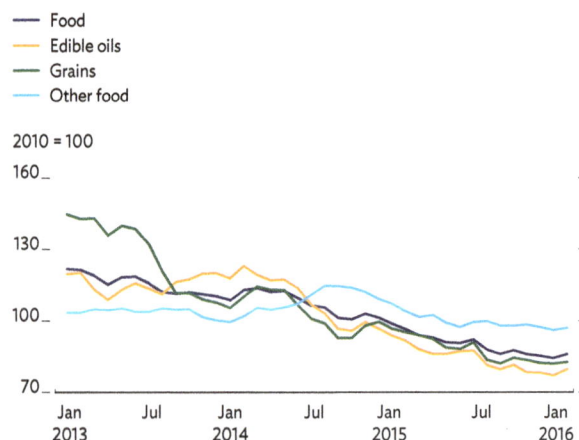

Source: World Bank. Commodity Price Data (Pink Sheet). http://www.worldbank.org (accessed 4 March 2016).
Click here for figure data

El Niño peaked in November 2015 but remains strong and will fade to neutral only in June. However, global supplies (stocks plus production) of the three major grains remain healthy. The latest prospects from the March 2016 report of the US Department of Agriculture show global supplies of these three crops reaching 2.70 billion tons in the 2015/16 crop year, 0.2% higher than the previous year. Global production of wheat in 2015/16 is expected to be 0.9% higher, resulting in a 14-year high in the stock-to-use ratio (Figure A1.19). On the other hand, the market for maize is forecast to be tight, as global production in 2015/16 is seen declining by 4.0% on account of severe drought attributed to El Niño. Despite these cuts in production, the stock-to-use ratio will rise slightly on lower consumption and higher stock carryover.

Also affected by El Niño, global rice production is expected to fall by 1.6%. Production by major rice exporters India, Pakistan, Thailand, and Viet Nam is forecast to drop by 3.4%, but the stock-to-use ratio will remain close to its 10-year average at 18.7%.

The outlook for edible oils remains positive. Production of the 10 major edible oils is projected to rise by 1.3%. Supplies are expected to remain high because of elevated stock carryover, especially for soybeans, for which production increased by almost 30% from 2013/14.

Recent weather forecasts suggest that the current El Niño could be one of the strongest on record. However, it is unlikely to cause a spike in global agricultural prices because supplies of major agricultural commodities are ample and energy prices low. Current and past periods of El Niño show the weak link between El Niño episodes and global food prices, during which food price indexes either declined or changed very little (Figure A1.20). Regarding La Niña, a weather disruption that can follow El Niño, the March report of the Agricultural Market Information System of the Food and Agriculture Organization puts the probability of experiencing La Niña in the latter part of 2016 at 50%. In view of well-supplied markets for most grains, oilseeds, and edible oils, the food commodity price index is expected to decline a further 1% in 2016 before rebounding by 1% in 2017.

External environment in sum

The much-anticipated improvement in the global outlook has yet to materialize. In particular, despite some promising signs from the US, growth in the industrial economies will remain flat. As such, they cannot provide a fillip for developing Asia's exports and growth. The US Federal Reserve is likely to raise interest rates further, but the cautious and gradual nature of the hikes will cushion the adverse effect on the region's financial stability. Subdued oil prices will contain inflationary pressures but are unlikely to boost growth, as they partly reflect weak global demand. In sum, developing Asia must navigate a challenging and uncertain external environment, looking to itself to reignite growth.

A1.19 Stock-to-use ratio

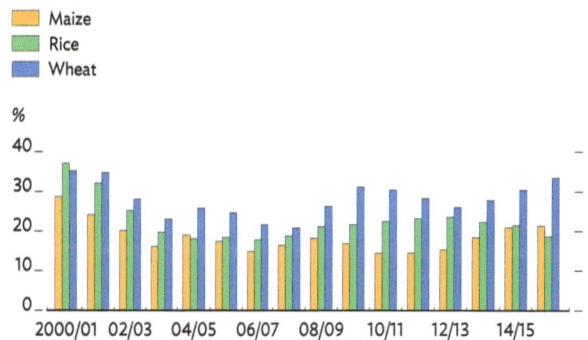

Legend: Maize, Rice, Wheat

Source: US Department of Agriculture. Production, Supply, and Distribution Online. http://www.fas.usda.gov/psdonline/psdQuery.aspx (accessed 10 March 2016).
Click here for figure data

A1.20 Change in price indexes during El Niño peak periods

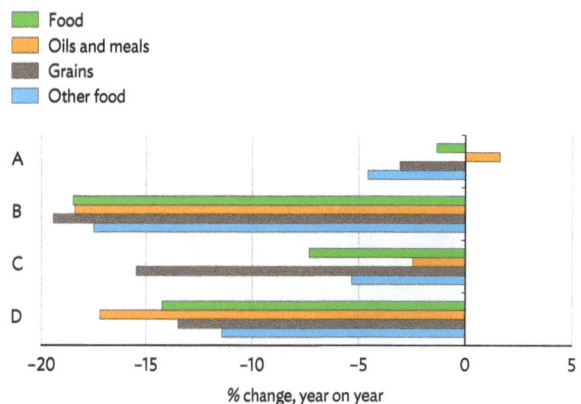

Legend: Food, Oils and meals, Grains, Other food

A = Aug 1964–Jan 1965 versus Aug 1965–Jan 1966,
B = Sep 1981–Feb 1982 versus Sep 1982–Feb 1983,
C = Aug 1996–Feb 1997 versus Aug 1997–Feb 1998,
D = Sep 2014–Feb 2015 versus Sep 2015–Feb 2016.
Sources: World Bank. Commodity Price Data (Pink Sheet). http://www.worldbank.org (accessed 4 March 2016); Golden Gate Weather Services. El Niño and La Niña Years and Intensities. http://ggweather.com (accessed 11 March 2016).
Click here for figure data

2

ASIA'S POTENTIAL GROWTH

Asia's potential growth

Many Asian economies have registered remarkably high output growth rates in the past 3 decades. This achievement came about despite disruptions caused by economic crises. Arguably, the most serious downturn was the Asian financial crisis of 1997–1998, which severely affected Southeast Asia and the Republic of Korea. By comparison, the global financial crisis (GFC) of 2008–2009 has had much less impact on Asia. The main reason why the region's economies were not directly affected was their low exposure to United States (US) subprime mortgages. The region was nevertheless affected indirectly as demand for its exports from its main trading partners contracted significantly.

This was enough to disrupt growth momentum in Asia, and as a result economic growth in Asia slowed in the aftermath of the GFC. From an average of 8.3% during 2006–2010, gross domestic product (GDP) growth in the region fell to 5.9% in 2015 (Figure 2.1.1). This downward trend in regional growth follows 6 years of accelerating growth in the interval 2001–2007. The People's Republic of China (PRC), which accounts for a large share of the region's GDP, has been the main driver of regional economic growth. Given the recent slowdown in the PRC, some observers have started talking about a "new normal" of substantially lower growth in the region.

While developing Asia is not alone in this regard—growth also declined in Africa, Latin America, and Eastern Europe—its slowdown is likely to have repercussions for the region and the rest of the world. Developing Asia's success in lifting 1 billion individuals out of poverty during 1990–2012 hinged on its ability to sustain high rates of economic growth. Moreover, as the region currently accounts for more than a quarter of world GDP as valued at market exchange rates, a persistent slowdown in developing Asia threatens to undermine the fragile global recovery.

This theme chapter aims to reveal the factors underlying the growth slowdown and the extent to which the slowdown reflects changes in the region's productive capacity. What has happened to developing Asia's productive capacity—its so-called potential growth—and how can policy makers respond?

2.1.1 Average GDP growth in selected regions

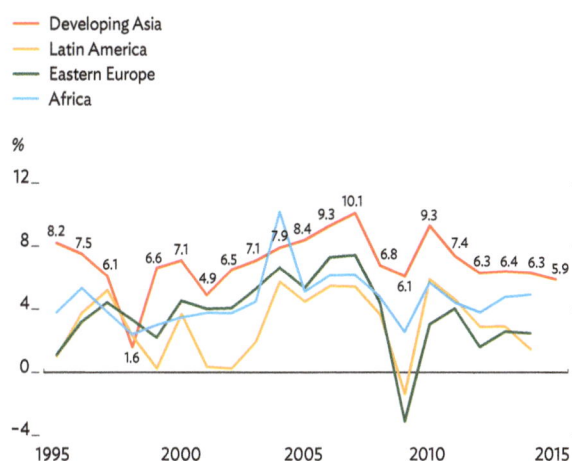

— Developing Asia
— Latin America
— Eastern Europe
— Africa

Source: ADB estimates.
Click here for figure data

This chapter was written by Jesus Felipe of the Economic Research and Regional Cooperation Department, ADB, Manila; Matteo Lanzafame of the University of Messina; and Miguel León-Ledesma of the University of Kent. Contributions from Bart Verspagen and Neil Foster-McGregor of the United Nations University–Maastricht Economic and Social Research Institute on Innovation and Technology, Kunal Sen of the University of Manchester, as well as from Noli Sotocinal of the Economic Research and Regional Cooperation Department, are acknowledged.

Understanding the growth slowdown

The issues posed by the decline in Asia's growth rate, and the nature of that decline, are important from a policy perspective. The right policy response depends on the nature of the region's slowdown. Is it a temporary—albeit prolonged—effect of the business cycle? Or are more persistent changes under way? If weaker growth reflects slack demand such as softening export orders or a downturn in private investment, then fiscal or monetary stimulus may be needed for temporary support. But if supply-side factors are at play, and growth moderation stems from slowing expansion of the region's productive capacity, then any revival of growth prospects may depend on structural policy reform.

The concepts of potential GDP and potential growth, which are grounded in a view of an economy's productive capacity under conditions of stable inflation and full employment, can be used to distinguish temporary deviations from the underlying trend in actual GDP growth. This chapter provides the theoretical foundation for potential growth, develops a simple framework to estimate it from readily available macroeconomic indicators, and applies the framework to a sample of developing economies in Asia.

Conceptualizing potential growth

Standard economic theory assumes that transitory shocks to the actual growth rate do not significantly affect the dynamics of the underlying trend or the potential growth rate. Several studies have recently challenged this view, however, and have proposed arguments and provided empirical evidence that support the hypothesis that there is a significant relationship between the short-run cyclical behavior of economic growth and long-term performance (e.g., Stiglitz 1993, Cerra and Saxena 2008). This suggests that the GFC may indeed have a significant impact on the future growth trajectory of individual economies.

The possibility of a permanent downward shift affects prospects for sustained increases in output. This is an important medium-term concern for policy makers, particularly in less developed countries where intense pressure exists to deliver sustained increases in living standards. Rodrik (2009), for example, argued that the world after the 2008–2009 crisis would be significantly different from its pre-crisis incarnation, in particular as a milieu for East Asian economies thriving as they did in the 20th century. This is because the crisis has permanently reduced growth in both productivity and the labor force.[1] Likewise, Pritchett and Summers (2014) argued that the days of fast growth in Asia might be numbered because regression to the mean is empirically the most robust feature of economic growth. The statistical analysis showed that rapid growth episodes in developing countries are frequently followed by significant slowdowns. Moreover, the historical distribution of growth has an average of 2% with a standard deviation that is also 2%.

One approach to addressing the main issues is to examine the supply side of the economy through the concept of potential or natural output growth. The notion of potential output was initially formulated to quantify the ability of an economy to produce output, i.e., its productive capacity. "Potential output" is therefore the highest level of real GDP that can be attained over the long term. By translating levels to growth rates, one obtains the rate of growth of potential output. A limit to output growth exists because of technical, natural, and institutional constraints on the ability to produce.

Growth theory indicates that in the long run economies tend to grow at a rate consistent with the full utilization of productive resources, i.e., the natural or potential growth rate. Short-term shocks can induce temporary deviations from potential growth rate, which give rise to changes in unemployment and inflation, but over time these changes are corrected by price adjustments and growth returns to its potential. What this means is that the high growth rates enjoyed by Asian economies reflected their high potential growth rates. Nevertheless, the precise meaning of this term has evolved over time (Box 2.1.1).

The approach followed in this chapter is consistent with Harrod's definition of potential growth—the sum of the growth rates of labor productivity and of the labor force—and with Okun's concept of potential output (Harrod 1939, Okun 1962). Hence, potential output growth is defined as the maximum rate of growth that an economy can achieve consistent with macroeconomic stability, in which there are neither inflationary nor deflationary pressures.

There is broad agreement that Asia's spectacular growth in recent decades was enabled by its rapid structural transformation, i.e., its capacity to shift resources out of agriculture into sectors of higher productivity (ADB 2013). The speed of an economy's structural transformation depends largely on institutional barriers that affect, among other things, the reallocation of factors of production, e.g., restrictive labor laws. Given that these barriers are pervasive in many Asian countries and that agriculture is still a large employer (employing 50% of all workers in India and about 30% in the PRC), Asia's prospects to reengineer high growth will depend largely on eliminating these barriers. Arguably, a significant share of the high growth registered by the Republic of Korea and Taipei,China from the mid-1960s to the mid-1990s, and in the PRC after 1980, is accounted for by the weakening of these barriers, which facilitated the absorption of labor by the manufacturing and service sectors. But most Asian economies still have significant barriers that prevent the development of modern manufacturing and services. Moreover, there are important obstacles that make it difficult to efficiently reallocate factors across firms.

This leads to the important point that potential growth consistent with stable inflation as used in this chapter is conditional on the economy's institutions and economic structure. Suppose that one could measure additional growth over and above this potential growth that could be achieved with the removal of all institutional barriers

2.1.1 Evolving notions of potential output growth

The idea of potential output has evolved historically. There are four main stages in the progression.

First stage. When Harrod (1939) discussed the "natural growth rate," this was probably the first formal reference in the literature to the idea of an economy's full-employment growth rate. Harrod defined an economy's natural growth rate ($\hat{g}^N$) as the sum of the growth rates of labor productivity ($\hat{y}^N$) and of the labor force ($\hat{n}^N$), i.e., $\hat{g}^N = \hat{y}^N + \hat{n}^N$. It represents the maximum sustainable rate of growth that technical conditions make available to the economic system. At any particular time, actual growth can diverge from the natural growth rate because of various restrictions, rigidities, and constraints, as well as the effect of positive and negative transitory shocks. Nonetheless, actual growth cannot persistently exceed $\hat{g}^N$ as this would eventually create inflationary pressures, including an excessively tight labor market. With wages rising relative to the price of capital, the economy would adopt more capital-intensive techniques, unemployment would rise again to a comfortable approximation of full employment, and growth would converge on the natural rate. On the other hand, if actual growth were consistently lower than the natural growth rate, the resulting rise in unemployment would trigger the opposite price adjustment process, and falling wages would in due course restore higher employment through the adoption of more labor-intensive production techniques until equilibrium in the labor market was achieved, and actual and natural growth rates were brought into line.

Second stage. It was not until the 1960s that these ideas gave rise to an active body of empirical work around the idea of potential output. Since then, there have been essentially two concepts of potential output in the literature. The first is based on Okun (1962), and the second on Friedman (1968). Okun was interested in the question how much output the economy could produce under conditions of full employment and answered it by introducing the concept of potential gross national product. Okun's work harked back to Harrod but also accommodated Keynes and the Phillips curve. He argued that potential output is a supply concept of the level of output under the full utilization of factor inputs. However, Okun stressed that the social target of maximum production and employment is constrained by a social desire for price stability. This did not imply, however, that inflation had to be stabilized at a low rate. Okun's aim was to specify the appropriate fiscal policy to maximize employment subject to the constraint that inflation should not be excessive. The implied relationship—referred to as Okun's Law—had practical policy implications under conditions of a stable trade-off between inflation and unemployment (the Phillips curve) and the direct responsiveness of employment to demand (as explored by Keynes).

Third stage. Okun was seriously questioned in the 1970s. The reason was not his concept of potential output. Rather, the rise of inflation during that decade caused disappointment with full employment policies. Friedman (1968) and Phelps (1967) questioned the stability of the inflation–unemployment trade-off embodied in the Phillips curve. They argued that the rate of wage increases was stable at only one rate of unemployment, which was termed its "natural rate" or the "nonaccelerating inflation rate of unemployment." If unemployment were beneath this natural rate, expectations of rising wages would cause inflation to accelerate without limit. The Friedman–Phelps critique of the Phillips curve had clear significance for the labor market and cast doubt on the feasibility of full employment, which was the touchstone of Okun's work.

Fourth stage. The result was a radical shift in thinking in the 1980s and 1990s about the relationship between demand pressure and inflation. The outcome was Okun's concept of the output gap being superseded by variants of Friedman's natural rate hypothesis. The central bank reaction function presented in Taylor (1993), for example, became a rule observed by many central banks when setting interest rates. This work led by the end of the 1990s and early 2000s to the so-called New Consensus Macroeconomics, also referred to as the New Keynesian Perspective. Essentially, this is a three-equation model consisting of (i) the relationship between interest rates and the output gap, (ii) the Phillips curve relationship between inflation and the output gap, and (iii) the so-called Taylor Rule, which sets interest rates according to the output gap and the difference between actual and targeted inflation. In these models, prices or real wages adjust toward their long-run equilibrium values but do so slowly, with the result that actual output may deviate from the short-term measure of potential output. Consequently, the output gap measures the deviation of actual from potential output that arises as a result of rigidities in prices and wages that prevent them from responding freely to changes in demand and supply.

and distortions in the economy: market imperfections, collusion, rent-seeking, externalities, and government policies that obstruct the mobility of factors, both capital and labor. This would then be the true maximum rate at which the economy can grow. This concept is referred to as the economy's *frontier potential growth*. It cannot be quantified, but the idea is clear and useful for developing economies.

While the difference between potential growth and frontier potential growth is not large in advanced economies, the distinction is important for economies riddled with inefficiencies. Policies and reforms that ease some of these constraints in the latter group can have salutary effects on potential growth, especially if it languishes far from the frontier. Understanding these constraints can help policy makers propel their economies closer to their true limit.

Estimating potential growth

Potential output is not directly observed. As such, the first step in analyzing developing Asia's potential is to develop an empirical model. This section develops a simple empirical model and applies it to a sample of 22 developing economies in Asia (Box 2.1.2). While limited data availability constrained selection for the sample, the group includes the three largest economies—the PRC, India, and Indonesia—and representatives of all subregions in developing Asia. As the sample accounts for more than 98% of GDP in the region in 2014, the aggregate results should broadly represent the region's experience.

At present, most economists view economic growth as the sum of a cyclical component and a permanent component. The former captures the business cycle or demand fluctuations and the latter the long-run trajectory of growth. This is the "natural" or potential growth rate of the economy, consistent with the full utilization of productive resources—in particular full employment of the labor force accompanied by stable inflation. There are various methods to estimate the potential growth rate, which are summarized in Box 2.1.3.

From the methods listed in the box, this chapter uses a multivariate estimate that relies on information on GDP growth and inflation. This is obviously an improvement over the univariate filters. Unlike the growth accounting approach, it does not require a series of capital stock, which is lacking in most Asian economies. And, unlike the output identity approach, the method employed in this chapter provides an explicit link with concepts of macroeconomic stability. Before the model is estimated, univariate filters are applied to the data series to extract the underlying trends of each variable.

As noted above, deviations of actual growth from the potential rate cause resources to be either overutilized or underutilized, giving rise to changes in the unemployment rate and, consequently, to inflationary or deflationary pressures. Consequently, potential output growth is associated with a stable inflation environment. The framework used in this chapter to estimate the potential growth rate of the Asian economies builds on this intuition.

Potential growth as modeled in this chapter is consistent with the Harrod (1939) concept of the natural rate of growth. The natural rate of growth is described as both the potential growth rate toward which the economy tends in the long-run and the short-term upward limit to growth, which turns cyclical expansions into recessions.

2.1.2 Sample economies

Azerbaijan	Pakistan
Bangladesh	Papua New Guinea
Cambodia	Philippines
People's Republic of China	Singapore
	Sri Lanka
Fiji	Taipei,China
Hong Kong, China	Tajikistan
India	Thailand
Indonesia	Turkmenistan
Kazakhstan	Uzbekistan
Republic of Korea	Viet Nam
Malaysia	

2.1.3 Methods to estimate potential growth

Potential growth, unlike actual growth, is not directly observable and hence has to be estimated. Some of the most widely used methods are as follows:

Univariate filters. These are statistical procedures that are not based on any underlying economic theory and use information only on GDP. Their objective is to statistically remove the cyclical component of a series from the raw data. The most widely used is the Hodrick–Prescott, but some other filters are the Baxter–King, Christiano–Fitzgerald, Beveridge–Nelson, and Corbae–Ouliaris.

Multivariate estimates. These approaches use information from several economic series to obtain estimates of potential output. The models are typically based on a structural theory. For example, they estimate the rate of economic growth consistent with "macroeconomic stability." One simple model is a bivariate structural time series linking temporary fluctuations in output to inflation, and postulating that the output gap is positively related to inflation pressures. An extended version could add an Okun's Law equation relating unemployment and output growth.

Growth accounting approach. This is also a multivariate approach in that it uses information on variables related through an aggregate production function: output, employment, capital, and residually measured total factor productivity. Typically, authors derive a decomposition of the sources of growth using a Cobb–Douglas production function such as $Y_t = A_t K_t^\alpha (L_t H_t)^{(1-\alpha)}$. In most cases it is not estimated econometrically; rather, factor markets are assumed to be competitive, so the labor and capital elasticities equal the factor shares in national income, and these are imposed to derive total factor productivity growth.

Output identity. This approach decomposes output (Y) multiplicatively as the product of a series of terms, e.g., labor productivity in hours (Y/H), hours per employee (H/L), the employment rate (L/P), and working-age population (P), such that $Y = \left(\frac{Y}{H}\right) * \left(\frac{H}{L}\right) * \left(\frac{L}{P}\right) * P$. These series can also be filtered to calculate their trend, which is then interpreted as the potential level. Like the production function approach, this method does not explicitly link the estimation of trend growth to the estimation of the output gap and inflation.

Since by definition it is the sum of the growth rates of labor productivity and the labor force, potential growth can be usefully decomposed into these two elements once it is estimated. Note that when actual growth is equal to potential, employment grows at the same rate as the labor force, keeping the unemployment rate constant. As such, when actual growth is consistently slower than the natural rate, unemployment will rise, and vice versa.

As a consequence, a convenient method to estimate the natural growth rate relies on the relationship between unemployment and output growth formalized in Okun's Law (e.g., León-Ledesma and Thirlwall 2002). Such a choice is complicated, however, by the lack or unreliability of labor market data for many Asian economies. This problem is addressed by noting that a natural extension of the concept of the natural growth rate is the link with the relationship between unemployment and inflation typified in the Phillips curve. The process, as described in Box 2.1.4, is to estimate the relationship of the gap between actual and expected inflation to the gap between actual growth and its natural rate. The model that relates output growth and inflation generates annual estimates of the potential growth rate.

Potential growth trends in developing Asia

When applied to developing economies with significant surplus labor, the model suggests that they can grow fast until the surplus is eliminated. Economies with surplus labor have relatively high labor force growth rates, many unemployed and underemployed workers, and low wages. Under these circumstances, there is room to grow

2.1.4 Multivariate estimates of potential growth

The model used for estimation has three underlying pillars: (i) Harrod's notion of the natural growth rate, (ii) Okun's Law relating unemployment to output, and (iii) the Phillips' curve relating inflation to output.

Since the natural growth rate is defined as the sum of the growth rates of labor productivity and the labor force, unemployment will rise whenever the actual rate of growth ($\hat{g}_t$) falls below the natural rate ($\hat{g}_t^N$), and it will fall when $\hat{g}_t$ rises above $\hat{g}_t^N$. This yields the following specification of Okun's Law:

$$\Delta U_t = \sigma - \varsigma \hat{g}_t \tag{1}$$

where ΔU_t is the percentage change in the unemployment rate and the natural growth rate given by (σ/ς). This specification and its variants have been widely used in the literature to estimate $\hat{g}_t^N$ for countries and regions and also to investigate its possible endogeneity (e.g., León-Ledesma and Thirlwall 2002, Lanzafame 2010). The specification in equation (1) presents two issues that are addressed in this chapter. First, the model produces only a single estimate of the potential growth rate for the time period under analysis. Since its evolution over time is what is important, a time-varying parameter approach is applied to estimate a time series for $\hat{g}_t^N$. Second, the unemployment rate and, more generally, labor market data are notoriously unreliable for some of the economies in the sample.

To deal with this data problem, Harrod's definition of $\hat{g}_t^N$ is linked to the relationship between unemployment and growth. The potential growth rates of the Asian economies are then estimated based on an aggregate supply model. In the long run, unemployment will be constant when it is equal to the nonaccelerating inflation rate of unemployment (NAIRU). Therefore, the potential growth rate can be defined as that growth rate consistent with $U_t = U_t^N$, which implies $\Delta U_t = 0$. Okun's relation in terms of the NAIRU can be rewritten as follows:

$$U_t = U_t^N - \beta_t(\hat{g}_t - \hat{g}_t^N) \tag{2}$$

where the Okun coefficient (β_t) and the NAIRU (U_t^N) are assumed to vary over time.

The relationship between inflation and unemployment is given by the following Phillips curve:

$$\pi_t = \pi_t^e - \gamma_t(U_t - U_t^N) \tag{3}$$

where π_t and π_t^e are, respectively, the actual and expected inflation rates, while γ_t is a time-varying parameter. By substituting (3) into (2), the following equation is obtained:

$$\pi_t = \pi_t^e + \phi_t(\hat{g}_t - \hat{g}_t^N) \tag{4}$$

where $\phi_t = \beta_t\gamma_t$. The specification in (4) formalizes an aggregate supply model with time-varying parameters.

To estimate the model in (4), an estimate of the expected inflation rate π_t^e is required. Because of limited data for expected inflation, π_t^e is modeled as a function of the actual inflation rate π_t with two possible specifications. One specification, expected inflation in time t, is a time-varying function of actual inflation in t plus a random shock:

$$\pi_t^e = \alpha_t\pi_t + \varepsilon_t \tag{5}$$

The estimated model in this case is as follows:

$$\hat{g}_t = \hat{g}_t^N + \frac{(1-\alpha_t)}{\phi_t}\pi_t + \varepsilon_t \tag{6}$$

The second specification assumes an extreme form of adaptive expectations (a random walk), with expected inflation in t equal to actual inflation in t–1 plus a random shock:

$$\pi_t^e = \pi_{t-1} + \varepsilon_t \tag{7}$$

The second model is as follows:

$$\hat{g}_t = \hat{g}_t^N + \frac{1}{\phi_t}\Delta\pi_t + \varepsilon_t \tag{8}$$

The constant term $\hat{g}_t^N$ in equations (6) and (8) provides an estimate of potential growth over time. To take account of the possible effects of the degree of openness on the slope of the Phillips curve, equations (6) and (8) are augmented with the share of imports in GDP. These equations are specified in state-space form, and the Kalman filter is used for estimation. This is a statistical procedure that can produce time-varying coefficients (Harvey 1989).

faster without stoking inflationary pressures. When surplus labor is eliminated, wages and possibly inflation start increasing. That is when growth is at its potential. It is true that a country with surplus labor can have rising inflation, but the likely explanation in such a situation is that constraints are creating bottlenecks that hamper the reallocation of labor. This implies that an economy's potential growth rate could be higher if such bottlenecks were eased or eliminated.

Meanwhile, in the case of the Central Asian economies, their dependence on natural resources can affect the estimates through the effect of commodity price shocks on domestic inflation. However, it is

2.1.5 How well does the aggregate supply model of potential growth perform?

To gauge whether the model produces sensible estimates of potential output growth, test its key insight: Inflationary pressures should arise when the gap between actual and potential growth rates widens. The test is carried by pooling all data. The following regression is estimated using a fixed effects model:

$$\Delta\pi_{it} = \vartheta_i + \omega(\hat{g}_{it} - \hat{g}_{it}^N) + \varepsilon_{it}$$

where $\Delta\pi_{it}$ is the change in the inflation rate and $(\hat{g}_{it} - \hat{g}_{it}^N)$ is the difference between actual and potential growth rates.

The expectation is that $\omega > 0$ and statistically significant. The model is first estimated for a large sample of 71 economies across the world, and then for the sample of 22 developing Asian economies plus Japan. Results confirm the hypothesis that, when the gap between actual and potential growth widens, inflationary pressures emerge. In the larger sample, results confirm that, where inflation rates are below 25%, for each percentage point of actual growth in excess of the natural growth rate, the inflation rate increases by about 0.12 percentage points. Where inflation is above 25%, the relationship breaks down. Meanwhile, in the sample of Asian economies, results show that, where inflation rates are below 45%, for each percentage point of actual growth in excess of the natural growth rate, the inflation rate increases by about 0.2 percentage points.

difficult to state a priori the sign of this relation, which possibly should be stronger in more open economies. This can be controlled for, if only indirectly, by including in the model the share of imports in GDP (Romer 1993). The problem is the lack of sufficiently long time series, with the consequence that meaningful results are difficult to obtain. The model being estimated is therefore based on certain assumptions that may not exactly fit oil-dependent economies. Box 2.1.5 discusses how well the model performs with the given sample.

Graphs of estimated potential growth rates and actual growth rates are presented in Figure 2.1.2. These are for 12 of the 22 developing economies in Asia under consideration.[2]

These graphs show that the potential growth rate was more stable than actual growth, and that it was fairly high and/or increasing in the 1980s and 1990s in most economies. The pattern aligns with expectations. The graphs also suggest that, in most cases, the estimated potential growth rate was higher in 2000 than in 2014. Moreover, the trend was either stable or declining during 2008–2014. Figure 2.1.3 shows the difference between the period average rates for potential growth and actual growth between 2000–2007 (pre-crisis) and 2008–2014 (post-crisis).

It is worth noting that during 2008–2014, potential growth declined in Asia's advanced economies as well as in some of the major economies, including the PRC and the Republic of Korea. Thailand suffered a significant decline in its potential growth rate, which is the lowest in Southeast Asia. Potential growth increased, however, in Indonesia, Pakistan, the Philippines, and Uzbekistan. Meanwhile, Bangladesh, Fiji, and India maintained the same pace in both subperiods. Overall, comparing pre-crisis and post-crisis periods, the decline in potential growth accounts for 39.6% of the decline in actual growth.[3] This implies that about 60% of the decline appears to be a temporary effect of the business cycle.

2.1.2 Potential growth rate estimates and actual growth rates

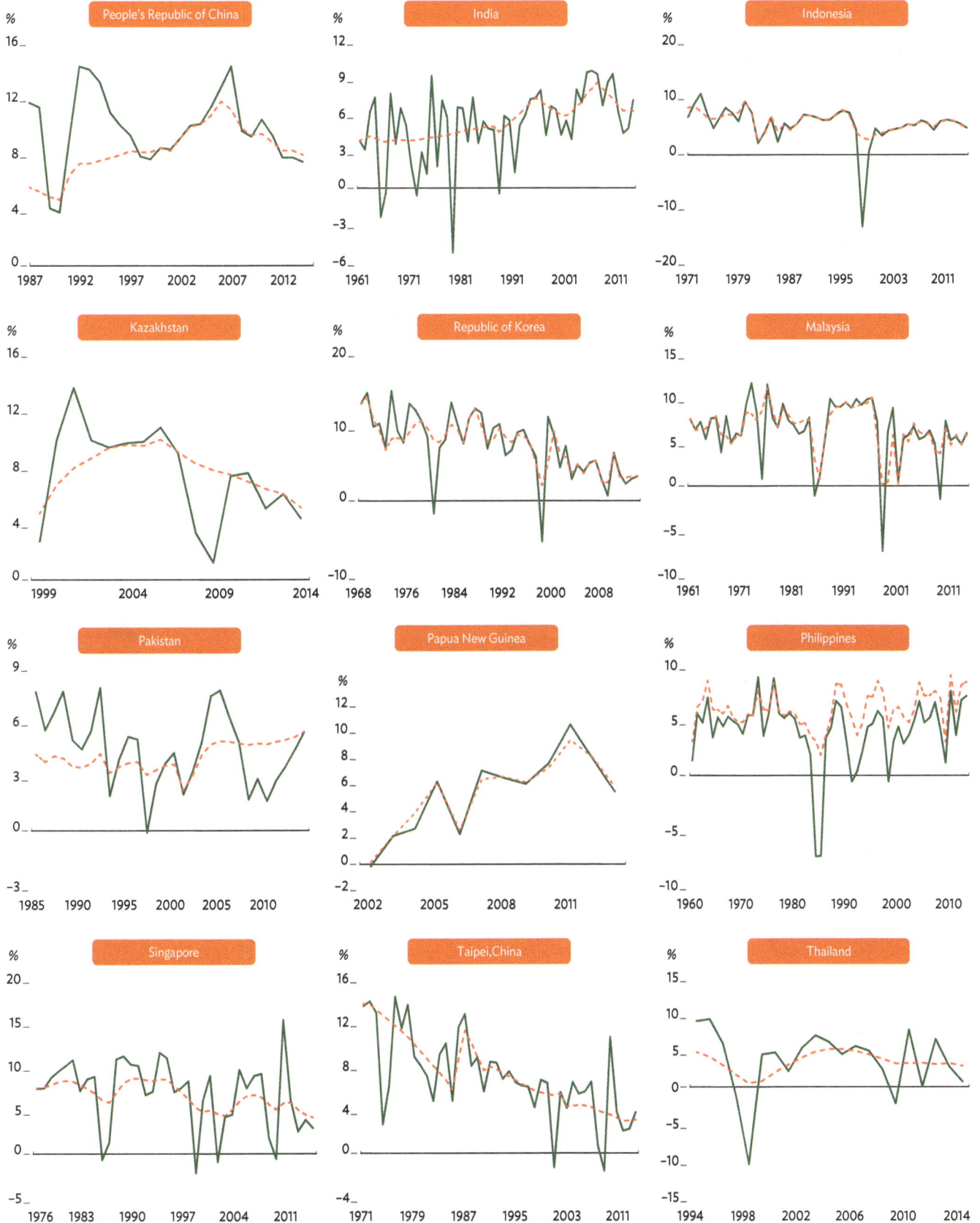

People's Republic of China

India

Indonesia

Kazakhstan

Republic of Korea

Malaysia

Pakistan

Papua New Guinea

Philippines

Singapore

Taipei,China

Thailand

Note: Broken lines show potential growth, solid lines actual growth.

Source: ADB estimates.

Click here for figure data

Key features of potential growth trends in the four largest economies in the sample, which accounted for about 80% of developing Asia's actual GDP in 2014, were as follows:

People's Republic of China. During the expansionary phase up to 2007, before the GFC, the PRC economy operated at potential or slightly above it. From 2008, a gradual decline in potential growth is observed to be about 7.9% in 2014, just slightly above actual growth at 7.4%. Post-crisis average potential growth declined by 1.11 percentage points relative to the pre-crisis average. During 2008–2014, inflation slowed as the deviation of actual growth from potential growth was only slightly negative. This is consistent with the theoretical framework underlying the model, which states that a decline in the inflation rate is associated with the actual growth rate being below potential.[4]

India. For most of the estimation period, India's potential growth rate was quite stable.[5] A substantial increase starting in the early 2000s is observed, with potential growth peaking in 2007 at 8.6%. As with the PRC, potential growth declined in the aftermath of the GFC, falling to 6.3% in 2014. However, the average in 2008–2014 was only 0.06 percentage points lower than in 2000–2007. The average deviation of actual from potential growth was slightly negative. Also as with the PRC, this indicates that India's economy grew at close to its potential during this period.

Republic of Korea. The economy's potential growth rate has been declining for quite some time. It experienced a significant decline during the Asian financial crisis of 1997–1998, after which it recovered slightly. However, the broader trend since 2001 has been negative. The 2008–2014 average was 2.09 percentage points lower than in 2000–2007. The 2008–2014 averages of actual and potential growth were also very close to each other, the deviation being slightly negative. This is consistent with a slightly declining inflation rate. In 2014, the Republic of Korea's potential growth rate was estimated at 3.3%, very close to actual growth.

Indonesia. For most of the estimation period, Indonesia's potential growth rate was stable. However, its potential growth rate declined during the Asian financial crisis of 1997–1998 to 3% from a peak of 8.4% in 1995. It then recovered to an average of almost 5% in 2000–2007 and increased to 5.8% during 2008–2014. During this period, actual and potential growth rates were close, so that the average change in inflation was stable. Among developing Asia's four largest economies, only Indonesia registered a significant increase in potential growth during 2008–2014, rising 0.86 percentage points higher than the 2000–2007 average.

In Figure 2.1.4, the weighted average of the estimated potential growth rates of 13 Asian economies (Asia-13) for which consistent estimates since 1988 are available is calculated. These economies—Bangladesh, Fiji, India, Indonesia, the Republic of Korea, Malaysia,

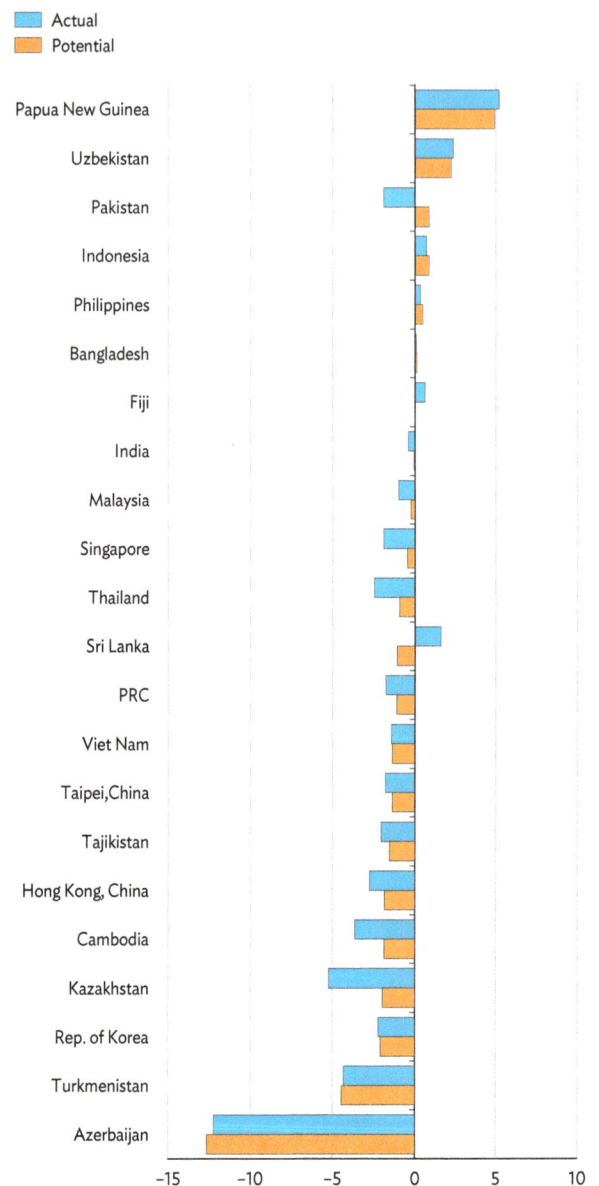

2.1.3 Differences in average actual and potential growth rates, 2000–2007 versus 2008–2014

PRC = People's Republic of China.

Notes: For Fiji, pre-crisis growth rates are for 2001–2007. For Papua New Guinea, post-crisis growth rates are for 2008–2013. Singapore and Thailand used a model augmented with financial factors (Felipe et al. 2015). For Tajikistan, pre-crisis actual growth is for 2001–2007, and potential growth is for 2002–2007.

Source: ADB estimates.

Click here for figure data

Pakistan, the Philippines, the PRC, Singapore, Sri Lanka, Taipei,China, and Hong Kong, China—represent almost 94% of developing Asia's actual GDP in both 1988 and 2014. The weighted average provides a more aggregate picture of these growth dynamics and will help answer the question whether there is evidence that Asia is entering a new normal of lower potential growth. Average potential growth for two other subgroups is also plotted: One is the same group of economies but excluding the PRC (Asia-12) and the other includes only the Republic of Korea, Singapore, Taipei,China, and Hong Kong, China (Asia-4). A comparison of Asia-13 and Asia-12 averages allows the assessment of the influence of the PRC on the potential growth performance of the region as a whole.

In the case of Asia-4, potential growth declined from an average of about 9% in 1988 to just over 3% in 2014. The aggregate behavior of Asia-13 provides a more complex and nuanced view of Asia's potential growth. First, potential growth increased prior to the Asian financial crisis of 1997–1998. The series peaked at a range of 7.3%–7.4% in 1994–1996. Potential growth declined during the crisis and bottomed out in 1998 at 5.36%. It then recovered and increased from 1999 to 2007, peaking at 8.45%. After the GFC in 2008, potential growth started declining, falling to 6.7% in 2014, almost 2 percentage points below the peak. The significant decline from the peak indicates that the region may have entered a new normal of lower potential growth, an issue that will be explored further in the third section of this theme chapter.

It is also important to note that developing Asia's dynamics of potential growth are increasingly determined by the growth performance of the PRC. The PRC share in regional GDP increased to almost 55% in 2014 from only 25% in 1988. In this context, the surge in regional potential growth between 1998 and 2007 was mostly the result of the phenomenal growth performance by the PRC (Figure 2.1.5). The consequence was that the PRC contributed about three-quarters of the overall rise in potential output growth during this period. Specifically, the PRC contributed 2.31 percentage points out of the total increase of 3.09 percentage points. Of that 2.31 percentage points, 1.09 is derived from its rising potential growth rate, and 1.22 can be attributed to the growing PRC share in developing Asia's GDP. Most of the remaining increase in potential growth was contributed by India and the Republic of Korea, while several economies made negative contributions to the regional average.

In the same vein, the decline from the onset of the GFC to 2014 was determined primarily by events in the PRC, India, and the Republic of Korea. However, the latter two economies played a bigger role in this episode. Specifically, about one-third of the 1.78 percentage point fall in average

2.1.4 Estimates of average potential growth rate

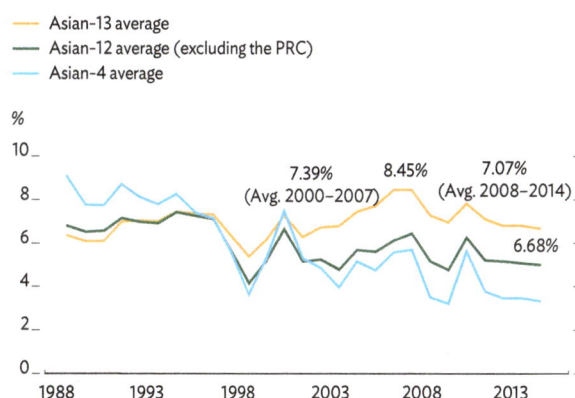

Asia-4 = Republic of Korea, Singapore, Taipei,China, and Hong Kong, China; Asia-12 = Asian-13 minus the People's Republic of China; Asia-13 = Bangladesh, the People's Republic of China, Fiji, India, Indonesia, the Republic of Korea, Malaysia, Pakistan, the Philippines, Singapore, Sri Lanka, Taipei,China, and Hong Kong, China.
Notes: Regional potential growth rate is the average of the individual economies' growth rates, weighted by their share in actual GDP. The regional average including the 22 economies that constitute developing Asia (i.e., the 22 in the study, excluding Japan) since 2000 is as follows (Tajikistan is not included in 2000 and 2001 as its weight is only 0.3%): 2000: 7.04%; 2001: 6.18%; 2002: 6.65%; 2003: 6.75%; 2004: 7.40%; 2005: 7.69%; 2006: 8.40%; 2007: 8.38%. 2008: 7.21%; 2009: 6.87%; 2010: 7.68%; 2011: 7.00%; 2012: 6.70%; 2013: 6.71%; 2014: 6.56%.
Source: ADB estimates.
Click here for figure data

2.1.5 Contributions to change in potential growth

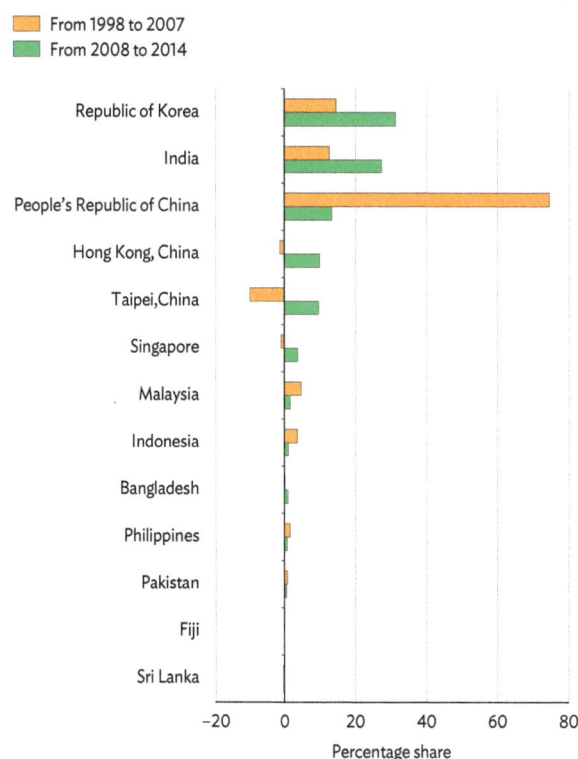

Source: ADB estimates.
Click here for figure data

potential growth can be attributed to the Republic of Korea, which experienced a large fall in both potential growth and GDP share—nearly 7 percentage points—from 2007 to 2014. India's GDP share and potential growth rate also declined, by 2 and 2.3 percentage points, respectively. As a result, its contribution to the aggregate decline was also approximately a third. Meanwhile, the decline in potential growth in the PRC was offset by the rise in its regional share of GDP, so that its net contribution to the regional decline was only 0.24 percentage points, or 13% of the total.

The picture without the PRC (Asia-12) is very similar to that of the Asian-13 but, as expected, potential growth without the PRC is lower both before and after the GFC. As with Asia-13, the decline during 2008–2014 was significant. The substantial decline in Asia-12 average potential growth with respect to the earlier part of the 1990s is also noted. Another common feature is that Asia-12 average potential growth during the Asian financial crisis was lower than during the GFC. With or without the PRC, the behavior of potential growth clearly shows a turning point after the GFC.

The question remains whether this slowdown in potential growth is a new normal for the region—and what, if anything, policy makers can do to counteract this trend. Future gains in living standards and poverty elimination rest on a grasp of potential growth. Identifying the institutional and policy constraints that keep an economy from achieving its frontier potential growth will be critical to counteract the current slowdown. Knowing which factors have driven potential growth in the past can guide policy makers' efforts to meet today's growth challenge.

Determinants of potential growth

Several approaches are used to tease out what is behind the recent slowdown in potential growth. First, the time-series estimates of potential growth for the 22 developing economies in Asia can be decomposed using a set of simple techniques that stem from the definitions of the key concepts. From the Harrod (1939) concept of the natural growth rate, potential growth is the sum of labor force growth and potential labor productivity growth—that is, growth in potential output per worker. Potential labor productivity growth itself can be decomposed to show it driven by such factors as within-sector productivity growth, the effect of employment reallocation across sectors, capital accumulation, and total factor productivity growth.

Second, an econometric model is estimated using cross-country data for a larger sample of countries including those outside of Asia to establish the determinants of potential growth. The objective is to obtain robust and reliable estimates of variables significantly correlated with the potential growth rate.

Finally, firm-level data are used to study the role of institutional obstacles in generating distortions that cause resource misallocation. This exercise can help shed light on policies that could help shift an economy closer to its frontier potential growth.

Potential labor productivity growth

Following Harrod's definition of the natural growth rate, potential labor productivity growth is potential growth less the growth rate of the labor force. Because labor market data in many developing economies in Asia are unreliable, working-age population, which is the population aged 15–64, is used as a proxy for the labor force. These data are filtered using appropriate statistical techniques to purge short-term variability, which is caused largely by transitory migration flows.

Figure 2.2.1 shows both potential and actual labor productivity growth rates for the 12 Asian economies whose potential growth was graphed in the previous section. The PRC displays a high potential labor productivity growth rate—significantly higher than that of India. This explains a large part of the difference in potential output growth between these two economies. Consistent with their transition into high-income economies, the Republic of Korea and Taipei,China show marked declines in potential labor productivity growth. This is less obvious in Singapore. Actual and potential labor productivity growth tend to track each other quite closely in most economies. However, the Philippines is a notable exception, with actual labor productivity growth lagging potential for most of the period.

Figure 2.2.2 reports the breakdown of potential output growth into potential labor productivity growth and filtered labor force growth for the periods 2000–2007 and 2008–2013. With a few exceptions— Malaysia, Pakistan, and Singapore—potential labor productivity growth

2.2.1 Potential and actual labor productivity growth rates

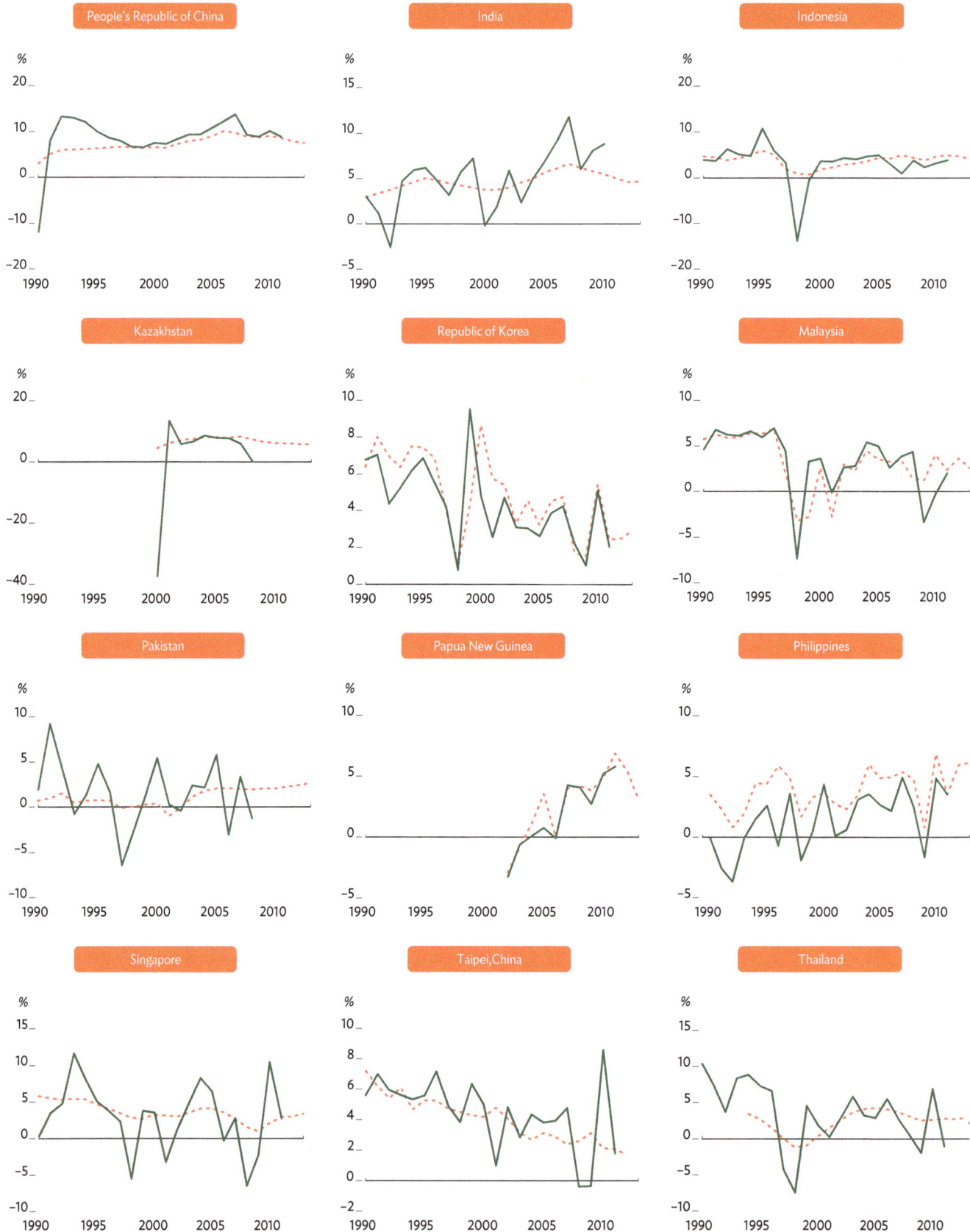

Note: Broken lines show potential growth, solid lines actual growth.
Source: ADB estimates.
Click here for figure data

was the main contributor to potential output growth. On average, potential labor productivity growth accounted for 78% of potential output growth during 2000–2007 and 86% during 2008–2013.

Meanwhile, Figure 2.2.3 shows the change in annual average potential output growth between the periods 2000–2007 and 2008–2013. There is a decline in most economies. The figure also shows in each bar the change in the two components. In the PRC, potential output growth declined by about 1 percentage point between the two subperiods. Most of the decline is accounted for by the slowing of working-age population growth, with potential labor productivity growth actually increasing slightly. On the other hand, India saw a very small increase in potential output growth between the two periods. This was accounted for by the increase in potential labor productivity growth, which was slightly larger than the decline in working-age population growth. In the Republic of Korea, most of the decline in potential growth is accounted for by the decline in potential labor productivity growth. And, in Indonesia, most of the increase in potential output growth was accounted for by the increase in potential labor productivity growth.

Decomposition of potential labor productivity growth

Using shift-share analysis, the estimates of labor productivity growth are decomposed into productivity growth within the sector, changes in the employment structure, slack in the economy, capital deepening, and total factor productivity growth (Foster-McGregor and Verspagen 2016). This provides a simple but very useful way to assess which component of potential labor productivity growth is the largest and matters the most in explaining labor productivity growth. Box 2.2.1 shows how these decompositions are interpreted.

Equation (3) in Box 2.2.1 shows that potential labor productivity growth can be decomposed into the sum of the within, static, and dynamic effects, plus two terms that capture an *output gap* and a *labor gap*. This decomposition allows the comparison of the changes in the two gaps with the three structural effects. Results are presented in Figure 2.2.4 along with the average potential labor productivity growth for 1990–2011.

In most economies, the contribution of the combined gaps to potential labor productivity growth is relatively small compared to those of the structural effects. Kazakhstan, the Philippines, and Sri Lanka are the main exceptions, all with gaps making positive contributions. The positive contribution means that potential labor productivity growth has been faster than actual labor productivity growth.

2.2.2 Contributions to potential output growth

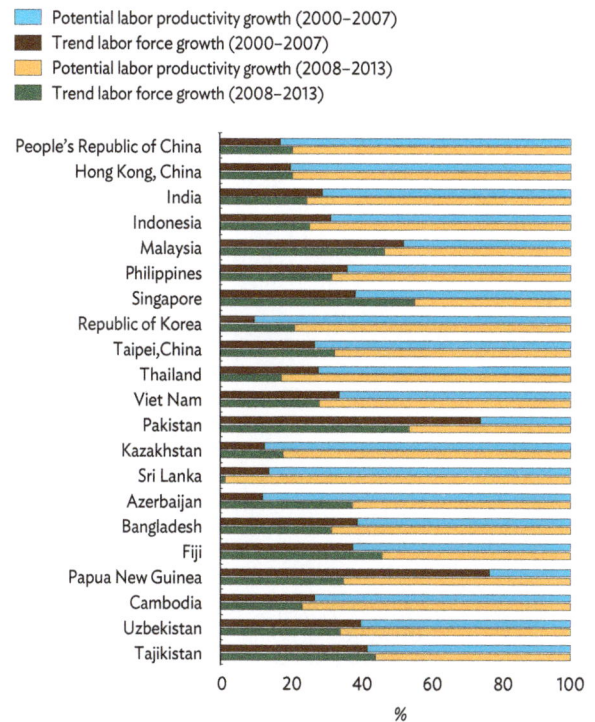

Note: For Fiji and Papua New Guinea, first period refers to 2002–2007. For Taipei,China, Cambodia, and Uzbekistan, second period refers to 2008–2012. For Tajikistan, first period refers to 2002–2007 while second period refers to 2008–2012.
Source: ADB estimates.
Click here for figure data

2.2.3 Change in potential output growth and its components between 2000–2007 and 2008–2013

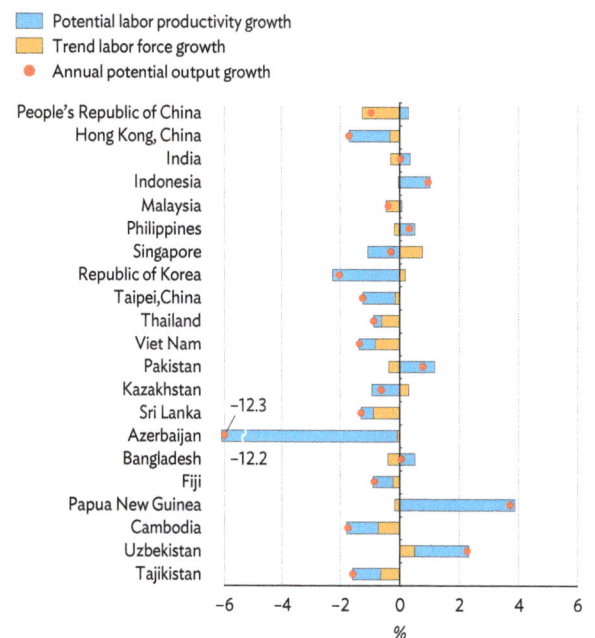

Note: For Fiji and Papua New Guinea, first period refers to 2002–2007. For Taipei,China, Cambodia, and Uzbekistan, second period refers to 2008–2012. For Tajikistan, first period refers to 2002–2007 while second period refers to 2008–2012.
Source: ADB estimates.
Click here for figure data

2.2.1 Decomposition of labor productivity growth, potential labor productivity growth, and total factor productivity growth

The procedure for decomposing potential labor productivity growth can be depicted in stages:

1. Decomposition of actual labor productivity growth.

A well-known structural decomposition of labor productivity growth is given by the following equation (omitting the subscript 't' for time):

$$\hat{g}-\hat{l} \equiv \hat{y} \equiv \sum_i \frac{(y_i^1-y_i^0)}{y^0}s_i^0 + \sum_i \frac{(s_i^1-s_i^0)}{y^0}y_i^0 + \sum_i \frac{(y_i^1-y_i^0)(s_i^1-s_i^0)}{y^0} \quad (1)$$

where $\hat{g}$ is the growth rate of GDP, $\hat{l}$ is the growth rate of aggregate labor input, y is labor productivity and $\hat{y}$ denotes actual labor productivity growth, and s_i denotes the share of industry i in aggregate employment. The three terms on the right hand side are the *within effect*, or the contribution of productivity growth rates within each sector i; the *static effect*, or the productivity effect of relocating labor that results from differences in productivity levels at the start of the period; and the *dynamic effect*, or the productivity effect that results from relocating labor from one sector to another, at the same time taking into account the change in the productivity growth rate over the period. The sum of the last two is equal to the effect of employment reallocation across sectors. The symbol Σ denotes summation with this operation carried out for each of the three effects across the nine sectors for which data are available: agriculture, mining, manufacturing, construction, utilities, trade, transport and commerce, the public sector, and finance, insurance, and real estate.

2. Potential labor productivity growth and the output and labor gaps.

The same structural decomposition of labor productivity growth is applied to the potential rate of labor productivity growth ($\hat{y}^N$) by rewriting the definition of potential growth rate (g^N) as follows:

$$\hat{y}^N \equiv \hat{g}^N - \hat{n}^N \equiv (\hat{g}-\hat{l})-(\hat{g}-\hat{g}^N)+(\hat{l}-\hat{n}^N), \quad (2)$$

where $\hat{n}^N$ is the growth rate of potential labor force, $(\hat{g}-\hat{l}) \equiv \hat{y}$ is the growth rate of actual labor productivity, $(\hat{g}-\hat{g}^N)$ is the difference between the actual rate of output growth and the potential rate (or the *output gap*), and $(\hat{l}-\hat{n}^N)$ is the difference between actual employment growth and the growth rate of the potential labor force (and equal to the growth rate of the participation rate). This is called the *labor gap*. These last two terms reflect slack in an economy that is not operating at its potential.

Substituting equation (1) into equation (2), yields a decomposition of potential labor productivity growth:

$$\hat{y}^N \equiv \sum_i \frac{(y_i^1-y_i^0)}{y^0}s_i^0 + \sum_i \frac{(s_i^1-s_i^0)}{y^0}y_i^0 +$$

$$\sum_i \frac{(y_i^1-y_i^0)(s_i^1-s_i^0)}{y^0}-(\hat{g}-\hat{g}^N)+(\hat{l}-\hat{n}^N) \quad (3)$$

The first three terms have the same interpretation as in equation (1), while the last two are the output and labor gaps. A negative output gap and a positive labor gap add to potential labor productivity growth.

3. Total factor productivity growth.

Total factor productivity (TFP) is often used as a measure of the efficiency with which both labor and capital are used and is sometimes preferred to labor productivity. The growth rate of TFP can be decomposed into the same three terms as labor productivity growth by replacing labor productivity in equation (1) with TFP (ϕ). The resulting decomposition is as follows:

$$\hat{\phi} \equiv \sum_i \frac{(\phi_i^1-\phi_i^0)}{\phi^0}s_i^0 + \sum_i \frac{(s_i^1-s_i^0)}{\phi^0}\phi_i^0 + \sum_i \frac{(\phi_i^1-\phi_i^0)(s_i^1-s_i^0)}{\phi^0} \quad (4)$$

The same three terms representing the within, static, and dynamic contributions to TFP growth ($\hat{\phi}$) in this case are present.

4. Extended decomposition of potential labor productivity growth: the role of TFP growth and of capital deepening.

Combining TFP growth decomposition with decomposition of potential labor productivity growth provides a more detailed decomposition of the latter that allows an estimation of the effects of both capital deepening and TFP growth. From a production function that assumes perfectly competitive factor markets, actual labor productivity growth can be written as follows:

$$(\hat{g}-\hat{l}) \equiv \hat{\phi}+(1-\alpha)(\hat{k}-\hat{l}) \quad (5)$$

where $\hat{k}$ is the growth rate of aggregate capital, $(1-\alpha)$ is the share of capital in GDP, and $\hat{\phi}$ is the growth rate of TFP. This equation states that the growth rate of actual labor productivity is equal to TFP growth plus the weighted growth rate of the ratio of capital over labor, with the weight being the share of capital in GDP. Replacing $\hat{\phi}$ in equation (5) with the expression in equation (4) and inserting this into equation (2) results in the following decomposition of potential labor productivity growth:

$$\hat{y}^N \equiv \sum_i \frac{(\phi_i^1-\phi_i^0)}{\phi^0}s_i^0 + \sum_i \frac{(s_i^1-s_i^0)}{\phi^0}\phi_i^0 +$$

$$\sum_i \frac{(\phi_i^1-\phi_i^0)(s_i^1-s_i^0)}{\phi^0}+(1-\alpha)(\hat{k}-\hat{l})-(\hat{g}-\hat{g}^N)+(\hat{l}-\hat{n}^N) \quad (6)$$

This relates potential labor productivity growth to the within, static, and dynamic contributions to TFP growth, capital deepening, and the output and labor gaps.

The analysis implies that, on average, the within effect accounts for 91% percent of potential labor productivity growth, and the static effect for 15%. Meanwhile, the dynamic effect is small, and the contribution of the two gaps is negative. It can therefore be concluded that the failure to realize potential because of the two gaps has a minimal role in explaining potential labor productivity growth.

Subsequent decomposition accounts for capital deepening and TFP growth (Figure 2.2.5). As shown in Box 2.2.1, the contribution of TFP growth is equal to the sum of the within, static, and dynamic effects. Interestingly, the contribution of capital deepening is always positive and high in many countries. Hence, a significant portion of overall labor productivity growth comes from capital deepening rather than from pure efficiency improvements. This also implies that actual labor productivity growth is higher than TFP growth in all cases. As in the previous decomposition, the within effect is found to make the dominant contribution to potential labor productivity growth.

Factors affecting structural transformation

The findings show that the structural transformation effects (that is, the static and dynamic effects) contributed much less than the within effect. This raises the question what has prevented the faster reallocation of labor. Felipe et al. (2014) documented that the share of agricultural employment in the Republic of Korea recorded a 1.23 percentage point decline per annum during 1962–2013, falling from 69% to 6%. Meanwhile, the corresponding decline for the PRC was 1 percentage point per annum, from a share of 82% to 31%, and for Taipei,China 0.88 points, from a share of 50% to 5%. These are among the fastest declines in history, even faster than the declines experienced by the advanced economies in the 19th and 20th centuries. Meanwhile, India, Pakistan, and many other economies still have very high agricultural employment shares, which are declining very slowly.

Figure 2.2.6 shows the employment structure of typical low-, middle-, and high-income country. Probably, the most salient feature is the different shares of agriculture: 39% of total employment in low-income economies, 17% in middle-income economies, and 2% in high-income economies. The flip side of this is the share of services.

Structural transformation has been much faster in some Asian economies than in others. Differential paces of economic growth can, by themselves, generate different speeds of structural change that reflect the relative productivity growth of different sectors, or changes in the composition of demand (Herrendorf, Rogerson, and Valentinyi 2014). Impediments to the reallocation of factors of production are also important. These can be related to government failure or market failure caused by coordination problems and underdeveloped financial markets (Sen 2016).

2.2.4 Structural decomposition of potential labor productivity growth, 1990–2011

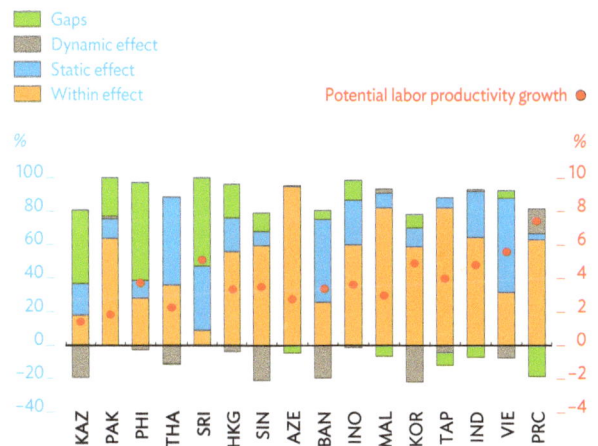

AZE = Azerbaijan, BAN = Bangladesh, HKG = Hong Kong, China, IND = India, INO = Indonesia, KAZ = Kazakhstan, KOR = Republic of Korea, MAL = Malaysia, PAK = Pakistan, PHI = Philippines, PRC = People's Republic of China, SIN = Singapore, SRI = Sri Lanka, TAP = Taipei,China, THA = Thailand, VIE = Viet Nam.
Note: For Kazakhstan, 1999–2008. For Pakistan, 1995–2008. For Thailand, 1994–2011. For Sri Lanka, 1995–2011. For Azerbaijan, 2001–2011. For Bangladesh, 2003–2009. For Viet Nam, 1996–2011.
Source: ADB estimates.
Click here for figure data

2.2.5 Extended decomposition of potential labor productivity growth, 1990–2011

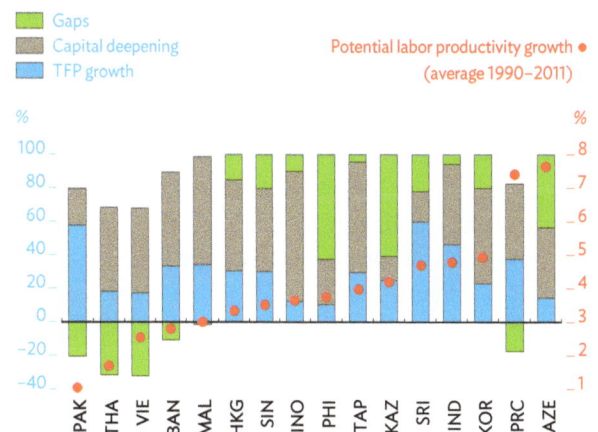

AZE = Azerbaijan, BAN = Bangladesh, HKG = Hong Kong, China, IND = India, INO = Indonesia, KAZ = Kazakhstan, KOR = Republic of Korea, MAL = Malaysia, PAK = Pakistan, PHI = Philippines, PRC = People's Republic of China, SIN = Singapore, SRI = Sri Lanka, TAP = Taipei,China, TFP = total factor productivity, THA = Thailand, VIE = Viet Nam.
Source: ADB estimates.
Click here for figure data

2.2.6 Typical employment structures by type of economy

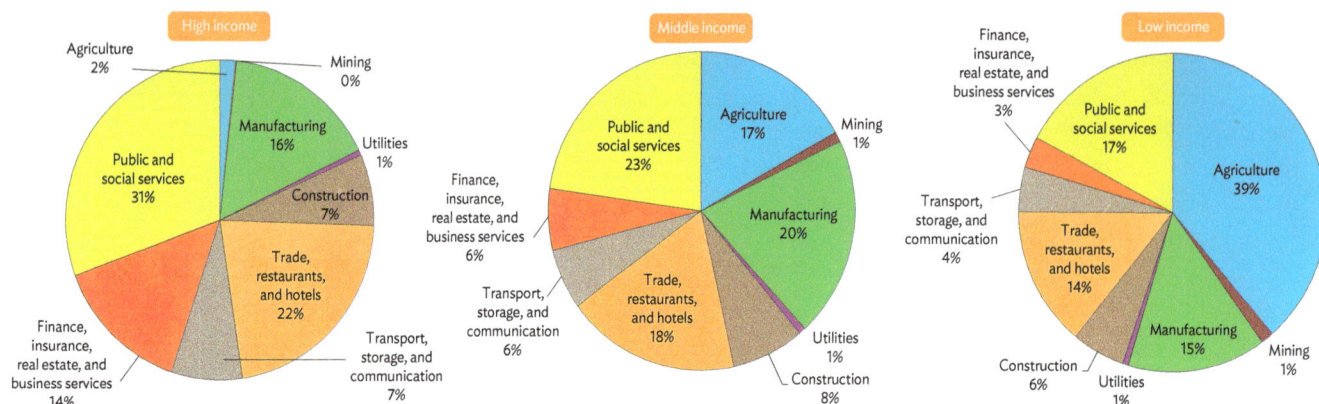

Notes: These are derived from Lowess regressions (Foster-McGregor and Verspagen 2016). The shares in the three charts are the predicted values of these regressions at three distinct values of GDP per capita: $24,189 (the 2011 value for Taipei,China as the high-income reference), $8,737 (the 2011 value for the People's Republic of China as the middle-income reference), and $3,372 (the 2010 value for India as the low-income reference). To be precise, the employment structure of these three economies is not used, but instead the predicted values of the employment structure derived from the Lowess regression at these levels of GDP per capita.

Source: ADB estimates.

Click here for figure data

Government failures that slow down the rate of structural transformation often occur in four policy areas. First, land reform and land-use policies affect the reallocation of labor resources from low- to high-productivity sectors, albeit indirectly. Widespread land reform through the fair redistribution of agricultural land can boost agricultural productivity and provide surplus labor that may be reallocated to industry. Agrarian reform can also effect income redistribution that encourages the formation of human capital and increase aggregate demand. The Republic of Korea and Taipei,China successfully implemented widespread land reform prior to industrialization, allowing their economies to undergo rapid structural transformation from the 1970s to the 1990s. Other economies in Asia attempted to implement land reform but with few tangible results.

Second, labor policies that are geared toward protecting labor welfare impose rigidities in nominal wages and introduce barriers to labor reallocation. These regulations provide incentive to substitute capital for labor and can slow down the pace of investment. As such, labor market regulations potentially impede structural transformation when they are overly rigid. One problem partly responsible for India's slow pace of structural transformation is its rigid labor market as stipulated in the Industrial Disputes Act, 1947.

A third government failure is migration policy that restricts worker mobility. Limiting the mobility of labor directly affects the availability of this resource and can create geographic imbalance between the availability of qualified workers and demand for them. An example of a restrictive migration policy is the *hukou* system of residency permits in the PRC, which constrains the free flow of labor between urban and rural areas and consequently slows the pace of structural transformation.

Lastly, governments inadvertently raise the cost of business by imposing product and market regulations. These slow structural transformation through their negative effects on investment and, consequently, firms' scale of operations. While governments often impose labor market and product market regulations to mitigate market failures, the failure of regulatory reform to keep pace with economic development can introduce barriers to structural transformation.

The other set of determinants involve market failures such as coordination problems that result from the high cost of collating and processing information on new products, technologies, and industries, and credit market failures. Both of these market failures involve externalities and information asymmetries.

Coordination problems typically arise when externalities create significantly large differences between private and social returns. In particular, a problem arises when externalities depress private returns. Investment in new technology, for example, is risky, with the first mover typically bearing the brunt of the risk. Meanwhile, successful investment invites the entry of other investors and undercuts the first mover's effective rate of return on the investment. To avoid exposure to this risk, the investor may forego the investment unless it is possible to prevent or delay the entry of competition, even though society would view competition as beneficial. This state of affairs discourages investment in new technology and the adoption of new production processes unless governments intervene.

Credit market failures often stem from bad choices and moral hazards in the allocation of loans. Developing economies typically have underdeveloped financial markets and suffer severe information asymmetries. In addition, misguided government policies can force the misallocation of credit, making it difficult to obtain financing for new projects with promise and to scale up operations that have already proven their worth (León-Ledesma and Christopoulos 2016). The resulting low rate of investment and small scale of operations in high-productivity sectors slows the pace of structural transformation. To overcome credit market failures, governments can implement selective credit policies by providing credit directly to targeted sectors and indirectly through loan guarantees.

Macroeconomic determinants of potential growth

The panel of Asian countries under study is augmented by including other economies, both emerging and advanced, to arrive at a total of 69 economies studied over the period 1960–2014 (the list is reported in Table 2.2.1). As potential growth is the sum of the growth rates of potential labor productivity and the labor force, the analysis needs to account for both components. Moreover, the decomposition analysis indicates that potential labor productivity growth is attributed mostly to productivity growth within sectors.

The search for the determinants of productivity growth is complex because the literature provides a long list. To overcome this difficulty, various procedures for model selection were devised with the objective of determining which variables robustly correlate with economic growth (e.g., Sala-i-Martin, Doppelhofer, and Miller 2004). One such methodology is applied in this chapter: the Bayesian model-averaging

2.2.1 Economies included in the analysis

Developing Asia	Azerbaijan, Bangladesh, Cambodia, the People's Republic of China, Fiji, India, Indonesia, Kazakhstan, the Republic of Korea, Malaysia, Pakistan, Papua New Guinea, the Philippines, Singapore, Sri Lanka, Tajikistan, Thailand, Turkmenistan, Uzbekistan, Viet Nam, Taipei,China, and Hong Kong, China
Other emerging economies	Algeria, Argentina, Bolivia, Brazil, Colombia, Costa Rica, Dominican Republic, Ecuador, Egypt, Hungary, Mexico, Morocco, Panama, Peru, Poland, Qatar, Saudi Arabia, South Africa, Turkey, Uruguay, and Venezuela
Advanced economies	Australia, Austria, Belgium, Canada, the Czech Republic, Denmark, Estonia, Finland, France, Germany, Greece, Iceland, Ireland, Israel, Italy, Japan, Luxembourg, the Netherlands, New Zealand, Norway, Portugal, the Slovak Republic, Slovenia, Spain, Sweden, Switzerland, the United Kingdom, and the United States

approach to estimating classical linear regression models when uncertain about the choice of the explanatory variables (e.g., Magnus, Powell, and Prüfer 2010). Of the long list of 35 possible determinants, details of which are in Lanzafame et al. (2016), the process identified nine robust variables. Two other important institutional variables are included, but only as interactions with two of the robust variables. The definitions and sources of the variables are in Table 2.2.2.

2.2.2 List of variables

Variable name	Definition and explanation	Source
Robust variables		
Working-age population growth rate	This is the trend growth rate of the working-age population aged 15–64, obtained by filtering the data with the Corbae–Ouliaris filter.	Calculations using World Bank's World Development Indicators data
Initial GDP per capita	The value of GDP per capita in the initial period is used to test for convergence.	World Bank's World Development Indicators
Technological gap with the United States	This variable captures the advantage enjoyed by the country that introduces new goods into a market. It is computed as 1 minus the ratio of the level of productivity to that of the United States in purchasing power parity. Closing the gap—that is, taking the variable toward zero—is a sign of progress and catch-up with the frontier. The expected impact is positive since the advantage of backwardness dissipates as the gap closes.	Calculations using Penn World Tables 8.1 data
Gross enrollment ratio in tertiary education	This is the ratio of total enrollment, regardless of age, to the population of the age group that officially corresponds to the tertiary level.	CANA Database for cross-country analyses of national systems, growth, and development (v. Jan 2011). Original source: United Nations Educational, Scientific, and Cultural Organization
Index of labor market rigidity	This index varies from 0 (most flexible) to 3.5 (most rigid). It has four components that are equally weighted: minimum wage, rigidity of hours, the difficulty of laying off redundant workers, and the cost of laying off redundant workers.	World Bank's *Doing Business* database; LAMRIG database by Campos and Nugent (2012)
Voice and accountability index	This index reflects perceptions of the extent to which a country's citizens are able to participate in selecting their government. It incorporates freedom of expression, freedom of association, and freedom in the media. The index ranges from –2.5 (low) to +2.5 (high).	World Bank's Worldwide Governance Indicators, 2014 Update
Government effectiveness index	This index reflects perceptions of the quality of public services, the quality of the civil service, and the degree of civil service independence from political pressures; the quality of policy formulation and implementation; and the credibility of the government's commitment to such policies. The index ranges from –2.5 (low) to +2.5 (high).	World Bank's The Worldwide Governance Indicators, 2014 Update
Trade ratio	This is the sum of exports and imports of goods and services as a percentage of GDP.	World Bank's World Development Indicators national accounts data; Organisation for Economic Co-operation and Development national accounts data
Financial capital integration Index	This is the sum of total foreign assets and liabilities as a percentage of GDP.	Updated and extended version of data set constructed by Lane and Milesi-Ferretti (2007)
Supplementary interaction variables		
Regulatory quality	This index reflects perceptions of the ability of the government to formulate and implement sound policies and regulations that permit and promote private sector development. It varies from –2.5 (low) to 2.5 (high). The variable interacts with financial capital integration.	World Bank's Worldwide Governance Indicators, 2014 Update
Political stability	This index reflects perceptions of the likelihood that the government will be destabilized or overthrown by unconstitutional or violent means, including politically motivated violence and terrorism. It varies from –2.5 (low) to 2.5 (high). This variable interacts with the technology gap with the United States.	World Bank's Worldwide Governance Indicators, 2014 Update

Source: ADB.

The working-age population growth rate is a proxy for the growth rate of the labor force. As the estimates control for labor force growth, the other independent variables are essentially determinants of potential labor productivity growth. A model with country fixed effects is estimated to quantify the effect of these variables on potential growth. Results of the benchmark model estimates are in line with expectations (Table 2.2.3).

2.2.3 Model estimates

Variable	Benchmark	Macro stability
Initial GDP per capita	–0.00033**	–0.00033**
Working-age population growth	1.15725**	1.22262**
Gap with the US	0.07306*	0.07345*
Gap with the US × political stability	–0.00613*	–0.00759*
Tertiary enrollment ratio	0.16284**	.122695**
Tertiary enrollment squared	–0.00160**	–0.00140**
Labor market rigidity	–2.92375**	–2.76644**
Voice and accountability	1.65097^	2.0438*
Government effectiveness	1.36106**	1.15356**
Trade ratio	0.06488**	0.08178**
Trade ratio squared	–0.00007**	–0.000097**
Financial capital integration	0.00452*	0.00415*
Financial capital × regulatory quality	–0.00313**	–0.00289**
Break in 2008–2014	–2.72717**	–2.82251**
Actual–potential growth gap		0.05946
Growth gap volatility		–0.19208**
Number of economies	61	61
Number of observations	425	421

Notes: ** indicates significance at the 1% level, * at 5%, and ^ at 10%. Variables instrumented with first lag. Driscoll and Kraay (1998) standard errors. Fiji and Papua New Guinea were not included in the regression analysis for lack of data, but the model estimates include the other 20 developing economies in Asia.
Source: ADB estimates.

Benchmark model results

The coefficient of working-age population growth is the elasticity of potential output with respect to that variable. It is statistically significant and at the same time not significantly different from 1. This is consistent with the definition of the natural or potential growth rate used in this chapter. The results also indicate that working age is a good proxy for the potential growth rate of the labor force.

The process of capital accumulation has as its proxy initial income per capita. The rationale is that a poor country has a low ratio of capital to labor, which translates into potential to grow quickly. This is driven primarily by the greater opportunity to accumulate capital. The coefficient in the benchmark model implies that an additional $1,000 of initial income per capita lowers potential output growth by 0.33 percentage points.

Using the preferred specification shown in the left column of Table 2.2.3, it is determined that the gross enrollment ratio in tertiary education and an economy's openness to international flows of goods and services have quadratic effects. This means that the effect of these two variables on potential growth increases but only up to a limit.

Meanwhile, coefficients on the technology gap and the three proxies for institutional quality are statistically significant. The positive sign of the technology gap variable is consistent with the observation that the advantage of backwardness dissipates as the gap narrows. The possibility that institutional quality may also affect potential growth indirectly is also considered. For example, Kose et al. (2009) suggested that the effect of integration on international financial markets may be dependent upon institutional quality. To explore this possibility, interaction variables are specified involving the technological gap with the US and political stability, and financial capital integration and regulatory quality. If the impacts of the technological gap and of the integration index depend on institutional quality, then the interaction terms should turn out to be significant.

The empirical results show that the gap with the US has a positive and significant impact on potential growth for the entire range of values of the index of political stability, and its effect is smaller for countries with greater political stability. A 1 percentage point reduction in the gap with the US raises potential output growth by 0.085 percentage points for the least politically stable countries and 0.055 percentage points for the most politically stable.[6] This means that economies that are far from their productivity frontiers and that also have lower political stability can be expected to reap larger benefits from technological spillovers.

Institutional quality also affects the impact of financial integration. Moreover, the effect becomes higher for small values of regulatory quality, with a maximum of 0.0115 percentage points for countries with the lowest regulatory quality.[7] This result may seem counterintuitive at first. From a policy viewpoint, however, it means that financial integration acts as a substitute for high-quality institutions. For emerging economies with low-quality institutions, including some in Asia, the implication is that successful integration into international financial markets may bring about significant long-term growth benefits by raising the potential growth rate.

Incorporating macro stability

The benchmark model is extended by including two variables that capture business cycle features. The first is the actual–potential growth gap, the average of the deviation between an economy's actual growth rate and its potential in the previous 5 years. This variable measures the average distance between actual and potential growth rates. A statistically significant coefficient implies that expansionary or recessionary phases affect the potential growth rate.[8] The second is growth gap volatility, measured as the standard deviation of the actual–potential growth gap during the previous 5 years. This variable measures the volatility of actual growth with respect to the potential growth rate. This captures the possible effects of business cycle features, such as growth volatility, on potential growth.

The coefficient on growth gap volatility is significant with the expected negative sign. The results suggest that reducing volatility by 1 percentage point brings about an increase in potential growth of about 0.193 percentage points. This outcome is in line with other evidence in the literature (e.g., Ramey and Ramey 1995) and indicates that higher growth volatility may harm the potential growth rate and, consequently, that demand-management policies aiming to stabilize actual growth near potential growth can benefit the economy's long-term performance.

Potential growth, misallocation, and institutional obstacles

The impact of reducing or eliminating institutional barriers to factor mobility is examined in this section. The analysis considers the factors that affect structural transformation. The concept of *frontier potential growth* is related to activities and operations at the level of the firm that misallocate factors of production. This analysis complements the results on determinants of potential growth, particularly the importance of institutional variables. Better institutions facilitate the efficient allocation of productive resources, bringing potential growth closer to the frontier and pushing up the frontier itself.

A further motivation for the firm-level analysis is that differences in income per capita across economies are explained mostly by differences in productivity (Caselli 2005). According to the recent literature, differences in productivity and their persistence are attributed in turn to resource misallocation (Kalemli-Ozcan and Sorensen 2012). Factors of production are said to be misallocated if a different allocation of the current aggregate endowment of capital and labor across firms would increase the economy's aggregate productivity.

Misallocation is generated by obstacles. These create in turn distortions or wedges in the marginal products of capital and labor across firms. For example, subsidized credit makes the marginal product of capital artificially low for firms receiving the subsidy and artificially high for other firms. The result is that subsidized firms are more capital intensive than they otherwise would be, and unsubsidized firms are more labor intensive. The outcome is a misallocation of resources. Eliminating the credit subsidy and other distortions allows resources to be better allocated, resulting in faster productivity growth.

Surveys reveal a list of issues that firms consider to be important for them: inspection rules, access to credit, corruption, and labor regulations, among others. The implication is that an economy's potential rate of growth is not independent of policy. Understanding the role of these obstacles is therefore important from a policy and institutional perspective.

Two types of wedges or distortions on the marginal product of capital and labor across firms are calculated by comparing each firm's factor shares of labor and capital with the average of the economy. The measures are explained in more detail in Box 2.2.2. The first is a measure of *output distortion*, wherein the marginal products of capital and labor increase by the same proportion. An example is inspection rules that affect firms beyond a certain size. If there are no distortions, the share of labor in total value added is equal across all firms. However, if a firm avoids inspection rules by being smaller than the optimal size, it will employ fewer workers and hence the labor share will be smaller than the average. Therefore, the ratio of the firm's labor share to the average of the economy is a useful measure of output distortion.

The second is a measure of *factor market distortion*. These distortions alter the use of capital relative to labor, making the ratio different from what is optimal. As noted above, lack of access to credit reduces firms' use of capital, making them more labor intensive than they would otherwise be. Note that, if there were no distortions, the ratio of the shares of capital and labor would be the same across firms. Factor market distortion is therefore measured by comparing the firm's labor to capital ratio with the average ratio in the economy.

Firm-level data for 62 developing economies obtained from World Bank Enterprise Surveys data—the Standardized Data for 2006–2014—are used for empirical analysis. This is a stratified survey of firms that contains financial and business environment information. The original data set contains 134 surveys that cover a total of 61,669 firms. However, the sample is considerably reduced when the data are cleaned. Since multiple cross-sectional surveys are available for some economies, only those with the largest number of firms are kept, such that every economy is represented only once. The final sample is made up of 62 economies and a maximum of 21,539 firms. Details are provided in León-Ledesma (2016). The empirical analysis will determine to what extent certain obstacles to a firm's operations explain the two distortions.

Since the distortion is measured as the difference from the country mean, the average distortion within an economy is zero by construction. Therefore, to see how distortions differ across economies, one needs to look at some other aspect of the distribution such as the standard deviation. The standard deviation, a measure of how dispersed the distortion is within an economy, is calculated using the sample of firms within each economy. As shown in Table 2.2.4, the output distortion is more dispersed on average than the factor market distortion in the full sample of 62 economies and in the subsample of 13 Asian ones. Also, the dispersion of both distortions is slightly wider in the Asian economies.

2.2.4 Within-economy dispersion of the misallocation measures

	Mean	Min	Max
All 62 economies (21,539 firms)			
Output distortion	1.6288	0.7257	2.3836
Factor distortion	1.3958	0.8579	3.0764
13 Asian economies (10,593 firms)			
Output distortion	1.7110	1.3639	2.2137
Factor distortion	1.4966	1.0342	2.1345

Note: Within-economy dispersion is the standard deviation of the distortion across the sample firms within each economy.

Source: ADB estimates based on data from the Standardized Data 2006–2014, World Bank Enterprise Survey.

2.2.2 Distortion measures and misallocation

Measures of distortion are derived from the Hsieh and Klenow (2009) theoretical framework. The framework proposes a model with heterogeneous firm productivity and two types of distortions: output distortions (τ_y) and factor market distortions (τ_k). Output distortions increase the marginal products of capital and labor by the same proportion, and factor market distortions raise the marginal product of capital relative to that of labor. Because these distortions are specific to individual firms and different for each one, they introduce dispersion in firms' incentives to employ factors of production.

The framework assumes that output (Y) is produced using labor (L) and capital (K) with a Cobb–Douglas technology as $Y_i = A_i K_i^\alpha L_i^{1-\alpha}$, where A_i is firm-specific total factor productivity (TFP). With competitive markets, α and $(1-\alpha)$ are the aggregate capital and labor shares, respectively, in total value added (or total costs). Firms maximize profits (subject to this production technology):[a]

$$\pi_i = \max_{K,L}\left[(1-\tau_{y,i})P_iY_i - wL_i - (1+\tau_{k,i})rK_i\right], \tag{1}$$

where w and r are the wage rate and the rental price of capital, respectively, and they are assumed to be equal across firms since factor markets are competitive. Note that the output distortion $\tau_{y,i}$ affects output, while factor-market distortion $\tau_{k,i}$ affects the cost of capital. Also note that TFP and the two distortions are firm-specific, thus causing misallocation as explained in the main text. To obtain measures of the two distortions with a counterpart in the data, Hsieh and Klenow (2009) uses the first order conditions of the maximization problem. After a few transformations, they are as follows:

$$1+\tau_{k,i} = \frac{\alpha}{(1-\alpha)}\frac{wL_i}{rK_i} \tag{2}$$

$$1-\tau_{y,i} = \theta\frac{wL_i}{(1-\alpha)P_iY_i} \tag{3}$$

where $(1+\tau_{k,i})$ and $(1-\tau_{y,i})$ are the measures of the two distortions. Equation (2) indicates that if $\tau_{k,i} = 0$, i.e., if there is no misallocation, the left-hand side equals 1, which implies that $\frac{wL_i}{rK_i}$ (the firm's relative share) is equal to $\frac{(1-\alpha)}{\alpha}$, or the economy's relative share; that is, in the absence of distortions, all firms have the same relative factor share. On the other hand, when there is a factor market distortion, the ratio of labor to capital compensation is higher if the distortion is positive, or smaller if the distortion is negative, than the ratio of the aggregate shares, and the firm is more labor intensive or capital intensive than would be otherwise be optimal. For example, $\tau_{k,i}$ will be high for firms with problems accessing credit, and low otherwise. Likewise, equation (3)

indicates that if $\tau_{y,i} = 0$, i.e., if there is no misallocation, all firms should have the same labor share, $(1-\alpha)$ (θ is a term that captures the effect of the price elasticity of demand). On the other hand, when there is an output distortion, the firm's labor share is higher if the distortion is negative, or smaller if the distortion is positive, than the aggregate labor share, so the firm will be either larger or smaller than is optimal. For example, $\tau_{y,i}$ will be high for firms that face restrictions on size, and low for firms that benefit from output subsidies.

At the level of the individual economy, the dispersion of the distortions, as measured by the standard deviation, is an index of misallocation. This is because, as noted above, in the absence of distortions all firms have the same shares and hence the dispersion is zero.

The empirical strategy follows from the framework. The logarithms of the two distortions $(1+\tau_{k,i})$ and $(1-\tau_{y,i})$ are regressed on 15 obstacles that are declared by firms to affect their operations. To quantify the effect of the obstacles, a dichotomous or dummy variable is created; it takes a value of 1 if a firm answered that the obstacle was "major" or "very severe," and otherwise it takes 0 (i.e., it was "no obstacle," "minor," or "moderate"). This is done separately for the large sample containing 21,539 firms and for the reduced sample of 10,593 Asian firms (the exact number of firms varies depending on whether all firms replied or not). The regressions take the form

$$\log Distortion = a + \sum_{i=1}^{15}\gamma_i X_i + \delta Firm\ size_i + \sum country\ dummies$$

for each of the two distortions, and for the firms in the complete sample of countries and for the firms in the sample of Asian countries (i.e., a total of four regressions). X_i denotes the 15 obstacles considered, and the proxy for firm size is the number of employees, full-time equivalent. The complete sample includes 62 country dummies (fixed effects) and the Asian sample 13 country dummies. Of interest would be whether the coefficients γ_i are statistically significant or not. Note that, in the absence of misallocation, all factor shares should be equal and so the obstacles should not be good predictors of the distortions. If, on the other hand, there is misallocation and it relates to firms' declared obstacles, then the latter should be good predictors of the distortions.

---

[a]   The model assumes that all firms use the same Cobb–Douglas production function. Therefore, in equilibrium, α is the "average" capital share in the economy. In practice, Hsieh and Klenow (2009) allow for α to differ across sectors.

Reference:
Hsieh and Klenow 2009.

Measures of institutional obstacles are also obtained from the same database. Fifteen such obstacles to firms' operations are considered. Firms are asked whether a specific obstacle is important for their operations. Table 2.2.5 presents the list of 15 obstacles and their prevalence in the data set for all economies and for the 13 in the Asian subsample. Generally, Asian firms declare that they face lower obstacles than their counterparts in other regions, especially in terms of informal competitors, corruption, and access to finance. The exceptions are in customs regulations and access to land.

2.2.5 Institutional obstacles by firm

Description	% of firms declaring an obstacle[a]	
How much of an obstacle are the following?	All	Asia
Electricity supply	38.7	35.3
Transportation of goods, supplies, and inputs	17.1	13.8
Customs and trade regulations	11.4	13.3
Informal competitors	24.4	17.4
Access to land	17.0	19.2
Theft and other crime	16.5	9.6
Tax rates	31.5	24.2
Tax administration	20.8	15.3
Business licensing and permits	14.6	11.1
Political instability	30.2	26.6
Corruption	36.5	25.6
Courts	12.2	10.8
Access to finance	24.9	19.8
Labor regulations	12.8	8.1
Inadequately educated workforce	19.9	16.7

[a] Percentage of firms that declare that the obstacle is "major" or "severe." The total number of firms is 21,539, of which 10,593 are in Asia.

Source: ADB estimates based on data from the Standardized Data 2006–2014, World Bank Enterprise Survey.

Do these declared obstacles explain output distortion, factor market distortion, or both? Are there differences between the firms that declare these obstacles to be major or severe and those that declare them only moderate or minor? To answer these questions, the empirical strategy summarized in Box 2.2.2 is carried out.

Regression coefficients of the obstacle dummy variables, together with their 95% confidence intervals, are plotted for each of the 15 obstacles in Figures 2.2.7 and 2.2.8. Results in blue correspond to the regressions using firms in all economies, and results in orange refer to Asian firms. Each regression coefficient times 100 indicates the differential, as percentage change in the distortion, between a firm that declares that an obstacle is major or very severe and a firm that declares that it is not important, minor, or moderate. A statistically insignificant coefficient should be interpreted as evidence that the obstacle is not a significant determinant of misallocation. Conversely, a statistically significant coefficient on a given obstacle means that firms that declare it as major or severe are different from those that do not. In other words, the obstacle is a good predictor of distortion.

A positive coefficient in the regressions for the output distortion implies that firms that declare the obstacle as serious have a larger labor share than the average. Therefore, these firms are larger than they would be if both factors were not misallocated. This is the case for infrastructure obstacles such as poor electricity and transportation, and for customs and trade regulations. This indicates that firms are forced to grow beyond their optimal size to overcome the negative effects of lack of infrastructure. A similar result was obtained for tax rates, the efficiency of tax administration, corruption, and labor regulations. Overall, the largest coefficients are those of customs and trade and labor regulations, at approximately 0.2. This can be interpreted to mean that firms that declare these two obstacles as major or severe have a labor share that is 20% higher than firms that declare these two obstacles not important.

Meanwhile, a negative coefficient in these regressions indicates that the labor share of the firms that declare an obstacle as major or severe is smaller than the average. Therefore, these firms are smaller than they would be without the distortion. This is the case for informal sector competitors, access to land, theft and other crime, courts, access to finance, and poor education. These obstacles act as a tax that holds firm size below optimal. Firms that declare these two obstacles to be major or severe have a labor share 20%–30% less than those firms that declare that these obstacles are not important.

For the factor market distortion regressions, a positive coefficient implies that the share of labor relative to capital is higher than the economy average and that firms are therefore more labor intensive than they would be without the distortion. This is the case for courts, access to finance, labor regulations, and inadequate education. For these obstacles, the difference in the share of labor relative to capital between firms that are affected and those that are not is approximately 10%. On the other hand, a negative coefficient implies that the share of labor relative to capital is lower than the average and that firms are therefore more capital intensive than they would be without the distortion. This is the case for electricity and corruption, with coefficients also at about 10%.

These results lead to the conclusion that the institutional obstacles predict both output and factor market distortions. In aggregate, these factors are key determinants of productivity differences across economies. The evidence shows clear dispersion in the distortions faced by firms in the sample of 62 developing economies. These distortions strongly correlate with institutional obstacles that prevent the efficient allocation of resources between firms. Removing these obstacles would facilitate substantial factor reallocation at the micro level.

2.2.7 Coefficients of output distortion regressions

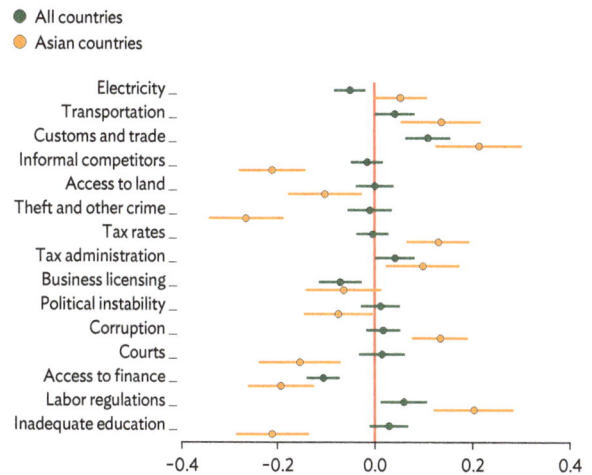

● All countries
● Asian countries

Note: Estimated coefficients on the horizontal axis show the differential as a percentage change in the distortion between a firm that declares that an obstacle is major or very severe and one that declares it not important, a minor obstacle, or moderate. Statistically significant coefficients are good predictors of the output distortion.

Source: ADB estimates.

Click here for figure data

2.2.8 Coefficients of the factor market distortions regressions

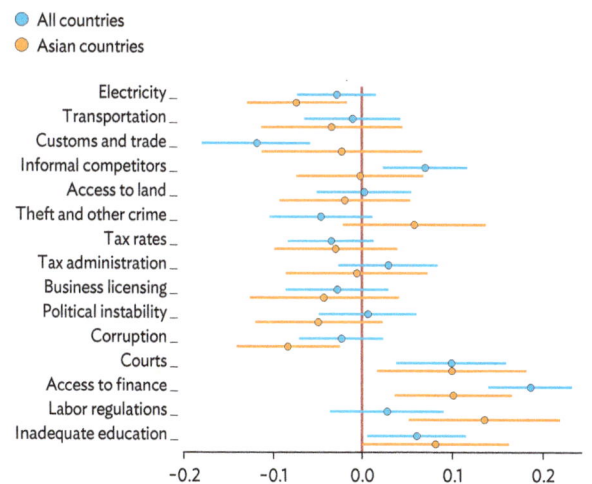

● All countries
● Asian countries

Note: Estimated coefficients on the horizontal axis show the differential as a percentage change in the distortion between a firm that declares that an obstacle is major or very severe and one that declares it not important, a minor obstacle, or moderate. Statistically significant coefficients are good predictors of the factor-market distortion.

Source: ADB estimates.

Click here for figure data

The analysis indicates that most of the 15 obstacles appear to affect distortions that influence the optimal size of firms. On the other hand, many of the obstacles appear to be statistically insignificant in the analysis of factor market distortions. Only courts, access to finance, labor regulations, inadequate education, electricity, and corruption are significant.

The top three obstacles mentioned by the Asian firms are generally significant determinants of distortions in the regressions discussed above. Electricity, corruption, labor laws, access to finance, education, and courts are significant drivers of distortions affecting both output and factor markets. Policy aiming to alleviate misallocation should prioritize addressing these obstacles. For instance, infrastructure obstacles such as electricity appear to be very important drivers of misallocation in the poorest countries. In the PRC, fewer obstacles are declared major or severe. However, tax rates appear to be an important determinant of misallocation by acting as a subsidy on size. In Indonesia, Bangladesh, and Pakistan, access to electricity, which distorts both output and factor markets, is a priority area to reduce misallocation and enhance potential growth through productivity gains.

Asia's aggregate productivity growth would increase through the efficient reallocation of resources at the firm level. This could be achieved through reform to policy on financial and labor markets and on land access, as well as from infrastructure improvements. Such reform could offset part of the natural decline in potential growth that arises as Asian economies become more developed.

A "new normal" for potential growth?

Potential growth since the global financial crisis of 2008–2009 differs sharply from before it. Is this a new normal for Asia? The macro model in the previous section (Table 2.2.2) gives some indication that the period since the global financial crisis has turned less favorable for potential growth. The model includes a binary variable equal to 1 for the period 2008–2014 and 0 otherwise. The statistically significant coefficient on this variable in both the benchmark model and the macro stability model indicates that potential growth in the global sample was lower in the post-crisis period than its historical trend. Even after controlling for changes in the other determinants of potential growth, it was down 2.7 percentage points in the benchmark model. The decline is less for Asia at about 2.2 percentage points, but this too is a sizeable drop.[9]

While the region's potential remains above the trough hit during the Asian financial crisis of 1997–1998, internal factors suggest that the current moderation has yet to run its course. An important implication drawn from the analysis of the determinants of potential growth is that the region's potential has started to decline because the factors that allowed Asia to grow quickly in earlier decades have started to fade. This is true of both the demographic dividend (at least in some economies) and factors that affect labor productivity, such as education, trade, and financial capital integration. As a result, without structural reform, potential growth in many regional economies will slide further because of unfavorable demographics, convergence with advanced economies, and spillover from growth moderation in the PRC.

The fading demographic dividend

Economic theory and the evidence presented in this chapter indicate that the growth rate of the working-age population has a direct proportional impact on the potential growth rate. Recalling the definition of the potential growth rate as the sum of labor productivity growth and labor force growth, and using World Bank projections of the growth rate of the Asian working-age population in 2015–2020, the contribution of this element of potential growth can be assessed as either increasing or decreasing relative to 2008–2014. Figure 2.3.1 shows that, in most Asian economies under consideration, working-age population growth is projected to be lower in 2015–2020 than in 2008–2014. The average annual decline between the two periods is projected at 0.43 percentage points.[10]

These growth forecasts of working-age population can be used to forecast potential output growth. The potential

2.3.1 Working-age population growth rates (%)

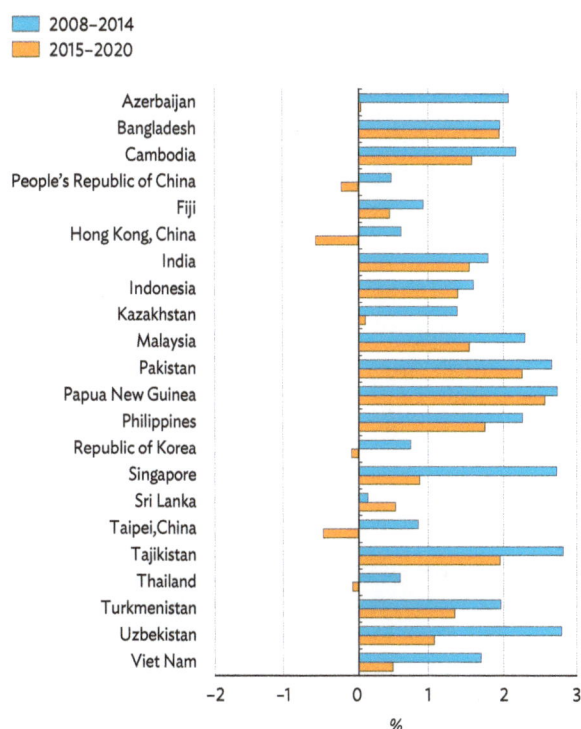

Source: ADB estimates based on World Bank, World Development Indicators online database. Data for Taipei,China are from http://eng.stat.gov.tw/lp.asp?ctNode=2265&CtUnit=1072&BaseDSD=36

Click here for figure data

2.3.1 Annual potential growth rate in 2015–2020 adjusted for the effects of working-age population trends

	Forecast based on the 2008–2014 average	Forecast based on the 2014 estimate
Azerbaijan	3.25	1.02
Bangladesh	5.96	6.11
Cambodia	6.81	6.48
People's Republic of China	8.11	7.23
Fiji	1.25	3.27
Hong Kong, China	1.84	1.08
India	6.72	6.04
Indonesia	5.59	4.79
Kazakhstan	5.56	3.80
Republic of Korea	2.68	2.52
Malaysia	4.27	5.06
Pakistan	4.53	5.00
Papua New Guinea	7.14	5.74
Philippines	6.55	7.39
Singapore	3.25	2.24
Sri Lanka	5.96	7.22
Taipei,China	2.04	1.76
Tajikistan	6.06	5.88
Thailand	2.62	2.25
Turkmenistan	10.40	9.65
Uzbekistan	6.60	6.40
Viet Nam	4.81	4.86
Average	**6.40**	**6.01**

Note: The first estimate is the sum of each economy's estimated average potential growth rate in 2008–2014 plus the change in working-age population growth rate between 2015–2020 and 2008–2014. The second estimate is the sum of each country's estimated average potential growth rate in 2014 plus the change in working-age population growth rate between 2008–2014 and 2015–2020.

Source: ADB estimates.

growth rate projections are shown economy-by-economy in Table 2.3.1. Two forecasts of potential output growth are constructed: one based on the estimated potential growth rate over 2008–2014 and the other based on the estimated potential growth rate in 2014. Both can be considered good proxies for the current potential growth rate. The impact of the projected change in working-age population growth between 2008–2014 and 2015–2020 is then incorporated by adding the change in working-age population growth to the current potential growth rate. Depending on the assumption made about the starting potential output growth value, developing Asia's 2015–2020 potential output growth varies from 6.01% to 6.40%.

To evaluate how this average decline in potential growth will affect living standards in Asia, measures of potential growth per capita for 2015–2020 are calculated, relying on the potential growth rate estimates and World Bank projections for population growth.

2.3.2 Potential growth per capita estimated for 2015–2020

Economy	(1) Population growth rate difference between 2015–2020 and 2008–2014	(2) Potential growth per capita in 2008–2014	(3) Based on the 2008–2014 average	(4) (3) – (2)	(5) Based on the 2014 estimate	(6) (5) – (2)
Azerbaijan	-0.72	3.74	2.45	-1.29	0.22	-3.52
Bangladesh	-0.02	4.80	4.80	0.01	4.95	0.16
Cambodia	-0.04	5.83	5.26	-0.57	4.93	-0.90
People's Republic of China	-0.08	8.30	7.70	-0.61	6.82	-1.49
Hong Kong, China	-0.33	2.35	1.28	-1.07	0.52	-1.83
Fiji	-0.10	0.85	0.72	-0.13	2.74	1.89
India	-0.18	5.63	5.55	-0.07	4.87	-0.75
Indonesia	-0.20	4.50	4.48	-0.02	3.68	-0.82
Kazakhstan	-0.64	5.22	4.61	-0.61	2.85	-2.37
Republic of Korea	-0.13	2.96	2.28	-0.68	2.12	-0.84
Malaysia	-0.28	3.41	2.94	-0.47	3.73	0.32
Pakistan	-0.12	2.81	2.53	-0.28	3.00	0.19
Papua New Guinea	-0.23	5.06	5.12	0.06	3.72	-1.34
Philippines	-0.05	5.50	5.04	-0.46	5.88	0.38
Singapore	-1.15	2.56	1.85	-0.71	0.84	-1.72
Sri Lanka	0.20	5.15	5.33	0.18	6.59	1.44
Taipei,China	-0.19	3.05	1.94	-1.11	1.66	-1.39
Tajikistan	-0.11	4.68	3.92	-0.76	3.74	-0.94
Thailand	-0.08	2.98	2.41	-0.57	2.04	-0.94
Turkmenistan	-0.12	9.76	9.25	-0.51	8.50	-1.26
Uzbekistan	-0.76	6.40	5.42	-0.98	5.22	-1.18
Viet Nam	-0.32	4.94	4.06	-0.88	4.11	-0.83
Average	**-0.24**	**5.89**	**5.72**	**-0.17**	**5.31**	**-0.58**

Source: ADB estimates.

Column 1 of Table 2.3.2 reports the population growth rate differential between 2015–2020 and 2008–2014. It shows that, with the exception of Sri Lanka, average population growth is expected to be lower in 2015–2020 than in 2008–2014 in all developing economies in Asia.

Also reported in Table 2.3.2 are estimates of potential growth per capita for 2015–2020. Using the estimated average potential growth rate and actual population growth in 2008–2014, an estimate of potential growth per capita in this period is first constructed and shown in column 2. Next, based on the two projected estimates of potential growth in 2015–2020 combined with population growth projections, measures of potential growth rate per capita in 2015–2020 are constructed. These estimates are based on the 2008–2014 average value of the estimated potential growth rate (column 3) and on the 2014 estimated potential growth rate (column 5). Results indicate that the average potential growth rate per capita will be between 5.31% and 5.72%. Columns 4 and 6 show the difference with respect to average potential growth in 2008–2014, with negative values indicating that annual potential growth per capita is projected to be lower in 2015–2020 than in 2008–2014.

The results in Table 2.3.2 suggest that, notwithstanding the projected slowing of population growth in 2015–2020, potential growth per capita in Asia is expected to fall relative to 2008–2014 by an average of 0.17–0.58 percentage points annually. This is because the fall in working-age population growth over the period outstrips the fall in total population growth. Living standards will rise more slowly over the next few years than in 2008–2014.

Fading advantage of backwardness

Developing Asia's past success has narrowed the gap with the advanced economies. The econometric results in the previous section show that a smaller technological gap relative to the US will reduce potential growth. The so-called advantage of backwardness, which allowed developing economies in Asia to grow by adopting existing technologies, is fading as they converge in sophistication with the advanced economies. With less scope for playing catch-up with the advanced economies, growth in many Asian economies will depend more on some other determinants of potential growth, such as tertiary education and trade. On the other hand, low- and middle-income economies still have scope to benefit from the convergence effect.

Spillover from PRC growth moderation

Actual growth in the PRC is forecast to moderate further, from 6.9% in 2015 to 6.5% in 2016 and 6.3% the year after. The trend is an adjustment to several important structural changes, notably the end of the stage in development during which less productive labor can be drawn from rural areas into more productive manufacturing. This kept wages down in the past and helped the PRC attract considerable foreign direct investment, but now wages have begun to rise. A legacy of past population policies is particularly unfavorable demographics, as the benefits from a relatively youthful population turn rapidly into a burden as the population ages. Moreover, the economy is shifting its growth model from a heavy reliance on investment to one in which consumption is the primary driver.

As Asia's largest economy, and the second largest in the world, the PRC exerts a significant role as an engine of global growth, so concerns about slowdown in the PRC are certainly warranted. However, whether the consequences of the slowdown persist for years or decades will depend critically on its relationship with potential output growth and, in particular, with productivity growth in other economies. It is thus important to understand whether natural rates of growth in other Asian economies move significantly in tandem with the PRC. Theoretically, there are several possible channels that can underpin such a relationship. Trade relations with the PRC could foster productivity-enhancing structural change in other economies, accelerate technological transfer, and foster competition-driven efficiency gains, for example. Change could also reflect the global demand effects.

The benchmark model is augmented to test whether actual growth in the PRC has an effect on potential growth in the global sample.

Similarly, actual growth in the US is included as the world's largest economy may have an even bigger impact on growth than the PRC. The estimate of the model including these spillovers is shown in Table 2.3.3.

The results shown in Table 2.3.3 can be interpreted as estimates of the degree of co-movement between actual growth rates in the PRC and the US and potential growth rates in the rest of the world.[11] PRC and US growth rates both turn out to be positive and significant. Results from the model indicate that each 1 percent of actual growth in the PRC is associated with a rise of about 0.2 percentage points in average potential growth in the global sample. The corresponding effect from the US is nearly twice as great, at 0.39 percentage points.

Concluding remarks

It is important to emphasize that the natural rate of growth is contingent on policies that affect the mobilization and reallocation of resources in the economy. As the regression results show, policies can change an economy's potential growth rate, possibly counterbalancing the effects of factors that lead to a decline in equilibrium growth. Thus, the "new normal" should not be taken as a natural constant but one that can reflect policy decisions, for better or worse. As the organization of markets and governments changes over time, potential growth may move closer to the frontier potential growth rate.

The empirical evidence shows, however, that deviations of actual from potential growth do not significantly affect the latter. This implies that policies that aim to raise the actual growth rate above the potential have only a temporary effect. Demand-side policies are less effective than supply-side policies in restoring potential output. Policy decisions that affect factor reallocation and productivity gains can reactivate growth for long periods, thus offsetting any potential growth losses from the exhaustion of growth patterns typical of the initial stages of economic development.

2.3.3 Modeling the impact of slower growth in the PRC and the US

	Spillover
Initial GDP per capita	–0.00034
Working-age population growth	1.0228**
Gap with the US	0.081924^
US gap x political stability	–0.00395
Tertiary enrollment ratio	0.08522
Tertiary enrollment squared	–0.00109^
Labor market rigidity	–3.0915**
Voice and accountability	1.6002
Government effectiveness	1.55105**
Trade ratio	0.057578**
Trade ratio squared	–0.00005*
Financial capital integration	0.00099
Financial capital x regulatory quality	–0.00206^
Break in 2008–2014	–1.93914**
PRC growth	0.20185**
US growth	0.39016*
Number of economies	59
Number of observations	411

PRC = People's Republic of China, US = United States.
Notes: ** indicates significance at 1%, * at 5%, and ^ at 10%. The PRC and the US are excluded from the panel used for the estimations. Variables, including the PRC and US growth, instrumented with first lag. Driscoll and Kraay (1998) standard errors.
Source: ADB estimates.

Policies to invigorate potential growth

Simulations to evaluate the implications of changes in the determinants of potential growth can provide a quantitative basis for policy recommendations. In the previous section, the effect of demographics on potential output growth was calculated (Table 2.3.2). The effects of the other determinants are assessed by way of a simulation that uses the estimates of the determinants of potential output growth reported in the two models in Table 2.2.2.

Future potential growth: a simulation

This section builds on the intuition that, for most of the determinants of potential growth that were found to be significant, it is possible to define a *frontier value*—that is, a particular value for which the impact on potential growth is maximized or, as in the case of the technological gap, has been completely exhausted.[12] Building on this and a number of additional assumptions, a scenario for a 10-year period is considered over which the effects of the assumed changes in the determinants of potential growth are evaluated. Specifically, for each one of the relevant variables included in the exercise, the frontier values and specific assumptions are as follows:

Initial income per capita. This variable remains constant.

Gap with the US. The technological gap with respect to the US is assumed to remain stable over the period considered. This is consistent with a scenario in which the pace of technological innovation in the US is fairly similar to the rate of technological spillover into Asian economies.[13]

Tertiary enrollment ratio. The frontier value is a ratio of 51%, i.e., the threshold beyond which any additional increase in the share of population with tertiary education has a negative effect on potential growth.

Labor market rigidity. The frontier value of this index is 0, which corresponds to the most flexible labor market regulatory framework.

Voice and accountability. The frontier value of this index is 2.5, at which people's perceptions about political freedoms and accountability are most favorable.

Government effectiveness. The frontier value for this index is 2.5, at which people's perceptions about the quality and effectiveness of the public sector are most favorable.

Trade ratio. The frontier value is 443%, beyond which the effects of trade on potential growth become negative. It is assumed that the value of the trade ratio increases by 25 percentage points over 10 years.

Integration index. Because of the interaction with regulatory quality, the frontier value of the integration index cannot be uniquely defined. It is assumed that the value of the financial integration index increases by 25 percentage points over 10 years.

Based on these assumptions and definitions, the simulation is conducted as follows:

1. For each variable the difference between the latest available value and the respective frontier value as defined above is calculated, and the distance from the frontier (DfF) is calculated.

2. It is assumed that countries close half of the DfF for each variable over a 10-year period.

3. For the tertiary enrollment ratio, labor market rigidity, voice and accountability, government effectiveness, and the trade ratio, the impact on potential growth is constructed as the product of the respective values of half of the DfF times the corresponding coefficients in the benchmark model (Table 2.2.2). For the tertiary enrollment ratio and the trade ratio, nonlinearities are taken into account by setting to zero the potential gain if the economy has already achieved the frontier value.

4. As mentioned above, it is assumed that the gap with the US remains constant for the 10-year period, so its impact in the simulation is set at zero.

5. For the trade ratio and the integration index, the assumption is a 25% increase over the initial value. The impact of this change on potential growth is calculated using the relevant coefficient estimates from the benchmark model (Table 2.2.2), holding constant the regulatory quality indicator for the integration index and taking into account nonlinearities in the case of trade.

Two additional channels are considered, through which policy intervention can affect the potential growth rate. The first is the possible effects of policies to counteract the slowdown in working-age population growth, such as postponing retirement age and relaxing immigration restrictions. Specifically, a scenario is considered in which policy is able to halve the projected annual decline in working-age population growth. The effect of this is reported in the line labeled "Demographics" in Table 2.4.1. (Among the sampled Asian economies, only Sri Lanka shows positive demographic changes.)

The other channel incorporates the expected gains from macroeconomic stabilization policies, the proxy for which in the framework is lower volatility of actual growth with respect to potential growth. Specifically, it is assumed that the 5-year standard deviation of actual growth with respect to the potential growth rate (i.e., variable growth gap volatility introduced in the macro stability model) declines by 25% with respect to its mean value over the 1960–2014 period, as a consequence of better macro-management policies. The impact of this change is reported in the line labeled "Stable macroeconomy" in Table 2.4.1, and for each economy is constructed as the product of the 25% fall in growth gap volatility times the relevant coefficient in the macro stability model in Table 2.2.3.[14]

The simulation is conducted to answer this question: By how much would potential output growth increase over the 10-year period if economies could close through reform half of the distance between their

2.4.1 Simulated future contributions to potential growth, percentage points

Item	Contribution
Demographics	−0.33
Reform	0.98
Stable macroeconomy	0.09
Total	0.73

Note: The table shows the weighted average annual contribution of each determinant of potential growth to the increase in potential growth over a decade, as calculated in a simulation for 22 Asian economies in the sample.

Source: ADB estimates.

current values for each determinant and the highest possible value, and thereby reduce macroeconomic volatility? It is assumed that governments introduce policies that mitigate the negative effect of lower working-age population growth.

Simulation results are shown in Table 2.4.1, which provides the results of the three effects discussed earlier: the effect of reducing the negative impact of working-age population growth by half, the positive effect of supply-side reform, and the positive effect of demand-management policies to stabilize actual growth around potential, effectively reducing volatility. If governments manage to successfully introduce policies that reduce the projected decline in working-age population, then the negative impact of this effect could be as small as −0.33 percentage points on average.[15]

Reform could add about 0.98 percentage points per annum to developing Asia's growth. The largest increases— experienced by Uzbekistan, Azerbaijan, and Cambodia— exceed 1.2 percentage point per annum (Figure 2.4.1). The reforms that seem to provide the largest boost to potential output growth address the labor market and institutional quality.

Finally, demand-management policies could reduce the volatility of actual versus potential growth and boost developing Asia's potential growth by about 0.1 percentage points per annum on average. The sum of all these reforms and policies is shown in Table 2.4.1 in the line "Total." The average estimated impact on developing Asia's potential growth is 0.73 percentage points per annum.

2.4.1 Impact on potential growth

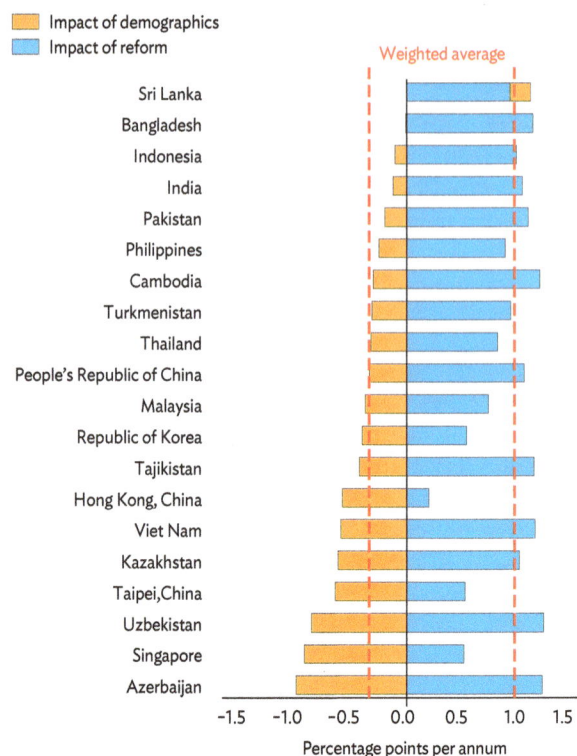

Source: ADB estimates.
Click here for figure data

Policy implications

Economies with a particularly negative demographic outlook should aim to enlarge their labor force and working-age population by adopting more flexible immigration policies or incentives to increase the fertility rate. In the short to medium term, measures to increase female participation in the workforce and to postpone retirement age can be effective as well.

Since the long-term growth rate of the labor force is largely determined by demographic factors, the focus of policy interventions to increase potential growth should be on productivity enhancement. Indeed, the evidence presented in this chapter indicates that whether the projected decline in potential growth actually materializes hinges not alone on working-age population growth, but also on the implementation of effective economic policies and institutional transformation, as well as on changes to other determinants of potential growth that affect potential labor productivity growth.

The estimates of the determinants of potential output growth indicate that closing the technological gap with respect to the US, boosting the gross enrollment ratio in tertiary education up to about 51%, raising labor market flexibility, strengthening voice and accountability and government effectiveness, opening up to trade to about 443% of GDP, and advancing financial integration into the world economy can raise potential growth. These are fundamental pillars of a successful growth strategy. Naturally, larger improvements in these factors will support more substantial positive effects, so the straightforward policy recommendation for Asian economies is to focus on devising the most efficient and effective measures to bring about economic and institutional change that enhances potential growth.

As stated in the first section of this chapter, the estimate of an economy's potential growth depends on its institutions and structure. Frontier potential growth was defined as the growth rate that the economy could achieve if all institutional barriers and distortions that obstruct factor mobility were removed. The analysis indicates that the removal of firm-level obstacles that affect firm size and the efficient allocation of capital and labor can move developing Asia's economies closer to their frontier potential growth. Particular attention should be paid to correcting deficient judicial systems, unequal access to finance, excessive labor regulation, inadequate education, poor electricity supply, and corruption, which can cause distortions within firms and in factor markets. For example, tax system reform that is neutral with respect to firm size can improve productivity. Deepening the development and outreach of the financial system can advance productivity growth through the efficient allocation of capital.

During the transition to improved allocation, economies will already enjoy a higher potential growth rate. Benefits will derive from structural reforms to financial and labor markets, policies to improve access to land, strengthened governance, an improved business environment, and significant infrastructure investments to secure basic needs such as electricity and water supply.

Infrastructure should remain a priority for Asian policy makers. As the needs are large, governments must find creative financing solutions such as public–private partnership. Toward facilitating private investment, policy can incentivize companies to purchase new assets by, for example, accelerating depreciation.

Likewise, higher potential and frontier potential growth can be achieved by relaxing government policies and addressing market imperfections that impede the more efficient allocation of labor, especially where agricultural employment remains above a high 30%: Azerbaijan, Bangladesh, the PRC, India, Indonesia, the Philippines, Sri Lanka, Thailand, and Viet Nam.

While increasing potential growth might seem to be an objective exclusive to economic policy, an appropriate policy mix can be deployed to correct imbalances between actual and potential growth, and to avoid them where they threaten to emerge. The existence of a significant gap between actual and potential growth, and the resulting economic performance that is other than optimal, create either inflationary pressures or unemployment. Indeed, inappropriate policy interventions may widen gaps or make them more persistent, exacerbating the associated problems. Moreover, wider gaps are bound to bring about greater growth volatility that, as indicated by empirical evidence presented in this chapter, negatively affects potential growth.

This reinforces the view that effective demand management and stabilization policies may have significant positive effects.

The analysis indicates that such measures, and economic policy more generally, can play a growing role in boosting long-term growth in developing Asia. As developing Asia continues its convergence with the advanced economies, the advantages of backwardness will fade until they are finally extinguished. The potential for technological spillover from economies on the technological frontier will decline as the technology gap narrows, and the demographic dividend will turn into a demographic debt as growth in working-age population slows. For long-term growth to continue in Asia, and for living standards to improve at rates similar to the past, effective policy measures and improvements in the quality of institutions will have to compensate for the lost advantages of yesterday. In the aftermath of the global financial crisis, developing Asia's progress toward high-income status will increasingly depend on how fast it can close the gap in policy and institutions with respect to the advanced economies.

Asia's new normal today need not be its future normal. To ensure a healthy future for potential growth, Asia must employ the full range of policy responses to augment labor supply, improve labor productivity, and maintain macroeconomic stability.

Endnotes

1   A first reason, Rodrik argued, was that industrialization in the style of the Republic of Korea seemed to be impossible in today's world because technological change was rendering manufacturing more capital and skill intensive. Second, some Asian economies would experience declining labor force growth rates (e.g., the PRC and Japan), though others would still enjoy a demographic dividend (e.g., India). In the former group, productivity growth would have to accelerate to compensate for the shift in demographics (McKinsey Global Institute 2015). Third, the World Trade Organization has begun to disallow many industrial policies widely used in the past to push growth (Felipe 2015), and developed countries would not be as willing in the years ahead to run current account deficits so that the developing world could run surpluses. In the Asian context, Lin and Zhang (2015) has argued in reference to the PRC that the GFC would not have long-lasting effects and that the decline in growth was only transitory.

2   Two versions of the model are available: closed economy and open economy augmented with the ratio of imports to GDP, the latter following Romer (1993). In total, three different versions are estimated: (i) actual inflation (equation [6]) and closed economy for the PRC, Fiji, Japan, the Philippines, Sri Lanka, and Viet Nam; (ii) adaptive expectations (equation [8]) and open economy augmented for Azerbaijan, India, and Taipei,China; and (iii) adaptive expectations (equation [8]) and closed economy for Bangladesh, Cambodia, Indonesia, Kazakhstan, the Republic of Korea, Malaysia, Pakistan, Papua New Guinea, Tajikistan, Turkmenistan, Uzbekistan,

Viet Nam, and Hong Kong, China. The model with actual inflation and open economy did not fit any of the economies well. The results shown for Singapore and Thailand are derived from a different model that includes financial factors (Felipe et al. 2015).

3   This estimate is derived by dividing the percentage point change in potential growth by the percentage point change in actual growth for the 22 developing Asian economies, and then taking the average.

4   It should be noted that the statistical procedure used to generate a time-varying estimate of potential output growth (the Kalman smoother) updates the complete series every time a new estimate is added—see details in Lanzafame et al. (2016). After adding the PRC growth rate estimate for 2015, which is 6.9%, the estimates since 2010 become lower, with a potential growth rate of 7.69% for 2014 (instead of 7.91%) and 7.29% for 2015.

5   India released an updated GDP series that contains very few years, so the old series was used in the model estimates. Adjusting up the growth rate based on the years where the two series overlap (2012–2014) yields a slightly higher potential growth rate of 6.94% in 2014.

6   The direct impact of reducing the gap with the US, as indicated by the coefficient of this variable, shows that a country with a gap that is narrower by 1 percentage point has potential growth that is slower by 0.07 percentage points. However, the gap with the US is also interacted with the index of political stability in the model, and this interaction term needs to be taken into account to fully quantify the impact of the gap on potential growth. Ignoring the effects of all other variables in the model, potential output growth is computed as $g^n = 0.07 \times \text{gap} - 0.006 \times \text{gap} \times \text{political stability}$. Recall that the index of political stability ranges from –2.5 to 2.5, with higher positive numbers indicating greater political stability. The total effect of reducing the gap by 1 percentage point is therefore calculated as $0.07 + (0.006 \times 2.5) = 0.085$ percentage points for the least politically stable and $0.07 - (0.006 \times 2.5) = 0.055$ percentage points for the most politically stable economies.

7   This is calculated as $0.004 + (0.003 \times 2.5) = 0.0115$ for the lowest regulatory quality. For values of regulatory quality above –0.41 the impact is not statistically significant. Note that this is the impact of financial integration through regulatory quality. The direct impact of financial capital integration is simply given by the coefficient of this variable (0.004), which means that countries with financial integration 1 percentage point higher will have potential growth higher by 0.004 percentage points.

8   This is approach is similar to that of León-Ledesma and Thirlwall (2002).

9   Regressions for the Asian economies alone (not shown for reasons of space) are less reliable since the sample size is significantly smaller. Nevertheless, the Asian dummy for the 2008–2014 structural break is always negative, with values that oscillate between –2.0 and –2.3.

10 This is the difference between the average growth rate of the actual working-age population growth rate in 2008–2014 and the projected growth rate for 2015–2020. This weighted average is computed using population shares as weights.

11   The spillover model for the subpanel of Asian economies is estimated as well, but the results are not as reliable because the sample size is small.

12   The methodology and terminology employed in this section are akin to those used by the World Bank in its Distance to Frontier exercise (http://www.doingbusiness.org/data/distance-to-frontier).

13   This is a plausible assumption for the purposes of this simulation. Obviously, it cannot be assumed for the longer term, over which many Asian economies should continue to enjoy the so-called advantage of backwardness.

14   This means that coefficients from two different regressions are being used. Even if all coefficients from the macro stability model were used, results would be very similar.

15   This is the reduction in the region's potential output growth solely due to a lower projected trend growth rate in working-age population growth during 2015–2020, and assuming that countries implement measures (e.g., increase fertility rates, increase females labor participation, etc.) to reduce the negative impact of declining working-age population growth rates by 50%. It is computed using individual countries' trend growth rates of working-age population (not actual growth rates as in endnote 10), weighted by their respective GDP shares.

References

ADB. 2013. *Key Indicators for Asia and the Pacific 2013: Asia's Economic Transformation: Where to, How, and How Fast?* Asian Development Bank.

Campos, N. and J. B. Nugent. 2012. The Dynamics of the Regulation of Labor in Developing and Developed Countries since 1960. *IZA Discussion Papers* 6881. Institute for the Study of Labor.

Caselli, F. 2005. Accounting for Cross-Country Income Differences. In Aghion, P. and S. Durlauf, eds. *Handbook of Economic Growth*. 1(1). Elsevier.

Cerra, V. and S. C. Saxena. 2008. Growth Dynamics: The Myth of Economic Recovery. *American Economic Review* 98(1).

Driscoll, J. C. and A. Kraay. 1998. Consistent Covariance Matrix Estimation with Spatially Dependent Panel Data. *The Review of Economics and Statistics* 80(4).

Felipe, J, ed. 2015. *Development and Modern Industrial Policy in Practice: Issues and Country Experiences.* Asian Development Bank and Edward Elgar.

Felipe, J., N. Sotocinal, and C. Bayudan-Dacuycuy. 2015. The Impact of Financial Factors on the Output Gap and Estimates of Potential Output Growth. *ADB Economics Working Paper Series* No. 457. Asian Development Bank.

Felipe, J., C. Bayudan-Dacuycuy, and M. Lanzafame. 2014. The Declining Share of Agricultural Employment in the People's Republic of China: How Fast? *ADB Economics Working Paper Series* No. 419. Asian Development Bank.

Foster-McGregor, N. and B. Verspagen. 2016. The Role of Structural Transformation in the Potential of Asian Economic Growth. *ADB Economics Working Paper Series* No. 479. Asian Development Bank.

Friedman, M. 1968. The Role of Monetary Policy. *American Economic Review* 58(1).

Harrod, R. F. 1939. An Essay in Dynamic Theory. *The Economic Journal* 49(193).

Harvey, A. 1989. *Forecasting, Structural Time Series Models and the Kalman Filter*. Cambridge University Press.

Herrendorf, B., R. Rogerson, and A. Valentinyi. 2014. Growth and Structural Transformation. In Aghion, P. and S. Durlauf, eds. *Handbook of Economic Growth*. 1(2). Elsevier.

Hsieh, C. and P. Klenow. 2009. Misallocation and Manufacturing TFP in China and India. *The Quarterly Journal of Economics* 124(4).

Kalemli-Ozcan, S. and B. Sorensen. 2012. Misallocation, Property Rights, and Access to Finance: Evidence from Within and Across Africa. *NBER Working Paper* 18030. National Bureau of Economic Research.

Kose, M. A., E. Prasad, K. Rogoff, and S.-J. Wei. 2009. Financial Globalization and Economic Policies. *CEPR Discussion Papers* 7117. Centre for Economic Policy Research.

Lane, P. and G. M. Milesi-Ferretti. 2007. The External Wealth of Nations Mark II: Revised and Extended Estimates of Foreign Assets and Liabilities, 1970–2004. *Journal of International Economics* 73(2).

Lanzafame, M. 2010. The Endogeneity of the Natural Rate of Growth in the Regions of Italy. *International Review of Applied Economics* 24(5).

Lanzafame, M., J. Felipe, N. Sotocinal, and C. Bayudan-Dacuycuy. 2016. The Pillars of Potential Growth and the Role of Policy: A Panel Data Approach. *ADB Economics Working Paper Series* No. 482. Asian Development Bank.

León-Ledesma, M. 2016. Potential Growth, Misallocation, and Institutional Obstacles: Firm-level Evidence. *ADB Economics Working Paper Series* No. 480. Asian Development Bank.

León-Ledesma, M., and D. Christopoulos. 2016. Misallocation, Access to Finance, and Public Credit: Firm-Level Evidence. *Asian Development Review* 33(2).

León-Ledesma, M. and A. P. Thirlwall. 2002. The Endogeneity of the Natural Rate of Growth. *Cambridge Journal of Economics* 26(4).

Lin, J. and F. Zhang. 2015. Sustaining Growth of the People's Republic of China. *Asian Development Review* 32(1).

Magnus, J. R., O. Powell, and P. Prüfer. 2010. A Comparison of Two Model Averaging Techniques with an Application to Growth Empirics. *Journal of Econometrics* 154(2).

McKinsey Global Institute. 2015. *Global Growth: Can Productivity Save the Day in an Aging World?* McKinsey & Company.

Okun, A. 1962. Potential GNP: Its Measurement and Significance. *Proceedings of the Business and Economic Statistics Section*. American Statistical Association.

Phelps, E. 1967. Philips Curves, Expectations of Inflation and Optimal Unemployment Over Time. *Economica* 34(135).

Pritchett, L. and L. H. Summers. 2014. Asiaphoria Meets Regression to the Mean. *NBER Working Paper* 20573. National Bureau of Economic Research.

Ramey, G. and V. A. Ramey. 1995. Cross-Country Evidence on the Link Between Volatility and Growth. *American Economic Review* 85(5).

Rodrik, D. 2009. Growth after the Crisis. *CEPR Discussion Papers* 7480. Centre for Economic Policy Research.

Romer, D. 1993. Openness and Inflation: Theory and Evidence. *The Quarterly Journal of Economics* 108(4).

Sala-i-Martin, X., G. Doppelhofer, and R. I. Miller. 2004. Determinants of Long-Term Growth: A Bayesian Averaging of Classical Estimates (BACE) Approach. *American Economic Review* 94(4).

Sen, K. 2016. The Determinants of Structural Transformation in Asia: A Review of the Literature. *ADB Economics Working Paper Series* No. 478. Asian Development Bank.

Stiglitz, J. 1993. Endogenous Growth and Cycles. *NBER Working Paper* 4286. National Bureau of Economic Research.

Taylor, J. B. 1993. Discretion versus Policy Rules in Practice. *Carnegie-Rochester Conference Series on Public Policy* 39(1).

3

ECONOMIC TRENDS AND PROSPECTS IN DEVELOPING ASIA

CENTRAL ASIA

ARMENIA
AZERBAIJAN
GEORGIA
KAZAKHSTAN
KYRGYZ REPUBLIC
TAJIKISTAN
TURKMENISTAN
UZBEKISTAN

Armenia

Despite an unfavorable external environment, the economy managed to grow by 3.0% in 2015. Weak domestic demand helped contain inflation and improve external accounts but exacerbated the budget deficit. Demand will likely remain sluggish in 2016 and 2017, reducing growth and inflation and moderately widening the current account deficit. The challenge is to make growth inclusive across regions.

Economic performance

The economy grew by 3.0% in 2015, down from 3.5% in 2014. On the supply side, growth was driven by agriculture and industry as expansion in services moderated (Figure 3.1.1).

Agriculture grew by 11.4%, aided by favorable weather and continued government support to farmers that provided preferential loans, diesel fuel, seeds, and fertilizers, as well as by expansion of the cultivated area. Industry excluding construction grew by 6.3%. Much of this growth came from export-oriented mining and metallurgy, reflecting expansion in late 2014 at the Teghut copper mine, the country's second largest mine. Construction contracted by 4.2% following the 4.6% decline in 2014.

The expansion in services, which generate about half of GDP, slowed sharply to 1.1% from 5.8% a year earlier, reflecting a 7.1% slump in the remittance-supported trade subsector. Growth in services came mainly from higher growth in information technology, finance, insurance, and recreation.

On the demand side, most of the expansion stemmed from a narrower deficit in net exports of goods and services. Public consumption improved by an estimated 5.4% in 2015 on higher government spending. However, total consumption declined as private consumption contracted, for the first time since 2009, by an estimated 5.0%. This reflected a 35.8% fall in remittances, mainly from the Russian Federation, from which remittances plunged by 42.2% (Figure 3.1.2). Total investment decreased by an estimated 6.4% in 2015, exceeding the 2.6% decline in 2014.

Inflation was subdued in 2015 as private consumption contracted, agricultural output rose, global commodity prices fell, the exchange rate remained relatively stable, and the Central Bank of Armenia tightened monetary policy in the first half of the year. For the first time since 2005, deflation was recorded at the end of 2015 as the 12-month inflation rate December over December fell to −0.1%, well below the inflation target band of 2.5%–5.5% set by the central bank. Average annual inflation nevertheless rose slightly to 3.7% from 3.0% in 2014, reflecting larger increases for food and other goods (Figure 3.1.3).

3.1.1 Supply-side contributions to growth

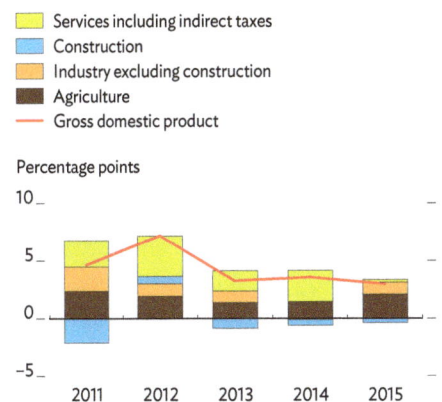

- Services including indirect taxes
- Construction
- Industry excluding construction
- Agriculture
- Gross domestic product

Percentage points

Source: National Statistical Service of the Republic of Armenia. http://www.armstat.am (accessed 1 March 2016).
Click here for figure data

3.1.2 Sources of remittances

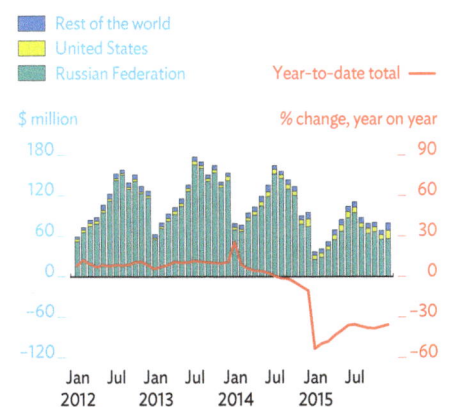

- Rest of the world
- United States
- Russian Federation
- Year-to-date total

$ million   % change, year on year

Source: Central Bank of Armenia. http://www.cba.am (accessed 1 March 2016).
Click here for figure data

This chapter was written by Grigor Gyurjyan of the Armenia Resident Mission, ADB, Yerevan.

Monetary policy helped not only to contain inflation but also to limit the decline in the Armenian dram as the ruble depreciated, with the central bank intervening only to avoid disorderly exchange rate movements. In line with price and market developments, it adjusted policy rates periodically throughout the year. With inflation expectations well anchored, it gradually eased its policy rate from 10.50% in February 2015 to 8.75% by year-end, and to 8.50% in February 2016. Low inflation and only mild depreciation of the Armenian dram against the US dollar, by less than 2% in 2015, caused the dram to appreciate during the year against the currencies of Armenia's leading trade partners by 2.8% in nominal effective terms and 2.9% in real effective terms (Figure 3.1.4).

Strong inflows of foreign financing helped, along with higher exports, to raise foreign exchange reserves and offset the drop in remittance inflows. Foreign exchange reserves rose by 19% to $1.8 billion at the end of 2015, estimated to equal 4.4 months of imports, versus 3.3 months at the end of 2014.

Fiscal policy was mildly expansionary in 2015, supporting growth through public consumption. The ratio of revenue to GDP declined to 22.7% in 2015 from 23.6% in 2014 as economic growth and transfers from the Eurasian Economic Union customs pool disappointed and as domestic and external trade slipped. Expenditure rose to 27.3% of GDP from 25.5% a year earlier, mainly reflecting higher capital spending (Figure 3.1.5). The fiscal deficit rose from 1.9% of GDP in 2014 to 4.6%, double the budget target of 2.3%.

Higher borrowing for infrastructure development and to cover the budget deficit raised the ratio of public debt to GDP from 43.6% in 2014 to 48.6% at the end of 2015 (Figure 3.1.6). Heavy reliance on external financing saw external public debt climb in nominal terms by more than $0.5 billion to $4.3 billion, or 41.3% of GDP. Domestic public debt increased by more than $100 million to $762 million.

As exports rose and weak domestic demand slowed import growth, the current account deficit narrowed to an estimated 4.6% of GDP in 2015 from 7.3% a year earlier (Figure 3.1.7).

The trade deficit shrank to an estimated 13.3% of GDP from 17.7% in 2014. Imports of goods plummeted by an estimated 15.5%, while exports held steady and export destinations diversified somewhat. The services account continued to improve, reflecting gains in construction, telecommunications, and travel.

Economic prospects

Although economic performance in 2015 beat expectations, the outlook remains very uncertain. Armenia is highly vulnerable to exogenous shocks, particularly from the Russian Federation, its main trading partner. With continued recession there during 2016, growth is projected to slow to 2.0% in 2016 before recovering slightly to 2.3% in 2017 (Figure 3.1.8).

The growth outlook will worsen if the economy in the Russian Federation deteriorates further. No consensus exists on how the lifting of international sanctions against Iran will affect Armenia.

3.1.3 Inflation

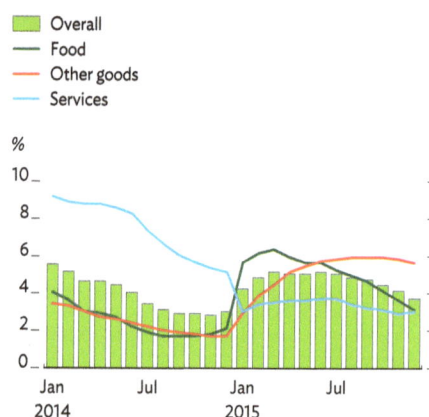

Source: National Statistical Service of the Republic of Armenia. http://www.armstat.am (accessed 1 March 2016).
Click here for figure data

3.1.4 Reserves and effective exchange rates

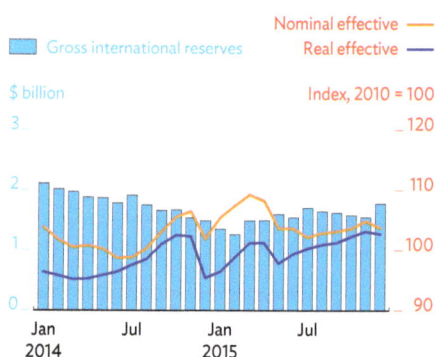

Sources: Central Bank of Armenia. http://www.cba.am; International Monetary Fund. International Financial Statistics online database (accessed 1 March 2016).
Click here for figure data

3.1.5 Fiscal indicators

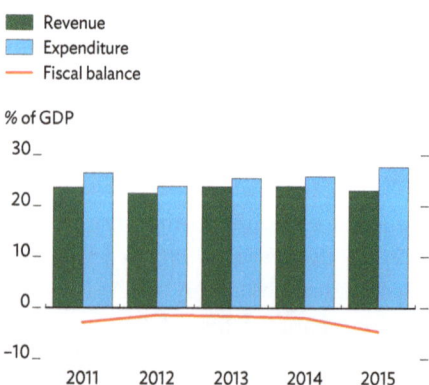

Sources: Ministry of Finance. http://www.minfin.am; National Statistical Service of the Republic of Armenia. http://www.armstat.am (accessed 1 March 2016).
Click here for figure data

Agriculture is expected to remain the key supply-side driver of growth, followed by moderate expansion in services and industry. If the weather remains favorable, agriculture should continue to grow over the forecast period, though more slowly than in 2015. Government support for such inputs as seed, fuel, and fertilizer should spur expansion, as should subsidized credit and measures to promote the development of value chains and enhance the productivity and efficiency of farming, such as establishing cooperatives. Also promoting growth will be greater interest from the private sector in agriculture using greenhouses.

Growth in industry is expected to remain sluggish, reflecting subdued domestic and external demand. The government's renewed emphasis on stimulating exports will provide further impetus for industry, which will also benefit from moderate growth in construction, mostly from progress in externally financed infrastructure projects for roads, water supply, and school rehabilitation.

A projected decline in retail trade will likely slow the rise in services, in which most growth is expected to come from gains in tourism, finance, information, and communications.

On the demand side, investment and private consumption are both projected to contract, though less than in 2015, with growth coming from a further narrowing of the deficit in net exports.

Fiscal policy will be tightened gradually in the medium term, following the fiscal slippage and rise in external debt during 2015. The government projects the fiscal deficit at 3.5% of GDP in 2016, with expenditure remaining unchanged to accommodate lower revenue from weaker economic activity. The volume of transfers from the Eurasian Economic Union customs pool will likely be unchanged in 2016. Moreover, high and rising public debt will require further fiscal consolidation to reduce the debt-to-GDP ratio and contain external imbalances.

Monetary policy will likely support growth. Average annual inflation is projected to remain subdued, at 3.8% in 2016 and 4.0% in 2017, reflecting slow growth and output below potential. While modest growth should put downward pressure on prices, inflation would likely be higher if external developments cause significant dram depreciation.

The current account deficit is projected to widen to 5.2% of GDP in 2016 and then narrow to 5.0% in 2017 (Figure 3.1.9). The trade deficit is forecast to continue narrowing, while the income deficit will remain small. Exports are forecast to expand by only 0.2% in 2016 and then by 1.0% in 2017 as efforts to diversify markets largely offset drag from recession in the Russian Federation. Imports are projected to decline by 1.5% in 2016, reflecting the lagged effect of smaller remittances, and then rise by 2.0% in 2017 as lower fuel and commodity prices support consumption. Renewed trade with Iran could mean more trade overall, in particular higher exports.

An uncertain external environment will require using domestic measures to sustain growth, in particular rebuilding fiscal and external buffers, and implementing structural reforms to further enhance the business environment, boost competitiveness, diversify exports and markets, and improve governance and transparency.

3.1.1 Selected economic indicators (%)

	2016	2017
GDP growth	2.0	2.3
Inflation	3.8	4.0
Current account balance (share of GDP)	−5.2	−5.0

Source: ADB estimates.

3.1.6 Public debt

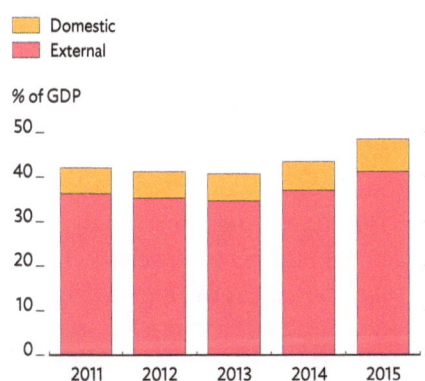

Sources: Ministry of Finance. http://www.minfin.am; National Statistical Service of the Republic of Armenia. http://www.armstat.am (both accessed 1 March 2016).
Click here for figure data

3.1.7 Current account components

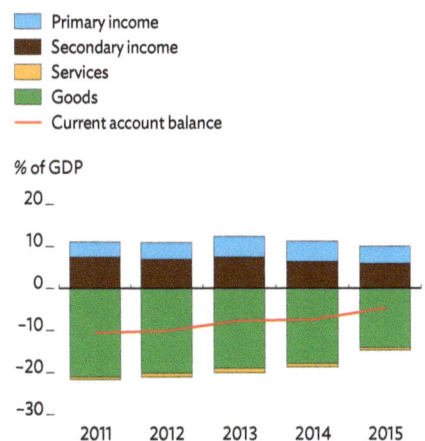

Sources: Central Bank of Armenia. http://www.cba.am (accessed 1 March 2016); ADB estimates.
Click here for figure data

Policy challenge—attaining balanced regional development

Widening disparity between the capital city and the regions is a major threat to inclusive growth over the long term. Economic activity is heavily concentrated in the capital, Yerevan, which accounts for more than 40% of industrial production and more than 80% of trade and services but has only a third of the country's population and a quarter of its poor. By contrast, the regions enjoy little economic opportunity or diversification and endure much worse poverty, dependence on worker remittances, and physical infrastructure.

The government recognizes that the high concentration of wealth in Yerevan hampers economic and human development and exacerbates large and persistent regional disparities. The Armenia Development Strategy to 2025, approved in 2014, aims to overcome regional disparity in development and prioritize over the medium and long term regionally targeted development policies. The resulting programs should ensure faster economic development in the most depressed regions, enabling them to largely close their development gaps with national norms.

A development initiative approved in 2011 emphasizes the creation, rehabilitation, and development of economic infrastructure and the improvement at the regional and community level of the quality and accessibility of public social services for education, health care, cultural enrichment, and environmental protection.

Scaling up targeted economic development initiatives that build on each locality's comparative advantages, and therefore offer potential for longer-term impact, is critical for diversifying rural households' sources of income and enhancing the structure of regional economies. Along with measures to promote private sector development, especially through small and medium-sized enterprises, such development initiatives can promote job creation and thereby raise living standards toward levels enjoyed in the capital.

Investing in social and economic infrastructure, including health and education facilities and transport, can also promote more uniform growth across the regions. Programs to improve access to markets and social services in poor regions can serve this objective, as can incentives for private firms to invest in these areas.

Public–private partnership in infrastructure can be pursued to reduce government expenditure while allowing more projects that promote equity across regions.

3.1.8 GDP growth

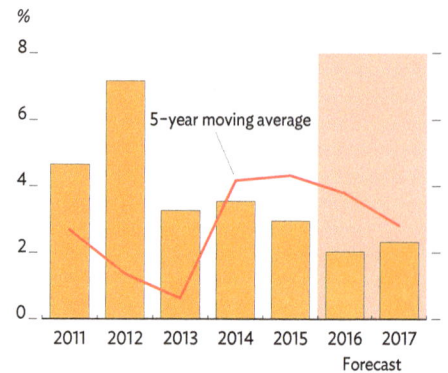

Sources: National Statistical Service of the Republic of Armenia. http://www.armstat.am (accessed 1 March 2016); ADB estimates.
Click here for figure data

3.1.9 Current account balance

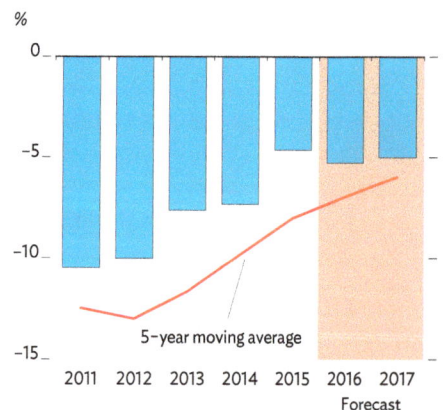

Sources: National Statistical Service of the Republic of Armenia. http://www.armstat.am (accessed 1 March 2016); ADB estimates.
Click here for figure data

Azerbaijan

Plunging oil prices in 2015 cut export earnings, and sharp currency depreciation reduced household consumption and public investment, slowing growth to 1.1%. Continued weakness in oil prices is projected to cause GDP to contract by 1.0% in 2016 before recovering to 1.0% growth in 2017 as oil prices revive. Only by financing the expansion of diverse sectors can Azerbaijan move away from heavy dependence on hydrocarbons.

Economic performance

Economic growth slowed to 1.1% from 2.8% in 2014 as oil prices plummeted and a 50% depreciation of the Azerbaijan manat reduced nominal GDP by 8.0% (Figure 3.2.1). The oil sector is reported to have expanded by 1.2%, following a 3.7% contraction in 2014, while cuts in public investment constrained the economy outside the oil sector, which expanded by only 1.1%, down from 7.0% in 2014.

On the supply side, industry shrank by 1.9%, versus 0.5% growth in 2014, as a decline in construction outweighed improvements in mining and manufacturing (Figure 3.2.2). Cuts in public investment and lower demand for real estate reversed 9.1% expansion in construction in 2014 to 13.4% contraction. Growth in services decelerated to 4.5% from 7.4% in 2014, owing to a slowdown in social and other services. Agriculture had the strongest increase, as government concessions on inputs contributed to 6.6% growth following 2.6% decline in 2014.

On the demand side, private and public consumption are believed to have declined because of currency depreciation and some tightening of lending later in the year, even as household savings grew by 31.7% in 2015, more than double the 12.4% growth rate in 2014. Net exports fell sharply because of lower oil prices, as hydrocarbons constitute more than 90% of exports.

Declining energy prices and the drop in export earnings forced the central bank to devalue the manat by 25% on 21 February 2015 and then, on 21 December, abandon the peg to the US dollar, which precipitated another plunge. The manat ended the year down by half against the US dollar after repeated interventions cost the central bank more than two-thirds of its foreign exchange reserves, which stood at $4.4 billion at the end of January 2016, down from $13.8 billion a year earlier.

Official reports suggest that average annual inflation accelerated to 4.0% from 1.4% in 2014, reflecting devaluation in February 2015 and higher inflation in trading partners, and despite a decline in global food prices. The inflation rate month on month reached 7.7% in December, when the manat peg was abandoned (Figure 3.2.3).

3.2.1 Exchange rate and average crude oil price

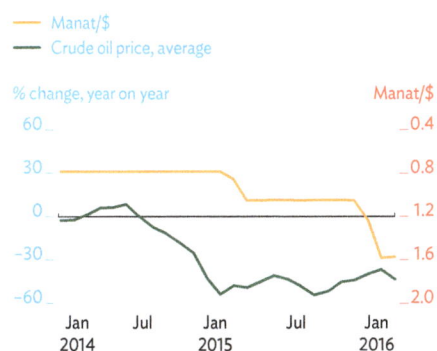

Sources: Central Bank of the Republic of Azerbaijan; Haver Analytics.
Click here for figure data

3.2.2 GDP growth by sector

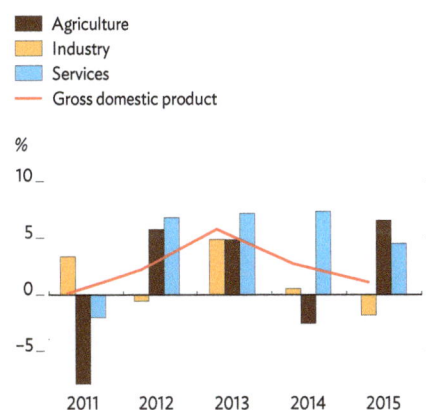

Source: State Statistical Committee of the Republic of Azerbaijan.
Click here for figure data

This chapter was written by Nail Valiyev of the Azerbaijan Resident Mission, ADB, Baku.

Food prices rose by 6.1% over the whole of 2015, while prices for other goods increased by 3.8%.

Plunging oil prices forced a tightening of fiscal policy. Despite rising as a share of GDP because of the decline in nominal GDP, both revenue and expenditure fell in nominal terms. Revenue, including from the state oil company, dropped by 6.7% to the equivalent of 31.5% of GDP, slightly above 31.2% in 2014 (Figure 3.2.4). Receipts were mainly transfers from the sovereign wealth fund, whose assets fell by $3.5 billion to $33.6 billion at the end of 2015 (Figure 3.2.5). Total expenditure declined by 4.9% as the government deferred some investment projects but still rose as a percentage of GDP to 32.7%, from 31.7% in 2014. The budget recorded a deficit equal to 1.1% of GDP, less than the 3.0% budgeted. Total government and government-guaranteed debt more than doubled to 28.1% of GDP from 11.2% at the end of 2014, largely because of depreciation.

Monetary policy aimed to stabilize the exchange rate for most of the year while supporting growth. In July, the central bank cut its policy rate from 3.5% to 3.0%, where it stayed for the rest of the year, to boost investment in the non-oil economy. This helped maintain credit growth at 20.5%, with lending rates unchanged. However, the drop in international reserves caused broad money to contract by 1.1% after having grown by 11.8% in 2014 (Figure 3.2.6). As almost half of the loan portfolio is denominated in foreign currencies, depreciation caused nonperforming loans to rise to 6.9% of all loans in 2015 from 5.2% a year earlier.

Dollarization increased as foreign exchange deposits reached 82.5% of all deposits in January 2016, against 51.6% a year earlier. Moreover, banks have come under severe pressure from depreciation and the resulting sharp increase in their foreign currency liabilities. Fraud was alleged at the country's largest bank, and the authorities announced the creation of a new supervisory body for the financial sector. As part of an announced consolidation, six banks were closed in early 2016 for not meeting capital requirements.

Lower oil prices slashed the current account surplus to an estimated 0.4% of GDP from 13.9% in 2014, with exports falling by more than 40%. According to the State Statistical Committee, the trade surplus narrowed by 65.2%, or $13.7 billion, as the February 2015 devaluation did little to boost exports other than oil. Imports, 40% of them electronics and vehicles, grew by 0.4%, reversing a 14.2% decline in 2014.

Economic prospects

Without strong fiscal stimulus, the economy is projected to contract by 1.0% in 2016 because of continued low oil prices, followed by 1.0% growth in 2017 as an expected revival in oil prices facilitates economic recovery (Figure 3.2.7). Higher social spending should limit the downturn in 2016. Despite a 10% salary increase for civil servants introduced in early 2016, real household spending is expected to slow as sharply higher inflation, at 12%, reduces real incomes.

On the supply side, industry is forecast to contract in 2016 because of slowing oil production, but it could improve in 2017 and raise incomes

3.2.3 Monthly inflation

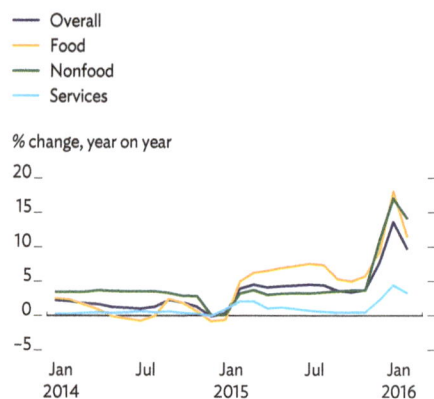

Source: State Statistical Committee of the Republic of Azerbaijan.
Click here for figure data

3.2.4 Fiscal balance

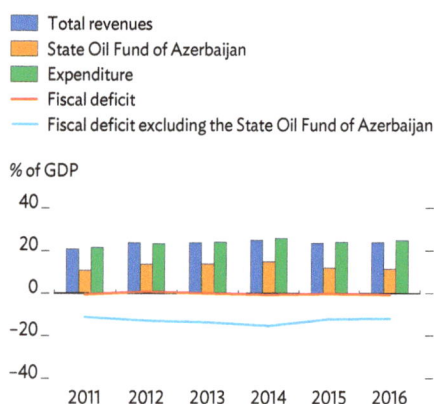

Source: Ministry of Finance of the Republic of Azerbaijan.
Click here for figure data

3.2.5 Strategic reserves

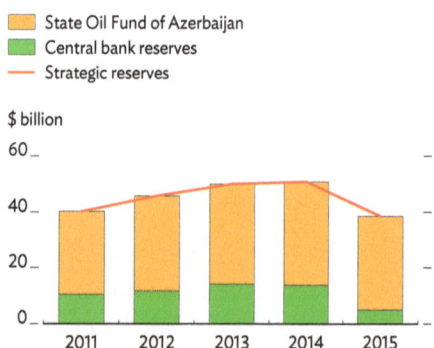

Sources: Central Bank of the Republic of Azerbaijan; State Oil Fund of Azerbaijan. http://www.oilfund.az (accessed 21 March 2016).
Click here for figure data

if oil prices rebound. Public investment, including assistance from development partners for infrastructure, should stabilize construction in both years. Some growth in agriculture is also anticipated each year with continued government support for farmers, including the anticipated completion of reservoir and irrigation networks.

On the demand side, private consumption and investment, both public and private, will be the main sources of growth. Net exports should narrow in 2016 and recover in 2017 along with oil prices, but the growth outlook remains vulnerable to any further energy price shock.

A projected inflation spike to 12.0% in 2016 reflects the impact of currency depreciation on imports, which supply nearly half of consumption. A projected decline in global food prices, slower income growth, and the waning effects of the currency realignment are projected to slow inflation to 5.2% in 2017 (Figure 3.2.8). However, inflation will likely be higher if the manat depreciates further.

Weak oil prices pose a severe challenge to fiscal policy, as revenues depend heavily on oil taxes and transfers from the state oil fund. Revenue as a percentage of GDP is projected to decline to 30.2% in 2016. However, the budget aims to support the economy with higher social spending on pensions, targeted social assistance, and stipends, raising expenditure to 33.3% of GDP and the deficit to 3.1%. Following amendment of the legal ceiling on external debt, total government and government-guaranteed debt is projected to climb to 40.9% of GDP in 2016 with investment in the Southern Gas Corridor, other power-related infrastructure, and transport.

The uncertain outlook for oil prices also affects the current account, which is projected to run a small deficit equal to 0.6% of GDP in 2016 as exports decline by 12.2%, outpacing the decline in imports. The current account is forecast to return in 2017 to a surplus of 1.5%, with some recovery of oil prices and exports rising by 7.0% while imports decline again, by 1.5% (Figure 3.2.9). The trade surplus is likely to remain small over the medium term until oil prices recover significantly.

Policy challenge—diversification through a stronger financial sector

The economic repercussions of declining oil prices underscore Azerbaijan's vulnerability as it continues to depend mainly on hydrocarbon revenues. With oil prices projected to remain low for some time and oil production already likely at its maximum, sustainable growth is possible only through significant economic diversification.

Diversification will require, among other things, greater access to credit from a more resilient financial sector. Small and medium-sized enterprises (SMEs) in particular need financing if they are to contribute to higher growth outside of the oil sector. Credit expansion requires stronger financial institutions, financial markets that are deeper and more liquid and efficient and thus able to handle larger volumes, broader domestic sources of finance, and better access for more users of banking and other financial services. In tandem with greater financial

3.2.6 Contributions to money supply growth

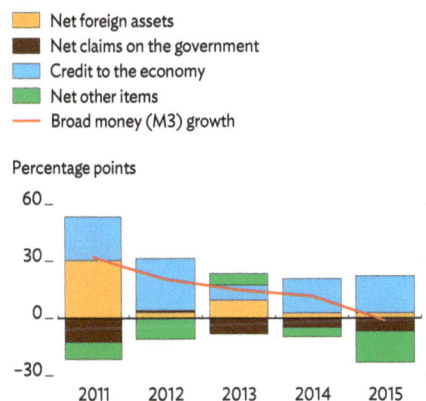

Source: Central Bank of the Republic of Azerbaijan.
Click here for figure data

3.2.7 GDP growth

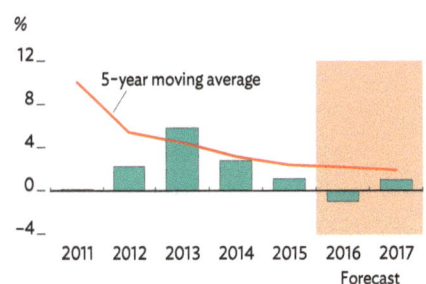

Sources: Central Bank of the Republic of Azerbaijan; ADB estimates.
Click here for figure data

3.2.1 Selected economic indicators (%)

	2016	2017
GDP growth	–1.0	1.0
Inflation	12.0	5.2
Current account balance (share of GDP)	–0.6	1.5

Source: ADB estimates.

intermediation, Azerbaijan needs stronger competition among financial institutions and closer regulation of their activities.

Persistent dollarization has greatly squeezed liquidity in local currency. As the share of loans and deposits in foreign currency rises, so does the risk posed to banks by their foreign exchange liabilities and nonperforming loans. Poor banking practices and the proliferation of nonperforming loans challenge the soundness of banks and their efforts to maintain market liquidity. Moreover, the central bank's lack of sufficient refinancing facilities undercuts commercial banks' ability to provide loans, particularly to SMEs, as does the weakness of bankruptcy law and other protections for creditors. Access to finance is particularly constrained outside of the capital.

The decision in January 2016 to provide full deposit insurance will likely boost confidence in the banking system. Capping interest rates on foreign currency deposits at 3% while retaining a higher ceiling of 12% on manat deposits should encourage the holding and use of manat, as should the government's recent issue of local currency bonds. The central bank's lengthening of secured loans to banks from 1 to 7 days and the reduction in reserve requirements for local currency deposits from 2.0% to 0.5% ought to enhance local currency liquidity while easing banks' liquidity management. These moves, together with the central bank's direct provision of finance to SMEs, should make financing more available, especially in manat, thereby promoting the use of the local currency.

The government's decision to close inadequately capitalized banks and to encourage bank consolidation could strengthen the banking system by simultaneously raising capitalization and reducing costs, thereby enabling narrower spreads between deposit and lending rates. If the emergence of several stronger and more effective banks ensues, the sector could become more competitive. Steps to reduce the government's presence in the sector could also help if implemented in a way that augments rather than inhibits competition.

The authorities have decided to introduce a single overarching financial market supervisor to regulate banks, insurers, other lenders including microfinance institutions, and the capital market. The new regulator can strengthen the financial sector if it proves effective at supervising a wide array of financial institutions with diverse characteristics.

Other measures worth pursuing would be to reform the bankruptcy law and reinforce creditors' rights, making banks more willing to lend and thus broadening access to finance. The authorities should avoid any measures that would unduly constrain lending, especially by the microfinance institutions that provide services in remote areas.

3.2.8 Inflation

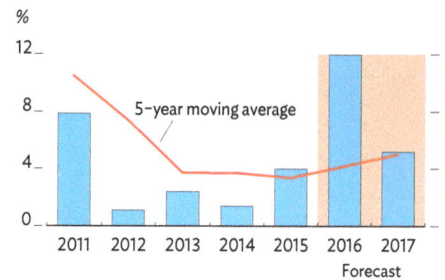

Sources: Central Bank of the Republic of Azerbaijan; ADB estimates.
Click here for figure data

3.2.9 Current account balance

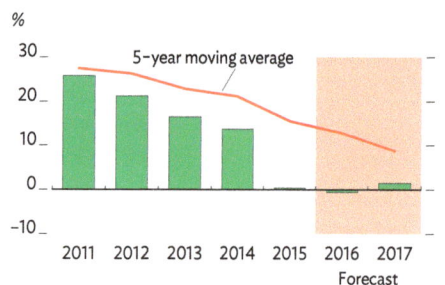

Sources: Central Bank of the Republic of Azerbaijan; ADB estimates.
Click here for figure data

Georgia

Growth slowed to 2.8% as a weak external environment curbed investment, exports, and remittances. Currency depreciation fueled inflation. With continued external weakness, growth is expected to remain low in 2016 before recovering in 2017 on stronger global expansion. Inflation is expected to rise in 2016 before reverting, while the current account deficit should narrow in both years.

Economic performance

GDP grew by an estimated 2.8% in 2015, down from 4.6% in 2014, as recession in the Russian Federation and weakness in other trading partners slowed investment growth and reduced manufacturing, exports, and remittances.

On the supply side, growth was driven by increases of 12.4% in construction and 13.7% in mining that offset a 2.8% decline in manufacturing (Figure 3.3.1). Industry overall rose by 3.3%. Services expanded by 3.0%, reflecting strong performance in finance and tourism, and agriculture grew by 2.8%.

On the demand side, domestic demand was the main driver, with private consumption rising by an estimated 11.9%. Investment growth halved to 13.7% from nearly 28.0% a year earlier, reflecting in part a decline in foreign direct investment from the record set in 2014. With weak external demand and continued sluggishness in regional growth, the net exports deficit worsened by 15.4%.

Inflation accelerated again in 2015, particularly during the second half, to 4.0% (Figure 3.3.2). Higher import prices resulted from a 27.3% depreciation in the Georgian lari vis-à-vis the US dollar in 2015 that more than offset declines in global food and energy prices. Price increases for alcoholic beverages and tobacco (11.0%), health care (10.5%), and furnishings, household equipment, and maintenance (9.2%), and a one-time rise in electricity tariffs, were partly mitigated by lower transport prices from cheaper fuel.

The budget deficit is estimated to have reached 3.7% of GDP in 2015, above the 2.9% recorded in 2014 (Figure 3.3.3). Revenues increased by 10.1% to equal 28.4% of GDP as both tax and nontax revenue rose, while only modest growth in spending on goods and services, and a similarly modest rise in social spending despite significant health care outlays, held public expenditure to 32.1% of GDP. Total public debt rose to 45.4% of GDP from 34.8% in 2014, reflecting in part the impact of lari depreciation. External debt amounted to 78% of all debt, comprising concessional multilateral or bilateral loans with an average interest rate of 1.9% in 2015.

3.3.1 GDP growth by sector

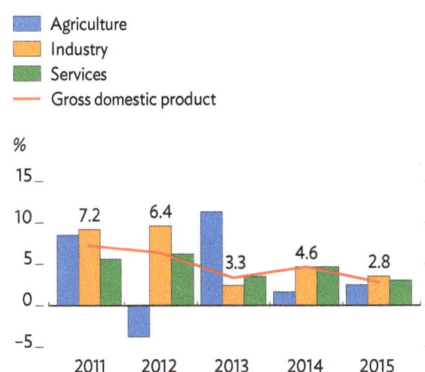

Note: Sector growth in 2015 is for the first 9 months over the same period in 2014.
Source: National Statistics Office of Georgia. http://www.geostat.ge (accessed 3 March 2016).
Click here for figure data

3.3.2 Inflation

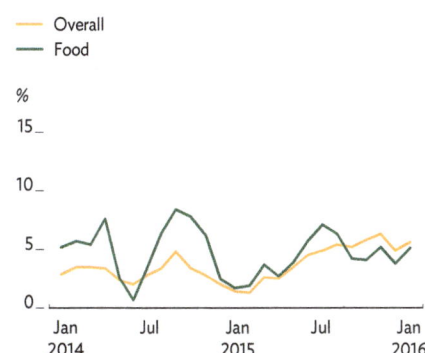

Source: National Statistics Office of Georgia. http://www.geostat.ge (accessed 3 March 2016).
Click here for figure data

This chapter was written by George Luarsabishvili of the Georgia Resident Mission, ADB, Tbilisi.

Monetary policy was tightened in response to depreciation and rising inflationary expectations. The National Bank of Georgia, the central bank, raised the policy rate in several steps from 4% in January to 8% at year-end (Figure 3.3.4). Interest rates on domestic government debt rose, and average rates on lari loans increased by 2.9 percentage points to 20.4%, while those in foreign currency decreased slightly to 10.3%. Deposit interest rates followed a similar trend. Dollarization, as measured by the share of foreign currency deposits in the banking system, rose by 9.6 percentage points to 66.7%. Broad money (M3) grew by 19.3%, more than in 2014, as foreign currency deposits expanded by some 44% while domestic currency deposits contracted (Figure 3.3.5). Credit to the economy grew by 19.4%. The share of nonperforming loans in all loans remained virtually unchanged at 2.7%. Although banks' prudential ratios remained comfortable, sector growth in profits slowed to 13% from 22% in 2014.

Recession in Georgia's main trading partners, including the Russian Federation and Ukraine, has seriously affected external trade. The current account deficit remained sizeable at an estimated 10.5% of GDP, down slightly from 10.6% in 2014, as a 20.9% drop in exports widened the trade deficit. Exports to the Russian Federation in particular fell by 40.7%, while vehicle re-exports plunged by nearly 65%. Meanwhile, exports to the European Union rose by 3.6%. Imports fell by 15.2%, as the lari depreciated against some trading partners' currencies (while appreciating by 11.0% against the ruble). Recession in the Russian Federation and Ukraine contributed to a 25% decline in remittances. A rise in transit tourists including transit traffic raised tourism receipts.

The current account deficit was financed mainly by foreign direct investment, which nevertheless fell by some 23.2% to about $1.35 billion. To smooth exchange rate fluctuations, the central bank sold during the year $287 million in foreign exchange, up from $100 million in 2014. Gross international reserves declined by 6.6% to $2.5 billion, equivalent to 3.4 months of imports.

Economic prospects

Growth is expected to remain near 2.5% in 2016 before rising to 3.5% in 2017 (Figure 3.3.6). Domestic demand is expected to be the main source of growth, reflecting fiscal support for consumption and investment. Anticipated hikes in social expenditure and capital outlays are likely to support expansion in 2016 and beyond, thereby aiding growth prospects. A projected 16.5% yearly rise in credit should also promote growth.

On the supply side, industry is forecast to expand by 2.1% in 2016 and 4.0% in 2017, as the government is considering further tax measures to support business, such as a zero tax on reinvested profit. Services are projected to grow by 2.6% in 2016 and 3.4% in 2017 on continued expansion in tourism. Agriculture is expected to grow modestly, by 2.4% in 2016 and 3.4% in 2017, assuming favorable weather and continued government support.

External demand is expected to improve only modestly in 2016. Recovery is projected to be slow in Georgia's main trading partners as

3.3.3 Fiscal indicators

- ■ Tax revenue
- ■ Nontax revenue and grants
- ■ Total expenditure
- — Fiscal balance

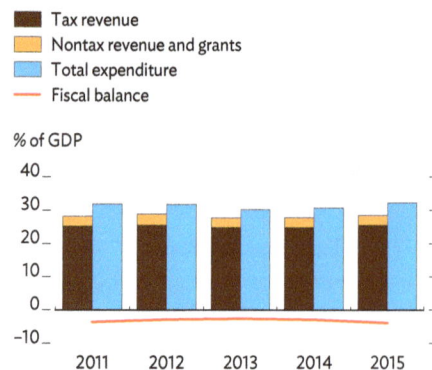

Sources: International Monetary Fund. www.imf.org; Ministry of Finance of Georgia. www.mof.ge (both accessed 3 March 2016).
Click here for figure data

3.3.4 Interest rates

- — Policy
- — Lending
- — Deposit

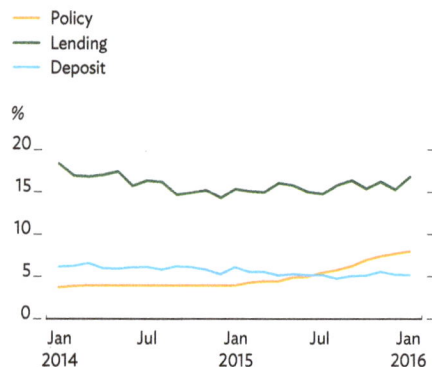

Source: National Bank of Georgia. https://www.nbg.gov.ge (accessed 3 March 2016).
Click here for figure data

3.3.5 Contributions to money supply growth

- ■ Net foreign assets
- ■ Net claims on the government
- ■ Credit to the economy
- ■ Net other items
- — Broad money (M3) growth

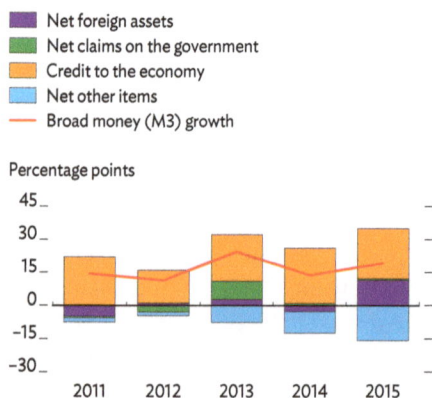

Source: National Bank of Georgia. https://www.nbg.gov.ge (accessed 3 March 2016).
Click here for figure data

recession persists in the Russian Federation. Growth should strengthen in 2017 with a pickup in global expansion, including stronger recovery in the euro area, as Georgia stands to benefit from its 2014 Association Agreement with the European Union to create an extensive free trade area with that market.

Average annual inflation is projected to reach 5.0% in 2016 as the lari continues to depreciate against a strong US dollar on global currency markets and further declines in global prices for food and energy limit the impact of depreciation. Inflation should slow to 4.0% in 2017 as the effect of a one-time rise in utility tariffs wanes. It will be greater than forecast if foreign prices are higher than expected, lari depreciation steeper, or economic growth stronger. The central bank is likely to continue raising the refinancing rate, albeit gradually. Broad money growth is forecast to decelerate to 14.5% in 2016 as private credit growth slows, and then rebound to 19.0% in 2017 on further government efforts to improve firms' access to long-term finance in local currency.

The upcoming cut in profits tax will likely keep the budget deficit above 4.0% of GDP in 2016, despite strong revenue performance that should offset higher spending for pensions and other social programs. The deficit is expected to fall slightly in 2017 as revenue is boosted by higher excise taxes on tobacco and alcoholic beverages, by reform to customs duties, and by improvements in tax administration. Public debt is expected to increase to 45.8% of GDP in 2016 before easing to 44.8% in 2017 as foreign debt decreases (Figure 3.3.7).

The current account deficit is expected to narrow to 9.5% of GDP in 2016 and 9.2% in 2017, reflecting higher exports and remittances (Figure 3.3.8). Exports are expected to rise by 8.5% in 2016 and 14.3% in 2017 as vehicle re-exports and service exports accelerate. Imports are projected to grow at a lower rate than exports, by 4.6% as depreciation depresses imports and then by 11.6% in 2017. Net services should rise by 10.9% in 2016 and 15.8% in 2017. However, the trade balance will remain negative because of a high import bill and weak external demand. Assuming careful debt management and limited volatility in foreign inflows, gross reserves are projected to stay at $2.5 billion in 2016 before rising to $2.6 billion in 2017 (Figure 3.3.9).

The forecast above is subject to downside risks. Weaker-than-expected recovery among trading partners would reduce exports, and further lari depreciation would stiffen inflationary pressures.

Policy challenge—raising productivity to boost growth

Georgia's economy operated below potential in 2015, reflecting the difficult external environment. A key challenge is to reignite growth and restore economic output to its potential.

Boosting growth will depend mainly on improving productivity through structural reform, given Georgia's aging population and the limited scope for countercyclical stimulus. Raising investment remains critical, especially in the context of low oil prices and dampening

3.3.1 Selected economic indicators (%)

	2016	2017
GDP growth	2.5	3.5
Inflation	5.0	4.0
Current account balance (share of GDP)	−9.5	−9.2

Source: ADB estimates.

3.3.6 GDP growth

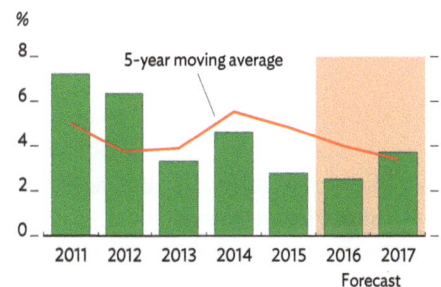

Source: ADB estimates.
Click here for figure data

3.3.7 Public debt

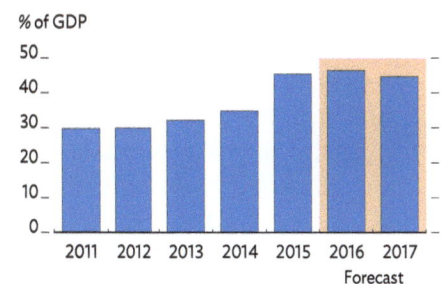

Source: International Monetary Fund, World Economic Outlook database. https://www.imf.org/external/pubs/ft/weo/2015/02/weodata/index.aspx (accessed 3 March 2016).
Click here for figure data

investor appetite in the oil-exporting countries that provide most of Georgia's foreign direct investment.

Structural transformation to boost research and development (R&D) and innovation, aided by declining commodity prices, can help the economy return to trend growth. International assessments have highlighted Georgia's need to improve R&D and education. Georgia ranked 101 out of 140 economies in the quality of higher education and 128 for university–industry collaboration in the *Global Competitiveness Report 2015–2016* of the World Economic Forum. Moreover, education expenditure remains low, at under 3% of GDP, despite high enrollment. Low spending constrains educational attainment, hampering efforts to develop a workforce with the skills needed for a dynamic economy. Besides gradually raising education expenditure, the government plans to prioritize job growth and increase investment in R&D. Doing so would raise productivity while making growth more inclusive.

To narrow rural–urban disparities, the government has adopted a more proactive strategy to promote rural growth through investment in agriculture and to make reform more inclusive by targeting smallholder farmers and industrial startups with concessional funds. Specialized agencies have been created to facilitate exports and upgrade entrepreneurial skills, bolster production capacity through job creation, support innovation and technology transfer, and promote the application of new technologies in business to help commercialize innovative R&D for a knowledge-based economy.

To strengthen governance, quality assurance, and finance for professional education, the government has established a framework for professional competence in line with market trends and demand for professional qualifications. To smooth the transition from training to work, it has strengthened employment policies and introduced an integrated information portal for labor market management that helps identify mismatches between employable skills and available labor, thereby helping educational institutions expand training for professions in greater demand.

A shrinking and aging population limits the size of the workforce, constraining growth. Providing education and training to enhance older workers' facility with information technology and communications could help. The government's new Solidarity Fund encourages voluntary contributions to aid older people, particularly those in need.

Productivity could be further enhanced by improving efficiency in both rural and urban areas. The government's development strategy helps enterprises and farmers with innovative financial products that include preferential credit and leasing programs.

Continued productivity improvements will depend on structural, policy, and institutional reforms to encourage investment in export-oriented activities. Government initiatives in these areas would help accelerate productivity growth and harness the potential of the export sector.

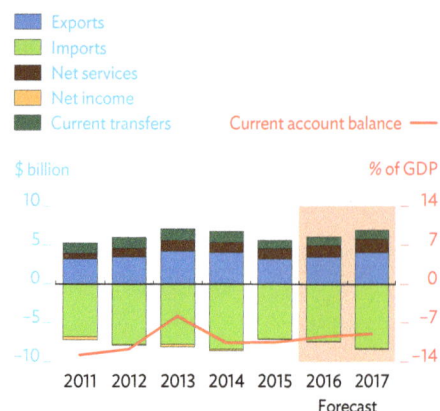

3.3.8 Current account components

- Exports
- Imports
- Net services
- Net income
- Current transfers
- Current account balance

Sources: National Bank of Georgia. https://www.nbg.gov.ge (accessed 3 March 2016); ADB estimates.
Click here for figure data

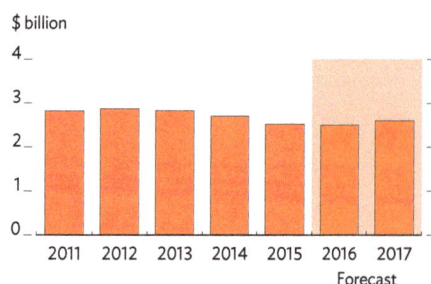

3.3.9 Gross international reserves

Sources: National Bank of Georgia. https://www.nbg.gov.ge (accessed 3 March 2016); ADB estimates.
Click here for figure data

Kazakhstan

Continued weak oil prices slashed growth and pushed the current account into deficit for the first time since 2009. Growth is expected to remain low at 0.7% in 2016 but recover slightly to 1.0% in 2017, reflecting higher countercyclical outlays. Policy must address financial vulnerabilities that stem from low oil prices, persistent problems with nonperforming loans, and further dollarization.

Economic performance

Growth slowed sharply to 1.0% from 4.3% in 2014 on low prices for oil, the economy's main export. On the supply side, data for the first 9 months show that industry contracted by 0.6%, reversing 0.1% growth during the same period in 2014, as utilities and mining declined. Agriculture expanded by 2.9%, doubling from 1.4% in the same period in 2014 on increases of 5.6% for crops and 3.2% for livestock. Growth in services slowed to 2.4% from 5.8% a year earlier because of lower growth in trade, transport, and real estate.

On the demand side, during the first 9 months of 2015 consumption expanded by 2.8%, slightly above the 2.5% recorded during the same period of 2014 (Figure 3.4.1). This reflected a jump in private consumption in the first half, as consumers rushed to buy imported goods in anticipation of a sharply lower Kazakh tenge, which came in August as the authorities abruptly abandoned an exchange rate band for a floating rate. Growth in public consumption in the first 9 months of 2015 slowed to 2.5% from 11.2% a year earlier, as lower oil-based revenue restrained expansion of current expenditure. Expansion of investment, however, rose to 5.0% from 0.2%, as higher public investment more than offset a slowing in private investment associated with lower oil prices. Net exports fell by 1.5%, versus a 7.5% increase in the same period of 2014, as exports fell more than imports (8.2% versus 6.7%).

Average annual inflation eased to 6.6% from 6.7% in 2014. However, sharp depreciation of the tenge fueled inflation in the last quarter of the year, driving the 12 month inflation rate December over December to 13.6% from 7.4% in 2014. Goods other than food, mainly imports, were the primary source of inflation, rising by 8.2% over the year, as price controls for utilities and some food items constrained other price increases (Figure 3.4.2).

Lower revenue attributable to weak oil prices forced cuts in planned spending, as the republican budget deficit narrowed to 2.2% of GDP from 2.7% in 2014. Revenue, which included transfers of oil earnings from the National Fund for the Republic of Kazakhstan amounting to 6.3% of GDP, rose to 14.8% of GDP from 14.5% in 2014.

3.4.1 GDP growth by demand components

- Private consumption
- Public consumption
- Gross fixed investment
- Net exports of goods and services
- Gross domestic product

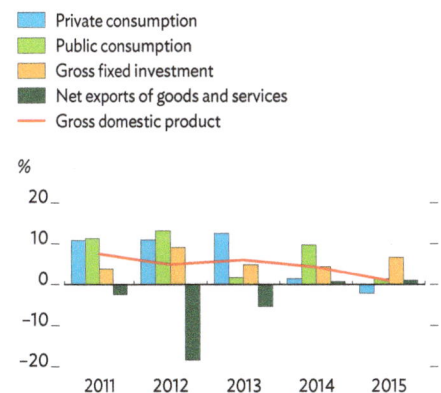

Source: Republic of Kazakhstan. Ministry of National Economy. Committee on Statistics.
Click here for figure data

3.4.2 Monthly inflation

- Food and nonalcoholic beverages
- Clothing and footwear
- Housing, water, electricity, gas, and other fuels
- Furnishings, household equipment, and maintenance
- Transport
- All goods and services

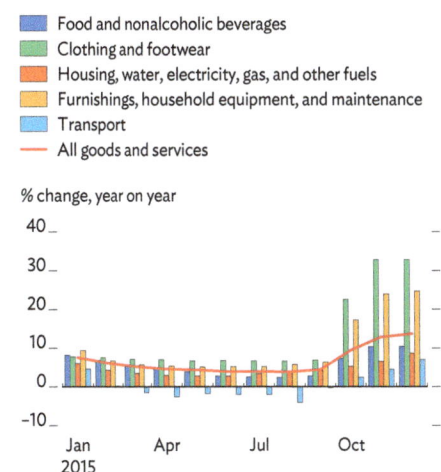

Source: Republic of Kazakhstan. Ministry of National Economy. Committee on Statistics.
Click here for figure data

This chapter was written by staff of the Central and West Asia Department.

Reduced economic activity and lower prices for commodity exports constrained tax yields, though the sharp depreciation of the currency boosted receipts somewhat during the last quarter. The budget was amended several times during 2015 in light of the plunge in oil prices, combining cuts in certain spending categories with countercyclical government programs that included a post-devaluation pay rise, higher pensions and social transfers, price adjustments for government programs, and preparations for Expo 2017. Total expenditure was 16.3% of GDP, up from 15.9% in 2014 (Figure 3.4.3).

Monetary policy during 2015 tried to strike a balance between stemming the decline in growth attributable to low oil prices and curbing the inflation that followed the adoption of a floating exchange rate and the resulting plunge in the value of the currency. On 19 August 2015, Kazakhstan announced a move from a tightly managed exchange rate band of T155–T188 per $1 to a floating rate regime. This triggered an immediate plunge to T252 per $1 and a subsequent depreciation to T340 by the end of the year, despite an effort to stem the decline that contributed to a net reduction of $1.2 billion in international reserves from August to December (Figure 3.4.4). To contain inflation, the National Bank of Kazakhstan, the central bank, introduced a base interest rate of 12% on 2 September 2015 and raised it to 16% a month later and to 17% in February 2016. However, extensive dollarization, with more than 65% of bank deposits in foreign currency, limits the effectiveness of monetary policy (Figure 3.4.5). The growth of broad money tripled to 34.3% from 10.5% in 2014, in part because currency depreciation raised the domestic currency value of foreign exchange deposits. Local currency deposits grew by only 7.9%. Nonperforming loans (NPLs) remain a significant issue facing banks, though the ratio of NPLs to all loans was reined in to below 10% by the end of 2015.

For the first time since 2009, Kazakhstan's current account turned negative in 2015, with an estimated deficit equal to 2.8% of GDP following a surplus of 2.6% in 2014. Exports plunged by 42.4%, far more than the 6.2% decline in 2014. This largely reflected low oil prices, which fell still further in the last quarter of the year, but slow growth in trading partners hurt other exports as well. Imports fell by 22.9%, more than the 14.2% drop in 2014, as slow growth and the sharp rise in domestic prices for imported consumer goods curbed demand. Imports of services fell by 8.5%, versus an increase by 5.8% in 2014, as demand from mining and related activities decreased. However, the deficit in the income account narrowed by 50.6% as foreign investors' earnings from oil exports declined sharply. The year saw the assets of the National Fund for the Republic of Kazakhstan fall by 13.3%, and international reserves by 4.6% (Figure 3.4.6).

Economic prospects

Growth is forecast to remain subdued at 0.7% in 2016 and 1.0% in 2017. Higher countercyclical expenditure, the Expo 2017 in Astana, and the anticipated entry into production of the long-delayed Kashagan oilfield mitigate the prospective drop in private consumption. With commodity prices expected to show little improvement, however, growth could be

3.4.3 Fiscal indicators

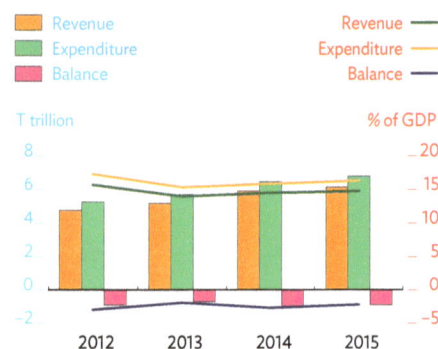

Sources: Ministry of Finance of the Republic of Kazakhstan; ADB estimates.
Click here for figure data

3.4.4 Exchange rate

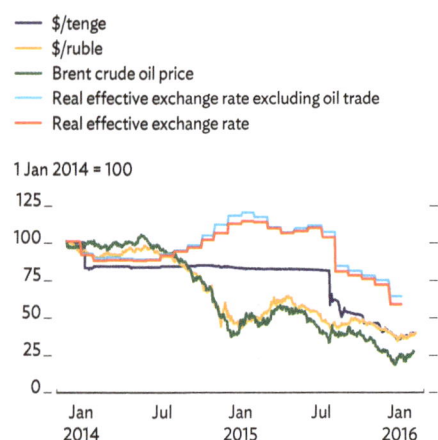

Sources: National Bank of the Republic of Kazakhstan; Bloomberg (accessed 9 March 2016).
Click here for figure data

3.4.5 Dollarization in the banking system

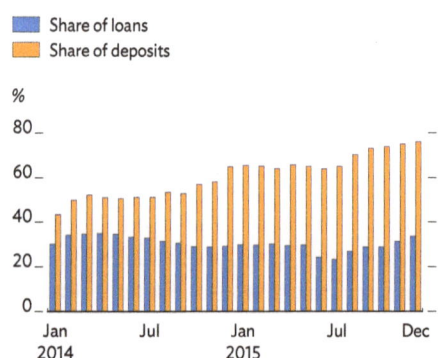

Source: National Bank of the Republic of Kazakhstan.
Click here for figure data

lower than forecast if oil prices fall further or expansion in regional trading partners disappoints.

On the supply side, construction and industry are forecast to expand by 1.4% in 2016 and 4.2% in 2017, as construction should benefit from public contracts, and higher oil production should boost industry in 2017 (Figure 3.4.7). With depreciation raising the competitiveness of agricultural exports and reducing demand for imported food, agricultural production can expect to grow by 3.0% in both 2016 and 2017. Services, the driver of economic growth during the past 5 years, are projected to grow by only 0.9% in 2016 and contract by 1.0% in 2017, as the slump in trade from declining domestic demand offsets expected growth in transport.

On the demand side, private consumption should contract by 4.0% in 2016 and another 3.7% in 2017 in response to high prices, particularly for imports. Public consumption is forecast to grow by 4.0% in 2016 and 5.0% in 2017, reflecting higher general service outlays to prepare for Expo 2017 and the implementation of countercyclical projects. Together, public and private investment are projected to expand by 7.3% in 2016 and 6.1% in 2017 as public projects are used to offset sluggish private investment in extractive industries and low growth elsewhere in the economy. Net export volumes are forecast to rise by 2.0% in 2016 and 5.0% in 2017 as volumes of mostly commodity exports contract less than imports, which are mainly price-sensitive consumer goods. In 2017, a rise in oil production attributable to the Kashagan oilfield should also boost exports.

Average annual inflation is projected to accelerate to 12.6% in 2016, reflecting the impact of currency depreciation and a low base during the first 3 quarters of 2015, and then slow to 4.6% in 2017 as higher interest rates, weak domestic demand, and price controls restrain further increases. Imports other than food are expected to remain the main source of inflation.

Over the next 2 years, fiscal policy is expected to support growth. The republican budget is projected to record a deficit equal to 1.8% of GDP in 2016 and 1.2% in 2017, after accounting for expected income transfers of 8.1% of GDP in 2016 and 8.0% in 2017 from the National Fund for the Republic of Kazakhstan. Tax receipts are projected to decline from the equivalent of 8.0% of GDP in 2015 to 6.9% in 2016, and then rebound to 7.4% in 2017 as higher prices add to value-added tax collections (though revenue may suffer from possible corporate tax rate cuts). Expenditure is forecast equaling 16.9% of GDP in 2016 and 18.0% in 2017 with planned outlays for countercyclical projects and Expo 2017 preparations. Total public and publicly guaranteed debt is projected to rise from 17.4% of GDP in 2015 to 17.8% in 2016 and 19.9% in 2017 with projected borrowing from multilateral development banks and the impact of tenge depreciation on external public debt.

Over the next 2 years, monetary policy is expected to focus on containing inflation, though high dollarization and a shallow financial system will limit its effectiveness. Broad money growth is projected to rise by 33.5% in 2016, assuming an average exchange rate of T350 per $1, and by 7.5% in 2017, assuming an average rate of T370. These projections assume a small rise in local currency deposits and, as a result of

3.4.1 Selected economic indicators (%)

	2016	2017
GDP growth	0.7	1.0
Inflation	12.6	4.6
Current account balance (share of GDP)	−3.5	−3.1

Source: ADB estimates.

3.4.6 Foreign currency reserves and oil fund assets

Source: National Bank of the Republic of Kazakhstan.
Click here for figure data

3.4.7 Supply-side contributions to growth

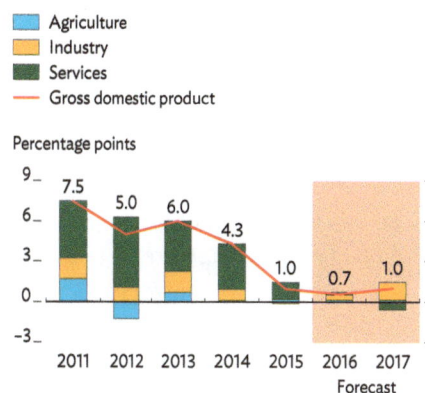

Sources: Republic of Kazakhstan. Ministry of National Economy. Committee on Statistics; ADB estimates.
Click here for figure data

depreciation, a much larger increase in the local currency value of foreign currency deposits.

The current account is forecast to record deficits equal to 3.5% of GDP in 2016 and 3.1% in 2017, mainly reflecting continued weak oil prices (Figure 3.4.8). Exports are projected to decline by 24.5% in 2016 and then rise by 10.4% in 2017 as international oil prices recover somewhat and the Kashagan oilfield starts producing in 2017. Imports are expected to fall by 23.3% in 2016 and, with some increase in imports for Expo 2017, rise by 3.5% in that year. Trade in services should record a deficit equal to 2.6% of GDP 2016 and 3.2% in 2017 because of some substitution of domestic for imported services to avoid higher costs from tenge depreciation. The deficit in the income account should move in line with oil price developments.

Public and publicly guaranteed external debt is projected to rise slightly, from the equivalent of 10.3% of GDP at the end of 2015 and 2016 to 10.6% at the end of 2017, reflecting planned loans from multilateral development banks and the impact of depreciation. Total external debt is expected to increase from 84.6% of GDP at the end of 2015 to well above 100.0% at the end of 2016.

Policy challenge—strengthening a weak financial system

The sudden move to a floating exchange rate from a tightly managed band revealed financial vulnerabilities that stem not only from persistently high NPLs but also from high and growing dollarization and much lower oil prices. Since the global financial crisis of 2008–2009, old and new NPLs attributable to construction and real estate have inhibited private sector lending, with NPLs reaching 37.6% of total lending in 2012. By 1 January 2016, NPLs had fallen to 8.0%, meeting a central bank target of less than 10% after it took on some NPLs and eased writing them off. Besides NPLs, the country also suffers from a highly concentrated financial sector in which banks held more than half of sector assets at the end of 2015, and the top five banks held nearly 60% of all banking assets.

Currency depreciation has further increased the cost in tenge of foreign currency borrowing, undercut bank capitalization, worsened the risk of borrower default, and consequently hurt the market value of banks' equity and deterred their lending. Depreciation has greatly increased the tenge value of private external debt, which totaled $8.6 billion for banks and $54.2 billion for other private firms at the end of September 2015. In addition, refinancing has become difficult. Possibilities for foreign refinancing suffered from a downgrade in the country's sovereign credit rating to BBB–, the lowest investment grade. Moreover, a 17% central bank policy rate and shallow interbank and bond markets make domestic refinancing very costly. As a result, there has been no new lending in real terms. Loans as a percentage of GDP hardly changed during 2014 and 2015 (Figure 3.4.9). To provide finance to small and medium-sized enterprises, the consolidated pension fund

3.4.8 Current account balance

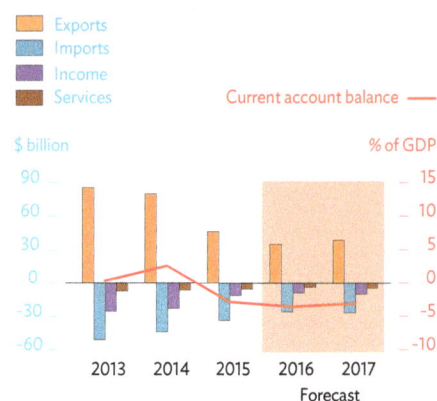

Sources: Republic of Kazakhstan. Ministry of National Economy. Committee on Statistics; ADB estimates.
Click here for figure data

3.4.9 Loan portfolio

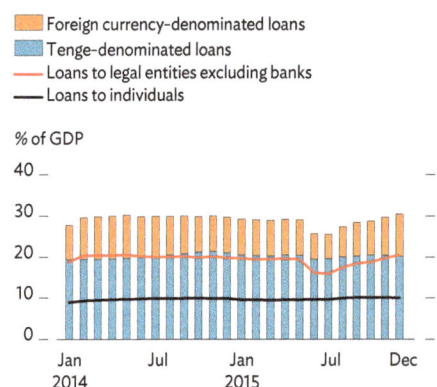

Source: National Bank of the Republic of Kazakhstan.
Click here for figure data

started making loans at concessional rates as part of a T600 billion injection into banks and national companies to stimulate retail lending.

The government and the central bank have taken some steps to address these problems. The government helped reduce NPLs by introducing the prudential requirement that NPLs cannot exceed 10% of all loans, legal amendments to facilitate writing off NPLs, and special purpose vehicles to shift NPLs from bank balance sheets to the central bank. In 2015, the capital adequacy ratio was raised slightly. All banks must now measure credit risk by external ratings, while market risk and operational risks are assigned by set formulas.

Beyond these measures, the financial system requires considerable support. To provide it, the central bank needs credibility, autonomy, and the resources to fill this role, especially as high dollarization hinders its ability to serve as a lender of last resort in foreign currency. As of 1 January 2016, four of the country's 35 banks failed to comply with central bank prudential requirements. Banks may still overstate NPL provisions, which are based partly on collateral that has not been revalued since 2008. Moreover, most banks serve only small customer bases, and the loan portfolios of the smaller banks in particular are concentrated in a few sectors. As a result, the banking system suffers from highly concentrated lending, with individual banks' exposure to their single largest borrower averaging 19.6% in January 2016. This is worryingly close to the 25% prudential norm in Kazakhstan, which is higher than in some other countries.

Further, the banks' net open foreign exchange positions (foreign exchange liabilities exceeding assets) rose dramatically during 2015 (Figure 3.4.10), and prudential requirements current in 2014 were relaxed for 2015 but not for 2016. Recapitalizing much of the banking system, both in tenge and foreign currency, might become necessary as risk-weighted provisions against unhedged foreign currency loans to corporations are often inadequate.

To stabilize the banking system, the government plans as medium-term measures to further develop noncash payments, reduce turnover in lightly regulated shadow banks, and ban foreign currency pricing. To achieve stability in the long run, the government will try to accelerate economic diversification and increase the local content of goods and services as far as possible under World Trade Organization regulations. In the short run, the size of guaranteed tenge deposits will be doubled from T5 million to T10 million, while interest rates on foreign currency deposits will be cut to 3%. The central bank also plans to provide more liquidity and continue to implement reforms to improve supervision and comply fully with Basel III requirements. A program to consolidate banks could minimize fiscal costs if banks require recapitalization. In addition, reining in dollarization is crucial to make both tenge intermediation and monetary policy more effective.

3.4.10 Change in banks' net open foreign exchange positions

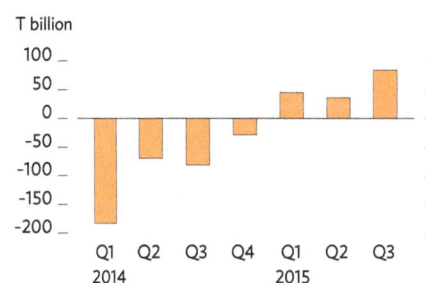

Q = quarter.
Source: National Bank of the Republic of Kazakhstan.
Click here for figure data

Kyrgyz Republic

Growth declined to 3.5% from 4.0% in 2014 as slower expansion in industry offset gains in agriculture and services. Growth is projected to plunge to 1.0% in 2016 as the external environment weakens before recovering to 2.0% in 2017 with some improvement in the Russian Federation and other trade partners. Currency depreciation is fueling inflation and exacerbating a debt problem that needs urgent attention.

Economic performance

Continued recession in the Russian Federation and a slowdown in neighboring Kazakhstan weighed heavily on the economy. Growth slowed to 3.5% from 4.0% in 2014. Outside the troubled gold sector, growth was 4.5%, reflecting strong performance in agriculture and services.

On the supply side, growth in industry slowed to 1.4% from 5.7% in 2014 as gold production halved and output fell in textiles and electricity (Figure 3.5.1). Expansion in construction halved to 13.9% from 27.1% in 2014 with less growth in investment, and growth in services declined to 3.7% from 4.6%, reflecting slowdowns in transport and retail trade. Agriculture grew by 6.2% after a 0.5% decline in 2014.

On the demand side, private consumption is estimated to have grown by 6.9%, down from 7.7% in 2014, as currency depreciation and lower remittances hurt retail trade. The same factors slashed capital investment growth to 8.0% from 24.9%.

Average annual inflation slowed to 6.5% from 7.5% in 2014 despite currency depreciation, while the 12 month inflation rate December over December dropped to 3.4% from 10.5% as food prices fell by 4.2% (Figure 3.5.2). Inflation came mainly from increases of 50.0% for electricity, 26.0% for thermal energy, and 12.3% for goods other than food.

The fiscal deficit declined to the equivalent of 3.0% of GDP from 3.9% in 2014 as about half of expected capital projects did not materialize. Revenues reached 37.4% of GDP, up from 35.9% in 2014, mainly on the sale of a mining license. Meanwhile, underspending on goods and services and delays in implementing public investment projects limited expenditure. Public debt nevertheless climbed to an estimated 68.8% of GDP, as external public debt expanded to 63.0% of GDP with sharp depreciation of the Kyrgyz som.

Monetary policy remained cautious as the central bank intervened to stabilize the local currency. The som depreciated by a modest 5.4% during the first half of 2015 but became highly volatile after the 20 August float

3.5.1 GDP growth by sector

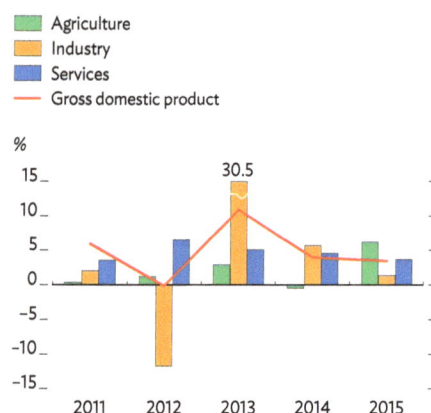

Source: National Statistics Committee of the Kyrgyz Republic. http://www.stat.kg (accessed 3 March 2016).
Click here for figure data

3.5.2 Monthly inflation

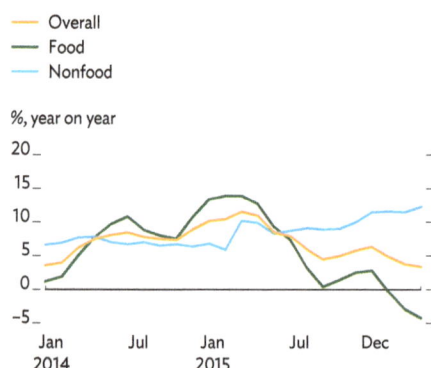

Source: National Statistics Committee of the Kyrgyz Republic. http://www.stat.kg (accessed 14 March 2016).
Click here for figure data

This chapter was written by Gulkayr Tentieva of the Kyrgyz Resident Mission, ADB, Bishkek.

of the Kazakh tenge. By the end of the year, the som had depreciated by 28.9% (Figure 3.5.3). The central bank intervened repeatedly in 2015 to stabilize the som, at a cost of $261 million. The policy rate was reduced slightly to 10.0% at year-end from 10.5% a year earlier. However, monetary policy can do little under extensive dollarization, and 55.2% of loans and 68.3% of deposits were in foreign currency at the end of 2015. The average deposit interest rate increased marginally to 4.95% from 4.84% in 2014, while the average lending rate increased to 18.61% from 17.58%. Deposits rose by 16.1%, and credit by 18.9%, while broad money grew by 14.9%, up from 3% in 2014. At the end of December, nonperforming loans reached 7.1%, up from 4.5% in 2014.

The 2015 current account deficit is estimated to equal 17.0% of GDP, up from 16.8% in 2014. The trade deficit narrowed to $2.4 billion from $2.9 billion as imports plunged by 29.0% and exports fell less sharply, by 11.0%. Remittances declined by 25.8% (Figure 3.5.4). At the end of 2015, international reserves were $1.78 billion, cover for 3.7 months of imports, down from $1.96 billion at the end of 2014.

External public debt as a percentage of GDP is estimated to have risen sharply to 63.0% from 51.0% at the end of 2014, mainly reflecting the depreciation of the som (Figure 3.5.5).

Economic prospects

Growth is expected to slow to 1.0% in 2016, with continued weakness in the external environment, and recover slightly to 2.0% in 2017, assuming some improvement in the Russian Federation and other trade partners (Figure 3.5.6). However, the economy remains vulnerable to shocks from its largest enterprise, the Kumtor gold mine, where a drop in output cut 1% from growth in 2015 and disputed mine ownership could disrupt production in 2016.

On the supply side, processing, light industry, and to some extent construction should lift the economy. In addition, accession to the Eurasian Economic Union (EEU) may boost trade and transportation, though demand in the EEU is weakening and the need to raise tariffs to EEU levels may shrink trade with economies outside the union (Box 3.5.1). On the demand side, lower remittances may further reduce household incomes and private consumption in 2016, though remittances should eventually rise with recovery in the Russian Federation and other trade partners.

3.5.1 The impact of economic union

The Kyrgyz Republic joined the EEU in 2014, and the borders with Kazakhstan have been open since 12 August 2015. Accession has clouded the country's growth prospects. While the country may ultimately benefit from higher trade, more efficient flows of labor and capital, and a decline in nontariff trade barriers, its average tariffs will likely rise toward the common external tariff of the EEU. Moreover, inflation may rise because of the large import content of intermediate and final consumer goods. The government is working to implement challenging reforms to comply with EEU technical regulations on plant diseases, pest control, and veterinary requirements, to boost opportunities for exporters of agricultural products.

3.5.3 Exchange rate

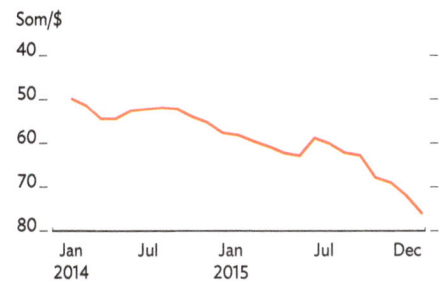

Source: National Bank of the Kyrgyz Republic. http://www.nbkr.kg (accessed 3 March 2016).
Click here for figure data

3.5.4 Remittances

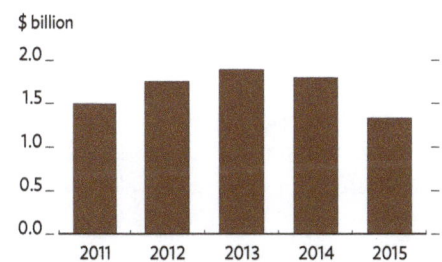

Source: National Bank of the Kyrgyz Republic. http://www.nbkr.kg (accessed 3 March 2016).
Click here for figure data

3.5.5 External debt

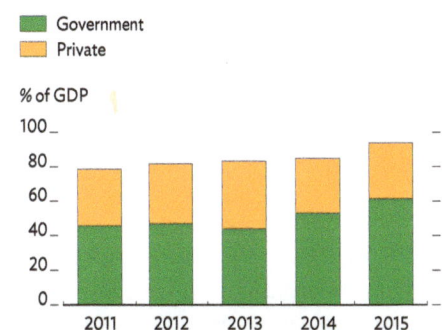

Note: Government debt is both government and government-guaranteed debt.
Sources: Ministry of Finance; National Statistics Committee of the Kyrgyz Republic. http://www.stat.kg; National Bank of the Kyrgyz Republic. http://www.nbkr.kg (both accessed 3 March 2016).
Click here for figure data

Inflation could jump in 2016 to 10.0% because further som depreciation is expected in response to weakness in the tenge and the ruble, and because tariffs on imported goods must rise to EEU levels. Inflation should ease to 8.0% in 2017 in line with smaller exchange rate and tariff adjustments.

Monetary policy will remain cautious in 2016 as the central bank aims to stabilize the local currency and contain inflation, probably raising the policy interest rate if inflation accelerates. Interest rates would rise more with further depreciation of the som.

The fiscal deficit is projected to equal 9.1% of GDP in 2016 and 4.1% in 2017. The government aims to limit the deficit by restraining expenditure. With slow growth, revenue is projected at around 35.0% of GDP in 2016 and 2017, while expenditure is forecast at 40.2% or more, pending cuts. Tax revenue could be higher if EEU accession yields more customs revenue than now forecast. However, the ratio of public debt to GDP will likely increase in 2016, possibly to the brink of high debt distress as defined by the International Monetary Fund.

The current account deficit is forecast to remain near 17.0% in 2016 but ease to 15.0% in 2017 with some improvement in the external environment (Figure 3.5.7). Exports are forecast to grow by 5%–9% in both 2016 and 2017, mainly from gains in agricultural products and textiles. However, weaker consumer demand in 2016 in the EEU could worsen the trade outlook. The government, using $1 billion from the Russian Kyrgyz Development Fund, is working to restructure the economy by supporting export-oriented industries and taking other measures to smooth entry into the EEU. Imports are expected to grow by about 5% in both 2016 and 2017 because of planned infrastructure projects. Remittances will likely fall another 10% in 2016 with continued recession in the Russian Federation, where nearly all Kyrgyz migrants work, and possible further ruble depreciation.

Policy challenge—achieving fiscal and debt sustainability

The public debt situation worsened notably in 2015 as further sharp depreciation of the som raised the ratio of external public debt to GDP to an estimated 63.8% by year-end, well above the current legal ceiling of 60.0% (Figure 3.5.8). Moreover, slowing growth, rising inflation, and reserve depletion threaten to exacerbate the debt problem.

Although the government has introduced amendments to raise the public debt ceiling, its goal is to bring the ratio of debt to GDP below 65% in the medium term. Reducing the debt ratio will require prioritizing and rescheduling public investment, cutting the wage bill and other spending, and better managing debt.

Besides these measures, greater care when contracting and guaranteeing new debt would require a moratorium on commercial borrowing and improved debt monitoring to minimize risks from public enterprises.

Fiscal consolidation is essential to restore debt sustainability while funding programs that address poverty and boost growth.

3.5.6 GDP growth

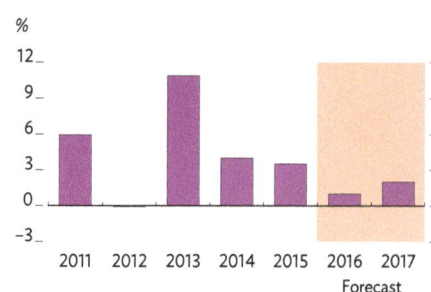

Sources: National Statistics Committee of the Kyrgyz Republic. http://www.stat.kg (accessed 3 March 2016); ADB estimates.
Click here for figure data

3.5.1 Selected economic indicators (%)

	2016	2017
GDP growth	1.0	2.0
Inflation	10.0	8.0
Current account balance (share of GDP)	-17.0	-15.0

Source: ADB estimates.

3.5.7 Current account balance

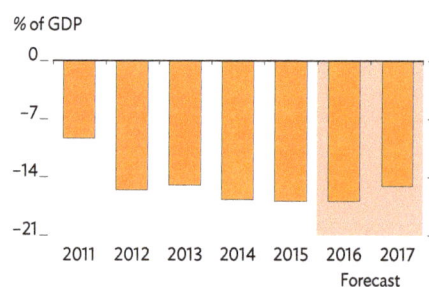

Sources: National Bank of the Kyrgyz Republic. http://www.nbkr.kg (accessed 3 March 2016); ADB estimates.
Click here for figure data

The government is developing measures—held back in 2015 because of parliamentary elections—for fiscal consolidation in 2016, to be accelerated in 2017 and 2018.

Tax revenue should be raised by improving tax administration and widening the tax base by removing exemptions and simplifying tax procedures. On the revenue side, the government plans to (i) strengthen the administration of value-added taxes, (ii) let exemptions expire on schedule while eliminating other exemptions and avoiding new ones, (iii) raise excise rates on alcohol and tobacco, (iv) introduce stamp duties on some domestic goods, and (v) enact a luxury tax on high-value real estate. On the expenditure side, it plans to (i) refrain from ad hoc wage increases and prepare a plan to gradually reduce the wage bill to 8% of GDP by 2018, (ii) streamline purchases of goods and services while keeping outlays at the 2015 level in som terms, (iii) rationalize and better target existing subsidies, (iv) review electricity tariffs to ensure sector sustainability, (v) reduce duplication in social benefits and improve their targeting, and (vi) keep domestically financed public investment below 3% of GDP.

If these measures are implemented, public and publicly guaranteed debt is projected to peak at 66% of GDP in 2017, then fall below 65% by 2018. However, as the risks to debt sustainability remain high, it is critical to improve debt management and mobilize domestic sources of financing. Measures to stimulate growth include using the Russian Kyrgyz Development Fund to support export-oriented industries and improving the business environment to attract investments.

3.5.8 Public debt

■ Public debt
— Fiscal deficit

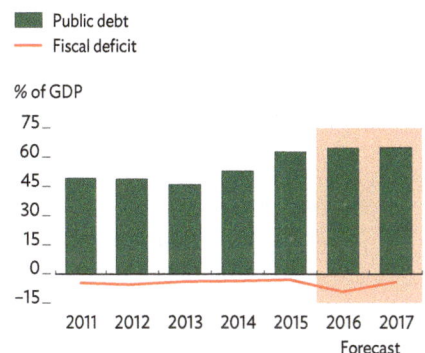

Sources: National Bank of the Kyrgyz Republic. http://www.nbkr.kg (accessed 3 March 2016); ADB estimates.
Click here for figure data

Tajikistan

Reported growth slowed to 6.0% and trade declined, reflecting lower commodity prices, weak private investment, and remittance shortfalls. Growth is projected to fall to 3.8% in 2016 as recession continues in the Russian Federation and activity remains weak in other trading partners, then recover slightly to 4.0% in 2017. A better business environment would boost local production and employment, alleviating excessive dependence on remittances.

Economic performance

Growth decelerated to 6.0% in 2015 from 6.7% a year earlier as recession in the Russian Federation and a plunge in the ruble caused remittances, Tajikistan's main source of income, to fall by a third (Figure 3.6.1). About 135,000 Tajik migrant workers returned home as a result of tightened immigration control in the Russian Federation. Other constraints on growth were lower prices for primary Tajik exports aluminum and cotton, weak private investment, and the depreciation of the Tajik somoni by nearly a third.

On the supply side, a 21.2% rise in construction fueled by public investment was the main driver, offsetting a 7.0% decline in services due mainly to the drop in remittances (Figure 3.6.2). Growth in industry slowed to 11.2% from 13.3% in 2014 despite significant gains in electricity generation and mining. Growth in agriculture slowed to 3.2% from 4.5% in 2014 as late spring frosts reduced exports of dried fruit.

On the demand side, low remittances and currency depreciation constrained private consumption. Higher investment from the People's Republic of China (PRC) partly offset lower private consumption.

Inflation slowed, despite the depreciation, to 5.1% from 6.1% in 2014, reflecting the drop in private consumption, lower global prices for petroleum and wheat, and currency depreciation in Tajikistan's main trade partners. Prices rose by 4.3% for food, 7.8% for other goods, and 2.3% for services.

Fiscal policy was generally expansionary over the year, though lower private consumption and a 20% drop in imports constrained tax revenue. In response, the government deferred a salary increase but maintained social spending. Despite the slowdown, total revenue including grants rose from the equivalent of 28.4% of GDP in 2014 to an estimated 30.1%, reflecting better tax administration (Figure 3.6.3). Expenditure also rose, to 32.4% from 29.0% in 2014, as capital spending was expanded to maintain economic activity. The overall budget deficit reached 2.3% of GDP. Public and publicly guaranteed debt (all external) rose to 27.8% of GDP at the end of 2015 from 22.7% a year earlier as the somoni depreciated.

This chapter was written by Muhammadi Boboev of the Tajikistan Resident Mission, ADB, Dushanbe.

3.6.1 Remittances and exchange rate

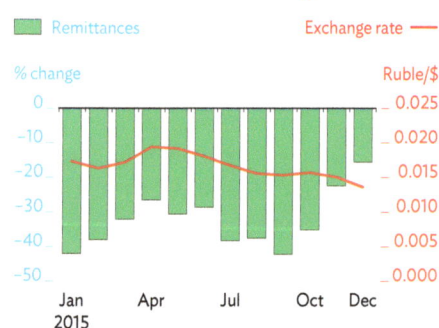

Note: Remittances fell by 33.3% in 2015 as the ruble depreciated by 27% against the dollar.
Sources: National Bank of Tajikistan; Bloomberg.
Click here for figure data

3.6.2 GDP growth by sector

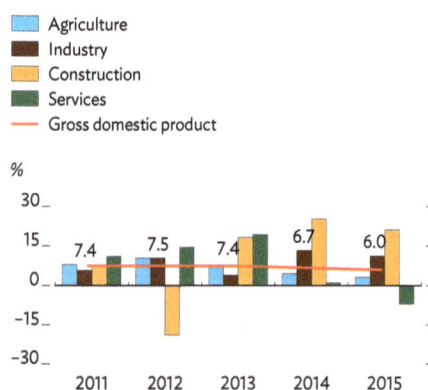

Source: Tajikistan State Statistical Agency.
Click here for figure data

Monetary policy aimed to ensure macroeconomic stability and rein in inflation. To facilitate lending, reserve requirements were cut for financial institutions that met capital adequacy standards: by 0.5 percentage points to 1.5% for local currency deposits, and by 1.0 percentage point to 7.0% for foreign. In response, broad money grew by 18.7% during the year, up from 7.1% in 2014 (Figure 3.6.4). At the same time, the National Bank of Tajikistan, the central bank, used open market operations to reduce liquidity. In March 2016, it raised the refinancing rate by 1.0 percentage point to 9.0% to dampen inflation.

Depreciation intensified financial sector problems because of extensive dollarization. Nonperforming loans reached 30%, while average bank capital fell to 12% of assets. Efforts to consolidate microfinance organizations by raising their minimum capital requirements induced some to merge or close when their licenses were withdrawn.

Lower remittances and export receipts, along with currency depreciation in Tajikistan's main trade partners, caused the somoni to depreciate, despite sizable interventions to stabilize exchange rates, by 31.7% against the dollar and 16.1% against the ruble (Figure 3.6.5). At the end of 2015, reserves totaled $494.3 million, covering only about 1.6 months of imports, which is well below prudential norms and constrains the central bank's ability to defend the currency against any further depreciation (Figure 3.6.6).

To ease currency pressures, foreign exchange control was strengthened. In April 2015, the operations of private exchange offices were brought under the control of banks. In September, the central bank signed a $500 million currency swap agreement with its counterpart in the PRC. In December, authorization for foreign exchange operations was restricted to financial institutions. In February 2016, the central bank sought to shield the currency from ruble fluctuation by asking all financial institutions to convert incoming ruble remittances into somoni.

The current account deficit narrowed from the equivalent of 9.1% of GDP in 2014 to an estimated 5.9% despite the plunge in remittances. Exports fell by 8.9%, mainly because of weak demand and lower world prices for the country's main exports, while imports dropped by 20.1% due to lower private consumption. External debt equaled 27.8% of GDP at the end of 2015, mainly because of depreciation.

Economic prospects

Growth is forecast to slow to 3.8% in 2016, reflecting the continuing recession in the Russian Federation, before recovering to 4.0% in 2017 with some recovery in the external outlook. Second-round effects of developments in 2015, along with weaker economic performance in Tajikistan's other main trade partners (the PRC, Kazakhstan, and Turkey) and continued low global commodity prices, will limit remittances and foreign investment, constraining demand and consumption in 2016. Expected recovery in the Russian Federation and better performance in other regional partners in 2017 should improve growth prospects.

On the supply side, industry is forecast to grow moderately in 2016 as construction picks up and to accelerate in 2017 on increases in mining

3.6.3 Fiscal balance and public debt

- Domestic debt
- Public and publicly guaranteed external debt
- Expenditures
- Revenue and grants
- Fiscal balance including the public investment program

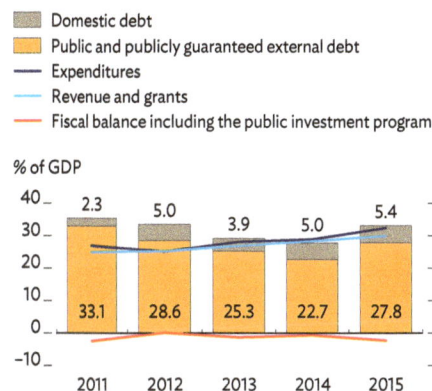

Sources: National Bank of Tajikistan; Tajikistan State Statistical Agency.
Click here for figure data

3.6.4 Monetary indicators

- Credit to the private sector
- Broad money
- Reserve money
- Refinancing rate (period average)

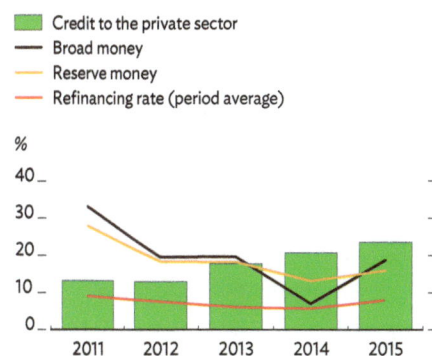

Sources: National Bank of Tajikistan; International Monetary Fund.
Click here for figure data

3.6.5 Exchange rates

Somonis to the US dollar   Somonis to the ruble

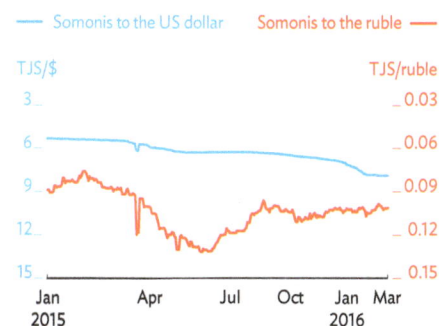

Source: National Bank of Tajikistan.
Click here for figure data

and processing, as well as the opening of Tajikistan's segment of a regional high-voltage power line and a gas pipeline from Turkmenistan to the PRC. Agriculture should grow modestly as repatriating migrants return to their farms. However, services are projected to contract further as weak remittances hold down household income.

On the demand side, weak remittances, low foreign exchange earnings, and likely continued depreciation of the currency will limit gains in private consumption and investment, though a possible hike in civil service salaries during 2016 would support consumption. With private investment shrinking, the government is likely to expand public investment.

Inflation is projected to accelerate to 8.5% in 2016 and slow to 7.5% in 2017, reflecting the lagged effect on import prices of depreciation in 2015 and somewhat less depreciation in 2016 (Figure 3.6.7). Weak demand should limit price hikes in services. Higher inflation could result if foreign exchange restrictions are further tightened, or if depreciation exceeds expectations.

Fiscal policy is expected to be expansionary over the next 2 years given the challenges facing the economy. The budget is projected to record deficits equal to 2.5% of GDP in 2016 and 1.5% in 2017, but deficits could be higher with further depreciation or pressure to clear arrears at public enterprises. The projected growth slowdown is expected to limit revenues despite ongoing reform to tax administration. Revenue is forecast equal to 29.0% of GDP in 2016 and 30.5% in 2017. Total expenditure is forecast at 31.5% of GDP in 2016 and 32.0% in 2017, with increases for capital investment but not current outlays. Higher public investment should raise public debt above 35% of GDP.

Monetary policy will likely aim to curb inflation while preventing recession. Broad money growth will rise mainly as foreign exchange deposits gain value in local currency terms. Exchange rate policy is expected to move gradually to a floating rate regime because of limited reserves. Banks face serious risks from ongoing depreciation, tightened foreign exchange regulations, and stagnant retail trade and services.

The current account deficit is forecast to narrow to 4.8% of GDP in 2016 and then widen to 5.5% in 2017 (Figure 3.6.8). Exports are projected to rise by 5% in 2016 and 7% in 2017 as depreciation boosts competitiveness. Imports are expected to contract by 7% in 2016 in tandem with lower demand before rising by 5% in 2017 with higher capital spending and some growth in remittances with recovery in the Russian Federation.

Policy challenge—developing a new growth model

Tajikistan is highly vulnerable to external shocks, particularly from commodity prices and remittances (Figure 3.6.9). Output and exports are constrained by limited production and low value added. This leaves remittance-financed consumption as the main source of growth.

Tajikistan needs a new growth model based more on domestic production and exports. Research suggests that the economy's potential growth rate has fallen by 2 percentage points since 2007, raising concerns about growth prospects over the medium to long term.

3.6.1 Selected economic indicators (%)

	2016	2017
GDP growth	3.8	4.0
Inflation	8.5	7.5
Current account balance (share of GDP)	−4.8	−5.5

Source: ADB estimates.

3.6.6 Gross international reserves

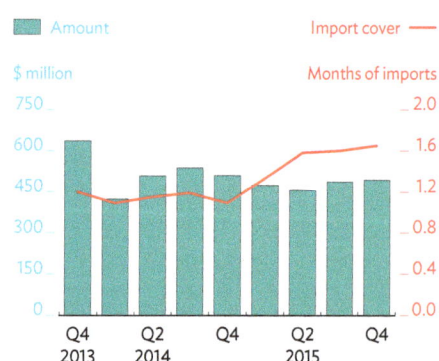

Source: National Bank of Tajikistan.
Click here for figure data

3.6.7 Inflation

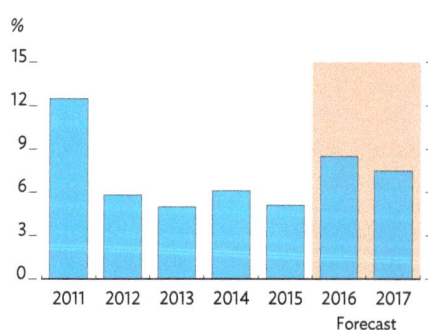

Sources: Tajikistan State Statistical Agency; ADB estimates.
Click here for figure data

While stimulating demand may help in the short run, sustained growth will require supply-side reform to revive the country's industrial base and boost employment.

The government is considering a number of measures in its National Development Strategy to 2030 to boost economic activity: securing stable access to energy resources, attaining self-sufficiency in food production, integrating international and national transport links, developing communication networks, and broadening access to social services.

Further, Tajikistan would do well to address important obstacles facing businesses. According to the World Bank's *Doing Business 2016* report, Tajikistan ranks exceptionally poorly on getting electricity, at 177 out of 189 economies surveyed; taxation at 172; and getting construction permits at 152. Moreover, the complexity of tax regulation is the second highest concern among firms in Tajikistan, according to the *Global Competitiveness Report 2015–2016* of the World Economic Forum. During the past year, many firms have been pressured to make advance tax payments. Tight foreign exchange controls have further complicated doing business.

In the short run, a few measures would make private investment more attractive: adopting more stable and transparent investment incentives; reducing the number of surprise business inspections, in part by halving the number of government units conducting them; limiting advance tax payments to 3 months' worth of annual liabilities; streamlining the granting of construction permits; and simplifying regulations on certifying product quality, toward boosting exports.

Over the medium term, a sequenced approach to growth should start small in carefully selected locales. Private investment should be encouraged to improve identified urban growth nodes, value chains in priority areas, and connections with external markets. This approach would build on the four special zones the government has created to increase exports, which otherwise risk becoming enclaves because of weak links with the local economy. Simple, infrastructure-driven economic corridor development anchored on the strongest center, Dushanbe, could magnify current growth potential, propelling expansion in the Kurgan–Tube area. Economic corridor development—featuring improved transportation and small but clustered investments in energy, information and computer technology, or urban infrastructure—could also create the jobs that Tajikistan needs, in particular for returning migrants.

3.6.8 Current account balance

% of GDP

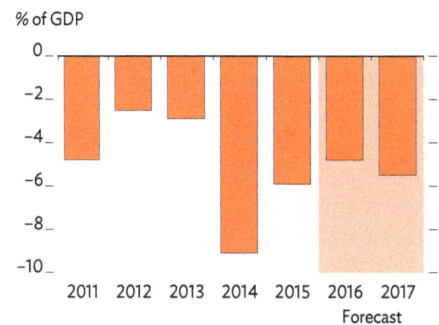

Sources: International Monetary Fund; National Bank of Tajikistan; ADB estimates.
Click here for figure data

3.6.9 Remittances and GDP growth

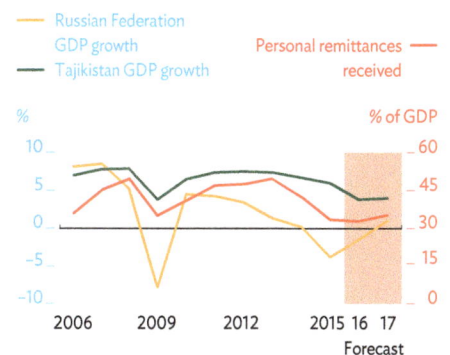

Sources: World Bank, World Development Indicators online database; National Bank of Tajikistan; ADB estimates.
Click here for figure data

Turkmenistan

Growth slowed to 6.5% in 2015 with the decline in global energy prices, and the current account deficit widened to 11.8% of GDP with exports falling more than imports. Growth is forecast to remain at 6.5% in 2016 on reduced energy earnings, then recover to 7.0% in 2017 with expected higher petroleum prices. Diversifying the highly concentrated export sector would help smooth output volatility and create jobs to absorb a young and growing working-age population.

Economic performance

The government reported growth at 6.5% in 2015, down from 10.3% a year earlier (Figure 3.7.1). The slowdown reflected declines in energy prices, but growth found support from investments in social and industrial development, which picked up to 7.8% from 6.7% in 2014.

On the supply side, slower growth in hydrocarbons cut expansion in industry to 3.1% from 11.4% in 2014. Growth in agriculture accelerated to 7.9% from 4.2% a year earlier, reflecting good harvests of wheat and cotton and increased livestock farming. Expansion in services diminished slightly, to 10.0% from 10.6% in 2014, mainly due to slower growth in services related to construction.

Average annual inflation is estimated to have held steady at 6.0% (Figure 3.7.1). Despite the 19% devaluation of the Turkmen manat at the beginning of the 2015, prices for food and services stabilized during the second half with price controls, state subsidies, and the absence of further depreciation. The government's import-substitution policy contributed by helping to fill the market with less expensive locally produced food and household goods. Broad money growth slowed to 8.4% from 11.4% in 2014. However, growth in private credit is estimated to have risen to 30.0% from 20.9% in 2014, reflecting mainly import substitution and construction by small and medium-sized enterprises.

The government budget is estimated to have moved from a surplus equal to 0.8% of GDP in 2014 to a deficit of 1.0% (Figure 3.7.2). This reflects continued spending on social programs, including a 10% rise in public wages, pensions, and students' stipends, along with higher investment outlays. Lower hydrocarbon exports limited revenues, but the government's Stabilization Fund helped smooth revenue volatility. As in past years, energy revenues largely covered the fiscal deficit in the non-hydrocarbon economy, estimated at 10.3% of GDP in 2015. Public debt rose slightly, to 18.7% of GDP from 16.8% in 2014.

Lower prices and slack demand for energy products—especially natural gas, Turkmenistan's main export—sharply reduced export earnings. Export revenues are estimated to have fallen by 34% as hydrocarbon exports plunged by 36.5%. Imports dropped by 22.4%.

This chapter was written by Jennet Hojanazarova of the Turkmenistan Resident Mission, ADB, Ashgabat.

3.7.1 GDP growth and inflation

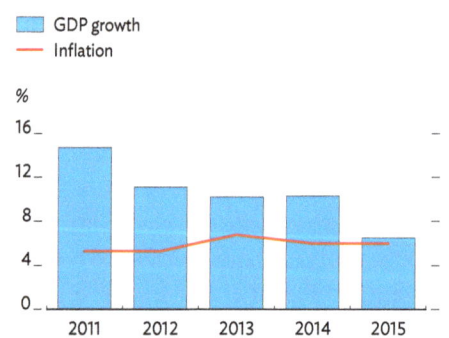

Sources: International Monetary Fund. 2015. *Regional Economic Outlook, Middle East and Central Asia.* October; ADB estimates.
Click here for figure data

3.7.2 Government fiscal balances

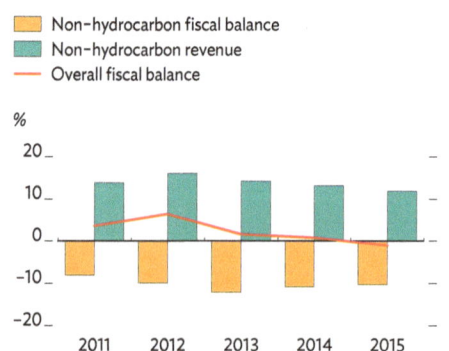

Note: Non-hydrocarbon fiscal balance and revenue are percentages of non-oil gross domestic product, and the overall fiscal balance is a percentage of total gross domestic product.
Sources: International Monetary Fund. 2015. *Regional Economic Outlook, Middle East and Central Asia.* October; ADB estimates.
Click here for figure data

The current account deficit widened to 11.8% of GDP from 5.8% in 2014 as exports declined more than imports. Foreign direct investment, mainly in hydrocarbons and construction, rose slightly to 9.6% of GDP. External debt, all of it public, stayed below 20% of GDP, while foreign exchange reserves were estimated at 30 months of import cover at the end of 2015.

Economic prospects

The economy relies heavily on oil and gas exports, the earnings from which are envisioned to remain weak with lower prices. This may prompt the government to cut spending, but a low public debt ratio and considerable fiscal reserves allow it to adjust gradually and sustain growth through social spending and public investment that support the non-hydrocarbon economy.

Growth is projected steady at 6.5% in 2016, rising to 7.0% in 2017. However, it could be lower if external weakness persists, requiring the government to implement more stringent fiscal adjustment.

To limit inflation, the government will continue import-substitution policies and price controls. Inflation is nevertheless projected rising to 6.6% in 2016 before returning to 6.0% in 2017, assuming no further manat depreciation. The Central Bank of Turkmenistan will likely tighten monetary policy by restraining credit expansion. Broad money growth is expected to slow further to 7.2% in 2016.

The state budget for 2016 projects a deficit equal to 1.2% of GDP. The Stabilization Fund will continue to support domestic development projects to build social and industrial infrastructure. With lower natural gas prices, export earnings should diminish further in 2016, widening the current account deficit to 12.3% of GDP. A modest recovery in global energy prices in 2017 is expected to narrow the current account deficit to 10.0% of GDP. Foreign direct investment will likely remain strong in both years. External debt is projected at 16.6% of GDP in 2016 and 15.9% in 2017.

Policy challenge—diversification for sustainable growth

Turkmenistan has one of the highest ratios of trade to GDP in Central Asia. Trade generates nearly 84% of GDP, and hydrocarbons account for over 90% of exports, making Turkmenistan's exports the most concentrated in the subregion (Figure 3.7.3). Such reliance on earnings from hydrocarbons leaves the economy highly exposed to developments in the global oil and gas market.

The current deterioration in the external environment, and especially falling energy prices, highlight the economy's vulnerability from dependence on energy exports (Figure 3.7.4). While fiscal measures can offset external shocks over the near term using savings accumulated in sovereign wealth funds, a prolonged period of low energy prices could diminish these buffers. Greater diversification would help smooth output volatility, create jobs to absorb the country's young and

3.7.1 Selected economic indicators (%)

	2016	2017
GDP growth	6.5	7.0
Inflation	6.6	6.0
Current account balance (share of GDP)	−12.3	−10.0

Source: ADB estimates.

3.7.3 Export structure, 2014

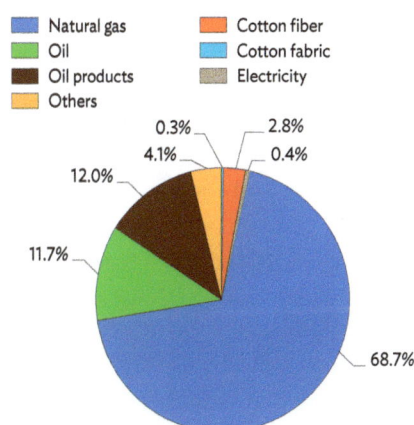

Source: State Committee of Statistics of Turkmenistan. 2015. Statistical Yearbook.
Click here for figure data

3.7.4 GDP growth and exports

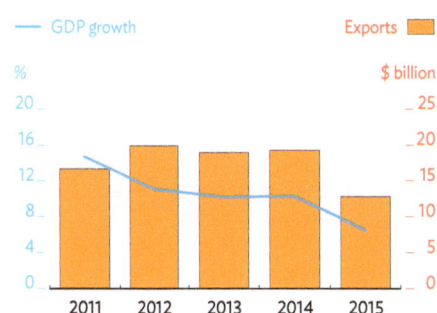

Sources: International Monetary Fund. 2015. Regional Economic Outlook, Middle East and Central Asia. October; ADB estimates.
Click here for figure data

growing working-age population, and develop the economy outside of the hydrocarbon sector.

The government initiated programs within the National Program for Socio-Economic Development, 2011–2030 to diversify the economy through state-led industrialization and private sector development. The priority sectors—oil and gas, electric power, chemicals, construction, transport and communications, light industry, food processing, textiles, and agribusiness—received targets and government allocations with the aim of boosting growth in the non-hydrocarbon economy and in hydrocarbon processing. Heavy public investment and strong foreign direct investment (Figure 3.7.5) support the government's industrial policy with gross investment that in 2015 equaled 36.6% of GDP.

As the share of processing in all industry rose from 29% in 2012 to a provisional 42% in 2015, diversification has been most evident in hydrocarbons, and a dynamic tradable sector beyond hydrocarbons has yet to emerge. Gaining more from diversification requires balanced investment management, with adequate support to manufacturing and agriculture in addition to expanding hydrocarbons and services, making investments more efficient, and deepening structural reforms.

The magnitude of public investment provides ample opportunity to improve its management. A well-coordinated multiyear investment plan should balance growth in hydrocarbons and the rest of the economy. Raising the quality of investment depends on introducing a strong medium-term fiscal framework, careful prioritization, and thorough appraisal and selection of investment projects.

As the capital-intensive hydrocarbon sector employs little labor—only 1.7% of total employment (Figure 3.7.6)—industrial policy should dedicate adequate support to productive sectors outside of hydrocarbons that can generate export income and employment. Investment in highly productive industrial clusters would strengthen value chains throughout the economy, create networks of local suppliers, and expand the employment potential of the export sector. Industrializing agriculture, which provides 43% of all employment, by developing agribusiness and adopting advanced technology would likely boost its productivity and add value to its products. Productivity can be further enhanced, and more jobs created, by developing a high-quality service sector where large potential exists: transport and communications, logistics, finance, trade and marketing, and tourism.

Policies should aim to create an environment conducive to private sector expansion, encouraging firms to develop export markets, upgrade workers' skills, and promote technology transfer through foreign capital. Investments in education and health would create the human capital needed for structural transformation and improve social development in the country, whose current Human Development Index ranking is 109 out of 188. Investing in research and development for innovation, and providing local businesses with information and financial support, would help them acquire the critical mass needed to enter the global market.

Reform to strengthen institutions and governance, the legal and regulatory framework, and the protection of property rights—and to render public finance more open and transparent—would enable hydrocarbon revenues to be invested more efficiently and productively, thereby furthering diversification.

3.7.5 Foreign direct investment

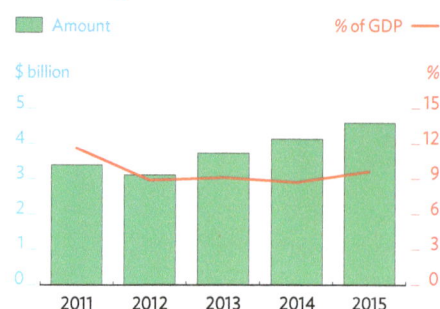

Sources: United Nations Conference on Trade and Development. 2015. *World Investment Report.* New York and Geneva; United Nations; European Bank for Reconstruction and Development. 2015. *Transition Report 2015–16.* London.
Click here for figure data

3.7.6 Employment by sector, 2014

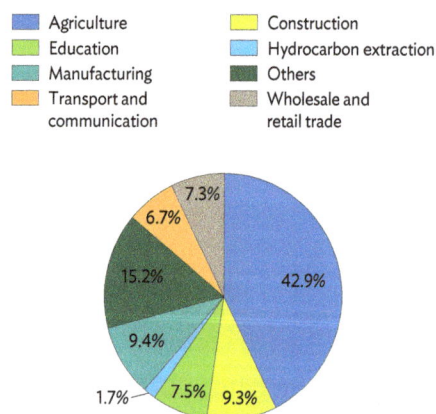

Note: Others include health care, public administration and defense, arts and entertainment, real estate, professional and scientific work, distribution of utilities, finance, and rest of employment.
Source: State Committee of Statistics of Turkmenistan. 2015. *Statistical Yearbook.*
Click here for figure data

Uzbekistan

Despite a challenging external environment, rising public investment buoyed growth at 8.0% in 2015. Trade contracted sharply, and the current account surplus narrowed. Growth is expected to slow to 6.9% in 2016, reflecting continued weakness in trade partners, before recovering to 7.3% in 2017 as the global outlook improves. Strengthening competitiveness in diverse markets will require further efforts to promote innovation.

Economic performance

The economy grew by 8.0% in 2015, the ninth consecutive year of expansion at 8.0% or higher. Growth was expected to be lower because of a slowdown in the Russian Federation, Uzbekistan's largest trade partner and source of remittances. This slowdown has profoundly affected Uzbekistan in two ways: It reduced bilateral trade and remittances, thereby diminishing foreign exchange revenues and private consumption, and it accelerated the depreciation of the Uzbek sum against the US dollar. In response, the government tightened import controls while expanding public investment and commercial lending to sustain domestic demand.

On the supply side, the main contributors to growth were industry at 8.0%, down from 8.3% in 2014, and services (including construction) at 14.0%, down from 15.4%. In industry, public investment boosted output in metallurgy, construction materials, and food processing. Export-oriented machinery and energy—traditional locomotives of industrial growth—showed little or no expansion despite receiving more than a quarter of all investment. Public investment also supported robust construction, which expanded by 17.0%. In services, telecommunications expanded by 15.4% and finance by 30.0%, mainly on higher domestic lending and sustained demand. Transport, including logistics, grew by 5.1%, down from 8.9% in 2014 in line with weaker external trade. Agriculture grew by 6.8%, slightly down from 6.9% in 2014, supported by favorable weather and good harvests of grain and cotton (Figure 3.8.1).

On the demand side, growth found support in public investment and, to a lesser extent, consumption. The government reported that gross investment, a fifth of which came from abroad, rose by 9.5%, while gross fixed capital formation rose by 9.6%. Energy received the largest share of investment at 24.0%, followed by petrochemicals at 2.6%. In 2015, a consortium involving Uzbekistan and the Republic of Korea completed a $4.0 billion petrochemical plant on the Surgil natural gas deposit that produces polymers high in demand, generating exports and replacing

3.8.1 Supply-side contributions to growth

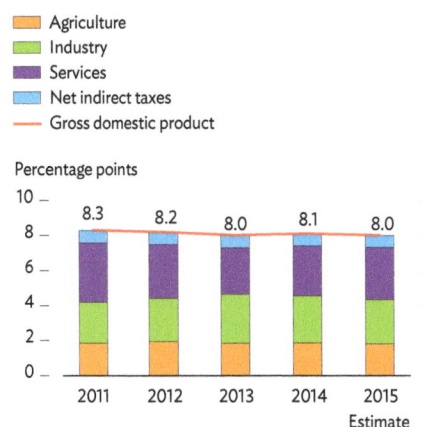

- Agriculture
- Industry
- Services
- Net indirect taxes
- Gross domestic product

Percentage points

Sources: State Statistics Committee; ADB estimates.
Click here for figure data

This chapter was written by Iskandar Gulamov of the Uzbekistan Resident Mission, ADB, Tashkent.

imports. Other projects expanded power plants and constructed a new production facility at General Motors Uzbekistan. Despite a 17% rise in public sector wages, a massive drop in remittances limited growth in private consumption. According to the Central Bank of the Russian Federation, in the first 9 months of 2015 (the latest for which data are available), remittances to Uzbekistan sent via money transfer systems fell by 59% from the same period in 2014, to $1.8 billion (Figure 3.8.2). Recession in the Russian Federation, the sharp depreciation of the ruble, and the return of 330,000 Uzbek migrant workers in 2014 and 2015 precipitated the plunge in remittances.

The government reported inflation at 5.6%, well within the target range of the Central Bank of Uzbekistan. The International Monetary Fund, using the same data but a different methodology, estimated inflation at 9.3% in the year to September 2015, down from the previous year (Figure 3.8.3). Average annual inflation for 2015 is estimated at 9.0%. Despite higher public wages and pensions, tariff hikes, and currency depreciation, inflation slowed in 2015, reflecting lower global food prices and import costs. Inflationary pressures came largely from greater depreciation of the sum, which lost 37% of its value against the US dollar on the parallel market in 2015, reflecting the depreciation of the ruble against the US dollar and lower global petroleum prices.

The central bank continued its policy of steadily lowering the official rate of the sum against the US dollar, as the unofficial rate fell even faster on the parallel market. Taking into account weaker currencies across the Commonwealth of Independent States (most notably the ruble and Kazakh tenge), the sum is estimated to have appreciated in real terms in 2015, making exports less competitive. The government responded by restricting imports and strengthening foreign exchange controls. The gap between official and parallel market exchange rates more than doubled in 2015.

The central bank cut its policy interest rate from 10.0% in 2014 to 9.0% while keeping strict control over payment arrears and cash in circulation by promoting noncash payments through debit cards. Broad money growth is estimated to have risen slightly, to 20.7% in 2015 from 18.0 % a year earlier, in line with expanding domestic credit.

The augmented budget balance—which includes the surplus of the Uzbekistan Fund for Reconstruction and Development, the sovereign wealth fund—is estimated to have recorded a surplus equivalent to 0.2% of GDP for 2015, down from 2.1% a year earlier (Figure 3.8.4).

The state budget was reported in deficit as tax cuts for firms and individuals and lower international prices for gas, copper, and cotton reduced revenues. Early in 2015, the government announced a new 5-year public investment program to upgrade industry and infrastructure. The $40.8 billion program raised capital spending to an estimated 4.7% of GDP from 4.1% in 2014. Total government debt, all of it external, rose to 11.0% of GDP from 8.7% in 2014, in line with higher foreign borrowing for domestic infrastructure. Holding substantial foreign exchange reserves of around $24 billion, the government has no plans to borrow domestically over the medium term.

The government reported a $455.1 million surplus in external trade in goods and services in 2015, triple the $149.5 million surplus

3.8.2 **Remittances from the Russian Federation**

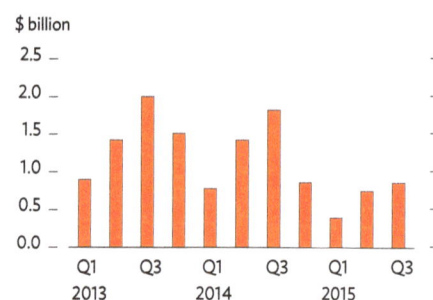

Q = quarter.
Source: Central Bank of the Russian Federation.
Click here for figure data

3.8.3 **Broad money and inflation**

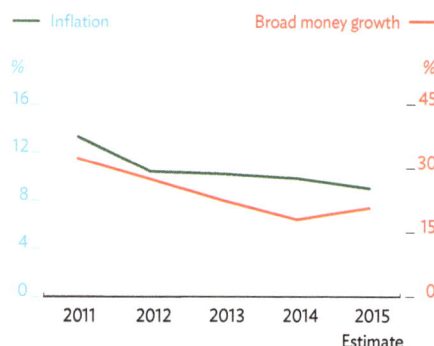

Sources: International Monetary Fund; ADB estimates.
Click here for figure data

3.8.4 **Fiscal performance**

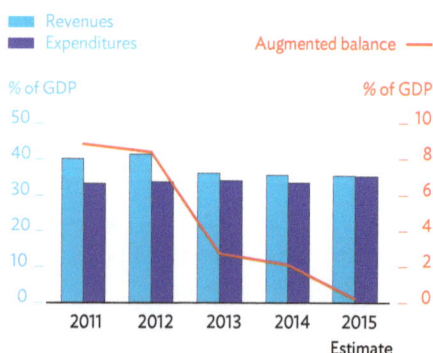

Note: Augmented budget includes the Fund for Reconstruction and Development.
Sources: International Monetary Fund; ADB estimates.
Click here for figure data

reported a year earlier (Figure 3.8.5). Excluding services, the trade balance recorded a deficit of $1.7 billion, and the current account surplus narrowed to 0.3% of GDP from 1.4% in 2014. Exports of goods and services plunged by 8.8% as global prices for the country's export commodities (natural gas, gold, copper, and cotton) hit historic lows and slowdowns in Kazakhstan, the Republic of Korea, and the Russian Federation constrained trade. Total trade with these three partners dropped by 22% from 2014. Exports of energy declined by 30%, cotton by 9%, and metals by 16%.

Developments in the Russian Federation since mid-2014 have profoundly affected Uzbekistan's export performance. Weak consumer demand there and rapid appreciation of the sum against the ruble hurt bilateral trade, which fell by 25%. These factors had a particularly negative effect on machinery exports, mainly General Motors automobiles, which plunged by 71%. The local market absorbed some of the surplus vehicles, often as investments to preserve the value of savings.

Imports of goods and services fell by 12.2% from 2014, mainly due to lower global prices and tighter import controls, with imports of energy falling by 16.2% and metals by 17.4%. External debt, mostly medium to long term, was estimated at 15.8% of GDP at the end of 2015, up from 13.4% in 2014.

Economic prospects

Growth is forecast to slow to 6.9% in 2016 because of the weak external outlook and recover to 7.3% in 2017, led by public investment and government spending (Figure 3.8.6). On the supply side, investment-led industry will remain the key driver of growth, supported by domestic lending. Planned wage and pension increases that exceed inflation should, along with social transfers, support private consumption and growth in services.

Agriculture is projected to grow at 6.0% in 2016 and 6.5% in 2017 as vegetable harvests improve and wheat production holds its own. Early in 2016, the government announced a gradual reduction in output and state procurement of cotton fiber, from 3.4 million tons in 2015 to 3.0 million by 2020. It also announced the reallocation of substantial cropland from cotton to vegetables. These two measures reflect a shift from energy- and water-intensive cotton to more sustainable crops with higher valued added.

In March 2015, the government announced a program of structural reform, modernization, and diversification of industry to 2019, which carries forward policies initiated in 2010 (Box 3.8.1). The program will boost investments to develop high-tech industry, make production less energy intensive, and expand the output of goods with high valued added, potentially generating a more advanced export mix. Public investment will rise substantially to achieve program objectives. The sovereign wealth fund is expected to finance an increasing share of domestic investment. Gross fixed capital formation is forecast to rise by 13% in 2016 and 11% in 2017.

3.8.5 Current account components

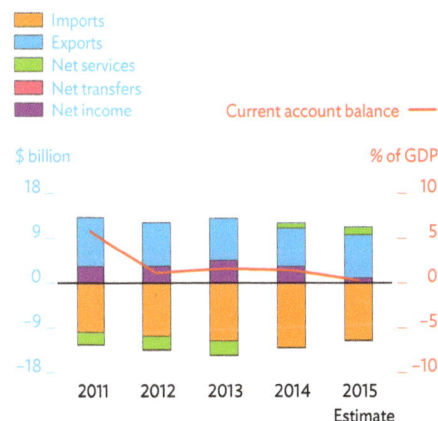

Sources: International Monetary Fund; ADB estimates.
Click here for figure data

3.8.1 Selected economic indicators (%)

	2016	2017
GDP growth	6.9	7.3
Inflation	10.0	11.0
Current account balance (share of GDP)	0.2	0.8

Source: ADB estimates.

3.8.6 GDP growth

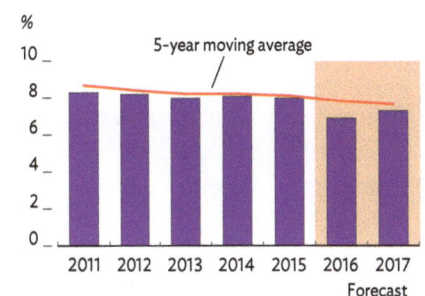

Source: Asian Development Outlook database.
Click here for figure data

The government will continue to support domestic consumption in 2016 and 2017, most likely by raising public sector wages, welfare payments, and pensions. However, the continued economic slowdown in the Russian Federation and associated losses in remittances will restrain growth in consumption, at least during 2016. Private consumption is forecast to rise by only 1.5% in 2016 but 3.0% in 2017.

Inflation is forecast at 10.0% in 2016 and 11.0% in 2017 (Figure 3.8.7). Inflationary pressures will emanate from higher government spending and, from 2017, anticipated faster depreciation of the currency. Continued declines in global prices for food and other imports could partly offset these pressures. Nevertheless, over the medium term, inflation will remain a key challenge, requiring close coordination of monetary, exchange rate, and fiscal policy.

The government has projected a consolidated budget deficit of 1.0% of GDP in 2016, supporting economic expansion. Including expected sovereign wealth fund surpluses, the augmented budget is projected to post a surplus of 0.1% of GDP in 2016 and 0.3% in 2017. Expenditure is forecast to increase in 2016 and 2017 as the government raises health and education outlays, along with capital spending. It announced that expenditures for health and education will rise by 16% in 2016 and together comprise 59% of total budget outlays.

The current account surplus is forecast to narrow to 0.2% of GDP in 2016 before widening to 0.8% in 2017 with some improvement in the global environment. Falling international prices for the country's main exports, weak global trade, and the deteriorating economic situation in the Russian Federation and the People's Republic of China will reduce the trade surplus and transfers. Merchandise exports are projected to rise by 2.0% in 2016 and 4.0% in 2017.

Merchandise imports are projected to rise more gradually, by 2.0% in 2016 and 2.5% in 2017. Demand will come mostly from public infrastructure spending and the industrial modernization program. Lower global commodity prices and import controls should limit import payments.

Policy challenge—improving competitiveness through innovation

The weak global environment and historically low energy prices will continue to restrain activity in Kazakhstan, the People's Republic of China, and, along with ongoing trade sanctions, the Russian Federation, undermining Uzbekistan's primary trade flows. Uzbekistan's exports depend heavily on prices for a few major commodities and developments in a handful of countries. A more diverse and sophisticated export base is essential to minimize external shocks and ensure export competitiveness, highlighting the importance of securing the continued transfer of technology along with capital equipment procured under the state-led industrial development program.

Important as technology transfer may be, economic growth in Uzbekistan still comes mainly from factor accumulation, notably increases in the capital stock. State-led industrialization and the ensuing

3.8.1 Overview of industrial policy for 2015–2019

In March 2015, the government adopted an ambitious program of structural reform, industrial modernization, and diversification for 2015–2019. The program carries forward government industrial policies initiated in 2010 and follows a program for 2011–2015. It targets developing high-tech industrial sectors, reducing the energy intensity of production, and expanding the production of finished goods. The program has 846 investment projects totaling $40.8 billion for modernization and technological renovation, including $19.6 billion of committed financing and $21.2 billion in potential projects. The government aims to mobilize a rising share of foreign investment to finance the new program using infrastructure support, tax exemptions and preferences, and other incentives. Successful implementation of this program is expected to raise the share of industry in GDP to 27% by 2020 (from 24% in 2015) and enable average growth of 9% per year in industry during 2015–2019.

3.8.7 Inflation

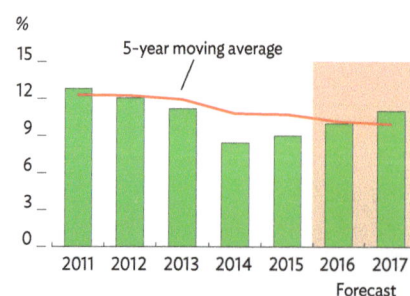

Source: Asian Development Outlook database.
Click here for figure data

capital accumulation have not produced significant technology transfer or productivity gains, probably because of policy-based allocation of capital and labor and distortions in prices and exchange rates. In addition, most investment goes to capital-intensive state-owned enterprises, in which management preferences and government support provide little incentive for innovation. The lack of innovation also reflects low spending on research and development (R&D), equal to only 0.2% of GDP, compared with more than 2.5% in advanced economies.

State-owned research institutions dominate the financing of R&D for lack of interest among enterprises and foreign investors in innovative products, which represent only 7% of industrial output. Moreover, barely 0.5% of enterprises use innovative technologies for production, and the number of patent applications has languished for over a decade (Figure 3.8.8). Three-quarters of firms interviewed in a recent World Bank industrial survey had not introduced any new products in the past 3 years, and only 1% had contracts with local R&D institutes. Constraints on innovation include the high costs and economic risks of innovation, a shortage of qualified personnel, and the lack of financial resources, incentives, and information about new technologies.

Innovation needs support from appropriate interventions to strengthen technological capacity in domestic firms. The speed and depth of technological upgrading are closely linked to how domestic firms acquire technological knowledge: through informal learning, foreign direct investment, or licensing.

Liberalizing foreign trade and promoting foreign investment facilitate access to global technology and innovation. Though exposing the country to more volatility, a more open economy promotes the adoption of external knowledge through trade and foreign investment. It also facilitates the absorption of foreign technology, which helps developing countries catch up with more advanced economies and grow. Uzbekistan's high costs of external trade (as evidenced by consistently low ratings for trading across borders in the World Bank's annual *Doing Business* surveys) and inadequate access to foreign exchange hamper knowledge acquisition and, thus, economic restructuring. Accordingly, measures to lower trade barriers and liberalize access to foreign exchange would promote innovation and long-term competitiveness.

While learning and technological absorption occur at the firm level, the extent to which countries upgrade their technological prowess also depends on institutional linkages. Innovation depends critically on facilitating interaction between enterprises and science and research institutions, expanding public funding for R&D and education, and enacting measures to reduce the cost of innovation for private firms. Science and research institutions and universities in Uzbekistan currently develop 72% of all innovations, versus industrial enterprises' 7%. Thus, facilitating interaction between research institutes and firms should raise the share of innovative products in industry and accelerate the adoption of innovative processes.

3.8.8 Uzbekistan patent applications to World Intellectual Property Organization

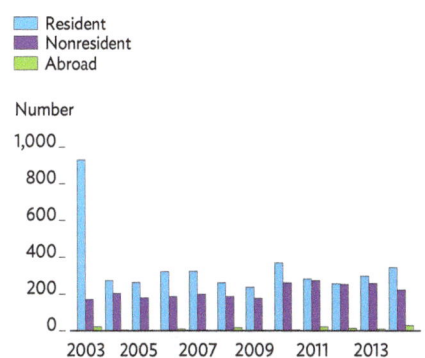

Source: World Intellectual Property Organization statistics database. www.wippo.int (accessed 3 March 2016).
Click here for figure data

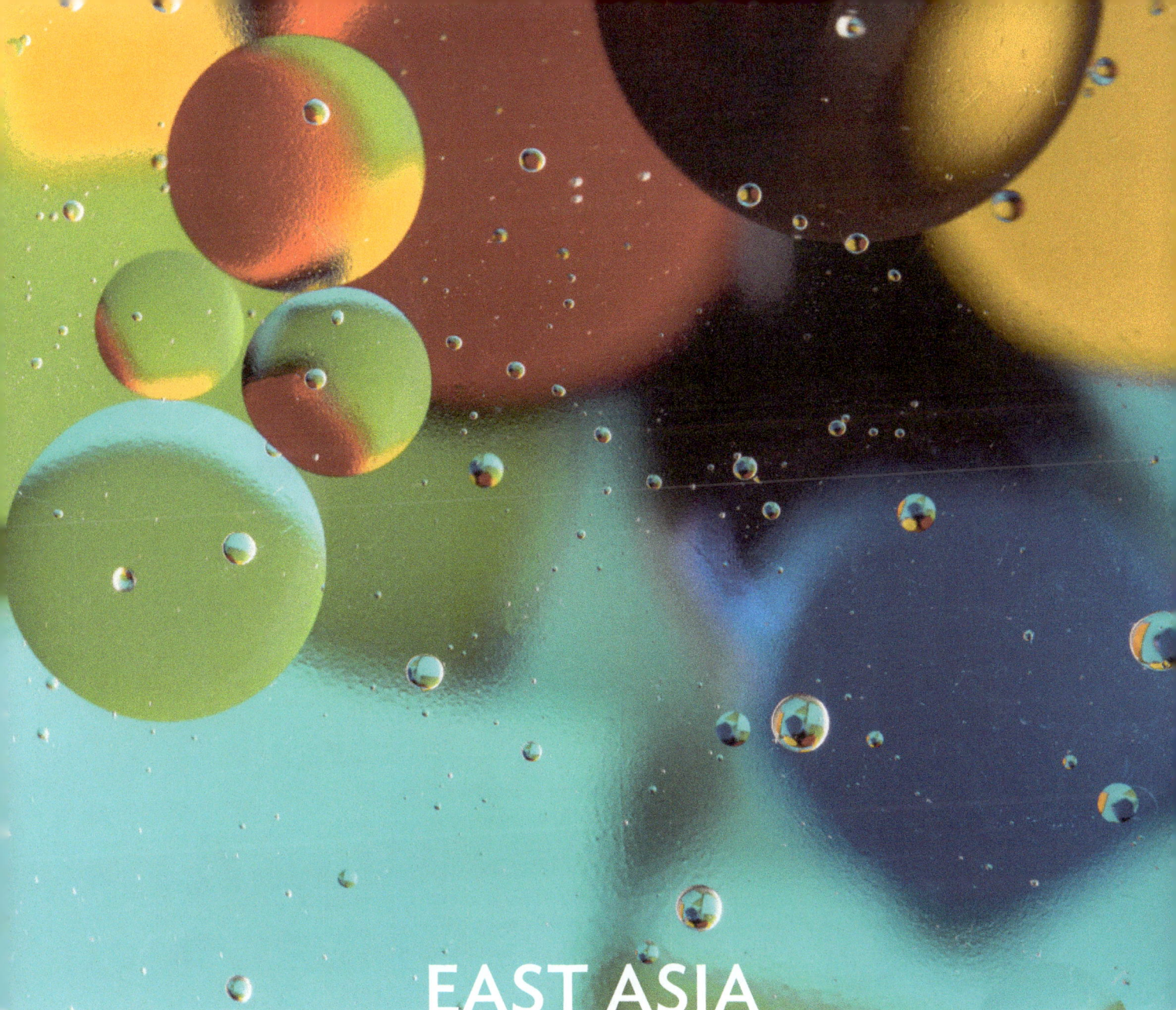

EAST ASIA

PEOPLE'S REPUBLIC OF CHINA
HONG KONG, CHINA
REPUBLIC OF KOREA
MONGOLIA
TAIPEI,CHINA

People's Republic of China

Economic growth continues to decelerate and is increasingly driven by services and consumption. Inflation will rise but remain low in 2016 and 2017, and the current account surplus will stay broadly stable. The authorities need to intensify supply-side structural reform to improve economic resilience in the face of a darkening international environment, financial market volatility, and financial and social challenges associated with industrial transformation.

Economic performance

Growth slowed further from 7.3% in 2014 to 6.9% in 2015 (Figure 3.9.1), continuing a trend since 2010 as the economy of the People's Republic of China (PRC) shifts further toward a new normal in which domestic consumption and services are the main engines of growth, with the government increasingly focused on growth quality over quantity. Despite growth moderation, the PRC has doubled its GDP since 2009 to reach $10.8 trillion in 2015, thus continuing to account for about a third of global growth in 2015, almost the same as in 2010 when its then smaller economy was growing by double digits. Apart from the difficulty of sustaining the high growth rates of the past in today's much larger economy, the moderation mainly reflects growth in the workforce slipping from its peak in recent years and the short-term adverse impact of measures to alleviate economic, environmental, and social imbalances. Delay in the global recovery played a role by suppressing export growth, though the PRC benefited from lower commodity prices.

On the supply side, rebalancing progressed further toward growth driven by the service sector. Services contributed an estimated 3.7 percentage points to GDP growth, while industry contributed 2.8 points and agriculture 0.3 points. The share of services in nominal GDP increased to 50.5% (Figure 3.9.2). Financial services performed particularly strongly, growth of retail sales remained robust, and the hospitality sector stabilized after 2 lean years in which an anticorruption initiative limited scope for lavish entertainment. Within industry, consumer-oriented manufacturing outperformed heavy industry, which continued to suffer from excess capacity, spillover from an ailing housing sector, and lower commodity prices. Heavy industry was the main factor behind the decline in aggregate industrial profits by 2.3% in 2015. Profits fell in 12 of 41 industrial subsectors, particularly affecting coal mining, petroleum and natural gas, and metals. Five northern provinces where these industries are concentrated reported growth substantially below the country average. They also reported job losses, though the labor market remained stable countrywide with 13.1 million new jobs in cities and healthy wage growth.

3.9.1 Economic growth

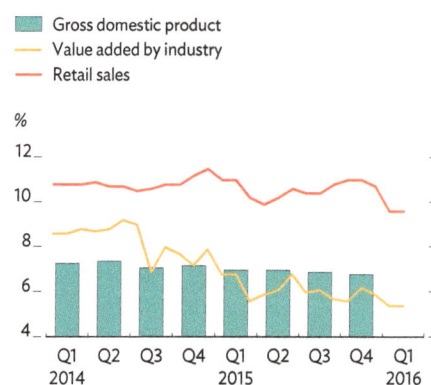

Q = quarter.
Note: GDP data for the first quarter of 2016 are not yet available.
Source: National Bureau of Statistics.
Click here for figure data

3.9.2 Share of sectors in nominal GDP

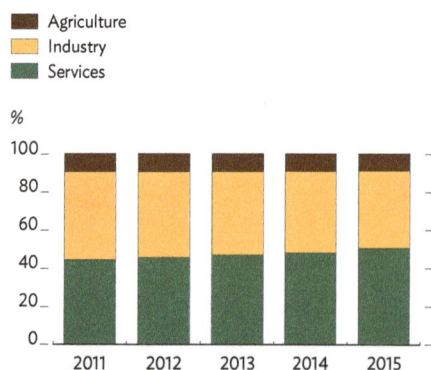

Source: National Bureau of Statistics.
Click here for figure data

This chapter was written by Jurgen Conrad and Jian Zhuang of the People's Republic of China Resident Mission, ADB, Beijing.

On the demand side, consumption was the main growth engine, contributing 4.6 percentage points to GDP growth, up from 3.7 in 2014 (Figure 3.9.3). Investment contributed 2.5 percentage points, down from 3.4 in 2014, while the contribution of net exports turned negative. The continuing structural slowdown in investment growth was most pronounced in real estate, which suffers from a large housing overhang. The government cushioned the correction by removing purchase restrictions, improving access to mortgages, relaxing down-payment requirements, and accelerating public housing construction and shantytown redevelopment. Real estate sales grew in recent months and prices increased, even as unsold floor space kept rising (Figure 3.9.4).

Growth in manufacturing investment decelerated further due to an uncertain business outlook, particularly for capital-intensive industries, and a high corporate debt burden weighing most heavily on state-owned enterprises. Investment in infrastructure slowed less, benefiting from government support. Consumption remained robust, supported by strong growth in households' real disposable income, which rose by 7.4% year on year, driven by higher wages and social transfers. Stock market volatility since mid-2015 did not affect consumption, as stocks are only a fraction of financial wealth even for the small 7% of the urban population with trading accounts (Figure 3.9.5). Indeed, urban depositors' propensity to spend increased markedly in the second half of the year, according to a survey by the People's Bank of China, the central bank. The disparity between urban and rural household incomes narrowed further from 2.75 times in 2014 to 2.73 in 2015 (Figure 3.9.6), edging the official Gini coefficient of inequality further down to 0.462 from 0.469 in 2014 and 0.473 in 2013.

Consumer price inflation averaged 1.4% year on year in 2015, down from 2.0% in 2014 and 2.6% in 2013, and substantially below the central bank's inflation ceiling of 3.0% (Figure 3.9.7). This moderation mainly reflected lower prices for imported food and other commodities in line with global trends and renminbi appreciation in real effective terms. Core inflation, which excludes energy and food, remained stable at 1.6%. Average producer price deflation intensified from 1.9% in 2014 to 5.2% in 2015 as falling global commodity prices reduced industrial input costs, which have a large weight in the PRC producer price index. Persistent excess capacity in a number of industries likely did not affect the producer price index, as it was broadly stable during the year.

Fiscal policy became more expansionary in 2015 and was instrumental to achieving the official GDP growth target of "about 7%." The deficit in the official consolidated budget of the central and local governments nearly doubled from 1.8% of GDP in 2014 to 3.5% as growth in expenditure outpaced revenue (Figure 3.9.8). Consolidated government expenditure grew by 11.8% year on year in the first half of 2015 and by 19.4% in the second half, to average 15.9% in 2015. Only part of the increase can be explained by the inclusion in consolidated expenditure of sizable off-budget spending by local governments. Budgetary revenue growth accelerated to 8.5% year on year, after a slow start. Personal income tax revenues increased particularly strongly, suggesting better collection.

3.9.3 Demand-side contributions to growth

- Consumption
- Investment
- Net exports
- Gross domestic product

Percentage points, year to date

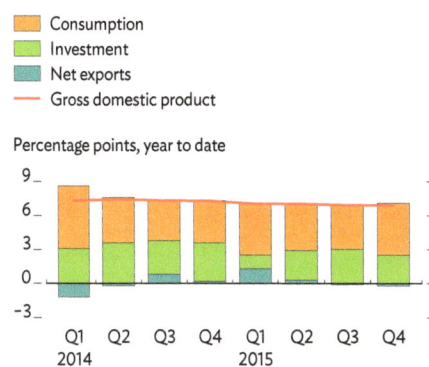

Q = quarter.
Source: National Bureau of Statistics.
Click here for figure data

3.9.4 Real estate markets

- Floor space sold
- Floor space waiting for sale
- Residential property price

Million square meters   CNY/square meter ('000)

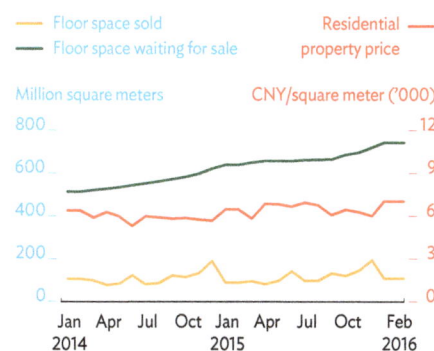

Sources: National Bureau of Statistics; National Development and Reform Commission; ADB estimates.
Click here for figure data

3.9.5 Stock markets

- Shanghai Stock Exchange: A share
- Shenzhen Stock Exchange: A share

19 Dec 1990 = 100 ('000)   20 Jul 1994 = 100 ('000)

Sources: Shanghai Stock Exchange; Shenzhen Stock Exchange.
Click here for figure data

As a result, public sector debt likely increased beyond the 57% of GDP estimated by the International Monetary Fund for 2014. Public debt sustainability was improved as local governments, which are the main holders of public debt, transformed into bonds CNY3.2 trillion in principal payments that came due in 2015 (4.7% of GDP), thus reducing servicing costs and lengthening maturity. Nevertheless, according to the Ministry of Finance, many sub-provincial governments still have debt-to-revenue ratios above the official ceiling of 100%, and some still violate restrictions imposed on off-budget borrowing.

To keep funding costs stable in light of moderating inflation, the central bank cut regulatory reserve requirements and benchmark loan and deposit rates on several occasions and injected liquidity into the banking system through open market operations and refinancing facilities for selected banks. As a result, money market rates fell to historic lows in nominal terms, as did benchmark deposit, lending, and mortgage rates (Figure 3.9.9). Lending rates declined a bit if deflated by the consumer price index but increased if deflated by the producer price index. Despite increased capital outflows, broad money (M2) supply growth averaged 11.9% in 2015, only marginally down from 12.7% in 2014, and was 5.5 percentage points above nominal GDP growth, up from a 4.6 point difference in 2014 and 4.7 points in 2013 (Figure 3.9.10). Hence, debt and its associated risks continued to mount. Bank lending grew strongly, particularly in the second half of the year. The estimated stock of total social financing (a broader gauge of financing provided to nonfinancial enterprises and households from banks, nonbank financial institutions, and capital markets) expanded by an average of 15% in 2015. These developments suggest that economic activity was not constrained by credit supply.

Financial intermediation became more transparent as banks and capital markets gained ground at the expense of nonbank financial institutions, mainly due to regulatory tightening and policy initiatives including central bank lending facilities provided through banks. Bank loans accounted for almost 70% of total social financing provided in 2015, up from 61.8% in 2014, while credit from trust funds and other nonbanks plunged to only 3.8% from 17.6% in 2014 and a peak of 29.8% in 2013 (Figure 3.9.11). The role of equity in enterprise finance continued to grow despite a setback after midyear stock market turbulence, and it accounted for 5.0% of total social financing in 2015, up from 2.7% in 2014 and only marginal contributions in preceding years. Similarly, corporate bonds contributed 18.5% of total social financing, up from 12.3% in 2014. Local governments' off-budget financing vehicles continued to account for a substantial share of corporate bond issuance.

The renminbi is pegged to a basket of currencies that is undisclosed but was estimated in 2014 to be weighted 90% in US dollars. It has thus risen in tandem with the strong appreciation of the US currency since late 2014. By July 2015, according to the Bank for International Settlements, the renminbi appreciated by more than 14% year on year in nominal effective terms (against a trade-weighted basket of currencies) and in real effective terms, taking inflation into account (Figure 3.9.12). On 11 August 2015, the government moved to make the official exchange rate more market oriented by basing its determination

3.9.6 Growth of urban and rural per capita incomes

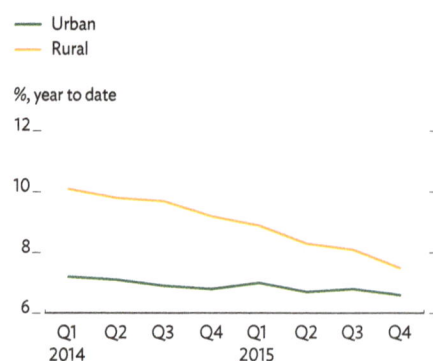

Q = quarter.
Source: National Bureau of Statistics.
Click here for figure data

3.9.7 Monthly inflation

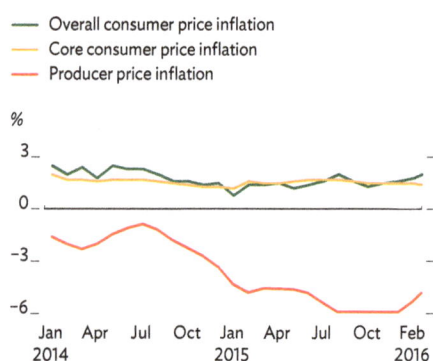

Sources: National Bureau of Statistics; People's Bank of China.
Click here for figure data

3.9.8 Fiscal indicators and nominal GDP

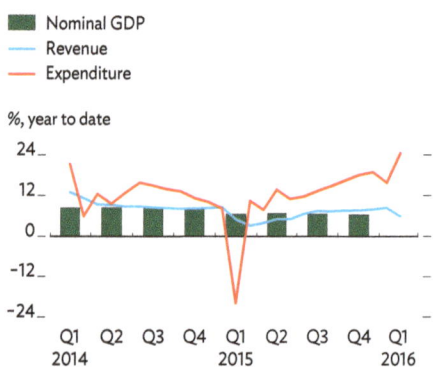

Q = quarter.
Sources: Ministry of Finance; National Bureau of Statistics.
Click here for figure data

on daily market quotes, thus taking another step toward the declared policy objective of full exchange rate flexibility. As a result, the appreciation of the renminbi against trade partner currencies moderated to about 1.5% year on year by January 2016 in both nominal and real terms. The government also improved foreign central banks' access to the currency market and its reporting about official reserves, which facilitated the decision of the Executive Board of the International Monetary Fund in November 2015 to include the renminbi in special drawing rights by September 2016. The authorities have recently indicated that they will pay more attention to the nominal effective rate as a benchmark, which suggests that they will change the composition of the basket and lower the weight of the US dollar. This expectation has already generated more exchange rate volatility against that currency.

Exports fell by 4.4% year on year in dollar terms in 2015 as global demand remained soft. However, real export growth was stronger than the dollar figures suggest, given the weakness of other invoicing currencies like the euro and the Japanese yen. Further, while a stronger renminbi might have narrowed the competitive edge of the PRC relative to its trade partners, the PRC has not lost global market share, according to the central bank, and the share of high-tech products in overall exports increased.

The import bill also fell, by 13.4% in US dollar terms, owing to lower commodity prices and important structural changes: Imports of raw materials declined as domestic demand for construction materials and energy weakened, while robust demand for consumer goods, including cars, and for intermediate products and machinery is increasingly met by domestic suppliers. Imports would have fallen even more if oil import volume had not increased by 8.8%, most likely to build up reserves.

The result was a trade surplus one-third above 2014. This propelled the current account surplus up to $293.2 billion, or 2.7% of GDP, despite a sharp increase in the services deficit caused by substantial overseas expenditure by outbound tourists (Figure 3.9.13). Nevertheless, the balance of payments was pushed into deficit by smaller net inflows of foreign direct investment and larger net outflows of other investment, including repayment of trade credits and other foreign currency loans, and by PRC exporters' retention abroad of foreign currency proceeds in expectation of further renminbi depreciation (Figure 3.9.14). Gross international reserves declined accordingly by $513 million (including valuation changes caused by US dollar strength vis-à-vis other reserve currencies) at the end of 2015 but remained sizable at $3.4 trillion, or 31.2% of GDP.

Economic prospects

Further weakening of economic growth momentum in early 2016 and the likely adverse short-term impact of structural reform, including reduced investment in industries with excess capacity, point to continued deceleration in economic growth over the forecast period, albeit somewhat mitigated by fiscal stimulus targeted to maintain social and financial stability. GDP growth is forecast to ease to 6.5% in 2016,

3.9.9 Interest rates and interbank offered rate

— Shanghai interbank offered rate overnight
— Lending rate
— Deposit rate

Source: People's Bank of China.
Click here for figure data

3.9.10 Money supply and nominal GDP

■ Nominal GDP
— Broad money (M2)

Q = quarter.
Note: GDP data for the first quarter of 2016 are not yet available.
Sources: National Bureau of Statistics; People's Bank of China; ADB estimates.
Click here for figure data

3.9.11 Total financing provided

■ Bank loans
■ Corporate bonds
■ Equity
■ Nonbank loans

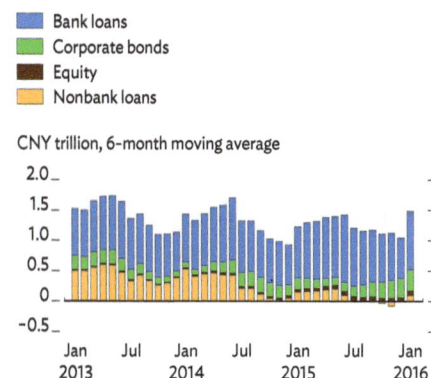

Sources: People's Bank of China; ADB estimates.
Click here for figure data

within the government target range of 6.5%–7.0%, and to 6.3% in 2017 before stabilizing or rising again (Figure 3.9.15).

Investment will remain the main drag on growth. Investment in real estate and capital-intensive industries with excess capacity will show particularly weak growth over the forecast period. This can be only partly compensated by sustained government spending on infrastructure and by higher investment in services and consumer-oriented manufacturing— two areas where growth is likely to hold up. Infrastructure investment will continue to enjoy strong government support, though its growth rate will likely decline further (Figure 3.9.16). Moreover, with only a 22% share in overall investment, infrastructure investment cannot contribute as much to GDP growth as does investment in manufacturing or real estate. Government support for investment activity indicates that reducing the high share of investment in GDP (perhaps 45%), in line with the strategy of rebalancing GDP toward consumption, will be managed over several years to avoid a hard landing in the short term.

Consumption growth will remain more robust. However, with incomes in poorer parts of the country still heavily dependent on slowing investment on large projects, consumption may weaken somewhat along with decelerating income growth. As in previous years, net exports are unlikely to make a significant contribution to growth.

Inflation is projected to rise over the forecast period as administered prices are further deregulated, and as commodity prices recover from current lows, but it will be held below the government ceiling of 3.0% by decelerating GDP growth (Figure 3.9.17). Thus, there is still room for interest rate cuts to stimulate growth, but the authorities may opt instead to reduce regulatory reserve requirements, which are still very high at 17.0% for large banks after the last cut on 1 March 2016. The central bank seems to be moving toward a monetary policy oriented to interest rates but is likely to maintain quantitative tools to control credit supply for priority sectors. High growth in lending and associated risks, particularly related to a high debt burden in those parts of industry that are most affected by decelerating economic activity, will continue to deserve close attention. With continuing liberalization of capital movements, more flexibility in exchange rate policy will be needed over time to make monetary policy more effective.

The government has announced that fiscal policy will stay expansionary. Efforts to curb local government spending will continue over the forecast period toward achieving the strategic objective of rendering local government finance more efficient, accountable, and sustainable. Official budget deficits will widen as more off-budget activities of local governments are brought on budget. Legislative and institutional preparations for a national property tax that will raise local government revenues have made progress but will take time to complete. Therefore, further increases in central government transfers can be expected. An alternative would be to redistribute personal income and consumption tax receipts from the center to local governments. Further, responsibility for financing and implementing major projects will be shifted away from local governments, thus ameliorating their need for unorthodox financing. Ceilings on bond issuance by provincial governments will be raised to help finance a larger share of deficits and

3.9.12 Exchange rates

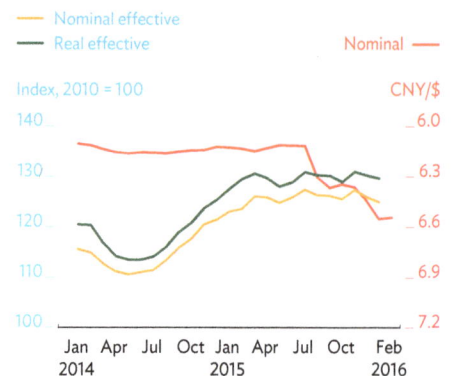

Sources: Bank for International Settlements; State Administration of Foreign Exchange.
Click here for figure data

3.9.13 Current account balance

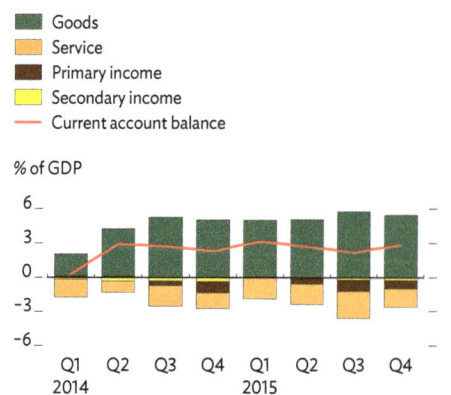

Q = quarter.
Sources: State Administration of Foreign Exchange; ADB estimates.
Click here for figure data

3.9.14 Capital and financial account

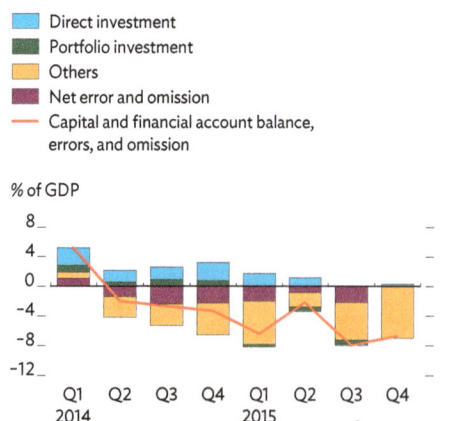

Q = quarter.
Note: "Others" include capital account balance, financial derivatives, and other investment for data before Q4 2015. As some data are unavailable, "others" in Q4 2015 include capital account balance, portfolio investment, financial derivatives, other investment, and error and omission.
Sources: State Administration of Foreign Exchange; ADB estimates.
Click here for figure data

to transform all principal debt payments due over the forecast period into bonds. If bond ratings and yields further diverge according to how creditworthy the issuers are, this would signal that the program is becoming increasingly market driven.

The current account surplus will be maintained in 2016 but decline somewhat in 2017. Imports, following the pattern set by commodity prices, are forecast to be lower in 2016 but higher in 2017, while exports are unlikely to pick up strongly in light of lackluster global growth and trade. Exports with higher value added will continue to grow, however, compensating for diminished exports with lower value added. The services deficit will continue to widen, especially in the absence of substantial additional progress toward service sector deregulation.

The government is expected to peg the renminbi to a more diversified basket of currencies over the forecast period and thereby keep it broadly stable in trade-weighted terms. Capital flows are thus likely to become even more a function of progress toward opening the capital account and reforming the domestic financial sector. The authorities are expected to improve equity market governance, streamline procedures for share issuance, and license more private banks to improve resource mobilization and allocation. Administrative measures taken in late 2015 and early 2016 to slow capital outflows are likely to be only temporary. The government will continue to pursue its strategic objective of further opening the capital account by improving cross-border capital movement, but not at the expense of financial stability. It will retain sufficient controls to limit potentially destabilizing short-term capital flows. In February 2015, the government substantially broadened and simplified foreign private investors' access to the domestic bond market, which at $7.3 trillion is the third largest in the world. This has potential to increase net capital inflows; foreigners currently hold less than 2% of domestic bonds. Additional channels for private cross-border capital transfer would likely facilitate capital outflow. A reduction in low-yielding official reserves could be in the interest of the PRC, particularly if it results from an increase in higher-yielding outbound foreign investment.

The principal international risks to the projections arise from the worsening global investment climate, considerable volatility in financial markets, and another dip in global commodity prices since the beginning of 2016. Complicating these developments is uncertainty about the economic trajectory of the PRC, which could affect investor and consumer sentiment worldwide and put the global recovery at risk, thereby reverberating back on the PRC.

The principal domestic risk is that uncertainty about PRC exchange rate policy could create expectations of further renminbi depreciation, which would accelerate capital outflows and invite additional administrative measures to stem them. Wavering on renminbi internationalization could erode confidence in PRC market reform more broadly, exacerbating negative sentiment. This risk could be defused by better explaining the new PRC exchange rate regime and policy, as well as the composition of the peg basket, which should include only currencies that are sufficiently liquid.

3.9.15 GDP growth

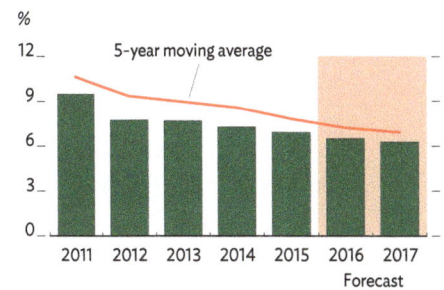

Source: Asian Development Outlook database.
Click here for figure data

3.9.16 Nominal growth in key components of fixed asset investment

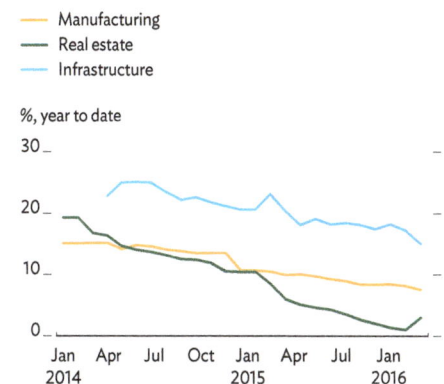

Source: National Bureau of Statistics.
Click here for figure data

3.9.17 Inflation

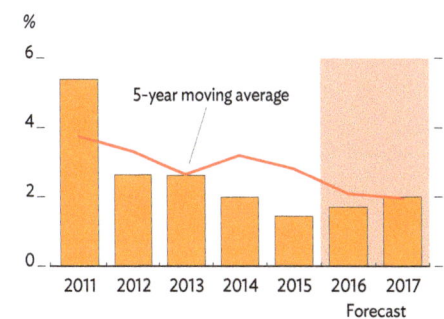

Source: Asian Development Outlook database.
Click here for figure data

Another domestic risk is that consumer sentiment could be undermined if income growth decelerates further and labor market conditions become more complicated as industrial restructuring progresses, changing consumption patterns in ways that are difficult to predict. Continued close attention to labor market conditions and income growth will be needed.

Slower economic growth and rapid credit expansion, including credit to inefficient firms, harbor risks to the quality of bank assets. Nonperforming loans officially account for less than 2% of the loan portfolio, but an increasing number of loans overdue for more than 90 days are not classified as problem loans. Further, continuing strong credit growth may mask more serious repayment problems. These risks are, however, still manageable. Recent interest rate cuts have reduced financing costs, loan-loss reserves are still twice as high as the official nonperforming loan total, and banks are well capitalized and further strengthening their capital base by issuing shares and subordinated loans. In addition, safeguarding financial stability is a key motivation for the government's policy favoring a managed slowdown in economic growth.

Policy challenge—trimming excess property inventory and industrial capacity

Since the Central Economic Work Conference in December 2015, the government has stressed the need to accelerate "supply-side reform." This emphasis is not new. Reform in the PRC over the past 35 years has been mostly about supply-side reform, or how to use existing human and physical resources more efficiently by reforming prices, company ownership, and the financial sector while opening up to trade and foreign investment, streamlining the role of the government in the economy, and strengthening markets. The reform agenda outlined in November 2013 consists mainly of structural reform aiming to increase productivity and ensure that high growth over the long term propels the PRC toward high-income status. Reemphasizing supply-side reform now highlights the government's policy that, although targeted demand-side support through monetary and fiscal policy will continue, structural reform will remain the priority going forward.

Two key supply-side reforms among several identified by the government are reducing the housing overhang to reenergize the real estate sector and alleviating excess capacity in manufacturing. Strengthening local government finances is a precondition for success in both areas.

The way to move the property inventory is to generate demand for housing by deepening land reform in rural areas and liberalizing the household registration (*hukou*) system. Rural land reform, which aims to facilitate land sales to give rural residents the seed money they need to successfully establish themselves in cities, should be accelerated even though some pilot projects reportedly met local resistance. The government's plan to expand low-rent public housing programs could benefit some migrant workers, but implementing *hukou*

3.9.1 Selected economic indicators (%)

	2016	2017
GDP growth	6.5	6.3
Inflation	1.7	2.0
Current account balance (share of GDP)	2.7	2.5

Source: ADB estimates.

reform would be more effective. If provided with full urban resident rights through *hukou* reform, and with better access to credit, many of the 274 million rural migrants currently in urban areas could take up unsold properties. The government's urbanization plan foresees 100 million more migrants permanently settling in urban areas. For this urbanization program to succeed, migrants must have full access to public services in cities, which requires stronger local government finances. Another challenge is to ensure that the migrants are trained appropriately for urban jobs.

Many companies with excess capacity, most of them state-owned enterprises (SOEs), use outmoded technology to generate meager profits, if not losses, and are deeply in debt. Because these companies are inherently inefficient, supporting them through stimulus programs to raise demand for their products has aggravated problems rather than solved them. However, reducing excess capacity by closing enterprises faces several challenges, including widespread layoffs and related increases of social spending, falling tax revenues, and loan losses.

ADB estimates that reducing excess capacity in iron and steel, coal mining, cement, shipbuilding, aluminum, and flat glass by 20% might eliminate 3.6 million jobs, or 0.7% of total nonfarm employment. These losses would be concentrated in cities and regions that specialize in mining and metal production. Concerned about how closing such firms could derail near-term growth, social stability, and local government finances, the government has set less ambitious targets to reduce production capacity for steel by 10%–15% and for coal by 10% within 3–5 years.

Many local governments are already struggling as revenues from land sales shrink and debt for infrastructure and social housing construction grows, leaving them dependent on taxes paid by state-owned enterprises. Closing these enterprises might squeeze local governments' revenues further while forcing them to spend more on social security. The central government has promised to help pay for social benefits and the retraining of laid-off workers, and intends to establish a special fund for this purpose, among other measures.

As most state-owned enterprises with excess capacity depend heavily on bank lending and have high ratios of debt to assets (estimated at 68% in the coal sector in 2015), forcing them into bankruptcy threatens banks' balance sheets with more nonperforming loans. This is one reason why the government encourages mergers rather than bankruptcy to meet the challenge of excess capacity. The merger process must be well managed to ensure that the merged enterprises run efficiently and are not burdened by unsustainable debt. The government should also make it easier for banks to acknowledge and write off nonperforming loans. For instance, it should rescind the policy of requiring a lower credit allocation to a region, city, and industry if a single industry or state-owned enterprise in it incurs excessive bad debt, as this policy penalizes enterprises that perform well. This would reduce local authorities' resistance to closing hopelessly indebted and inefficient enterprises, improve credit allocation, and support the development of well performing enterprises in their jurisdiction.

Hong Kong, China

Growth slowed to 2.4% in 2015, but inflation eased and the current account and fiscal position were healthy. Growth will be still slower in 2016 and 2017 with weak tourism and global trade. Inflation will remain subdued, and the current account surplus will narrow. The dollar peg can accommodate US interest rate hikes and growing ties with the People's Republic of China, but these developments foreshadow broader policy challenges.

Economic performance

GDP grew by 2.4% in 2015, down from 2.6% in 2014. Sluggish global trade and significant volatility in the financial markets of the People's Republic of China (PRC) halted the upward growth trajectory enjoyed in the first half of the year. Uncertainty about the timing of US interest rate hikes exerted downward pressure on domestic demand, asset prices, and market sentiment.

Domestic demand nevertheless remained the main engine of growth in 2015. Private consumption expanded by 4.8% and contributed 3.2 percentage points to GDP growth (Figure 3.10.1). Rising real incomes, moderating inflation, and low unemployment helped offset the drag from weak retail sales amid softening tourist arrivals. Government consumption also expanded, but its contribution to growth remained unchanged at 0.3 percentage points. Investment fell by 7.3%, shaving 1.7 percentage points from GDP growth. Investment in machinery and equipment acquisition declined, together with inventories, but private construction outlays remained resilient. Net exports broke their 4-year negative streak, contributing 0.7 percentage points to growth. Imports shrank by 1.8% year on year because of low consumption demand from visitors, while exports fell by 1.5% as external demand and inbound tourism weakened (Figure 3.10.2).

While expanding slower than in 2014, construction and services drove growth on the supply side. Construction grew by 1.7% on a buoyant private sector, and expansion in most services propelled growth in the service sector to 1.9%.

The current account surplus widened to 3.1% of GDP as the merchandise balance improved, though the services surplus narrowed on weak tourist arrivals and trade and cargo flows. The improved current account and large net inflows of direct and other investment offset net outflows of portfolio capital, enlarging the overall balance of payments surplus. Gross official reserves rose to $359 billion by the end of 2015, cover for 7.1 months of imports.

3.10.1 Demand-side contributions to growth

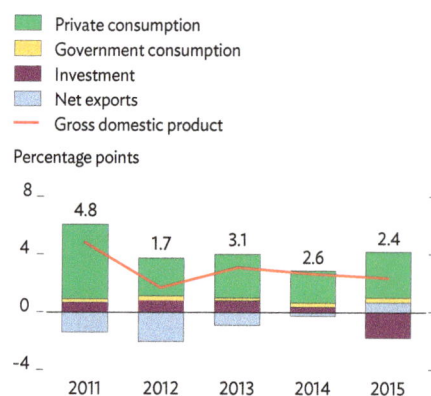

- Private consumption
- Government consumption
- Investment
- Net exports
- Gross domestic product

Percentage points

Source: CEIC Data Company (accessed 25 February 2016).
Click here for figure data

3.10.2 External trade

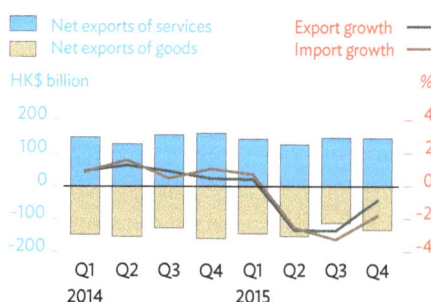

- Net exports of services
- Net exports of goods
- Export growth
- Import growth

HK$ billion / %

Q = quarter.
Source: CEIC Data Company (accessed 25 February 2016).
Click here for figure data

This chapter was written by Benno Ferrarini and Marthe Hinojales of the Economic Research and Regional Cooperation Department, ADB, Manila.

Consumer price inflation slowed to 3.0% from 4.4% the previous year (Figure 3.10.3). External price pressures continued to recede in light of subdued international prices for food and other commodities, low imported inflation, and a strengthening US dollar, to which the local dollar is pegged. Steady labor costs and softer rental growth helped contain domestic costs. After rising early in the year, residential property prices calmed in the fourth quarter, falling by 7% quarter on quarter.

On the fiscal front, the government expects the budget surplus to narrow to the equivalent of 1.3% of GDP in FY2015 (ending 31 March 2016), with fiscal reserves equal to 35.8% (Figure 3.10.4). Estimated revenues were below the original estimate mainly because land sales were lower and HK$45 billion was set aside for the Housing Reserve, established to finance public housing programs. Meanwhile, expenditures increased modestly along with higher social welfare services, which absorb 15% of government expenditure. Overall public expenditure in FY2015 is estimated to equal 19.2% of GDP, in line with the fiscal management guideline of holding public expenditure below 20.0% of GDP.

Monetary conditions remained loose, while macroprudential measures implemented in February 2015 helped bring down the average loan-to-value ratio and debt-servicing ratio of new mortgages. Meanwhile, a softening property market and the government's demand-management measures tamped down the volume and value of new mortgages and suppressed speculative buying (Figure 3.10.5). Domestic credit growth slowed to 3.9%, and growth in broad money (M2) supply further decelerated to 5.5% from 9.5% in 2014. The Hong Kong Monetary Authority (HKMA) raised its benchmark base rate in December 2015 to 0.75% from 0.50% in tandem with the US Federal Reserve's increase of its federal funds rate.

Uncertainty about the US interest rate hike and concern over the PRC economy wiped out early hefty gains on the Hang Seng Stock Exchange Index, pushing it 7.2% lower by year-end (Figure 3.10.6). Hong Kong, China remains a leading international fund-raising platform, raising in 2015 over HK$260 billion with initial public offerings, a 13% rise over 2014 that propelled it past New York and Shanghai to first place by this measure. Its role as the premier center for offshore renminbi trading has been strengthened with an additional issuance of PRC sovereign bonds and the opening of new channels for two-way financial flows with the PRC, including the mutual recognition of funds, which allows eligible locally domiciled funds in either market to be sold to retail investors in the other.

Economic prospects

GDP growth is projected to slow to 2.1% in 2016 and recover to 2.2% in 2017 (Figure 3.10.7). Domestic demand will remain the engine of growth. A survey in the first quarter of 2016 showed a pessimistic trend in business sentiment, particularly in trade and retailing (Figure 3.10.8). However, private consumption will benefit from stable labor market conditions. The government expects tax and short-term relief measures

3.10.3 Monthly inflation

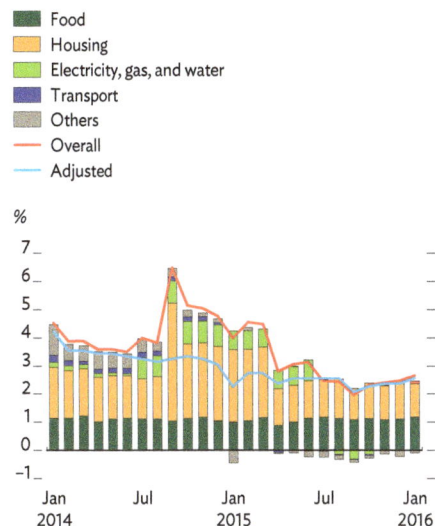

Note: Adjusted inflation refers to the overall rate once the effects of temporary government subsidies are removed.
Source: CEIC Data Company (accessed 11 March 2016).
Click here for figure data

3.10.4 Fiscal indicators

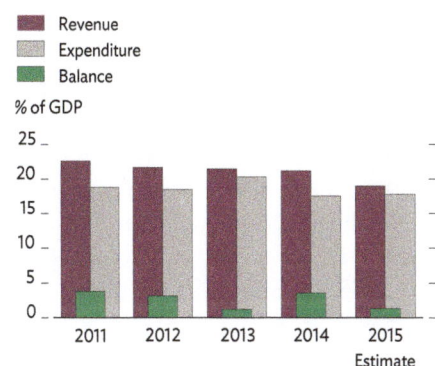

Sources: The Government of the Hong Kong Special Administrative Region of the PRC. The 2016–2017 Budget, and other years. http://www.budget.gov.hk; Hong Kong Monetary Authority; *Asian Development Outlook* database.
Click here for figure data

3.10.5 Confirmor sales in the secondary residential property market

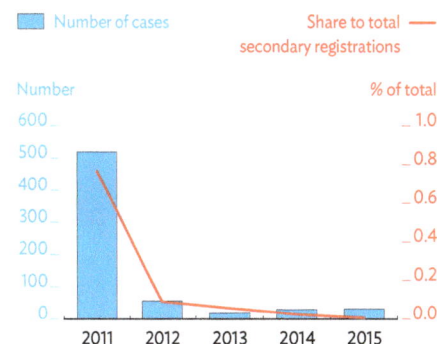

Note: A confirmor sale occurs when the property seller or buyer sells the property to a third party sub-buyer before the original transaction has been completed.
Source: CEIC Data Company (accessed 23 February 2016).
Click here for figure data

and spending initiatives in the FY2016 budget to boost 2016 GDP by 1.1%. Large public infrastructure projects will drive investment growth.

Trade is likely to offer little growth impetus in 2016 as manufacturing and trade remain subdued globally and economic rebalancing in the PRC weighs on exports. Imports will stay constrained by weakness in both retained imports and export-induced demand. The trade deficit will be offset by a modest surplus in the services account as demand for professional and financial services offsets weaker tourism. In the near term, the government's strategic focus on innovative technologies can, along with positive spillover from the new 5-year plan of the PRC, provide support to the local services account. The current account surplus is forecast to narrow to 2.0% of GDP in 2016 and 1.8% in 2017.

Inflation is forecast at 2.5% in 2016 and 2.7% in 2017. Soft international commodity prices will keep external price pressures at bay, and local cost increases will be restrained by slower economic growth and lower rents. These factors will counter a slight uptick in world oil and commodity prices in 2017.

The FY2016 budget is expected to post a small surplus of HK$11 billion. To boost the economy, it has as one-time measures tax reductions for households and firms and waivers of property rates, business registration fees, and fees for tourism-related trades. Recurrent measures include higher tax allowances and deduction ceilings for payers of salaries tax. Ample fiscal reserves will enable an increase in the fiscal stimulus should the economy show signs of weakening. Sufficient housing supply remains a core objective. Expenditure is thus expected to remain close to the government's guideline of 20% of GDP. To address the longer-term fiscal challenges arising from an aging population, the government is implementing a 3-year expenditure-control measure and, in January 2016, established its Future Fund by investing a portion of fiscal reserves in long-term assets for achieving higher returns.

One risk to growth is negative spillover from the PRC as it transitions to more sustainable growth, which could harm employment and business conditions but could also create higher demand from the PRC for services. The other main risk is unexpectedly sharp increases in US interest rates, which could tighten monetary conditions, deepen the current correction in residential property, and burden the private sector with potentially soaring debt service costs, further weakening domestic demand. The risk of a "perfect storm"—a sharp PRC downturn coinciding with heightened volatility from further US rate hikes—is small but significant. Yet the economy remains resilient, buffered by prudent economic management, ample fiscal resources to finance countercyclical measures, and a sound financial system able to withstand external headwinds.

Policy challenge—pressure on the exchange rate

The start of 2016 witnessed some downward pressure on the local dollar. In January, the currency dropped to its lowest value against the US dollar in nearly a decade. Deepening concern about the depreciating renminbi and a slowing PRC economy, and about interest rates in the US, caused outflows to mount, reversing the capital inflows that had

3.10.1 Selected economic indicators (%)

	2016	2017
GDP growth	2.1	2.2
Inflation	2.5	2.7
Current account balance (share of GDP)	2.0	1.8

Source: ADB estimates.

3.10.6 Stock market

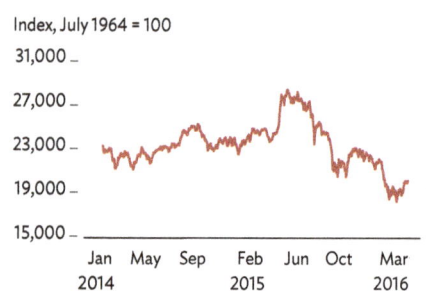

Source: Bloomberg (accessed 11 March 2016).
Click here for figure data

3.10.7 GDP growth

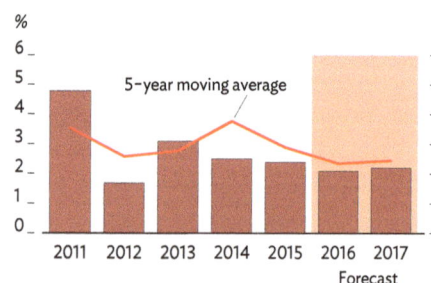

Source: Asian Development Outlook database.
Click here for figure data

pushed the exchange rate with the US dollar closer to the middle of the exchange rate band during much of the second half of 2015. The exchange rate and the Hang Seng stock index have moved broadly in tandem since the beginning of 2016 (Figure 3.10.9).

The currency peg to the US dollar and concomitant alignment with US monetary policy pose a challenge to Hong Kong, China in view of its close ties with the PRC, but the HKMA sees no need to modify or abandon the peg. It stands by the currency board, which has since 1983 been central to economic development and the emergence of Hong Kong, China as a global financial center. Proximity to the PRC is one thing, but the monetary link with the US has suited the local economy as an anchor and its financial system as a stabilizer. A fully backed monetary base and diligent fiscal management over the years have helped the linked exchange rate system outlast many past crises, including the Asian financial crisis of 1997–1998, when it survived severe speculative attack.

The argument for pegging to the renminbi is likely to solidify as financial ties with the PRC continue to grow. Changing the currency regime may deserve consideration when the PRC currency is freely convertible, its capital account fully liberalized, and its financial system well developed. These conditions are, however, not yet in view. In the meantime, financial integrity should be preserved by continuing to adhere to high regulatory and supervisory standards, deploying macroprudential measures as appropriate, and continuing prudent fiscal policies.

The government's fiscal reserves accumulated through sustained fiscal discipline and year after year of budget surpluses have kept the peg credible. Its fiscal health remains strong in the short term. However, fiscal reserves are seen gradually diminishing over the longer term, mainly because the government has earmarked additional provision over the medium term for health-care reform and retirement protection. Recurrent expenditures are set to increase in the coming years as an aging population requires expanded social services, and the tax base will likely become narrower with a shrinking workforce. Ensuring good fiscal management to support the peg depends on strengthening the revenue regime by broadening the tax base and avoiding any reliance on volatile and cyclical sources such as land sales.

3.10.8 Business tendency survey

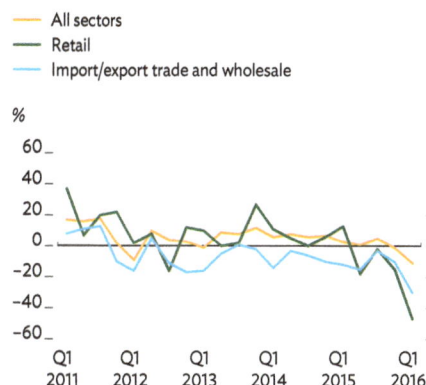

Q = quarter.
Note: Net balance of expected quarter-on-quarter changes in the business situation. A positive reading denotes a likely upward trend in the business situation.
Source: CEIC Data Company (accessed 22 January 2016).
Click here for figure data

3.10.9 Daily stock market index and exchange rates

Source: Bloomberg (accessed 11 March 2016).
Click here for figure data

Republic of Korea

Buffeted by a challenging external environment, exports and growth disappointed in 2015, but inflation was lower and the current account surplus higher. Growth will remain steady in 2016 before picking up modestly in 2017 on an improved global outlook. The current account surplus will shrink this year and next, and inflation will be higher. Deregulating the service sector can provide a much-needed fillip to the economy.

Economic performance

The economy suffered a tepid first half in 2015 but bounced back in the second half to grow by 2.6% for the year, down from the 3.3% recorded in 2014 as weak external demand and an outbreak of Middle East respiratory syndrome (MERS) took their toll. The recovery, supported by fiscal stimulus and an accommodative monetary policy, came as the impact of MERS on domestic demand began to fade in the third quarter (Figure 3.11.1).

Investment contributed 2.2 percentage points to GDP growth (Figure 3.11.2). Construction investment picked up after a subdued first half to record 4.0% growth for the year, and sustained growth in plant and equipment investment by 5.2% drove the surge in investment.

Consumption grew by 2.4% in 2015 and contributed 1.6 percentage points to GDP growth. Private consumption expanded by 2.1% and government consumption by 3.3%. Consumer spending surged in the second half as consumer sentiment reached a 14-month high in November and employment prospects improved (Figure 3.11.3). Job creation strengthened in the final quarter, and the labor participation rate reached 62.6% in 2015, the highest since 2000. The unemployment rate declined steadily, but the annual average unemployment rate remained at 3.6%. Net exports subtracted 1.2 percentage points from GDP growth as the volume of imports expanded but real exports of goods increased only by 0.4%, down from 2.8% in 2014 (Figure 3.11.4).

On the supply side, services posted 2.8% growth and contributed 1.5 percentage points to GDP growth. Expansion in finance and insurance accelerated and contributed the most to overall service sector growth, which found further support as the volume of retail sales rebounded from 1.7% growth in 2014 to 3.4% on a government-sponsored shopping promotion. Mirroring export weakness, manufacturing decelerated from 4.0% growth in 2014 to 1.4% in 2015, and its contribution to economic growth declined to 0.4 percentage points.

3.11.1 Quarterly GDP growth

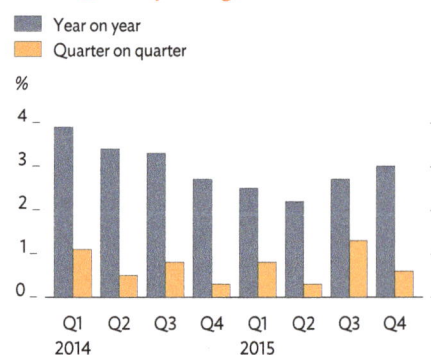

Q = quarter.
Source: Bank of Korea, Economics Statistics System, http://ecos.bok.or.kr/EIndex_en.jsp (accessed 29 January 2016).
Click here for figure data

3.11.2 Demand-side contributions to growth

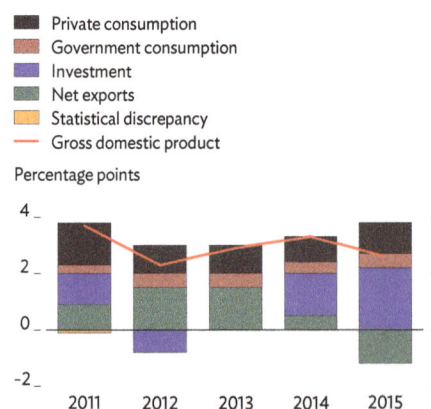

Source: Bank of Korea, Economics Statistics System, http://ecos.bok.or.kr/EIndex_en.jsp (accessed 29 January 2016).
Click here for figure data

This chapter was written by Gemma Esther Estrada and Donghyun Park of the Economic Research and Regional Cooperation Department, ADB, Manila.

In response to economic softness induced by MERS and the collapse of exports, the government introduced in July a supplementary budget equal to 0.8% of GDP to cover new spending plans and compensate for the tax shortfall. The fiscal deficit widened to 3.0% of GDP from 2.0% in 2014, raising government domestic debt to an estimated 36.6% of GDP from 33.9%.

Growth was also supported by an accommodative monetary policy. The Bank of Korea, the central bank, cut its policy rate in March and June 2015 to a record low of 1.5%. Nevertheless, monthly inflation remained below 1% in most months, and annual inflation averaged 0.7% as global oil prices languished, with core inflation averaging slightly above 2% during the year (Figure 3.11.5). Inflation slipped back to 0.8% in January 2016 from 1.3% in December as oil prices continued to fall.

The easy monetary policy has further deepened household debt, which amounted to a record $1.0 trillion, or 78.9% of GDP, at the end of 2015 (Figure 3.11.6). Mortgages accounted for 41.5% of household debt, confronting policy makers with a quandary over how to support the housing market while containing household debt.

Exports suffered as shipments to all major destinations declined. Exports to the People's Republic of China (PRC), accounting for about one-fourth of all merchandise exports, have contracted since early 2014 and dropped further by 5.6% in 2015 as that economy decelerated (Figure 3.11.7). Exports to the European Union also fell by 6.9% and those to the US slipped by 1.0%. In US dollar terms, merchandise exports declined by 10.5% in 2015, but imports contracted even more sharply by 18.2%, partly reflecting the steep decline in global commodity prices. In January 2016, imports fell further by 20.1%, while exports declined by 18.6%, the sharpest drop since 2009.

The current account surplus widened to an estimated 7.8% of GDP in 2015 from 6.0% in 2014, ensuring a healthy overall balance of payments surplus despite foreign portfolio outflows. Amid turbulence in global financial markets, the country posted net foreign portfolio equity and debt outflows by year-end of $7.3 billion, equal to 0.5% of GDP.

After mildly appreciating against the US dollar during the first 5 months, the won slid in the remaining months to close 5.8% lower by the end of the year. In real effective terms, it appreciated by 0.7% during the year, owing to an inflation rate higher than those of trade partners.

Economic prospects

Against a backdrop of subdued external demand, growth is likely to stagnate in 2016 at 2.6%. The forecast assumes sustained expansion in domestic demand, in particular private consumption, countering the difficult export environment. As the economy remains fragile, the broadly accommodative monetary and fiscal stance is expected to continue. Growth will edge up to 2.8% in 2017, assuming stable expansion in the global economy (Figure 3.11.8).

Growth in private consumption is expected to accelerate slightly this year on improving consumer sentiment. In the absence of a major shock, private consumption will rise by 2.2% in 2016, spurred by moderating price pressures, given low oil prices, the extension of the lower sales

3.11.1 Selected economic indicators (%)

	2016	2017
GDP growth	2.6	2.8
Inflation	1.4	2.0
Current account balance (share of GDP)	6.5	5.5

Source: ADB estimates.

3.11.3 Growth in private consumption

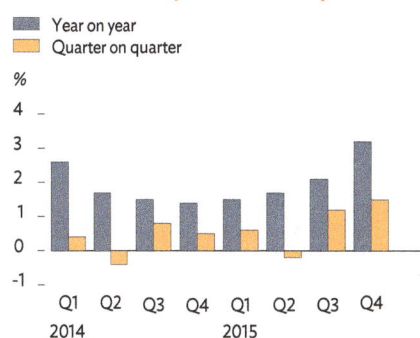

Q = quarter.
Source: Bank of Korea, Economics Statistics System, http://ecos.bok.or.kr/EIndex_en.jsp (accessed 29 January 2016).
Click here for figure data

3.11.4 Merchandise export and import volumes

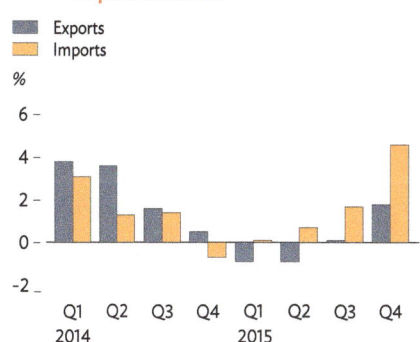

Q = quarter.
Source: Bank of Korea, Economics Statistics System, http://ecos.bok.or.kr/EIndex_en.jsp (accessed 29 January 2016).
Click here for figure data

3.11.5 Monthly inflation

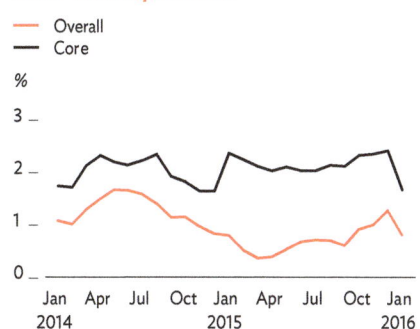

Source: CEIC Data Company (accessed 15 March 2016).
Click here for figure data

tax on vehicles, and steady growth in employment (Figure 3.11.9). The projections also assume effective policy to control mounting household debt, which threatens private consumption. To limit further buildup of household debt, the government has started to enforce stricter standards for screening mortgage applications and to closely monitor household lending by nonbank institutions.

Growth in investment, particularly gross fixed capital, will likely continue its moderate pace. Growth in construction will be buoyed by government plans to ease regulations and provide tax incentives for rental housing construction on a large scale. Investment in new industries will find encouragement in government support for investment by small- and medium-sized enterprises through a W2 trillion loan fund, tax incentives for research and development, and the frontloading of expenditure in the Corporate Investment Promotion Program. Growth in plant and equipment is nevertheless likely to slow as both external and domestic environments remain uncertain.

Exports may rebound on better global prospects in the second half, but import growth driven by stronger domestic demand is expected to outpace export growth to the forecast horizon. Although oil prices are expected to average lower this year, import values will increase as growth in import volume accelerates. As a result, the current account surplus will narrow to 6.5% in 2016 and further to 5.5% in 2017.

On the fiscal front, the government will maintain its expansionary stance to support consumption and investment. Proposed higher spending on welfare and employment will bolster domestic demand. The government's proposed spending and revenue program suggests the fiscal deficit equaling 2.3% this year—lower than last year though the government plans to raise spending by 2.9% in 2016 and expects fiscal revenues to increase by 2.3%. As in 2015, healthy public finances will allow the government to introduce supplementary budgets if economic conditions deteriorate. Meanwhile, to support growth, the government announced that first quarter spending will be W14 trillion higher than a year earlier.

In tandem with a sustained and moderate expansion in domestic demand and higher oil prices, inflation is likely to pick up this year to 1.4% and next year to 2.0%, which is the central bank's new annual inflation target for 2016–2018. With price pressures subdued, the central bank is likely to keep interest rates at current record lows to stimulate domestic demand, while remaining vigilant about any further buildup in household debt.

Downside risks to growth are both internal and external. Domestically, mounting household debt could tamp down consumption. Subdued business confidence, which has fallen from already low levels since November 2015 (Figure 3.11.10) owing to a difficult outlook for exports and low capacity utilization (Figure 3.11.11), may undermine prospects for investment.

Softer-than-expected external demand, especially in the slowing PRC, poses probably the single biggest risk to GDP growth. As the PRC is an important export market, a sharp growth slowdown there would be a major blow to growth in the short run. In addition, the Bank of Japan's decision in late January to move toward negative interest rates

3.11.6 Household debt to GDP

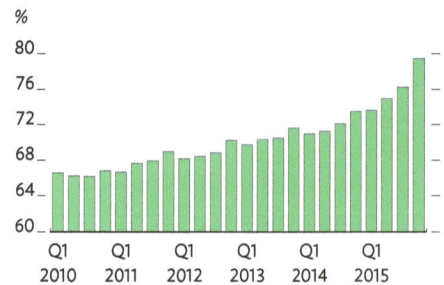

Q = quarter.
Source: Bank of Korea, Economics Statistics System, http://ecos.bok.or.kr/EIndex_en.jsp (accessed 15 March 2016).
Click here for figure data

3.11.7 Exports to the People's Republic of China

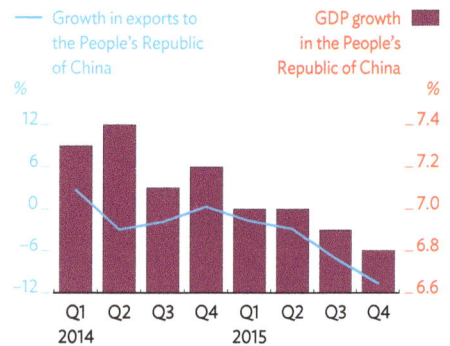

Q = quarter.
Source: CEIC Data Company (accessed 15 March 2016).
Click here for figure data

3.11.8 GDP growth

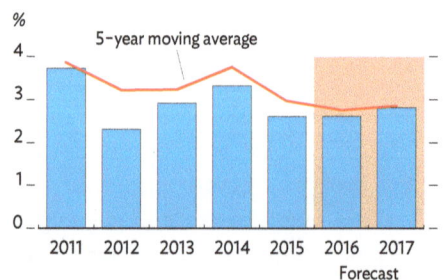

Sources: Bank of Korea, Economics Statistics System, http://ecos.bok.or.kr/EIndex_en.jsp (accessed 29 January 2016); ADB estimates.
Click here for figure data

could weaken the Japanese yen and thereby hurt the competitiveness of exports from the Republic of Korea, as many of them, including electronics and automobiles, compete directly with Japanese exports. While low oil prices will improve terms of trade and boost household income, they are not an unmixed blessing. They dampen demand in oil-exporting countries, which collectively account for 7.1% of exports from the Republic of Korea. Last year, such exports declined by 15.5%. Further, financial market turmoil in oil producers and other emerging markets could spill over into the Republic of Korea.

Uncertainties generated by US Federal Reserve rate hikes may destabilize financial markets and further dampen sentiment, especially in light of the country's highly open capital account. The stock market has not been immune to the recent selloff in regional equity markets. The Korea Composite Index fell by 8% about a month after the Fed hiked its federal funds rate by 25 basis points. Persistent uncertainty over asset prices could temper both business and consumer confidence. A particularly difficult risk to assess is the possibility of heightened tension with Democratic People's Republic of Korea arising from its nuclear program.

Policy challenge—strengthening the service sector as an engine of growth

For several decades, the Republic of Korea pursued export-oriented industrialization, and it successfully developed a globally competitive manufacturing sector. As manufacturing is now highly efficient, achieving further productivity gains is a challenge. Indeed, GDP growth that languished short of 3.0% in 3 of the past 4 years has fueled concerns that potential growth over the medium to long term may have declined. An effective response would be to unlock potential in the service sector, which could boost growth in the short term and beyond.

Service sector productivity in the Republic of Korea has lagged behind both domestic manufacturing and the service sectors of other members of the Organisation for Economic Co-operation and Development (OECD) (Figure 3.11.12). This indicates large scope for developing the service sector to reduce the economy's dependence on currently lackluster exports of manufactured goods. In the high-income, high-tech economy of the Republic of Korea, service sector development should center on services with high value added. These include financial intermediation, computer services, business services, communication, and legal and technical services, which currently account for a smaller share of service sector output than do traditional services with lower value added, such as public administration, wholesale and retail trade, and transport and storage.

The shift from a manufacturing-led economy to a more balanced one in which services play a larger role requires various reforms, the most crucial of which is deregulation. The service sector is highly regulated to protect small and medium-sized enterprises. Strict entry and licensing requirements, stringent approval requirements, and price controls have likely contributed significantly to low sector productivity.

3.11.9 Employment indicators

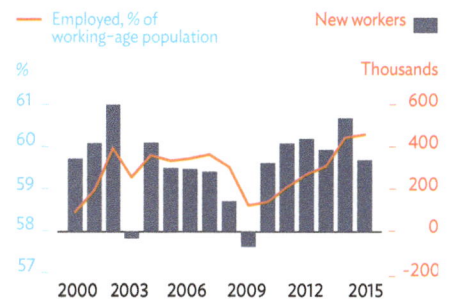

Source: ADB estimates based on data from Korean Statistical Information Service. http://kosis.kr/eng. (accessed 21 January 2016).
Click here for figure data

3.11.10 Business confidence

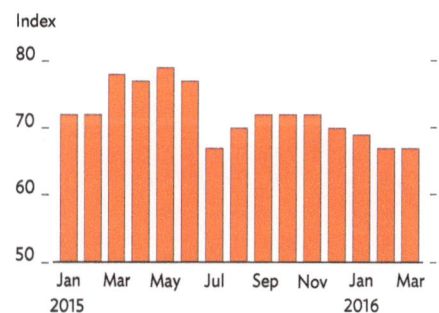

Note: A reading below 100 means that more firms answered negatively than positively.
Source: Bank of Korea, Economics Statistics System, available: http://ecos.bok.or.kr/EIndex_en.jsp (accessed 15 March 2016).
Click here for figure data

3.11.11 Manufacturing capacity utilization

Q = quarter.
Source: Korean Statistical Information Service. http://kosis.kr/eng/ (accessed 2 February 2016).
Click here for figure data

An indication of how regulation in the Republic of Korea fares vis-à-vis other economies is provided by product market regulation indicators, which measure regulations that are potentially anticompetitive and cover state control, barriers to entrepreneurship, and barriers to trade and investment. A lower score means fewer restrictions. The Republic of Korea does better than the OECD average in terms of state control and barriers to entrepreneurship, but scores poorly on barriers to trade and investment, and to entry in the service and network (information technology) sectors.

Enhancing services has been on the government's agenda. Its "creative economy" policy agenda, announced in 2014, emphasizes the role of the service sector, naming five service areas for government support: health and medical care, tourism, finance, education, and software. Little progress was made in 2015 due to legislative gridlock, but prospects are better for 2016 after the April elections. The government has announced that it will continue to provide support specific to the service sector, correct unfair regulatory practices against the service sector, and promote exports of services.

It will try to push through deregulation of the hotel industry, encourage remote medical services, and allow home and vehicle sharing in selected locations. While challenging, these reforms will be major steps, if implemented, toward improving productivity in the service sector.

3.11.12 Labor productivity, % of OECD productivity, late 2000s

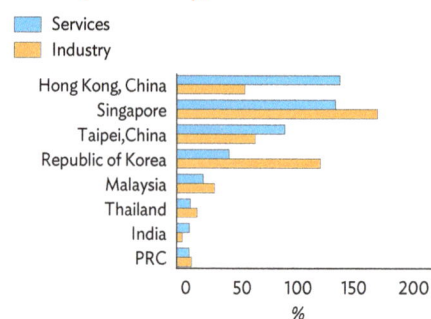

OECD = Organisation for Economic Co-operation and Development, PRC = People's Republic of China.

Note: Computed by dividing average labor productivity in an economy by the average labor productivity in the OECD.

Source: Noland, M., D. Park, and G. Estrada. 2013. Developing the Service Sector as an Engine of Growth for Asia: Overview. In D. Park and M. Noland, eds. *Developing the Service Sector as an Engine of Growth for Asia.* Asian Development Bank.

Click here for figure data

Mongolia

Economic growth decelerated sharply in 2015, but so did inflation, and the current account deficit narrowed. Growth will stagnate in 2016 under lower mining output and necessarily tight macroeconomic policies. Inflation will dip further before climbing again in 2017. Consistently pursuing fiscal policy, effectively continuing efforts to diversify the economy, and ensuring social protection are important challenges of economic management in Mongolia.

Economic performance

Growth decelerated sharply to 2.3% in 2015 from 7.9% in 2014 as macroeconomic policies became less expansionary, falling mineral prices and a strong currency eroded exports, and foreign direct investment declined by 33.8%. On the supply side, growth slowed in all sectors but remained robust in industry, which contributed 2.0 percentage points to growth, and agriculture, which contributed 0.9 points (Figure 3.12.1). Industrial output rose by 8.8%, supported by 13.0% expansion in mining as production at the vast Oyu Tolgoi copper and gold mine increased. However, a decline by 1.4% in construction dragged down growth in the rest of industry to 0.6%. Agriculture grew by 10.7% despite a drought. As trade and social sectors shrank, service sector growth fell to 1.1%, subtracting 0.7 percentage points from GDP.

On the demand side, a 27.7% fall in investment following a 30.1% decline in 2014 subtracted 9.9 percentage points from growth. Consumption growth slowed to 4.6% as government consumption declined, reducing its contribution to growth to 3.2 percentage points. Substantial import contraction turned net exports positive, which contributed 9.1 percentage points to growth (Figure 3.12.2).

Several factors caused average inflation to halve to 6.6% from 12.8% in 2014. Preemptive slaughtering of livestock in anticipation of a harsh winter sharply reduced meat prices, which have a large weight in the consumer price index. Subdued domestic demand, an insufficiently flexible exchange rate, and tight monetary policy also reduced price pressures.

In April 2015, the International Monetary Fund assessed Mongolia at high risk of debt distress. The ratio of public debt to GDP, including the central bank's foreign liabilities, swelled from 31.0% in 2010 to 77.4% in 2015, with public debt per capita quadrupling to over $3,000 (Figure 3.12.3). The budget deficit stabilized at 3.1% of GDP in 2015, and the consolidated deficit—including Development Bank of Mongolia expenditures—shrank to 7.9% of GDP from 11.4% in 2014. The move toward lower consolidated deficits is positive but also partly reflects

3.12.1 Supply-side contributions to growth

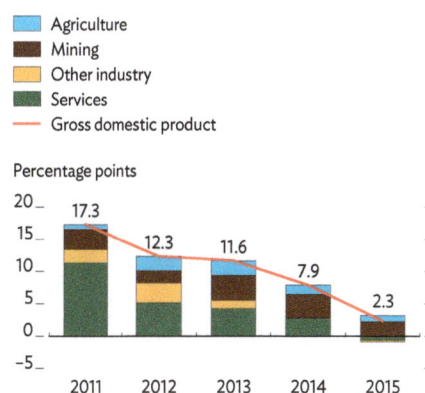

- Agriculture
- Mining
- Other industry
- Services
- Gross domestic product

Percentage points

Source: National Registration and Statistics Office.
Click here for figure data

3.12.2 Demand-side contributions to growth

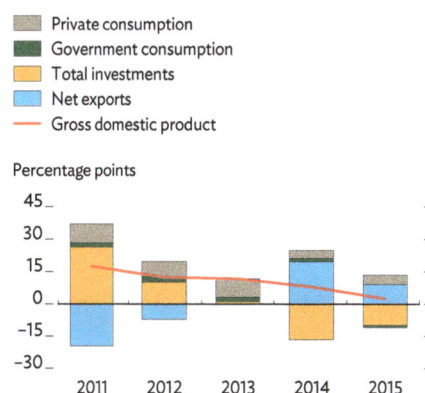

- Private consumption
- Government consumption
- Total investments
- Net exports
- Gross domestic product

Percentage points

Source: National Registration and Statistics Office.
Click here for figure data

This chapter was written by staff of the East Asia Regional Department.

difficulties in borrowing on favorable terms. Indeed, the Chinggis bond 2018 yield peaked at 13.3% in February 2016, following a multiyear low of 4.5% in 2015 (Figure 3.12.4). This development and a 16.9% revenue shortfall from optimistic assumptions forced a 48.9% cut in government investment (excluding investments by the Development Bank of Mongolia), limiting expenditure growth to 1.5%. To further fiscal consolidation, social welfare transfers are better targeted to the poor, and inefficiencies in public spending corrected.

The Economic Transparency Law, 2015 exposed substantial undeclared income or assets and waived evaded taxes, fines, and penalties (equivalent to 47% of GDP or 151% of government expenditures). The law expanded the tax base marginally but also rewarded tax evasion and may have strengthened incentives to conceal.

Monetary policy was tightened as the central bank sold foreign currency and raised its policy rate in August 2014 and January 2015 by 2.5 percentage points in total, and as the price-stabilization program was phased out. As price pressures receded, the central bank lowered its policy rate by 1 percentage point in January 2016. The broad money supply declined by 1.3% in 2015, following 24.6% growth in 2014. Outstanding loans declined by 6.5%, but nonperforming loans increased by 64.2% to 5.5% and loans past due by 217.8% to 7.5% (Figure 3.12.5). An asset management institution may be established. However, avoiding a recurrence of nonperforming loan proliferation depends on avoiding moral hazard, strengthening prudential regulation and supervision, and prudent monetary policy.

Bolstered by central bank interventions totaling $1.2 billion, equal to 10.2% of GDP, the exchange rate hovered in the range of MNT1,950–MNT2,000 per US dollar for most of last year, a depreciation of only 6% year on year. By its real effective exchange rate, the Mongolian togrog appreciated by an average of 7.8%. Exports declined by 19.2% as higher exports of copper concentrates, oil, and gold by volume failed to compensate for declining commodity prices and volume reductions in coal and iron ore shipments (Figure 3.12.6). As imports fell by 28.1%, the merchandise trade surplus increased and the current account deficit narrowed from 11.5% of GDP to 4.8%. With substantial external borrowing, this narrowed the overall balance of payments deficit to $268.1 million from $471.1 million in 2014.

As reported by the central bank, gross international reserves declined by $326.8 million to $1.3 billion, reduced by currency interventions but benefiting from external debt issuance by the central bank and the government, versus $1.9 billion in foreign liabilities. Public and publicly guaranteed external debt, including these foreign liabilities, rose by 21.5% to equal 65.3% of GDP, heightening the vulnerability of the fiscal and external accounts to currency risk and financial market volatility. Additional commercial external debt was reportedly incurred in March 2016 to finance infrastructure. The policy regarding the repayment or refinancing of over $1.8 billion in external debt due in 2017–2018 is yet to be made public. An equal amount withdrawn from the credit line provided under a currency swap facility with the central bank of the People's Republic of China will also eventually have to be reversed.

3.12.3 Public debt and GDP per capita

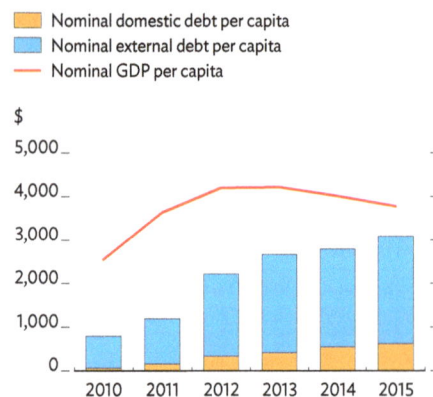

Notes: Nominal GDP per capita at current exchange rates. Estimates exclude state-owned enterprise debt, which amounted to $267 per capita in 2014.
Source: Ministry of Finance. http://www.mof.gov.mn
Click here for figure data

3.12.4 Benchmark bond yields

Source: Bloomberg (accessed 14 March 2016).
Click here for figure data

3.12.5 Bank asset quality

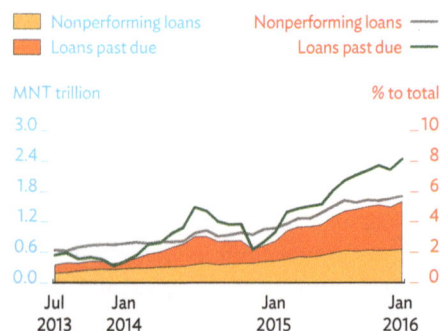

Note: Excluding banks in liquidation and non-depository financial institutions.
Source: Bank of Mongolia. http://www.mongolbank.mn
Click here for figure data

Economic prospects

Growth will stagnate at 0.1% in 2016 and 0.5% in 2017 as mining production declines and shrinking Development Bank of Mongolia disbursements, rising debt repayment, and mounting balance-of-payments pressures necessitate tighter macroeconomic policy (Figure 3.12.7). Agriculture will be the main growth driver, and services will be flat as demand falters. Industry will benefit from the midyear start of underground mine construction at Oyu Tolgoi, ramping up in 2017 and likely to generate $2.5 billion in domestic capital cost expenditure to 2022. However, the mine's ore quality is lower than originally expected, which will affect export values and budget revenues in 2016–2017. This factor—excluded from this forecast—will be captured when the government's GDP estimates are revised later and could lower growth by 1–2 percentage points each year.

Average inflation will stabilize at around 3.0% in 2016, with meat prices normalizing in the second half of the year (Figure 3.12.8). Inflation will pick up to 7.0% in 2017 with gradual currency depreciation as central bank interventions are expected to be phased out.

International reserves face pressure as debt repayments loom and the fiscal situation and the external environment hinder debt issuance. Moreover, the current account deficit will expand to equal 8.0% of GDP in 2016 and 15.0% in 2017, reflecting the lower quality of exported ore, weak external demand, and increased imports related to Oyu Tolgoi.

A delay in Oyu Tolgoi underground development would affect economic prospects and raise risk perceptions, thereby constraining debt refinancing options. Although a delay is unlikely because project financing is secured, the scenario brings to the fore the absolute necessity of maintaining policy buffers and prudent macroeconomic policy. Other external risks include lower commodity prices and tightened external financing conditions. Further, risks to fiscal and external accounts would accumulate if large external borrowing occurred at high interest rates (except for debt repayment).

Policy responses should include reducing consolidated deficits further, strengthening debt management, and—most urgently—resolving looming external debt repayments. Gradual currency depreciation in line with market fundamentals would restore competitiveness and contain balance-of-payments pressures while safeguarding foreign exchange reserves, but its adverse impact on the financial sector and the public debt ratio cannot be ignored. Loose monetary policy should be avoided, as it could aggravate balance-of-payments pressures. Special care needs to be taken with civil servant replacements, especially in key macroeconomic areas, to ensure that sufficient institutional memory and capacity are retained to address immediate challenges.

Policy challenge—maintaining social protection while restructuring

Endowed with vast mineral wealth, Mongolia has promising long-term prospects. Large mining projects are expected to generate fiscal and balance-of-payments surpluses in the future. Successfully managing this

3.12.6 Commodity export price and quantity changes

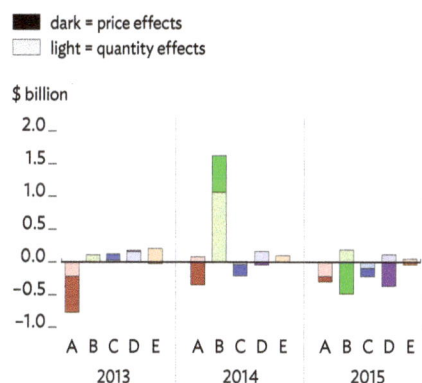

■ dark = price effects
▢ light = quantity effects

A = coal, B = copper concentrate, C = iron ore, D = crude oil, E = nonmonetary gold.
Source: Bank of Mongolia. http://www.mongolbank.mn
Click here for figure data

3.12.7 GDP growth

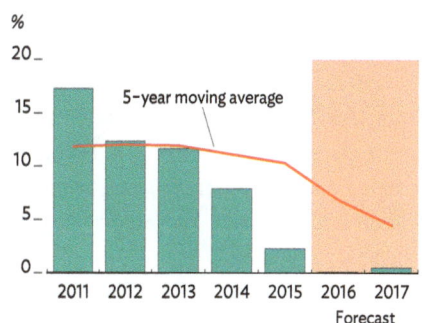

Source: Asian Development Outlook database.
Click here for figure data

3.12.1 Selected economic indicators (%)

	2016	2017
GDP growth	0.1	0.5
Inflation	3.0	7.0
Current account balance (share of GDP)	−8.0	−15.0

Source: ADB estimates.

mineral wealth is key to Mongolia's future. In this process, ensuring macroeconomic stability and making mining-led growth sustainable and inclusive are the greatest development challenges ahead.

Limited economic diversification has left Mongolia highly dependent on its mining sector, which relies heavily on inflows of foreign direct investment. This exposes the economy to external shocks caused by swings in commodity prices and the economic cycles of its trading partners. The current unfavorable external environment—characterized by plummeting foreign direct investment, falling commodity prices, and growth moderation in the PRC—is adversely affecting socioeconomic conditions in Mongolia. GDP growth has sharply decelerated, reducing employment.

A decade of heretofore strong economic growth has substantially boosted average incomes in Mongolia, reducing the incidence of poverty since 2010 by 17 percentage points to 21.6% in 2014. The poverty rate would be an estimated 10 percentage points higher today in the absence of Mongolia's social welfare programs. Income inequality as measured by the Gini coefficient was reduced from 0.36 in 2008 to 0.32 in 2014, but severe disparities remain between urban and rural areas, especially those in the remote western regions. Despite commendable progress, one in five Mongolians still lives in poverty and depends largely on welfare benefits for basic sustenance.

The current economic slowdown underscores the importance of strengthening social protection in Mongolia. This is particularly important in the context of the government's commitment to economic restructuring and adjustment. The fiscal consolidation and monetary tightening required to ensure macroeconomic stability could weaken the economy in the short term. A smaller welfare budget would reverse gains in poverty reduction by pushing people back below the poverty line, perhaps even creating some newly poor. Social welfare programs' past success in reducing poverty argues for their continuation and strengthening.

The government administers 71 social welfare programs that reached a third of the population in 2014. Expenditures for all programs have been increased since 2010 to reflect demographic trends in an expanding population, offset the impact of inflation on real incomes, and reduce poverty. However, challenges persist. Many social welfare programs are unnecessarily expensive because they do not target only the poor. Moreover, the fragmentation of programs results in the duplication of benefits and high administrative and implementation costs. Subsidies to support such programs would have greater impact if they were better targeted.

To reform these welfare programs, policy should improve poverty targeting and consolidate programs to reduce implementation costs and strengthen program impact. Better targeting and consolidation would ensure the fiscal sustainability of programs as the government strives to stabilize the macroeconomic situation and institute the structural reform that is essential to laying a foundation for sustainable growth.

3.12.8 Inflation

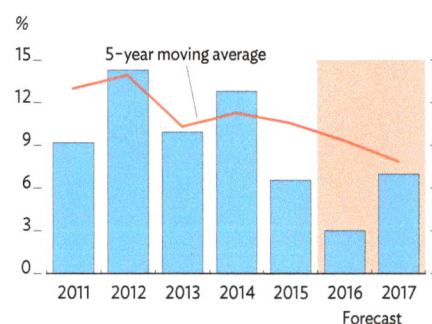

Source: Asian Development Outlook database.
Click here for figure data

Taipei,China

Growth slowed in 2015, prices fell, and the current account surplus widened. Growth will likely be higher in 2016 and 2017 on countercyclical government expenditure and robust private consumption, with rises also for inflation and the current account surplus. Ensuring sustainable export growth is the main policy challenge but cannot be achieved through competitive currency depreciation.

Economic performance

GDP expanded by 0.8% in 2015, down from 3.9% in 2014 and the weakest growth since 2010, dragged down by declines in government expenditure and exports (Figure 3.13.1). Government consumption contracted by 0.4%, subtracting 0.1 percentage points from growth. Private consumption was the driver of growth, boosted by subsidies for the purchase of energy-saving products, as well as for rents, transport services, and mobile phone upgrades. It expanded by 2.3%, adding 1.2 percentage points to growth as the unemployment rate improved, albeit only marginally and countered by a decline in average monthly earnings. Investment rose by 1.5% to contribute 0.3 percentage points to growth as private investment remained robust, compensating for declining government outlays (Figure 3.13.2). Exports of goods and services, which account for 64.5% of GDP, dropped by 0.2% as demand for industrial products weakened in all major trading partners. Imports of goods and services expanded by 0.9%, causing net exports to shrink by 8.5% and subtract 0.7 percentage points from GDP growth.

On the supply side, sector growth rates cannot be determined because of a large discrepancy in the preliminary data, but indications are that most sectors stagnated. Sizable declines in mining and quarrying, and in electricity and gas, are thought to have pushed down industrial output. The service sector, which is the largest contributor to GDP at 62.8%, is thought to have grown only marginally with increases in finance and insurance and in information and communication, but contraction in wholesale and retail trade. Agriculture is likely to have contracted, but its 1.8% share of GDP renders its impact on growth marginal.

The consumer price index fell by 0.3% year on year in 2015 as prices for electricity and gas, transportation and communication, and fuel declined significantly, outweighing a food price increase of 3.1%. However, core inflation, which excludes food and energy, remained unchanged at 0.4%. The average wholesale price index fell by 8.8% on account of large declines in the prices of mineral products, water supply,

3.13.1 Demand-side contributions to GDP growth

Private consumption
Government consumption
Investment
Exports of goods and services
Imports of goods and services
— Gross domestic product

Percentage points

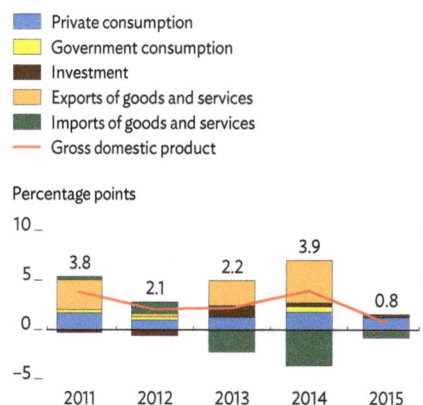

Sources: Directorate-General of Budget, Accounting and Statistics (DGBAS). http://eng.stat.gov.tw; Haver Analytics (accessed 24 February 2016).
Click here for figure data

3.13.2 Contributions to growth in gross fixed capital formation

Construction
Transport and equipment
Machinery
Intangible fixed assets
Total

Percentage points

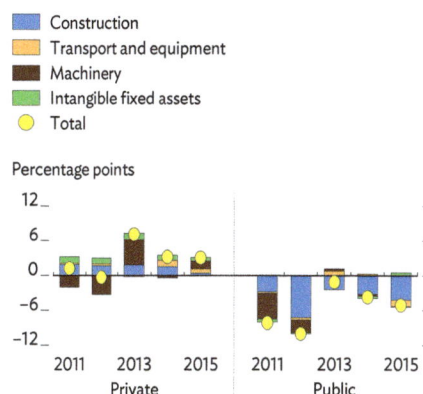

Source: Haver Analytics (accessed 24 February 2016).
Click here for figure data

This chapter was written by Xuehui Han and Nedelyn Magtibay-Ramos of the Economic Research and Regional Cooperation Department, ADB, Manila.

electricity, and gas (Figure 3.13.3). In response to emerging deflation and stalling growth, the central bank reduced the discount rate in two steps from 1.875% in September to 1.625% in December. The money supply (M2) rose by 5.8%, and credit to the private sector increased by 4.5%.

The budget deficit rose from the equivalent of 0.8% of GDP in 2014 to 0.9% in 2015. Central government revenue grew by 2.9% on the full-year impact of higher business tax rates for banks and insurance companies implemented in late 2014, and on proceeds from the sale of shares of some listed public companies. However, expenditure increased more, by 4.4%, as spending grew for education and—reflecting demographic trends—social security and pensions.

The current account posted a surplus equal to 14.5% of GDP in 2015 (Figure 3.13.4) as the balance on goods and services and net income increased, widening the overall balance of payments surplus to 2.9% of GDP, despite a decline in net capital inflows. Foreign exchange reserves increased by the end of December 2015 to $426 billion, or 81.4% of GDP. After local dollar appreciation by 2.3% against the US dollar during the first half of the year came depreciation by 6.1% in the second half. Following a similar trend, the currency depreciated in nominal effective terms by 1.3% and in real effective terms by 1.2% during 2015.

Economic prospects

GDP growth is forecast to rise to 1.6% in 2016 and 1.8% in 2017 on countercyclical investment planned by the government and on private consumption. Government outlays are expected to rise by the equivalent of 2.1% of GDP in 2016. Expansionary fiscal policy and the delayed impacts of past measures, such as facilitating companies' access to credit and investment in real estate, will be the main drivers of growth in 2017. Private consumption expenditure should rise modestly in 2016 and 2017, benefiting from consumer subsidies initiated in November 2015. Private investment will be less robust than in 2015 as sector sentiment indexes for manufacturing and services remain low, though the manufacturing purchasing managers' index signaled in January 2016 likely future expansion. Meanwhile, a sharp 12.4% decline year on year in export orders that same month extended contraction in export orders to 10 consecutive months, pointing to only a modest rise, if any, in exports this year (Figure 3.13.5). Weak external demand, especially from the People's Republic of China (PRC), and rising competition from the Republic of Korea and other economies will counter the potential benefit to export demand this year and next from higher growth in the US.

Fiscal policy is expected to be expansionary, keeping the deficit at 0.9% of GDP in 2016 but perhaps lower in 2017. The revenue base will expand in both years with the introduction of a unified tax on profits from land and other property sales, which raises the tax rate on land sales. Demographic trends will start to impose greater pressures on public finances, requiring further widening of the relatively narrow tax base.

Monetary policy is expected to remain expansionary during the forecast period, given the low growth prospects, helping to push inflation up this year and next. Likely further weakening of the local dollar and moderate food price increases will be tempered by falling oil prices to

3.13.1 Selected economic indicators (%)

	2016	2017
GDP growth	1.6	1.8
Inflation	0.7	1.2
Current account balance (share of GDP)	14.8	15.3

Source: ADB estimates.

3.13.3 Inflation

— Wholesale price index
— Core
— Food
— Overall

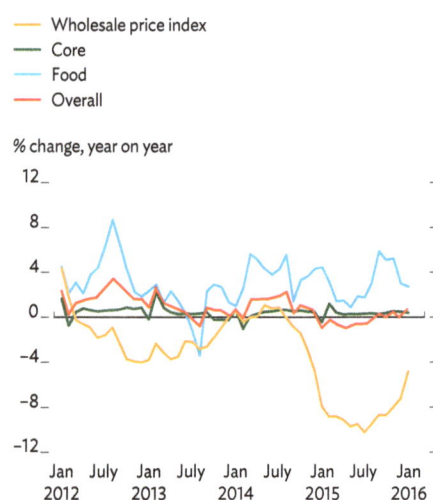

Sources: CEIC Data Company; Haver Analytics (both accessed 24 February 2016).
Click here for figure data

3.13.4 Current account indicators

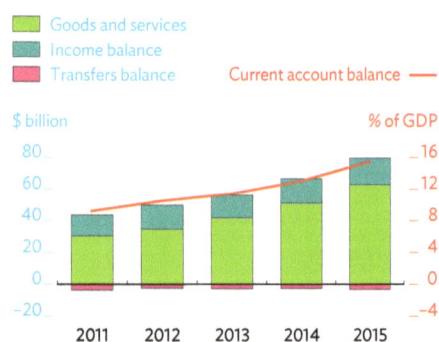

Sources: Central Bank of the Republic of [Taipei,China]. http://www.cbc.gov.tw; Directorate-General of Budget, Accounting and Statistics (DGBAS).
Click here for figure data

yield an inflation rate of 0.7% in 2016. Inflation will rise further to 1.2% in 2017 as oil prices recover. The current account surplus will grow to the equivalent of 14.8% of GDP in 2016 and 15.3% in 2017, as trade contraction is expected to affect imports more than exports.

The projections are subject to downside risks. The start of proposed fiscal stimulus is uncertain with a change of administration, the newly elected President taking office in May 2016. Any delay in implementing the stimulus would undercut growth prospects for 2016. Lower-than-expected growth in the PRC or the US, or volatility in global stock markets, would have adverse spillover.

Policy challenge—maintaining sustainable growth in exports

Taipei,China's economy depends heavily on exports to the US, the PRC, and Hong Kong, China (Figure 3.13.6).

Since 2001, when Taipei,China joined the World Trade Organization, the share of its exports to the PRC in its total exports has increased steadily, from 3% in 2000 to 26% in 2015. The share of exports to Hong Kong, China has grown to 14%, and exports to the US now amount to 12% of the total. With 52% of exports going to these three destinations and generating 33% of GDP in Taipei,China, developments in these economies strongly influence the sustainability of export growth. An empirical analysis of the sensitivity of these exports to growth rates in these trade partners shows that economic growth in the PRC and the US are the main determinants of export growth for Taipei,China (Table 3.13.2). A 1.0% increase in nominal GDP growth in the PRC raises the rate of export growth for Taipei,China by 2.0%, while a 1.0% increase in nominal GDP growth in the larger but slower-growing US economy increases it by 4.5%. Therefore, strengthening economic growth in the US over the coming years can be expected to offset any weakening of economic growth in the PRC in terms of the effect on the rate of export growth for Taipei,China.

However, Taipei,China cannot rely on growth in these economies alone to sustain its export growth momentum, as these relationships can erode over time with competition from other exporters. Indeed, correlation analysis indicates that depreciation of the local dollar against

3.13.5 Export orders

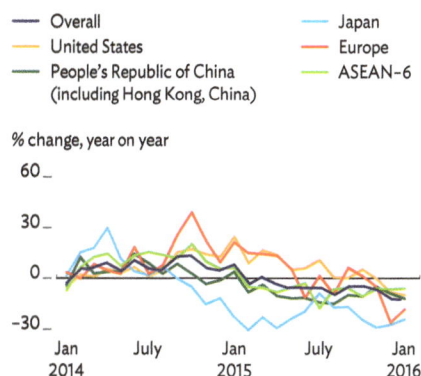

Note: ASEAN-6 comprises Indonesia, Malaysia, the Philippines, Singapore, Thailand, and Viet Nam.
Source: Haver Analytics (accessed 24 February 2016).
Click here for figure data

3.13.6 Export shares, 2015

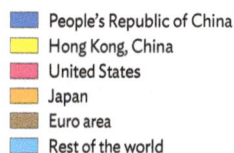

Source: Haver Analytics (accessed 24 February 2016).
Click here for figure data

3.13.2 Determinants of Taipei,China export growth rate (2001–2014)

Coefficient of GDP growth			
People's Republic of China	United States	Euro area	Japan
2.0*	4.5*	-1.6*	-0.3
Coefficient of Taipei,China export growth			Constant
lagged 1 period	lagged 2 periods	lagged 3 periods	-27.2*
-0.6*	-0.3*	-0.1	

* = significant at 5%.
Notes: All values in nominal terms. Adjusted R squared -0.9.
Source: ADB estimates.

the US dollar does not increase export orders for Taipei,China, and depreciation against the renminbi decreases export orders from the PRC and Hong Kong, China—as well as export orders overall (Table 3.13.3). This result implies that competitive devaluation by export competitors, especially the Republic of Korea, nullifies the effect of local dollar depreciation (Figure 3.13.7). On the other hand, the correlation results show that depreciation of the local dollar against the won increases PRC, US, and overall export orders (Table 3.13.3).

However, this finding should not be taken as evidence that depreciation against the currencies of competing exporters, rather than against the currencies of export partners, can promote exports. Indeed, monthly exchange rate data from January 2001 to December 2015 point to the futility of such a policy. During this period, local dollar depreciation against the renminbi was accompanied half of the time by its appreciation against the won. This indicates that depreciation of the local dollar against the renminbi or the US dollar will likely be followed by larger depreciation of the won against the same currencies, rendering futile any policy of promoting exports through currency depreciation.

To encourage export growth, Taipei,China should promote innovations to move from price competition to value competition, and to differentiate its products from competing exporters. For example, for its semiconductor industry, it can move toward producing wafers and manufacturing equipment rather than importing them as inputs for its own exports, thus reducing production costs and helping to develop more profitable capital-intensive industries.

3.13.7 Exports by major commodity, 2014

- 27
- 84
- 85 to the People's Republic of China
- 85
- 90
- Others

Share of exports, %

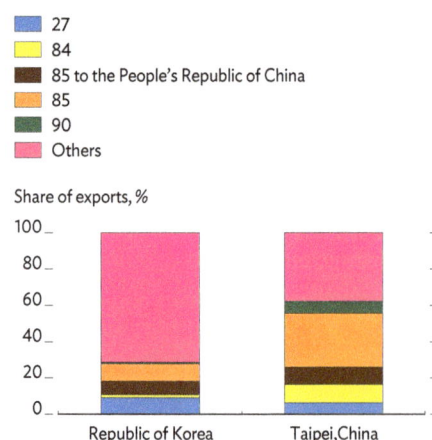

27 = mineral fuels, mineral oils and products of their distillation, bituminous substances, mineral waxes, 84 = nuclear reactors, boilers machinery and mechanical appliances, parts thereof, 85 = electrical machinery and equipment and parts thereof, sound recorders and reproducers, television image and sound recorders and reproducers, and parts and accessories of such articles, 90 = optical, photographic, cinematographic, measuring, checking, precision, medical or surgical instruments and apparatus, parts and accessories thereof.

Sources: ADB estimates using data from Bureau of Foreign Trade, Ministry of Economic Affairs, http://www.trade.gov.tw; UN Comtrade International Trade Statistics Database SITC Revision 3, http://comtrade.un.org (both accessed 1 March 2016).

Click here for figure data

3.13.3 Correlations between export orders and NT dollar depreciation against different currencies

Change in	NT$/$		NT$/CNY		NT$/W	
	A	B	A	B	A	B
Total export orders						
Month on month	−0.001	0.132	−0.037	0.045	0.082	−0.138
Quarter on quarter	−0.146*	−0.170	−0.180*	−0.266*	0.240*	0.331*
Semester on semester	−0.269*	−0.443*	−0.289*	−0.480*	0.346*	0.425*
Year on year	−0.249*	−0.292*	−0.306*	−0.411*	0.342*	0.424*
United States export orders						
Month on month	0.0250	0.129			0.043	−0.172
Quarter on quarter	−0.086	−0.136			0.162*	0.207*
Semester on semester	−0.189*	−0.393*			0.246	0.309*
Year on year	−0.233*	−0.258*			0.293*	0.399*
People's Republic of China and Hong Kong, China export orders						
Month on month			−0.065	0.112	0.097	−0.106
Quarter on quarter			−0.192*	−0.152	0.239*	0.331*
Semester on semester			−0.282*	−0.394*	0.346*	0.402*
Year on year			−0.270*	−0.363*	0.370*	0.435*

* = significant at 10% level, A = January 2001–December 2015, B = January 2009–December 2015.

SOUTH ASIA

AFGHANISTAN
BANGLADESH
BHUTAN
INDIA
MALDIVES
NEPAL
PAKISTAN
SRI LANKA

Afghanistan

The unity government formed after presidential elections in 2014 is beset by an escalation in the insurgency that undermines its efforts to boost growth and public confidence in the wake of the 2014 withdrawal of international security forces. Growth edged up in 2015, and the outlook is for a modest pickup. Improved security, political cooperation, and donor support are required for the economy to transition to a sustainable path.

Economic performance

Growth remained slow in 2015 as deteriorating security and continuing political uncertainty sapped consumer and investor confidence. GDP growth is provisionally estimated to have accelerated marginally to 1.5% from 1.3% in 2014 (Figure 3.14.1).

On the supply side, agricultural output is estimated to have fallen by 2.0% with less favorable weather, but production has remained relatively high since the record-breaking harvest in 2012. Growth in services picked up slightly to 2.8% on marginally higher demand, while expansion in industry slipped to 1.4% as investment dropped markedly and consumers spent less on manufactured goods. With the investment falloff, private and government consumption now appear to account for 85% of GDP.

Afghanistan experienced mild deflation in 2015, with consumer prices averaging 1.5% less than in 2014. Food prices averaged 1.9% lower and nonfood prices 1.2% lower, reflecting weak domestic demand as well as declining global prices for fuel and other commodities. Prices tended to recover after July, and by December the consumer price index was 0.2% higher than in December 2014 (Figure 3.14.2).

Fiscal policy was tight in 2015, holding current expenditure lower than in 2014 and cutting the discretionary development budget by almost half. The tighter fiscal stance was required by missed revenue targets, the accumulation of arrears, and the drawdown of cash reserves in 2014. New tax measures and better collection restored fiscal discipline and boosted budget revenue by 22.1%, allowing the budget to record a slight cash surplus in 2015 (Figure 3.14.3). Nevertheless, the budget continues to be heavily dependent on support, as grants funded 67% of national budget expenditures: 62% of recurrent expenses and 81% of development.

Reserve money is the nominal anchor for monetary policy, which continues to be conducted under a floating exchange rate regime largely through biweekly foreign exchange auctions that sell dollars for current account transactions and also to mop up excess local currency liquidity.

3.14.1 GDP growth by sector

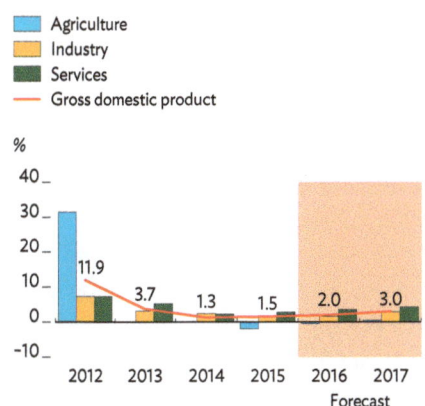

Note: Years are fiscal years ending on 21 December of the same calendar year.
Source: Asian Development Outlook database.
Click here for figure data

3.14.2 Inflation

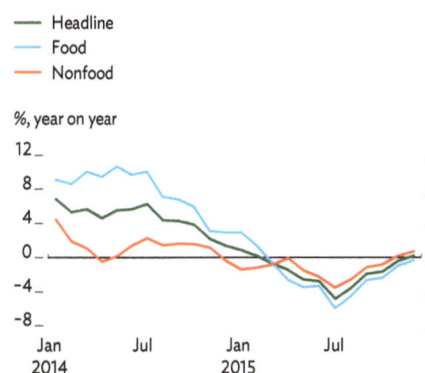

Sources: Central Statistical Office for primary data; ADB estimates for headline, food, and nonfood inflation.
Click here for figure data

This chapter was written by Rehman Gul of the Afghanistan Resident Mission, ADB, Kabul.

The deteriorating security situation has eroded trust in the local currency and left the economy even more highly dollarized. Growth in broad money declined to 5.7% from 8.3% in 2014. Increased private capital outflows in 2015, mostly accompanying a marked increase in emigration, put pressure on the foreign exchange market, resulting in a 17% depreciation of the afghani against the US dollar and a $300 million decline in gross international reserves to $7.0 billion (Figure 3.14.4).

The current account including official grants is estimated to have been a surplus equal to 4.5% of GDP in 2015, down from 6.4% in 2014 (Figure 3.14.5). The decline came with a 26.5% fall in exports of services mainly provided to international security forces, whose withdrawal was completed at the end of 2014, taking many local jobs and markedly reducing national personal income. Excluding grants, the current account is estimated to have recorded a deficit equal to 41.7% of GDP, widened from 37.8% in 2014.

Economic prospects

Economic growth is projected to accelerate slightly to 2.0% in 2016 and 3.0% in 2017, assuming that security and political conditions do not deteriorate, planned donor support holds firm, and the current positive trend of improved policy and governance reform continues. Raising investor confidence depends on improving the security and business environment, especially for the extractive industry, and strengthening governance and the rule of law. If the government implements measures to improve governance, moderate growth in industry and services is projected to the forecast horizon. Growth in agriculture, on the other hand, is forecast to remain flat in 2016 with unfavorable weather but likely to improve in 2017.

Fiscal policy will continue to focus on boosting revenue collection by at least 1% of GDP per annum, as well as on improving the execution of the development budget through reforms that strengthen policy and governance and build capacity. The overall fiscal position including grants is forecast to be about balanced, with no borrowing, in the forecast period as expected donor grants will supplement domestic revenue to fully fund recurrent and development expenditure requirements. The ratio of domestic revenues to recurrent spending is projected to improve to 47.1% in 2017 from 43.9% in 2014.

Headline inflation is forecast to be 3.0% in 2016 and 3.5% in 2017, based on *Asian Development Outlook* baseline assumptions and prudent fiscal and monetary policies. Monetary policy will continue to prioritize price stability and avoiding undue depreciation of the afghani, which is expected to remain under downward pressure because of uncertain political and security conditions.

Including grants, the current account surplus is projected to narrow to 2.0% of GDP in 2016 and cross to a 0.7% deficit in 2017 as growth in imports exceeds exports. This trend underscores the need to pass the extractive industry law and adopt reform to create an environment more friendly to business. Excluding grants, the current account deficit is projected to equal 42.0% of GDP in 2016 and 42.8% in 2017.

3.14.1 Selected economic indicators (%)

	2016	2017
GDP growth	2.0	3.0
Inflation	3.0	3.5
Current account balance (share of GDP)	2.0	−0.7

Source: ADB estimates.

3.14.3 Fiscal indicators

- Current expenditures
- Capital expenditures
- Domestic revenues
- Grants
- Overall balance

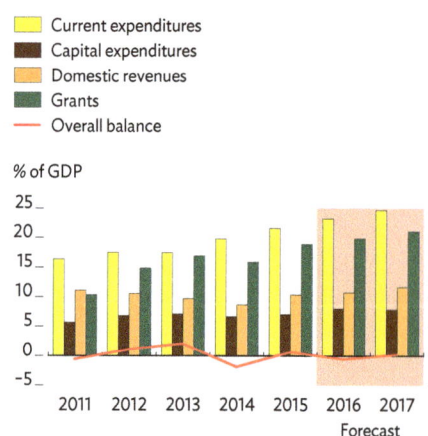

Note: Years are fiscal years ending on 21 December of the same calendar year.
Sources: World Bank, Afghanistan Economic Update; International Monetary Fund Country Report No. 15/324, November 2015 for 2015–2017; ADB estimates.
Click here for figure data

3.14.4 Nominal exchange rate

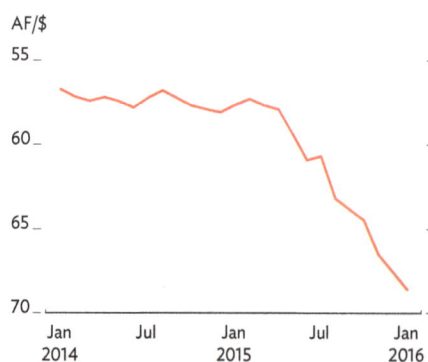

Sources: Da Afghanistan Bank (Central Bank of Afghanistan). http://www.centralbank.gov.af/ (accessed 10 March 2016); ADB estimates.
Click here for figure data

Policy challenge—narrowing the fiscal gap

Afghanistan faces major macroeconomic challenges, the greatest being to improve fiscal sustainability. Since 2012, the fiscal gap has been widening as growth in domestic revenues lagged rising expenditure, in large part because of markedly slower economic growth and also because of lapses in governance (Figure 3.14.6). Public spending is rising because of larger security expenditures following the withdrawal of international forces, necessary increases in social benefit spending, and higher outlays for operations and maintenance as donors transfer completed projects to the government. Nevertheless, Afghanistan must reduce its heavy dependence on foreign aid, as set out in the government's plan for its "transformation decade" from 2015 to 2024. At the least, this means fully financing operating expenditures from domestic revenues. If progress is not made toward improving revenue performance, budget deficits and public debt will rise, the delivery of essential public services will come under pressure, and donor fatigue will set in.

In 2015, the government took significant steps to improve revenue collection: doubling the tax on business receipts to 4% from 2%, introducing a 10% tax on mobile phone top-ups, increasing the fuel fee from AF1 to AF2 per liter, and raising fees for international airlines overflying national air space. As a result, domestic revenue grew by 22%. Moreover, the government began implementing broad reforms set out in agreements with the International Monetary Fund and the World Bank-administered Afghanistan Reconstruction Trust Fund.

Projections over the medium term, however, show government expenditures increasing faster than domestic revenues under the existing tax system. Revenues need to be boosted by expanding the rates and coverage of excise and property taxes, minimizing substantial tax exemptions, improving taxpayer compliance and enforcement, and stemming leakage. In particular, Parliament needs to approve the long-delayed value-added tax law as quickly as possible to replace the business receipts tax and institute a major source of revenue. The government also needs to develop a taxation structure and revenue-sharing framework specifically for the extractive industry. The sector enjoys investor interest and high potential for revenue generation if deficiencies in security and essential infrastructure are successfully addressed.

Steps can be taken on the expenditure side as well to narrow the fiscal gap. The execution of the development budget should be improved to accelerate the development of new infrastructure that will drive private investment and spur growth that can enlarge the tax base, create jobs, and reduce poverty. In addition, savings can come from improved transparency and accountability in the use of public funds achieved through efficient budget and expenditure management.

3.14.5 Current account balance

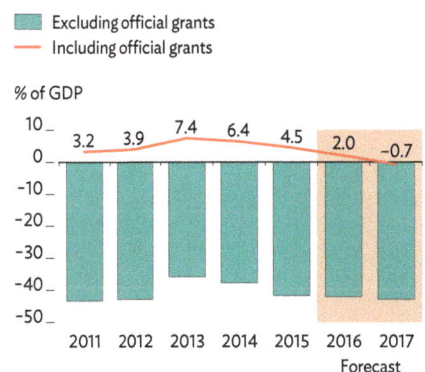

Note: Years are fiscal years ending on 21 December of the same calendar year.
Sources: World Bank, Afghanistan Economic Update; International Monetary Fund Country Report No. 15/324, November 2015 for 2013–2017; ADB estimates.
Click here for figure data

3.14.6 Fiscal sustainability indicators

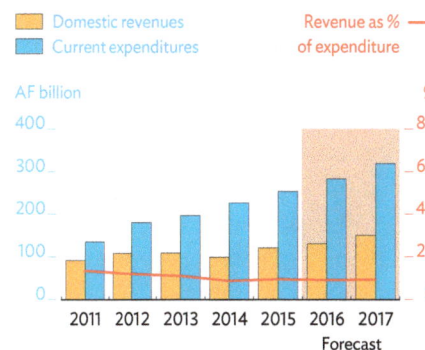

Note: Years are fiscal years ending on 21 December of the same calendar year.
Sources: World Bank, Afghanistan Economic Update; International Monetary Fund Country Report No. 15/324, November 2015 for 2015–2017; ADB estimates.
Click here for figure data

Bangladesh

Growth was resilient in FY2015 despite political protest that hindered exports and private investment. Global headwinds notwithstanding, growth is expected to edge up in the next 2 years on steady expansion in garment exports. The goal of graduating from low- to middle-income status requires much higher investment and thorough reform to improve the business environment, boost budget revenue, and strengthen financial discipline.

Economic performance

GDP growth in FY2015 (ended 30 June 2015) picked up to 6.6% from 6.1% in FY2014 despite a short period of political protest at midyear that disrupted transportation and services (Figure 3.15.1). Growth in agriculture moderated to 3.3% from 4.4% a year earlier because harvests of staple and horticultural crops were less favorable. Meanwhile, robust domestic demand pushed industry expansion to 9.7% from 8.2% the previous year, led by manufacturing for the domestic market and construction. Services growth advanced slightly to 5.8% from 5.6%.

On the demand side, the main contributor to growth was private consumption boosted by higher remittances. Net exports subtracted from growth as exports grew more slowly than imports. Investment rose only marginally to 28.9% of GDP in FY2015 from 28.6% the previous year, mostly on increased public investment. Private investment remained stagnant owing to investor caution, infrastructure and skill shortages, and a weak business environment. Foreign direct investment remains below 1.0% of GDP and 3.0% of total investment.

Average inflation moderated to 6.4% in FY2015 from 7.4% a year earlier, largely in response to lower global prices for food and other commodities (Figure 3.15.2). Year-on-year inflation eased throughout the year to end at 6.3% in June 2015, down from 7.0% a year earlier. Food inflation decelerated to 6.3% from 8.0%, while nonfood inflation edged up to 6.2% from 5.5%. Food inflation subsequently fell to 3.8% year on year in February 2016 on bountiful seasonal supplies, while nonfood inflation spiked to 8.5% on increases in administered prices for natural gas and electricity. These divergent trends offset each other to leave overall inflation hovering at just below 6%.

Growth in broad money supply slowed in FY2015 mainly as net credit to the government fell and expansion in net foreign assets decelerated. Broad money growth was, at 12.4%, lower than the FY2015 monetary program target of 16.5% (Figure 3.15.3). Private credit growth was also below the program target, at 13.2% versus 15.5%, as uncertainty held back demand for investment loans. Bank credit to the government

3.15.1 Supply-side contributions to growth

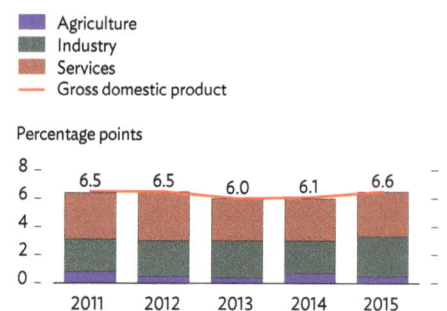

- Agriculture
- Industry
- Services
- Gross domestic product

Percentage points

6.5   6.5   6.0   6.1   6.6

2011   2012   2013   2014   2015

Note: Years are fiscal years ending on 30 June of that year.
Source: Bangladesh Bureau of Statistics.
http://www.bbs.gov.bd
Click here for figure data

3.15.2 Monthly inflation

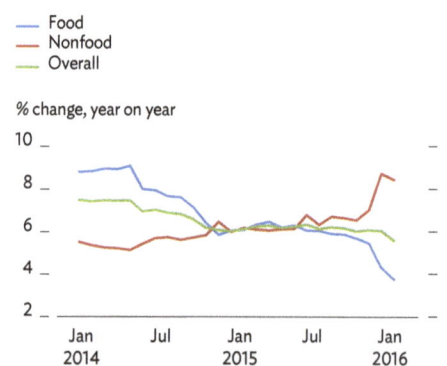

- Food
- Nonfood
- Overall

% change, year on year

Jan 2014   Jul   Jan 2015   Jul   Jan 2016

Source: Bangladesh Bank. 2016. *Economic Trends.* February.
http://www.bangladesh-bank.org
Click here for figure data

This chapter was written by Mohammed Parvez Imdad, Shamsur Rahman, Md. Golam Mortaza, and Barun K. Dey of the Bangladesh Resident Mission, ADB, Dhaka.

declined as the government turned increasingly to financing the deficit through sales of national savings certificates.

With ample liquidity in the banking system, interest rates trended downward. As inflation remained above its target, Bangladesh Bank, the central bank, kept the main policy (repo) rate unchanged. The average yield on 91-day Treasury bills declined to 5.4% in June 2015 from 6.9% a year earlier. Banks' weighted average interest rate for lending declined to 11.7% in June 2015 from 13.1% a year earlier as the deposit interest rate fell to 6.8% from 7.7%, narrowing banks' rate spread by 0.5 percentage points to 4.9%.

National Board of Revenue tax collection grew by 13.2% in FY2015, underperforming the budget target, particularly for income taxes because of subdued economic activity together with delayed reforms in revenue collection. The collection of nontax revenues was also weaker than expected because profit transfers from state-owned enterprises disappointed. Although social spending was maintained as budgeted, overall spending was under budget as fuel subsidy requirements and public investment were both lower than expected. As a share of GDP, revenue fell to 9.6% from 10.4% a year earlier, while spending slipped to 13.9% from 14.0%, holding the budget deficit to 4.3% (Figure 3.15.4). Three-quarters of the deficit was financed domestically, entirely from nonbank sources as demand for national savings certificates ballooned, their rates highly attractive as bank deposit rates fell.

Exports grew by only 3.3% in FY2015, down from 12.1% a year earlier. Disruption to production early in 2015 from political protest, weak demand from leading export destinations, and unfavorable exchange rate movements against the euro helped keep expansion tepid. Garments, which accounted for 81.7% of exports, grew by only 4.1%, down from 13.8%. Import growth accelerated from 8.9% in FY2014 to 11.2% on higher demand for capital goods, food grains, industrial raw materials, and petroleum products, expanding the trade deficit to $9.9 billion. Workers abroad remitted $15.3 billion as greater employment overseas pushed remittances 7.7% higher than a year earlier.

Despite the pickup in workers' remittances, the current account suffered as higher deficits in trade, services, and primary income reversed it to a deficit of $1.6 billion, equal to 0.8% of GDP, from the surplus of $1.4 billion recorded in FY2014 (Figure 3.15.5). The combined capital and financial accounts recorded a large surplus of $5.6 billion in FY2015, up from $3.4 billion in FY2014 because of a larger increase in net trade credit. However, the current account deficit pushed the overall balance of payments to a lower surplus of $4.4 billion from $5.5 billion in FY2014. The surplus lifted the central bank's gross foreign exchange reserves to $25.0 billion including valuation adjustments, or cover for 6.2 months of imports, by the end of June 2015 from $21.5 billion a year earlier (Figure 3.15.6).

The central bank's active exchange rate management kept the Bangladesh taka stable against the dollar, depreciating by only 0.2% in FY2015. However, trade partners' greater currency depreciation against the dollar and lower domestic inflation pushed the taka up in real effective terms by 14.0% year on year during the fiscal year, indicating some loss of export competitiveness (Figure 3.15.7).

3.15.3 Monetary indicators

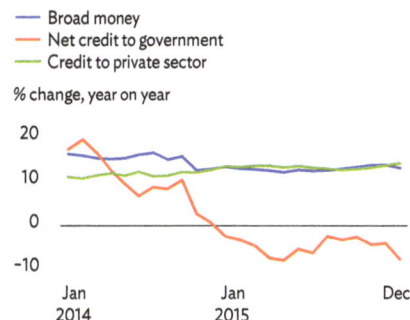

Source: Bangladesh Bank. 2016. *Major Economic Indicators: Monthly Update.* February. http://www.bangladesh-bank.org
Click here for figure data

3.15.4 Fiscal indicators

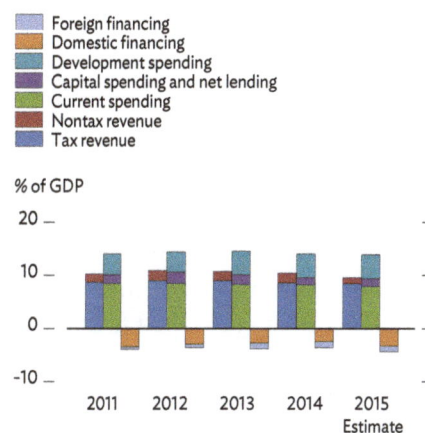

Note: Years are fiscal years ending on 30 June of that year.
Source: Asian Development Outlook database.
Click here for figure data

3.15.5 Current account components

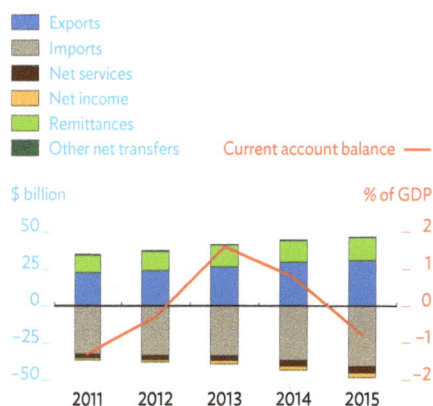

Note: Years are fiscal years ending on 30 June of that year.
Source: Bangladesh Bank. *Annual Report 2014–2015.* https://www.bb.org.bd
Click here for figure data

The Dhaka Stock Exchange broad index experienced some month-to-month volatility but rose moderately by 2.3% in the year to June 2015 (Figure 3.15.8). The ratio of market price to earnings declined over the fiscal year to 15.9 as market capitalization climbed by 10.3% to about $42 billion, mainly reflecting the listing of 19 new companies. Net foreign portfolio investment is estimated to have fallen by a third to $618 million. The capital market is becoming more stable and transparent as regulations are strengthened and demutualization progresses with the separation of trading rights from ownership and management in the Dhaka and Chittagong stock exchanges.

Economic prospects

Growth is expected to inch up to 6.7% in FY2016, underpinned by stronger garment exports and rising private consumption as government employees get wage increases (Figure 3.15.9). Despite macroeconomic stability, domestic demand remains restrained by consumer and investor caution. This is reflected in slower private credit growth, a decline in consumer and capital goods imports, and slow tax revenue collection in the first half of FY2016. Growth is expected to rise to 6.9% in FY2017, aided by higher remittance and export growth as the US and the euro area economies strengthen. Domestic political calm is seen to build confidence in consumers and investors and so support growth momentum.

Agriculture is expected to be little changed, growing at 3.2% in FY2016. Rising demand for agricultural products other than traditional crops—and improved infrastructure, connectivity, and marketing facilities—are projected to edge sector growth up to 3.4% in FY2017.

Industry is expected to expand slightly faster at 9.8% in FY2016. Though export growth is forecasted to rise, it will be partly offset by slackening consumer demand caused by a slowing of remittance growth. Industry will likely grow by 10.0% in FY2017 with a pickup in domestic and external demand, better safety standards and compliance in garment factories, some gains in electricity supply and infrastructure availability, and improved business confidence.

Services growth is projected to improve a bit to 5.9% in FY2016 as industry expands. With a pickup in external trade and domestic demand, services growth is projected to rise further to 6.1% in FY2017.

Inflation is seen to moderate slightly in FY2016 to average 6.2% despite an increase in public sector wages early in the fiscal year (Figure 3.15.10). Global fuel and commodity prices are expected to decline, the crop outlook is broadly favorable, and the central bank will follow prudent monetary policy without hampering output growth. Although nonfood inflation is on the rise, driven by higher wages and upward adjustments to administered prices of natural gas and electricity, continuing low food inflation will keep overall inflation in check. Inflation decelerated to 5.6% year on year in February 2016 from 6.1% a year earlier as food inflation declined to 3.8% from 6.1% and nonfood inflation rose to 8.5% from 6.2%. Inflation is expected to average higher at 6.5% in FY2017 on account of global fuel prices bottoming out, economic growth picking up modestly, and a new value-added tax coming into effect.

3.15.6 Gross foreign exchange reserves

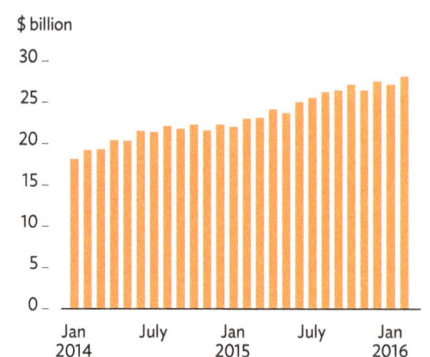

Source: Bangladesh Bank . http://www.bangladesh-bank.org/econdata/intreserve.php
Click here for figure data

3.15.7 Exchange rates

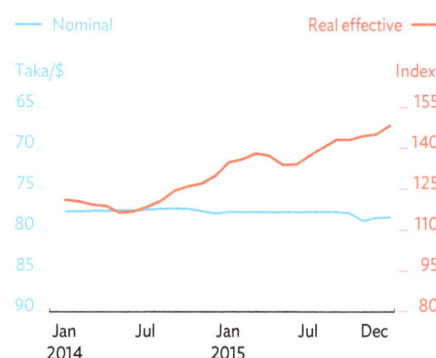

Source: Bangladesh Bank. 2016. *Economic Trends.* February. http://www.bangladesh-bank.org
Click here for figure data

3.15.8 Dhaka stock exchange indicators

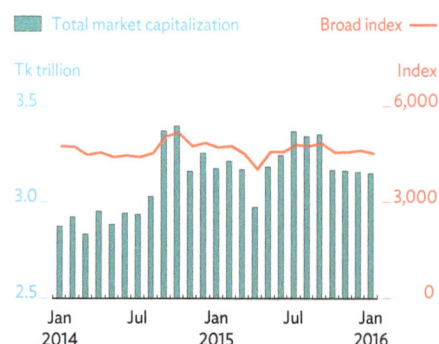

Source: Dhaka Stock Exchange Ltd. 2016. *Monthly Review.* January.
Click here for figure data

The monetary policy statement for the second half of FY2016 (January–June 2016) prioritizes stabilizing inflation and supporting inclusive and environmentally sustainable growth. In a bid to further ease market interest rates and stimulate investment, the central bank lowered in January 2016 its main policy rates by 50 basis points, taking the repurchase rate to 6.75% and the reverse repurchase rate to 4.75% (Figure 3.15.11). In view of prevailing excess bank liquidity, and to meet competition from private banks, seven state-owned banks jointly decided to lower lending rates by 1.5–2.0 percentage points from February 2016.

Exports grew by 8.9% in the first 8 months of FY2016, significantly up from 2.4% growth in the corresponding period of FY2015 as garment exports grew by 9.5%. This reflects in part improved safety standards and worker rights in the garment industry, which major buyers demanded following fatal factory collapses with severe loss of lives in 2012 and 2013. With a stable political environment, export growth is expected to be 8.0% in FY2016, markedly better than the 3.3% recorded in FY2015. Export growth is projected to accelerate further to 9.0% in FY2017 (Figure 3.15.12).

Imports rose by 7.0% in July–December 2015 as higher imports of chemicals, crude oil, pharmaceuticals, and raw materials for the garment industry were only partly offset by declining imports of food grains, sugar, fertilizer, and capital equipment. Imports are expected to pickup in the second half to grow by 9.0% in FY2016. Imports are expected to increase by 11.0% in FY2017.

Workers' remittances declined by 1.5% to $9.8 billion in the first 8 months of FY2016, reflecting stagnant wages and taka appreciation against host currencies. Overseas jobs for Bangladeshi workers surged by 55.7% in the first 8 months of FY2016 (Figure 3.15.13). This foreshadows in the following months a likely rise in remittances, which are expected to grow by 5.0% in FY2016 and a further 7.0% in FY2017.

The current account deficit is expected to improve slightly to 0.5% of GDP in FY2016 with a narrower trade deficit (Figure 3.15.14). However, the current account deficit is projected to widen to 1.0% of GDP in FY2017 as remittance inflows will not suffice to offset the larger trade gap that is projected.

The FY2016 budget targets 29.5% growth in tax revenue and 23.1% growth in total spending, including current spending and the annual development program. Achieving these large increases will be challenging, so shortfalls are likely on both sides of the ledger. Developments in the early months of FY2016 indicate that revenue as a share of GDP increased to 10.3%, while public spending rose to 15.0%. The projected fiscal deficit is, at 4.7% of GDP, slightly higher than the 4.3% outcome in FY2015. Just over 70% of the deficit is expected to be financed from domestic sources—again mostly not from banks.

Like other net oil-importing countries, Bangladesh enjoyed a windfall gain from lower global oil prices. Visible impacts are in the trade balance and in lower subsidy costs to the budget. The authorities' maintenance of retail fuel prices enabled the Bangladesh Petroleum Corporation to earn healthy operating profits and recoup some of its large past losses. Retail fuel prices may be lowered if international prices

3.15.9 GDP growth by sector

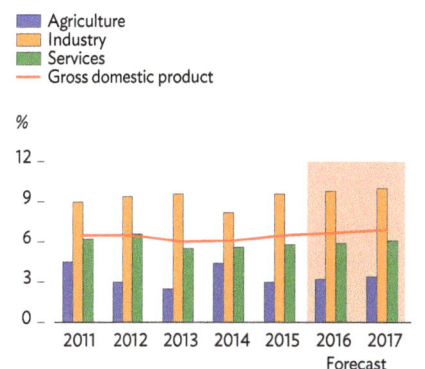

Note: Years are fiscal years ending on 30 June of that year.
Sources: Bangladesh Bureau of Statistics.
http://www.bbs.gov.bd; ADB estimates.
Click here for figure data

3.15.10 Inflation

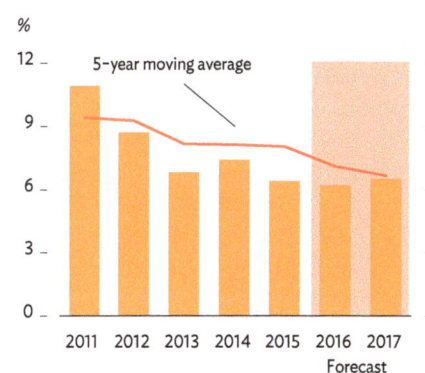

Note: Years are fiscal years ending on 30 June of that year.
Sources: Bangladesh Bank. 2016. *Economic Trends.* January.
http://www.bangladesh-bank.org; ADB estimates.
Click here for figure data

3.15.1 Selected economic indicators (%)

	2016	2017
GDP growth	6.7	6.9
Inflation	6.2	6.5
Current account balance (share of GDP)	−0.5	−1.0

Note: Years are fiscal years ending on 30 June of that year.
Source: ADB estimates.

fall further and all past liabilities of Bangladesh Petroleum Corporation are duly paid.

External and domestic debt does not pose a systematic risk to debt servicing. Debt as a percentage of GDP continued to improve in FY2015. Central government debt declined to 27.2% of GDP in FY2015 from 29.1% in FY2014 as the ratio of external debt to GDP continued its steady decline (Figure 3.15.15). The government's prudent decisions on borrowing from external sources were reflected as external debt stepped down annually to reach 12.0% of GDP in FY2015, for which the external debt service ratio is 2.3%. Domestic debt rose slightly to 15.2% of GDP in FY2015 from 15.0% in FY2014 as the sale of national savings certificates to the public expanded to cover a shortfall in revenue collection. The average interest paid on domestic debt is 10.6%.

Policy challenge—promoting investment and growth

The Seventh Five-Year Plan aims to achieve 8% GDP growth and scale up investment from the equivalent of 29% of GDP to 35% by FY2020. As in the past, momentum has to come from private investment. Indicative growth scenarios suggest that private investment needs to rise from 22% of GDP to at least 27%. However, it will be a challenge to achieve an increase in the private investment rate in the next 5 years that is equal to 5 percentage points of GDP, especially in view of stagnant private investment over the past 5 years. Despite a very favorable macroeconomic performance and political calm prevailing since the second quarter of 2015, investor confidence remains subdued.

To boost private investment it is necessary to address three binding constraints by improving electricity and gas supply, easing problems in property acquisition and registration, and strengthening logistics. Additionally, policy focus is required on resolving insolvency and lowering the cost of trading across borders. Bangladesh needs real progress toward greatly cutting the cost of doing business to boost private and foreign investment. It ranks 174 among 189 countries surveyed in the World Bank's *Doing Business 2016*—well below India at 130, Pakistan at 138, and Sri Lanka at 107. Streamlined tax payment procedures, improved access to credit, and better contract enforcement are priorities.

High transaction costs caused by inadequate supply of electricity and gas badly constrain investment and growth. Despite considerable new investment in power generation, getting electricity connections for new businesses is a challenge, according to surveys. Addressing the problem requires that regulatory procedures be further simplified by reducing their number and application response times. Capacity enhancement is critical to enable response to new requests for electricity and gas connections in the required volume and at lower cost. This will require substantial public investment and an effective strategy for primary energy supply in the medium term.

Long delays and the high cost of obtaining and registering land frustrate private investment, especially in manufacturing.

3.15.11 Interest rates

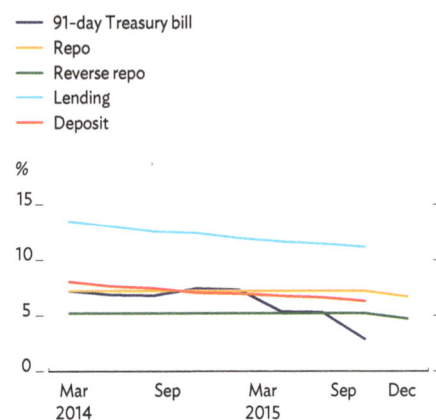

Source: Bangladesh Bank. 2016. *Major Economic Indicators: Monthly Update*. February. http://www.bangladesh-bank.org
Click here for figure data

3.15.12 Contribution to export growth

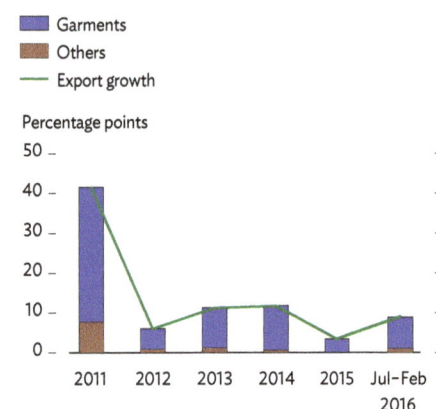

Note: Years are fiscal years ending on 30 June of that year.
Source: Export Promotion Bureau.
Click here for figure data

3.15.13 Growth in overseas employment

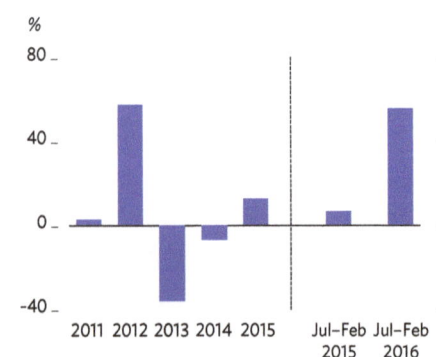

Note: Years are fiscal years ending on 30 June of that year.
Source: Bangladesh Bank. 2016. *Monthly Economic Trends*. February. http://www.bangladesh-bank.org
Click here for figure data

The land market is very inefficient because of weak land ownership documentation, institutional bottlenecks, poor zoning laws, and high transaction costs. The government has started digitizing land records in an initiative that needs to be scaled up and out across the country. Meanwhile, population pressure and rapid urbanization have made urban land increasingly hard to acquire. As land prices have skyrocketed, so have land disputes and various forms of corruption including land grabbing. The challenge for policy makers is acute, and it will take time and effort to simplify land transactions and registration through regulatory reform, improve land administration and record keeping through institutional reform, establish economic zones for private investors both domestic and foreign, and improve mechanisms to enforce zoning laws on land use.

The authorities must also address weak trade logistics and the long delays to trade transactions and associated costs that they cause. Much of the problem lies in getting goods from the factory gate to the port. Handling capacity at Chittagong port has improved, and port handling charges are now less of a concern. However, road and railway networks need their capacity enhanced in line with rising transport demand to capitalize on such gains.

More generally, boosting investment and sustaining growth momentum as Bangladesh approaches middle-income status require deep policy reform and strengthened institutions. Ensuring easier access to finance depends on a healthy banking sector with enhanced capital adequacy and fewer nonperforming loans. Continuing reform to the capital and insurance markets needs to be accelerated in tandem with regulatory strengthening to provide long-term loans for investment. Import tariff reform, stalled for the past 2 decades, must be tackled to enhance the economy's competitiveness. Revenue collection in Bangladesh is low even compared with other South Asian economies and must be markedly improved to provide resources for investment in infrastructure and social development. Operationalizing the new value-added tax is an essential first step toward significantly better revenue mobilization. Likewise, rationalizing energy and power subsidies is essential to improve fiscal flexibility. Finally, institutional capacity needs to be strengthened with a sharper focus on project implementation.

3.15.14　Current account balance

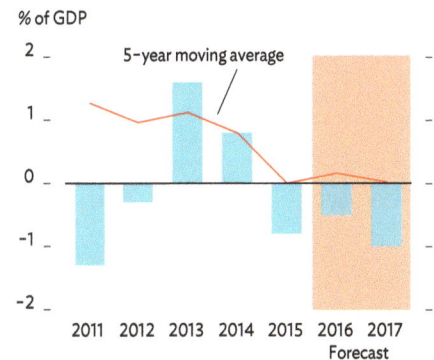

Note: Years are fiscal years ending on 30 June of that year.
Sources: Bangladesh Bank. *Annual Report 2014-2015*; ADB estimates.
Click here for figure data

3.15.15　Public debt

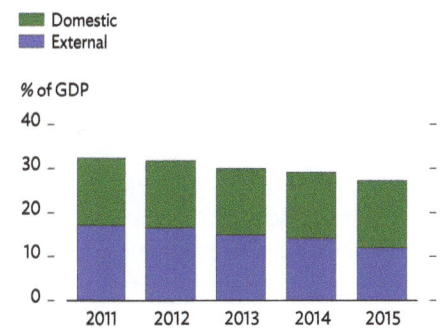

Note: Years are fiscal years ending on 30 June of that year.
Source: Bangladesh Bank. *Annual Report 2014-2015*.
http://www.bangladesh-bank.org
Click here for figure data

Bhutan

Growth accelerated in FY2015 on revived domestic demand and continued expansion of construction on large hydropower projects. The outlook is for moderately higher growth from new hydropower output, strong domestic demand, and strengthened fiscal programs for economic diversification and small enterprise development. Strategies to enhance education and labor skills that are more attuned to economic demands will help make growth in Bhutan more inclusive.

Economic performance

Growth quickened to an estimated 5.9% in FY2015 (ended 30 June 2015) after slowing in recent years as domestic demand faltered under import and credit restrictions imposed to alleviate shortages of Indian rupee reserves. With the restrictions lifted in September 2014 and hydropower construction back on track following an earlier delay, gross fixed investment strongly recovered, and imports of machinery and equipment markedly pick up.

On the production side, services and industry both accelerated (Figure 3.16.1). Faster growth in the service sector was broad based, led by the revival in wholesale trade and financial activities. Hotels and transport gained from double-digit growth in tourist arrivals, while socioeconomic services rose from increased public spending. Industrial growth advanced on a robust pickup in construction and import-related manufacturing. Agriculture also grew, benefitting from continuing government programs to enhance production.

Despite robust demand, inflation slowed markedly throughout the year as prices fell for both domestic and imported food, which together comprise 40% of the consumption basket (Figure 3.16.2). Bhutan's prices broadly follow movements in India's market prices, as most goods are imported from India and the Bhutanese ngultrum is pegged one-to-one to the Indian rupee. Domestic inflationary pressures were subdued by improved harvests and lower housing and transport costs courtesy of declining world oil prices. Average inflation eased to 6.6% in FY2015 from 9.6% in the previous year.

Government expenditure (excluding net lending) grew by 18.1%, rising by 1.2 percentage points as a share of GDP (Figure 3.16.3). In line with the goal in the Eleventh Five-Year Plan, FY2013–2018 of making growth more inclusive and diversified, spending supported crop and livestock production, infrastructure improvement, and the development of priority sectors. Despite a 7.1% increase in revenue, total government resources fell by 3.8% because grants declined by 21.7%, mainly reflecting the high base in FY2014 that included a large grant

3.16.1 Supply-side contributions to growth

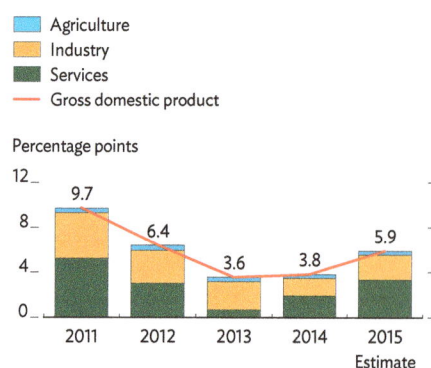

- Agriculture
- Industry
- Services
- Gross domestic product

Note: Years are fiscal years ending on 30 June of that year.
Sources: National Statistics Bureau. National Accounts Statistics 2015. http://www.nsb.gov.bt; ADB estimates.
Click here for figure data

3.16.2 Inflation

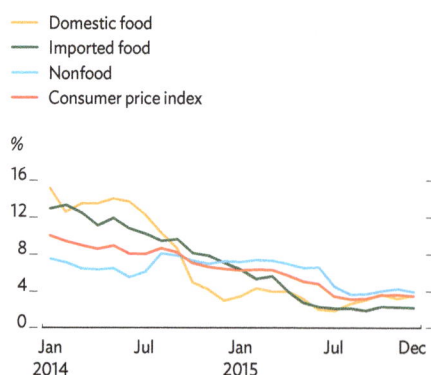

- Domestic food
- Imported food
- Nonfood
- Consumer price index

Source: National Statistics Bureau. Monthly Consumer Price Index Bulletin. December 2015. http://www.nsb.gov.bt
Click here for figure data

This chapter was written by Soon Chan Hong of the South Asia Department, ADB, Manila, and Elbe Aguba, consultant, South Asia Department, ADB, Manila.

from India to support priority sectors. The overall fiscal balance turned to a deficit of Nu2.8 billion, equal to 2.2% of GDP.

The Royal Monetary Authority introduced new macro-prudential regulations to improve monetary management and, early in FY2015, withdrew the foreign exchange and credit restrictions. With liquidity and credit building up, the cash reserve ratio was raised from 5% to 10% in March 2015, and the base rate for bank lending was revised up from 10.32% to 10.49% in May 2015. Priority sectors remained exempted from the base rating system to steer credit to them. By the end of FY2015, money supply had grown by 7.8%, well below the 26.0% monthly peak that fiscal year but outpacing the 6.6% recorded in the previous year (Figure 3.16.4). Credit to the private sector rose by 13.8% by the end of FY2015, double the expansion rate in FY2014, as credit growth in construction markedly quickened. Credit increased as well in trade and commerce—and to an extent in agriculture—supported by low lending rates for priority sectors.

The current account deficit remained high at the equivalent of 28.2% of GDP, up slightly from 26.4% in FY2014 (Figure 3.16.5). The rise was mainly from higher hydropower interest payments, which drove up the primary income deficit. The trade deficit, though still high on large hydropower-related imports and robust consumption, narrowed slightly to 20.3% of GDP owing to higher exports of hydropower and mineral-based construction goods, as well as moderating prices for imports from India.

As net capital and financial flows could not offset the current account deficit, gross official reserves fell slightly by $39 million to $959 million, equal to nearly 10 months of imports and well above the conventional benchmark of 3 months (Figure 3.16.6). The share of Indian rupee reserves, at about 18% of the total, remained adequate for cross-border payments.

Bhutan's external debt rose by $96 million to $1.85 billion in FY2015 on continued hydropower construction, and despite lower debts from the short-term line of credit, but fell as a share of GDP to 90% (Figure 3.16.7). The debt service ratio improved with the increase in export value. As most debt is for hydropower with large economic gains expected in the future, the International Monetary Fund estimates the risk of debt distress to be only moderate.

Economic prospects

Industry growth is expected to strengthen moderately in FY2016 as electricity output increases with the year-round operation of the new Dagachhu hydropower station, while construction of the new Nikachhu hydropower station will supplement ongoing investment. Manufacturing growth is expected to remain strong on robust demand for construction-related goods—iron, steel, and cement—for export and domestic use. Industry growth will ease slightly in FY2017 on base effects and because no new hydropower capacity is expected until at least 2018.

The service sector is projected to maintain momentum in FY2016 on robust domestic demand that will benefit retail trade, hotels and restaurants, and finance, and on strengthened wholesale trade supporting

3.16.1 Selected economic indicators (%)

	2016	2017
GDP growth	6.4	6.1
Inflation	4.0	5.0
Current account balance (share of GDP)	−28.8	−27.0

Note: Years are fiscal years ending on 30 June of that year.
Source: ADB estimates.

3.16.3 Fiscal indicators

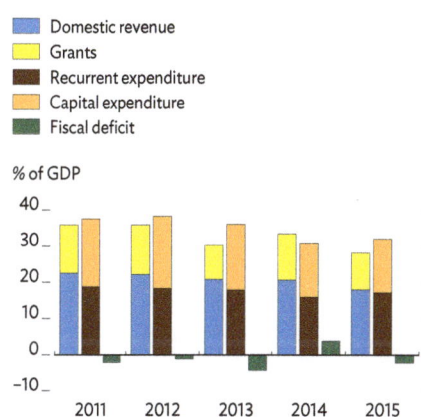

- Domestic revenue
- Grants
- Recurrent expenditure
- Capital expenditure
- Fiscal deficit

Note: Years are fiscal years ending on 30 June of that year.
Source: National Budget Financial Year 2015/16. Ministry of Finance. http://www.mof.gov.bt
Click here for figure data

3.16.4 Monetary indicators

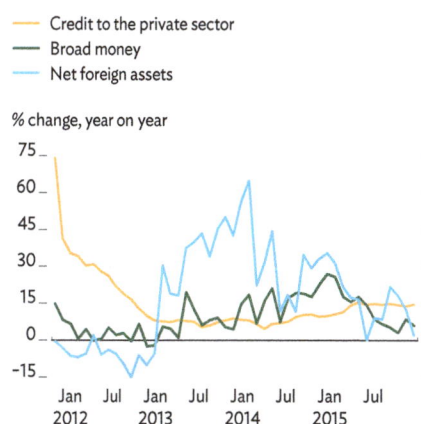

- Credit to the private sector
- Broad money
- Net foreign assets

Source: Royal Monetary Authority of Bhutan. Monthly Statistical Bulletin. March 2016. http://www.rma.org.bt
Click here for figure data

domestic construction and goods exports. Fiscal programs are expected to intensify and support growth in FY2016, as expenditures excluding net lending are projected to increase to 32.5% of GDP, and the deficit to widen to 3.1% before narrowing to 0.6% in FY2017. The government will strengthen diversification efforts with priority lending facilities and tax exemptions for sectors with potential: agribusiness, small cottage industries, and tourism.

Against this backdrop, GDP growth is expected to climb moderately to 6.4% in FY2016 before easing slightly to 6.1% in FY2017. Notwithstanding robust demand, inflation is projected to ease further to 4.0% in FY2016 in view of India's policy targeting inflation and a continued downward drift in global commodity prices. Inflation is projected to pick up to 5.0% in 2017 following projected price movements in India and in the world market.

The current account deficit is expected to remain large in the forecast period as imports for hydropower construction strengthen, hydropower interest payments build up, and consumption imports stay strong. The deficit is likely to shrink markedly beginning in 2018 as two large projects amounting to 1,740 megawatts are brought on line, essentially doubling current electricity export capacity.

Policy challenge—strengthening education for inclusive growth

Bhutan needs to improve its labor base to ensure that growth is sustainable and inclusive. The strength and quality of the workforce depends on its educational attainment and acquisition of the knowledge and skills needed for productive employment. As the economy has rapidly transformed over the decades from agriculture toward hydropower and services, it needs a strong workforce that responds to the demand from the growing sectors. Interventions will be challenged by low educational attainment, skills shortages and mismatch with labor demand, and employment disparity by region, gender, and age.

Over the past decade, Bhutan has invested 5.5% of GDP annually in education, which is higher than the regional average of 3.5%. Despite this high investment, considerable gaps remain in the country's educational achievement. Nationally, average years of schooling is very low by regional standards (Figure 3.16.8), with only 34% of the population at least 15 years old achieving at least a secondary education. Adult and youth literacy rates are the lowest in South Asia (Figure 3.16.9). Although primary school enrolment rates are high, many students do not continue to secondary and tertiary school, as access is limited and unequal because of high costs and a lack of higher-level schools, especially in rural areas. Some of those who leave school enter vocational training, but most work in low income-earning agriculture.

Among students that reach the tertiary level, 70% major in language, business, or commerce. Only 15% major in engineering or technology, with the rest in law or medical-related studies. By contrast, most jobs in the private sector require skills in construction, crafts, machinery operation, or engineering. Because of labor skills shortages, 60% of

3.16.5 Current account components

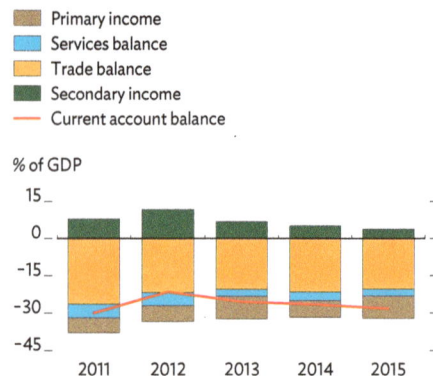

Note: Years are fiscal years ending on 30 June of that year.
Source: Royal Monetary Authority of Bhutan. Annual Report FY2014/15. http://www.rma.org.bt
Click here for figure data

3.16.6 Gross international reserves

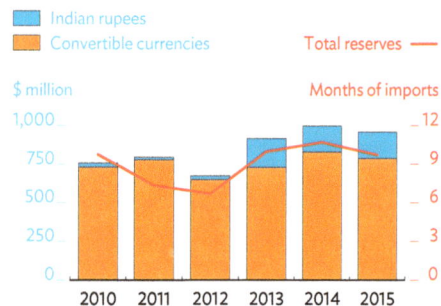

Note: Years are fiscal years ending on 30 June of that year.
Source: Royal Monetary Authority of Bhutan. Annual Report FY2014/15. http://www.rma.org.bt
Click here for figure data

3.16.7 External debt

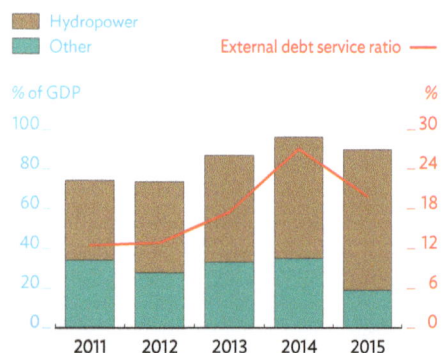

Notes: Years are fiscal years ending on 30 June of that year. The external debt service ratio excludes external debt service for loans received through an overdraft facility provided by India.
Source: Royal Monetary Authority of Bhutan. Annual Report FY2014/15. http://www.rma.org.bt
Click here for figure data

these jobs have been filled in the past 5 years by foreign workers. Various studies point to this mismatch of education and skills as a major constraint on private sector development.

Bhutan's high employment rate, averaging 97% over the past 10 years, masks regional and gender disparities, in particular high unemployment in urban areas and among women and youth, and underemployment in rural areas. Worker vulnerability is commonplace, as 58% of workers depend on subsistence agriculture, mostly as unpaid family workers or working on their own account. Only about 24% are employed in the private sector, and the remaining 19% are in government or the civil service.

If growth is to be inclusive, economic progress must translate into local employment and benefits. The country's growth path dictates higher investments in technical and skills-based infrastructure and better alignment of education with future labor demands.

Under the Bhutan Education Blueprint, 2014–2024 and its implementation plan for 2015, action is being taken to improve the quality of education, widen access to schooling especially in remote areas, address achievement gaps, and strengthen system efficiency. A three-stage approach is planned. It starts by upgrading school curricula and teaching quality, increasing the number of skill-based learning institutions, improving learning methods through information and communication technology, and enhancing skills training and employment programs for youth. The next two stages will accelerate these programs to achieve target outcomes. Close collaboration with the private sector is important to maximize capacity and the interventions implemented with limited resources. The goal is to transform education and strengthen the workforce to make it more responsive to needs in the sectors that drive economic growth.

3.16.8 Mean years of schooling, 2014

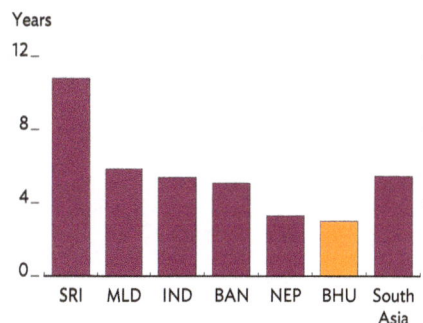

BAN = Bangladesh, BHU = Bhutan, IND = India, MLD = Maldives, NEP = Nepal, SRI = Sri Lanka.
Note: Mean years of schooling is the average number of years of education received by people aged 25 and older.
Source: United Nations Development Programme. *Human Development Report 2015.* http://hdr.undp.org
Click here for figure data

3.16.9 Literacy rates, 2005–2013

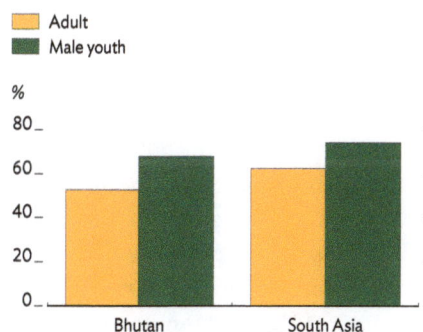

Note: Adults are aged 15 and older, and youth is defined as aged 15–24.
Source: United Nations Development Programme. *Human Development Report 2015.* http://hdr.undp.org
Click here for figure data

India

Growth accelerated in FY2015 despite a double-digit decline in exports. It is projected to dip marginally in FY2016 with a slowdown in public investment, stressed corporate balance sheets, and declining exports, then pick up in FY2017 as newly strengthened bank and corporate finances allow a revival in investment. Notwithstanding unexpected delays in enacting some economic reform, the prospects for continued rapid growth are undiminished.

Economic performance

Advance government estimates point to the economy growing at 7.6% in FY2015 (ending 31 March 2016), marginally above the forecast of 7.4% in *Asian Development Outlook 2015 Update*. The estimate could be a tad optimistic, however, as achieving it would require GDP to increase by 7.7% in the last quarter of the fiscal year (Figure 3.17.1).

Despite a weak monsoon for a second consecutive year, agriculture grew by 1.1% in FY2015, mainly on strong growth in livestock. Food grain production is estimated to have increased by 0.5% in FY2015, though there was lower production of rice, coarse cereals, oilseeds, and sugarcane.

After growing by 5.9% in FY2014, industry accelerated further to 7.3% in FY2015. Manufacturing growth rebounded to 9.5% with the aid of robust performance in the manufacturing operations of private corporations, whose margins have been inching up with lower input costs. Strong growth in manufacturing as measured by value added continues to be at variance with anemic growth in industrial production, which measures volume. Growth in other industry subsectors—mining, construction, and utilities—moderated in FY2015.

Expansion in services also moderated, to 9.2%, largely in line with slower growth in public administration, defense, and the "other services" category. An increase in bank deposit and credit growth in the second half of FY2015 helped financial, real estate, and professional services grow at a healthy 10.3%, while robust growth in airline passengers and sales of commercial vehicles bolstered expansion in trade, hotels, transport, and communications to 9.5%.

Private consumption growth is estimated to have picked up to 7.6% in FY2015 from 6.2% a year earlier (Figure 3.17.2). However, these estimates are likely to be optimistic, as achieving them would require private consumption to grow at 11.7% in the fourth quarter of FY2015, nearly double the 6.1% growth rate achieved in the first 3 quarters. Much of the improvement in private consumption stems from a pickup in urban consumption, while rural consumption has remained

---

This chapter was written by Johanna Boestel and Abhijit Sen Gupta of the India Resident Mission, ADB, New Delhi.

3.17.1 Supply-side contributions to growth

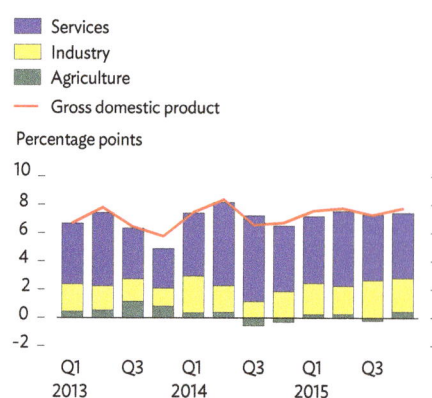

- Services
- Industry
- Agriculture
- Gross domestic product

Percentage points

Q = quarter.
Note: Years are fiscal years, Q1 is April–June.
Sources: Ministry of Statistics and Programme Implementation. http://www.mospi.nic.in; CEIC Data Company (accessed 22 February 2016).
Click here for figure data

3.17.2 Demand-side contributions to growth

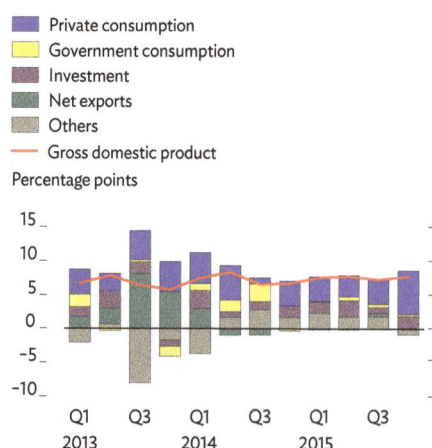

- Private consumption
- Government consumption
- Investment
- Net exports
- Others
- Gross domestic product

Percentage points

Q = quarter.
Note: Years are fiscal years, Q1 is April–June.
Sources: Ministry of Statistics and Programme Implementation. http://www.mospi.nic.in; CEIC Data Company (accessed 22 February 2016).
Click here for figure data

subdued as a result of two consecutive weak monsoons. Government consumption growth also stayed tepid as the central government boosted capital expenditure and curtailed current expenditure. A 20.9% increase in capital expenditure undertaken by the central government helped investment growth improve to 5.3% from 4.9% in FY2014. However, private investment remained weakened by overcapacity and Indian corporations' debt overhang.

Inflation has stayed subdued, averaging 5.0% in FY2015 (Figure 3.17.3). Despite 2 years with weak monsoons, food inflation continues to trend low, though it picked up in the second half of the year on higher prices for selected products such as pulses, onions, and sugar. The easing of food inflation overall was helped by lower global commodity prices, restrained increases in domestic procurement prices, and improved management of government food stocks. Despite soft global prices for crude oil, fuel inflation inched up to 5.5% from 4.1% in FY2014. The uptick came primarily from higher fuel inflation in rural areas, which commonly use domestically produced fuel such as firewood and biogas that are not affected by low oil prices. Even in urban areas, the decline in oil prices was only partly passed through to retail prices, as taxes were increased to bolster government revenues. After declining by nearly 300 basis points in FY2014, core inflation has remained relatively sticky, staying within the narrow range of 4.1% to 4.8% in FY2015, indicating entrenched inflation expectations.

Despite inflation declining by nearly 500 basis points from its peak in late 2013, key policy rates were reduced by a cumulative 125 basis points: 75 basis points in the last quarter of FY2014 followed by 50 basis points in September 2015 (Figure 3.17.4). Such calibrated policy rate reduction reflected concern about the prospect of the US Federal Reserve increasing interest rates and the resulting volatility in global financial markets, sharp price increases for some food products, and possibility of deviation from the path of fiscal consolidation.

Bank credit growth averaged less than 10% in FY2015 as falling inflation lowered firms' input costs and thereby reduced their working capital requirements, and as firms increased their use of nonbank financing (Figure 3.17.5). Banks' limited pass-through of cuts in policy rates meant the cost of funds fell only slowly, prompting firms to shift to other instruments such as corporate bonds and commercial paper, for which interest rates fell much more steeply. Moreover, a surge in foreign direct investment, low global interest rates, and ready access to credit allowed companies to source foreign funds at lower cost.

Weak balance sheets at public banks, which account for 70% of bank lending, continue to pose risks for economic growth as they limit banks' ability to fund investment. The ratio of nonperforming assets to total advances deteriorated from 4.6% in March 2015 to 5.1% in September 2015, though restructured loans declined a bit to 6.2% from 6.4%. Taken together, the ratio of stressed advances exceeds 11%, raising concern about the quality of bank assets (Figure 3.17.6). The government and the central bank have moved to revitalize public sector banks by recapitalizing selected banks, allowing others to raise capital from markets (thereby diluting the government's holding), and improving governance by appointing executives in a professional and

3.17.3 Inflation

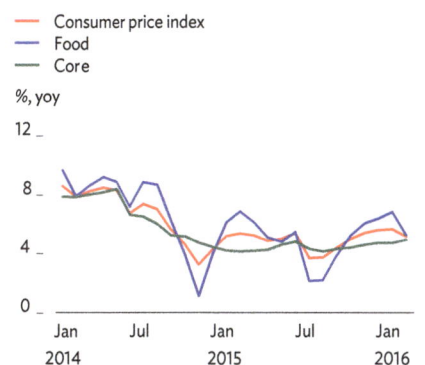

Sources: CEIC Data Company (accessed 15 March 2016); ADB estimates.
Click here for figure data

3.17.4 Policy interest rates

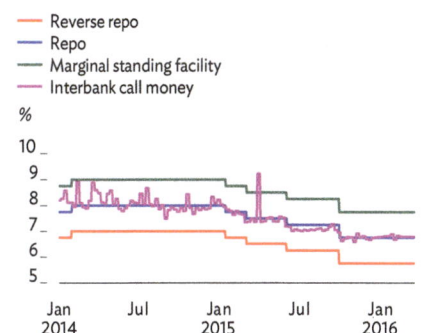

Sources: Bloomberg; CEIC Data Company (both accessed 15 March 2016).
Click here for figure data

3.17.5 Bank credit to businesses

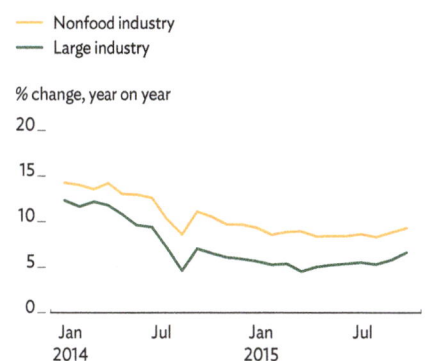

Source: Bloomberg (accessed 10 March 2016).
Click here for figure data

transparent manner. Moreover, bank lenders were given the option to convert their loans into equity in borrowers' companies under a specified pricing formula to collectively become majority shareholders, and to appoint new management if a company failed to meet milestones set up under a restructuring package.

The government was able to achieve its target of reducing the budget deficit to the equivalent of 3.9% of GDP from 4.1% in FY2014 (Figure 3.17.7). The reduction came through curtailed current expenditure and through tax revenue growth that exceeded the target. While corporate and personal income tax collection fell short of their targets, revenue from excise duties and taxes on services grew faster than planned, helped by hikes in excise duties on petroleum products. Despite receipts from planned asset sales falling well below their target, nontax revenue registered healthy growth at over 30% as public sector enterprises, including public banks, paid higher dividends.

Expenditure grew by 7.3% in FY2015, marginally higher than budgeted growth at 6.8%. Unlike in previous years, capital expenditure grew robustly, by 20.9%, such that the ratio of capital expenditure to GDP rose to 1.8% in FY2015. By contrast, current expenditure growth was tamed at 5.5%. The sharp drop in global oil prices, deregulation of diesel prices, and use of cash transfers to qualified recipients to rationalize the subsidized cooking gas benefit cut expenditures on the petroleum subsidy by more than half. However, there was an uptick in the outgo on account of fertilizer and food subsidies.

A national commission that reviews the salaries of the central government employees every decade recommended a 23.5% increase in salaries and pensions. According to the commission, the wage revision would cost the central government budget the equivalent of 0.46% of GDP. The government is waiting for a committee set up in late January 2016 to announce its final verdict on the commission's recommendations.

Imports are estimated to have contracted by 15.5% in FY2015, primarily aided by a sharply reduced oil import bill. With the price of imported crude oil declining by more than half in the course of FY2015, oil imports fell by more than 40% even as volume picked up by 8% over the previous year. Gold imports increased by 2.6%, despite lower prices, as import volumes registered a marked gain of 21.4% during the year. At the same time, imports other than oil and gold stabilized as consumption goods such as electronics and readymade garments registered growth, indicating improved domestic consumption demand. However, imports of capital goods such as machinery, transport equipment, and iron and steel remained weak.

Lower commodity prices and anemic global demand weighed on exports, which contracted by 18.0% in FY2015. While lower oil prices brought refined petroleum exports down by more than half, non-oil exports also declined by 9.4%. Exports of key products including engineering goods, electronics, leather, textiles, and gems and jewelry contracted as demand weakened in the advanced economies, the People's Republic of China, and oil-producing nations. Higher service exports and remittances helped to narrow the estimated current account deficit to the equivalent of 1.3% of GDP (Figure 3.17.8).

3.17.6 Nonperforming and restructured loans

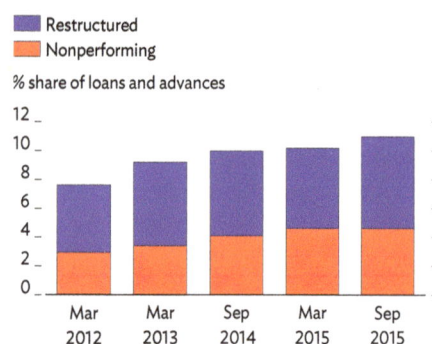

■ Restructured
■ Nonperforming

% share of loans and advances

Source: Reserve Bank of India. http://www.rbi.org.in
Click here for figure data

3.17.7 Federal budget indicators

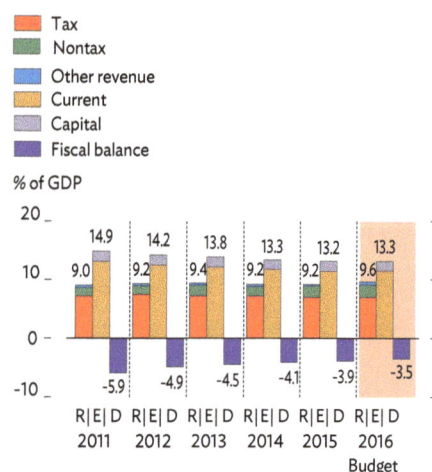

■ Tax
■ Nontax
■ Other revenue
■ Current
■ Capital
■ Fiscal balance

% of GDP

R = revenue, E = expenditure, D = deficit financing.
Note: Years are fiscal years, Q1 is April–June.
Source: Ministry of Finance Union Budget 2016–2017. http://indiabudget.nic.in
Click here for figure data

3.17.8 Trade indicators

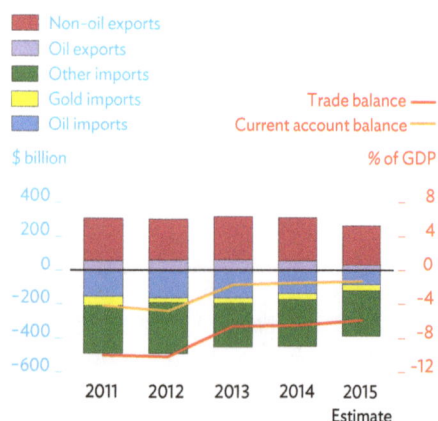

■ Non-oil exports
■ Oil exports
■ Other imports
■ Gold imports
■ Oil imports

Trade balance ——
Current account balance ——

$ billion   % of GDP

Note: Years are fiscal years ending on 31 March of the next year.
Sources: CEIC Data Company (accessed 17 March 2016); ADB estimates.
Click here for figure data

Buoyed by measures to enhance foreign direct investment—including raising the ceiling for investment in several important sectors such as broadcasting and defense, as well as rationalizing and simplifying procedures—net flows of foreign direct investment surged to an estimated $32 billion, nearly 26% higher than in the previous year. Inflows in the form of deposits by nonresident Indians also remained strong, growing to nearly $15 billion in FY2015. These inflows and continuing business and government loan inflows increased gross international reserves in FY2015 by $9.2 billion to over $350 billion (Figure 3.17.9).

Portfolio flows turned negative during the year with estimated net outflows of $3.7 billion from the equity market and $0.7 billion in debt, in line with the experience of other emerging markets. The selloff reflected concerns about interest rates rising in the US, the economic slowdown in key emerging markets, and slower-than-anticipated progress on politically difficult domestic economic reforms. The outflow from the equity market was a factor pushing stock prices on the Bombay Stock Exchange Sensex down by 13% over the year (Figure 3.17.10).

The Indian rupee depreciated by 8% against the US dollar in FY2015. However, it weakened in nominal effective terms by a smaller 5%, and in real effective terms by less than 3%, implying that it moved in parallel with the currencies of trading partners (Figure 3.17.11).

Economic prospects

While public investment and urban consumption were the major drivers of growth in FY2015, a revival of private investment and rural consumption is critical if growth is to remain strong in FY2016 and FY2017, given the likely sluggish recovery in the advanced economies and the anemic outlook for global trade. Urban consumption is expected to receive a boost from the impending salary hike for government employees in 2016. That salary hike is likely a factor in pushing private sector wages somewhat higher. However, reviving rural consumption will hinge on the quality of the monsoon, as a major part of the rural economy continues to depend heavily on agriculture. Nevertheless, budgetary support for programs to improve agricultural productivity and funding for the government employment scheme for poor rural families should boost rural incomes and spending.

Public investment will continue to be an important driver of growth, as the government is expected to use savings from oil to further boost government investment. However, the finances available to ramp up investment in FY2016 will be considerably smaller than in FY2015, given sharper fiscal tightening and increased outgo on account of a higher public sector wage bill. New investment announcements are just beginning to recover and inch higher (Figure 3.17.12). While the number of stalled projects has declined marginally, it remains elevated. Ongoing deleveraging by private corporations, reductions in policy rates, and public investment are likely to initiate a recovery in private investment. Further, the uptick in consumption could soak up excess capacity across sectors and invite fresh investment.

3.17.9 International reserves

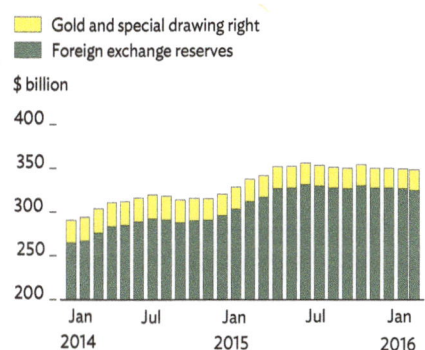

Source: CEIC Data Company (accessed 15 March 2016).
Click here for figure data

3.17.10 Stock price indexes

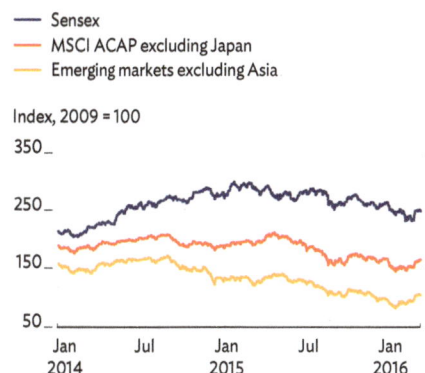

Source: Bloomberg (accessed 26 February 2016).
Click here for figure data

3.17.11 Exchange rate

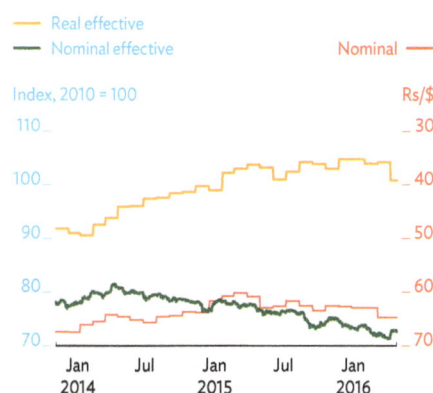

Source: Bloomberg (accessed 15 March 2016).
Click here for figure data

Various investment outlook surveys provide a mixed picture. The manufacturing purchasing managers' index declined for 6 consecutive months to December but turned higher in January and February 2016 on new orders and exports (Figure 3.17.13). The services index has been more robust, reaching a 21-month high in January but then falling in February on a marginal increase in output. At the same time, Nomura's index of composite leading indicators shows growth momentum stabilizing, while the central bank's industrial outlook survey points to strengthening business sentiment.

A normal monsoon would augur well for growth in agriculture, which has been depressed by weak rains in the past 2 years. The slowdown in advanced economies including the US, lower export commodity prices, and weaker currencies in some major trading partners vis-à-vis the Indian rupee are likely to hit merchandise exports and financial, telecom, business, and other tradeable services. Lower net exports could thus impinge on growth.

Limited policy headroom exists to bolster growth, given pressures from an uptick in inflation and plans for further fiscal consolidation. However, with new guidelines from the central bank requiring banks to set their lending rates based on marginal cost of funds or the rates offered to new deposits, there will be greater transmission of reduced policy rates to lending rates. The consequent reduction in the cost of borrowing is likely to boost aggregate demand.

On balance, growth is projected at 7.4% in FY2016, marginally lower than the 7.6% achieved in FY2015 as the expected decline in external demand offsets a pickup in domestic demand. Moreover, the weak balance sheets of public sector banks will hamper lending and growth prospects. Growth is expected to pick up a bit to 7.8% in FY2017, helped by the government's strengthening of public sector banks' capital and operations, private investment benefitting from corporate deleveraging, the financing of stalled projects, and an uptick in bank credit.

After 2 years of decline, consumer inflation is likely to accelerate slightly in both years. The salary hike for civil servants would boost consumption, perhaps fueling broad inflation. Meanwhile, somewhat higher global oil prices are likely in the second half of FY2016, some of which would transmit to retail prices. On the other hand, a normal monsoon would help mitigate some of the pressure on food prices, which firmed up in the second half of FY2015. Despite inflation declining substantially in the past 3 years, inflation expectations have remained elevated and even inched up since the beginning of FY2015, implying that core inflation is entrenched. Inflation is likely to average 5.4% in FY2016, rising to 5.8% in FY2017 as global oil prices firm up and domestic demand strengthens.

The central bank has signaled an accommodative monetary stance, though further cuts to key policy rates would be contingent on the evolving inflation trajectory and the implementation of planned budget consolidation. Thus, while aggressive rate cuts are unlikely, FY2016 may see some monetary easing.

The FY2016 budget displays fiscal prudence by reaffirming the path of fiscal consolidation and reducing the fiscal deficit to 3.5% of GDP. Gross tax revenue growth of 11.7% in FY2016 seems achievable with

3.17.12 New investment projects announced

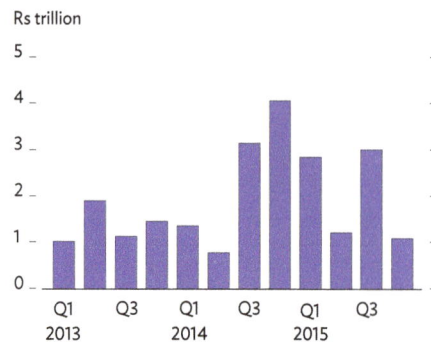

Q = quarter.
Source: Centre for Monitoring Indian Economy.
Click here for figure data

3.17.13 Purchasing managers' indexes

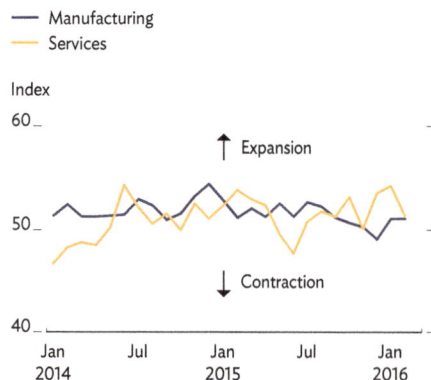

Note: Nikkei, Markit.
Source: Bloomberg (accessed 6 March 2016).
Click here for figure data

a tax buoyancy of 1.1. In fact, estimates of indirect tax growth appear to be conservative with excise duty growth pegged at 12.2% even after the government hiked the excise duty on petroleum products late in FY2015. Estimates of service tax revenue growth also appear to be more conservative than in previous years. By contrast, estimates of nontax revenue are optimistic. The government has targeted a 21% increase in the dividends of public sector companies excluding banks. Moreover, proceeds from telecommunications spectrum sales are expected to rise sharply from Rs560 billion in FY2015 to Rs990 billion, while the disinvestment target has been set at Rs565 billion, more than double the Rs253 billion achieved in FY2015. Reliance on asset sales makes achieving budget targets dependent on market conditions.

A focus of the budget is to revive rural demand, which has remained under stress for 2 consecutive years of weak monsoons. The budget also increases social sector spending and boosts infrastructure allocations for road transport, power generation, renewable energy, and railways. The expenditure mix is expected to deteriorate, however, with capital expenditure projected to grow by only 3.9% (and decline as a share of GDP), against 11.8% expansion for current expenditure. Within current expenditure, while petroleum subsidies are expected to decline further, allocations for food subsidies will increase. Outgo on account of salaries and pensions are budgeted to increase as the government implements recommendations from the national commission.

As crude oil prices are projected to decline by 32% in FY2016, refined petroleum exports, which account for nearly 20% of merchandise exports, are likely to contract by 28% during FY2016. Sluggish global growth and an appreciating rupee in real effective terms are likely to further impede exports. Encouragingly, exports by volume of metal and metal products, basmati rice, and drugs have been resilient, and higher prices for these key exports are likely to provide a boost. On balance, exports will likely contract by 1.5% in FY2016. Imports of crude oil are expected to decline by 24% on weak prices. Gold imports are likely to remain flat as volumes rise but prices decline. Other imports could inch up as domestic demand strengthens, increasing total imports by 3.5%. Consequently, the current account deficit is expected to widen a bit to the equivalent of 1.6% of GDP in FY2016, up from an estimated 1.3% in FY2015.

With growth in the large advanced economies edging up, and higher oil prices in 2017 helping exports of refined petroleum, overall merchandise exports are expected to recover to 5.0% growth. At the same time, imports are projected to rebound by 9.0% with higher growth and oil prices, causing the current account deficit to widen to 1.8% of GDP. The higher current account deficit will likely be easily financed by stable capital flows. In the medium term, a sustained pickup in exports would require a competitive currency, continued progress in reducing supply-side bottlenecks, and a lower cost of doing business.

Numerous measures enacted to attract foreign direct investment and further measures to improve the business environment will ensure that India remains a favored base for manufacturing and exporting. After registering an outflow of $4.4 billion in FY2015, portfolio investment is likely to pick up as Indian assets continue to look attractive vis-à-vis assets in emerging market peers.

3.17.1 Selected economic indicators (%)

	2016	2017
GDP growth	7.4	7.8
Inflation	5.4	5.8
Current account balance (share of GDP)	−1.6	−1.8

Note: Years are fiscal years ending on 30 June of that year.
Source: ADB estimates.

Policy challenge—fostering bank finance of infrastructure

The private sector has played a large role in infrastructure financing since 2005. The Twelfth Five-Year Plan, 2012–2017 envisioned 21% of infrastructure financing (and 42% of all debt financing) being sourced from banks. Infrastructure financing needs were estimated at around $200 billion per year to FY2017. Healthy banks are needed to ensure that the private sector can continue to play its desired role in infrastructure financing, as public infrastructure spending can be raised only so far, even in light of a substantial drop in government debt. However, high and rising nonperforming assets (NPAs) in the banking sector, coupled with an overleveraged corporate sector, could choke off this important source of infrastructure financing, leaving a speed bump on India's road to high and sustained economic growth. Since 2011, gross fixed capital formation has begun to decline as a share of GDP and is no longer a significant driver of economic growth (Figure 3.17.14).

The nexus of a highly indebted corporate sector and proliferating NPAs will be difficult to resolve quickly. The interest cover ratio, measuring companies' ability to pay interest on their debts, remains low in over 2,000 companies operating in such key sectors as electric power, steel, and construction, as regularly surveyed by the Reserve Bank of India, the central bank—though some sectors, such as manufacturing, experienced a decisive uptick in the last quarter of FY2014 (Figure 3.17.15). Credit growth has been slow, particularly at public sector banks, which still hold about 72% of all bank assets and are a vital source of infrastructure financing for India's corporate sector. Key financial indicators deteriorated rapidly (Figure 3.17.16). With banks understandably cautious about extending new loans while resolving their NPA issues and cleaning up their balance sheet, and with the highly leveraged corporate sector reluctant to undertake new investment, viable projects may go unfinanced, considerably impeding economic growth.

The causes for the sharp rise in NPAs are both internal and external: supply-side bottlenecks, a highly leveraged corporate sector, weak governance and project appraisal capacity within banks, and a slowdown in global and domestic demand. Moreover, loans to the electric power sector, to which banks are highly exposed, are beset with problems related to the deteriorating health of power distribution companies. However, the government is taking a wide range of steps to address these issues, tackling bank governance, recapitalization, debt restructuring, and NPA recognition. Its Indradhanush program, announced in early 2015, aims to recapitalize public sector banks with Rs700 billion over the next 4 years and strengthen internal governance.

A package to strengthen the financial health of state-owned electricity distributors was unveiled in November 2015, with states voluntarily taking over 75% of the debt of their distribution companies. The package provides incentives for electricity distributors to reduce their technical losses and debt service costs and to improve their financial discipline.

3.17.14 Investment indicators

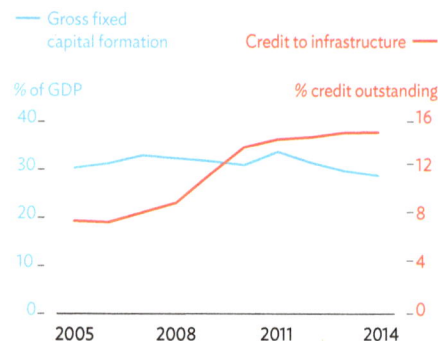

Sources: World Bank. World Development Indicators online database; CEIC Data Company (both accessed 17 March 2016).
Click here for figure data

3.17.15 Interest cover ratio of companies in key sectors

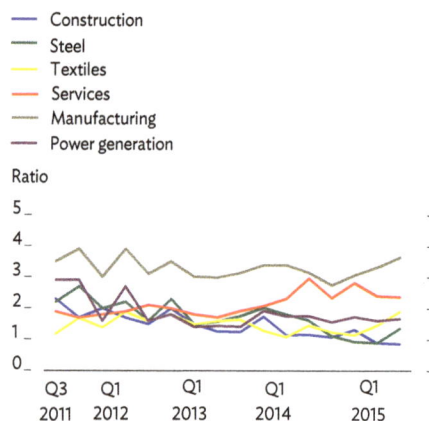

Q = quarter.
Note: Years are fiscal years, Q1 is April–June.
Source: CEIC Data Company (accessed 17 March 2016).
Click here for figure data

3.17.16 Key financial indicators of public sector banks

Note: Years are fiscal years, Q1 is April–June.
Source: CEIC Data Company (accessed 17 March 2016).
Click here for figure data

In December 2015, a bankruptcy law was introduced in Parliament that promises to substantially improve the quality and speed of debt restructuring, a process that has heretofore been slow and unstructured. The central bank undertook several measures to strengthen NPA disclosure, risk control, and the appointment process at public sector banks. In early February 2016, the central bank governor advocated "deep surgery" for banks in place of Band-Aids, encouraging all banks to disclose and fully provide for all NPAs by March 2017. This call for greater recognition of NPAs came after an intense review of asset quality conducted by the central bank in the last 2 months of 2015 and can be expected to push up the reported incidence of NPAs in the banking system (Figure 3.17.17). While the FY2016 budget provision to recapitalize banks generally disappointed industry observers and some international rating agencies, the central bank's revision on 29 February 2016 of how tier 1 capital is calculated is estimated to boost tier 1 capital by Rs350 billion to Rs400 billion. Meanwhile, the government is taking steps to revive flagging private sector investment: introducing a strengthened resolution mechanism for troubled public–private partnerships, setting up the National Infrastructure Investment Fund to attract private sector financing into infrastructure, and introducing tax-free infrastructure bonds.

Together, these measures should gradually unclog bank finance channels and increase private sector spending on infrastructure, provided that the legal changes are implemented properly and there is no further dramatic deterioration in the health of banks or corporations.

3.17.17 Nonperforming loans to all public sector bank loans

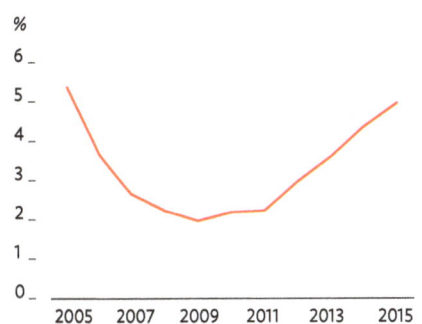

Note: Years are fiscal years, Q1 is April–June.
Source: CEIC Data Company (accessed 17 March 2016).
Click here for figure data

Maldives

A downturn in tourism brought markedly slower growth in 2015 and, combined with higher capital spending, enlarged budget and current account deficits, even as inflation fell to a record low. The outlook is for moderate growth on tepid recovery in tourism and on further infrastructure spending intended to foster economic diversification and higher, less volatile growth over the long term.

Economic performance

GDP growth braked to an estimated 1.5% in 2015 from 6.5% a year earlier as tourism contracted and transport growth slowed markedly (Figure 3.18.1). As most taxes are tied to tourism, growth was cut further as tax earnings net of subsidies fell. Growth came largely from robust public investment that propelled a doubling of construction growth to over 40%.

In sharp contrast with previous years, tourism contracted by over 4% as growth in arrivals slowed and bed-night occupancy slipped (Figure 3.18.2). Growth in tourist arrivals declined to 2% from 7% in 2014 despite upbeat tourism globally and in Asia. Arrivals from the People's Republic of China (PRC)—which provides 30% of the total—fell by 1% following 6 years of rapid growth and despite resilient outbound travel from the PRC. Arrivals from Europe—which has a 44% market share—picked up but only slightly. Despite some growth in arrivals, bed-night occupancy, which largely determines earnings, fell by 4.3% as the average stay continued to shorten.

With vibrant investment and construction, the related real estate sector expanded, and imports of wood, cement, and other construction materials jumped by about 40% over the year. Expansion in fishery-based sectors, mainly agriculture and manufacturing, fell with lower fish purchases by volume and output of processed fish. Growth in the other sectors was minimal.

Average inflation eased further from 2.1% in 2014 to 1.0%—the lowest rate in 10 years—as world food and oil prices declined. Monthly inflation rates were variable but fell in transport and remained low in fish, a staple, and in most other key items, including water and electricity (Figure 3.18.3). Also keeping prices low was the reversal of import duty hikes on some key items soon after they were introduced in April 2015.

The government embarked in 2015 on a highly expansionary path through its scaled-up public investment program for airport and harbor expansion, energy projects, and housing construction in Malé and

3.18.1 Supply-side contributions to growth

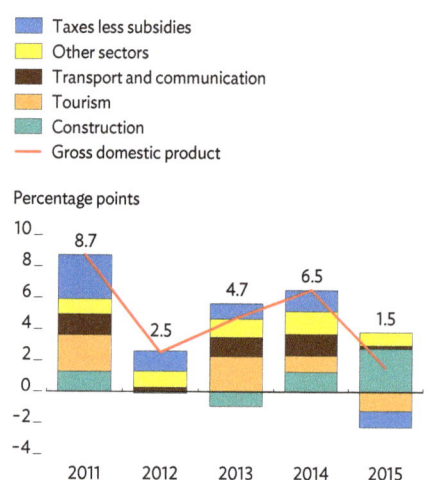

Source: Maldives Monetary Authority. 2016. Monthly Statistics. January. http://www.mma.gov.mv
Click here for figure data

3.18.2 Tourism indicators

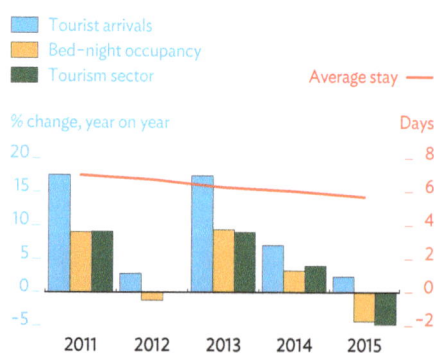

Source: Maldives Monetary Authority. 2016. Monthly Statistics. January. http://www.mma.gov.mv
Click here for figure data

This chapter was written by Masato Nakane of the South Asia Department, ADB, Manila, and Elbe Aguba, consultant, South Asia Department, ADB, Manila.

the east atolls to accommodate its program of voluntary population consolidation. Budget expenditures including net lending surged by 30%, their share of GDP rising in 2015 by 8.9 percentage points to 43.7% (Figure 3.18.4). Capital spending accounted for most of the growth, increasing by 5.2 percentage points while remaining below 30% of total expenditures. Revenue grew by only 11%, much lower than budgeted because increases in certain import duties were reversed and surprisingly low tourist arrivals depressed tourism goods and services taxes despite a rate hike from 8% to 12% in November 2014. The fiscal deficit swelled to equal 7.4% of GDP, from 2.7% the previous year.

Most of the fiscal gap was financed domestically, through issuances of bonds and Treasury bills, and borrowing from other financial corporations. For the second time since issuances were conducted through a tap system in 2014, Treasury bill interest rates were cut in November, by about 400 basis points across all maturities (Figure 3.18.5). The value of Treasury bill issuances in November fell by 35.1% and for the whole year by 17.2%, while growth in the outstanding value slowed markedly to 12.9% from 36.0% in 2014. As a percentage of GDP, domestic public debt stood at 47.4%, and external public debt at 20.5%, pushing total public debt to 67.9%, or 1.4 percentage points higher than in 2014 (Figure 3.18.6).

Monetary policy remained broadly expansionary, with policy rates of liquidity windows kept low (1.5% for the overnight deposits and 10.0% for the overnight Lombard) and the required reserve ratio halved to 10% in August. Domestic assets expanded by 27.4% after falling by 1.6% in 2014, with most of the growth in domestic credit derived from claims on the public sector, largely government securities (Figure 3.18.7). Growth in credit to the private sector quickened to 12.6% from 3.1% in 2014. Growth in money supply slowed slightly from 14.7% in 2014 to 13.6% as net foreign assets fell by 2.6% following 5 years of rapid growth.

A larger trade deficit and a decline in the services surplus from lower tourism receipts widened the current account deficit substantially to 12.6% of GDP, the largest in 4 years (Figure 3.18.8). The trade deficit widened as exports, mainly fish and re-exports of fuel, fell sharply by 19.6% and imports, which are nearly 9 times exports, grew by 9.1% on higher transport and construction-related imports, notwithstanding low global oil and commodity prices.

Inflows of direct and other investments were lower than in 2014, and the net capital and financial accounts fell short of covering the current account deficit. Gross international reserves fell by $50.7 million to $564 million at year-end, although usable reserves—funds available for foreign exchange requirements—increased slightly by $49.7 million (Figure 3.18.9), with import coverage at less than a month.

Economic prospects

The growth outlook rests heavily on prospects for tourism and public-led investments. Growth will be driven in the near term by investment, as external economic developments will likely keep recovery in tourism modest and gradual over the forecast period.

3.18.3 Inflation

— Overall
— Food, including fish
— Housing, water, electricity, and gas
— Transport

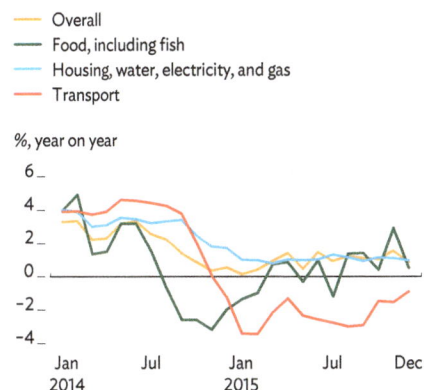

Sources: National Bureau of Statistics. 2016. *Consumer Price Index.* January. http://www.planning.gov.mv/; Maldives Monetary Authority. 2016. *Monthly Statistics.* January. http://www.mma.gov.mv
Click here for figure data

3.18.4 Fiscal indicators

■ Domestic revenue
■ Grants
■ Recurrent expenditure
■ Capital expenditure
— Fiscal deficit

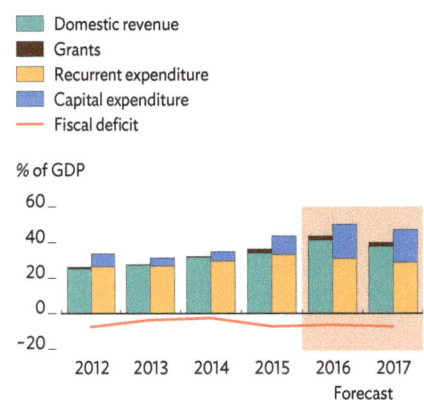

Source: Maldives Monetary Authority. 2016. *Monthly Statistics.* January. http://www.mma.gov.mv
Click here for figure data

3.18.5 Treasury bill interest rates

— 28 day
— 91 day
— 182 day
— 364 day

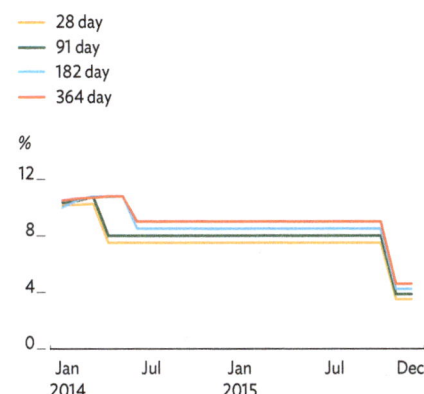

Source: Maldives Monetary Authority. 2016. *Monthly Statistics.* January. http://www.mma.gov.mv
Click here for figure data

Arrivals growth may pick up moderately to 5% in 2016, broadly in line with the tourism outlook for Asia. Bed-night occupancy and earnings are projected to recover to positive but minimal growth, held back by the short average stay preferred by Asian tourists.

The PRC will continue to lead arrivals growth, but less so in view of recent trends, notably moderating economic growth there and stronger competition from nearer destinations. A stronger pickup from Europe may be expected as economic recovery there gathers pace. Strengthened marketing, new flights, and the opening of 10 new resorts are seen to boost travel interest. Integrated resorts for the middle-income segment that are expected to open by 2017 would also help augment tourism numbers.

Growth will come largely from strong public investments fueling construction and real estate development. The government plans for its public sector investment program to grow by about 140% to Rf9.1 billion in 2016, with growth easing to 6% in 2017. Most of the investment surge is to be financed through external loans, while domestic borrowing is to be kept restrained. Correspondingly, budget expenditures are programmed to grow in 2016 by 23% and then moderate in 2017. The share of capital spending will rise to 39% in 2017 from 24% in 2015, while that of recurrent spending will decline to 61%. The budget deficit is expected to remain high at 6.5% of GDP in 2016 and 7.3% in 2017.

Assuming similar investment growth in 2015, construction-led industrial growth is projected to reach at least 20% in 2016 in conjunction with the public sector investment program before moderating slightly in 2017. Against this backdrop and the expected gradual recovery in tourism, GDP growth is projected to rise to 3.5% in 2016 and further to 3.9% in 2017. Growth could be much higher if tourism or foreign investment picks up faster than expected, or if oil prices and therefore fuel and electricity subsidies decline more than anticipated.

Inflation is expected to remain low at 1.2% in 2016, as the further easing of world oil and food prices will help offset upside pressures from expansionary policies. Inflation is seen edging up to 1.4% in 2017 as world prices recover modestly. The current account deficit is projected to remain large on strong construction-related imports and limited exports, despite likely higher tourism receipts and low world commodity prices.

Policy challenge—diversifying the economy

The economy depends heavily on tourism. In the last 10 years, tourism has come to account directly for around 30% of GDP—or nearly two-thirds if tourism-related sectors such as transportation and communications are included. This has increased the country's already high vulnerability to external shocks and GDP growth volatility. Tourism has created significant sources of government revenue, notably the goods and services tax on tourism. At the same time, though, the fiscal balance has become much more led by the business cycle. Stabilizing the economy and strengthening development depend on diversifying the economic base.

3.18.6 Public debt

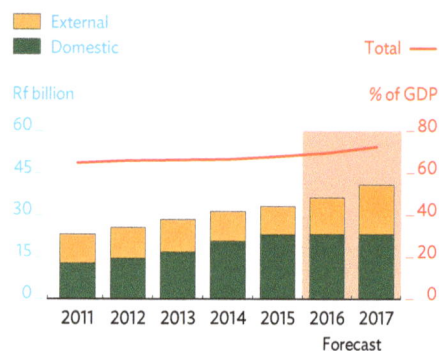

Sources: Maldives Monetary Authority. 2016. Monthly Statistics. January. http://www.mma.gov.mv; Ministry of Finance and Treasury. Budget in Statistics Financial Year 2016.
Click here for figure data

3.18.7 Contributions to money supply growth

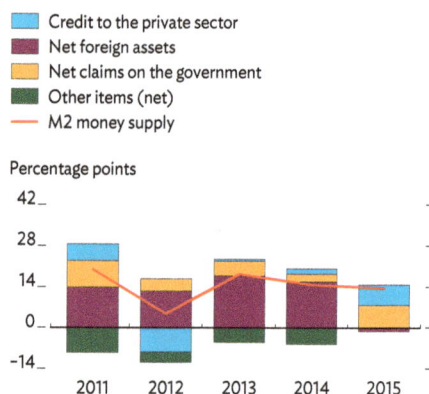

Source: Maldives Monetary Authority. 2016. Monthly Statistics. January. http://www.mma.gov.mv
Click here for figure data

3.18.8 Balance of payments

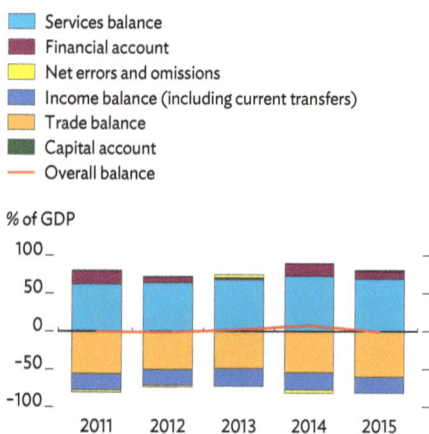

Source: Maldives Monetary Authority. 2016. Monthly Statistics. January. http://www.mma.gov.mv
Click here for figure data

In September 2014, the government introduced special economic zones (SEZs) for export processing, free trade, a high-technology park, and offshore financial services especially in Islamic finance. Early this year, the Maldives Monetary Authority began acquiring the capabilities necessary to screen and register companies for participation. SEZs can, if well managed, enable economic diversification into labor-intensive and strategic sectors, toward engendering economic stability and rapid growth. The country's existing liberal investment regime will help them succeed with a range of incentives, including 100% foreign ownership, long-term land leases, and freedom to employ foreign labor, among other rights. However, geographic and logistical conditions pose challenges to commercial viability.

The government plans to expand financial services through Islamic banking and a capital hub for channeling SEZ and tourism investments. The financial service sector is currently dominated by banks, which hold over 60% of financial assets (Figure 3.18.10). Although bank assets as a share of GDP are high, expansion has been volatile as most capital inflows and lending are connected with tourism. Sustained expansion has been restrained by sluggish credit to the private sector, a limited consumer market, high nonperforming loans, and the high cost of finance. The development of SEZs provides good potential to widen the market base—as can further development of a wider range of financial products and credit information and guarantee systems to help reduce credit risks.

Islamic finance was first introduced in 2005 through an insurance company that grew to become in 2011 a full-fledged bank offering various banking products and services in line with Islamic principles. Five licensed institutions currently offer Islamic finance, and traditional finance institutions have shown interest. The Maldives Monetary Authority is developing a legal, regulatory, and supervisory framework to facilitate further expansion of Islamic banking.

Institutional capacity for macroeconomic and fiscal management will likely need strengthening to enhance the SEZ growth strategy, as will expenditure management to ensure the sustainability of substantial external borrowing for infrastructure projects under expansionary fiscal programs for 2016 and 2017. Attracting more foreign direct investment for projects in the SEZs requires transparent and flexible currency convertibility and the honoring of contracts for existing foreign investments.

3.18.1 Selected economic indicators (%)

	2016	2017
GDP growth	3.5	3.9
Inflation	1.2	1.4
Current account balance (share of GDP)	–12.6	–10.5

Source: ADB estimates.

3.18.9 Gross international reserves

Source: Maldives Monetary Authority. 2016. *Monthly Statistics.* January. http://www.mma.gov.mv
Click here for figure data

3.18.10 Assets of financial corporations

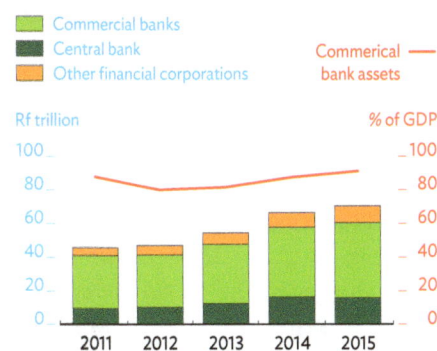

Source: Maldives Monetary Authority. 2016. *Monthly Statistics.* January. http://www.mma.gov.mv
Click here for figure data

Nepal

Devastating earthquakes late in FY2015 cut economic growth, and a surge in worker remittances expanded the current account surplus. Growth is expected to slide markedly in FY2016, affected by reconstruction delays, extended trade and transit disruptions as minority groups object to features of the newly announced constitution, and an unfavorable monsoon. Recovery in FY2017 is contingent on accelerating reconstruction and restoring trade and transit to normal.

Economic performance

GDP growth fell to 3.0% in FY2015 (ended 15 July 2015) from 5.1% a year earlier after earthquakes in April and May 2015 caused extensive damage to homes and other infrastructure and caused transport and supply disruptions (Figure 3.19.1). Growth in services, which account for over half of GDP, slowed to 3.9%, the lowest since 2012, as wholesale and retail trade, transport, tourism, and financial services were disrupted. Expansion in agriculture, which suffered earlier from an unfavorable monsoon, slowed to 1.9%. Persistent supply-side constraints, especially power shortages, held back growth in industry to a lackluster 2.6%.

Inflation averaged 7.2% in FY2015, down from 9.1% a year earlier and the lowest since FY2008, as prices moderated across the board (Figure 3.19.2). Despite a weak harvest and supply disrupted by the earthquakes in much of the country, food inflation eased to average 9.6%, which was still elevated but down from 11.6% in the previous year as food stocks proved adequate and relief operations effective, and as inflation fell in India, the country's major trading partner. Nonfood inflation also moderated to average 5.2%, down from 6.8% in FY2014 as the marked fall in global oil prices pulled down administered domestic prices aligned with them.

Although the FY2015 budget was announced in a timely manner, actual expenditure (equal to 20.0% of GDP) was just 81.0% of budget allocations, lower than the 84.0% achieved in the previous year. Expenditure was affected by disruptions from the earthquakes in the last quarter of the fiscal year, when expenditure bunching usually takes place, but the expenditure shortfall mainly reflected persistent procedural and procurement inefficiencies that impede capital spending and economic development. Actual capital spending fell 30.0% short of the budget allocation, a much larger shortfall than 21.6% a year earlier, and remained at only 4.0% of GDP (Figure 3.19.3).

Monetary conditions continued to be highly accommodative, as in the previous year. A surge in remittances bolstered bank deposits and reserves, but financial institutions struggled to find bankable projects

3.19.1 Supply-side contributions to growth

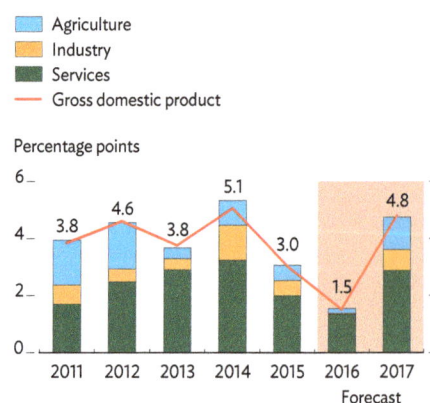

- Agriculture
- Industry
- Services
- Gross domestic product

Percentage points

Forecast

Note: Years are fiscal years ending on 15 July of that year.
Sources: Central Bureau of Statistics. 2015. *National Accounts of Nepal 2014/15.* http://cbs.gov.np/; ADB staff estimates.
Click here for figure data

3.19.2 Monthly inflation

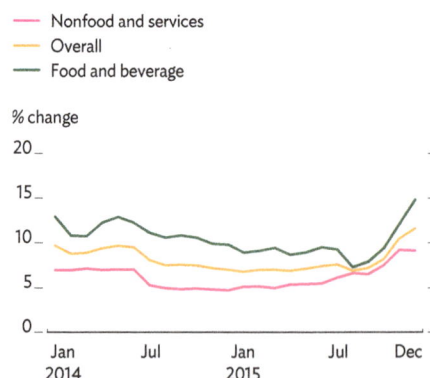

- Nonfood and services
- Overall
- Food and beverage

% change

Source: Nepal Rastra Bank. 2016. *Recent Macroeconomic Situation.* http://www.nrb.org.np
Click here for figure data

This chapter was written by Raju Tuladhar, Pradeep Singh, and Neelina Nakarmi of the Nepal Resident Mission, ADB, Kathmandu.

ready for investment. The average interbank rate increased to 0.70% from 0.22% the previous year, indicating that short-term liquidity management by Nepal Rastra Bank, the central bank, had become more effective (Figure 3.19.4). Weighted average deposit and lending rates continued to moderate, leaving real lending rates positive but real deposit rates negative. Growth in credit to the private sector picked up to 19.4% from 18.3% a year earlier (Figure 3.19.5). Although the central bank continued to direct financial institutions to channel credit to productive sectors to promote growth, private investment opportunities remained constrained by the persistent infrastructure deficit, other supply-side constraints, and political uncertainty.

A slowdown in imports combined with the surge in remittance inflows further expanded the current account surplus to 5.1% of GDP from 4.6% a year earlier (Figure 3.19.6). Despite the depreciation of the Nepalese rupee, which is pegged to the Indian rupee, exports declined by 3.9% as the currency appreciated in inflation-adjusted terms and because earthquakes disrupted production and transport services. Import growth slowed markedly to 8.0% from 13.9% in the previous year, mainly as imports of petroleum products declined by 19.0% from the combined effects of falling global oil prices and supply disruptions in the final months of the year. The trade deficit widened marginally to 31.2% of GDP from 30.7% in FY2014. Remittance inflows grew by 12.2% to equal a record 29.1% of GDP as migrant workers boosted their remittances to rebuild family homes and provide other post-earthquake support. The surplus in the overall balance of payments climbed to $1.5 billion, swelling gross foreign exchange reserves to $8.1 billion, enough to cover over 11 months of imports of goods and services (Figure 3.19.7).

Economic prospects

Economic growth is projected to slide further in FY2016 due to slow recovery from the earthquakes, political strife on the Terai plains bordering India, and an unfavorable monsoon for the second year running. Earthquake recovery has been dismayingly slow largely because the establishment of the National Reconstruction Authority was greatly delayed by political differences on its organizational structure and leadership. The high-powered authority—considered necessary for fast-tracking reconstruction through streamlined and prioritized program planning and implementation—was officially established only in December 2015 under revised legislation. While its head has been named, the organization has yet to become fully functional.

Although the Constituent Assembly, the second of which was elected in November 2013, finally enacted the long-pending new constitution on 20 September 2015, it did so amid protests from political parties on the Terai, which view as inadequate constitutional provisions for citizenship, provincial and electoral constituency delineation, and the representation of disadvantaged groups in state organizations. The protests escalated into disruptive strikes beginning in September that shut down trade through cross-border entry points with India, causing acute shortages of petroleum products, raw materials for construction and industry, and other essential commodities. Though Parliament (the successor

3.19.3 Fiscal indicators

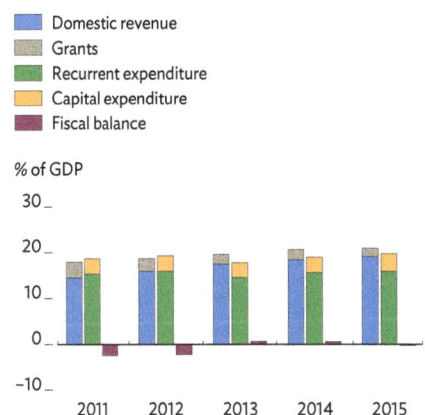

- Domestic revenue
- Grants
- Recurrent expenditure
- Capital expenditure
- Fiscal balance

Note: Years are fiscal years ending on 15 July of that year.
Source: Ministry of Finance. Budget Speech 2016.
Click here for figure data

3.19.4 Commercial banks' weighted average rates

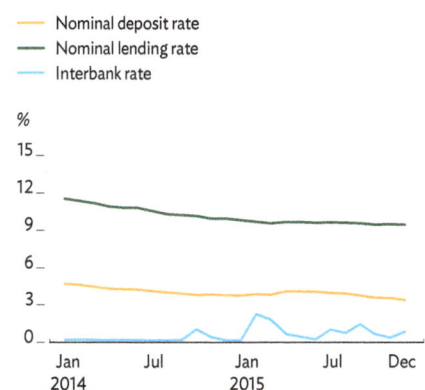

- Nominal deposit rate
- Nominal lending rate
- Interbank rate

Source: Nepal Rastra Bank. 2016. *Recent Macroeconomic Situation.* http://www.nrb.org.np
Click here for figure data

to the Constituent Assembly) passed several amendments to the new constitution on 23 January 2016 in response to demands for change, the Terai parties remain dissatisfied and continued their protests. On 8 February 2016, however, they withdrew their obstructions at the cross-border entry points, allowing trade to resume.

The constitutional dispute has adversely affected the ability of the new coalition government, formed soon after the enactment of the constitution, to roll out high-priority economic reforms committed to earlier in the reconstruction- and reform-oriented FY2016 budget. These include the enactment of a new electricity act, the electricity regulatory commission act, and the foreign investment and technology transfer act, which is essential for attracting private sector investment including foreign direct investment.

In light of the delayed implementation of reconstruction programs, trade and transit disruption, and the unfavorable monsoon, GDP growth is projected to slow further to 1.5% in FY2016, below the government's revised projection of 2.0%. Very low growth is seen in services, particularly in wholesale and retail trade, transport and communication, and tourism, which are worst affected by the supply disruptions. The Ministry of Agricultural Development expects harvests of paddy to drop by 10.0% and maize by 5.0%, slowing agriculture growth to a projected 0.5%. Industry is projected to see little or no growth owing to fuel shortages and the lack of raw materials for manufacturing and construction. GDP growth in FY2017 could rebound to 4.8%, but this assumes a normal monsoon, the National Reconstruction Authority becoming fully operational and accelerating reconstruction, normal cross-border trade, and progress in resolving domestic political tensions.

Inflation is projected to rise to 10.5%, higher than the target of 8.5% set by the central bank in its FY2016 monetary policy. Although lower global oil prices are being passed through to administered fuel prices (a policy adopted in September 2014), average inflation in FY2016 will be elevated on the combined effects of a smaller harvest, acute shortages of fuel and other essential commodities, and higher transport costs during much of the year. Food inflation is expected to average 11.8% and nonfood inflation 9.5%. Inflation is projected to subside to 8.2% in FY2017. This assumes a normal harvest, fuel and other commodity supplies returning to normal, and lower global prices for oil and other commodities.

Nepal's external position is expected to further strengthen in FY2016 with surpluses in both the current account and the overall balance of payments above the already high surpluses of FY2015. The trade deficit is expected to narrow sharply on an 8.0% decline in imports resulting from the trade and transit disruption and lower prices for petroleum imports. The narrowing will come despite a 15.0% fall in exports, which are much smaller than imports. The significant narrowing of the trade deficit coupled with a continued rise in remittances is expected to further expand the current account surplus to equal 10.3% of GDP. In FY2017, the current account surplus is expected to narrow again to 6.4% of GDP as import growth recovers on the resolution of trade obstruction and the increase in import demand with the acceleration of reconstruction programs, and with some slowdown in remittance inflows affected by weakening demand for labor in host countries.

3.19.1 Selected economic indicators (%)

	2016	2017
GDP growth	1.5	4.8
Inflation	10.5	8.2
Current account balance (share of GDP)	10.3	6.4

Note: Years are fiscal years ending on 30 June of that year.

Source: ADB estimates.

3.19.5 Credit to the private sector and money growth

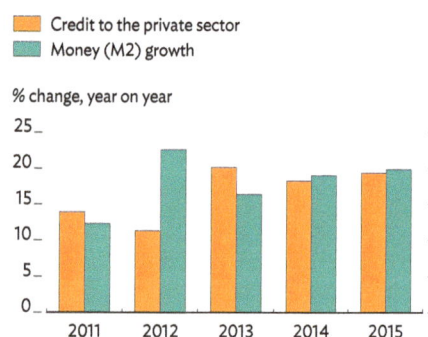

Credit to the private sector
Money (M2) growth

Note: Years are fiscal years ending on 15 July of that year.
Source: Nepal Rastra Bank. 2016. Recent Macroeconomic Situation. http://www.nrb.org.np
Click here for figure data

Policy challenge—accelerating reconstruction and capital expenditure

The devastating earthquakes challenged Nepal's growth and development prospects over the short to medium term. The disaster exacted a huge human toll, taking nearly 9,000 lives and destroying 750,000 homes, factories, and cultural heritage sites. It upended the livelihoods of 5.4 million, pushing an estimated 3.0% of the population into poverty. The government's post-disaster needs assessment estimated $5.2 billion in capital stock losses and another $1.9 billion in economic losses. The combined losses are estimated to equal one-third of GDP. The cost of recovery and rebuilding the lost capital stock is estimated at $6.7 billion (Table 3.19.1).

Notwithstanding the significant cost of reconstruction and recovery, the key policy challenge is not a dearth of resources. Nepal's development partners pledged $4.0 billion in reconstruction aid during the International Conference on Nepal's Reconstruction that the government successfully organized in the aftermath of the earthquakes. Further, in response to the earthquakes, the government presented an ambitious budget for FY2016, which calls for total spending to increase to equal 32.1% of GDP from 24.3% in FY2015, while capital expenditure is to more than double to 10.0% of GDP (Figure 3.19.8). The $910 million allocation for reconstruction is nearly half of the capital budget.

However, more than 8 months into the fiscal year, only a small fraction of the reconstruction budget has actually been spent, reflecting institutional and procedural bottlenecks that constrain the timely execution of capital works. Key factors holding back rapid reconstruction include (i) delay in establishing the National Reconstruction Authority, which particularly affected the speedy initiation of housing reconstruction; (ii) significant damage in vast rural areas with difficult access; (iii) the limited capacity of sector institutions that oversee private housing, schools, hospitals, roads, and other community infrastructure to assess damage, plan reconstruction, procure materials, and implement reconstruction with quality control; and (iv) the limited availability of such human resources as masons, engineers, and social workers.

There has nevertheless been progress in pre-construction activities, as the National Reconstruction Authority was finally established and its head appointed in December 2015 toward beginning significant physical reconstruction by April 2016. To make up for the delay, significant efforts are required toward (i) fully operationalizing the authority with a lean structure and autonomy to effectively monitor, coordinate, and enforce timely delivery by designated agencies; (ii) ensuring the quality of design and implementation toward building back better; (iii) building and supplementing capacity in relevant institutions through outsourcing and management support; (iv) assembling and training a sufficient number of skilled and semiskilled workers for reconstruction; and (v) ensuring transparency and accountability in program delivery with community participation.

3.19.6 Current account indicators

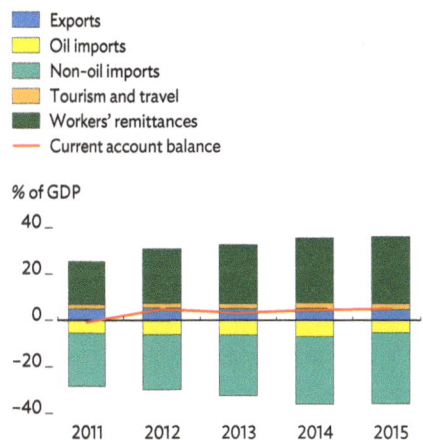

Note: Years are fiscal years ending on 15 July of that year.
Source: Nepal Rastra Bank. 2016. *Recent Macroeconomic Situation.* http://www.nrb.org.np
Click here for figure data

3.19.7 Gross international reserves and exchange rate

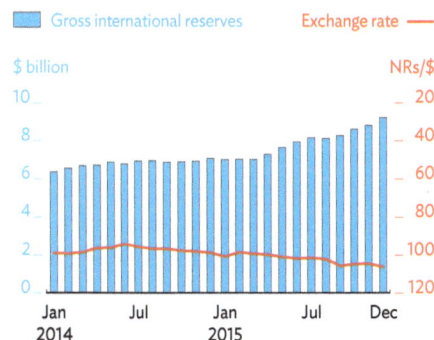

Source: Nepal Rastra Bank. 2016. *Recent Macroeconomic Situation.* http://www.nrb.org.np
Click here for figure data

3.19.1 Damage, losses, and reconstruction needs ($ billion)

Sectors	Damage	Losses	Reconstruction needs
Social: cultural heritage, education, health, housing and human settlements, and nutrition	3.6	0.5	4.1
Productive: agriculture, finance, industry, commerce, irrigation, and tourism	0.6	1.2	1.8
Infrastructure: communications, community infrastructure, electricity, transport, water, and sanitation	0.5	0.1	0.7
Cross-cutting: gender, social protection, employment and livelihoods, disaster risk reduction, environment and forestry, and governance	0.5	0	0.5
Total	5.2	1.9	7.1

Source: National Planning Commission.

Parallel to accelerating reconstruction, scaling up capital expenditure on critical infrastructure for energy, transport, urban amenities, and irrigation remains a key priority toward attaining higher economic growth that is inclusive and sustainable. Capital spending has been persistently weak at the equivalent of about 4.0% of GDP annually, but spending at 8.2%–11.8% of GDP is required to close existing infrastructure gaps within a decade. Nepal's robust fiscal balance in recent years suggests that there are substantial fiscal resources with which to expand capital expenditures. Current circumstances call for wider and longer-term reform and capacity development in investment planning, budget formulation and execution, and project management including design, procurement, and implementation that is timely and cost-effective and has good quality control.

Likewise, investment in human capital development needs to be enhanced in terms of both amount and quality. Despite substantial achievement of Millennium Development Goals related to education, Nepal's human capital base remains very weak, with only 14% of 16-year-olds earning school completion certificates. The country cannot afford to be complacent but needs to substantially improve its delivery of education services in primary schools, technical education and vocational training centers, and universities. This calls for accelerating reform to improve the quality of education and learning outcomes through the early enactment of the proposed education act, restructuring of school and examination systems, improvement of teacher management and development, and establishment of strong and regular mechanisms to guide the reform process.

These efforts to build critical infrastructure and human capital need to be accompanied by economic and sector reform as announced in the FY2016 budget. Reform can engender an enabling environment to attract private sector investments into the country's competitive industries such as high-value agriculture and agro-processing, hydropower, labor-intensive and other competitive manufacturing, and high-value services such as tourism and information and communication technology. Priorities include legislative reform to promote public–private partnership, efficient budgetary processes and management, industrial enterprise development, agribusiness promotion, and institutional and regulatory restructuring of the energy sector.

3.19.8 Budgeted and actual capital spending

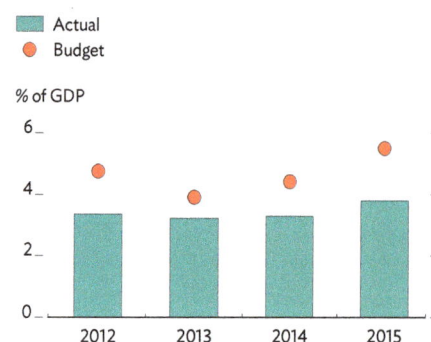

Sources: Central Bureau of Statistics. http://cbs.gov.np/; Ministry of Finance. Budget speech (various years).
Click here for figure data

Pakistan

The economy continued to pick up in FY2015 as economic reform progressed and security improved. Inflation markedly declined, and the current account deficit narrowed with favorable prices for oil and other commodities. Despite global headwinds, the outlook is for continued moderate growth as structural and macroeconomic reform deepens. Persistence will be required to overcome longstanding structural impediments to investment and enable faster growth.

Economic performance

GDP growth edged up slightly to 4.2% in FY2015 (ended 30 June 2015) but remained below the government target of 5.0% (Figure 3.20.1). Services expanded by 5.0% and remained the largest contributor to growth in FY2015, as agriculture and manufacturing posted more modest gains. Growth in services was led by recovery in finance and insurance that reflected higher profits and in general government services, which expanded on higher infrastructure spending and wages. Continued energy shortages, slowing external demand, and a base effect on food and fertilizers pushed down expansion in large-scale manufacturing to 3.3%. Continued resilience in small-scale manufacturing and a pickup in construction to double digits supported industry growth at 3.6% that was nevertheless nearly a full percentage point lower than a year earlier.

Consumption grew by 5.1% in FY2015 and remained the largest demand-side component in GDP. Private consumption expanded by 3.6%, benefitting from continued inflows of remittances, higher public sector salaries, and low inflation, while public consumption rebounded to grow by 16% (Figure 3.20.2). Total investment increased to equal 15.1% of GDP in FY2015, largely on higher public fixed investment. Private fixed investment edged lower to 9.7% of GDP from 10.0% a year earlier, hampered by continued energy constraints and the generally weak business environment that has depressed investment for several years. Net exports subtracted from growth for a second consecutive year as exports fell more sharply than imports.

Average consumer price inflation decelerated by almost half to 4.5% in FY2015 in line with lower global prices for oil and food. Inflation was down across all major groups. It fell to 3.2% year on year in June 2015 from 7.2% a year earlier (Figure 3.20.3). Food inflation was very slight for nearly a year to October 2015 if compared with high rates 12 months earlier. With the fading of a high base effect, inflation rose again in the first 7 months of FY2016, though in January 2016 it was a moderate 3.3%.

3.20.1 Supply-side contributions to growth

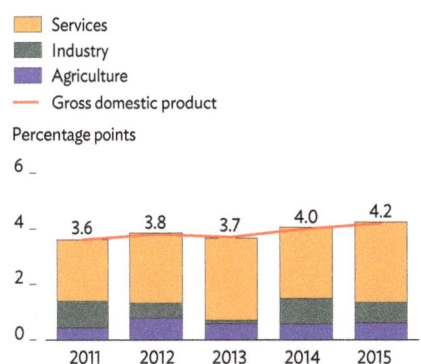

- Services
- Industry
- Agriculture
- Gross domestic product

Percentage points

Note: Years are fiscal years ending on 30 June of that year.
Source: Ministry of Finance. *Pakistan Economic Survey 2015–16.* http://www.finance.gov.pk
Click here for figure data

3.20.2 Demand-side contributions to growth

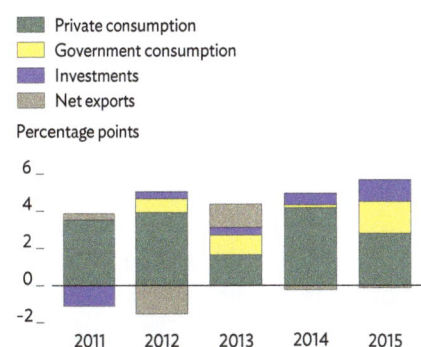

- Private consumption
- Government consumption
- Investments
- Net exports

Percentage points

Note: Years are fiscal years ending on 30 June of that year.
Source: Ministry of Finance. *Pakistan Economic Survey 2015–16.* http://www.finance.gov.pk
Click here for figure data

This chapter was written by Farzana Noshab of the Pakistan Resident Mission, ADB, Islamabad.

The State Bank of Pakistan, the central bank, significantly eased monetary policy in FY2015 as inflation fell and the government borrowed less from it. The central bank cut policy rates by a cumulative 300 basis points in four steps from November 2014 to May 2015 to lower its lending rate to banks (the reverse repurchase rate) to 7.0%. To improve transmission of monetary policy, the central bank introduced from 1 June 2015 the policy rate, a new target for operations in the money market that will be maintained 50 basis points below the reverse repurchase rate, as it narrowed the interest rate corridor to 200 basis points. Subsequently, to support domestic credit growth, it lowered in September all corridor rates by 50 basis points to bring the new policy rate to 6.0% (Figure 3.20.4).

The consolidated budget deficit excluding grants equaled 5.4% of GDP in FY2015, marginally lower than in the previous year (Figure 3.20.5). Nevertheless, recent performance is markedly better than the average deficit of 8.1% of GDP during FY2011–FY2013, as notable progress was achieved in reining in energy subsidies and boosting tax revenues by eliminating many concessions and exemptions. On the expenditure side, increases in power tariffs reduced total budget subsidies to 1.0% of GDP. Another achievement was to increase funding for the public sector development program to 3.7% of GDP from an average 3.4% during FY2012–FY2014. That the primary deficit (the overall deficit less interest payments) meanwhile fell more steeply than the overall deficit—to 0.7% of GDP from 4.1% in FY2013— underlines how rapidly interest payments on the public debt are expanding.

Government revenue was, at 14.4% of GDP in FY2015, marginally lower than in the previous year as larger tax collection was offset by the normalization of nontax revenue receipts, which had ballooned in the preceding year with one-off events. Tax collection by the Federal Board of Revenue enjoyed double-digit growth that still fell short of the ambitious budget target. Slower growth in both direct taxes and general sales tax reflected weakness in manufacturing, declining imports, and lower inflation crimping the tax base. Tax as a share of GDP is, at 11%, very low compared with other Asian economies. Ongoing reform aims to widen the tax net, improve tax administration, and eliminate distortions in the tax system.

The budget deficit was financed mostly by heavy borrowing from commercial banks (Figure 3.20.6). Nearly 80% of the expansion in banking system credit during FY2015 went to the government. Despite ample liquidity provided by the central bank, growth in private credit slowed to PRs209 billion from PRs371 billion a year earlier. Credit demand for working capital including trade finance slowed as commodity prices declined, power shortages continued, and external demand remained weak. Loans for fixed investment increased markedly, albeit from a small base.

Total public debt marginally declined to the equivalent of 64.8% of GDP in FY2015 from 65.1% the previous year, but it remained above the 60% threshold set under the Fiscal Responsibility Debt Limitation Act, 2005 (Figure 3.20.7). Foreign public debt fell to 20.3% of GDP from 21.6% as domestic public debt increased by 1 percentage point to 44.5%

3.20.3 Inflation

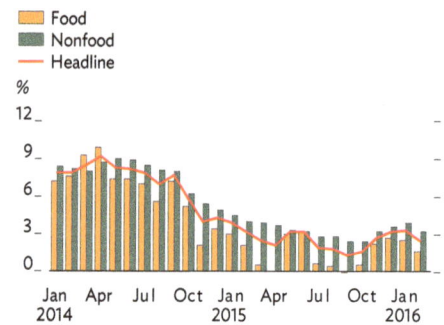

Source: State Bank of Pakistan. Economic Data. http://www.sbp.org.pk (accessed 21 March 2016).
Click here for figure data

3.20.4 Interest rates

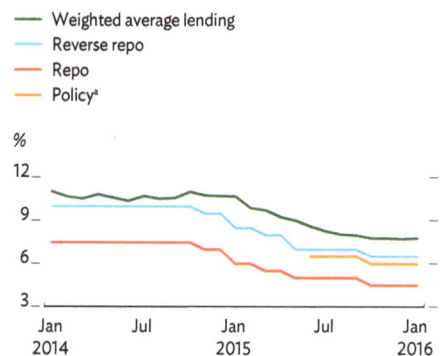

a The new policy or target rate was introduced by the State Bank of Pakistan on 15 May 2015.
Source: State Bank of Pakistan. Economic Data. http://www.sbp.org.pk (accessed 21 March 2016).
Click here for figure data

3.20.5 Government budget indicators

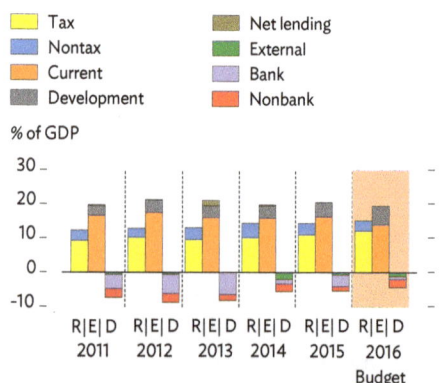

R = revenue, E = expenditure, D = deficit financing.
Notes: Years are fiscal years ending on 30 June of that year. Data refer to consolidated federal and provincial government finances. Net lending includes statistical discrepancy. Nonbank includes privatization proceeds.
Source: Ministry of Finance. Pakistan Economic Survey 2015–2016. http://www.finance.gov.pk
Click here for figure data

of GDP, excluding power sector arrears at 0.8%. Better public debt management has reduced the share of short-term domestic debt by 14% since 2013, lengthening the maturity profile. However, half of domestic debt is still short term and vulnerable to interest rate variation.

The current account deficit eased to the equivalent of 1.0% of GDP in FY2015 from 1.3% a year earlier (Figure 3.20.8). The trade deficit widened by 3.8% to $17.2 billion as exports fell by 4.0%, mainly from a marked drop in textile and cotton exports, while the large decline in oil import payments was largely offset by increased quantities of other imports—including consumer goods, textile raw materials, iron and steel, and selected food items—such that total imports fell by only 0.9%. Deficits in both services and primary income also widened, but an 18.2% gain in worker remittances to $18.7 billion nevertheless brought modest improvement in the current account deficit.

Economic prospects

GDP growth is expected to accelerate modestly to 4.5% in FY2016 and 4.8% in FY2017, assuming continued macroeconomic stability, expected improvement in energy supply, and planned infrastructure investment tied to an economic corridor project linking Pakistan with the People's Republic of China (PRC). Further implementation of structural reform will consolidate recent gains in macroeconomic stability and improve the investment climate as the security situation improves, especially in Karachi, the commercial hub of the country.

Growth in industry is expected to be driven by strong expansion in construction and continued moderate expansion in mining, utilities, and manufacturing. Growth in large-scale manufacturing accelerated to 3.9% in the first half of FY2016 from 2.7% in the same period of last year, supported by low prices for raw materials, improved gas and electricity supply, and expanded construction, as well as lower interest rates (Figure 3.20.9). However, textile production, the largest segment, grew by only 1.0% during the first half and is expected to constrain overall growth in large-scale manufacturing this year, partly because of weaker demand in export markets and rising competition. Strong construction that reflects government spending on development and large investments in power projects has pushed up cement production.

Agriculture is likely to continue to grow only moderately, as cotton output is projected to fall because of heavy rains in July 2015 and much lower global cotton prices. However, continued strong expansion in livestock, which accounts for over half of agricultural production, will partly offset reductions elsewhere. The government introduced an agriculture support package in September 2015 that offers cash transfers to cotton growers, tax concessions for imports of agricultural machinery, and subsidies for fertilizers. Growth in services will be led largely by transport improvements and higher profits for financial services, though retail and wholesale trade should also benefit from improved industrial activity.

Consumption will expand with low inflation, higher public sector salaries and pensions, and government employment schemes in the auto industry, but a slowdown in remittances and lower commodity

3.20.6 Budget borrowing from banks

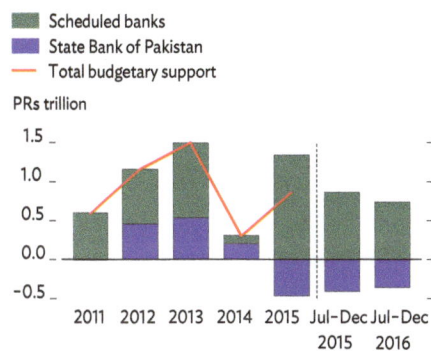

Note: Years are fiscal years ending on 30 June of that year.
Source: State Bank of Pakistan. Economic Data. http://www.sbp.org.pk (accessed 18 March 2016).
Click here for figure data

3.20.7 Public debt

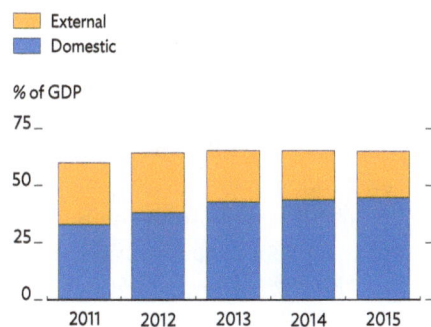

Note: Years are fiscal years ending on 30 June of that year.
Source: State Bank of Pakistan. Economic Data. http://www.sbp.org.pk (accessed 22 March 2016).
Click here for figure data

3.20.8 Current account components

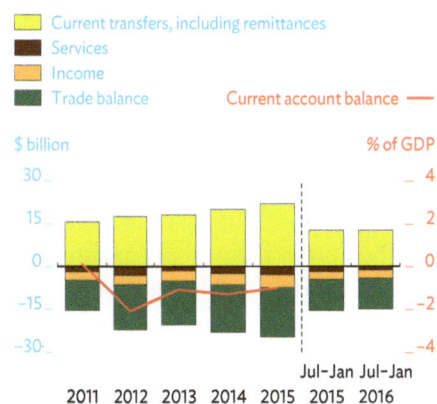

Note: Years are fiscal years ending on 30 June of that year.
Source: State Bank of Pakistan. Economic Data. http://www.sbp.org.pk (accessed 14 March 2016).
Click here for figure data

prices are expected to retard growth in rural incomes and spending. Private investment should pick up in line with monetary easing and the improved security situation. Military operations in parts of the country have significantly curtailed the terror attacks that had hampered economic activity in recent years. Net private credit flows more than doubled during the first 7 months of FY2016, mainly for fixed investment and working capital in manufacturing, electricity, and construction. Net exports will continue to be a drag on growth as exports falter and lower oil imports are offset by higher quantities of other imports.

Inflation is expected to average 3.2% in FY2016, reflecting lower global oil and commodity prices. In the first 8 months of the fiscal year, inflation averaged only 2.5%, with food inflation at 1.5% and other inflation at 3.2%. Tax adjustments on some imports in December 2015 are expected, however, to push inflation up marginally in the remaining months of the fiscal year. Inflation is expected to pick up to 4.5% in FY2017, mainly because of a slight recovery expected in global oil prices, firmer prices for other international commodities, and somewhat higher domestic demand.

The central bank stood by its accommodative monetary stance as inflation fell. In September, it reduced the policy rate, effective in October, by 50 basis points to 6%, the lowest in decades. Net credit to the private sector expanded by PRs310 billion during the first 7 months of FY2015 from PRs164 billion in the same period of the previous year, reflecting monetary easing and capacity improvements. The government borrowed heavily from commercial banks to finance the deficit and to retire its debt to the central bank.

The FY2016 budget targets a lower fiscal deficit equal to 4.3% of GDP, to be achieved by both boosting revenue and containing expenditure. Revenues are budgeted to increase by 17.6% and expenditure by 7.0%. Federal Board of Revenue tax collection during the first half of FY2016 fell below target partly because lower oil prices undercut import duty collection (Figure 3.20.10). To offset the revenue shortfall, the excise duty on cigarettes was increased, and regulatory duties and additional customs duties were imposed on a variety of products, especially luxury goods, effective on 1 December 2015. The government further curtailed tax concessions and exemptions in February 2016.

On the spending side, the government is selectively trimming current and capital spending, which includes absorbing the cost of the agricultural support package announced in September. Budgetary allocations for the public sector development program in FY2016 were increased by 50% over the amount actually spent in the previous year. The higher allocations include extending the Benazir Income Support Program to 5.3 million beneficiaries and the rollout of a conditional cash-transfer program for education that will benefit 1 million children by the end of the fiscal year. Moreover, 11% of spending is earmarked for transport projects under the economic corridor project with the PRC. Budgetary spending on untargeted subsidies, including for electric power, was reduced by a third over the past 3 years as the government raised power tariffs to bring them close to cost recovery.

3.20.9 Large-scale manufacturing

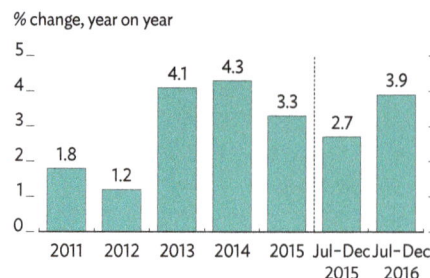

% change, year on year

Note: Years are fiscal years ending on 30 June of that year.
Source: State Bank of Pakistan. Economic Data. http://www.sbp.org.pk (accessed 26 January 2016).
Click here for figure data

3.20.10 Federal Board of Revenue tax collection

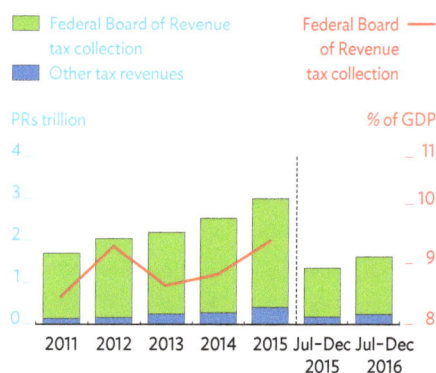

Note: Years are fiscal years ending on 30 June of that year.
Source: State Bank of Pakistan. Economic Data. http://www.sbp.org.pk (accessed 14 March 2016).
Click here for figure data

3.20.1 Selected economic indicators (%)

	2016	2017
GDP growth	4.5	4.8
Inflation	3.2	4.5
Current account balance (share of GDP)	–1.0	–1.2

Note: Years are fiscal years ending on 30 June of that year.
Source: ADB estimates.

Nevertheless, the past accumulation of inter-company arrears in the sector, or circular debt amounting to $3 billion at the end of June 2015, is a fiscal risk that will only worsen with any more buildup. However, low global prices for oil, which fuels a third of power generation in the country, have temporarily lifted some of the financial pressure on these high-cost producers. Construction on larger and more efficient plants is rapidly proceeding.

The current account deficit in FY2016 is projected to remain low at 1.0% of GDP for a second year in a row as prices for oil and other commodities stay low and inflows continue under the Coalition Support Fund—despite declining exports and slowing growth in remittances. The current account deficit fell to 1.2% of GDP during the first 7 months of FY2016 from 1.7% a year earlier as trade and services deficits narrowed. Import payments fell by 7.0% on divergent developments: food and petroleum products, which together account for about one-third of imports, fell by 32% because of high domestic wheat stocks and the drop in global oil prices. Meanwhile, all other imports grew by 8.3% on quantity increases for textile raw materials (reflecting the drop in domestic cotton production), fertilizers, and power generation machinery (reflecting major investment in the power sector). The savings from lower import payments were more than offset by an 11.4% fall in export receipts over the period, reflecting lower quantities and prices.

Challenges for export growth are generally weak external demand, growth moderation in the PRC, Pakistan rupee appreciation against the euro, lost textile market share to new competitors, and unfavorable terms of trade for exports with little value added. Persistent rupee appreciation, by 20% in real terms over the past 2 years, has adversely affected export competitiveness (Figure 3.20.11). The rupee continued to be a relatively strong currency as the US dollar strengthened in the first half of FY2016, depreciating by only 2.8% to PRs104.9 per dollar. Assuming some revival in prices for oil and other commodities, larger imports to support higher investment and growth, and some improvement in exports as factories enjoy better power supply, the current account deficit is projected to widen to 1.2% of GDP in FY2017.

Workers remittances expanded by only 6% in the first 7 months of FY2016, down from an average of 15% annually in the previous 6 years, the falloff likely reflecting reduced oil incomes in the Gulf, a major host region. As remittances significantly contribute receipts and buffer against external shocks, any sustained slowdown on top of falling exports would create concern for the stability of external accounts.

Official foreign exchange reserves expanded to $15.4 billion in January 2016 (Figure 3.20.12). The financial account was strengthened by a $500 million euro bond issued in September 2015 and larger multilateral disbursements in the first 7 months of FY2016. However, inflows that do not create debt continued to be limited, as foreign direct investment increased only slightly to $624 million, with inflows mainly into electric power and oil and gas, while portfolio investment amounted to only $155 million.

3.20.11 Exchange rates

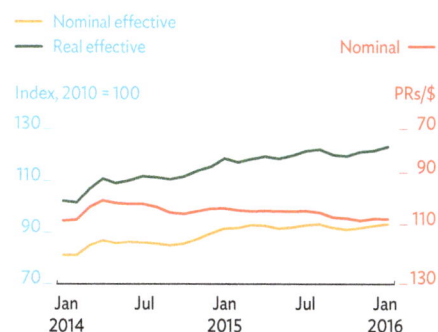

Source: CEIC Data Company (accessed 8 March 2016).
Click here for figure data

3.20.12 Gross international reserves

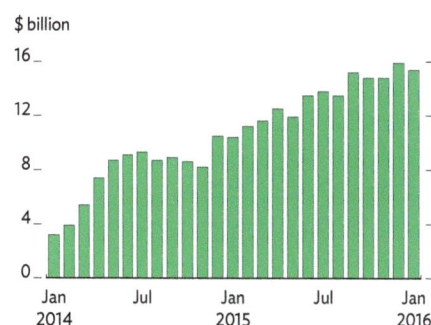

Source: State Bank of Pakistan. Economic Data.
http://www.sbp.org.pk (accessed 14 March 2016).
Click here for figure data

Policy challenge—economic reform to lift growth

Achieving high and sustainable growth has been a challenge for
Pakistan. Growth has been volatile, with periodic episodes of high
growth followed by spells of low growth as economic reform is
implemented only sporadically and incompletely (Figure 3.20.13).
GDP growth fell to an average of 2.8% during FY2009–FY2013 from
6.6% during FY2004–FY2008. Longer-term growth potential has also
declined. Studies that have disaggregated growth into supply-side
components suggest that the contributions of productivity gains and
capital accumulation have slipped.

Challenges that impede growth in Pakistan include weak
infrastructure and transport connectivity and inadequate workforce
skills, governance and institutions, service delivery, and access to finance.

Limited public resources constrain investment in infrastructure
for energy, transport, irrigation, and urban services. This impairs
connectivity, raises the cost of doing business, restrains productivity,
and blocks access to public services. Governance and institutional
challenges across all sectors undermine effective public service
delivery and obstruct private sector development. Operational losses
incurred by many large public enterprises drain already meager public
resources. These challenges are most obvious in the energy sector and
its deficient infrastructure. Inadequate investment has weakened human
development, and the resulting dearth of skills hampers the country's
ability to compete in global markets and transition to production with
higher value added. Access to finance is limited as the financial system
lacks depth because of constrains on both demand and supply.

These barriers are reflected in Pakistan's low ranking in the
World Bank's *Doing Business Report 2016*, at 138 out of 189 economies
surveyed. Policies to alleviate these constraints would help improve
the business climate, raise domestic savings and investment, boost
competitiveness and exports, and improve public service delivery,
thereby boosting productivity and growth.

The government is currently implementing a structural reform
program to relieve constraints on growth by improving service delivery
in energy and other infrastructure sectors, expanding fiscal space,
fostering a competitive business environment, liberalizing trade, and
restructuring or privatizing public enterprises.

Economic reform and an improving security environment should
further boost business confidence and foster private investment.
Ongoing reforms to address the power deficit, which is the greatest
impediment to manufacturing and growth, have shown progress.
Improved governance in the energy sector has reduced power outages
for industry, improved tariff revenue recovery, and curtailed line losses.
Initiatives to monitor the performance of power distribution companies
and to introduce multiyear tariffs aim to improve efficiency and
strengthen the regulatory environment.

With power tariffs gradually moving toward market-based
pricing, power sector subsidies are contained, thus leaving funds for
infrastructure spending. Reform is under way to raise tax revenues and
widen the tax base through improved governance of tax administration
supported by legislative action. The government has also initiated a

3.20.13 GDP growth

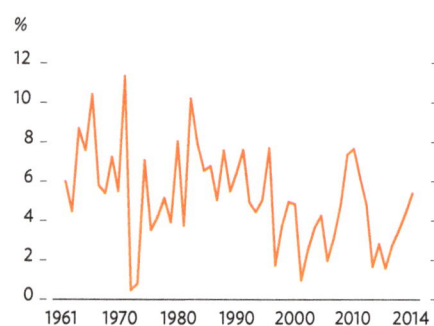

Note: Years are fiscal years ending on 30 June of that year.
Source: World Bank. World Development Indicators online
database (accessed 18 March 2016).
Click here for figure data

process for restructuring and possibly privatizing prioritized public enterprises under a dedicated reform strategy. Besides providing fiscal relief and improving service delivery, efficiency improvements thanks to these reforms are critical to improving the competitiveness of downstream industries that depend on production from these enterprises for inputs.

The government's plan to improve the business climate addresses issues across the board: obtaining construction permits, paying taxes, enforcing contracts, starting businesses, trading across borders, and accessing credit. As the first step, the government introduced one-stop shops online to facilitate new business registration, streamline firms' navigation of business regulations and bureaucratic procedures, and reduce the cost of doing business. It started to remove statutory tax concessions and exemptions, reduce maximum import tariff rates, and institute a simpler tariff system with fewer slabs. The National Financial Inclusion Strategy was launched in May 2015 to broaden access to finance. The enactment of the Credit Bureau Bill aims to support financial institutions' extension of credit to more small and medium-sized enterprises. The Deposit Protection Fund is being set up to establish a modern deposit insurance mechanism to strengthen financial stability.

A sustained reform effort will be required over the medium to long term to boost productivity and potential growth, building on the progress achieved so far. Reform needs to be supplemented by other policy measures, including the formulation of a well-coordinated industrial policy to support faster growth and revive exports. While the government is committed to its reform program, implementation challenges that include resistance from various stakeholders could slow progress. In addition, domestic security concerns remain despite improvement, and natural disasters are a perennial downside risk. The price of oil remains a wildcard.

Sri Lanka

Growth was marginally lower in 2015, but the current account deficit improved slightly and inflation moderated. Meanwhile, the budget deficit widened, and foreign exchange reserves dropped sharply. The government will have to work to realign fiscal policy toward putting the country on a high and sustainable growth track.

Economic performance

Economic expansion has markedly slowed in the past 3 years from the rapid pace of the post-conflict economic boom. Provisional estimates place growth at 4.8% in 2015, marginally lower than 4.9% expansion a year earlier (Figure 3.21.1). Weak global demand and political change characterized the year, as did an expansive fiscal policy following presidential elections in January and parliamentary contests in August that established a coalition cabinet. Investment faltered as investors decided to wait and see, and as the new administration cut capital spending and temporarily suspended some large investment projects approved by its predecessor. A surge in private and government consumption spending was left to sustain growth during the year.

On the supply side, 5.3% expansion in the large service sector was the main driver of growth as the contribution from industry declined. The higher outcome for services came from acceleration in financial activities and in transportation of goods and passengers. Agriculture expanded by 5.5%, up from 4.9% a year earlier as the paddy harvest recovered and the production of fruit and vegetables increased— and despite lower output of tea and rubber, two major export crops. Expansion in industry slowed to 3.0% from 3.5% a year earlier, dragging down growth. Apparel production stagnated on weak external demand, though the important food-processing industry expanded by 5.4% even as exports slumped. Weakness in industry mainly reflected a 0.9% decline in construction caused by a marked fall in public and private investment.

Preliminary demand-side estimates of real GDP are not available, but nominal expenditure was estimated by the Central Bank of Sri Lanka. Central bank projections of private and government consumption expenditure indicate much higher growth in 2015 than in 2014, while investment, exports, and imports fell (Figure 3.21.2). Government consumption accelerated to 25.3% growth from 15.9% in 2014, reflecting higher pay and allowances for public employees. Expansion in private spending picked up to 8.0% from 4.7% in 2014 on higher salaries and larger transfers. Fixed capital investment slowed to

3.21.1 GDP growth by sector

- Agriculture
- Industry
- Services
- Gross domestic product

Percentage points

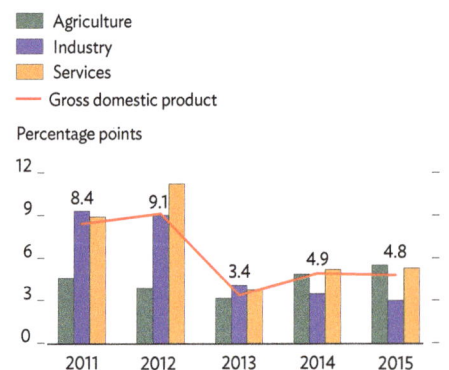

Source: Department of Census and Statistics Sri Lanka. http://www.statistics.gov.lk/ (accessed on 12 February 2016).
Click here for figure data

3.21.2 GDP growth by demand components

- 2014
- 2015 Central Bank of Sri Lanka projection

Percentage points

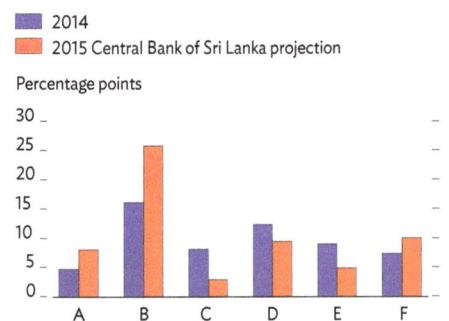

A = private consumption expenditure, B = government consumption expenditure, C = investment, D = exports of goods and services, E = imports of goods and services, F = GDP at market prices.
Source: Central Bank of Sri Lanka. Recent Economic Developments for 2014 and Prospects for 2015. http://www.cbsl.gov.lk
Click here for figure data

This chapter was written by Tadateru Hayashi, Nimali Hasitha Wickremasinghe, and Savindi Jayakody of the Sri Lanka Resident Mission, ADB, Colombo.

2.9% as spending on large infrastructure projects slowed and private investors adopted a cautious approach.

Average annual inflation, as measured by the national consumer price index, moderated to 3.8% in 2015 (Box 3.21.1). While food inflation was almost 20% in January and February 2015, it subsequently stabilized to bring average annual food inflation to 5.4%. At the same time, nonfood inflation hovered at around 2% in the first half of 2015. It trended up in the second half partly because of Sri Lankan rupee depreciation from September but averaged only 2.6% for the year. Overall inflation was 4.2% year on year in December 2015, but in January 2016 prices were 0.7% below those a year earlier because of a sharp fall in food prices from December highs and a large base effect (Figure 3.21.3).

Credit to the private sector accelerated sharply from mid-2014 to reach 25.1% in December 2015 (Figure 3.21.4). Much of the growth was from expansion in consumer credit fueled by excess liquidity in the domestic money market. In view of growing pressure on the balance of payments and foreign exchange reserves, the central bank tightened its monetary policy and in mid-January 2016 raised the statutory reserve ratio by 1.5 percentage points to 7.5% (Figure 3.21.5). As a result, excess liquidity declined to SLRs42 billion from SLRs90 billion in December 2015, causing a slight upward adjustment in market interest rates. In February 2016, the central bank firmed its policy rates by 50 basis points. Growth in credit to the private sector has slowed slightly.

The all share price index remained high at around 7,000 for most of 2015 (despite some overseas investors' withdrawal of capital) on the expectation that the new government would set an economic policy oriented to the private sector (Figure 3.21.6). However, deepening economic uncertainty and the government's announcement to suspend tax reforms announced in the 2016 budget caused the market to slump and likely put off new portfolio and foreign direct investment.

Efforts for fiscal consolidation were reversed in 2015. The new government's revised budget for 2015 aimed to provide more support for the poor and to collect more revenue from high-income groups and large commercial operations. The budget provided for a sizeable monthly allowance for public employees and higher transfers and subsidies. These changes combined with higher interest payments (which consume about one-third of budget revenue) to boost recurrent expenditure to 14.7% of GDP from 12.9% the previous year (Figure 3.21.7). Reversing recent trends, revenue increased to 12.2% of GDP from 11.6% in 2014 on increases in excise and custom duties on vehicle imports as imports surged in response to lower import tax rates set in the revised budget. The overall budget deficit excluding grants widened to the equivalent of 7.2% of GDP in 2015, well above both the 5.7% outcome in the previous year and the 4.9% budget target. Total government debt is estimated to have increased to equal 73.5% of GDP in 2015 (Figure 3.21.8).

Budget policy for 2016 sought to enhance tax revenue. The 2016 budget, presented to Parliament in November 2015, set a lower minimum threshold for liability under the value-added tax (VAT) to SLRs12 million from SLRs15 million, and revised the prevailing 11% single rate into three bands: 0%, 8%, and 12.5%. The threshold for the

3.21.1 National versus Colombo consumer price index

The national consumer price index was released in November 2015 with the series starting in January 2014. Compared with the Colombo consumer price index, it has broader coverage, including all the provinces and a larger basket that adds two new categories: alcoholic beverages and tobacco, and hotels and restaurants. The national index puts more weight on food, at 44% versus 41% on the Colombo index. While inflation measured by the national index in 2015 was on average 3.8%, it was much lower at 0.9% as measured by the Colombo index. This was because housing rent showed a decline in Colombo after a significant rise in 2013 and early 2014, which substantially pushed down inflation as measured by the Colombo index.

3.21.3 Inflation

— Food
— Nonfood
— Overall

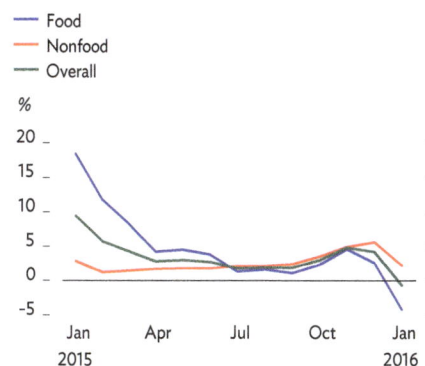

Source: Department of Census and Statistics of Sri Lanka. http://statistics.gov.lk (accessed on 24 February 2016).
Click here for figure data

nation building tax, a levy on gross business receipts, was also revised lower and the tax rate doubled from 2% to 4%. The budget also aimed to stop ad hoc and unproductive tax concessions offered by various government agencies. Moreover, tax concessions granted for any investment project were brought under the supervision and monitoring of the Ministry of Finance.

The implementation of major tax reform to the VAT and national building tax were deferred in January 2016. The latest fiscal projection taking into account these developments estimates a more modest increase in revenue equal to 13.2% of GDP, rather than 16.3% as proposed in the original budget, while the original ambitious public investment target is reduced. In this fiscal framework, recurrent expenditure is to be contained at 14.1% of GDP, while public investment will be 5.2%. The fiscal deficit excluding grants will narrow to 5.9% of GDP in 2016.

The balance of payments was under pressure in 2015 from a decline in exports, weak remittances from workers overseas, and large capital outflows. The current account deficit narrowed, however, on account of much lower spending on oil imports and robust tourist arrivals. Export earnings dropped by 5.6% in line with lower earnings from all major export categories as global demand weakened and prices fell. Exports of tea, rubber products, and garments largely accounted for the decline. Imports also fell during the year, by 2.5%, reflecting diverse developments. Imports other than oil—notably vehicles but other consumer goods as well—increased sharply by 10%, while oil imports fell by 41% because of lower prices to a total $1.9 billion less than a year earlier.

Earnings from tourism continued to expand robustly, growing by 17.8% to $2.9 billion. Overseas workers' remittances contracted by 0.5% to $6.9 billion, which seemed to be partly attributable to the fall in oil prices and weak growth in the Middle East, the main host destination. On balance, the current account recorded an estimated deficit equal to 1.9% of GDP in 2015, narrower than the 2.6% deficit in 2014 (Figure 3.21.9).

Capital outflow was the major factor in the deterioration of the balance of payments in 2015. Foreign investments in government securities recorded a net outflow of $1.1 billion, while foreign direct investment and portfolio inflows were well below levels a year earlier. The central bank estimates the overall balance of payments deficit to be $1.5 billion, reversing a surplus of $1.7 billion in 2014.

Gross international reserves fell to $7.3 billion in December 2015 from $8.2 billion a year earlier and declined further to $6.3 billion in January 2016 (Figure 3.21.10). Sri Lanka's latest sovereign bond, for $1.5 billion, was issued on 28 October 2015 at a coupon rate of 6.850% per annum. Fitch Ratings rated it BB–, Moody's Investors Service B1, and Standard and Poor's B+. Gross international reserves were supported by a $1.1 billion currency swap arrangement with India concluded in September 2015.

The Sri Lanka rupee was broadly stable against the US dollar for most of 2015 but weakened after September 2015, when the central bank stopped intervening on the foreign exchange market.

3.21.4 Interest rate, credit, and money growth

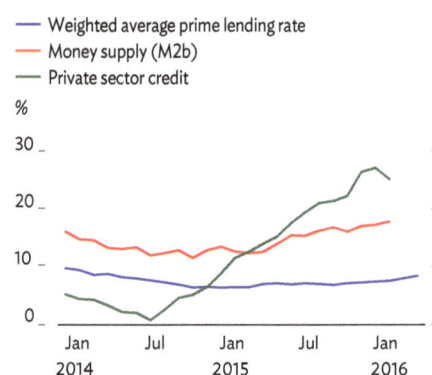

Source: Central Bank of Sri Lanka. Weekly Economic Indicators. http://www.cbsl.gov.lk
Click here for figure data

3.21.5 Deposit and lending rates and statutory reserve ratio

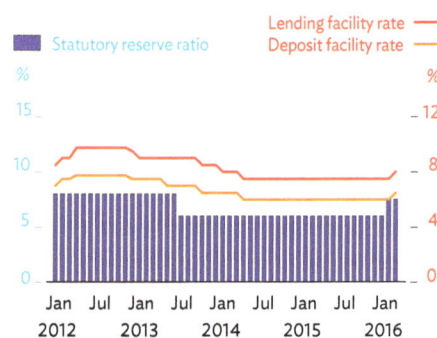

Source: Central Bank of Sri Lanka. http://www.cbsl.gov.lk (accessed on 8 March 2016).
Click here for figure data

3.21.6 Share prices and capital flows

Sources: Central Bank of Sri Lanka; CEIC Data Company (accessed 23 March 2016).
Click here for figure data

The rupee depreciated by 6.2% from SLRs137 to the dollar at the end of August 2015 to SLRs146 as of 11 February 2016 (Figure 3.21.11). In all of 2015, the rupee depreciated by 9% against the dollar and by nearly 4% in nominal and real effective terms, following a 3-year trend of gradual appreciation.

External debt in June 2015 was $43.5 billion, equal to 58.1% of GDP, of which 83% had a maturity of more than 1 year and was categorized as long term. The government's outstanding external debt amounted to $24.3 billion, or 56% of all external debt, of which $8.4 billion was in debt securities (Treasury bills and international sovereign bonds) and $6.8 billion was from multilateral lenders, $6.1 billion from bilateral lenders, and $3.0 billion from commercial sources.

Economic prospects

Weak global demand and uncertainty over policy will continue to hold down economic performance in 2016. Weak demand and low prices for Sri Lanka's major exports will constrain economic growth and exert pressure on the balance of payments, though somewhat lower oil prices projected for 2016 will alleviate this pressure, albeit less than in 2015. Continued concern over fiscal consolidation will hinder foreign investment and other capital inflows. Notably, in February 2016 Fitch Ratings downgraded Sri Lanka to B+ from BB– with a negative outlook because of rising refinancing risk and weaker public finances.

Fiscal consolidation is to be put back on track by a revision of the 2016 budget. Following the suspension in January 2016 of earlier plans for tax reform, the government has been preparing a revised budget for 2016. Its proposed tax reforms include a VAT rate increase to 15% from 11% and the introduction of a capital gains tax. The revised budget will be the basis for discussions with the International Monetary Fund (IMF) for possible support that interests the government. IMF support, once agreed, will protect against expected pressures from external imbalances as it builds international confidence and facilitates fiscal consolidation and tax reform.

A national development strategy will facilitate investment, both domestic and foreign. The Prime Minister outlined the government's strategy in his statement in November, which focused on job creation, rural development, linking up to global value chains, and attracting more foreign direct investment. The 2016 budget builds on these priorities and introduces some measures necessary to attract foreign investment. The master plan for the Western Region Megapolis Project, released in January 2016, elaborates on the development plan for Western Province, including Colombo, which will be a significant component of capital expenditure over the medium term. The public investment plan for 2016–2018 to be published in May 2016 will prioritize and streamline public projects, provide vision for economic development, and thus promote private sector investment.

Private investment can recover to drive economic growth in 2016, assuming that the revised budget is approved in mid-2016, the national development strategy is finalized, and agreement is reached with the IMF on possible support. Growth will be driven by domestic demand

3.21.1 Selected economic indicators (%)

	2016	2017
GDP growth	5.3	5.8
Inflation	4.5	5.0
Current account balance (share of GDP)	–2.0	–1.8

Source: ADB estimates.

3.21.7 Government finance

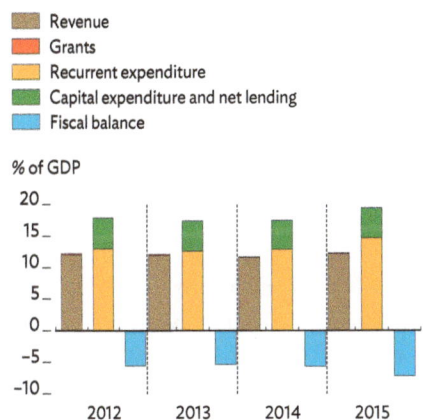

Sources: Central Bank of Sri Lanka, http://www.cbsl.gov.lk; Ministry of Finance and Planning and the Treasury of Sri Lanka, http://www.treasury.gov.lk
Click here for figure data

3.21.8 Government debt

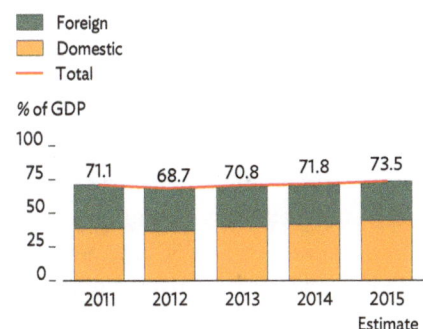

Sources: Central Bank of Sri Lanka. Recent Economic Developments for 2015 and Prospects for 2016. http://www.cbsl.gov.lk; Budget Speech 2016. Revised January 2016. http:www.treasury.gov.lk
Click here for figure data

as weak global economic recovery suppresses external demand. Consumption will increase only modestly after strong expansion last year. Public investment has potential to expand once additional revenue streams materialize. Under these circumstances, there is room for private sector investment to lead growth. In this scenario, economic growth is projected to pick up to 5.3% in 2016 and further to 5.8% in 2017 as the global environment improves.

Inflation will accelerate moderately under monetary tightening. While domestic demand remains restrained, the 9% depreciation of the Sri Lanka rupee in 2015 will exert upward pressure on import prices. The fading of base effects from several reductions to administered energy prices in 2015 may also cause some upward movement in inflation in 2016. Monetary policy will maintain a tight stance balanced between restraining price increases and fostering economic recovery. With global oil prices holding down domestic fuel prices, and assuming a steady supply of agriculture products, inflation is expected to rise only moderately. Accordingly, inflation is forecasted to pick up to 4.5% in 2016 and, as growth strengthens, to 5.0% in 2017.

The overall balance of payments will continue to be under pressure as exports stay weak during the global slowdown and remittances slacken from workers in the Middle East. Although exports will continue to struggle, a positive factor is the expected renewal in 2016 of concessions under the Generalized System of Preferences Plus scheme of the European Union. Imports will contract as oil prices decline and vehicle imports subside in response to the import tax. Receipts from tourism will continue to grow at a healthy rate in line with recent trends. Given this outlook, the current account deficit is projected to widen slightly to 2.0% of GDP in 2016 and improve in 2017 to 1.8% as exports pick up.

The government's commitment to fiscal consolidation is critical to ensure capital inflow. IMF support would help the government to maintain sufficient gross international reserves to sustain public and investor confidence. The overall balance of payments is likely to remain in deficit for the second consecutive year in 2016.

Policy challenge—tax reform

A persistently low revenue ratio has been a major challenge to Sri Lanka's efforts to achieve fiscal consolidation while meeting growing needs for social expenditure and public investment. The ratio of tax to GDP is, at 12%, uniquely low among countries at a similar stage of development. The tax system is quite complex, with a multiplicity of taxes. A relatively thin base reflects significant base erosion as various government offices granted an array of tax incentives. The government's repeated attempts to improve the tax system have had little impact. The Prime Minister's statement to Parliament in November 2015 indicated that he intended to address this issue partly by strengthening tax management and removing tax holidays and benefits. His policy includes minimizing regressive taxes and doubling the ratio of direct to indirect tax contributions from 20/80 to 40/60.

3.21.9 Current account components

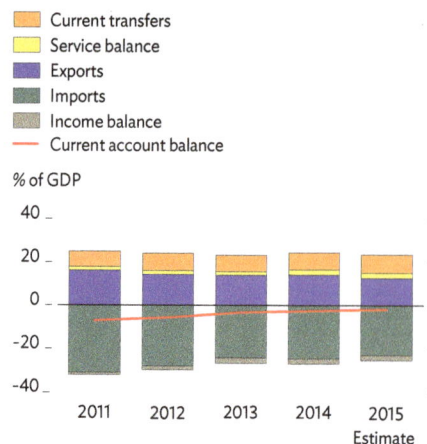

Sources: Central Bank of Sri Lanka. 2015. *Annual Report 2014*. http://www.cbsl.gov.lk; ADB estimates.
Click here for figure data

3.21.10 Gross official reserves

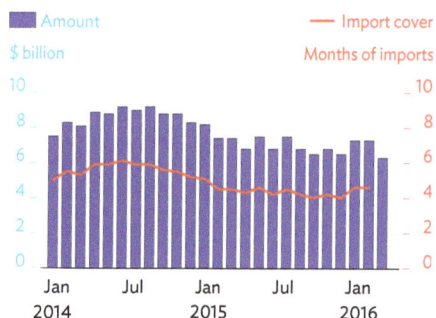

Source: Central Bank of Sri Lanka. http://www.cbsl.gov.lk
Click here for figure data

3.21.11 Exchange rates

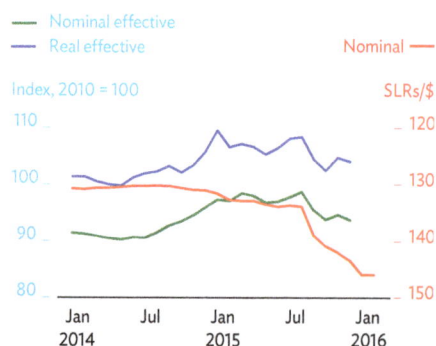

Source: Central Bank of Sri Lanka. http://www.cbsl.gov.lk
Click here for figure data

The 2016 budget nevertheless depended on expanded indirect taxes. It planned ambitious tax increases worth 2% of GDP, including increases in the nation building tax (NBT), excise duties, and taxes on external trade, while income taxes both personal and corporate are reduced marginally (Figure 3.21.12). The budget proposed expanding the tax base for the VAT and the NBT by lowering the minimum tax liability threshold and doubling the NBT rate. Indirect taxes in general place a smaller burden on tax administration and can immediately increase revenue, but they are regressive in that they impose a larger burden on the poor than the rich. Further, since the NBT is levied on turnover, the burden cascades and has a larger distortionary effect on the economy than does a VAT.

Moreover, personal income tax will became less progressive as the rate is unified at 15% from six bands: 4%, 8%, 12%, 16%, 20%, and 24%. Corporate tax rates were reformed to two bands—15% broadly and 30% applicable to a few selected activities including betting and gaming, liquor, tobacco, and banking and financial services—from the previous structure of 12% for incomes below SLRs5 million and 28% for higher incomes. The annual tax-free threshold for the personal income tax was increased to SLRs2.4 million from SLRs750,000, further narrowing the tax base. These proposals run counter to the policy outlined by the Prime Minister.

Proposed tax amendments in March 2016 address progressivity in the tax system. The Prime Minister announced to Parliament details of his proposed tax amendments. The proposal is to change the VAT to a 15% single rate that will not be imposed on essential commodities or electricity (though VAT concessions for telecommunications, private education, and private health expenditure will be removed), keep the NBT tax rate at 2%, and introduce a capital gains tax. The 2016 budget proposals on personal income tax and corporate tax are to be suspended. The statutory personal income tax rate to be applied from 2017 is increased from 15.0% to 17.5%.

The government has taken well-considered steps to enhance revenue. Further improving the tax system requires stronger policy analysis and more capacity in decision-making agencies. The Inland Revenue Department needs to set up a comprehensive tax policy analysis unit with the capacity to conduct statistical modelling and social surveys. Such analysis will inform policy makers on the impact of tax policy changes on revenue and the economy and facilitate tax administration policy analysis, intervention, and equitable revenue generation.

3.21.12 Government revenues

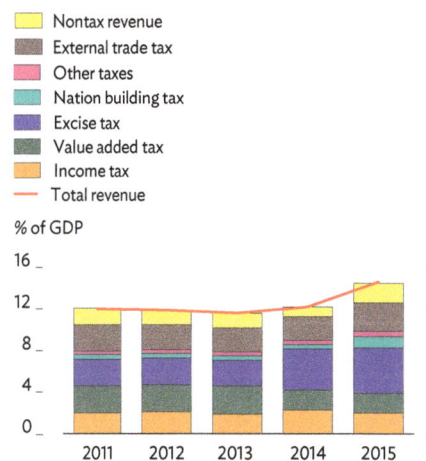

Legend:
- Nontax revenue
- External trade tax
- Other taxes
- Nation building tax
- Excise tax
- Value added tax
- Income tax
- Total revenue

Sources: Central Bank of Sri Lanka, http://www.cbsl.gov.-lk; Ministry of Finance and Planning and the Treasury of Sri Lanka, http://www.treasury.gov.lk
Click here for figure data

SOUTHEAST ASIA

BRUNEI DARUSSALAM
CAMBODIA
INDONESIA
LAO PEOPLE'S
	DEMOCRATIC REPUBLIC
MALAYSIA
MYANMAR
PHILIPPINES
SINGAPORE
THAILAND
VIET NAM

Brunei Darussalam

Slight gains in oil and gas production in 2015 slowed the pace of GDP contraction and, if maintained, are expected to restore GDP growth this year. Consumer prices, after easing in 2014 and 2015, are forecast to edge up. Lower oil and gas prices will likely push the current account into deficit in 2016. They also provide an opportunity to rein in energy subsidies.

Economic performance

Heavily dependent on exports of oil and natural gas, the economy contracted by an estimated 1.1% in 2015 (Figure 3.22.1). The pace of GDP contraction slowed from declines of 2.1% in 2013 and 2.3% in 2014 as oil and gas output edged up in 2015 after declining for several years. Crude oil production rose by 0.2% to 126,800 barrels per day and natural gas output by 4.9% to 1.4 billion cubic feet per day, owing largely to the completion of maintenance on some aging wells and pipelines (Figure 3.22.2).

Oil and gas accounts for more than 60% of GDP and 90% of both merchandise exports and government revenue. While hydrocarbon production rose a little last year, export prices plunged, sharply reducing export income and fiscal revenue. The rest of the economy—mainly services and construction—contracted by 2.3% in the first 3 quarters of 2015, the latest period for which data are available, and likely contracted in the full year (Figure 3.22.3). Services, particularly those provided by the government, contracted, but construction expanded as the government built infrastructure and housing projects.

On the demand side, investment, government consumption, and net exports all shrank in the first 3 quarters, but private consumption recorded solid growth.

Government spending was constrained by falling revenue from taxes, dividends, and royalties from oil and gas. Estimated revenue dropped by about half in FY2015 (ending 31 March 2016). The government responded by cutting expenditure by more than 25%, in part by postponing smaller capital outlays. The fiscal deficit in FY2015 is estimated at 14% of GDP, a sharp contrast with large surpluses exceeding 20% of GDP a few years ago (Figure 3.22.4). The deficit was financed by transfers from a fiscal stabilization fund.

Falling prices for oil and gas exports cut the trade surplus by more than half, and the current account surplus narrowed to an estimated 6.5% of GDP in 2015. Merchandise exports on a customs basis fell by 42.9% to $6.3 billion, and merchandise imports fell by 17.1% to $3.0 billion (Figure 3.22.5). International reserves were, at $2.9 billion, down by 16.9% from 2014 but still covered a high 11.4 months of imports.

3.22.1 GDP growth

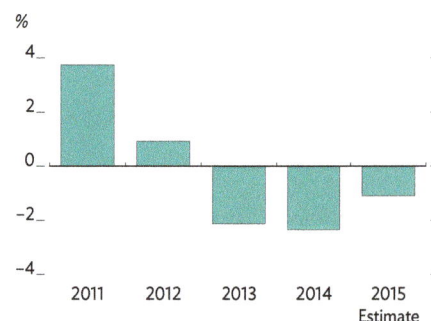

Source: Asian Development Outlook database.
Click here for figure data

3.22.2 Average daily production

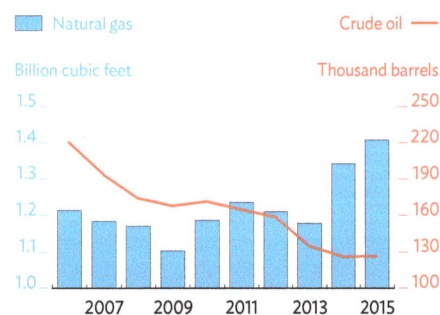

Sources: BP Statistical Review of World Energy 2015; Department of Energy.
Click here for figure data

This chapter was written by Shikha Jha and Pilipinas Quising of the Economic Research and Regional Cooperation Department, ADB, Manila.

Consumer prices declined for a second year in a row. Lower prices for transportation, clothing, education, and household equipment and maintenance more than offset small increases in prices for food, utilities, health care, and communications. Over the year, the consumer price index fell by 0.4%.

Growth in credit to the private sector slowed further to 3.1% at the end of 2015. Money supply (M2) declined by 1.8%. In October 2015, the monetary authority relaxed some conditions on unsecured personal credit. The Brunei dollar, which is pegged at par to the Singapore dollar, depreciated by 6.5% against the US dollar in 2015. Since 2006, the government has issued Islamic securities worth B$9.4 billion and plans to issue more with longer maturities. The monetary authority indicated that it might start a securities exchange in 2017.

Economic prospects

The economy is projected to return to growth this year on the assumption that oil and gas production continues to recover gradually as new technology extracts more oil from existing fields and that the government maintains significant investment in infrastructure. GDP is forecast to edge up by 1.0% this year and accelerate to 2.5% in 2017 if global demand and prices for hydrocarbons start to recover.

Construction will contribute to growth. The $100 million Sungai Kebun Bridge is to be completed this year, and construction on a bridge to Pulau Muara Besar, an island in Brunei Bay to be developed as an industrial hub, is expected to run through 2018. Work has started on the $1.1 billion Temburong Bridge to connect the Brunei Muara district with Temburong. This large project will continue through 2019. Site preparation and dredging is under way for a $2.5 billion oil refinery and aromatics cracker on Pulau Muara Besar. This project, planned by a company from the People's Republic of China, has been delayed, but construction could start during the forecast period. Commercial production is scheduled from 2019.

The impact that low oil and gas prices has on government revenue indicates that spending on public services and smaller capital projects will remain constrained. The FY2016 budget cuts total spending by 12.5% from the previous year's budget. Revenue is projected to fall further, and the budget is expected to post another deep deficit in FY2016. The budget puts a higher priority on spending that stimulates the economy, such as infrastructure construction and maintenance and the development of small and medium-sized enterprises. Accumulated financial assets provide a buffer against declines in revenue.

The government will push ahead with efforts to diversify the economy through foreign investment in export-oriented ventures. New foreign investments include a $52 million plant being built by Japanese companies to supply pipes and tubing for the petroleum industry and a $17 million organic farm proposed by investors from Singapore and Taipei,China. To attract investment the government has reduced the corporate tax rate to 18.5% and introduced a tax credit equal to 50% of salaries paid to new local employees in the first 3 years of employment. Progress has been made toward improving

3.22.3 Supply-side contributions to growth

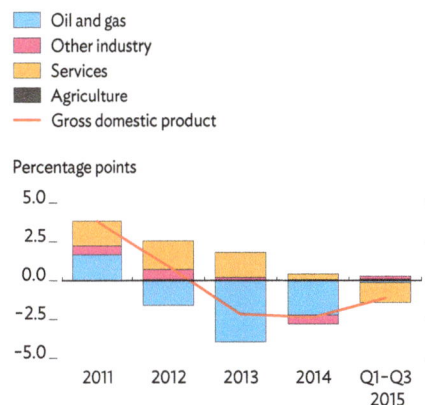

Q = quarter.
Source: CEIC Data Company (accessed 6 March 2016).
Click here for figure data

3.22.4 Fiscal indicators

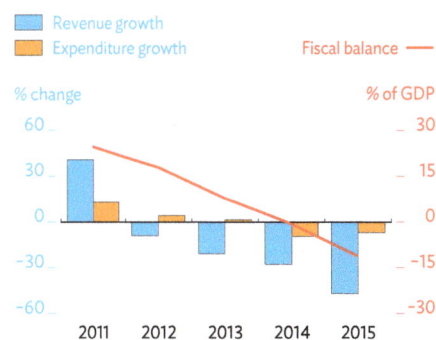

Note: Years are fiscal years ending 31 March of the next year.
Sources: Asian Development Outlook database;
Department of Economic Planning and Development. 2014.
Brunei Darussalam Key Indicators 2014.
Click here for figure data

3.22.1 Selected economic indicators (%)

	2016	2017
GDP growth	1.0	2.5
Inflation	0.2	0.4
Current account balance (share of GDP)	−1.3	2.0

Source: ADB estimates.

the business environment. Brunei Darussalam moved up 21 places to 84 among 189 countries ranked in the World Bank's *Doing Business 2016* report. The higher ranking followed government moves to improve online procedures and simplify registration requirements for starting a business and to make it easier and less costly to pay business taxes. Under new registration procedures, a business can be started in only 1 day. In addition, the government established its Brunei Darussalam Arbitration Center to resolve commercial disputes and drafted a new competition law that it said aligns with international best practice.

Consumer prices are forecast to rise slightly as economic growth picks up. The depreciation of the Brunei dollar against the US dollar will exert some upward pressure on prices. The consumer price index fell by 1.2% year on year in January 2016 but, for the year as a whole, is forecast to rise by 0.2% (Figure 3.22.6). Subsidies and price controls keep inflation low in this economy.

Lower global oil and gas prices this year will further diminish the value of merchandise exports. Next year, some recovery in oil prices should see exports start to recover. Imports are expected to rise a little in 2016 and more so in 2017. The current account is forecast to fall into deficit this year, returning to surplus in 2017.

Policy challenge—reducing fuel subsidies

International studies show that subsidies on fossil fuels and electricity not only impose a burden on government budgets but also divert funds from more productive investment in physical and social infrastructure. Moreover, subsidies artificially lower the price of energy, encouraging higher consumption and discouraging the development of alternative energy sources. They disproportionately benefit higher-income earners who own cars and air-condition their homes.

Brunei Darussalam's subsidies on fuel and power cost almost $400 million in 2014, or $900 per person, based on estimates by the International Energy Agency. The subsidy on gasoline has kept the retail price, in US dollars, around $0.40 per liter over the past decade. That compares with a retail price per liter of $0.98 in the US and $1.58 in Singapore in 2014 (Figure 3.22.7).

The sharp decline in oil prices provides an opportunity to rein in subsidies without causing steep increases in fuel prices for consumers. Indeed, the minister of energy and industry noted in 2015 that subsidies left people with little awareness of the true value of energy, adding that it was important to educate people away from dependence on subsidies and to find innovative alternatives to traditional approaches.

The government has started to address the issue by introducing progressive electricity tariffs for residential users. This system charges B$0.01 per kilowatt hour (kWh) for consumption up to 500 kWh, B$0.10 per kWh for higher consumption to 1,500 kWh, and B$0.15 per kWh for consumption beyond 1,500 kWh. Thus, electricity is still subsidized but less so for bigger consumers. The government says this system has encouraged consumers to use electricity more efficiently and reduced electricity consumption by 15%. It is considering extending progressive tariffs to commercial users.

3.22.5 Merchandise trade

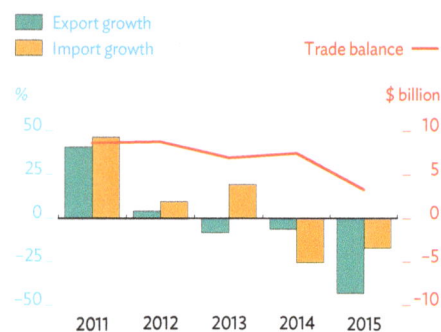

Source: CEIC Data Company Ltd (accessed 15 Feb 2016).
Click here for figure data

3.22.6 Inflation

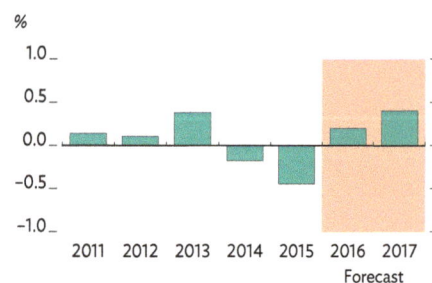

Source: Asian Development Outlook database.
Click here for figure data

3.22.7 Oil and gasoline prices

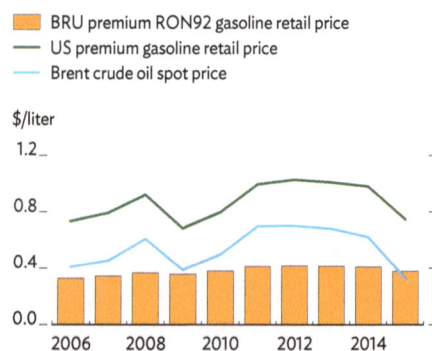

BRU = Brunei Darussalam, RON = research octane number, US = United States.
Sources: Ministry of Finance; Bloomberg; *IMF Statistical Appendix on Brunei Darussalam* (various years); US Energy Information.
Click here for figure data

Cambodia

Expansion in industry and services sustained solid economic growth in 2015. Inflation slowed to its lowest rate since 2009 but picked up at the end of the year. The outlook is for further robust growth led by garment and footwear manufacturing, construction, and services, and for moderate inflation. Rapid growth in credit and a real estate boom have heightened risks in the financial sector. Another challenge is to improve the quality of employment.

Economic performance

Industry, particularly garment and footwear manufacturing and construction, contributed strongly to 7.0% economic growth in 2015, as did services (Figure 3.23.1). Agriculture was virtually flat because of drought.

Cambodia's large supply of inexpensive, low-skilled labor has attracted substantial foreign direct investment (FDI) into the production of garments and footwear for export. Growth in such manufacturing accelerated to 9.8% last year. Meanwhile, growth in construction moderated from 2014 but was still buoyant at 19.2% in 2015. With expansion estimated at 11.7%, industry overall was the biggest contributor to GDP growth last year.

Services, the second biggest contributor to growth, grew by an estimated 7.1%. Strong domestic demand spurred expansion in real estate and business services at almost 12%. Finance, transport and communications, and wholesale and retail trade all grew by about 8%. Tourist arrivals rose by 6.1% in 2015, which was somewhat slower than in the previous year owing to declines in visitors from Japan, the Republic of Korea, and the Lao People's Democratic Republic, as well as slower growth in arrivals from other major markets (Figure 3.23.2).

Agriculture, by contrast, grew by just 0.2% as El Niño brought dry weather. The rice harvest was broadly unchanged from 2014. Production of maize and soya beans fell, but cassava output jumped by half, and natural rubber output rose slightly.

Domestic demand remained strong, accommodated by low inflation and high credit growth. Inflation averaging 1.2% in 2015, the lowest since 2009, was restrained by falling global oil prices and subdued food prices. By the end of the year, though, inflation had picked up to 2.8% (Figure 3.23.3).

Net FDI rose to an estimated $1.8 billion last year, up by 8% from 2014 and equal to 10% of GDP. Higher foreign investment in banks and microfinance institutions was notable.

3.23.1 Supply-side contributions to growth

- Agriculture
- Industry
- Services
- Taxes on products less subsidies and financial intermediation services indirectly measured
- Gross domestic product growth

Percentage points

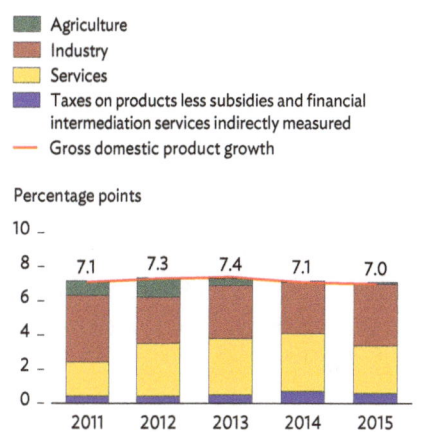

Sources: National Institute of Statistics; ADB estimates.
Click here for figure data

3.23.2 Tourism indicators

- Arrivals
- Growth

Million visitors

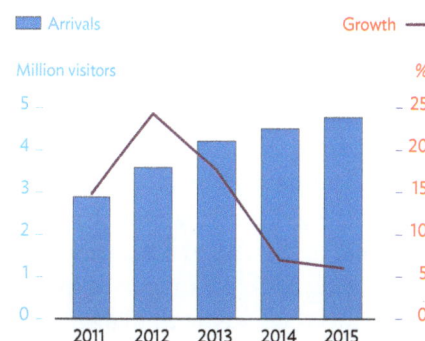

Source: National Institute of Statistics.
Click here for figure data

This chapter was written by Jan Hansen and Samphors Khieu of the Cambodia Resident Mission, ADB, Phnom Penh. The policy challenge section draws on a joint ADB and International Labour Organization report available at http://www.adb.org/publications/cambodia-addressing-skills-gap

The government's fiscal consolidation efforts narrowed the deficit, excluding grants, to an estimated 2.4% of GDP in 2015 from 3.5% in 2014 (Figure 3.23.4). Public revenue as a share of GDP was little changed at 17.1%, after having increased significantly in 2014 with improved tax collection. Expenditure as a share of GDP fell to an estimated 19.5% of GDP from 20.7%, partly the result of underspending in the capital budget. Government deposits in the banking system, which can be drawn down during economic shocks to implement fiscal policy in the absence of a domestic bond market, continued to rise last year, reaching an estimated KR6.7 billion, equal to 9.1% of GDP.

The monetary authorities kept the reserve requirement on foreign currency bank deposits, the main monetary policy tool, at 12.5% last year. However, they expanded reserve requirements to cover banks' foreign borrowings, to stem high growth in credit. Estimates indicate that growth in credit to the private sector moderated to 27.1% from 31.3% in 2014, and growth in the money supply (M2) halved to 14.7% from 29.9% (Figure 3.23.5). The Cambodian riel was broadly stable against the US dollar. Dollarization remained high, with a ratio of foreign currency deposits to broad money at 83% in 2015.

Merchandise exports increased by an estimated 14.1% to $8.5 billion in 2015. Shipments of garments and footwear, which comprise 70% of total exports, rose by an estimated 10.2%. Rice exports also rose. Merchandise imports increased by an estimated 11.9% to $11.9 billion, despite lower oil prices, as imports for the garment industry rose steeply. A smaller trade deficit and higher remittances narrowed the current account deficit excluding official transfers to an estimated 11.1% of GDP. This gap was largely financed by FDI.

Gross international reserves rose by 16% to $5.1 billion. While reserves equivalent to 4.4 months of imports appear adequate, high dollarization and financial vulnerabilities in the economy argue for building additional reserves to strengthen resilience under external shocks.

An International Monetary Fund analysis of debt sustainability in November 2015 found Cambodia at low risk of debt distress but vulnerable to shocks to growth, exports, and the budget. External public debt rose from $5.3 billion in 2014 to an estimated $5.7 billion in 2015, equal to 31.1% of GDP. Cambodia has practically no domestic debt.

Economic prospects

Steady economic growth of 7.0% is projected for 2016, with the pace quickening slightly in 2017 (Figure 3.23.6). Services are forecast to expand by 7.8% this year on robust growth in wholesale and retail trade, real estate and business services, and finance. Industry is seen growing by 9.5%, supported by diversification in garments and footwear toward products with higher value added. Growth in construction is expected to continue slowing from the very rapid pace of recent years. Agriculture should have a better year, projected to grow by 1.6% as El Niño fades.

Fiscal policy will likely be more expansionary. The 2016 budget targets a fiscal deficit, excluding grants, equal to 4.3% of GDP, considerably wider than last year's actual deficit. Public expenditure is

3.23.3 Monthly inflation

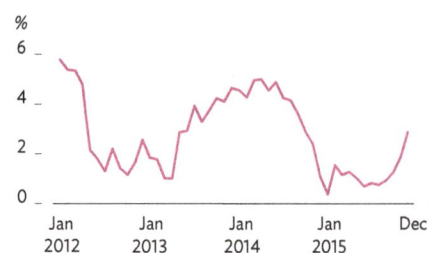

Source: National Institute of Statistics.
Click here for figure data

3.23.4 Fiscal indicators

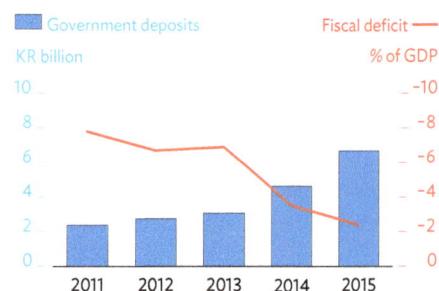

Source: National Bank of Cambodia.
Click here for figure data

3.23.5 Money supply and private sector credit

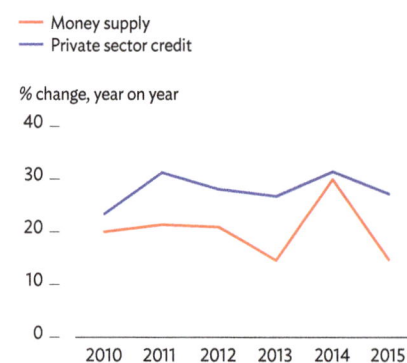

Source: National Bank of Cambodia.
Click here for figure data

projected to increase by 16.1% over the 2015 budget, mainly through a hike in civil service wages. Higher revenue is projected from improved tax collection.

While the economy shows signs of becoming more diversified within and across sectors, including garments and light manufacturing, and in export destinations, the base for growth remains narrow. Structural changes in the People's Republic of China and the relocation of some factories to Southeast Asia offer Cambodia opportunities to diversify production and exports. However, pressures for higher wages, US dollar appreciation, and stagnating productivity may weigh on Cambodia's competitiveness, in particular with other low-cost garment producers such as Myanmar.

To support diversification, the government launched last August an industrial development policy to 2025 aimed at upgrading industry from low-cost, labor-intensive manufacturing to production with higher value added. The strategic pillars of the policy are the promotion of foreign and domestic investment, the expansion and modernization of small and medium-sized enterprises, stronger regulations and enforcement, and a better business-enabling environment.

Subdued global food and fuel prices are expected to contain inflation to an average of 2.5% in 2016. Next year, the projected pickup in growth and higher global oil prices are seen lifting inflation to 3.0% (Figure 3.23.7). The external position is expected to remain stable, with the current account deficit financed mainly by FDI and official inflows. The current account gap is forecast to be little changed this year but narrower in 2017 in line with better export opportunities (Figure 3.23.8).

Domestic risks to the outlook stem from financial sector vulnerabilities that have emerged during a period of rapid growth in credit and a real estate boom, despite some moderation last year in lending and construction. Growth in bank lending for construction and real estate-related activities eased from a very rapid 45.0% year on year in the first quarter of 2015 but was still high at 34.3% in the fourth quarter, comprising 19% of total credit. The ratio of private sector credit to GDP almost doubled in 4 years to over 60%, and banks' average loan-to-deposit ratio breached 100 in February 2015. Rapid expansion of the financial system and the large number of banks and microfinance institutions have stretched the supervisory capacity of regulators.

External risks include disappointing growth in major export markets and a stronger US dollar that, under high dollarization, would further erode Cambodian competitiveness. Weaker-than-expected growth in the PRC could have spillover through investment, banking, and tourism channels. As banks and microfinance institutions increasingly rely on external funding, increased volatility in global financial markets could exacerbate funding costs and liquidity pressures. To counter external shocks, the government has rebuilt some fiscal space, but room for monetary policy to support growth is constrained by high dollarization and a consequent lack of monetary control. Efforts to build policy buffers and resilience should therefore continue.

3.23.6 GDP growth

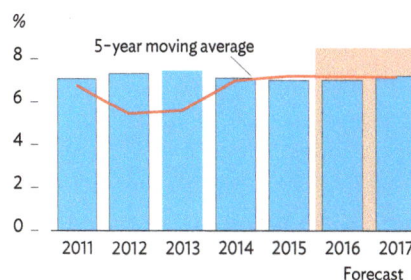

Source: Asian Development Outlook database.
Click here for figure data

3.23.7 Inflation

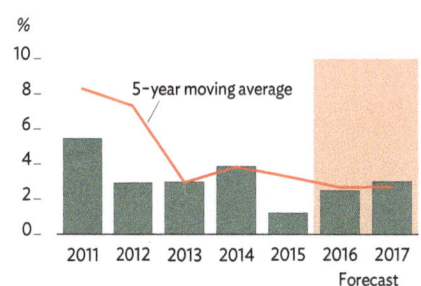

Source: Asian Development Outlook database.
Click here for figure data

3.23.1 Selected economic indicators (%)

	2016	2017
GDP growth	7.0	7.1
Inflation	2.5	3.0
Current account balance (share of GDP)	−11.1	−10.0

Source: ADB estimates.

Policy challenge—improving the quality of employment

Cambodia has achieved sustained high growth that averaged 7.9% from 2000 to 2015. However, the growth model of attracting FDI to take advantage of inexpensive, low-skilled, and abundant labor may not be viable for much longer. Generating more good jobs to sustain growth and raise incomes depends on diversifying the economy with new industries that will require a different and wider range of skills.

Labor force participation is high and a large proportion of the labor force is employed, but many jobs are informal, vulnerable, unstable, and poorly rewarded. To improve the quality of employment there is a critical need to address shortcomings in education and training and to help children complete school.

While 98% of children attend primary school, many drop out for lack of funds or because they expect low economic returns from education. Only 30% of young people complete high school. Low enrollment in secondary and higher education, and its poor quality, has left a mismatch between young workers' skills and employers' needs. Substantial benefits would likely result from improving the skills of those already in the workforce.

As for children still in school, preparing them for technical and vocational education and training, higher education, and employment will require upgrading the physical infrastructure of schools, modernizing curricula and textbooks, and improving teaching skills, particularly at the secondary level in math and science.

Coordinating general education with technical training would ensure that the two streams are complementary options for students. Better implementation of the qualification framework that was approved by the government in 2014 and collaboration with the private sector could link education and training across all levels and respond better to the skills needs of industry.

3.23.8 Current account balance

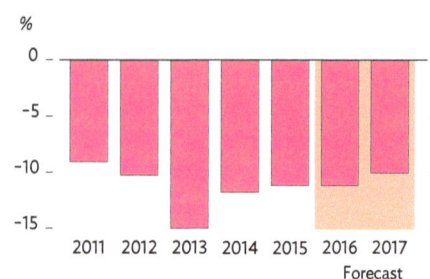

Source: Asian Development Outlook database.
Click here for figure data

Indonesia

Stronger public investment is expected to pull the economy out of a slowdown that persisted in 2015. The government has increased infrastructure funding and unveiled policy reforms to stimulate private investment. Lower interest rates will help. Inflation is forecast to decelerate by almost 2 percentage points this year. Further reforms are needed to boost productivity, attract investment, and stimulate new sources of growth.

Economic performance

Despite a pickup in government spending that lifted economic growth in the second half of 2015, the pace of GDP growth for the year was, at 4.8%, the slowest since 2009.

Growth in private consumption, by far the biggest contributor to GDP growth, decelerated to 4.8% last year on a decline in rural incomes, higher inflation, tighter consumer credit, and a weaker labor market (Figure 3.24.1). Rural incomes were hurt by lower prices for agricultural products and drought caused by El Niño. Private consumption got some support in the second half from increases in government funding for village funds and pay rises for civil servants.

Growth in fixed investment improved to 5.1% as the government ramped up investment in infrastructure and introduced a series of reforms to revive private investment (Figure 3.24.2). After facing delays in the first half, public investment rose sharply in the second, assisted by the government's improved performance in executing capital expenditure. Encouragingly, the ratio of fixed investment to GDP increased to 33.2%. Government consumption spending also rose, recovering from a slowdown in 2014 to expand by 5.4% in 2015 on improved budget execution.

Even though exports of goods and services fell by 2.0% in real terms, net external demand made a small contribution to GDP growth in 2015 as imports in real terms contracted by 5.8% on lackluster domestic demand and Indonesian rupiah depreciation.

Services, the biggest supply-side contributor to GDP growth, grew by 5.5% in 2015, easing from 6.0% in 2014. In particular, growth slowed sharply in wholesale and retail trade, reflecting moderation in private consumption. By contrast, information and communications maintained double-digit expansion. Manufacturing grew by 4.2%, the slowest pace in several years. As the property market softened, growth in construction moderated to 6.6% despite the upturn in infrastructure spending. Growth in agriculture slowed to 4.0% as the drought and forest fires struck on top of weak global prices for palm oil and

3.24.1 Demand-side contributions to growth

- Personal consumption
- Government consumption
- Gross fixed capital formation
- Stocks
- Net exports
- Statistical discrepancy
- — Gross domestic product

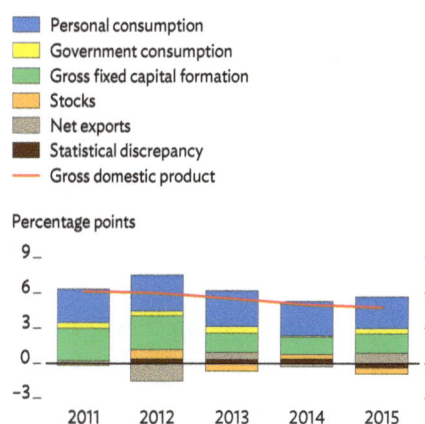

Source: CEIC Data Company (accessed 2 March 2016).
Click here for figure data

3.24.2 Fixed investment

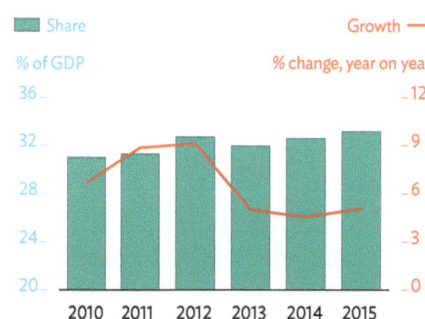

Source: CEIC Data Company (accessed 14 March 2016).
Click here for figure data

This chapter was written by Priasto Aji and Emma Allen of the Indonesia Resident Mission, ADB, Jakarta.

natural rubber. Mining actually contracted by 5.1% due to declining crude oil extraction and low mineral prices.

The labor market weakened in 2015 (Figure 3.24.3). Fewer than 200,000 jobs were created in the 12 months to August 2015, during which the working-age population aged 15 years and over increased by 3.1 million. The labor force participation rate fell to 65.8% in August 2015, the lowest on record, and the unemployment rate rose to 6.2% in August 2015 from 5.9% a year earlier, with youth unemployment climbing to 22.6%.

Inflation ebbed gradually from 8.4% at the end of 2014, then decelerated sharply in late 2015 as the impact of a 2014 fuel price hike faded (Figure 3.24.4). By December, inflation had subsided year on year to 3.4%. Core inflation, excluding food and fuel, eased to 4.0% in December. Nevertheless, year-average inflation remained high at 6.4% in 2015 owing to the 2014 fuel price hike, El Niño-induced drought, import restrictions on some food staples, and rupiah depreciation.

Higher food prices, lower rural incomes, and the weaker labor market caused the incidence of poverty to worsen to 11.1% in September 2015. Inequality as measured by the Gini coefficient remained elevated at 0.41 nationally.

Bank Indonesia, the central bank, reduced its policy interest rate by 25 basis points to 7.50% in February 2015, then kept the policy rate unchanged for 11 months to foster exchange rate stability and combat capital outflows. Growth in credit slowed to 10.5%. After inflation decelerated in the last quarter of 2015, the central bank reduced the policy rate by 75 basis points to 6.75% in the first quarter of 2016. The monetary authorities also cut the reserve requirement for banks in December 2015 and March 2016 to stimulate bank lending.

The government pushed ahead with planned spending on infrastructure and social development in 2015 even as subdued economic activity and lower commodity prices caused budget revenue to decline. This widened the fiscal deficit to 2.5% of GDP from 1.9% in the budget and 2.1% in 2014. Standard & Poor's, citing improved fiscal policy credibility, revised up its credit rating outlook for Indonesia to positive from stable in May 2015.

Merchandise exports fell by 15.4% in US dollar terms, weighed down by sagging demand in major markets and lower prices for export commodities. Merchandise imports fell in US dollar terms by an even steeper 19.8% because of subdued investment, rupiah depreciation, and lower oil imports. Consequently, the trade surplus almost doubled to $13.3 billion, which, coupled with lower deficits in services and primary income, narrowed the current account deficit to $17.8 billion, equal to 2.1% of GDP (Figure 3.24.5).

Foreign direct investment inflows were, at $15.5 billion in 2015, the lowest in 5 years, and net portfolio investment of $16.7 billion was down by just over one-third from 2014. A smaller surplus in the capital and financial account relative to the previous year tipped the balance of payments into deficit by $1.1 billion. Gross international reserves declined by 5.3% to $105.9 billion in 2015, sufficient to cover 7.5 months of imports and government debt payments (Figure 3.24.6).

3.24.3 Labor indicators

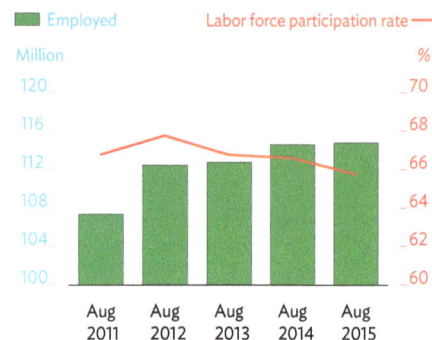

Source: CEIC Data Company (accessed 14 March 2016).
Click here for figure data

3.24.4 Inflation and policy rate

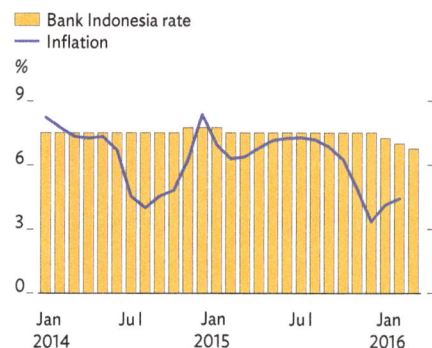

Source: CEIC Data Company (accessed 14 March 2016).
Click here for figure data

3.24.5 Current account balance components

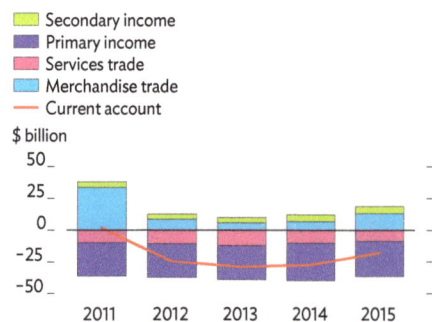

Source: CEIC Data Company (accessed 14 March 2016).
Click here for figure data

The rupiah depreciated by 10.2% against the broadly strengthening US dollar in 2015. In response to heightened rupiah volatility in August and September, the central bank moved to stabilize the currency by lengthening the maturity of its deposit facility.

Economic prospects

Public investment is projected to increase in 2016 as infrastructure projects initiated last year gather momentum and new projects get under way. Higher public capital spending should provide additional opportunities for private investment, which, together with the implementation of structural reform, will improve the investment climate. Household spending is projected to pick up, but net external demand could weigh on economic growth. On balance, the economy is seen expanding by 5.2% in 2016 and 5.5% next year (Figure 3.24.7).

The 2016 budget sees further improvement in the composition of public spending (Figure 3.24.8). Energy subsidies are projected to decline by 14% from 2015, freeing up resources for infrastructure, health care, and social protection. To this end, the government has raised its allocation for infrastructure by 7.4% from 2015. Local governments will receive higher transfers from the central government and are being encouraged to use accumulated surpluses for public investment. The 2016 budget also injects additional capital into state-owned enterprises involved in infrastructure, and some state enterprises get government guarantees to facilitate borrowing from international financial institutions.

Aiming for higher rates of budget realization, officials advanced the bidding process for public investment projects. By the end of January 2016, the government had completed the bidding process for 53% of the capital spending planned by central government ministries. Several infrastructure projects, notably in telecommunications and roads, commenced in the first quarter of 2016.

The government targets an ambitious 21% increase in revenue over the outcome in 2015, which will require significant improvements in tax collection. Excise tariffs have been raised, and a partial tax amnesty is planned for those who declare and repatriate offshore funds. Against this, low oil and commodity prices will continue to constrain revenue this year. The government anticipates a fiscal deficit equal to 2.2% of GDP in 2016—though, as in 2015, the outcome is expected to exceed the target.

Policy reforms are expected to stimulate private investment, particularly over the medium term. The government has unveiled 10 packages of such reforms since September 2015. The central bank is expected to maintain its focus on macroeconomic stability, though slower inflation over the forecast period could provide room for further reductions in interest rates to spur growth.

Household consumption is projected to improve slightly on easing inflation, tax cuts for lower-income workers from July 2015, and higher government allocations for village funds, which hire rural workers to build village infrastructure. These factors will help to mitigate the lingering impact of El Niño on farm incomes. The latest consumer

3.24.6 **Gross international reserves and exchange rate**

Sources: CEIC Data Company; Bloomberg (both accessed 14 March 2016).
Click here for figure data

3.24.7 **GDP growth**

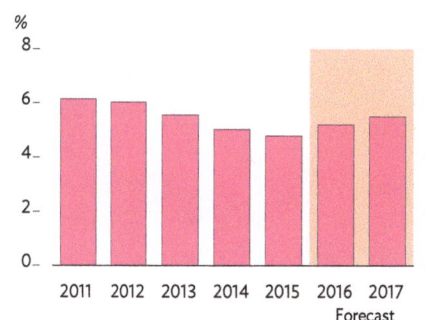

Source: Asian Development Outlook database.
Click here for figure data

3.24.8 **Government expenditures**

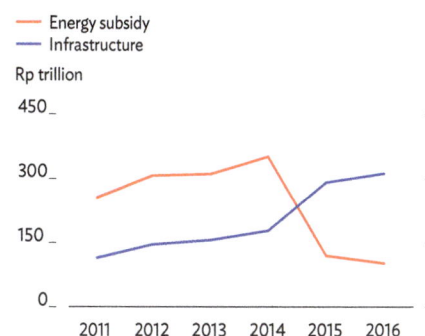

Source: Ministry of Finance.
Click here for figure data

survey by the central bank shows that consumers generally remained optimistic in February 2016, but less so than in January (Figure 3.24.9).

The outlook for exports is weak, however, in light of lackluster economic performance in many of Indonesia's trade partners. The decline in exports that started in 2012 is projected to continue, but at a much slower pace than in 2015 (Figure 3.24.10). Likewise, the decline in imports that has been under way since 2013 is expected to slow as investment gathers momentum. The current account deficit is forecast to widen over the next 2 years, but the balance of payments may well return to surplus on stronger capital inflows that should follow a better economic performance and strong implementation of investment reforms. Foreign holdings of rupiah bonds rose by $2.9 billion in the first 11 weeks of 2016, and the rupiah appreciated by 5.1% against the US dollar in this period.

By sector, services are expected to benefit this year as lower inflation and interest rates bolster consumer and business sentiment. Stronger spending on infrastructure will lift construction. The manufacturing purchasing managers' index in February appears to have bottomed out, and this indicates a potential upturn in the months ahead (Figure 3.24.11). As for agriculture, farmers postponed crop sowing late in 2015 to wait out the drought, which will hurt harvests in the first half of 2016.

Damage to agriculture from drought has put upward pressure on food prices, with inflation edging up to 4.3% year on year in the first 2 months of 2016. The government has approved imports of rice to dampen price increases. The rupiah's depreciation in 2015 is expected to have a modest impact on inflation this year. Year-average inflation is seen at 4.5% in 2016, down almost 2 percentage points from 6.4% in each of the past 3 years (Figure 3.24.12).

Domestic risks to the outlook are posed by delays in public infrastructure projects, including from possible shortfalls in government revenue. Delays in implementing infrastructure projects would hurt business confidence. In this regard, it will be important that reforms announced in 2015 are firmly implemented. An unexpected spike in inflation, perhaps caused by tight food supplies, could dent consumption and investor sentiment. External risks include weaker-than-anticipated growth in trading partners, which would further depress exports, and continued weakness in prices for export commodities. Current account and budget deficits reinforce the importance of maintaining capital inflows, which would be put at risk by renewed volatility in global financial markets.

Policy challenge—spurring new engines of growth

Development of commodity production for export has been an important driver of Indonesia's economic growth. Now that the global commodities boom has faded, the challenge is to spur other sources of growth. The expansion of manufacturing holds great promise. Others areas with potential for strong growth include tourism, marine fisheries, aquaculture, e-commerce to serve the growing middle class, and agricultural commodities with higher value added.

3.24.9 Consumer and business confidence indexes

Q = quarter.
Source: CEIC Data Company (accessed 14 March 2016).
Click here for figure data

3.24.10 Merchandise trade

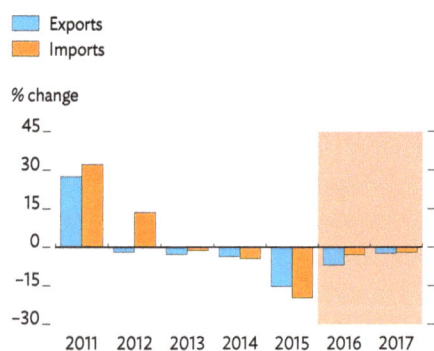

Sources: CEIC Data Company (accessed 2 March 2016); ADB estimates.
Click here for figure data

3.24.1 Selected economic indicators (%)

	2016	2017
GDP growth	5.2	5.5
Inflation	4.5	4.2
Current account balance (share of GDP)	−2.6	−2.8

Source: ADB estimates.

Recent reforms are designed to diversify growth sources and address growth constraints. From September 2015 to February 2016, the government unveiled 10 packages of reforms to attract investment, particularly in manufacturing. It opened an additional 35 sectors to foreign ownership, eliminated or simplified various regulations, improved procedures for land title registration, and accelerated business licensing. A new formula for setting minimum wages aims to make annual adjustments more simple and predictable. Tax breaks are provided to new manufacturing and labor-intensive industries, while credit subsidies are expanded for small and medium-sized enterprises. Port logistics services are to be reformed, and special economic zones further developed.

The next priority should be to forcefully implement the reforms to ensure a positive impact on investor perceptions. In this respect, decisions last year to raise tariffs on 5,000 products and require that all transactions be made in rupiah may have countered some of the gains.

The reform agenda is incomplete. For example, policies are needed to foster micro and small enterprises. One in three such manufacturing enterprises cites inadequate finance as its main constraint. Interventions to address the main issues—high interest rates, cumbersome procedures, and lack of collateral—have important roles to play in structural reform, as do upgrading technology and encouraging micro and small enterprises to form clusters to promote cooperation and economies of scale.

Indonesia's working-age population is projected to increase steadily through 2030. To take full advantage of this demographic dividend, further investment is needed in education and training that will help the economy make the transition to activities that add more value. Longer term, changes are required to improve the quality and relevance of education and training, and to address skill shortages and mismatches in the labor market (Figure 3.24.13).

The GDP share of trade in goods and services has declined over the past decade, even as it has increased in most other Southeast Asian economies. Although Indonesia is a large producer of palm oil, coal, rubber, and coffee, its total exports are less than 2% of global trade in goods and services. This points to the tremendous potential that expanding trade has for boosting demand for Indonesian goods and services, provided that a firm commitment to openness and global competitiveness is maintained. The growing use of nontariff measures such as import and export restrictions, and of state interventions to stabilize domestic commodity markets, ultimately weakens external competitiveness and should be reconsidered.

Economic integration under the auspices of the Association of Southeast Asian Nations will add to competitive pressures but also create opportunities to integrate Indonesia more closely into one of the world's most rapidly growing regions.

3.24.11 Manufacturing purchasing managers' index

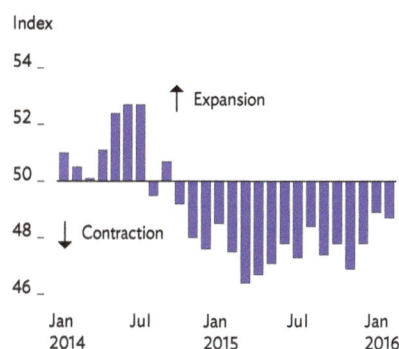

Note: Nikkei, Markit.
Source: Bloomberg (accessed 18 March 2016).
Click here for figure data

3.24.12 Inflation

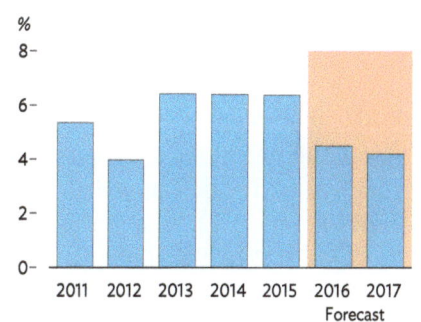

Source: Asian Development Outlook database.
Click here for figure data

3.24.13 Skills mismatch, August 2015

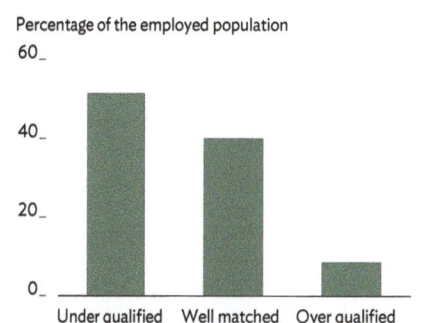

Source: Statistics Indonesia. 2015. Labor force survey, Statistics Indonesia. Jakarta.
Click here for figure data

Lao People's Democratic Republic

Having decelerated since 2013, growth is projected to pick up over the next 2 years, lending support to the economy's eligibility for graduation from least-developed status by 2020. Inflation has ebbed to its lowest in 6 years and is forecast to remain modest. Lower global oil prices have helped to bolster a fragile external position, but international reserves provide only a thin buffer against external shocks.

Economic performance

Expansion in services and electricity generation sustained solid economic growth in 2015, though the pace moderated for a second year in a row to an estimated 6.7%, largely owing to fiscal constraints and lackluster global demand for minerals (Figure 3.25.1).

Services, the biggest supply-side contributor to GDP growth, slowed a little in 2015 but still grew by an estimated 8.5%. The number of bank branches and microfinance institutions continued to increase, and telecommunications recorded moderate expansion. Tourism-related services such as accommodation and transportation benefitted as tourist arrivals rose by 12.6% to 4.7 million and revenue from tourism increased by 13.1% to $725.4 million (Figure 3.25.2).

Industry grew by an estimated 8.0%, also coming off the pace set in 2014. Inflows of foreign direct investment supported the construction of power plants, residential and commercial property, and projects in special economic zones. However, fiscal constraints dampened public construction. Output of electricity, mostly sold to Thailand, rose after the Hongsa lignite-fired power plant and new hydropower plants started commercial production (Figure 3.25.3). Production of copper, gold, and silver from the major mines edged up, but some potash mines closed.

Also slowing from 2014, agriculture expanded by an estimated 2.0% in 2015. Dry weather suppressed the production of rice, vegetables, and fish in some parts of the country, and rice output nationwide rose by less than 1%. Exports of forestry products fell by over 20%.

Government spending has been constrained over the past 2 years by the need to curb the fiscal deficit and repay arrears. Because the fiscal gap, including grants but excluding off-budget items, widened sharply to equal 5.6% of GDP in FY2013 (ended 30 September 2013), the government has since postponed some infrastructure investment, curbed off-budget spending, and cancelled a hike in civil service wages and allowances. These measures started to rein in the deficit in FY2014. However, as lower commodity prices weighed on revenue in FY2015, the fiscal gap widened to an estimated 4.7% of GDP.

3.25.1 Supply-side contributions to growth

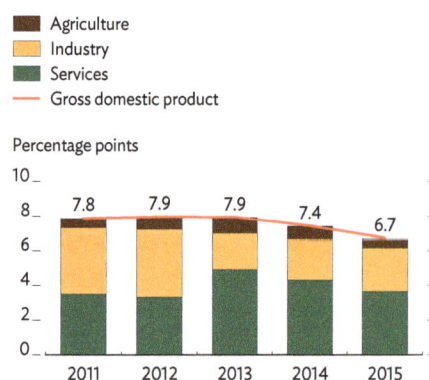

Sources: Lao Statistics Bureau; *Asian Development Outlook* database.
Click here for figure data

3.25.2 Tourism indicators

Source: National Tourism Administration.
Click here for figure data

This chapter was written by Rattanatay Luanglatbandith and Soulinthone Leuangkhamsing of the Lao PDR Resident Mission, ADB, Vientiane.

At about 16% over the past 2 years, credit growth has decelerated from almost 36% in 2013, and the central bank has phased down its direct lending for public infrastructure (Figure 3.25.4). Growth in the money supply has also slowed. To stimulate lending to small and medium-sized enterprises, the central bank directed commercial banks to lower interest rates effective from August last year. The Lao kip depreciated by 0.7% against the US dollar over 2015 but appreciated by 8.3% against the Thai baht.

Lower global fuel and food prices brought down inflation from 2.5% at the start of 2015 to 0.9% by December (Figure 3.25.5). Slower credit growth and firmer control over fiscal spending have helped to dampen inflation over the past 2 years. In 2015, the average inflation rate was, at 1.3%, the lowest since 2009.

Merchandise exports, mainly electricity and minerals, fell by an estimated 7.1% in US dollar terms in 2015. Imports also fell in US dollar terms, by an estimated 5.8%, due to lower oil and commodity prices and more subdued domestic demand. The trade deficit improved by an estimated 3% to $3.1 billion, and the current account deficit narrowed to equal 20.3% of GDP. Inflows of foreign direct investment and earnings from tourism contributed to an increase in gross international reserves to an estimated $986.8 million in December 2015, which covers less than 2 months of goods and services imports.

Expenditure and consumption surveys show that the poverty rate fell from 33.5% in 2003 to 23.2% in 2013, the latest available data. After gross national income per capita surpassed $1,000 in 2011, the World Bank reclassified the Lao People's Democratic Republic (Lao PDR) as lower-middle income. The government aims to meet income, quality of life, and economic vulnerability criteria by 2020 for eligibility to graduate from United Nations status as a least-developed country.

Economic prospects

Electricity production is expected to maintain growth as more new hydropower plants come online this year and the 1.9 gigawatt Hongsa lignite-fired plant makes a full-year contribution to GDP.

Growth in construction will be underpinned by work on additional hydropower plants, including the 1.3 gigawatt Xayaburi project scheduled for commissioning in 2019, as well as by new commercial, industrial, and residential developments. Robust expansion is projected for services, driven by growth in tourism and development in finance and telecommunications. Agriculture is projected to pick up in 2016, assuming better weather. However, mining is likely to be subdued in light of soft global demand and prices for minerals.

The impact of slowing growth in the People's Republic of China (PRC) on Lao PDR trade and investment is countered in part by gradual recovery forecast for Thailand—which will lift Lao PDR exports, tourism, and remittances—and by robust growth in Viet Nam. GDP growth could get a lift from next year if a planned $6.8 billion railway to link Vientiane with Yunnan Province in the PRC goes ahead. This project, to be built and largely funded by the PRC, would stimulate other investment from that source. It would also add to Lao PDR external debt.

3.25.3 Electricity output

Billion kilowatt-hours

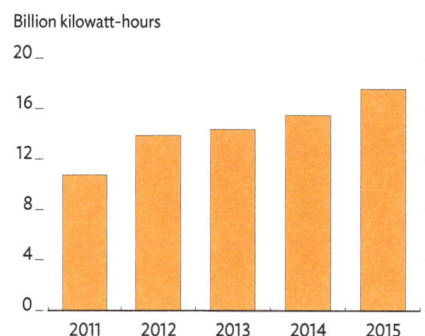

Source: Ministry of Energy and Mines.
Click here for figure data

3.25.4 Monetary indicators

— Domestic credit
— Money supply
Domestic credit ■

% change, year on year   KN trillion

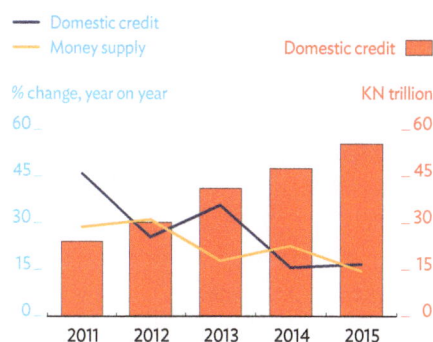

Source: Bank of the Lao People's Democratic Republic.
Click here for figure data

3.25.5 Monthly inflation

%, year on year

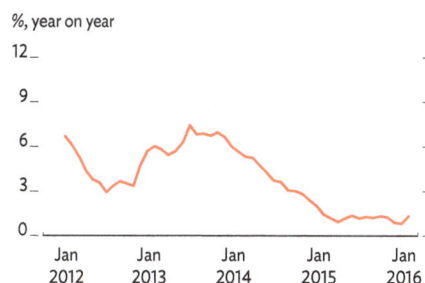

Source: CEIC Data Company (accessed 8 March 2016).
Click here for figure data

The government has committed to restrain growth in administrative spending, including civil service salaries. It will continue to repay arrears and has budgeted for additional expenditure related to a series of meetings to be hosted by the Lao PDR as the chair of the Association of Southeast Asian Nations in 2016. To address shortfalls in revenue, the government has stepped up efforts to strengthen tax collection, and it raised excise tax rates on vehicles and luxury goods from October 2015. Still, the fiscal deficit is expected to widen to 5.0% of GDP in FY2016 before narrowing in FY2017.

Taking these factors into account, GDP growth is forecast to pick up to 6.8% this year and 7.0% in 2017.

Lower oil prices and stable food prices forecast globally in 2016 will keep inflation subdued. The consumer price index rose by 1.1% year on year in the first 2 months of 2016. Inflation is forecast to quicken in the months ahead to average 1.8% in 2016 and edge higher in 2017 if oil prices turn up as projected (Figure 3.25.6).

Meanwhile, lower oil prices will help to sustain downward pressure on merchandise imports this year, though exports are seen edging up mainly on increased sales of electricity to Thailand. The current account deficit is forecast to narrow in 2016 but widen again in 2017 if the planned railway project is at a stage that requires sizable imports of materials and equipment (Figure 3.25.7).

Policy challenge—strengthening the external position

Measures to curtail the fiscal deficit and curb rapid growth in credit have succeeded, with substantial help from the drop in global oil prices, in lowering inflation and narrowing the external deficit. Nevertheless, the external position remains fragile. International reserves that cover less than 2 months of imports of goods and services provide only a thin buffer against external shocks.

Further, rising external debt has increased the risk of external debt distress, according to a 2014 debt-sustainability analysis by the International Monetary Fund and the World Bank. The analysis estimated total public and private external debt at the equivalent of 85% of GDP in 2013, projected to rise to 90%. Most of the external debt was long term. About half was public and publicly guaranteed debt, much of it on concessional terms.

Sustained fiscal and monetary discipline should go some way toward addressing external vulnerabilities. Higher and more diverse exports could make an important contribution but would require an improved domestic business environment to spur production, as well as greater exchange rate flexibility. Kip appreciation in real effective terms has hurt exports and stimulated imports, worsening the external deficit.

3.25.1 Selected economic indicators (%)

	2016	2017
GDP growth	6.8	7.0
Inflation	1.8	2.5
Current account balance (share of GDP)	–17.0	–20.0

Source: ADB estimates.

3.25.6 Inflation

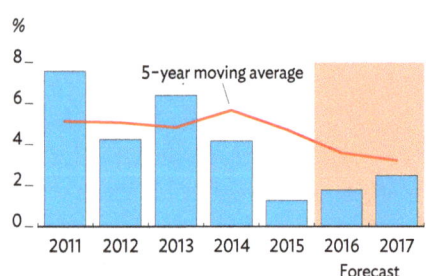

Source: Asian Development Outlook database.
Click here for figure data

3.25.7 Current account balance

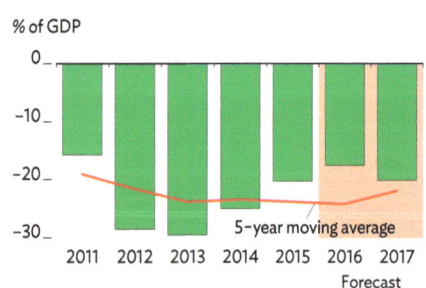

Source: Asian Development Outlook database.
Click here for figure data

Malaysia

A broad economic slowdown last year is expected to continue through 2016 before growth starts to pick up in 2017. Inflation is forecast to rise after moderating in 2015. The current account surplus is seen narrowing further this year. Significant progress has been made toward strengthening the fiscal position, but achieving a balanced budget by 2020 may require further action on both revenue and expenditure.

Economic performance

Though facing weaker global demand for exports and steep price declines for oil and other commodities, the economy grew by 5.0% in 2015 against average growth of 5.4% over the 4 previous years (Figure 3.26.1). Compared with 2014, GDP growth decelerated by 1.0 percentage point, with slowdowns in consumption and fixed investment and a decline in net exports.

Private consumption moderated last year, after several years of rapid expansion, to record growth at 6.0%, still robust enough to generate 3.1 percentage points of the growth in GDP. Household spending was dampened by the introduction of a goods and services tax (GST) in April 2015 together with softening in the labor market as the unemployment rate edged up from 2.9% to 3.2% in 2015, as well as by slowing growth in credit to households.

Growth in government consumption spending eased to 4.3%, and government fixed investment fell for a second year in a row, reflecting the completion of some large public projects and efforts to narrow the fiscal deficit. Private fixed investment decelerated, partly on the weak outlook for exports, but it still grew by 6.4%. Fixed investment overall rose by 3.7% in 2015, maintaining a slowing trend since 2012 (Figure 3.26.2). A rise in inventories contributed to GDP growth last year, but net external demand subtracted from growth as imports of goods and services rose in real terms by 1.3%, faster than the 0.7% real increase in exports of goods and services.

By sector, growth in services eased to 5.1% from 6.5% in 2014 as government services, finance, insurance, and retailing slowed, the last area dampened by the GST. Transport and communications maintained robust growth on demand for data communication services. The service sector generated more than half of GDP growth.

Vigorous 8.2% expansion of construction came from residential and civil engineering projects. Mining output rose by 4.7% on higher hydrocarbon production, but growth in manufacturing slowed to 4.9% as both domestic and external demand slackened. Industry as a whole

3.26.1 Demand-side contributions to growth

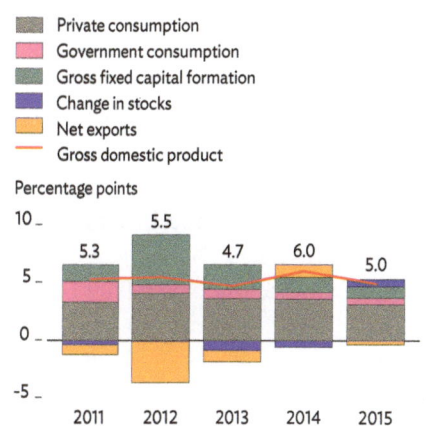

- Private consumption
- Government consumption
- Gross fixed capital formation
- Change in stocks
- Net exports
- Gross domestic product

Percentage points

Sources: Haver Analytics; Bank Negara Malaysia. 2016. *Monthly Statistical Bulletin.* February. http://www.bnm.gov.my (accessed 18 February 2016).
Click here for figure data

3.26.2 Fixed investment growth

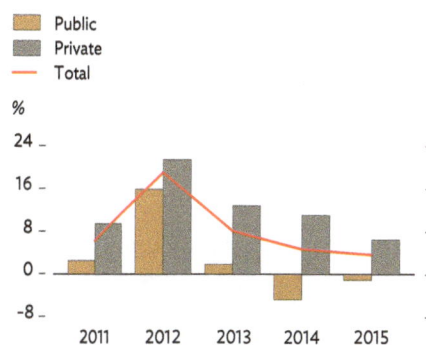

- Public
- Private
- Total

%

Sources: Haver Analytics; Bank Negara Malaysia. 2016. *Monthly Statistical Bulletin.* February. http://www.bnm.gov.my (accessed 15 March 2016).
Click here for figure data

This chapter was written by Akiko Terada-Hagiwara and Shiela Camingue-Romance of the Economic Research and Regional Cooperation Department, ADB, Manila.

grew by 5.2% in 2015, marginally faster than services but decelerating from 2014. Agriculture output increased by only 1.0%, held down by floods and haze.

After decelerating sharply in the first quarter of 2015 in line with lower oil prices, inflation picked up as the GST took effect and bad weather pushed up food prices (Figure 3.26.3). Depreciation of the Malaysian ringgit added to inflationary pressures. Nonetheless, inflation slowed on a year-average basis to 2.1% in 2015 from 3.1% the previous year, when the government cut fuel subsidies.

The government, committed to reining in its fiscal deficit, reduced public expenditure by 0.7% last year. Subsidy reductions and the new GST from April helped to shield the 2015 budget from steep falls in revenue from hydrocarbons, but total revenue still fell by 0.7%. The budget deficit continued to shrink gradually, narrowing to 3.2% of GDP (Figure 3.26.4).

The central bank kept its policy interest rate at 3.25% through 2015. Concerns over ringgit depreciation and capital outflows inhibited monetary easing. The rate of increase in broad money (M3) slowed to 2.7% by year-end. Growth in credit also decelerated, to 7.7% for credit to households and to 8.0% for businesses.

Malaysia recorded lower trade and current account surpluses last year. Merchandise exports fell by 15.5% in US dollar terms on declines in resource-based manufactures such as refined petroleum and natural rubber products, and in commodities, largely the result of lower prices for oil, liquefied natural gas, and some agricultural commodities. Merchandise imports fell by 14.7% in US dollar terms. Imports of intermediate and capital goods fell, reflecting weaker export demand and investment, while imports of consumer goods remained buoyant. The merchandise trade surplus fell by 19.5% to $27.9 billion.

Trade in services posted a wider deficit, partly from a decline in tourist arrivals, but the income deficit narrowed. The outcome was a 40% decline in the current account surplus to $8.7 billion, equal to 2.9% of GDP. Net outflows on the capital and financial accounts, taking into consideration large positive errors and omissions last year, totaled $7.7 billion, compared with larger outflows of $25.6 billion in 2014. Portfolio investment recorded net outflows of $7.2 billion, down by 39%, and for the first time since 2006 net direct investment turned slightly positive, taking into account reduced investment abroad by Malaysians. The balance of payments recorded a small surplus (Figure 3.26.5).

Gross international reserves fell by 18% to $95.3 billion, sufficient to cover 7.6 months of retained imports of goods. Lower reserves reflected central bank efforts to support the ringgit, which came under downward pressure in 2015 from falling oil prices and volatile global capital flows. Investor concerns about the finances of the government-owned investment company 1Malaysia Development added to pressure on the ringgit, which depreciated by 19% against the US dollar last year after 6% depreciation in 2014.

External debt fell to $194.3 billion but, as a ratio to GDP, rose to 72.1% from 67.5% owing to foreign exchange valuation effects. About 58% of the external debt was medium and long term and 36% was denominated in ringgit. Foreign investors pared holdings of government and corporate

3.26.3 Monthly inflation

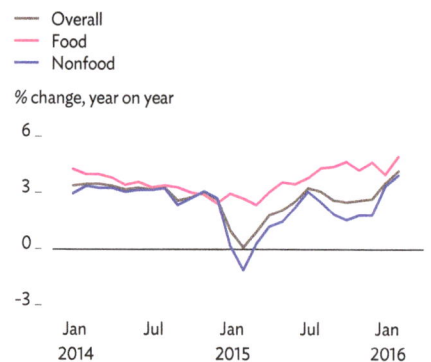

Sources: Haver Analytics; Bank Negara Malaysia. 2016. *Monthly Statistical Bulletin*. February. http://www.bnm.gov.my (accessed 14 March 2016).
Click here for figure data

3.26.4 Fiscal performance

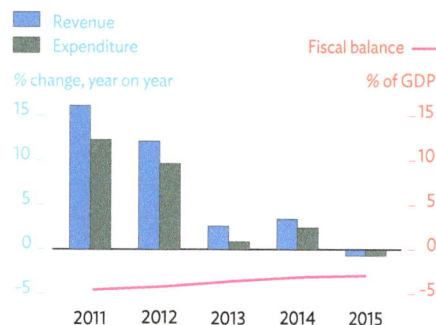

Sources: Ministry of Finance Malaysia. 2016. *Quarterly Update on the Malaysian Economy—4th Quarter 2015*. March. http://www.treasury.gov.my; CEIC Data Company (both accessed 15 March 2016).
Click here for figure data

3.26.5 Balance of payment components

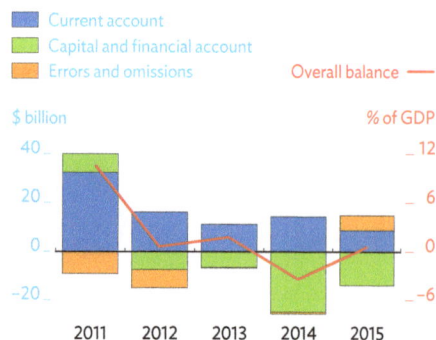

Sources: Haver Analytics; Bank Negara Malaysia. 2016. *Monthly Statistical Bulletin*. February. http://www.bnm.gov.my (accessed 15 March 2016).
Click here for figure data

debt securities as global oil prices weakened and expectations mounted that US interest rates would start to move higher.

The government unveiled in May 2015 its Eleventh Malaysia Plan, 2016–2020, which targets average annual GDP growth of 5.0%–6.0%. Average growth during the previous plan period, 2011–2015, was 5.3%. Inflation for the new 5-year plan period is targeted at below 3.0%. The goal of the plan is to raise gross national income per capita from $10,200 in 2015 to $15,690 in 2020, lifting Malaysia into the ranks of high-income nations.

Economic prospects

Economic growth is projected to moderate further in 2016 to 4.2% before it starts to recover next year (Figure 3.26.6). External demand will remain subdued in 2016 as growth slows in the People's Republic of China, Malaysia's second biggest export market, and economic activity stays sluggish in major industrial economies. Domestic demand will drive growth, but it is dampened this year by softer labor and property markets, lower earnings from hydrocarbons and other commodities, higher inflation, high household debt, slower growth in credit, and fiscal tightening.

These factors will weigh on private consumption, which is projected to grow at a slower pace than in 2015. The government has taken steps to cushion the slowdown in household spending. To bolster incomes it reduced mandatory employee contributions to the national retirement fund from March 2016, trimmed some personal tax rates from January 2016, and maintained a range of cash transfers. Further, the government increased the number of items exempted from the GST. The national minimum wage will rise from July 2016. Nevertheless, consumer confidence was low at the start of 2016 (Figure 3.26.7).

Slowing domestic demand and lackluster global prospects have taken their toll on business sentiment. The business conditions index declined through last year, though it steadied in the fourth quarter (Figure 3.26.7). The manufacturing purchasing managers' index shows little sign of sustained recovery after falling last year (Figure 3.26.8). In February 2016, manufacturers indicated renewed deterioration in operating conditions, led by a fall in new domestic orders. Moreover, the government's leading economic indicator pointed in January 2016 to slowing economic growth in the months ahead.

On the bright side, semiconductor book-to-bill ratios in North America and Japan are trending up, which suggests improving demand for electronic and electrical products (Figure 3.26.9).

Infrastructure projects under the Eleventh Malaysia Plan will support growth in fixed investment. Government-linked companies, particularly those in transportation and utilities, are expected to make substantial investments in the next 2 years. The government committed to push ahead with major infrastructure projects including mass rapid transit and light railway systems. However, prospects are bleak for investment in oil and gas exploration and production, considering the plunge in hydrocarbon prices. The state oil company Petronas reported that it will cut $11.4 billion in capital and operating expenditure over the

3.26.6 Annual GDP growth

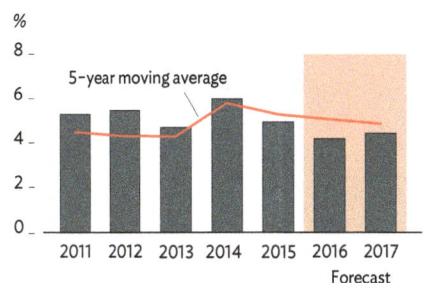

Source: Asian Development Outlook database.
Click here for figure data

3.26.1 Selected economic indicators (%)

	2016	2017
GDP growth	4.2	4.4
Inflation	2.7	2.5
Current account balance (share of GDP)	1.2	2.3

Source: ADB estimates.

3.26.7 Consumer and business confidence indexes

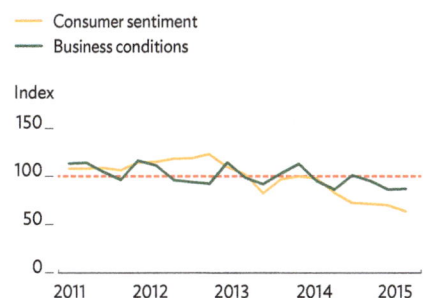

Note: Above 100 indicates improvement in business conditions and rising consumer confidence.
Sources: Malaysian Institute of Economic Research. https://www.mier.org.my; Haver Analytics (both accessed 15 March 2016).
Click here for figure data

3.26.8 Manufacturing purchasing managers' index

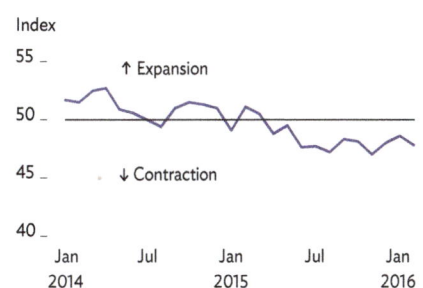

Note: Nikkei, Markit.
Source: Bloomberg (accessed 15 March 2016).
Click here for figure data

next 4 years. A fall in manufacturing capacity utilization last year from 79.8% to 75.0% indicates slack capacity overall in manufacturing, though investment is continuing to expand in oil refining and petrochemicals and is expected to pick up in electronic and electrical products.

Fiscal policy intends to further narrow the budget deficit in 2016 to 3.1% of GDP. Falling oil prices prompted the government in January 2016 to revise down its revenue expectations and reduce budgeted operating and development expenditures.

As for monetary policy, the central bank lowered in January 2016 its reserve requirement for banks to support economic growth. In March, it reiterated that the policy interest rate at 3.25% supports economic activity, suggesting the rate may remain there for some time.

Inflation is seen rising to average 2.7% in 2016 (Figure 3.26.10). Lower energy prices are expected to be offset by increases in prices of administered goods, higher road tolls, and higher prices for imports from ringgit depreciation. Dry weather from El Niño is expected to lift food prices. Inflation jumped to 4.2% in February 2016, largely on a temporary base effect caused by sharply lower inflation in the first few months of 2015. From April, the impact of the GST will drop out of the year-on-year inflation rate.

The outlook for exports this year remains weak. External demand is subdued and prices for export commodities remain low (Figure 3.26.11). In January 2016, customs-recorded exports fell by almost 20% in US dollar terms. Exports of mineral fuels and lubricants dropped by 48%, and shipments of manufactured goods fell by 21%, including an 11% fall in electronic and electrical products. The export performance is seen improving in 2017, assuming firmer global demand and help from the more competitive ringgit exchange rate. Prices for export commodities, too, are expected to rise next year.

Merchandise imports continued to decline in January but are expected to rise over this year, with the pace quickening in 2017 if investment picks up. Inbound tourism is likely to get a lift from relaxed visa requirements starting in February 2016 for tourists from the People's Republic of China. The current account surplus is forecast to decline this year before rising in 2017 (Figure 3.26.12).

Domestic and external uncertainties pose risks to the outlook, notably disappointing demand for exports and renewed weakness in oil and commodity prices. However, the economy's resilience under such developments is supported by its increasingly diversified economic structure (services and manufacturing now account for 75% of GDP), adequate international reserves, a flexible exchange rate, well-developed capital markets, and steps taken to bolster the budget.

Policy challenge—strengthening the fiscal position

Malaysia's budget has depended heavily on income from oil and gas, leaving it vulnerable to sharp declines in global prices for hydrocarbons. Until recently, oil and gas revenue accounted for about a third of total budget revenue. In the past 2 years, the government has taken two important steps to strengthen the fiscal position: It introduced the GST to broaden the tax base and cut subsidies, particularly on fuel, to free up budget resources for more productive purposes.

3.26.9 Semiconductor book-to-bill ratios

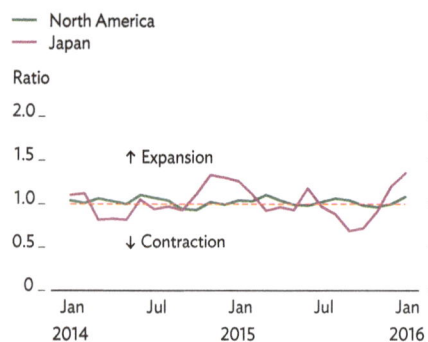

Note: The series is calculated as the ratio of the 3-month average of bookings (orders) to the 3-month average of billings (shipments). A ratio below 1 suggests industry contraction.
Source: Bloomberg (accessed 15 March 2016).
Click here for figure data

3.26.10 Annual inflation

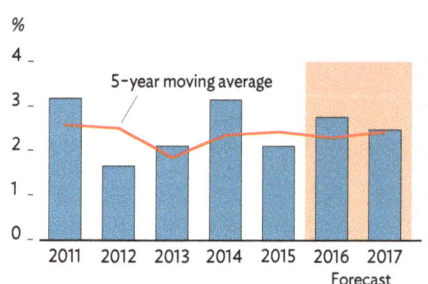

Source: Asian Development Outlook database.
Click here for figure data

3.26.11 Selected commodity prices

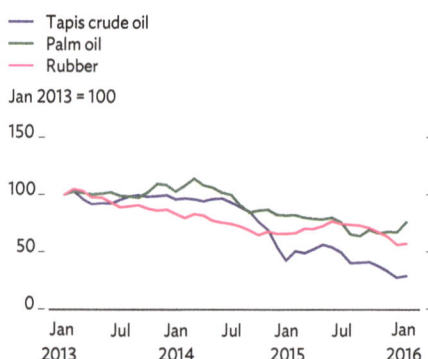

Sources: Haver Analytics; Bloomberg (accessed 15 March 2016).
Click here for figure data

Fuel subsidies were cut from RM21 billion, or 10% of total operating expenditure, in 2014 to RM2 billion, or 1%, in 2015. This saving offset a significant drop in revenue caused by lower oil and gas prices. The GST, introduced at a relatively low rate of 6% in April 2015, replaced sales and services taxes that raised the equivalent of 1.6% of GDP in 2014. The GST yielded about 3% of GDP in 2015. Nevertheless, the non-oil fiscal deficit in 2015 was still substantial at 7.0% of GDP, as the gain from the GST was offset by higher development expenditure (Figure 3.26.13).

The GST should improve the non-oil fiscal balance starting in 2016, though the near-term gains may be limited given the more subdued domestic demand. The government plans to make the GST more effective by lowering the registration threshold to broaden the tax base. Meanwhile, however, it also has foregone revenue by extending the number of items that are excluded from GST.

The 2016 budget includes other revenue-raising measures: The excise tax on tobacco was raised by 40% in November 2015, and personal income tax rates for high-income earners were increased from January 2016. The government's aim of a balanced budget by 2020 may require further action on both revenue and expenditure. Among other possibilities, higher revenue could come from improving the administration of personal and corporate income tax, raising the GST rate, or reducing tax exemptions.

The expenditure side would benefit from further reductions and improved targeting of subsidies, which include subsidies on cooking oil, assistance for education expenses, and cash transfers. These and other subsidies still absorb 10% of budget operating expenditure. For example, the BR1M cash transfer program for needy families could be targeted more tightly. In March 2016, 7.1 million people, or almost a quarter of the population, were approved to receive the cash transfer for this year, which is expected to cost RM5.9 billion.

3.26.12 Current account balance

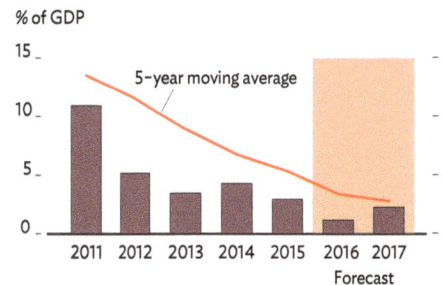

Source: Asian Development Outlook database.
Click here for figure data

3.26.13 Fiscal balance

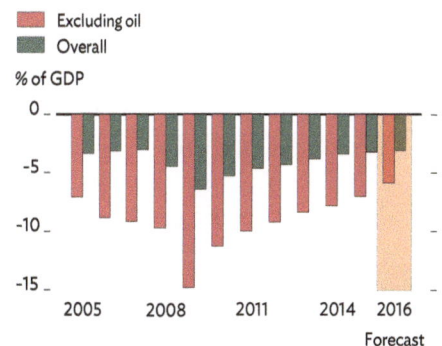

Sources: ADB estimates using data from Ministry of Finance Malaysia. 2016. *Quarterly Update on the Malaysian Economy—4th Quarter 2015.* March. http://www.treasury.gov.my; CEIC Data Company (both accessed 15 March 2016).
Click here for figure data

Myanmar

Despite severe flooding, the economy continued to perform well in the closing fiscal year. Growth is forecast to accelerate during 2016 on recovery in agriculture and increases in foreign direct investment. Among the near-term challenges facing the incoming government are high inflation and wide fiscal and external deficits. Upgrading the transport system is one of many longer-term challenges.

Economic performance

Economic growth eased to an estimated 7.2% in FY2015 (ending 31 March 2016) owing to severe floods and landslides that damaged agriculture, as well as to slower growth in the People's Republic of China (PRC) that hit trade and investment.

In July–August 2015, a cyclone and intense monsoonal rains caused widespread flooding and landslides that displaced more than 1.6 million people, killed 132, and devastated one-fifth of all cultivated land. The economic cost was estimated at $1.5 billion, equal to 3% of GDP. It was a disaster for agriculture, which contributes almost 30% of GDP and more than 60% of employment. International partners joined the reconstruction and rehabilitation efforts.

Construction, manufacturing, and services nevertheless continued to expand, and the government pushed ahead with structural reform to raise investment in social and physical infrastructure and improve the business climate. Growth in services was spurred by further increases in tourist arrivals to 4.7 million in 2015, about 70% entering overland (Figure 3.27.1). Spending by tourists rose by 19% to $2.1 billion in 2015.

Garment manufacturing maintained solid growth with new foreign-owned garment factories in Pathein, Bago, and Thilawa. Exports of garments rose by 28% to an estimated $2 billion. Exports of natural gas in volume terms increased by an estimated 2.9%, a much slower pace than in the previous year, and the value of gas exports likely fell by about 18% to $3.5 billion.

In a sign that business confidence remained robust despite the floods and political uncertainty ahead of national elections in November 2015, the number of business registrations in the first 9 months of FY2015 was, at 4,825, comparable to that in the same period of FY2014 (Figure 3.27.2). Approvals of foreign direct investment (FDI) totaled $4.9 billion from April to December 2015, down by 26% from the same period a year earlier. Most of the FDI was channeled into telecommunications, oil and gas, and manufacturing, primarily garments. None went into agriculture. FDI disbursements in FY2015 likely eased as well.

3.27.1 Tourism indicators

Note: Data refer to calendar year. Tourist arrivals include border tourism.
Source: Ministry of Hotels and Tourism.
Click here for figure data

3.27.2 Domestic business registrations

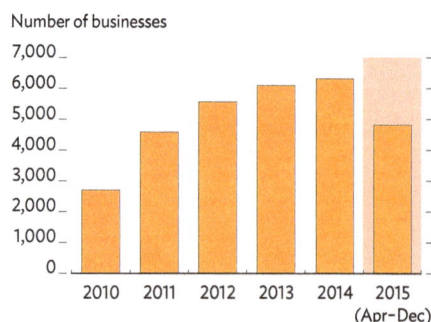

Note: Years are fiscal years ending 31 March of the next year. Data in FY2015 cover the first 9 months, from April to December 2015.
Source: Directorate of Investment and Company Administration.
Click here for figure data

This chapter was written by Peter Brimble of the Myanmar Resident Mission, ADB, Yangon, and Aung Tun, consultant, Myanmar Resident Mission, ADB, Yangon.

Hikes in food prices after the floods and depreciation of the Myanmar kyat propelled inflation to 16.2% in October 2015 (Figure 3.27.3). For FY2015 the average inflation rate was estimated at 11.0%. A widening current account deficit contributed to the kyat depreciating by 26% against a firming US dollar from April 2014 to January 2016. Rapid growth in credit to the private sector, estimated at 45% year on year, and 17.9% growth in the monetary base added to inflationary pressures.

Higher government spending during the election year widened the consolidated fiscal deficit to an estimated 4.8% of GDP in FY2015 from 2.9% in FY2014. Treasury bill auctions introduced in January 2015 broadened options for funding the deficit, but the auctions have yet to raise the amounts targeted. When fully implemented, the auction system should end the inflationary practice of monetizing the deficit through the sale of government debt to the central bank.

The government is also addressing the fiscal gap through tax reform that aims to raise the ratio of tax to GDP from its current low level of about 8%. A new tax law approved by Parliament is the centerpiece of wider reform that covers income tax, commercial tax, and stamp duty, among other levies.

Merchandise exports increased only marginally in FY2015 owing to softer demand for gems and minerals from the PRC, lower gas prices, and a fall in rice exports after the floods. Imports decelerated from the previous year but still grew at a double-digit rate as vigorous economic growth spurred demand for consumer and capital goods (Figure 3.27.4). Consequently, the trade deficit jumped by almost half, and the current account deficit widened to an estimated 8.9% of GDP. Official reserves are estimated at 2.5 months of imports, down from 2.8 months in FY2014. Declining foreign reserves likely prompted the central bank's move in mid-2015 to intensify measures to curb the use of US dollars.

External debt increased to an estimated $9.7 billion, equal to 14.7% of GDP. The International Monetary Fund and the World Bank have assessed Myanmar as being at low risk of debt distress. Public debt management, both external and domestic, has been strengthened through a new public debt law ratified by Parliament in early 2016 and a recently established debt management office. The government is encouraged to pursue further structural reform to broaden the base of economic growth and expand its finances.

Economic prospects

GDP growth is forecast to recover to 8.4% in FY2016 and record a similar pace in FY2017 (Figure 3.27.5). The impact of the floods on agriculture will fade during this year. FDI is expected to get a lift from the successful completion of national elections. Additional FDI is seen flowing into newly established special economic zones and the rapidly expanding transport and energy industries.

Government policy makers taking office in April 2016 have committed to continuing reform, which is necessary if Myanmar is to achieve its long-term growth potential, estimated at 8.0% annually. The new administration is expected to press for more transparency and

3.27.3 Monthly inflation

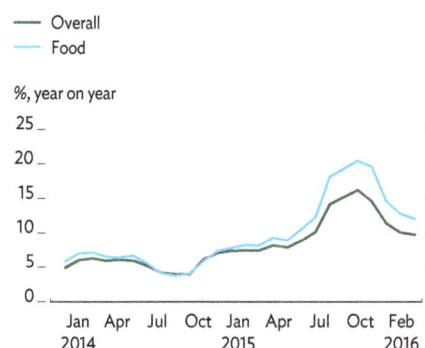

Source: Central Statistical Organization.
Click here for figure data

3.27.4 Trade indicators

Note: Years are fiscal years ending 31 March of the next year.
Sources: International Monetary Fund; ADB estimates.
Click here for figure data

3.27.5 GDP growth

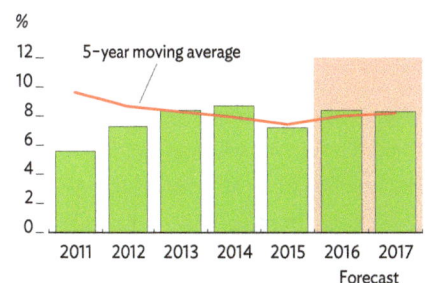

Note: Years are fiscal years ending 31 March of the next year.
Sources: International Monetary Fund; ADB estimates.
Click here for figure data

3.27.1 Selected economic indicators (%)

	2016	2017
GDP growth	8.4	8.3
Inflation	9.5	8.5
Current account balance (share of GDP)	−8.3	−7.7

Note: Years are fiscal years ending on 30 June of that year.
Source: ADB estimates.

deregulation, less red tape, improved education and training, and more effective and efficient government services. Its focus is likely to be on creating jobs largely by stimulating economic growth, in particular for the 70% of the population living in rural areas.

Cross-border economic integration will be an important driver of growth. Factors dampening the outlook—moderating growth in the PRC and weak global prices for gas and commodities—are partly offset by improving economic prospects in neighboring India and Thailand.

On the fiscal front, the FY2016 budget passed by Parliament in February 2016 calls for a modest reduction in the fiscal deficit. Revenue and expenditure are expected to fall in FY2016. The government has laid out an ambitious fiscal plan to, among other things, raise tax revenue, make spending more efficient, and restructure state economic enterprises.

Inflation will moderate as agricultural recovery from the floods brings down food prices, but it is still projected to remain high at 9.5% in FY2016 and 8.5% in FY2017 (Figure 3.27.6).

To manage rapid growth in credit, the central bank is preparing to strengthen bank supervision and prudential controls and to improve the functioning of the interbank money market to provide benchmarks for short-term lending rates. More reforms for finance and business are expected in 2016 (Box 3.27.1). Maintaining exchange rate flexibility will be crucial, as measures to resist depreciation have so far been largely counterproductive and a drain on reserves. The incoming government has indicated it will strengthen the autonomy of the central bank and develop stronger monetary policy tools.

The current account deficit is seen narrowing to 8.3% of GDP in FY2016 (Figure 3.27.7). Stronger economic growth will drive up imports, but this will be countered somewhat by lower prices for imported oil. Exports of agricultural products will rebound, and those of manufactured products will continue to grow, but gas export prices remain under downward pressure. Vulnerabilities in the fiscal and external accounts call for stronger efforts to build up official reserves to more comfortable levels.

External debt is projected to rise to $11.2 billion in FY2016, equal to 15.7% of GDP. Myanmar's risk of debt distress is expected to remain low, however, as most debt is on concessional terms and the government has been cutting back on commercial borrowing.

Despite significant economic reform since 2011, the new government faces daunting challenges. One is to maintain stability on the macroeconomic front and in regions affected by conflict. Another is to address deficits in infrastructure and in human resources and capacity that constrain social and economic development. A third challenge is to maintain and advance progress on reform to improve governance and strengthen public sector management, private sector development, and regional cooperation and integration. Combating poverty and child malnutrition remain high priorities, and anecdotal evidence suggests that income inequality is worsening. The economy is narrowly based, with growth depending on natural resource exports, construction, and tourism.

3.27.1 Reforms for finance and business

In January 2016, Parliament passed the amended Banks and Financial Institutions Law, which lays the foundations for more efficient licensing of financial institutions, a modern financial sector, and its enhanced supervision. The law sets guidelines for domestic and foreign banks, including more stringent rules on paid-up capital and reserve requirements. Four foreign banks received licenses in March 2016, adding to the nine that were licensed in 2014.

An important reform for the business environment will be the ratification expected in 2016 of a new company law that incorporates international standards of corporate governance. The law will define a foreign company according to a threshold of investment from overseas, which will allow foreign equity investment in Myanmar companies that are not joint ventures, as well as enable foreign firms to participate in capital markets.

The new Yangon Stock Exchange started trading in March 2016, initially with one company listed. Five more have been approved for listing, and others have applied.

3.27.6 Inflation

%

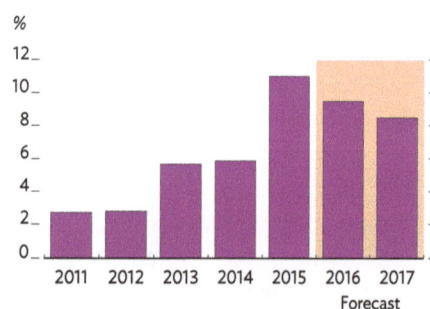

Note: Years are fiscal years ending 31 March of the next year.
Sources: International Monetary Fund; ADB estimates.
Click here for figure data

Intensified efforts are needed to improve the business environment through legal and regulatory reforms, better access to finance, and targeted trade and investment promotion and facilitation.

Risks to the economic outlook come from thin external and fiscal buffers, ethnic and sectarian tensions, unproven capacity in the new government to maintain reform momentum, and vulnerability to bad weather. El Niño is expected to bring drought to the dry zone in central Myanmar and unseasonable rainstorms to lower Myanmar. Incoming policy makers have promised to redouble efforts to improve economic and social data, which is badly needed to inform policy formulation and planning.

Policy challenge—upgrading the transport system

After decades of underinvestment, Myanmar's transport infrastructure provides generally poor access to markets and services, perpetuates poverty and regional inequality, and hampers business development. The country could reduce by one-third its transport costs by upgrading infrastructure, according to one estimate.

Only 40% of Myanmar's road network is paved. At least 60% of its trunk highways need maintenance or rehabilitation, as do most of its railways (Figure 3.27.8). Some 20 million people lack even basic access by rural road, and river transport infrastructure hardly exists. Demand is growing fast, with the number of vehicles on the roads more than doubling to 5 million from 2012 to 2015, and international air passengers more than doubling to 3.2 million from 2011 to 2014.

Investment estimated at $60 billion is needed through 2030 to upgrade transport systems to a standard in line with other countries at a similar stage of development. This means increasing transport sector investments to the equivalent of 3%–4% of GDP from little more than 1% in recent years.

The government's newly developed National Transport Master Plan envisages an efficient, modern, safe, and environmentally friendly system that covers all modes of transport. Under the plan, investment is required to upgrade the trunk road and rail networks, improve links with neighboring countries, develop access to rural areas, provide public transport in urban areas, and enhance intermodal transport networks and logistics.

Toward policy reform, a single transport ministry will help to coordinate policy, planning, investment, management, and regulation. Given the immense funding required, private sector resources could be mobilized through the restructuring of concessions to operate toll roads, competitive outsourcing of civil works, and corporatizing or privatizing of state-owned enterprises and activities that operate in competitive markets.

3.27.7 Current account balance

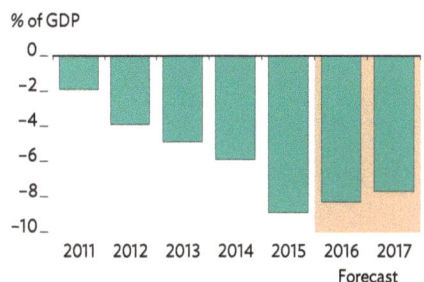

% of GDP

Note: Years are fiscal years ending 31 March of the next year.
Sources: International Monetary Fund; ADB estimates.
Click here for figure data

3.27.8 Transport challenges

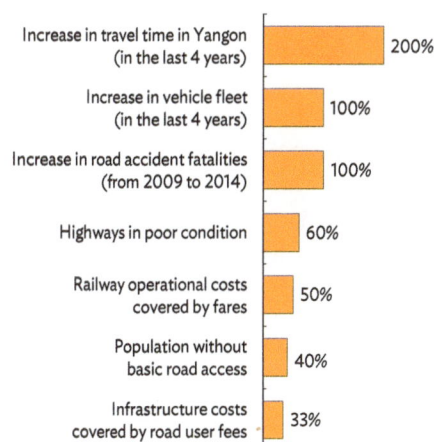

Increase in travel time in Yangon (in the last 4 years)	200%
Increase in vehicle fleet (in the last 4 years)	100%
Increase in road accident fatalities (from 2009 to 2014)	100%
Highways in poor condition	60%
Railway operational costs covered by fares	50%
Population without basic road access	40%
Infrastructure costs covered by road user fees	33%

Source: ADB. *Myanmar: Transport Sector Policy Note.*
Click here for figure data

Philippines

The economy posted solid growth last year generated by strong domestic demand, despite drag from net exports. Growth is projected to pick up with higher investment and consumption. Inflation is forecast to rise moderately as dry weather from El Niño presses upward on food prices and utility rates. Sustaining strong growth will require policy continuity supporting the development of infrastructure and human capital, improvements to the investment climate, and governance reform.

Economic performance

Economic growth moderated to 5.8% in 2015, a solid performance in the face of weak external demand and damage to agriculture inflicted by typhoons and drought from El Niño. Growth strengthened in the second half, reaching 6.3% in the fourth quarter.

Broad-based domestic demand underpinned growth last year. Growth in private consumption, which accounts for nearly 70% of GDP, accelerated to 6.2% and made the biggest contribution to overall growth from the demand side (Figure 3.28.1). Household spending benefitted from higher employment, remittance inflows from overseas workers, and low inflation. The unemployment rate fell from 6.6% in January 2015 to 5.8% in January 2016, and 752,000 new jobs were created in that period. Remittances rose by 4.4% to $28.5 billion, equal to 9.8% of GDP. The increase was 5.8% in peso terms.

Government expenditure, particularly on construction, accelerated during the year, helped by improved budget execution. Growth in government consumption quickened to 9.4%, and public construction jumped by 20.6%. A 5.4% rise in private construction and higher purchases of machinery and commercial vehicles reflected robust private fixed investment. Total fixed investment grew by 14.0%, more than double the pace of 2014, and significantly contributed to GDP growth. The ratio of fixed investment to GDP improved to 21.7%, though at that pace it still lagged some other Southeast Asian economies (Figure 3.28.2).

Net exports exerted considerable drag on GDP growth as imports of goods and services rose much faster than exports in real terms. Exports of services, particularly business process outsourcing (BPO), remained buoyant, but goods exports were lackluster.

By sector, services growth accelerated to 6.7%, which contributed nearly two-thirds of total growth. Trade, tourism-related services, and BPO were among the major contributors. Growth in manufacturing slowed to 5.7% on soft external demand but still generated about

3.28.1 Demand-side contributions to growth

- Private consumption
- Government consumption
- Fixed investment
- Change in inventories
- Net exports
- Statistical discrepancy
- Gross domestic product

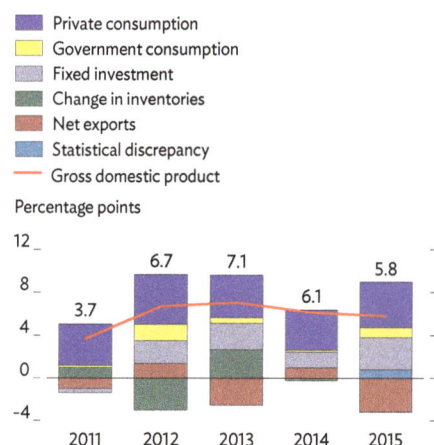

Source: CEIC Data Company (downloaded 7 March 2016).
Click here for figure data

3.28.2 Fixed investment

- Indonesia
- Malaysia
- Philippines
- Thailand

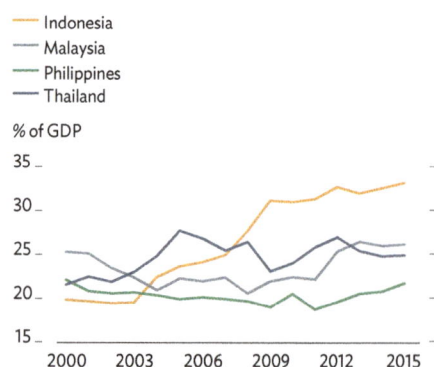

Source: CEIC Data Company (downloaded 7 March 2016).
Click here for figure data

This chapter was written by Sona Shrestha and Teresa Mendoza of the Philippines Country Office, ADB, Manila. The policy challenge section draws on ADB. Forthcoming. *Youth Situation in the Labor Market.*

one-fourth of the increase in GDP. Domestic demand supported manufacturing subsectors like food processing, chemicals, communication and transport equipment, and construction-related products. However, agricultural production was flat last year as typhoons and drought damaged crops, particularly rice and maize.

Inflation eased to below 1.0% for several months and averaged a low 1.4% in 2015 (Figure 3.28.3). Lower global oil and food prices dampened inflation, and rice imports to augment domestic supplies also helped. The central bank kept policy interest rates steady at 4% for overnight borrowing and 6% for overnight lending. Growth in broad money (M3) decelerated to 9.4% year on year in December 2015 from 11.2% a year earlier.

While the government ramped up public expenditure excluding interest by 15.7% in 2015, spending still fell short of the budget target. Revenue rose by 10.5% owing to higher tax income from tobacco and alcohol and more stringent tax enforcement. The budget deficit widened from 0.6% of GDP in 2014 to 0.9% in 2015, well below the 2.0% deficit ceiling in the budget. Reflecting a strengthening of the fiscal position in recent years, the ratio of government debt to GDP declined to 44.8% in 2015, the lowest in over a decade (Figure 3.28.4). Foreign debt comprised just over one-third of the total.

In the external accounts, merchandise exports fell by 13.1% in US dollar terms, with declines in exports of manufactured goods, minerals, and fruit and vegetables. Merchandise imports declined by 3.2% in US dollars, largely from lower oil prices. Buoyant imports of capital and consumer goods underlined the strength of private consumption and investment.

These developments widened the trade deficit by 25.2% to $21.7 billion. Nevertheless, earnings from BPO and tourism, together with remittances, generated a current account surplus of $8.4 billion, equal to 2.9% of GDP (Figure 3.28.5). The balance of payments, tempered by outflows of portfolio investment, recorded a surplus of $2.6 billion. Gross international reserves totaled $81.9 billion as of February 2016, cover for 10.2 months of imports of goods and services and income payments (Figure 3.28.6). The peso depreciated by 4.7% against the broadly strengthening US dollar in 2015.

Economic prospects

Growth in domestic demand is expected to drive higher rates of economic growth this year and next. Election-related spending will support growth through May 2016 when national elections are scheduled. Net external demand will likely remain a drag on growth in 2016, though less than in 2015, and add to growth in 2017. On balance, GDP is seen rising by 6.0% this year and 6.1% in 2017.

The acceleration in government spending in the second half of 2015 is projected to continue this year. The government has maintained its budget deficit ceiling at 2.0% of GDP in 2016, which accommodates a larger deficit than that realized in 2015. Budget allocations for infrastructure are boosted to the equivalent of 5.0% of GDP, including investments in roads, agricultural infrastructure, and schools.

3.28.3 Inflation and policy rate

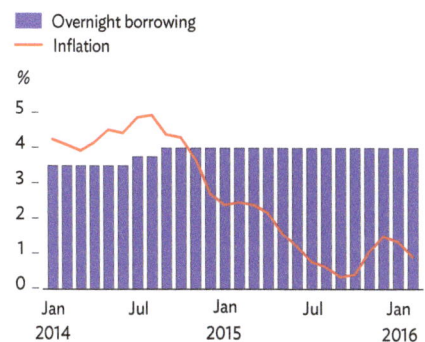

Source: CEIC Data Company (downloaded 14 March 2016).
Click here for figure data

3.28.4 National government debt outstanding

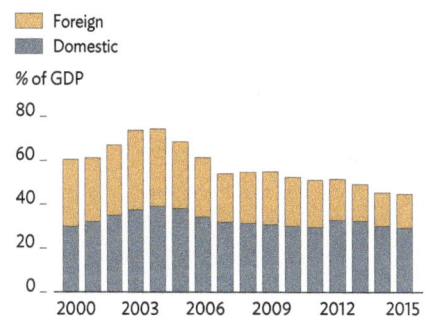

Source: CEIC Data Company (downloaded 14 March 2016).
Click here for figure data

3.28.5 Current account components

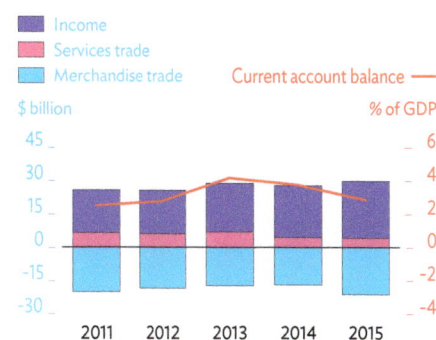

Source: CEIC Data Company (downloaded 14 March 2016).
Click here for figure data

Moreover, the government has accelerated the release of budget allocations and enhanced bidding and procurement processes to step up project implementation. Spending is raised on social services including funding for health, education, and conditional cash transfers to poor households. Civil service salaries are also raised this year.

Private consumption will be the main growth driver again this year. Rising employment, higher government salaries, modest inflation, and remittance inflows all point to robust consumer spending. Consumer confidence rose in the first quarter of 2016 (Figure 3.28.7). Nevertheless, the pace of increase in private consumption could moderate this year. Slower economic activity in the Middle East, where about one-fourth of overseas Filipinos work, has dampened growth in remittances (Figure 3.28.8). Still, diversity in sources provides a cushion as remittances flow from a broad range of countries (Figure 3.28.9).

Buoyant imports of capital goods in 2015 and higher foreign direct investment in the past 2 years suggest that private investment will maintain solid growth. Net inflows of foreign direct investment totaled $5.7 billion in 2015, similar to the 2014 figure but more than double the annual average from 2010 to 2013 (Figure 3.28.10). Growth in credit to business picked up to 16.0% in January 2016.

However, subdued global economic prospects indicate that merchandise exports will decline slightly this year before turning up in 2017. Exports fell by 3.9% year on year in January 2016, moderating from double-digit declines in most of 2015. The outlook for major markets Japan (receiving 21% of total merchandise exports in 2015) and the People's Republic of China (11%) is lackluster, but Philippine exports to the European Union (12%) are benefiting from expanded duty-free access granted in 2014, and exports to the US (15%) are expected to grow. Exports of services, mainly BPO, should perform well. Imports are projected to rise on growing consumption and investment, such that net external demand is seen weighing on GDP growth in 2016.

As inflation is projected to be within the official target range of 2%–4%, the central bank is expected to maintain an accommodative monetary policy. Inflation is forecast to trend up this year to average 2.3%, from 1.1% in the first 2 months (Figure 3.28.11). Drought from El Niño will likely raise food prices and utility rates, while peso depreciation and buoyant domestic demand will also contribute to inflation. The government has imported rice and expanded irrigation to mitigate the impact of El Niño. Next year, inflation is seen rising to 2.7%, assuming an upturn in global oil and commodity prices.

On the supply side, services such as transportation and communications are benefitting from election-related spending. Strong private consumption is driving growth in wholesale and retail trade, and the outlook is favorable for BPO and tourism. BPO revenue rose from $18.9 billion in 2014 to $22.0 billion in 2015, according to an estimate by the BPO industry association, with employment at 1.2 million. Tourism generated $5 billion in revenue from 5.4 million international tourists in 2015. The official target for 2016 is 6.0 million tourists. Tourism employed 5 million workers in 2015, or 12.7% of national employment.

3.28.6 Gross international reserves

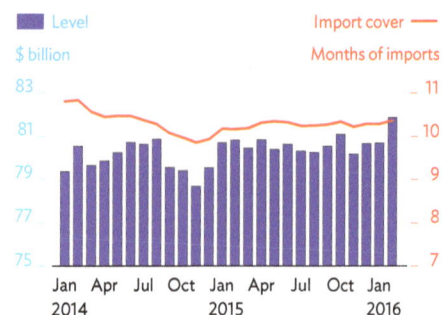

Source: CEIC Data Company (downloaded 14 March 2016).
Click here for figure data

3.28.7 Consumer expectations for the next 12 months

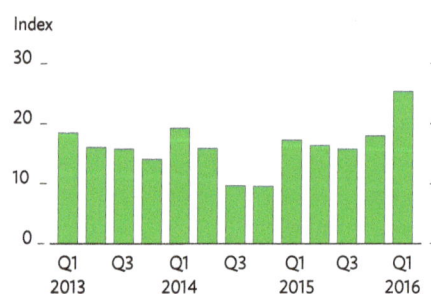

Q = quarter.
Note: The index is computed as the percentage of households that were optimistic less those that were pessimistic. A positive index indicates a favorable view.
Source: Bangko Sentral ng Pilipinas. www.bsp.gov.ph (accessed 22 March 2016).
Click here for figure data

3.28.8 Personal remittances

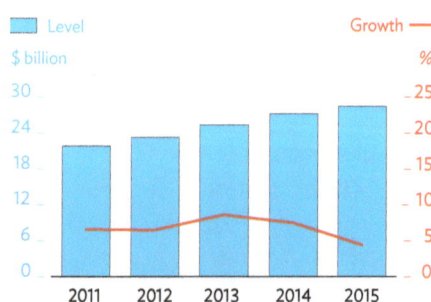

Source: Bangko Sentral ng Pilipinas. www.bsp.gov.ph (accessed 22 March 2016).
Click here for figure data

Private construction, while moderating from the rapid pace of recent years, is projected to expand through the forecast period. Public construction, including public–private partnership (PPP) projects, is expected to post vigorous growth. Many of the 12 PPP projects awarded since 2010, involving investment of about $4 billion, are under construction. They include highways, railways, an airport terminal, and water supply facilities. Another 14 projects with total investment estimated at $12 billion are being prepared for bidding. Sustaining progress on PPPs requires the program's continued development through the enactment of proposed legislation to improve the framework for PPP, better project appraisal and monitoring, and strengthened capacity in the agencies involved.

The government is putting more emphasis on manufacturing, illustrated by fiscal incentives for automobile production approved in 2015 that have attracted more investment into this industry. Over the past 4 years, the government and industry groups have worked together to develop roadmaps for the expansion of several manufacturing subsectors, among them the automotive industry, electronics, cement, chemicals, furniture, and some agro-based products. Since mid-2015, the manufacturing production index has edged higher, and in January this year it rose sharply. But for agriculture, dry weather is hurting prospects for expansion.

Slightly stronger GDP growth is forecast for 2017, in part on expectations of better economic performance in the US, the Philippines' second biggest export market and a significant source of foreign direct investment and remittances. Net external demand is projected to add to GDP growth in 2017. Private investment is expected to pick up if efforts to improve the investment environment are sustained.

The current account surplus is forecast to narrow this year. A wider merchandise trade deficit and slower growth in remittances are seen to outweigh a lower oil import bill and higher income from services exports.

Risks to the forecasts come from the impact on agriculture and food prices if El Niño is more severe than anticipated, and from weaker-than-expected economic performances in major trading partners. Potential risks from global financial market volatility are cushioned by the country's economic fundamentals: a surplus in the current account, high international reserves, low inflation, and an improved fiscal position. External debt as a share of GDP, at 26.5% in 2015, has been trending smaller since 2003. The economic outlook is subject to more uncertainty than usual as the outcome of the national elections will have an important bearing on policy. Sustaining the strong growth performance will require policy continuity in key areas, including the development of infrastructure and human capital, improvements to the investment climate, and governance reform.

Policy challenge—tackling youth unemployment

After some years of what was characterized as "jobless growth," a pickup in economic growth to 6.2% on average since 2010 has lifted the pace of job creation. The unemployment rate at 5.8% in January 2016 is historically low. The unemployment rate of young people aged

3.28.9 Sources of remittances, 2015

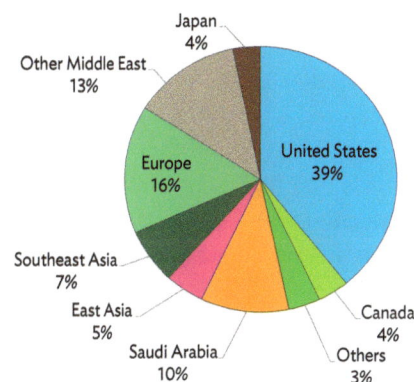

Source: Bangko Sentral ng Pilipinas. www.bsp.gov.ph (accessed 22 March 2016).
Click here for figure data

3.28.10 Net foreign direct investment inflows

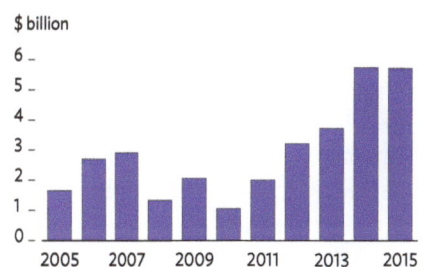

Source: Bangko Sentral ng Pilipinas. www.bsp.gov.ph (accessed 22 March 2016).
Click here for figure data

3.28.11 Inflation

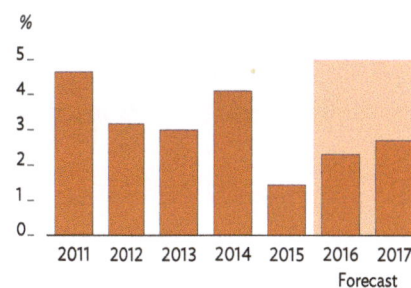

Source: Asian Development Outlook database.
Click here for figure data

15–24 years is higher at 14.4%, though this too has fallen since 2010 (Figure 3.28.12). The rate of underemployment also remains high at 19.7%. In large part reflecting the lack of good jobs, poverty remained elevated at 26.3% of the population in the first half of 2015, though declining from 28.8% in 2006.

A survey found that college graduates took about a year to find work, and high school graduates took up to 3 years. Many drift into informal work, often part time and poorly paid, or remain unemployed. One in four young people is neither working nor pursuing education or training.

The Philippines has a relatively young population, as half of all Filipinos last year were younger than 25 years, and the median age was estimated at 23. This offers an opportunity to raise potential growth, but the demographic dividend can be realized only if young people are employed in productive jobs.

A number of factors keep youth unemployment high. On the demand-side, the number of jobs generated each year falls short of what is needed to both absorb new entrants into the labor force and the 2.5 million unemployed, half of them young people. Almost 80% of new jobs in the past 6 years have been generated by the service sector, particularly BPO, tourism, and retail trade. Industry contributed about 20% of the new jobs, while employment in agriculture fell in most years (Figure 3.28.13). Stronger employment generation will require more broad-based growth driven by productivity gains across all sectors.

Mismatches between the education and skills young people acquire and the needs of the labor market are a constraint. Improving the relevance and quality of technical and vocational training programs and strengthening certification frameworks will help overcome such mismatches. More programs are needed to provide employment services, such as career guidance and coaching for young people when they leave school.

Following a successful pilot, the government is rolling out nationally the JobStart Philippines program, which aims to provide a full range of employment services to help students who have at least completed high school become job ready and find decent employment. These services include life skills and technical training, career guidance, and on-the-job training or internship. Other measures cover improving the quality of labor market databases to reduce job search costs and enable students and job seekers to make more informed decisions.

The effective implementation of these initiatives will require strengthening the capacity of local government employment offices and boosting their budget resources. Improving policies on the national apprenticeship program, temporary work agencies, and labor dispute resolution will also be needed to help young people gain longer-term and better paying jobs, rather than temporary ones.

3.28.1 Selected economic indicators (%)

	2016	2017
GDP growth	6.0	6.1
Inflation	2.3	2.7
Current account balance (share of GDP)	2.7	2.8

Source: ADB estimates.

3.28.12 Unemployment rates

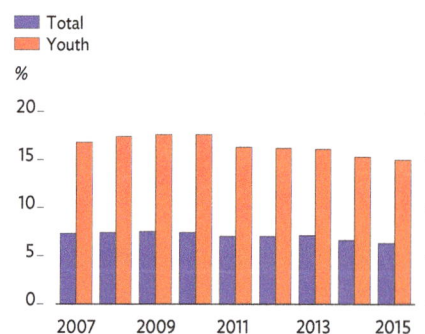

Source: Philippine Statistics Authority. www.psa.gov.ph
Click here for figure data

3.28.13 Change in employment by sector

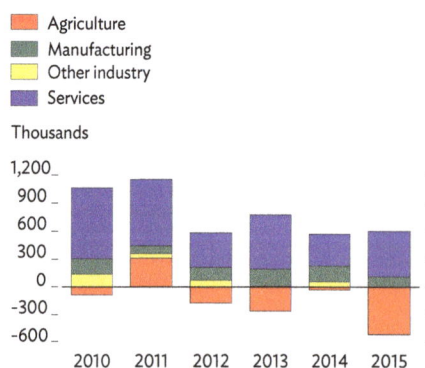

Source: Philippine Statistics Authority. www.psa.gov.ph
Click here for figure data

Singapore

Economic growth slowed in 2015, prices declined, and the current account improved. Growth is seen unchanged in 2016, and prices will be lower, but an uptick in both is forecast for 2017. The external surplus is expected to narrow in 2016 and widen next year. An important policy challenge is to rein in high household debt, as mortgage interest rates and falling property values could impinge on financial stability.

Economic performance

GDP growth slowed to 2.0% in 2015, the weakest growth rate since the global financial crisis in 2008. The main driver of growth was services, contributing 2.6 percentage points. Services expanded by 3.5% on strong performances in wholesale and retail trade and in finance and insurance. Sluggish private construction moderated growth in the sector to 2.5%, reducing its contribution to growth to 0.1 percentage points. Manufacturing, the biggest sector, has contracted for 5 consecutive quarters, pulling down GDP growth by 1.0 percentage point (Figure 3.29.1). Manufacturing output fell by 5.2%, mainly because of a slowdown in rig building and weaker demand for oil and gas equipment.

On the demand side, total consumption expenditure grew by 4.9% to contribute 2.1 percentage points to growth, driven primarily by private consumption expenditure on transport, goods and services, housing, and utilities (Figure 3.29.2). Exports of goods and services grew by 2.5% and imports by 2.1%, both lower than in 2014. Net exports therefore increased by 4.6%, contributing 1.3 percentage points to growth. However, investment declined by 6.2%—largely from decreases in private construction, intellectual property products, and machinery and equipment—to subtract 1.7 percentage points from growth.

Consumer prices fell by 0.5% on average in 2015 as rents declined and transport costs dropped in line with lower oil prices (Figure 3.29.3). Core inflation, which excludes accommodation and private road transport, remained subdued at 0.5% year on year.

The Monetary Authority of Singapore (MAS) continued to manage monetary policy by adjusting the Singapore dollar's nominal effective exchange rate within an undisclosed trading band. In response to expected further decline in consumer price index, the MAS eased monetary policy in October 2015, slowing the rate at which the Singapore dollar can appreciate by lowering the slope of the policy band but without changing its width. The currency appreciated by 0.2% on average in 2015 by its nominal effective exchange rate, as calculated

3.29.1 Contributions to growth, by industry

- 2014
- 2015

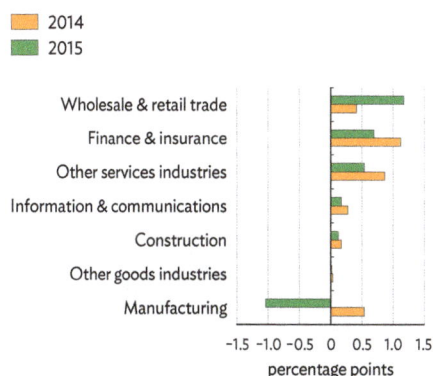

Notes: Other goods industries include agriculture, fishing and quarrying, and utilities. Other services industries include transportation and storage, accommodation and food services, business services, ownership of dwellings, and other services.
Source: Ministry of Trade and Industry. Economic Survey Singapore 2015 (accessed 24 February 2016).
Click here for figure data

3.29.2 Demand-side contributions to growth

- Private consumption
- Government consumption
- Investment
- Net exports
- Statistical discrepancy
- Gross domestic product

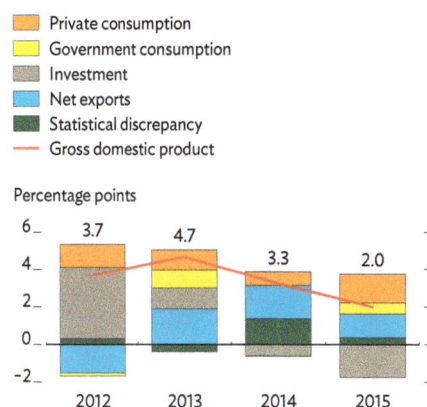

Source: Ministry of Trade and Industry. Economic Survey Singapore 2015 (accessed 24 February 2016).
Click here for figure data

This chapter was written by Minsoo Lee and Mai Lin Villaruel of the Economic Research and Regional Cooperation Department, ADB, Manila.

by the Bank for International Settlements, but depreciated by 1.6% by its real effective exchange rate. In nominal terms, the Singapore dollar depreciated by 8.5% against the US dollar on average to reach its lowest value since 2010 (Figure 3.29.4). The 3-month Singapore interbank offered rate rose gradually from 0.5% in December 2014 to 1.2% in December 2015 and, following the hike in the US federal funds rate, to 1.3% in February 2016 (Figure 3.29.5).

Merchandise exports contracted in US dollar terms by 12.2% in 2015 as exports of oil and goods other than electronics fell. Imports declined by 14.7% as oil imports shrank, widening the trade surplus to $78.7 billion. The current account surplus widened, to $57.6 billion, equal to 19.7% of GDP, despite a deficit in the services account. The overall balance of payments surplus narrowed to $1.1 billion, or 0.4% of GDP, owing to a rising deficit in the capital and financial accounts (Figure 3.29.6).

The budget for FY2015 (ending 31 March 2016) projected a primary deficit of S$4.0 billion, or 1.0% of GDP, following an actual primary surplus of 1.1% of GDP in FY2014, with expenditure rising by 19.3% and revenue by 4.8%. During the first 3 quarters of FY2015, revenue increased by 5.9% and expenditure by 11.8%, including developmental expenditure up by 19.6%. The budgetary outcome for FY2015 is therefore likely to be a primary surplus. Revenues increased as the number of certificates of entitlement for private car purchases grew and receipts rose from corporate and personal income tax, as well as from customs and excise taxes. Expenditures on social security and pensions were strengthened, and incentives were offered for investing in innovation. Outlays for celebrating Singapore's 50 years of independence, the Southeast Asia Games, and the ASEAN Para Games of the Association of Southeast Asian Nations also increased, but development expenditure in FY2015 is likely to be below the budgeted amount.

Economic prospects

Growth is forecast to remain stable at 2.0% in 2016 as expansion in services outweighs weakness in manufacturing and construction, which will be held back by low external demand and higher borrowing costs. The fall in the manufacturing purchasing managers' index below the 50 threshold in February 2016 indicates likely contraction in the first half of the year (Figure 3.29.7). Moreover, slower momentum in construction is expected as private construction contracts dropped in 2015. In 2017, GDP growth is expected to improve to 2.2% as services remain resilient and manufacturing rebounds moderately.

Consumption will drive growth in 2016 as the government increases spending on social welfare, health infrastructure, public transport, and the development of the Changi Airport and a planned high-speed rail link with Malaysia. Household spending will benefit from lower inflation and moderate wage increases but, given high household debt, be crimped by rising interest rates. Gross fixed investment will be weaker, as investment commitments reported by the Economic Development Board declined for most sectors in 2015 (Figure 3.29.8).

3.29.1 Selected economic indicators (%)

	2016	2017
GDP growth	2.0	2.2
Inflation	−0.6	0.4
Current account balance (share of GDP)	18.8	19.5

Source: ADB estimates.

3.29.3 Inflation

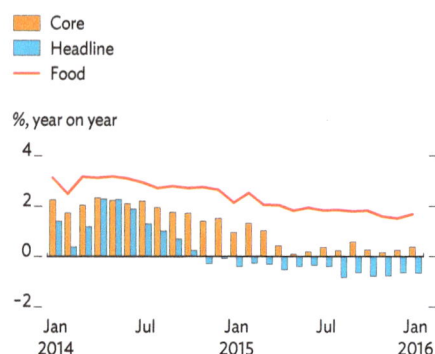

Source: CEIC Data Company (accessed 29 February 2016).
Click here for figure data

3.29.4 Exchange rates

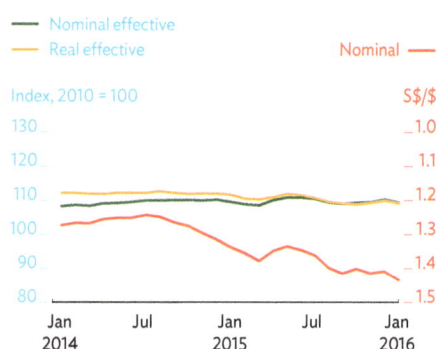

Sources: Bureau of International Settlement; CEIC Data Company (accessed 29 February 2016).
Click here for figure data

3.29.5 Interest rates

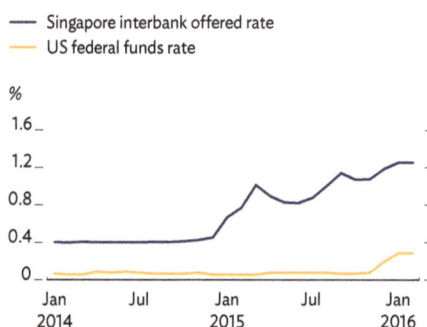

Source: CEIC Data Company (accessed 29 February 2016).
Click here for figure data

In January 2016, exports fell by 15.1% year on year and imports by 13.6%, pointing to continued weakness in external demand, including for oil. As Singapore is one of the world's top refiners of crude, low demand for petroleum products will drag down export growth. The trade balance is nevertheless expected to be in surplus in 2016, as imports will decline more than exports in US dollar terms, and net services will improve, despite weaker exports of energy services, with rising net exports of financial and tourism services. The current account surplus will narrow to 18.8% of GDP and widen again to 19.5% in 2017 as external demand recovers.

Lower certificate of entitlement premiums, continuing declines in rents and property prices that began in 2014, and falling utility prices will dampen prices in 2016 (Figure 3.29.9). The decline in consumer prices is projected to reach 0.6%, which is within the range of the forecast by the MAS. Inflation will return at 0.4% in 2017, assuming oil prices rise and food and social services costs continue to increase.

Despite deflationary expectations for 2016, the MAS is expected to continue to manage the nominal effective exchange rate along a moderately appreciating trend, but the nominal value of the Singapore dollar, which fell to S$1.41 to the US dollar in February 2016, is expected to decline further in 2016. On the fiscal front, the new government is expected to continue a prudent fiscal policy in view of the constitutional requirement that the budget be balanced over a government's full term.

Downside risks to the forecast stem from the uncertain global economic outlook and domestic property price movements. Lower oil prices and a sharper growth slowdown in the People's Republic of China could dampen export growth in 2016, and persistent weakness in the residential property market could choke investment growth. Further tightening of the labor market could, together with declining labor productivity since 2014, pose another risk to growth projections.

Policy challenge—restraining household debt

Household debt in Singapore rose from the equivalent of 65% of GDP in 2010 to 75% in 2015 (Figure 3.29.10). Tight macroprudential policies implemented by the MAS in the past few years have effectively dampened domestic credit growth, but household debt in Singapore is still among the highest in the region, at more than 220% of household disposable income in 2015. Twin reasons are the high rate of homeownership and high real estate prices. Mortgages account for more than 74% of household debt and are the main avenue of rising household debt (Figure 3.29.11). Low interest rates on mortgages and long maturities fueled a rapid rise in property loans, with a corresponding increase in locally incorporated banks' exposure to the property sector. Property-related lending accounts for 28% of banking system loans, and many other loans are collateralized with property.

Soaring household debt may not pose an immediate risk to economic activity or bank soundness, but it sows vulnerability. Borrowers may default if domestic income growth falters or, as 70% of mortgages have floating rates, global interest rates rise abruptly. This could mean

3.29.6 Balance of payments

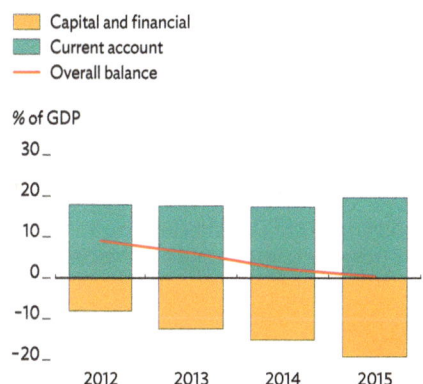

Source: Ministry of Trade and Industry. Economic Survey Singapore 2015 (accessed 24 February 2016).
Click here for figure data

3.29.7 Manufacturing purchasing managers' index

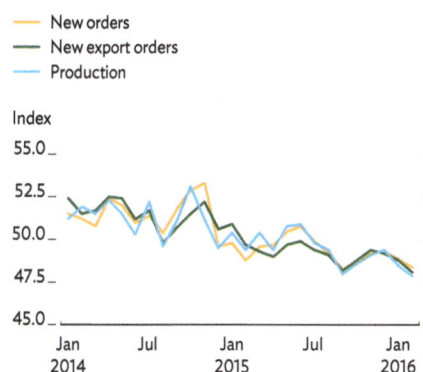

Sources: Singapore Institute of Purchasing and Material Management; Haver Analytics (accessed 29 February 2016).
Click here for figure data

3.29.8 Fixed asset investment commitments by sector

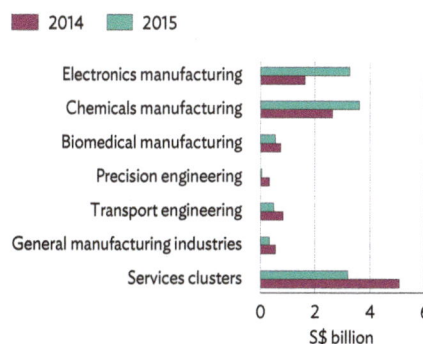

Source: Ministry of Trade and Industry. Economic Survey Singapore 2015 (accessed 24 February 2016).
Click here for figure data

more nonperforming loans. According to the MAS, the number of borrowers who had missed payments on unsecured credit for 2 or more months rose by 6% in September 2015, bringing the increase over the previous 12 months to 18%. Systemic risk could intensify, as higher borrowing costs are likely to dampen the housing market and construction, slowing domestic growth already weakened by a challenging external environment. This could further crimp consumer spending and hurt household finances. Housing price corrections also pose risks, and prices have fallen by more than 8% over the past 2 years following the 2013 introduction by the MAS of tighter macroprudential policies, including a 70% limit on the ratio of loan to value for new loans.

Continuing moderation in residential property prices has tempered growth in household wealth and spending. A sharp correction would likely hamper economic growth further, as real estate activity contributes substantial employment and value added. A buildup of macroeconomic risks and vulnerability could pose a systemic risk to the financial sector. Property foreclosures and personal bankruptcies could amplify pressures on bank balance sheets and impair the health of financial institutions and broader financial stability.

Risk stemming from a correction in property prices and payment defaults appear to be manageable because the banking system is strong. Nonperforming housing loans are currently only 0.4% of the loan portfolio and are adequately provisioned. Further, banks meet their minimum regulatory capital adequacy ratio of 10%, and the overall loan-to-value ratio was less than 50% in 2014, with just 5% of outstanding housing loans showing a ratio of above 80%. A financial stability review in 2015 therefore stated that only a huge fall in real estate prices could pose widespread debt-servicing problems. However, the adequacy of the existing substantial buffer against mortgage risk depends on how rapidly loan rates increase, house prices falter, or economic growth slackens. Policy makers should be vigilant of mounting vulnerability because domestic banks are exposed to the property sector to the tune of at least 46% of their loan portfolio. Continuous monitoring of bank activities and risks are essential to detect bank fragility, and preemptive macroprudential policies are needed to avert financial instability.

3.29.9 Property price index

Q = quarter.
Source: Haver Analytics (accessed 8 March 2016).
Click here for figure data

3.29.10 Household debt

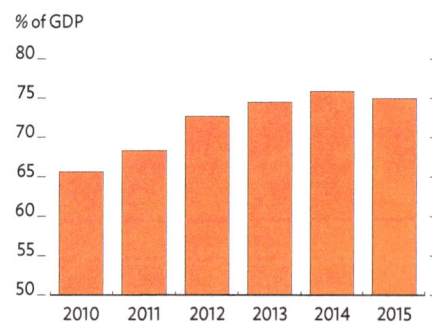

Source: Singapore Statistics (accessed 29 February 2016).
Click here for figure data

3.29.11 Household balance sheet

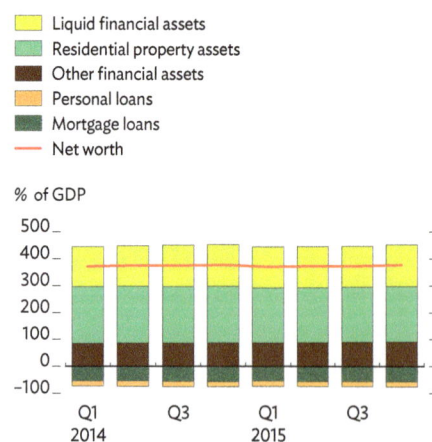

Q = quarter.
Source: Singapore Statistics (accessed 29 February 2016).
Click here for figure data

Thailand

Government spending revived economic growth in 2015, while private sector activity and exports lagged. Growth is seen picking up this year and next if planned infrastructure investment proceeds as scheduled. Lower farm incomes from drought and weak agricultural prices are weighing on private consumption. Consumer prices, having declined last year, are forecast to nudge up. Falling imports are leaving sizable trade and current account surpluses while exports remain weak.

Economic performance

Higher government spending, particularly on capital works, drove economic growth in 2015, assisted by a modest pickup in private consumption. GDP rose by 2.8%, compared with just 0.8% in 2014, when political unrest and a military coup disrupted the economy (Figure 3.30.1).

Public fixed investment rebounded by 29.8% from contraction in 2014 as the government accelerated budget disbursements for water-management, road, and community projects (Figure 3.30.2). State-owned enterprises also boosted spending on construction projects after public investment slumped in 2014 because of political disruptions and legal challenges. Government consumption spending rose by 2.2% in 2015, a pace similar to that of the 2 previous years.

In contrast with the rebound in public sector investment, fixed investment by the private sector fell by 2.0% in 2015 owing to lackluster prospects for exports, subdued private sector demand, and slack industrial capacity. The end of the year brought signs of improved private investment, mainly in buildings.

Private consumption picked up from 2014 to grow by a modest 2.1% last year. A major reason for tepid spending was contraction in agriculture caused by drought and low commodity prices, which cut farm incomes by 11.0% and reduced total employment by 0.2%. Another dampening factor was high household debt, equal to 81% of GDP. Consumer confidence sagged through the first 3 quarters before turning up at the end of 2015. The government launched two stimulus packages in the second half of 2015 to spur consumption. The first aimed to lift incomes and spending in rural areas through funding for village and community projects. The second provided tax rebates on consumer spending in the last week of 2015. Tax breaks for home purchase were also offered last year.

Net external demand contributed to GDP growth in 2015, largely because imports of goods and services declined in real terms for a second year in a row, reflecting subdued domestic demand.

3.30.1 Demand-side contributions to growth

- Private consumption
- Government consumption
- Total investment
- Net exports
- Statistical discrepancy
- Gross domestic product

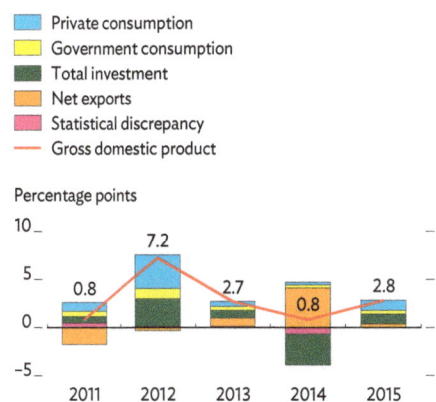

Source: National Economic and Social Development Board. http://www.nesdb.go.th (accessed 8 March 2016).
Click here for figure data

3.30.2 Fixed investment growth

- Private
- Public
- Total

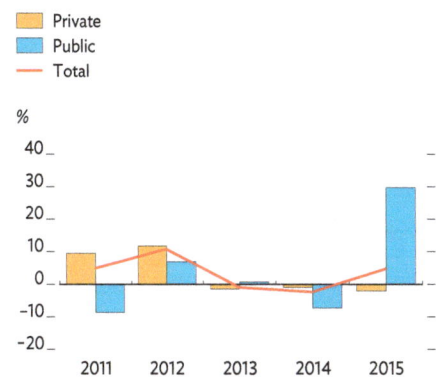

Source: National Economic and Social Development Board. http://www.nesdb.go.th (accessed 8 March 2016).
Click here for figure data

This chapter was written by Luxmon Attapich of the Thailand Resident Mission, ADB, Bangkok.

Exports of goods and services rose slightly in real terms as higher earnings from tourism more than offset a slide in merchandise exports.

From the supply side, GDP growth was driven by 5.0% expansion in services. Much of the growth in services stemmed from a 20.4% leap in tourist arrivals, a recovery from 2014 when street protests and military intervention hurt tourism (Figure 3.30.3). In particular, arrivals from the People's Republic of China (PRC) jumped last year. Solid expansion was recorded in tourism-related services including hotels, restaurants, and retail trade, as well as in finance and transport and communications.

Construction rebounded by 15.8% in 2015 as the government ramped up spending on capital works. Weak domestic and external demand held manufacturing growth to only 0.9%, which still improved on 2014. Car manufacturing and food processing performed relatively well, and electronics started to improve. Industry as a whole recorded growth at 2.2%.

Agriculture including fisheries had a particularly bad year, the sector shrinking by 4.2% because of drought and low prices for farm commodities. Rice and palm oil production fell, but shrimp culture recovered after a fall in 2014. Thailand's capture fishing industry was disrupted by a crackdown on foreign boats working Indonesian waters and by the threat of a ban on seafood exports to the important European Union market unless it tackled illegal, unreported, and unregulated fishing.

Economic growth did get support from fiscal and monetary policies. The government improved its budget disbursement rate to 94% in FY2015 (ended 30 September 2015) from 89% in FY2014, though still short of the 97% target. The fiscal outcome was a deficit equal to 2.5% of GDP. The central bank, confronted with an unexpectedly sluggish economy and declining consumer prices, lowered its policy rate in March 2015, and again in April, to 1.5%. Commercial banks reduced lending rates, and growth in credit to the private sector from deposit-taking institutions picked up to increase by 5.6%. Lending to small and medium-sized enterprises (SMEs) jumped in the last quarter when the government offered them low-interest loans and loan guarantees.

The consumer price index slipped by 0.9% in 2015 on lower prices for fuel and food, along with lackluster domestic demand (Figure 3.30.4). Core inflation remained positive, this measure of consumer prices that excludes fresh food and energy rising by 1.1%.

Thailand recorded large trade and current account surpluses, largely because imports slumped. Merchandise exports and imports have declined in US dollar terms for 3 consecutive years (Figure 3.30.5). In 2015, merchandise exports fell by 5.6% to $212.1 billion, with steep falls in agricultural and fishery products, as well as in oil and chemical products, but higher shipments of passenger cars. Exports declined to the PRC, Japan, and the larger economies in Southeast Asia but rose to the group of neighboring countries: Cambodia, the Lao People's Democratic Republic, Myanmar, and Viet Nam.

Merchandise imports dived by 11.3% to $177.5 billion, reflecting slack domestic demand and lower prices for imported oil and commodities. As a result, the trade surplus jumped by 40.7% to $34.6 billion. Trade in services was also in surplus, by $9.9 billion, contributing to

3.30.3 Tourism Indicators

Source: Bank of Thailand. http://www.bot.or.th (accessed 11 March 2016).
Click here for figure data

3.30.4 Inflation and policy interest rate

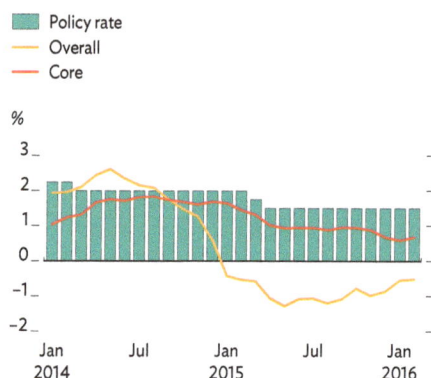

Sources: Bank of Thailand. http://www.bot.or.th; CEIC Data Company (both accessed 11 March 2016).
Click here for figure data

3.30.5 Trade indicators

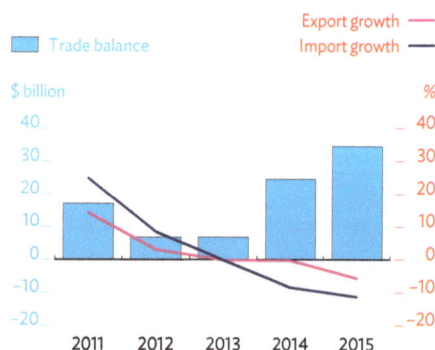

Source: Bank of Thailand. http://www.bot.or.th (accessed 8 March 2016).
Click here for figure data

a large current account surplus of $34.8 billion, equal to 8.8% of GDP. By contrast, capital and financial accounts registered a deficit of $19.0 billion, mainly from outflows of portfolio investment and Thai foreign investment abroad. Outward foreign direct investment doubled in 2015 from 2014, as foreign direct investment into Thailand rose by 29%.

Gross international reserves were, at $156.5 billion, little changed from 2014, covering 8.2 months of imports of goods and services, and standing at 2.9 times short-term external debt. The Thai baht depreciated by 8.6% against the broadly strengthening US dollar in 2015.

Economic reform in 2015 encompassed state-owned enterprises, special economic zones, and fuel subsidies. The government is forming a holding company to supervise state firms and improve their performance. The State Enterprise Supervisory Board ordered state enterprises to withdraw investment from 44 subsidiaries with business in areas unrelated to the parent firm. New special economic zones along borders with neighboring countries are being prepared. Lower global oil prices facilitated a phasing out of subsidies on diesel, cooking gas, and natural gas for vehicles.

Economic prospects

Growth is forecast to rise over the next 2 years, assuming that substantial public infrastructure investments proceed on schedule and the political climate is calm around national elections proposed for the second half of 2017. On these bases, GDP is projected to edge up to 3.0% this year and accelerate to 3.5% in 2017 (Figure 3.30.6).

Investment will pick up in 2016 under the government's Transport Infrastructure Master Plan, which runs through 2022. Implementation of 20 projects costing $51 billion will make headway in 2016. These projects include motorways, railways, mass transit rail lines, seaports, and expansion of Suvarnabhumi International Airport in Bangkok. The Ministry of Finance projects that almost $2 billion will be disbursed for these projects in FY2016. Thailand is also negotiating with the PRC to build two railway lines, but the timing of construction is uncertain.

The FY2016 budget increases public expenditure by 7.8% from the previous year's budget. The government has added B56 billion to the original FY2016 budget, with additional revenue sourced partly by auctioning 4G spectra for mobile phone services. Almost 39% of expenditure under the original budget was disbursed in the first 4 months of FY2016, ahead of target. The fiscal deficit is expected to widen to the equivalent of 3.0% of GDP in FY2016.

Good progress on the major investment projects would lift business confidence and private investment. The private sector can participate in infrastructure projects through fast-tracked public–private partnerships that so far include mass rapid transit lines, motorways, and a renewable energy power plant. The government's nascent Thailand Future Fund is another channel for equity investment in infrastructure.

Following up on stimulus rolled out last year for rural areas, consumers, and SMEs, the government declared 2016 to be a special investment-promotion year supported by a raft of tax breaks intended to revive private investment. A corporate tax rate cut to 20% originally

3.30.1 Selected economic indicators (%)

	2016	2017
GDP growth	3.0	3.5
Inflation	0.6	2.0
Current account balance (share of GDP)	7.5	4.0

Source: ADB estimates.

3.30.6 GDP growth

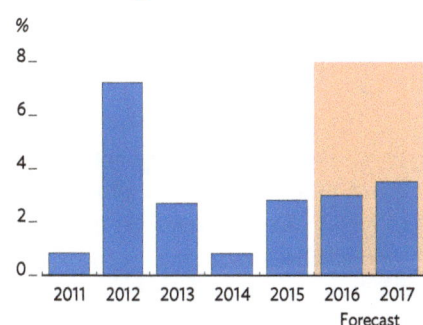

Source: Asian Development Outlook database.
Click here for figure data

3.30.7 Private consumption and investment

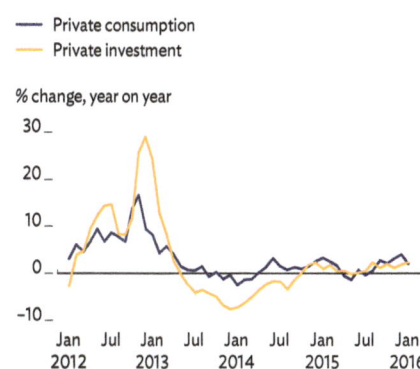

Note: Seasonally adjusted, 3-month moving average.
Source: Bank of Thailand. http://www.bot.or.th (accessed 11 March 2016).
Click here for figure data

for 2013–2015 is now permanent. SMEs pay a lower income tax rate for 2 years, and additional tax concessions are available for capital investment and for investments in special economic zones and in research and development. Investment in 10 industries targeted as new growth engines is exempt from corporate income tax for up to 15 years. The industries include biofuels, biotechnology, logistics, and robotics.

Private consumption is expected to increase at a modest pace in 2016 but then quicken next year. The stimulus measures will help, but consumption remains suppressed by household finances battered by drought, low prices for agricultural products, and already high household debt. Lower rice production curtailed by drought is unlikely to push up rice prices much because large stockpiles overhang the market. Rubber and palm oil face soft global demand and large inventories. Still, rural incomes are getting some support from government subsidies on both production costs and crop insurance, soft loans, and the funding for village projects. Planned tax restructuring in 2017 is expected to provide personal income tax relief, which should prod consumption.

Economic data for January 2016 indicate a lackluster start to this year (Figure 3.30.7). Private consumption decelerated in January, particularly for durable goods, as tax rebates for spending in 2015 expired and the excise tax on cars rose at the start of this year. Private investment and manufacturing continued to languish in January. Business sentiment for the near term declined, but most respondents to a Bank of Thailand survey in February expected business conditions to improve in the months ahead (Figure 3.30.8).

The consumer price index fell by 0.5% year on year in the first 2 months of 2016. Nevertheless, prices are projected to nudge higher during the year from the low base set in 2015. Baht depreciation puts some upward pressure on import prices while supporting economic growth. Inflation is forecast to average 0.6% in 2016, picking up to 2.0% in 2017 as domestic demand firms and oil prices turn up (Figure 3.30.9). Low inflation suggests that the Bank of Thailand will maintain an accommodative monetary stance.

External trade started 2016 on a weak note. Merchandise exports contracted in value terms in January and are projected to post a small decline this year before turning up in 2017. Tourist arrivals remained a bright spot in January, rising by 15%, with further gains expected. Merchandise imports slumped on lower oil prices and weak demand for raw materials and intermediate goods. Imports are seen rising slightly this year and accelerating in 2017 as investment gathers momentum. Another large current account surplus is forecast for this year before it subsides in 2017 (Figure 3.30.10).

Risks to the outlook come from a possible worsening of the drought, which would hit incomes, private consumption, and exports. The timely implementation of government investment projects is crucial. Delays would reduce public investment and damage consumer and business confidence alike. External risks stem from slower-than-anticipated growth in major trading partners and volatile global capital flows. Sizable current account surpluses, relatively low external debt, and substantial international reserves mitigate downside risks (Figure 3.30.11).

3.30.8 Consumer confidence and business sentiment indexes

— Consumer confidence: next 3 months
— Business sentiment: next 3 months

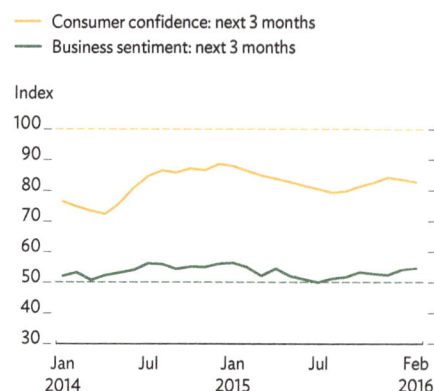

Note: A reading of less than 50 denotes a deterioration in business sentiment; a reading of less than 100 denotes deterioration in consumer confidence.
Sources: Bank of Thailand. http://www.bot.or.th (accessed 11 March 2016); CEIC Data Company.
Click here for figure data

3.30.9 Inflation

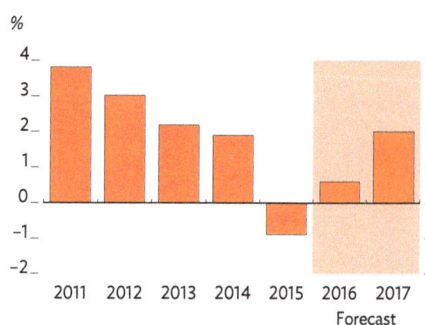

Source: Asian Development Outlook database.
Click here for figure data

3.30.10 Current account balance

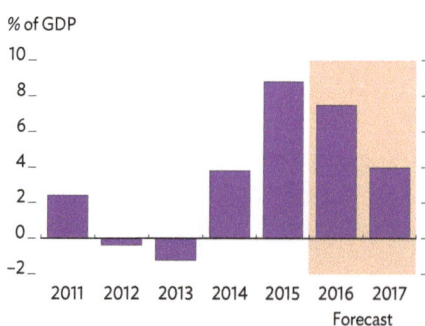

Source: Asian Development Outlook database.
Click here for figure data

Policy challenge—supporting growth in smaller businesses

SMEs comprise 99% of Thailand's businesses but generate less than 40% of GDP (Figure 3.30.12). A study last year found that poor access to finance keeps SMEs from making a bigger contribution to economic growth.

The state-owned Small and Medium Enterprise Development Bank of Thailand and the Thailand Credit Guarantee Corporation help to fund SMEs, but government resources alone are insufficient. Commercial banks are wary about lending to SMEs out of concern that their accounts are unreliable and they lack collateral for loans.

The government has started a program to encourage SMEs to keep a single set of financial statements to improve their chances of accessing bank finance. Under the program, past accounts of eligible businesses with revenue of less than B500 million in 2016 are exempt from audits by tax officials. Eligible businesses with revenue of up to B30 million and paid-up capital of up to B5 million get tax breaks for 2 accounting years.

To address inadequate collateral, the new Business Security Act allows businesses to use as collateral for borrowing from banks assets other than land, such as inventories and trademarks.

Start-ups can find it especially challenging to raise funds. In response, the government is offering new businesses exemption from corporate income tax for 5 years through 2020, and it wants state-owned banks to set up venture capital funds. It will be important that such funds focus on entrepreneurial and technologically innovative firms that will eventually be able to compete in international markets. The government is also looking to remove legal and regulatory obstacles to the development of new businesses, including through better enforcement of competition law.

Another constraint on SMEs is their lack of capacity and resources for research and development or to penetrate overseas markets. The government could help by investing in infrastructure and facilities that foster research and development. Thailand invested only 0.25% of GDP on research and development in 2011, comparing unfavorably with 1.1% in Malaysia, 2.0% in the PRC, and 4.0% in the Republic of Korea. On the issue of access to overseas markets, the Ministry of Commerce will support and arrange business introductions for SMEs that join international trade shows.

3.30.11 Gross international reserves

Source: Bank of Thailand. http://www.bot.or.th (accessed 11 March 2016).
Click here for figure data

3.30.12 Output of small and medium-sized enterprises

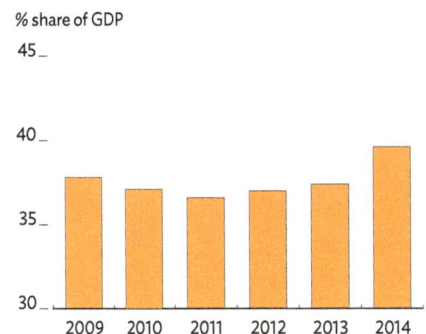

Source: The Office of SMEs Promotion.
Click here for figure data

Viet Nam

Vigorous expansion of manufacturing and construction in 2015 spurred the fastest economic growth in 7 years. Foreign direct investment is seen supporting strong growth through the forecast period. Inflation will revive but remain relatively modest. The current account is forecast to slide into a small deficit. Reforms to banks and state enterprises continue to make gradual progress, but an emerging need is better management of rapid urbanization.

Economic performance

Economic growth accelerated to 6.7% in 2015, the fastest clip since 2008. Industry expanded by 9.6% and contributed nearly half of total growth (Figure 3.31.1). Powered by high foreign direct investment (FDI), the manufacturing subsector rose by a rapid 10.6%, and construction grew by 10.8% on foreign investment in factories, a recovery in the property market, and higher spending on infrastructure. FDI disbursements, which have increased substantially over the past decade, swelled by 17% to $14.5 billion in 2015 (Figure 3.31.2).

Growth in services was maintained at 6.3% last year. Wholesale and retail trade grew by 9.1% on strong private consumption, and banking and finance expanded by 7.4% as growth in credit quickened. However, a 0.2% decline in tourist arrivals dampened growth in tourism-related services. Agriculture recorded lower growth at 2.4% as global food prices fell and El Niño brought drought.

By expenditure, private consumption accelerated to 9.3%, spurred by rising employment and incomes and lower inflation. Investment also strengthened as buoyant FDI inflows and expansion in credit supported a 9.0% rise in gross capital formation. Net external demand weighed on GDP growth, though, as imports of goods and services in real terms rose faster than exports.

Notwithstanding stronger domestic demand, inflation slowed to average just 0.6% last year, the lowest since 2001, mainly on lower food and fuel prices (Figure 3.31.3). The State Bank of Viet Nam, the central bank, kept policy interest rates steady in 2015 after reducing them over recent years, but commercial banks trimmed lending rates by 0.2–0.5 percentage points on average. Lending rates have dropped by half since 2011. Lower rates for borrowers complemented recovering consumer and investor confidence to spur credit growth to an estimated 18%, exceeding the government's initial target of 13%–15%. Broad money supply increased by an estimated 14% (Figure 3.31.4).

3.31.1 Supply-side contributions to growth

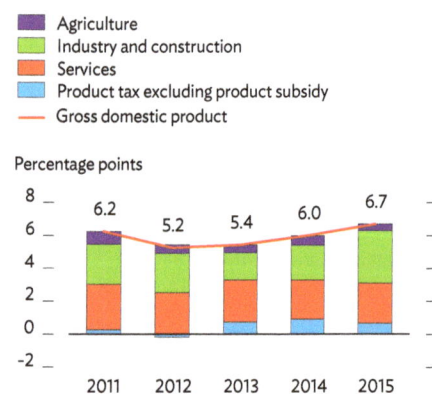

- Agriculture
- Industry and construction
- Services
- Product tax excluding product subsidy
- Gross domestic product

Source: General Statistics Office of Viet Nam.
Click here for figure data

3.31.2 Disbursed foreign direct investment

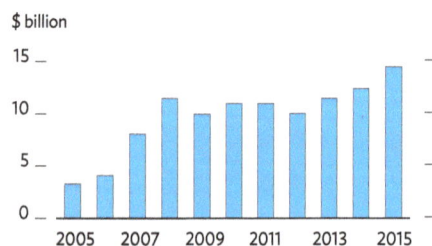

Source: General Statistics Office of Viet Nam.
Click here for figure data

This chapter was written by Aaron Batten, Chu Hong Minh, and Nguyen Luu Thuc Phuong of the Viet Nam Resident Mission, ADB, Ha Noi. The policy challenge section draws on an ADB capacity development technical assistance report available at http://www.adb.org/sites/default/files/project-document/176515/49153-001-tar.pdf

To support exports, and in response to depreciation affecting other Asian currencies, the central bank devalued the Viet Nam dong against the US dollar three times in 2015, adjusting the reference rate by 1% each time. The central bank also moved to enhance exchange rate flexibility by expanding the trading band from 1% to 3% on either side of the reference rate and changing to a daily reference rate announcement system. The monetary authority tightened regulations on foreign currency and discouraged foreign currency hoarding by mandating zero interest rates for US dollar deposits. Over 2015, the dong depreciated by 5% against the US dollar (Figure 3.31.5).

After several years of large external surpluses, the current account came under pressure in 2015 as imports rose faster than exports. Merchandise imports rose on a balance-of-payments basis by an estimated 12% to $155 billion. Imports of machinery, equipment, and electronic components surged by more than 25%, reflecting strong demand for capital goods and inputs into export-orientated manufacturing. Imports of consumption goods rose by 10%, lifted by buoyant consumer spending.

Merchandise exports increased by an estimated 7.9% to $162 billion. Customs data show that the biggest gains were in exports of mobile phones and their components, which jumped by 30% and comprised 19% of total exports. Viet Nam's imports and exports together now exceed 165% of GDP, compared with less than 70% when the government started economic reforms in the mid-1990s.

The result was a 39% fall in the trade surplus, which, along with an estimated 17% decline in remittances, cut the current account surplus to an estimated 0.3% of GDP from 4.9% in 2014. After taking into account a smaller surplus in the capital account and sizable negative net errors and omissions, the overall balance of payments recorded a deficit equal to 3.1% of GDP (Figure 3.31.6). Foreign exchange reserves fell to an estimated 2 months of import cover (Figure 3.31.7).

Efforts to rein in the fiscal deficit had limited impact last year. The government reported that the budget deficit equaled 5.4% of GDP, narrowing slightly from 5.7% in 2014. Revenue rose by 10.0% and would have increased faster if not for lower oil prices and a cut in the corporate income tax rate. Government expenditure grew by 7.3%. Public debt, including debt guaranteed by the government, was projected to equal a record 62% of GDP, approaching a 65% limit set by the National Assembly (Figure 3.31.8).

Progress on economic reform remains slow. The government sold minority equity stakes in some 160 state-owned enterprises in 2015, well below its target of 289. Many individual equitizations fell short of targets.

As for banking reforms, the central bank supported the mergers of several banks, following through on its plan for banking sector consolidation. Reported nonperforming loans (NPLs) declined to 2.7% of outstanding loans by the end of 2015, largely through their transfer from banks to the Viet Nam Asset Management Company. This company, established by the government in 2013 to acquire, restructure, and sell NPLs, had acquired $11.0 billion in bad loans by the end of 2015, up from $6.1 billion a year earlier. But with a limited capital base and lacking an adequate legal framework for resolving NPLs, it had sold or recovered by the end of December last year just 9% of the NPLs it held.

3.31.3 Inflation

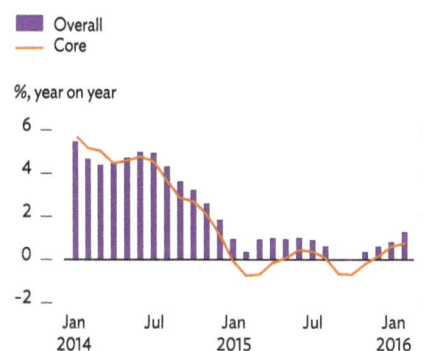

Note: Core excludes food inflation.
Source: General Statistics Office of Viet Nam.
Click here for figure data

3.31.4 Credit and money supply growth

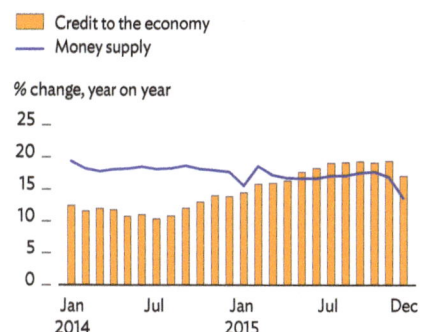

Sources: State Bank of Viet Nam; ADB estimates.
Click here for figure data

3.31.5 Exchange rate

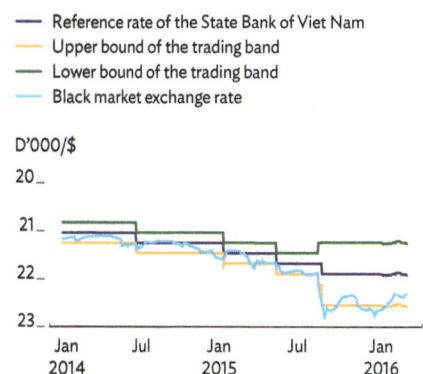

Sources: State Bank of Viet Nam; ADB observations.
Click here for figure data

Economic prospects

The economy is projected to sustain growth at 6.7% in 2016 before the pace moderates to 6.5% in 2017 (Figure 3.31.9). Strong export-orientated manufacturing, FDI inflows, and domestic demand will be partly offset by the effect of slowing expansion in the People's Republic of China (PRC). New FDI commitments came in relatively flat at $22.8 billion in 2015, which suggests that disbursements of FDI could level out this year and decline in 2017. About 60% of the FDI commitments are for export-orientated manufacturing.

Rising incomes and modest (though quickening) inflation are expected to buoy private consumption. Sharply rising sales of automobiles—up by 55% in 2015—illustrate the recovery in consumer confidence. Viet Nam has become the fastest-growing auto market in Southeast Asia. Business sentiment is similarly buoyant. A survey in December 2015 showed that 41% of businesses expected conditions to improve in 2016, and a further 40% expected stable conditions.

Prospects for growth in private investment are enhanced by a proliferation of trade and investment agreements concluded over the past 18 months. These include trade agreements with the European Union and the Republic of Korea, and commitments to participate in both the Trans-Pacific Partnership led by the US and the Eurasian Economic Union led by the Russian Federation. Viet Nam is expected to benefit as well from the ASEAN Economic Community, whose members in the Association of Southeast Asian Nations collectively form Viet Nam's third-largest export market after the US and the European Union.

These agreements will be implemented over several years but are expected to stimulate investment in the near term as businesses prepare for expanded trade opportunities. The agreements also signal to the business community the government's renewed commitment to liberalize the economy. In recent years, it has eased restrictions on foreign ownership of property and corporate shares and has said it would reduce from 51 to 6 the number of industries closed to foreign ownership. The VN Index of share prices rose by 6.1% in 2015, building on a 8.1% gain in 2014.

Manufacturing and construction are projected to maintain solid expansion. The purchasing managers' index showed in the first 2 months of 2016 improving business conditions for manufacturers, including a rise in new orders (Figure 3.31.10). Services are projected to expand at a robust pace, though prospects have dimmed for tourism from the PRC, the source of one-quarter of Viet Nam's inbound tourists. Visitor arrivals from the PRC fell by 8.5% in 2015. Subdued growth will continue for agriculture in the near term under soft global food prices and the effects of El Niño.

Inflation picked up to average 1.3% in the first 3 months of 2016 and is forecast to average 3.0% this year and 4.0% in 2017 (Figure 3.31.11). The government is expected to raise administered prices for education and health care and boost public sector minimum wages. Import prices will rise this year with dong depreciation, and higher global food and fuel prices in 2017 will add to inflation next year.

The central bank targets credit growth at 18%–20% in 2016 to accommodate strong economic growth. Lending interest rates might

3.31.6 Balance of payments indicators

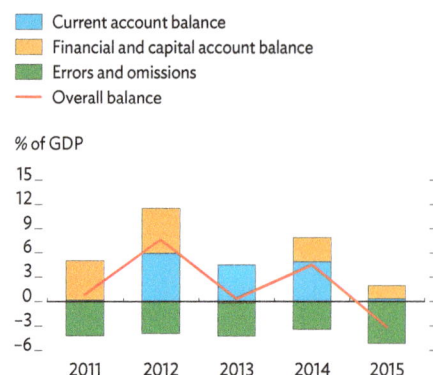

Sources: State Bank of Viet Nam; International Monetary Fund; ADB estimates.
Click here for figure data

3.31.7 Gross international reserves

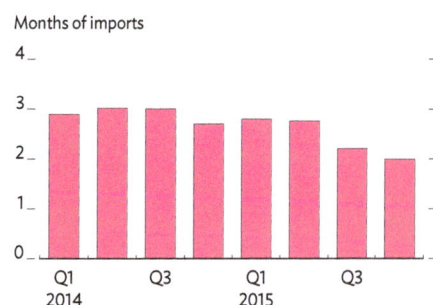

Q = quarter.
Note: Data exclude government foreign exchange deposits at the State Bank of Viet Nam and the foreign exchange counterpart of swap operations. Imports are on free-on-board basis.
Sources: State Bank of Viet Nam; International Monetary Fund; ADB estimates.
Click here for figure data

3.31.8 Public debt and debt servicing costs

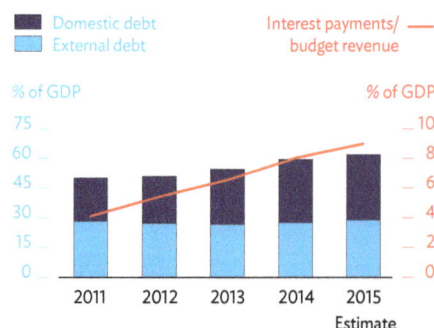

Sources: Government of Viet Nam; World Bank; International Monetary Fund; ADB estimates.
Click here for figure data

come under upward pressure in the forecast period as inflation gradually turns up and rising demand for credit collides with tighter bank liquidity.

Fiscal policy looks set to tighten gradually but to remain supportive of growth. The government aims to narrow the budget deficit to 4.9% of GDP in 2016 and 4.0% in 2017. Continuing a shift started in 2015, the budget for 2016 puts greater emphasis on capital expenditure, which is slated to rise by 25.5%. Current expenditure is set to rise by a more modest 6.5%.

Plans for fiscal consolidation are at risk, however, from shortfalls in revenue. Over the past 5 years, reductions in corporate income tax rates, the removal of tariffs, and tax exemptions for favored firms have eroded the tax base. Low oil prices are dragging on resource tax revenue, which comprises 10% of the total. Central government revenue and grants fell from the equivalent of 27.6% of GDP in 2010 to 22.0% in 2015. The government could use funds from the equitization of state-owned enterprises and issue more short-term securities to support the budget in the near term, but achieving a more sustainable fiscal position is likely to require tax reform to reverse falls in the ratio of tax to GDP.

Merchandise exports are seen rising by 10% in US dollar terms this year and by 14% in 2017 as new production from foreign-invested factories comes online and trade agreements take effect. Imports will also continue to grow in response to strong demand for both consumption and capital goods, and to supply inputs for manufacturing. Modest recovery is expected in remittances. The current account is forecast to slip into deficit this year and recover to balance in 2017 (Figure 3.31.12).

Sluggish progress on reforming banks and state-owned enterprises poses risks to the outlook. Undercapitalized banks with deficient financial transparency remain exposed to shocks. The upswing in credit growth could spark a new round of speculation in risky real estate. To mitigate such risks, the central bank took steps early in 2016 to tighten lending requirements for real estate and reduce the potential for maturity mismatch in bank lending. Further progress on bank consolidation and enhanced transparency, asset classification, NPL resolution, and disclosure requirements will be vital for strengthening the sector.

Policy challenge—managing rapid urbanization

Urbanization has been relatively recent in Viet Nam. Until the 1980s, the government's focus on agriculture encouraged workers to stay in rural areas, and as late as 1990 only 20% of the population lived in cities (Figure 3.31.13). Deeper economic reform and less-constrained rural–urban migration from the mid-1990s triggered rapid growth in cities, which developed as centers for services and manufacturing. Over the past 2 decades, the number of urban dwellers has jumped to 31 million, or 34% of the population, and is projected to reach 46 million, or 44%, by 2030.

Growth in urban centers and formal employment are important drivers of the economy, as illustrated by estimates that show at least

3.31.1 Selected economic indicators (%)

	2016	2017
GDP growth	6.7	6.5
Inflation	3.0	4.0
Current account balance (share of GDP)	−0.2	0.0

Source: ADB estimates.

3.31.9 GDP growth

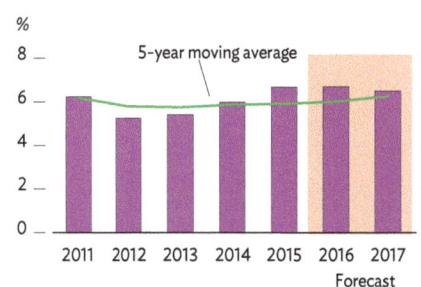

Source: Asian Development Outlook database.
Click here for figure data

3.31.10 Purchasing managers' index

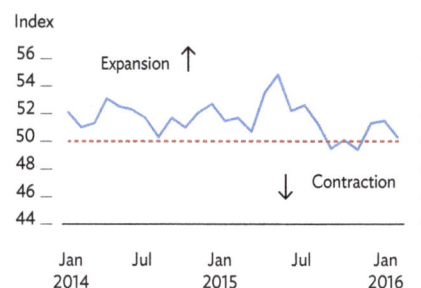

Note: Nikkei, Markit.
Source: Bloomberg (accessed 1 March 2016).
Click here for figure data

3.31.11 Inflation

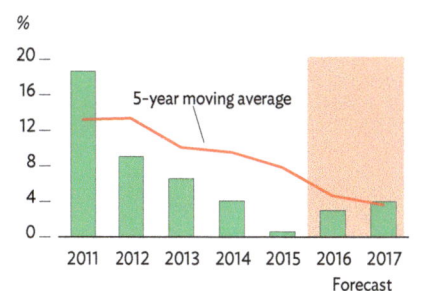

Source: Asian Development Outlook database.
Click here for figure data

70% of GDP is now generated in cities. However, urban transportation networks, water and sanitation systems, health and education services, and other physical and social infrastructure have struggled to keep pace. Moreover, rapidly rising urban populations strain natural resources and pollute the environment. To remain a vibrant industrializing economy, Viet Nam will need to develop more efficient urban centers that can support much larger populations. Achieving this will require progress on three fronts.

The first is urban planning. The current planning law stresses decentralized urban planning and stakeholder consultation, which requires more urban planning and management capacity in provincial and local governments. Too often, masterplans are idealized visions of future cities that do not take into account the real needs of households, businesses, or local governments.

Second is the funding of urban infrastructure. Outside of Ha Noi and Ho Chi Minh City, few urban governments can raise enough revenue for infrastructure on their own, leaving many heavily dependent on the central government annual budget. This inhibits infrastructure development because local governments need multiyear funding commitments to complete projects such as upgrades to citywide drainage systems. Funding can be even more difficult for critical projects that generate little revenue, such as sewerage, which typically require significant official development assistance from abroad.

For lack of own-source funding, urban authorities sometimes rely on private developers to provide infrastructure through land-for-development deals. Such deals can undervalue public land and build low-quality infrastructure. Further, a model of urban development driven by developers can distort supply by, for example, overinvesting in higher-end housing and underinvesting in homes for the urban poor. These issues can be addressed by strengthening provincial planning, creating medium-term frameworks for funding urban services, and encouraging provincial governments to deemphasize their role as investors and focus more on planning and regulating urban services, land use, and the stewardship of natural resources.

Finally, urban development needs to take the environment into account. Land-for-development deals often create urban sprawl and build inappropriately in high-risk areas, including floodplains. Moreover, the present planning system does not encourage governments to effectively incorporate climate change into urban plans. As a result, cities often focus on expansion and give inadequate attention to climate and disaster risks.

3.31.12 Current account balance

% of GDP

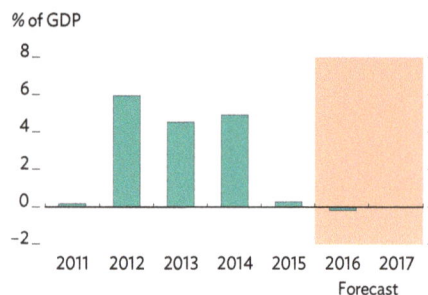

Source: Asian Development Outlook database.
Click here for figure data

3.31.13 Urban population

■ Urban population
■ Population in cities of more than 1 million

% of total population

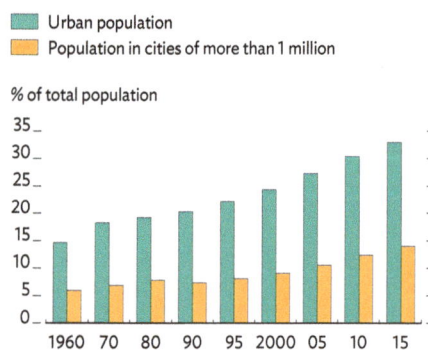

Source: World Bank, World Development Indicators online database (accessed 9 March 2016).
Click here for figure data

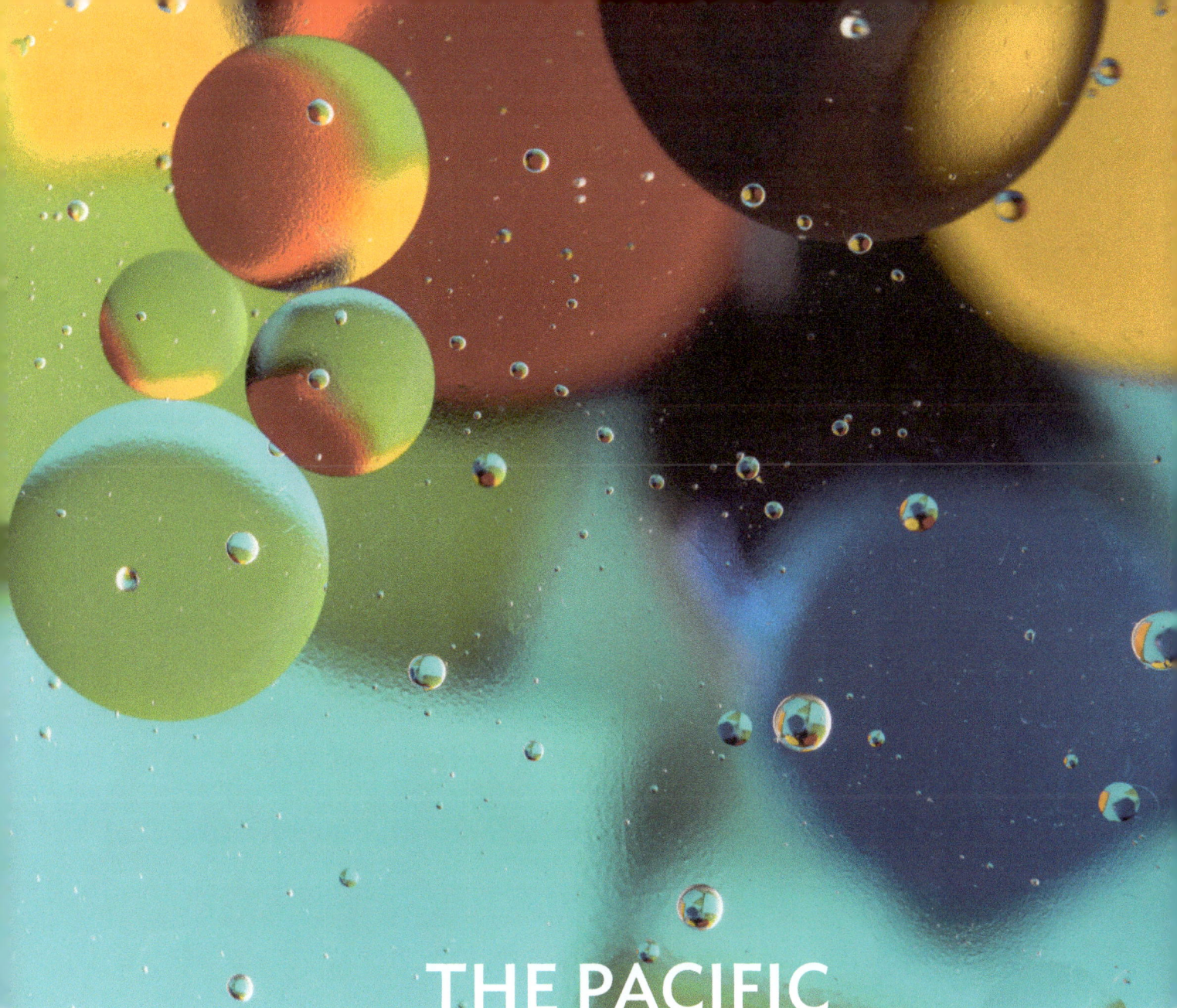

THE PACIFIC

FIJI
PAPUA NEW GUINEA
SOLOMON ISLANDS
TIMOR-LESTE
VANUATU
NORTH PACIFIC ECONOMIES
SOUTH PACIFIC ECONOMIES
SMALL ISLAND ECONOMIES

Fiji

Recent strong growth driven by a favorable domestic environment and rising investor confidence suffered a setback in February 2016 when a category 5 cyclone struck. Early assessment shows agriculture, especially sugar, was hard hit. Tourism faces headwinds from cancellations as high as 25% immediately following the cyclone. Damage and losses initially estimated to exceed $500 million, equal to roughly 11% of GDP, are likely to constrain growth in 2016.

Economic performance

Economic growth moderated to 4.0% in 2015 from 5.3% a year earlier as agricultural activity in sugar, fisheries, and timber slowed under a strong El Niño weather system that affected the country for most of the year (Figure 3.32.1). Tourism, which is Fiji's main earner of foreign currency, exceeded expectations with arrivals growing by 9.0% (Figure 3.32.2). While this likely reflected displacement of some tourists from Vanuatu following Cyclone Pam in early 2015, it was noteworthy that Fiji attracted larger numbers of visitors from Asia. Arrivals from the People's Republic of China were up by 41% during the year. Fiji Airways is actively targeting Asian markets with flights to the Republic of Korea and Hong Kong, China. The airline plans to start a new route to Singapore in April following the delivery of a new A330-300 aircraft in December 2015.

Growth in personal remittances at 28.3% and improved labor market conditions also helped to drive recent growth. Consumption spending remained strong as evidenced by a 12.4% increase in value-added tax (VAT) collections over the previous year and a 2.3% increase in domestic credit. Lending for investment surged by 77.7% in 2015, driven by strong growth in construction. Total investment equaled 29% of GDP in 2015 and has now surpassed the government target of 25% for 3 years in a row. Investment shows little sign of abating in the near term.

Fiscal policy remained expansionary and focused on road, water-supply, and sanitation infrastructure and human capital development pursued mainly by providing free primary and secondary education. Despite spending increases, the fiscal deficit declined from the equivalent of 4.1% of GDP in 2014 to 2.5% in 2015 following sales of state assets (Figure 3.32.3).

The Reserve Bank of Fiji maintained an accommodative monetary policy during 2015 to support domestic private sector investment and consumption. Interest rates across the banking sector were kept at historic lows, and the policy rate remained at 0.5% throughout 2015. Annual inflation was 1.4% at the end of 2015, kept low by falling international food and fuel prices. The government's downward adjustments to controlled fuel prices ensured that much of the decline in the global oil price was passed on to consumers.

This chapter was written by Caroline Currie of the South Pacific Subregional Office, ADB, Suva.

3.32.1 Supply-side contributions to growth

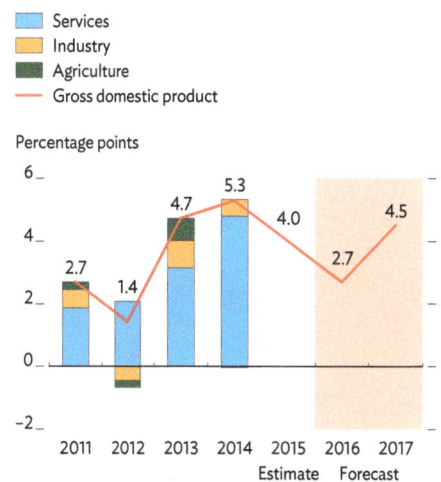

Legend:
- Services
- Industry
- Agriculture
- Gross domestic product

Percentage points

Sources: Fiji Bureau of Statistics; ADB estimates.
Click here for figure data

3.32.2 Visitor arrivals, by source

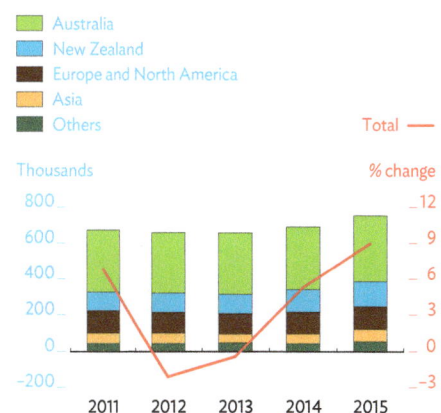

Legend:
- Australia
- New Zealand
- Europe and North America
- Asia
- Others
- Total

Thousands   % change

Source: Fiji Bureau of Statistics.
Click here for figure data

The current account deficit narrowed from the equivalent of 7.4% of GDP in 2014 to 4.0% in 2015 as declining international commodity prices reduced the import bill. Export revenues also fell, particularly from sugar and gold (Figure 3.32.4). Foreign exchange reserves held steady and currently cover 5.7 months of retained imports of goods and services.

Economic prospects

Following Tropical Cyclone Winston, the forecast for growth in 2016 is 2.7%, revised down from a pre-cyclone forecast of 4.0%. The late-February cyclone was the most powerful storm on record in the Southern Hemisphere. The worst damage occurred in rural areas and the islands to the north and west of the main island of Viti Levu. The cyclone caused severe damage to homes, schools, crops, and livelihoods. The sugar industry was particularly badly hit, and production in 2016 is expected to fall sharply. Damage was heavy but could have been much worse. The cyclone bypassed the capital city, Suva, and its central business district, as well as important tourist centers around Nadi. Major infrastructure was virtually unscathed.

Growth is expected to recover to 4.5% in 2017 boosted by reconstruction. The outlook for exports is positive except for sugar, which faces loss of preferential access to European markets in 2017. Fiji Airways' opening of a Singapore route in April 2016 will facilitate tourist access from Asia. Discussions over a new direct Beijing–Nadi route are also well advanced. These flights will likely boost tourism and could enhance opportunities for manufacturers and farmers to airfreight cargo to Asian markets. Fijian businesses are already exploring opportunities to expand exports of perishable goods such as fresh fish, other seafood, and flowers. Niche markets, including high-value garments and bottled water, are also expected to benefit from the new routes.

Aggregate demand is expected to remain strong in 2016 and 2017. The VAT reduction from 15% to 9% in the 2016 budget and strong growth in personal remittances following Cyclone Winston should boost spending. To aid families hurt by the cyclone, the Fiji National Provident Fund is allowing members to withdraw deposits of $500–$2,500 for disaster recovery. While helpful now, this could deplete savings and leave people vulnerable to poverty in old age.

Fiscal consolidation planned for 2017 is expected to have broad impact. The required extent of consolidation will depend on the government's success in partly divesting selected public assets. If the sales do not go ahead, the government could face a much larger budget deficit than the forecast 2.9% of GDP in 2016 and 2.5% in 2017.

Inflation is expected to rise to around 3.0% in 2016 and 2017 (Figure 3.32.5). Continuing low international fuel prices and the lower VAT are expected to be offset somewhat by upward pressure on prices from continuing strong domestic demand, and from local food prices driven higher by the cyclone and drought under El Niño.

The current account deficit is forecast to widen to the equivalent of 7.0% of GDP in 2016 as imports rise and sugar exports are lost in the wake of Cyclone Winston. The deficit is seen to narrow to 4.4% in 2017 as agricultural exports recover and post-cyclone imports subside.

3.32.3 Fiscal accounts

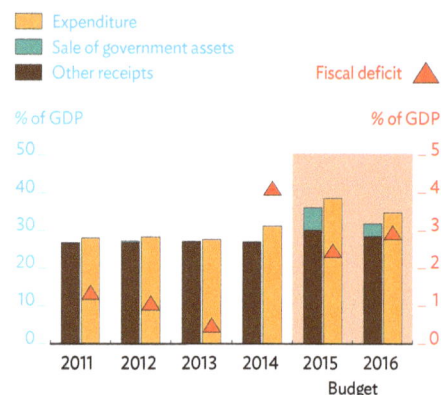

Source: Fiji Ministry of Finance. Economic and Fiscal Update: Supplement to the Budget Address (various years).
Click here for figure data

3.32.4 Exports

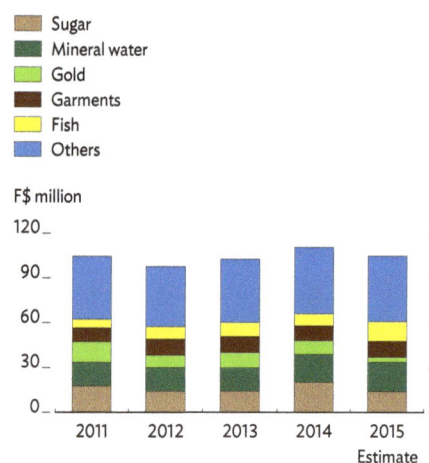

Note: Includes re-exports. Data for 2015 are estimates based on the year to November data.
Sources: Fiji Bureau of Statistics; ADB estimates.
Click here for figure data

3.32.1 Selected economic indicators (%)

	2016	2017
GDP growth	2.7	4.5
Inflation	3.0	3.0
Current account balance (share of GDP)	-7.0	-4.4

Source: ADB estimates.

Policy challenge—balancing cyclone recovery with long-term reform

In the immediate aftermath of Cyclone Winston, the government must work to sustain economic growth momentum while maintaining fiscal discipline. While the economic costs of the cyclone are high, social protection costs soared in March with the announcement of about $10 million in targeted assistance to people who are most vulnerable to falling into poverty. The aid is being made available as immediate relief assistance to be paid out over 3 months to 44,169 households currently receiving aid through three social protection programs.

Higher social protection costs press on the government's fiscal position as it reallocates spending to finance emergency relief efforts, including reorienting planned capital spending toward the rehabilitation of infrastructure and basic services in the worst affected areas. Despite an expected growth pickup in 2017 and beyond, the government will need to reduce expenditure in other areas to control fiscal deficits and keep its debt manageable during recovery (Figure 3.32.6).

In the medium-term, the government's focus on private sector development is vital to stimulating domestic and foreign investment, and to putting Fiji on a higher growth path. With this in mind, the government has been reforming its tax policies to stimulate private investment and consumption, and to enhance tax system transparency and compliance. The 2016 budget removed VAT exemptions and introduced new service and environment taxes, but further reforms are needed to foster private investment and expand the private sector.

The government has also introduced worthwhile business environment reforms, including financial reforms to encourage growth in small and medium-sized enterprises. For example, the new Companies Act, approved by the Cabinet in January 2016, and streamlined company registration are easing businesses' access to credit and to financial information on business partners and customers, as well as lowering startup costs. The government is working on further legislative and regulatory reforms, including secured transactions reform, to encourage greater private sector investment and public–private partnership, and to reduce ownership and control over a number of state-owned enterprises in 2016. Continuing progress will be vital to sustain Fiji's growth momentum.

3.32.5 Inflation

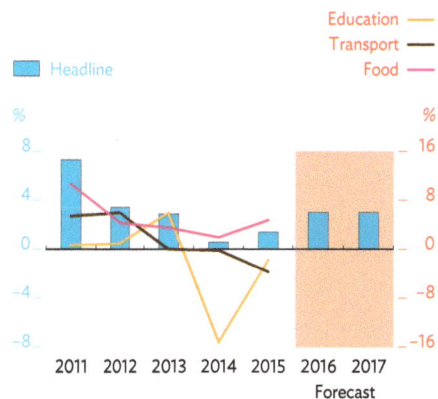

Sources: Fiji Bureau of Statistics; ADB estimates.
Click here for figure data

3.32.6 Public debt

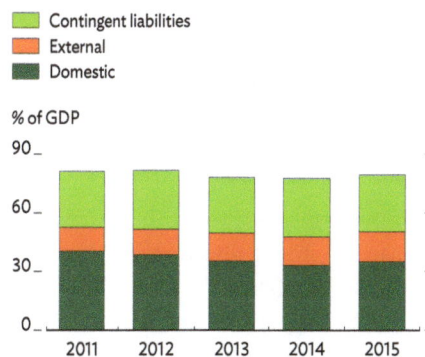

Note: Contingent liabilities data for 2015 are as of June.
Sources: Fiji Ministry of Finance. *Economic and Fiscal Update: Supplement to the Budget Address* (various years).
Click here for figure data

Papua New Guinea

Following strong growth in 2015, the first full year of gas production, the economy is forecast to grow by only 4.3% in 2016 and 2.4% in 2017. Non-mineral GDP, which better indicates underlying trends and how growth affects people's livelihoods, is projected to grow by 3.4% in 2016 and 3.6% in 2017. Increasing reliance on resource extraction raises volatility in the economy.

Economic performance

In 2015, the first full year of liquefied natural gas (LNG) production, the economy of Papua New Guinea (PNG) grew by 9.9% (Figure 3.33.1). Growth was considerably lower than initially forecast, however, due to lower energy prices, unfavorable weather for agriculture, and reduced mining output from the closure of the Ok Tedi gold and copper mine. Moreover, the early start of LNG production in 2014 reduced the statistical impact of the first full year of production. This performance followed more than a decade of strong, uninterrupted growth—averaging 6.8% per annum—supported by high global commodity prices and large private investments in the mineral sector.

The agriculture, forestry, and fisheries sector was affected by drought and low commodity prices in 2015. Growth in the sector decelerated to 2.1% in 2015 from 3.3% in 2014. Output from mining contracted by 3.7%. However, utilities continued to achieve strong growth, up by 6.0% in 2015, as did transport with 5.0% growth. Both outcomes reflected increased business activity in Port Moresby. Meanwhile, growth in wholesale and retail trade slowed from 4.0% in 2014 to 2.5%.

Inflation was steady in 2015 as prices increased by an average of 5.1%, down only slightly from the previous year's 5.2%. Although prices for imported oil fell steeply—by more than the PNG kina depreciated—the transmission of lower oil prices to the rest of the economy was constrained by market rigidities in sectors outside of mining.

Low commodity prices depressed export receipts (Figure 3.33.2). This, along with disappointing revenue from mining and petroleum operations, created serious fiscal challenges in 2015 (Figure 3.33.3). The original 2015 budget projected a fiscal deficit equivalent to 4.4% of GDP, but the government's 2015 midyear outlook projected an $800 million revenue shortfall and a deficit of $1.5 billion, equivalent to 9.4% of GDP, in the absence of fiscal adjustments. Preliminary estimates of the final budget outcome in 2015—which excludes loans and grants—suggests that the government was able to cut spending by the equivalent of $1.3 billion, leaving a deficit equal to 3.2% of GDP (Figure 3.33.4).

3.33.1 Economic growth and inflation

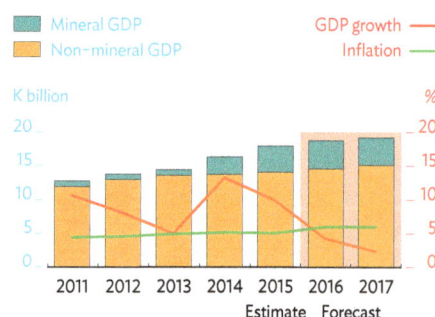

Sources: Bank of Papua New Guinea; Papua New Guinea 2016 National Budget; ADB estimates.
Click here for figure data

3.33.2 Export price indexes

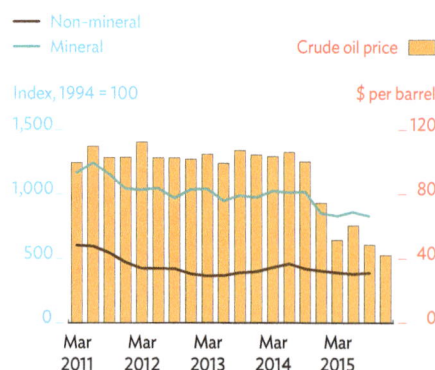

Sources: Bank of Papua New Guinea; World Bank Commodity Price Data (Pink Sheets).
Click here for figure data

This chapter was written by Yurendra Basnett of the Papua New Guinea Resident Mission, ADB, Port Moresby.

The smaller deficit reflected weak budget execution and payment deferrals, but these risk a buildup of expenditure arrears in the future.

In June 2014, the Bank of Papua New Guinea, the central bank, fixed the kina exchange rate some 20%–30% above the market rate and set a trading band with the aim of stemming what it saw as excessive kina depreciation. Although the rate has since been allowed to adjust gradually, most observers believe the kina is still overvalued relative to the currencies of the country's major trading partners. This has worsened foreign currency shortages and drained foreign exchange reserves, thereby heightening the risk of a forced and disorderly currency depreciation.

LNG exports pushed the current account balance into a surplus equivalent to 4.6% of GDP in 2015 (Figure 3.33.5). However, this did not translate into higher foreign reserves or tax revenue because offshore debt repayments climbed and investors were allowed to accelerate depreciation on the gas pipeline when calculating concession payments. Foreign exchange reserves actually fell from $2.3 billion at the end of 2014 (cover for 6.3 months of imports) to $2.1 billion a year later (5.6 months). Dollar shortages at commercial banks have persisted since 2015, such that the current backlog of exchange requests reportedly amounts to $500 million.

Economic prospects

Growth is expected at 4.3% in 2016, less than half the 2015 rate, reflecting base effects from last year's first full year of LNG exports and fiscal contraction. Although some recovery in oil and gas prices is expected over the next 2 years, average prices in both 2016 and 2017 are expected to remain below 2015 levels, to say nothing of earlier years. Food prices are also expected to continue to decline in 2016 before increasing modestly in 2017. These factors will likely push growth even lower in 2017, to 2.4%.

Continuing weakness in oil prices has dampened investment in the mineral sector, which has been the main driver of growth in recent years. The sector is nevertheless expected to remain important to economic growth in the medium term with the start of a few large mining projects. Firms appear to be continuing to consolidate their operations, however, to improve efficiency and reduce operating costs. This is expected to constrain private sector activity and consumption, as well as public revenue from payroll and corporate taxes. Fiscal consolidation is also likely to suppress domestic demand and formal employment.

With the return of normal rainfall following El Niño-induced drought in 2015, agriculture is projected to grow by 3.8% in 2016 and 3.4% in 2017. The sector projects higher output of coffee, cocoa, and palm oil, but further unfavorable weather in 2016 could pose downside risks. Oil and gas extraction is forecasted to grow by 7.1% in 2016 but then contract by 3.9% in 2017 as the sector enters decline from diminishing reserves. Construction is expected to grow by 3.0% in 2016 and 3.5% in 2017 ahead of the Asia-Pacific Economic Cooperation summit that PNG will host in 2018. Wholesale and retail trade is

3.33.3 Revenue performance and projections

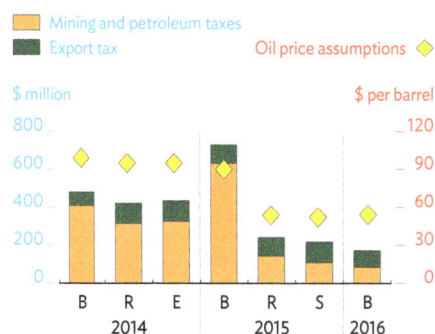

B = budget, R = revised, E = estimate, S = supplement.
Source: National budget documents (various years).
Click here for figure data

3.33.4 Fiscal performance

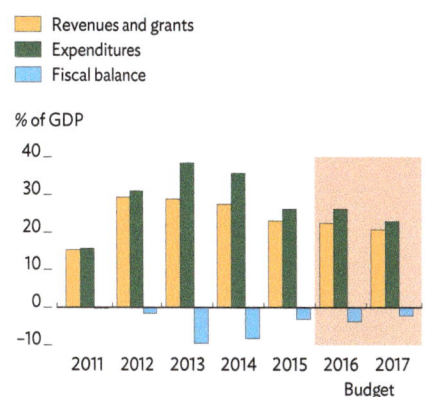

Note: 2015 figures as of the 2015 supplementary budget.
Source: National budget documents (various years).
Click here for figure data

expected to grow by 3.0% in 2016 and 5.0% in 2017, and the transport sector by 4.0% in both years.

Upside risks to the growth forecast include the expected resumption of production at the Ok Tedi mine and the Puma Oil Refinery in 2016, as well as the potential start of construction to extend the Papua LNG project. Despite falling commodity prices, LNG export volumes are expected to remain stable in 2016. Papua LNG is currently appraising gas resources, and a report due later this year will inform the company's investment plan and the possible start of new construction. The coffee harvest could be particularly large in 2016, as past experience suggests that coffee plants tend to bounce back after a year of drought stress.

Inflation is expected to accelerate to 6.0% in 2016 and 2017. The persistence of high inflation reflects government efforts to sustain public spending and expected kina depreciation. In 2017, recovering international oil prices are seen to compound inflationary pressure in PNG.

Rising fiscal deficits and cash flow concerns weigh heavily in the government's near-term policy concerns. Public expenditure is budgeted at $4.8 billion in 2016 (equivalent to 26.2% of GDP) and revenue at $4.1 billion. With lower revenue projections, the government plans fiscal deficits equal to 3.8% of GDP in 2016 and 2.2% in 2017. The primary deficit—estimated without revenues from resource exports, capital spending related to them, or interest payments—was estimated to equal 8.5% of non-mineral GDP in 2015. This deficit is seen to narrow modestly to 5.7% in 2016. Planned capital expenditures account for about 10% of total expenditure, and operational expenditure the remainder. Direct government financing covers 60% of capital expenditure, while the remaining 40% is financed from concessional loans and grants from development partners.

The government is likely to continue to face pressing cash-flow problems in 2016 with the buildup of expenditure arrears from deferred obligations, difficulties in financing its deficit, and higher debt servicing costs. Any unplanned expenditures, including cost overruns, would further strain cash-flow problems. Expenditures for hosting a meeting of African, Caribbean, and Pacific leaders in 2016, national elections in 2017, and the Asia-Pacific Economic Cooperation summit in 2018 also pose risks to budget integrity and fiscal balances. In light of fiscal constraints, the government plans to prioritize the completion of ongoing capital projects over starting new ones.

Cash-flow management is growing more difficult for the government as commercial banks reach their technical limits for exposure to government debt. The government is exploring options to float a $1 billion sovereign bond in 2016 to help refinance current borrowing, but this could prove costly. External debt servicing costs also appear likely to increase given downward pressure on the kina.

In 2016, the cost of domestic debt servicing is likely to increase significantly. Domestic debt stands at about 28% of GDP, while external debt equals 12% of GDP. Nearly half of the domestic debt (48.1%) is in Treasury bills for which yields have risen and maturity dates shortened. In 2014, no Treasury bills matured in less than 100 days, but at the start of 2016 such short-term Treasury bills accounted for an estimated 24%

3.33.5 Trade performance and current account balance

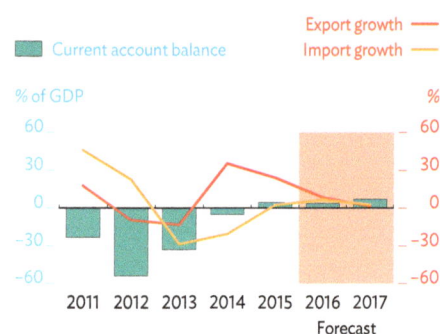

Sources: International Monetary Fund Article IV staff reports (various years); ADB estimates.
Click here for figure data

3.33.1 Selected economic indicators (%)

	2016	2017
GDP growth	4.3	2.4
Inflation	6.0	6.0
Current account balance (share of GDP)	3.8	7.2

Source: ADB estimates.

of the portfolio outstanding. As domestic debt has shifted to shorter maturities, interest costs and refinancing risks have risen. The 2016 budget estimates domestic debt repayments coming due this year will reach $3.0 billion, equal to a worrying 93.1% of projected current revenue (Figure 3.33.6).

LNG exports are projected to contribute to a current account surplus equal to 3.8% of GDP in 2016. This is a smaller surplus than in 2015, in line with lower projections for commodity prices. The current account surplus is seen to increase to the equivalent of 7.2% of GDP in 2017 with modest recovery in commodity prices. Coffee and palm oil will likely boost agricultural exports and support the surplus in coming years. Import growth is seen to ease in 2016 and 2017 with an expected slowdown in public and private investment.

Policy challenge—fostering economic diversification to tame growth volatility

The PNG economy has grown more dependent on resource exports in recent years with the rise of LNG and other extractive industries. This has elevated the influence of global commodity price volatility on the PNG economy. Strong global commodity prices attracted large investment in mineral extraction, triggering episodes of high growth. While this has significantly boosted government revenues and enabled large increases in public spending, the distribution of benefits has tended to be narrow. To encourage inclusive and sustainable growth, the government needs to ensure that other sectors—agriculture, manufacturing, and services—do not suffer as a result of growth in the mineral sector and are able to operate at their full potential. However, inadequate infrastructure, inflated operating costs, and an unfavorable business environment have deterred investors and kept productivity low in these sectors, inhibiting broad-based, sustainable economic growth.

Analysis suggests that past increases in output have resulted largely from increases in the labor force, and that the contributions of capital and new technology have been negligible except during periods of high investment in mining. Total factor productivity is estimated to have stagnated during the first 3 decades after independence. This highlights the deterioration in the operating environment and the extent of productivity stagnation in sectors other than mining.

Deteriorating infrastructure is an important constraint on productive capacity in agriculture, manufacturing, and services. It also hampers the government's ability to expand its delivery of basic health care, education, and other services. The poor quality of the transport network limits producers' access to markets and raises costs for service providers in remote communities. Although large investments in infrastructure development over the past few years have begun to address the problem, emerging fiscal pressures make it difficult to sustain recent progress.

3.33.6 Domestic debt repayments

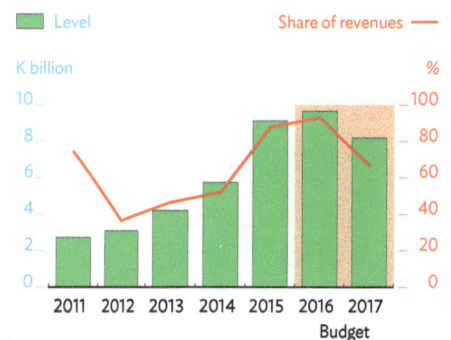

Sources: National budget documents (various years); ADB estimates.
Click here for figure data

Light manufacturing using domestically sourced agricultural inputs appears to be a promising area for improving labor productivity in PNG. Over the past decade, the agro-processing industry has grown by an average of 6.7% per year despite the challenges posed by kina appreciation and inflation tied to capital inflows for LNG development. Agro-processing now provides about a quarter of jobs in the formal sector and involves small producers as well as large global companies including Coca Cola and Nestlé. However, the high cost of doing business, poor connectivity, and human capital shortages impede further growth in this promising industry.

Tourism is another industry with strong potential in PNG that would benefit from infrastructure investments and could create tens of thousands of private sector jobs. Recognizing this potential, the 2016 budget more than triples to $19.9 million government expenditures to develop tourism. Developing the potential of PNG as a tourist destination first requires rehabilitating the image of the country as a safe destination for visitors. It also requires creating a business environment in which private developers can view PNG as a sound and secure place to invest in hotels and related businesses.

Fiscal constraints on the delivery of basic services and public infrastructure limit diversification in the PNG economy. Contracting out the maintenance and management of recently developed public infrastructure assets offers opportunities to reduce expenditures and the administrative burden on the public sector while promoting private sector growth and employment.

Diversifying the sectors of the economy that can create jobs, and from which the government can collect revenues, is clearly a policy priority if the country is going to avoid the cycles of boom and bust associated with reliance on mining exports. However, the approach to fostering diversification requires a rethink to emphasize institutional arrangements that rely on private sector enterprises to provide the bulk of the capital and know-how needed to develop businesses, and to keep the public sector focused on providing basic infrastructure and essential services.

Solomon Islands

Economic growth has recovered following severe floods in 2014, but longer-term prospects for sustaining growth are uncertain. Exports have been weak, and logging and development assistance are expected to decline over the medium term. The government hopes to use fiscal policy to drive economic growth. Policy should continue to safeguard macroeconomic stability while ensuring that increased spending is directed to areas that promote sustainable growth.

Economic performance

Economic growth rebounded to 3.2% in 2015 from 2.0% in 2014, led by investment (Figure 3.34.1). Construction picked up from rebuilding after the April 2014 floods and on strong business investment. Imports of capital goods increased by an estimated 27.4% over the previous year. Credit to the private sector expanded by 16.7%, with personal loans accounting for most of the increase and manufacturing also absorbing a large share.

Fiscal expansion contributed significantly to growth. After coming to power late in 2014, the government used its first budget to signal a shift toward expansionary fiscal policy after years of budget surpluses. Despite its late approval, the budget left a deficit estimated to equal 2.2% of GDP. Cash reserves built up in the past fell significantly, drawn down to finance deficit spending and to repay SI$154 million in domestic debt early. Cash reserves nonetheless remain substantial, equal to about 8.0% of GDP.

Consumer prices fell by 0.3% in 2015. Domestic prices normalized after increasing in the aftermath of the 2014 floods. Imported inflation was contained by lower global commodity prices and the continued appreciation of the Solomon Islands dollar against the currencies of Australia and New Zealand, the main sources of imports.

Exports continued to be weak, with total merchandise export receipts falling by an estimated 3.6%. This reflected, in part, the cessation of gold exports following the closure of the country's sole gold mine after the 2014 flood. Logging exports, which account for about two-thirds of export earnings, remained at record levels. However, other major export commodities saw volume declines, while softening international prices deepened the slump in export earnings.

Lower global oil prices provided significant relief to the balance of payments. Solomon Islands depends heavily on imported fuel, which is used to power electricity generation in the country. Lower oil prices saw the fuel import bill fall from the equivalent of 10.2% of GDP in 2014 to 7.2% in 2015 (Figure 3.34.2), but the effect of lower prices on

3.34.1 Supply-side contributions to growth

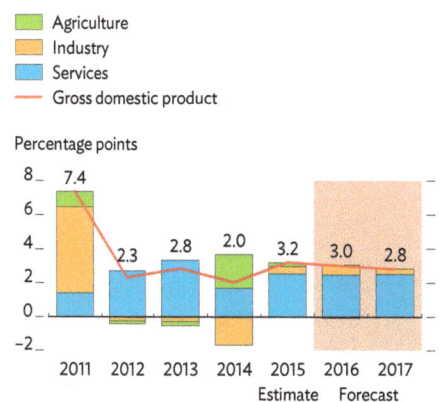

Sources: Ministry of Finance and Treasury; ADB estimates.
Click here for figure data

3.34.2 Fuel import bill and global oil price

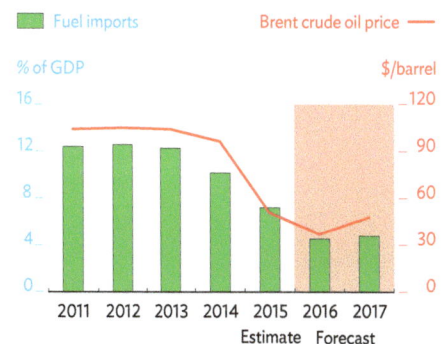

Sources: Central Bank of Solomon Islands; World Bank Commodity Price Data (Pink Sheets); ADB estimates.
Click here for figure data

This chapter was written by Roland Rajah of the Pacific Liaison and Coordination Office, ADB, Sydney.

the balance of payments was partly offset by higher import volumes. Merchandise import costs rose modestly on increased imports of capital goods, but imported business services fell significantly, which allowed the current account deficit to narrow slightly to 4.6% of GDP.

The central bank maintained its accommodative stance, capping its issuance of Bokolo Bills to SI$710 million and leaving the required reserve ratio unchanged at 7.5%. Foreign exchange reserves increased modestly in 2015, rising to an estimated 10.3 months of import cover (Figure 3.34.3). Broad money growth increased to 15% as strong growth in credit to the private sector continued and government spending of cash reserves injected significant additional liquidity. The Solomon Islands dollar continued to appreciate in nominal effective terms as the US dollar, which the Solomon Islands dollar closely tracks, rose against the currencies of Solomon Islands' major trade partners.

Economic prospects

As current growth drivers fade, growth is forecast to slow to 3.0% in 2016 and 2.8% in 2017. The pace of investment is expected to ease but remain elevated. Fiscal expansion is also expected to slow. Weak exports are seen to continue to detract from growth. Low oil prices are, however, supporting consumption while easing pressure on the balance of payments and providing the authorities with room to continue to pursue expansionary policy.

The government plans to continue to increase development spending as part of its growth strategy. It is targeting a fiscal deficit equal to 5.8% of GDP in 2016, financed by drawing down cash reserves. As in 2015, about 30% of government-funded expenditure will be directed toward its development budget, up significantly from 18.3% in the 2014 budget, and focused on infrastructure, rural development, and health. However, weak execution will likely continue to hamper spending in 2016 and 2017, and the fiscal deficit will likely be much smaller than budgeted (Figure 3.34.4).

Inflation is expected to rise to 4.4% in 2016 and 5.7% in 2017 (Figure 3.34.5). Domestic inflation is expected to pick up, reflecting elevated broad money growth and the fading of base effects from the 2014 floods. Imported inflation should remain contained in 2016 but will likely contribute to higher inflation in 2017 with a projected rise in global commodity prices.

Merchandise exports are seen to continue to contract as logging output falls. Copra and cocoa exports will likely continue to decline as other exports remain broadly flat. The import bill is expected to ease slightly in 2016 on account of lower average oil prices before rising in 2017 in line with forecasted increases in global commodity prices. The trade balance is expected to deteriorate, widening the current account deficit to the equivalent of 5.9% of GDP in 2016 and 7.2% in 2017.

Monetary policy is seen to remain accommodative. Broad money growth is expected to accelerate as the government spends its cash reserves and growth in credit to the private sector remains robust. The central bank has some scope to accommodate these developments. Foreign exchange reserves are expected to fall but remain at a

3.34.3 Foreign exchange reserves

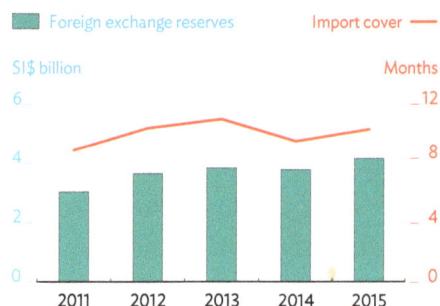

Source: Central Bank of Solomon Islands.
Click here for figure data

3.34.4 Fiscal balance

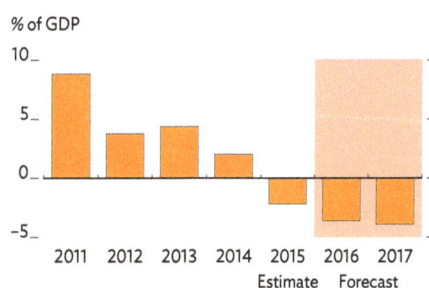

Sources: Ministry of Finance and Treasury; ADB estimates.
Click here for figure data

3.34.1 Selected economic indicators (%)

	2016	2017
GDP growth	3.0	2.8
Inflation	4.4	5.7
Current account balance (share of GDP)	-5.9	-7.2

Source: ADB estimates.

very comfortable level. However, given the government's fiscal targets, the central bank will need to carefully monitor developments and consider tightening monetary policy if fiscal expansion or other inflationary pressures prove greater than expected.

Policy challenge—fiscal policy for development

The government aims to increase public spending to lay the foundation for sustainable economic growth. The strategy takes advantage of fiscal buffers accumulated in recent years, and low global oil prices allow monetary policy to remain broadly accommodative. Preserving fiscal buffers and ensuring that increased spending is well targeted to promote sustainable growth will be critical. Results will likely be better if spending is increased gradually.

If fully implemented, the 2016 budget would largely exhaust government cash reserves. Even a rate of budget execution similar to last year would significantly erode cash reserves and constrain the government's ability to respond to future economic shocks. Excessive fiscal expansion also risks crowding out private sector activity, especially if the central bank is forced to tighten monetary policy to contain inflation. Meanwhile, a weak outlook for revenues argues for conserving fiscal reserves for future use. Setting a floor for cash reserves and strengthening policy coordination between the government and the central bank would be useful measures to safeguard stability.

Expenditure quality will be critical. Containing payroll costs would save money for higher-priority expenditures. Prioritizing public capital investment would likely yield the greatest growth impact. While the share of spending directed to the development budget has increased dramatically, it still contains significant recurrent expenditures. Tightening its focus on capital investment would benefit growth while ensuring that all recurrent spending is tracked and treated consistently. Effective recurrent budget management is particularly important as revenue growth is expected to slow, and funding requirements for the operation and maintenance of new capital investments need to be properly assessed and provided for in future budgets.

Line ministries' weak execution of budgets—particularly their low execution rates of development budgets—has been a perennial problem. This largely reflects systemic capacity constraints, so improving execution will take time, particularly to avoid impairing expenditure quality or weakening expenditure controls. In the interim, the government can target more implementation-ready projects and consider gradually scaling up public investment in line with improvements in implementation capacity.

3.34.5 Inflation

— Overall
— Domestic
— Imported

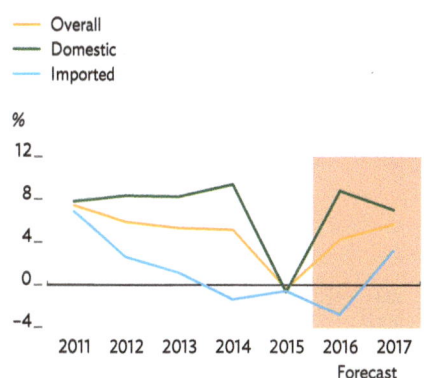

Sources: Central Bank of Solomon Islands; ADB estimates.
Click here for figure data

Timor-Leste

Economic growth slowed in 2015 as fiscal stimulus eased. Growth is expected to accelerate in 2016 and 2017 on rising public and private investment, but declining oil production highlights the need to diversify the economy. A young population lends Timor-Leste great potential to raise its long-term growth prospects by investing in human capital and encouraging broader participation in the labor market.

Economic performance

Growth slowed in 2015 as GDP excluding the large offshore petroleum sector expanded by an estimated 4.1% (Figure 3.35.1). Public spending, which has been the major driver of growth since 2007, declined modestly in 2015 with total expenditures excluding grants falling by an estimated 1.5% (Figure 3.35.2). Despite this decline, public spending excluding grants still equaled 91.2% of non-oil GDP (hereafter GDP).

The composition of public spending changed significantly in 2015 as increased transfers offset declines in purchases of goods and services and in capital investment. Growth in spending on salaries and wages halved from an average of 12.4% per annum in 2009–2014 to an estimated 6.3% in 2015. Spending on goods and services was cut by an estimated 9.1% year on year to $389.7 million in 2015. Savings on fuel from lower oil prices accounted for 39.8% of the reduction in goods and services purchases, and there were also significant cuts to spending on operational expenses, building and vehicle maintenance, and domestic and international travel by government officials.

Public transfers increased by 48.1% and accounted for almost one-third of public spending in 2015. This increase was driven by a doubling of payments to veterans of the fight for independence to $124.6 million and a $133.4 million transfer payment to the newly established Special Administrative Region of Oe-Cusse Ambeno. The region has been granted significant autonomy and is working to establish a special economic zone that will encompass the Oe-Cusse exclave and Atauro Island. It allocated 85.6% of its budget to capital investments in roads, the airport, electricity upgrades, a small aircraft, and a passenger ferry.

Capital investment through Timor-Leste's multiyear Infrastructure Fund fell by 22.8% to $239.4 million in 2015, though total capital investment is likely to have increased once investment by Oe-Cusse is included. Road and bridge upgrades took more than half of all Infrastructure Fund spending, and the electricity system a further 17.8%. Despite efforts to improve budget execution, a strong seasonal trend still marked capital disbursements (Figure 3.35.3).

3.35.1 Supply-side contributions to growth

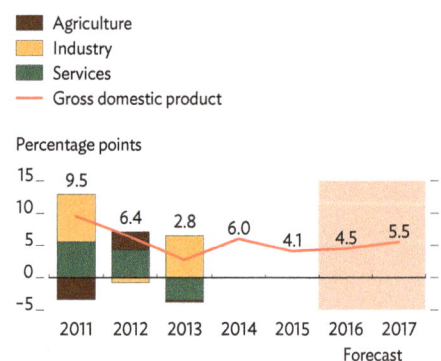

- Agriculture
- Industry
- Services
- Gross domestic product

Percentage points

Sources: Statistics Timor-Leste; ADB estimates.
Click here for figure data

3.35.2 Actual and budgeted expenditures

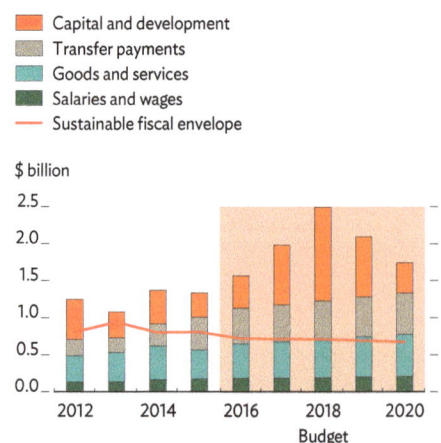

- Capital and development
- Transfer payments
- Goods and services
- Salaries and wages
- Sustainable fiscal envelope

$ billion

Source: Government of Timor-Leste. *Budget Book* (various years).
Click here for figure data

This chapter was written by David Freedman, consultant, Timor-Leste Resident Mission, ADB, Dili.

Income from offshore petroleum fell significantly in 2015 but still supplied 84.9% of government revenues excluding grants. The volume of petroleum production exceeded the budget forecast by 16.6%, but petroleum revenues were 19.8% less than forecast. Investments through Timor-Leste's Petroleum Fund recorded a net loss of $21.4 million in 2015—far below the forecast net income of $915.8 million—due to stock market volatility and foreign exchange losses caused by the appreciation of the US dollar, the official currency. Domestic revenues equaled 12.8% of GDP in 2015 and grew by 1.2% year on year as a small decline in tax receipts was offset by improved collection of fees and charges for government services such as electricity. Lower petroleum income and poor investment returns saw Timor-Leste's fiscal position swing from a surplus equal to 79.9% of GDP in 2014 to a deficit estimated at 14.2%. The Petroleum Fund balance consequently edged down to $16.2 billion by year-end, or $13,000 per capita.

The consumer price index rose by 0.4% in Dili and 1.3% elsewhere to yield a weighted annual national inflation rate of 0.6% (Figure 3.35.4). Price stability stemmed from falling international prices for key commodity imports, including rice and fuel, and the continued appreciation of the US dollar against the currencies of Timor-Leste's major trading partners in Southeast Asia.

Heineken broke ground on a new brewery and bottling plant due to begin operations late this year, and several economic indicators suggest good business conditions in 2015. Lending to the private sector increased by 10.5% with strong growth in construction and services. Business deposits in banks rose by 9.0%. Commercial electricity consumption climbed by 7.6%. International passenger arrivals rose by 5.3% year on year in the first 3 quarters.

Initial analysis suggests that recent increases in the planted area of rice and maize were sustained in 2015 and that high rainfall allowed good grain harvests in the first half. An improved coffee harvest saw export volume increase by an estimated 51% from a low base in 2014, but depressed international prices sent earnings marginally lower.

Merchandise imports increased by an estimated 10.9% despite lower commodity prices and a stronger US dollar. The resulting merchandise trade deficit of $537.9 million equaled 36.6% of GDP, in line with recent years. Lower income from petroleum production and the poor performance of Petroleum Fund investments saw the current account surplus tumble from 75.1% of GDP in 2014 to an estimated 14.2% in 2015 (Figure 3.35.5).

Economic prospects

GDP growth is forecast at 4.5% in 2016, rising to 5.5% in 2017 on large public and private investments. A public–private partnership to build a new international seaport west of Dili is expected to break ground in 2017 and will require an investment of $290 million, equivalent to 19.8% of GDP in 2015. Private sector financing is set to cover more than half of this cost. The government is planning major investments in other economic infrastructure, while private consortia are preparing to invest in cement manufacturing and tourism. The onset of El Niño in late 2015

3.35.3 Infrastructure fund disbursements

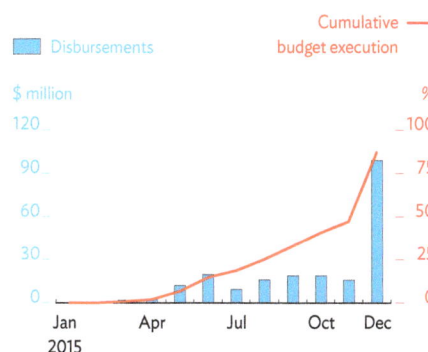

Source: Timor-Leste Budget Transparency Portal.
Click here for figure data

3.35.4 Inflation

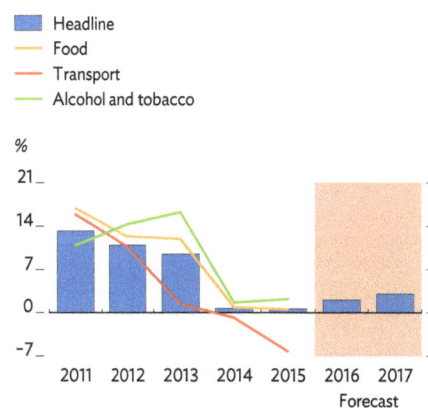

Sources: Timor-Leste National Statistics Directorate; ADB estimates.
Click here for figure data

3.35.5 Current account components

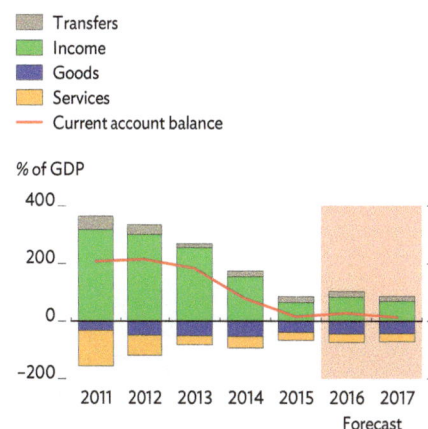

Sources: Banco Central de Timor-Leste; ADB estimates.
Click here for figure data

is expected to hurt 2016 grain harvests enough to require increased food imports, but the coffee harvest is expected to be significantly better in 2016 than in 2015.

Inflation is projected to increase modestly to 2.0% in 2016 and 3.0% in 2017 as the deflationary effects of the strong dollar and low commodity prices ease. Declining oil income has highlighted the challenge of balancing public investment needs with the twin goals of long-term fiscal sustainability and intergenerational equity. The 2016 budget trimmed forecasts for petroleum production volumes and reduced the undiscounted forecast for petroleum revenues during 2016–2022 by 56.4% relative to the 2015 budget forecast (Figure 3.35.6). This has reduced the estimate of sustainable annual income from the Petroleum Fund to $544.8 million from the 2015 estimate of $638.5 million. Yet the 2016 budget assumes an average oil price of $71.2 per barrel in 2016–2020, without taking into account the sharp decline in oil prices since mid-2015.

The government had initially targeted a significant fiscal adjustment for 2016 and 2017 to cut budgeted expenditures excluding grants from $1.57 billion in 2014 to $1.30 billion in 2016 and $1.20 billion in 2017. However, this adjustment has been deferred, and the 2016 budget has spending at $1.56 billion this year and projects average annual spending at $2.08 billion for 2017–2020 to complete major capital investments. Reforms to boost non-oil revenue collection are being prepared but are unlikely to mobilize significant domestic revenues in the short term. Domestic non-oil revenues are expected to average 10.8% of GDP in 2016 and 2017.

While total budgets in 2015 and 2016 are very similar, the composition of planned spending has changed significantly. The allocation to Oe-Cusse in 2016 rose sharply by 63.3% as the region's capital investment budget expanded by 49.6%. This compares with a 6.9% increase in budgeted capital investment for the rest of the country. These commitments are accommodated by cutting the recurrent budgets of most line ministries, which has contributed to lower budgets for health (–21%), education (–10%), and agriculture (–32%).

The capital investment budget for major projects during 2016–2020 is equivalent to 248.8% of last year's GDP. More than three-quarters of this budget is allocated to roads and bridges, expanding Dili's airport, new public buildings, and the Tasi Mane project to develop a petrochemical industry on the south coast (Figure 3.35.7). Fully implementing this investment program would strain government management capacity and risk wasting scarce public resources (Figure 3.35.8). The weak outlook for oil prices may threaten the commercial viability of new state-sponsored petrochemical developments, so careful appraisal of the proposed investment is warranted.

The 2016 budget law includes reform to restructure the Infrastructure Fund as an autonomous agency. Legislation specifying the details of the reform has yet to be tabled but could provide a timely opportunity to strengthen public investment management. In the short term, disruption associated with reform may delay the implementation of the 2016 capital budget. Over the longer term, reform may smooth budget execution and improve the quality of spending. The government

3.35.1 Selected economic indicators (%)

	2016	2017
GDP growth	4.5	5.5
Inflation	2.0	3.0
Current account balance (share of GDP)	26.1	11.8

Source: ADB estimates.

3.35.6 Adjustment to projected petroleum revenues

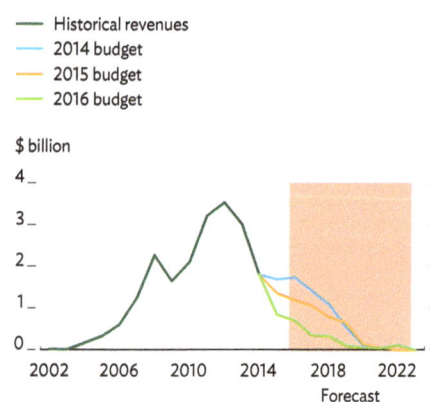

Sources: Budget Book, 2014–2016; ADB estimates.
Click here for figure data

3.35.7 Major infrastructure fund programs

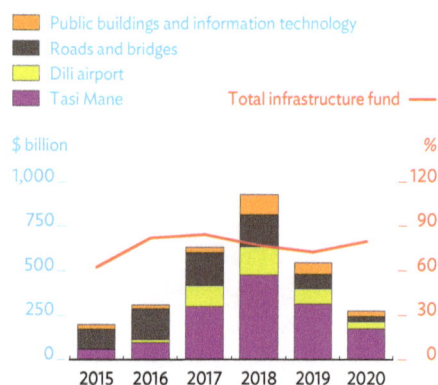

Source: National budget 2016.
Click here for figure data

also aims to complete reforms to improve the business enabling environment and stimulate financial sector development before national elections in mid-2017.

Income from petroleum production and Petroleum Fund investments will continue to be important to the current account balance. Improved returns on Petroleum Fund investments will partly offset declining petroleum production. As a result, the current account surplus is seen to rise to 26.1% of GDP in 2016 as investment returns improve, before falling to 11.8% in 2017 as petroleum production declines.

Policy challenge—realizing a demographic dividend

Timor-Leste can raise its potential growth rate by strengthening human capital formation and fostering labor market participation. Rapid population growth since independence has created a youthful nation, with 42% of citizens younger than 16. Timor-Leste's dependency ratio—the number of children and retired adults for each working-age adult—is one of the highest in the world. At the same time, adult participation in the labor force is relatively low.

As the young mature, Timor-Leste's working-age population will expand by 2.8% compounded annually from 2015 to 2050, which is forecast to rein in the dependency ratio from 0.89 in 2015 to 0.61 in 2050 (Figure 3.35.9). These trends can provide powerful economic stimulus if policy makes the most of Timor-Leste's demographic potential.

Expanded access to health care and education have produced clear gains since independence, with infant mortality halving from 2003 to 2009 and primary school enrolment rising from 65.6% in 2007 to 91.9% in 2013. However, malnutrition among young children remains high, and assessments of learning outcomes highlight the need to further strengthen preschool and primary education (Figure 3.35.10).

Investments to improve maternal and child health and strengthen education will raise long-term growth potential by improving future labor productivity. In the short term, growth may be enhanced and formal employment stimulated by reducing the costs employers face when hiring new workers. Timor-Leste's labor code imposes a range of restrictive and costly conditions on employers. The minimum wage of $115 per month may be high, given current workforce productivity and the large number of unskilled workers without jobs who may be willing to work for less.

At present, only 11.2% of the working-age population is formally employed, and half of these workers are directly employed by the government. Regulations that impede workers' move from informal to formal employment can be counterproductive and should be reviewed. It is also important to consider how social assistance transfers, equal to 11.8% of GDP in 2015, modify incentives for human capital accumulation and labor force participation.

3.35.8 Actual and forecast Petroleum Fund balances

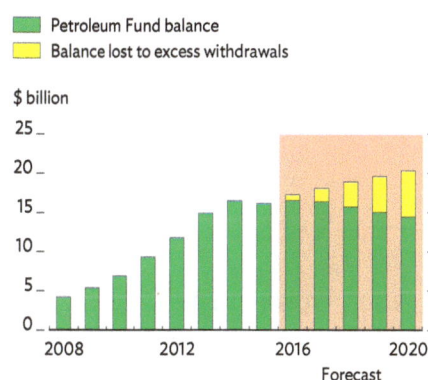

Sources: National budget 2016; ADB estimates.
Click here for figure data

3.35.9 Demographic projections, 2010–2050

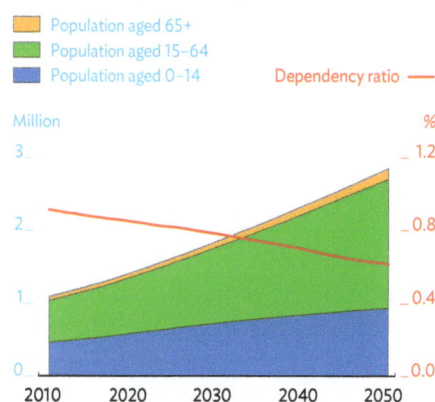

Source: Timor-Leste census, 2010.
Click here for figure data

3.35.10 Incidence of stunting in children aged under 5

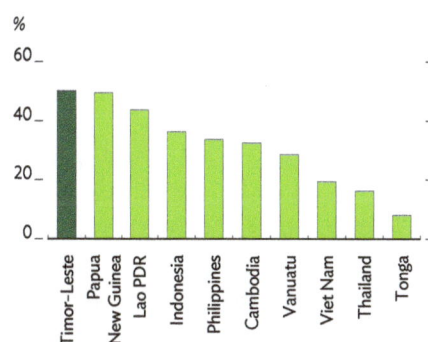

Lao PDR = Lao People's Democratic Republic.
Note: Most recent data during 2010–2014 are shown for each country.
Sources: World Development Indicators; Timor-Leste Food and Nutrition Survey 2013.
Click here for figure data

Vanuatu

The economy has been buffeted by a series of negative shocks, including a tropical cyclone, severe El Niño conditions, and problems at the international airport. Cyclone reconstruction has suffered significant delays. Following a corruption scandal and snap elections, a new government was formed. Meanwhile, much-needed infrastructure investment is getting under way, which should help improve the country's appeal as a tourist destination.

Economic performance

The economy is estimated to have contracted by 1.0% in 2015 (Figure 3.36.1). Tropical Cyclone Pam struck Vanuatu in March 2015, causing extensive damage and losses estimated to equal 64.1% of 2013 GDP. About a third of the damage was to private housing, but agriculture and tourism were badly affected. Planned reconstruction projects suffered long delays that limited their possible stimulus to growth in 2015.

In the aftermath of the cyclone, the authorities adopted a number of policies to support economic recovery. Parliament passed a budget revision that waived value-added tax and import duties on building materials and relief items, and doubled the allowances parliamentarians received for projects in their constituencies. Further, the Vanuatu National Provident Fund allowed members to withdraw up to 20% of their retirement account to fund rebuilding and livelihood reconstruction. The Reserve Bank of Vanuatu eased monetary settings by linking its policy rate to its 91-day note rate (effectively slashing the policy rate from 5.2% to 1.8%) and reducing bank reserve requirements.

The budget recorded a surplus equivalent to 1.4% of GDP. Strong revenue collection, which exceeded budget estimates by 8%, more than offset expenditures, which were only slightly greater than the budgeted amounts. As the bulk of cyclone reconstruction is being financed by development partners, external grants rose dramatically to reach about $75 million. Nonetheless, approval delays meant that major reconstruction projects did not break ground in 2015 and the expected boost to growth was delayed.

The tourism industry was badly affected by the cyclone but recovered more quickly than anticipated. In the immediate aftermath of the cyclone, tourist arrivals dropped significantly. Arrivals by air in March–June were down by 26% from the previous year, and cruise ship arrivals were 52% lower. However, arrivals recovered in the second half of the year, such that visitors by air in the whole of 2015 declined by only 17.3% and by ship by only 10.3% (Figure 3.36.2). Both shortfalls were less severe than initially feared. However, the extent to which the tourism

3.36.1 GDP growth

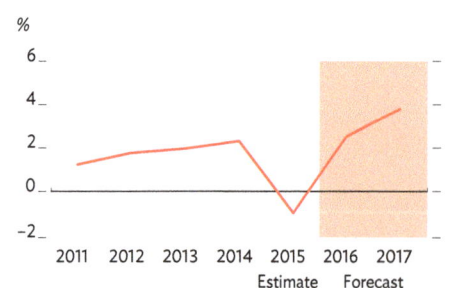

Sources: Vanuatu National Statistics Office; ADB estimates.
Click here for figure data

3.36.2 Visitor arrivals by mode of travel

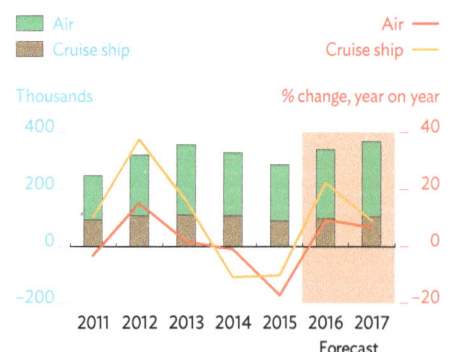

Source: Vanuatu National Statistics Office.
Click here for figure data

This chapter was written by Roland Rajah of the Pacific Liaison and Coordination Office, ADB, Sydney.

recovery has benefitted the local economy is unclear. This is because recovery was concentrated in cruise ship arrivals, and those arriving by ship tend to spend less locally than do other tourists. Many local tourism operators continued to report weak market conditions.

In the aftermath of the cyclone, inflation jumped to 5.7% in the second quarter, driven by a 12.3% increase in food prices. However, inflation subsequently eased and for 2015 as a whole prices were up by only 2.5%. Costs of transport, health, education, food, and clothing led price increases.

Agriculture was badly affected by the cyclone and suffered further setbacks from dry conditions associated with El Niño. Consequently, production volumes for most major agricultural export commodities fell (Figure 3.36.3). Overall export earnings contracted by an estimated 5.5% as softer international prices for most major exports worsened the decline.

The import bill rose sharply on higher imports of manufactured goods, food, and livestock after the cyclone, which outweighed the effects of lower prices for imported oil. The trade balance is estimated to have deteriorated to a deficit equal to 36.2% of GDP (from 25.3% in 2014), driving the current account deficit to an estimated 10.4% of GDP (compared with a surplus of 2.1% in 2014).

Economic prospects

The economy is expected to grow by 2.5% in 2016 and by 3.8% in 2017. The commencement of major reconstruction and several large new infrastructure projects should provide a substantial boost to growth in 2016, but this may be offset by the recent cancellation of flights to Port Vila by major international airlines, which will likely weigh heavily on the tourism industry. In 2017, growth is expected to pick up as tourism recovers and infrastructure construction continues.

Snap elections held on 22 January 2016, which were prompted by a corruption case that saw 14 members of Parliament convicted in late 2015, led to the formation of a new government in February. A new Prime Minister was elected unopposed by the new Parliament, which had most legislative districts represented by new representatives. The new government is focusing on political and electoral reform, as well as on more immediate issues such as passing the 2016 budget and addressing concerns about runway safety at the international airport.

In late January, two major airlines operating in the region, Air New Zealand and Virgin Australia, announced they would stop flying to Port Vila over concern about the safety of the runway at Bauerfield International Airport. Qantas, a third major carrier, announced that it was ending its codeshare agreement with Air Vanuatu—the government-owned airline. The government is undertaking urgent runway repairs, but these will take time and the immediate impact on the tourism industry in 2016 is expected to be significant. Air New Zealand and Virgin Australia carry around 40% of inbound tourists, and the cancellation of the Qantas codeshare may hurt Air Vanuatu's customer base. However, Air Vanuatu has increased its flights and cut ticket prices, which may help to offset some of these effects. A broader

3.36.3 Principal exports

- Copra
- Coconut oil
- Kava
- Beef
- Cocoa
- Others

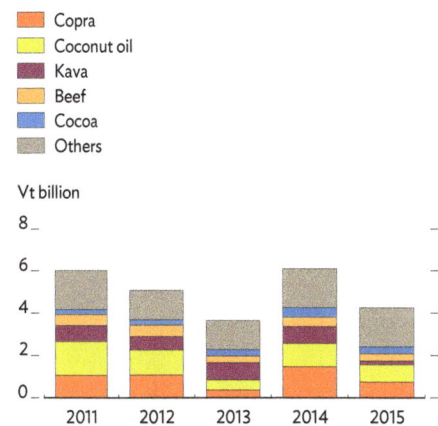

Sources: Vanuatu National Statistics Office; ADB estimates.
Click here for figure data

3.36.1 Selected economic indicators (%)

	2016	2017
GDP growth	2.5	3.8
Inflation	1.9	2.4
Current account balance (share of GDP)	–15.0	–11.0

Source: ADB estimates.

concern is the potential damage to Vanuatu's profile as a tourist destination, particularly coming on the back of Cyclone Pam last year.

Inflation is expected to remain subdued at 1.9% in 2016, reflecting lower international commodity prices as well as base effects from the jump in inflation in mid-2015 following Cyclone Pam (Figure 3.36.4). In 2017, inflation is projected to pick up to 2.4% in line with increased economic activity and rising international commodity prices.

The new government has yet to release its 2016 budget. The 2016 budget policy statement, approved under the previous government, targeted a balanced recurrent budget while taking on concessional debt to fund infrastructure investment and keeping the ratio of debt to GDP below 25%. The central bank is expected to maintain its accommodative stance through 2016, as both inflation and economic activity will likely remain relatively subdued.

The current account deficit is seen to widen further to the equivalent of 15.0% of GDP in 2016 as imported inputs for reconstruction and infrastructure works rise, and as tourism earnings remain depressed. In 2017, the current account is projected to improve to a deficit equivalent to 11.0% of GDP as tourism earnings recover.

Policy challenge—delivering infrastructure to boost tourism and lift potential growth

Growth has been lackluster over the past several years compared with the highs seen in the mid- to late-2000s. While private investment has been weak, the major difference has been lower public capital investment (Figure 3.36.5). The country's infrastructure has deteriorated for lack of maintenance. Inadequate funding for the operation of assets has further undermined economic returns on public investments.

Tourism, the country's key economic driver, has suffered as a result of deteriorating infrastructure. This is most evident in the cancellation of flights into Port Vila. However, the underlying issues run deeper. Visitor arrivals by air have been flat since 2012. While cruise ship visitation has risen significantly, its benefits to the local economy depend on passengers venturing onshore and purchasing local goods and services. Many point to deteriorating conditions in Port Vila and other areas as a key problem. Responses to a recent survey found the poor quality of public services and infrastructure cited most frequently as the least appealing aspect of visiting Vanuatu and the area where improvement was most needed. Meanwhile, improving connectivity remains crucial to developing tourism on the outer islands.

To address these problems and broader infrastructure deficiencies, the government recently approved the Vanuatu Infrastructure Strategic Investment Plan, 2015–2024, which plans $407 million in new projects. Ensuring adequate funding for operation and maintenance will be critical. Major projects funded by development partners are now getting under way, including upgrades to the international and domestic wharves in Port Vila and to Bauerfield International Airport, as well as urban development projects to improve public facilities in Port Vila.

3.36.4 Headline inflation and key components

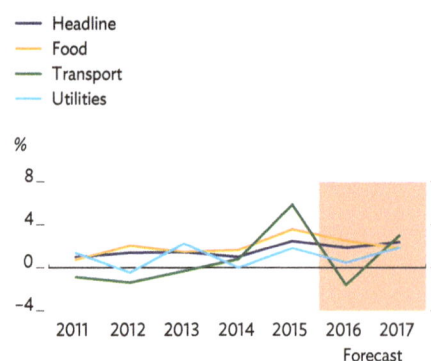

Sources: Vanuatu National Statistics Office; ADB estimates.
Click here for figure data

3.36.5 Government expenditures

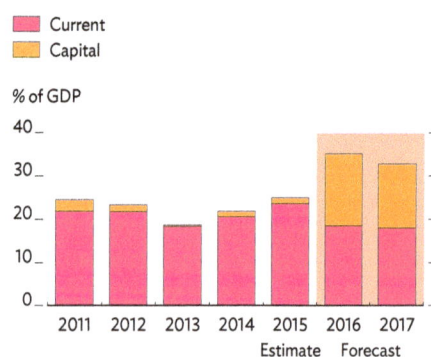

Sources: Vanuatu Department of Finance and Treasury; ADB estimates.
Click here for figure data

North Pacific economies

Recent performance across these economies was mixed and is expected to remain so. Strong growth continued in Palau driven by higher tourist arrivals, while GDP in the Republic of the Marshall Islands and the Federated States of Micronesia contracted in the absence of public investment. Growth is expected to slow this year in Palau as tourism faces capacity constraints. Recovery in the near term in the other two economies hinges on their ability to access capital grants to fund major infrastructure projects.

Economic performance

Growth accelerated to an estimated 6.7% in Palau (Figure 3.37.1) while the Republic of the Marshall Islands (RMI) and the Federated States of Micronesia (FSM) continued to contract in FY2015 (ended 30 September 2015), though by less than in FY2014. The improvement in Palau from 4.7% growth in FY2014 reflected strong performance in tourism (Figure 3.37.2). Tourism receipts in FY2015 were equivalent to 54.8% of GDP, up from 39.7% in FY2010. Visitor arrivals grew by 32.5% in FY2015 to reach 166,136, more than twice the number in FY2010. The increase in arrivals has been driven by expanded direct charter flights from Hong Kong, China and Macau, China. Arrivals from the People's Republic of China (PRC) accounted for 54.0% of all arrivals in FY2015, up from just 1.2% in FY2010. Despite a reduction in April of the number of charter flights allowed, from 48 per month to 32, arrivals remained strong as airlines adapted by flying larger aircraft.

The RMI and the FSM continue to rely on public infrastructure projects for growth, their economies otherwise characterized by small private sectors and widespread informal employment. The lack of new projects in these economies reflects continued problems in utilizing capital grants flowing from the compacts of free association that all three North Pacific economies have with the US. In addition, extreme weather exerted downward pressure on GDP growth.

Output in the FSM contracted for a fourth consecutive year, with GDP declining by an estimated 1.5% in FY2015 following a series of devastating typhoons that affected all four of its states (Figure 3.37.3). In March 2015, Typhoon Maysak destroyed an estimated 90% of food crops and hundreds of homes in Chuuk and on outlying islands in Yap. In May, Typhoon Noul struck the main islands of Yap, and Typhoon Dolphin caused severe flooding and damage in Pohnpei and Kosrae. Private consumption fell by 3.1%. Construction contracted by 16.6% with the completion of several compact-funded infrastructure projects, and capacity constraints hindered pickup through reconstruction.

3.37.1 Supply-side contributions to growth in Palau

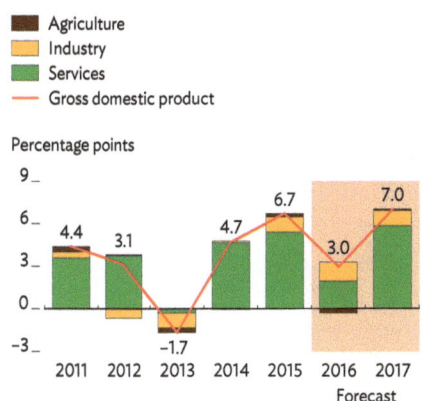

Note: Years are fiscal years ending on 30 September of the same calendar year.
Source: ADB estimates using data from the *Republic of Palau FY2014 Economic Review*.
Click here for figure data

3.37.2 Visitor arrivals in Palau by source

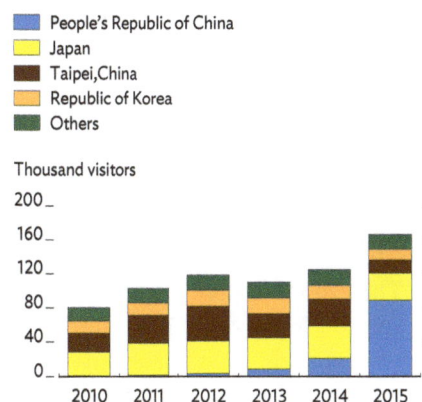

Note: Years are fiscal years ending on 30 September of the same calendar year.
Source: Palau Visitor's Authority and Office of Planning and Statistics, Ministry of Finance.
Click here for figure data

This chapter was written by Emma Veve and Cara Tinio of the Pacific Department, ADB, Manila; and Prince Cruz, consultant, Pacific Department, ADB, Manila.

The RMI economy contracted by 0.5% in FY2015 as election-related spending brought a slight improvement from a 1.0% decline in FY2014 (Figure 3.37.4). The most recent major infrastructure project, an airport road realignment, was completed in FY2013. Construction fell by 32.9% in FY2015 after an 11.9% decline in FY2014. The hotel and restaurant sector shrank by 4.3%, partly reflecting the government's purchase of a 36-room hotel to use as a campus for the University of the South Pacific. This reduced the number of rooms available in Majuro to around 150. Like the FSM, the RMI was affected by several typhoons, the strongest being Typhoon Nangka, which hit in July.

Lower international food and fuel prices pushed down inflation (Figure 3.37.5). In Palau, inflation fell to 2.2% in FY2015, the lowest since FY2010 (a year when GDP contracted). The second phase of a tobacco tax hike pushed up the prices of tobacco products by 14.6%. Cheaper fuel prices caused transportation and utility costs to fall by 5.0%, but food prices rose by 3.3% on strong demand. In the RMI, lower commodity prices pushed down utility and transportation costs, leaving inflation a minimal 0.5%. In the FSM, consumer prices declined by an estimated 1.1% in FY2015 as global food and fuel prices fell, despite supply shocks caused by typhoons. A decline in private consumption also drove deflation.

In FY2015, all three north Pacific economies continued to record fiscal surpluses (Figure 3.37.6). Additional revenues from fishing license fees provided much-needed revenue, especially for the FSM and the RMI (Figure 3.37.7). In the RMI, fishing license fees were estimated at 30.7% of total revenues excluding grants in FY2015, up from 11.4% the previous year. In the FSM, this share rose from 40.5% in FY2014 to 58.2%.

In October, Palau passed a law converting 80% of its territorial waters into a marine sanctuary, prohibiting commercial fishing, oil drilling, and seabed mining. To provide alternative livelihoods for affected households, the government will promote ecotourism. Fishing license fees, which accounted for 8.5% of total revenues excluding grants in FY2015, are expected to decline in the future.

The North Pacific economies lack manufacturing, so they depend on imports of goods. Their current account positions depend heavily on international commodity prices and the status of infrastructure projects. Cheaper global prices for fuel and other commodities, and higher fishing license revenues, pushed the current account balances of all these economies into surplus in FY2015 (Figure 3.37.8). In Palau, strong growth in tourism provided an additional push to achieve a small current account surplus. In the RMI and the FSM, the lack of construction helped reduce the import bill.

Economic prospects

The growth outlook in Palau remains positive because of tourism. In the RMI and the FSM, recovery will depend on their ability to resolve their access to capital investment funds under their compact agreements. Meanwhile, drought associated with El Niño could, if it intensifies, bring prolonged economic hardship.

3.37.3 Supply-side contributions to growth in the Federated States of Micronesia

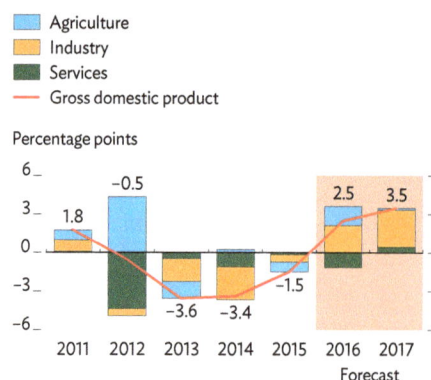

Note: Years are fiscal years ending on 30 September of the same calendar year.
Source: ADB estimates using data from the Federated States of Micronesia FY2014 Economic Review.
Click here for figure data

3.37.4 Supply-side contributions to growth in the Republic of Marshall Islands

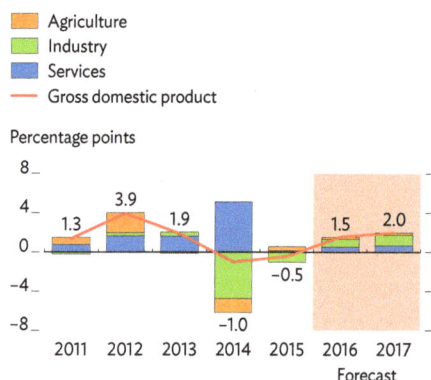

Note: Years are fiscal years ending on 30 September of the same calendar year.
Source: ADB estimates using data from the Republic of the Marshall Islands FY2014 Economic Review.
Click here for figure data

3.37.5 Inflation

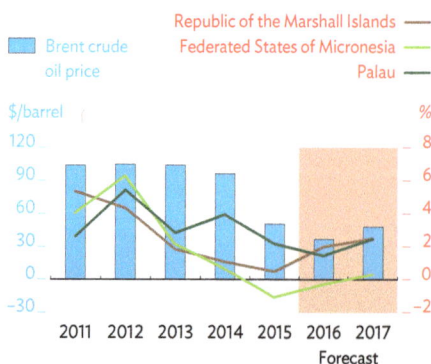

Note: Years are fiscal years ending on 30 September of the same calendar year.
Sources: Federated States of Micronesia FY2014 Economic Review; Republic of the Marshall Islands FY2014 Economic Review; Republic of Palau FY2014 Economic Review; ADB estimates.
Click here for figure data

3.37.1 Explaining changes in the Palau GDP forecasts

In *Asian Development Outlook 2015 (ADO 2015)*, published in March 2015, Palau's economy was projected to expand by 8.0% in FY2015 (ended 30 September 2015). In the October *ADO 2015 Update*, the projection was revised up to 10.0%. In this *ADO 2016*, GDP growth in FY2015 is now estimated at 6.7%. The main factor behind changes are recent trends in tourism.

Visitor arrivals reached a then record high of 125,427 in FY2014, up by 13.4% from the previous year. Rapid growth in arrivals from the PRC then pushed arrivals to 114,000 in the first half of FY2015. The Government of Palau was concerned by the steep increase in arrivals, especially in light of the low carrying capacity of public infrastructure and tourist attractions. Charter flights from Hong Kong, China and Macau, China—the main links from the PRC—were reduced from 48 to 32 per month. Final figures for FY2015 show arrivals at 166,136, up by 32.5% from the previous fiscal year.

When *ADO 2015* was being prepared, GDP growth for FY2014 was estimated at 6.9%. In mid-2015, official data for Palau was released, reflecting higher GDP growth at 8.0% in FY2014 with stronger contributions from wholesale and retail trade, financial intermediation, and information and communication technology. The latest data, released in October 2015, show growth in FY2014 revised down to 4.7%, partly because real estate, manufacturing, and financial intermediation contracted.

The latest revision also affected GDP growth figures for previous years, downgrading most of them, particularly from FY2011 to FY2014. This suggests unexpectedly weak transmission of growth in visitor arrivals into related economic activity. In view of this, the impact of the sharp increase in visitor arrivals in FY2015 is likely to be more muted, hence the lower estimate of GDP growth for the year.

Palau's economic expansion is expected to fall back to 3.0% in FY2016 as growth in tourist numbers slows (Box 3.37.1). This will be partly offset by growth in construction as hotel rooms are added to improve room availability. The double-digit growth rates for tourist arrivals in the past 2 fiscal years are unlikely to be sustained as hotels and tourist attractions operated nearly at capacity in FY2015. In the first quarter of FY2016, arrivals dropped by 11.7% from a year earlier, including a 13.6% drop in arrivals from the PRC, mainly because an aircraft flying from Hong Kong, China required maintenance. Visitor arrivals from other markets also fell significantly, notably Taipei,China down 22.0% and Japan down 6.4%. Lower arrivals are expected to persist through FY2016.

Palau is forecast to rebound in FY2017 with 7.0% GDP growth. The expected 9.2% increase in rooms is seen to enable business expansion in hotels and restaurants, retail trade, and transportation and communication. Infrastructure works such as the Koror-Airai sanitation project and a submarine broadband cable are expected to further spur growth.

The RMI economy is forecast to recover and grow by 1.5% in FY2016 and 2.0% in FY2017, supported by fisheries and projects financed by development partners, including a water supply and sanitation project in Ebeye. The recent election of a new government reflected public demands

3.37.6 Fiscal balance

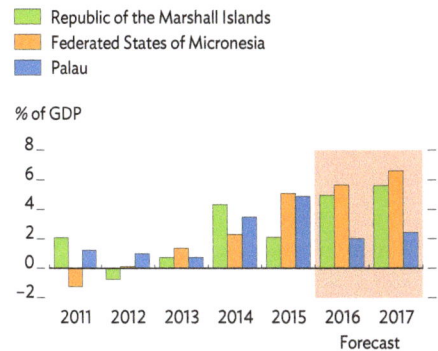

- Republic of the Marshall Islands
- Federated States of Micronesia
- Palau

Note: Years are fiscal years ending on 30 September of the same calendar year.

Sources: Federated States of Micronesia FY2014 Economic Review; Republic of the Marshall Islands FY2014 Economic Review; Republic of Palau FY2014 Economic Review; ADB estimates.

Click here for figure data

3.37.7 Revenues from fishing license fees

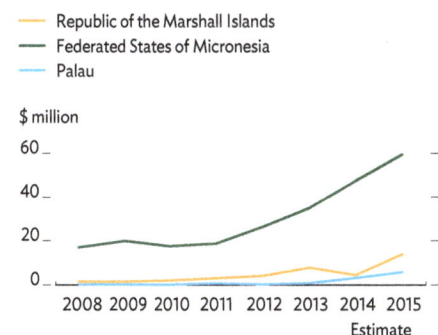

- Republic of the Marshall Islands
- Federated States of Micronesia
- Palau

Note: Years are fiscal years, ending on 30 September of the same calendar year.

Sources: Federated States of Micronesia FY2014 Economic Review; Republic of the Marshall Islands FY2014 Economic Review; Republic of Palau FY2014 Economic Review; ADB estimates.

Click here for figure data

for economic revitalization and job creation, but meeting high expectations will be a challenge. Support from development partners for reform to state-owned enterprises, in line with supportive legislation passed in 2015, could pave the way for private sector growth.

Growth in the FSM is forecast to reach 2.5% in FY2016 and 3.5% in FY2017 on expenditures from infrastructure grants connected to the compact agreement and on higher revenue from fishing licenses.

Low inflation is expected to persist in the North Pacific in FY2016 but then accelerate slightly in FY2017 in line with international fuel and food prices. The RMI is projected to run 2.0% inflation in FY2016, rising to 2.5% in FY2017, reflecting its weak economic performance. Reconstruction in the FSM is expected to temper deflation to 0.3% in FY2016 and contribute to inflation of 0.3% in 2017. Inflation in Palau is seen to ease further to 1.5% in FY2016, as the impact from the second phase of a tobacco tax hike in January 2015 fades, then climb to 2.5% in FY2017.

Current account surpluses are expected to continue except in Palau, where deficits equal to 2.3% of GDP in FY2016 and 1.3% in FY2017 are forecast as increased imports of construction materials for tourism ventures and lower tourism revenues more than offset lower fuel prices. The current account surplus in the RMI is projected to reach the equivalent of 11.1% of GDP in FY2016 and 8.9% in FY2017 as fishing license revenues rise. In the FSM, the current account surplus is seen to expand to 19.5% of GDP in FY2016 and 30.1% in FY2017.

Policy challenge—ensuring fiscal sustainability

Because their compact agreements with the US and the accompanying grants are scheduled to end in FY2023, the three North Pacific economies face a common challenge over the medium to long term of matching expenditure to expected revenues (including trust fund earnings) without the hefty grants that have supplemented revenues over the years (Figure 3.37.9). This must be achieved through fiscal consolidation and strengthened economic growth. The difficulty of achieving fiscal sustainability varies, however, among the economies.

Palau is arguably the best placed—through strong growth in tourism—to achieve sustainability. It is seeking to better manage its fast-growing tourism industry by controlling and coordinating multiple policy levers—foreign investment, public investment, taxation, small business development, environmental management—to translate high visitor demand into a flow of higher-value tourists and more local capture of their expenditure. This is an enormous challenge. Necessary tax reform has been delayed in the Senate and seems unlikely to progress in this election year. Effective policy implementation and enforcement will require political commitment, effort from the whole government, and an improved public understanding of the issues and the difficult choices they pose.

The FSM and the RMI require considerable effort to lift their growth rates while simultaneously managing expenditures closely. Key to boosting growth is the strategic use of capital investment funds supplied both through compact agreements and from development partners.

3.37.1 Selected economic indicators (%)

Marshall Islands	2016	2017
GDP growth	1.5	2.0
Inflation	2.0	2.5
Current account balance (share of GDP)	11.1	8.9
Federated States of Micronesia		
GDP growth	2.5	3.5
Inflation	−0.3	0.3
Current account balance (share of GDP)	19.5	30.1
Palau		
GDP growth	3.0	7.0
Inflation	1.5	2.5
Current account balance (share of GDP)	−2.3	−1.3

Note: Years are fiscal years ending on 30 June of that year.
Source: ADB estimates.

3.37.8 Current account balance

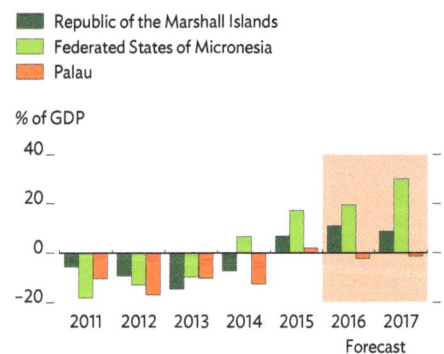

- Republic of the Marshall Islands
- Federated States of Micronesia
- Palau

Note: Years are fiscal years ending on 30 September of the same calendar year.
Sources: Federated States of Micronesia FY2014 Economic Review; Republic of the Marshall Islands FY2014 Economic Review; Republic of Palau FY2014 Economic Review; ADB estimates.
Click here for figure data

The FSM developed a strategic capital investment plan in 2015 that prioritizes public investment projects through a process coordinated by the national and state governments. The plan includes steps to improve implementation capacity and build upon public investment that has recently averaged $20 million annually. Any delay in investing the backlog in compact grants, which currently total over $140 million, would hamper local public expenditure and job generation, and ultimately require greater fiscal adjustment.

The RMI has maintained a steady flow of public investment projects and increasingly works to make operations more efficient and the business environment more attractive. The composition of the newly elected Parliament reflects increased public concern about economic performance. The passing of the State-Owned Enterprise Act in late 2015 provides a foundation for reinvigorating these economically essential entities. Certainly, change is needed because the Marshalls Energy Company, Air Marshall Islands, and the Marshall Islands Shipping Corporation all struggle financially. Further, internet penetration is only about 25% despite a broadband submarine cable, the use of which is being restricted by an unregulated monopoly public service provider.

3.37.9 Total revenues and grants

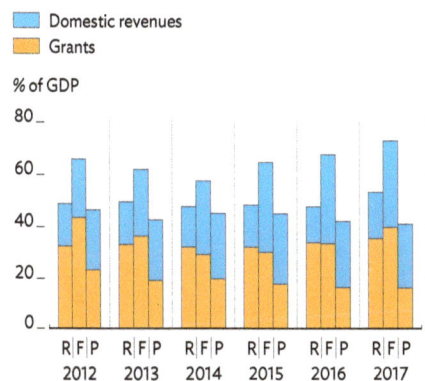

R = Republic of Marshall Islands, F = Federated States of Micronesia, P = Palau.

Note: Years are fiscal years ending on 30 September of the same calendar year.

Sources: Federated States of Micronesia FY2014 Economic Review; Republic of the Marshall Islands FY2014 Economic Review; Republic of Palau FY2014 Economic Review; ADB estimates.

Click here for figure data

South Pacific economies

Samoa and Tonga achieved higher growth as low oil prices helped boost activity in the transport and energy sectors, and as the implementation of public infrastructure projects improved. Growth in the Cook Islands slowed for lack of infrastructure projects and sufficient accommodation for tourists. Outward migration for employment supports consumption and helps alleviate poverty, but it also hampers economic growth. Opportunities in agriculture, related light industry, and tourism offer promise as potential growth engines.

Economic performance

In contrast with Samoa and Tonga, and despite growth in its own transport and energy sectors, the Cook Islands economy contracted by 0.5% in FY2015 (ended 30 June 2015) as activity in construction, finance, and business services slowed (Figure 3.38.1). A shortage of accommodation in the peak tourist season constrained visitor arrivals, and numbers from Australia and Canada, which jointly contribute one-fifth of all arrivals, were disappointing. Growth accelerated to 1.4% in Samoa and to 3.4% in Tonga as lower oil prices reduced input costs in the transport and electricity sectors. In Tonga, preparations for coronation celebrations in July 2015 and improved execution of public infrastructure projects contributed to higher growth. Samoa's relatively low growth rate reflects lower agricultural output, which declined by more than 11%, and sluggish construction.

Inflation in the Cook Islands accelerated to 3.0% in FY2015 as a result of higher alcohol and tobacco taxes and a weaker New Zealand dollar, its official currency (Figure 3.38.2). In Samoa, inflation averaged 1.9% as higher domestic food prices caused by lower agricultural output more than offset price declines for transport and imported food. This marked a sharp reversal of deflation in FY2014. Tonga experienced deflation at 0.7% as transport and utility prices fell because of lower fuel prices.

In the Cook Islands, the overall FY2015 fiscal deficit reached 1.7% of GDP, up from only 0.1% the previous year on increased infrastructure spending (Figure 3.38.3). In Tonga, a surplus equal to 1.7% of GDP in FY2014 turned into a small deficit of 0.2% in FY2015 with higher capital spending, including for cyclone reconstruction. In Samoa, a 19.3% decline in external grants prompted the government to cut expenditures, narrowing the deficit to the equivalent of 3.9% of GDP.

Debt sustainability is a concern across these economies. Public debt rose in all three economies in FY2015 and, by the end of the fiscal year, equaled 23.0% of GDP in the Cook Islands, 55.3% in Samoa, and 51.3% in Tonga (Figure 3.38.4). The increase in Tonga's ratio of debt to

3.38.1 GDP growth in the South Pacific

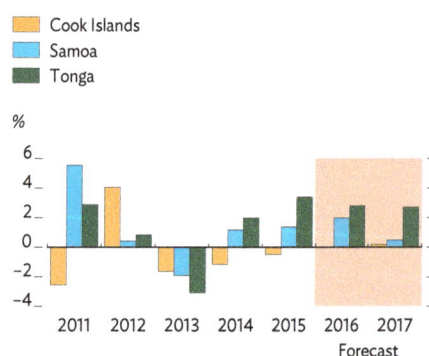

Note: Years are fiscal years ending on 30 June of that year.
Sources: Cook Islands Statistics Office; Samoa Bureau of Statistics; Tonga Department of Statistics; ADB estimates.
Click here for figure data

3.38.2 Inflation

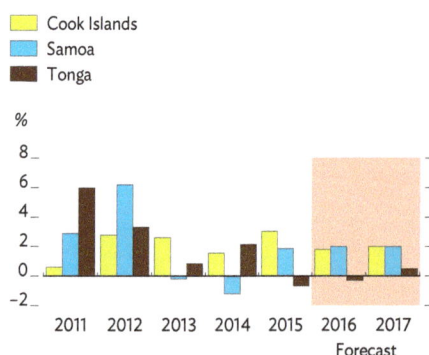

Note: Years are fiscal years ending on 30 June of that year.
Sources: Cook Islands Statistics Office; Samoa Bureau of Statistics; Tonga Department of Statistics; ADB estimates.
Click here for figure data

This chapter was written by Shiu Raj Singh of the South Pacific Subregional Office, ADB, Suva, and Cara Tinio, Laisiasa Tora, and Johannes Wolff of the Pacific Department, ADB, Manila.

GDP resulted from depreciation of the pa'anga against the renminbi and US dollar (the currencies in which most of Tonga's external debt is denominated) and increased borrowing, both domestically and from external concessional lenders.

Low growth and inflation in Samoa allowed the central bank to maintain an accommodative monetary policy in FY2015. Private sector credit grew by 17.6% year on year to June 2015 as credit to businesses and households increased. The National Reserve Bank of Tonga also maintained an accommodative monetary policy. Lending rates of around 8.5% (down from 12%–14% in the aftermath of the global financial crisis) and a government-managed fund scheme underpinned an 8.6% growth in credit to the private sector in FY2015 from 0.7% in the previous year. In the Cook Islands, credit from commercial banks grew by 1.1% in FY2015 despite relative stability in interest rates. This reflected a change in the banks' past preference for consolidating balance sheets, which succeeded in significantly reducing the prevalence of nonperforming loans in their portfolios.

Samoa's current account deficit was equivalent to 4.8% of GDP in FY2015, 2.2 percentage points narrower than the year before (Figure 3.38.5). This was the result of lower imports of services and higher remittances. The deficit was offset in part by external capital grants and drawdowns on loans. Foreign exchange reserves remained at a reasonable level, providing cover for 5.2 months of goods imports, despite declining from $155.2 million in FY2014 to $132.8 million. Tonga's current account deficit widened to the equivalent of 8.3% of GDP in FY2015 from 5.0% in FY2014, mainly due to increased merchandise imports related to coronation celebrations and lower earnings from exports of services. However, foreign exchange reserves ended FY2015 stable at $150.8 million, sufficient to cover 11.3 months of imports.

Economic prospects

Economic activity in the Cook Islands is expected to be flat in FY2016 and to grow modestly by 0.2% in FY2017, supported by public investment and a slight improvement in tourism. This forecast takes into account a downbeat outlook for economic growth in both New Zealand and Australia, which are important export destinations and source markets for tourists. Limited local capacity to implement capital projects and a shortage of tourist accommodation in the peak holiday seasons constrain growth in the near term. The loss of skilled workers to outward migration also hinders growth.

With fishing and tourism activity expected to increase, Samoa's economy is forecast to grow by 2.0% in FY2016 before slowing to 0.5% in FY2017 as nonfood manufacturing declines with the expected closure of a car parts factory. By contrast, the outlook for Tonga is positive, at least in the medium term. Preparations for the South Pacific Games and investments in tourism and government offices are expected to uphold growth at 2.8% in FY2016 and 2.7% in FY2017.

Inflation in the Cook Islands is forecast at 1.8% in FY2016 and 2.0% in FY2017 as import prices rise. In Samoa, prices are expected to increase by 2.0% in FY2016 in response to an expected decline in

3.38.3 Fiscal balance

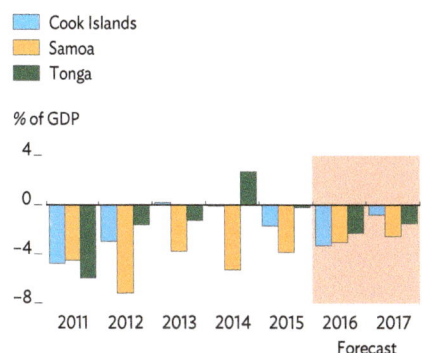

Note: Years are fiscal years ending on 30 June of that year.
Sources: Cook Islands Ministry of Finance and Economic Management; Samoa Ministry of Finance; Tonga Ministry of Finance.
Click here for figure data

3.38.4 Public debt

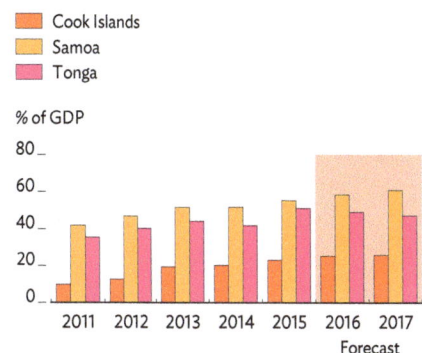

Note: Years are fiscal years ending on 30 June of that year.
Sources: Cook Islands Ministry of Finance and Economic Management; Samoa Ministry of Finance; Tonga Ministry of Finance.
Click here for figure data

domestic agricultural output and interruptions to local food supplies, and by the same rate in FY2017 as global fuel and food prices start to recover. In Tonga, deflation is seen to ease to 0.3% in FY2016 before returning to inflation, at 0.5%, in FY2017 in line with forecast global price rises for food and fuel. Demand generated by the South Pacific Games could exert additional upward pressure on prices.

The Cook Islands current account balance is forecast to improve on continued growth in tourism earnings. Surpluses are expected to equal 37.3% of GDP in FY2016 and 41.3% in FY2017 (Figure 3.38.5). Samoa's current account deficit is forecast to ease to 4.3% of GDP in FY2016 with lower payments for imports, then widen to 5.1% in FY2017 on higher import prices. In Tonga, the current account deficit is expected to narrow significantly (to the equivalent of 1.9% of GDP) in FY2016 as import costs decline. The deficit is seen to widen to 3.2% in FY2017. These deficits are expected to be largely offset by foreign grants and concessional loans.

Policy challenge—raising growth and creating jobs

A common policy challenge facing these three South Pacific economies is to achieve higher economic growth to generate new jobs. Their working-age populations have the option of emigrating to labor markets in New Zealand and Australia with relative ease. This migration brings in remittances—inflows that are particularly significant for Samoa and Tonga—but the associated labor drain stymies growth and creates a cycle of low growth that encourages further emigration, which further depresses economic activity.

The Cook Islands economy suffers from low tourism growth due to shortages of accommodation during the peak season. The lack of large new investments in hotels constrains tourism and broader economic growth. Without adding accommodation, tourism earnings can be raised only by increasing local inputs and attracting more high-end tourists, but these measures are unlikely to spur employment growth. Easing approval procedures for land leases and new tourism developments could expedite investment and facilitate growth in the private sector, thus creating jobs in the tourism industry.

Samoa has struggled with low growth following a series of disasters. Nonfood manufacturing has been contracting for some years, causing employment in the sector to dwindle. Growth in tourism has been slow as well. The availability of new sources of finance for agribusiness holds promise to create employment, both formal and informal, but may not be sufficient to catalyze sustained acceleration in economic growth.

A higher growth path for Tonga over the medium term requires sustained commitment to reform to improve the business environment. In the absence of reform, growth is expected to revert to a low trajectory—at or below the historical average growth rate of 1.7%—in the long run, once activity related to post-cyclone reconstruction and the hosting of the South Pacific Games is completed. As in Samoa, growth in agriculture and related light industry development, as well as efforts to attract more tourist spending, appear to be the most promising avenues for increasing employment in Tonga.

3.38.1 Selected economic indicators (%)

Cook Islands	2015	2016
GDP growth	0.0	0.2
Inflation	1.8	2.0
Current account balance (share of GDP)	37.3	41.3
Samoa		
GDP growth	2.0	0.5
Inflation	2.0	2.0
Current account balance (share of GDP)	−4.3	−5.1
Tonga		
GDP growth	2.8	2.7
Inflation	−0.3	0.5
Current account balance (share of GDP)	−1.9	−3.2

Note: Years are fiscal years ending on 30 June of that year.
Source: ADB estimates.

3.38.5 Current account balance

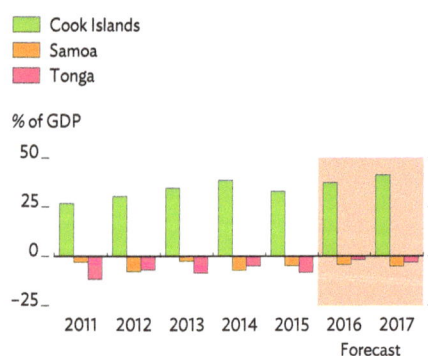

Note: Years are fiscal years ending on 30 June of that year.
Sources: Cook Islands Ministry of Finance and Economic Management; Samoa Ministry of Finance; Tonga Ministry of Finance.
Click here for figure data

Small island economies

Achieving fiscal sustainability despite dependence on volatile and uncertain revenue sources is a common challenge for the small island economies of Kiribati, Nauru, and Tuvalu. Record high fishing license revenues and investments from development partners have underpinned rising public expenditure and growth. However, in Nauru, damage to port facilities has disrupted phosphate exports and caused steep GDP contraction.

Economic performance

Kiribati's economy grew by 3.0% in 2015, driven by spending on infrastructure projects to upgrade a road and improve sanitation using development partner funds. Higher fishing license revenues that enabled increased government spending also contributed to growth (Figure 3.39.1). Nauru's economy is estimated to have contracted by 10.0% in FY2015 (ended 30 June 2015) after damage to the port's mooring system disrupted phosphate exports (which declined by two-thirds) and imports of fuel and other supplies. These losses were partly offset by increased government and consumer spending. Tuvalu grew by 2.0% in 2015 with stimulus from higher public spending on infrastructure projects and high fishing license revenues.

Inflation was lower in Kiribati as prices rose by only 1.4% in 2015 despite depreciation of the Australian dollar, the official currency (Figure 3.39.2). Inflation was slightly higher in Tuvalu at 2.0% in 2015. In both Kiribati and Tuvalu, lower food and fuel prices helped keep prices in check. In Nauru, inflation surged to 11.4% in FY2015 because of disrupted supply of consumer goods through the damaged port and the elimination of retail fuel subsidies.

The strongest El Niño in nearly 20 years has brought record tuna migrations to the region. As signatories to the Nauru Agreement, all three economies have benefited in recent years from higher licensing fees under the vessel day scheme. In 2015, fishing license revenues as a share of GDP were 99% for Kiribati, 21% for Nauru, and 64% for Tuvalu.

Government revenue declined by 14.3% in Kiribati, while expenditure increased by 3.5%. These trends replaced the large fiscal surplus in 2014 with a small deficit equivalent to 1.1% of GDP in 2015 (Figure 3.39.3). Nauru fell into fiscal deficit in 2015 as several revenue lines underperformed. In Tuvalu, revenues grew slower than expenditure to leave a much narrower fiscal surplus than in 2014.

Kiribati maintained its current account surplus with strong license fee and remittance inflows (Figure 3.39.4). Tuvalu, by contrast, saw declining inflows create a large current account deficit. No recent balance of payments data for Nauru are available.

This chapter was written by Roland Rajah of the Pacific Liaison and Coordination Office, ADB, Sydney, and Shiu Raj Singh of the South Pacific Subregional Office, ADB, Suva.

3.39.1 GDP growth

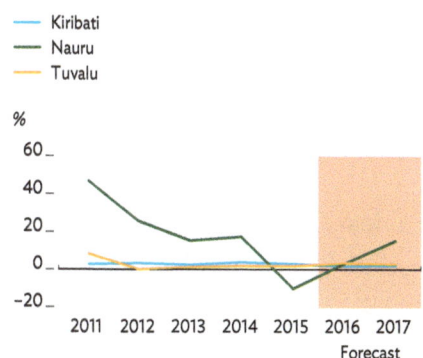

Note: Years are fiscal years ending on 30 June of that year for Nauru and coinciding with the calendar year for Kiribati and Tuvalu.

Sources: Kiribati National Statistics Office; Nauru budget documents; Tuvalu Central Statistics Division; ADB estimates.

Click here for figure data

3.39.2 Inflation

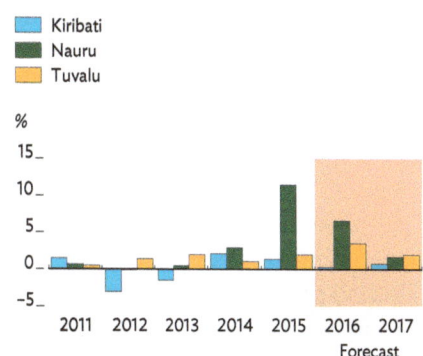

Note: Years are fiscal years ending on 30 June of that year for Nauru and coinciding with the calendar year for Kiribati and Tuvalu.

Sources: Kiribati National Statistics Office; Nauru budget documents; Tuvalu Central Statistics Division; ADB estimates.

Click here for figure data

Economic prospects

In Kiribati, the ongoing implementation of major projects, funded by development partners, in transport and in water supply and sanitation are expected to support growth at 1.8% in 2016, rising to 2.0% in 2017.

Growth in Nauru is expected to recover to 3.0% in FY2016 and then rise to 15.0% in FY2017 as phosphate exports recover following the full restoration of the moorings. Nauru will benefit as well from the gradual integration into the economy of about 850 refugees who recently cleared the Australian-run Regional Processing Centre. Most of these refugees are of working age and can significantly augment the existing labor force of 6,400. Many possess skills that could help address skills shortages, and some have already taken up local positions while others have opened new businesses.

Expansionary fiscal policy in Tuvalu in 2016 is expected to help boost growth to 3.5% as the government increases spending to develop new accommodation ahead of the Pacific Island Leaders Meeting in 2016. The government plans higher spending to build health centers and classrooms on outer islands and so make public expenditures more inclusive. Growth is expected to moderate to 3.0% in 2017 as the temporary boost to the economy from the leaders' meeting fades.

In Kiribati, inflation is expected to be low at 0.3% in 2016 as international prices remain depressed, then to rise to 0.8% as prices recover, particularly for oil. Inflation in Nauru is forecast to slow but remain elevated at 6.6% in FY2016 as problems with the moorings are likely to persist and continue to disrupt imports. However, inflation is seen to ease considerably in FY2017 to 1.7% after repairs to the mooring system are completed. In Tuvalu, inflation will likely accelerate to 3.5% in 2016, driven largely by demand created through fiscal expansion, then moderate to 2.0% in FY2017 in line with lower public spending.

The current account in Kiribati is projected to narrow in 2016 but maintain a surplus equal to 15% of GDP supported by fishing license revenues and remittances from workers overseas. A deficit equivalent to 10% of GDP is forecast for 2017 as fishing license fees are expected to moderate, and workers' foreign incomes and remittances to decline. In Tuvalu, the current account is projected to record a deficit equal to 21.4% of GDP in 2016 as public investments rise, before narrowing to 18.7% in 2017 with fiscal consolidation.

Policy challenge—achieving fiscal sustainability

The main macroeconomic challenge facing the small Pacific island economies is to achieve fiscal stability when existing revenue sources are volatile and highly uncertain. In early 2016, in response to falling prices for skipjack tuna, the three countries renegotiated the South Pacific Tuna Treaty with the US and agreed on lower access fees for 2016. Negotiations with the US are expected to continue. Further falls in skipjack tuna prices in 2017 pose a downside risk to fiscal and GDP growth projections for all three economies.

Fishing license revenues have contributed to annual budget surpluses in Kiribati in recent years. Since 2012, the government and development partners have worked to implement the Kiribati

3.39.3 Fiscal balance

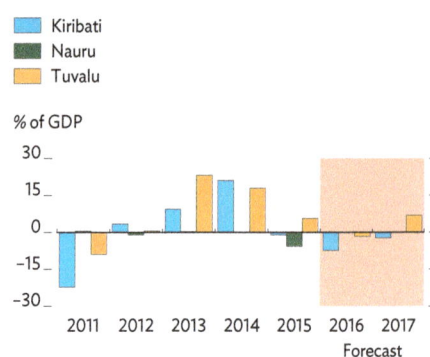

Note: Years are fiscal years ending on 30 June of that year for Nauru and coinciding with the calendar year for Kiribati and Tuvalu.
Sources: Kiribati National Statistics Office; Nauru budget documents; Tuvalu Central Statistics Division; ADB estimates.
Click here for figure data

3.39.4 Current account balance

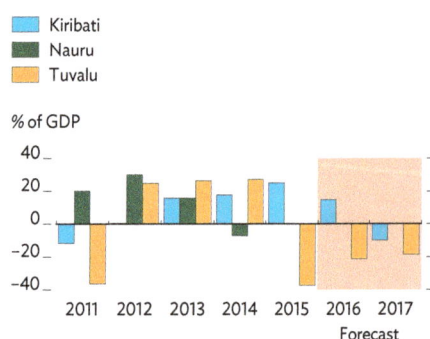

Note: Years are fiscal years ending on 30 June of that year for Nauru and coinciding with the calendar year for Kiribati and Tuvalu.
Sources: Kiribati National Statistics Office; Nauru budget documents; Tuvalu Central Statistics Division; ADB estimates.
Click here for figure data

Economic Reform Program, which aims to restore fiscal sustainability by improving revenue performance and containing public expenditure while safeguarding vital public services and infrastructure investments. The program reduces the amounts the government is allowed to draw down from its Revenue Equalization Reserve Fund, a sovereign wealth fund that was nearly depleted by high fiscal deficits in the wake of the global economic crisis. Development partners have encouraged the government to reinvest windfall fishing license revenues in the fund to build its real value per capita.

Nauru currently benefits from higher income associated with Australia's Regional Processing Centre and a related refugee resettlement program, fishing license fees, and, until recently, phosphate exports. In late 2015, the government established its new Nauru Intergenerational Trust Fund to deposit a share of windfall revenues in a long-term investment vehicle intended eventually to provide a stable source of budget financing. The current budget allocates A$20.4 million, or about 18% of total domestic revenue, for transfer to the fund once it becomes fully operational. Regular annual contributions are to follow a formula applied to Nauru's domestic revenues. The Government of Australia will also contribute to the fund annually and participate in its governing committee. Other partners have also been invited to join. The trust fund is a crucial step forward at a time when Nauru's budget relies increasingly on uncertain and unsustainable revenue sources. However, broader reforms remain critical. In particular, the government needs to establish a comprehensive fiscal framework to ensure that it can continue to contribute to the fund while maintaining adequate fiscal buffers, keeping consumption expenditure sustainable, and using a higher share of spending to develop human capital and infrastructure.

The substantial increase in fishing license revenues has been the driving force behind fiscal expansion in Tuvalu, where expenditures are up by 28% in the 2016 budget. With assistance from development partners, the government has restored the value of the Consolidated Investment Fund of the Tuvalu Trust Fund, from which the government sources supplementary financing to cover budget deficits. The value of the trust fund rose from A$6.2 million at the end of 2008 to A$25.6 million at the end of 2015. This places the government in a strong position to consolidate its finances without severely disrupting public service delivery. Fiscal consolidation is crucial to put future spending on a sustainable footing. Introducing a medium-term fiscal framework that targets a structural surplus would strengthen Tuvalu's capacity to manage revenue volatility, and placing more savings in the Tuvalu Trust Fund would help ensure resilience in the face of adverse shocks.

3.39.1 Selected economic indicators (%)

Kiribati	2015	2016
GDP growth	1.8	2.0
Inflation	0.3	0.8
Current account balance (share of GDP)	15.0	–10.0
Nauru		
GDP growth	3.0	15.0
Inflation	6.6	1.7
Current account balance (share of GDP)	...	...
Tuvalu		
GDP growth	3.5	3.0
Inflation	3.5	2.0
Current account balance (share of GDP)	–21.4	–18.7

... = data not available.

Note: Years are fiscal years ending on 30 June of that year for Nauru and coinciding with the calendar year for Kiribati and Tuvalu.

Source: ADB estimates.

STATISTICAL
APPENDIX

Statistical notes and tables

The statistical appendix presents selected economic indicators for the 45 developing member economies of the Asian Development Bank (ADB) in 18 tables. The economies are grouped into five subregions: Central Asia, East Asia, South Asia, Southeast Asia, and the Pacific. Most of the tables contain historical data from 2011 to 2015; some have forecasts for 2016 and 2017.

The data were standardized to the degree possible to allow comparability over time and across economies, but differences in statistical methodology, definitions, coverage, and practices make full comparability impossible. The national income accounts section is based on the United Nations System of National Accounts, while the data on balance of payments are based on International Monetary Fund (IMF) accounting standards. Historical data were obtained from official sources, statistical publications and databases, and documents of ADB, the IMF, and the World Bank. For some economies, data for 2015 are estimated from the latest available information. Projections for 2016 and 2017 are generally ADB estimates made on the bases of available quarterly or monthly data, though some projections are from governments.

Most economies report by calendar year. The following record their government finance data by fiscal year: Armenia; Azerbaijan; Brunei Darussalam; the Cook Islands; Hong Kong, China; Kazakhstan; the Kyrgyz Republic; the Lao People's Democratic Republic (Lao PDR); Samoa; Singapore; Taipei,China; Tajikistan; Thailand; and Uzbekistan. The Federated States of Micronesia, Nauru, the Republic of Marshall Islands, and Palau report government finance and balance-of-payments data by fiscal year. South Asian countries (except for the Maldives and Sri Lanka), Myanmar, Samoa, and Tonga report all variables by fiscal year.

Regional and subregional averages or totals are provided for seven tables (A1, A2, A6, A11, A12, A13, and A14). For tables A1, A2, A6, and A14, the averages are computed using weights derived from gross national income (GNI) in current US dollars following the World Bank Atlas method. The GNI data for 2011–2014 were obtained from the World Bank's World Development Indicators online. Weights for 2014 were carried over through 2017. The GNI data for the Cook Islands were estimated using the Atlas conversion factor. Myanmar and Nauru have no GNI data. For tables A11 and A12, the regional and subregional averages were computed on the basis of a consistent sum, which means that if there are missing country data for a given year, the sum of the prior year used for computing the growth rate excludes the corresponding country data. Data for Myanmar and Nauru are excluded from the computation of all subregional averages and totals.

Tables A1, A2, A3, A4, and A5. These tables show related data on output growth, production, and demand. Changes to the national income accounts series for some countries have been made to accommodate a change in source, methodology, and/or base year. The series for Afghanistan, Bhutan, India, Myanmar, and Pakistan reflect fiscal year data, rather than calendar year data, while those for Timor-Leste reflect the GDP excluding oil and United Nations inputs.

Table A1: Growth rate of GDP (% per year). The table shows annual growth rates of GDP valued at constant market prices, factor costs, or basic prices. GDP at market prices is the aggregation of the value added of all resident producers at producers' prices including taxes less subsidies on imports plus all nondeductible value-added or similar taxes. Constant factor cost measures differ from market price measures in that they exclude taxes on production and include subsidies. Basic price valuation is the factor cost plus some taxes on production, such as property and payroll taxes, and less some subsidies, such as labor-related subsidies but not product-related subsidies. Most economies use constant market price valuation. Fiji, Pakistan, and Sri Lanka use constant factor costs, while the Maldives and Nepal use basic prices. The series for Taipei,China has been changed to accommodate its adoption of the chain-linking method.

Table A2: Growth rate of per capita GDP (% per year). The table provides the growth rates of real per capita GDP, which is defined as GDP at constant prices divided by the population. The series for most of the Pacific countries were revised to accommodate a change of source for population data. Data on per capita gross national income in US dollar terms (Atlas method) for 2014 are also shown, sourced from the World Bank's World Development Indicators online.

Table A3: Growth rate of value added in agriculture (% per year). The table shows the growth rates of value added in agriculture at constant prices and its corresponding share in 2014 at current prices. The agriculture sector comprises agricultural crops, livestock, poultry, fisheries, and forestry.

Table A4: Growth rate of value added in industry (% per year). The table provides the growth rates of value added in industry at constant prices and its corresponding share in 2014 at current prices. This sector comprises manufacturing, mining and quarrying, construction, and utilities.

Table A5: Growth rate of value added in services (% per year). The table gives the growth rates of value added in services at constant prices and its corresponding share in 2014 at current prices. Subsectors generally include trade, banking, finance, real estate, public administration, and other services.

Table A6: Inflation (% per year). Data on inflation rates represent period averages. The inflation rates presented are based on consumer price indexes. The consumer price indexes of the following economies are for a given city or group of consumers only: Afghanistan is for Kabul (until 2011), Cambodia is for Phnom Penh, the Marshall Islands is for Majuro, Solomon Islands is for Honiara, and Nepal is for urban consumers.

Table A7: Growth in money supply (% per year). This table tracks the annual percentage change in the end-of-period supply of broad money as represented by M2 for most countries. M2 is defined as the sum of M1 and quasi-money, where M1 denotes currency in circulation plus demand deposits, and quasi-money consists of time and savings deposits including foreign currency deposits.

Tables A8, A9, and A10: Government finance. These tables give the revenue and expenditure transactions and the fiscal balance of the central government expressed as a percentage of GDP in nominal terms. For Cambodia (since 2006), the People's Republic of China, India, Kazakhstan, the Kyrgyz Republic, Mongolia, and Tajikistan, transactions are those reported by the general government.

Table A8: Central government revenues (% of GDP). Central government revenues comprise all nonrepayable receipts, both current and capital, plus grants. These amounts are computed as a percentage of GDP at current prices. For the Republic of Korea, revenues exclude social security contributions. For Singapore, revenues include the net investment returns contribution. For Kazakhstan, revenues include transfers from the national fund. Grants are excluded in Cambodia, the Lao PDR, Malaysia, Singapore, and Thailand; revenues from disinvestment are included for India; and only current revenues are included for Bangladesh.

Table A9: Central government expenditures (% of GDP). Central government expenditures comprise all nonrepayable payments to both current and capital expenses, plus net lending. These amounts are computed as a share of GDP at current prices. For Thailand, expenditures refer to budgetary expenditures excluding externally financed expenditures and corresponding borrowing. Those for Tajikistan include externally financed public investment programs. One-time expenditures are excluded for Pakistan.

Table A10: Fiscal balance of central government (% of GDP). Fiscal balance is the difference between central government revenues and expenditures. The difference is also computed as a share of GDP at current prices. Data variations may arise from statistical discrepancies, e.g., balancing items for both central and local governments, and from differences in the concept used in the individual computations of revenues and expenditures as compared with the calculation of the fiscal balance. For Fiji, the fiscal balance excludes total loan repayments. For Thailand, the fiscal balance is a cash balance composed of the budgetary and nonbudgetary balances. Some off-budget accounts are included in the computation of the fiscal balance for Turkmenistan.

Tables A11, A12, A13, and A14: Balance of payments. These tables show selected international economic transactions of countries as recorded in the balance of payments. These items cover annual flows.

Tables A11 and A12: Growth rates of merchandise exports and imports (% per year). These tables show the annual growth rates of exports and imports of goods. Data are in million US dollars, primarily obtained from the balance-of-payments accounts of each economy. Exports are reported free on board. Import data are reported free on board, except for the following economies, which value them on the basis of cost, insurance, and freight: Afghanistan; Bhutan; Cambodia; Hong Kong, China; India; the Lao PDR; Myanmar; the Philippines; Samoa; Singapore; Solomon Islands; and Thailand.

Table A13: Trade balance ($ million). The trade balance is the difference between merchandise exports and merchandise imports. Figures in this table are based on the exports and imports amounts used to generate tables A11 and A12.

Table A14: Current account balance (% of GDP). The current account balance is the sum of the balance of trade for merchandise, net trade in services and factor income, and net transfers. The values reported are divided by GDP at current prices in US dollars. In the case of Cambodia, the Lao PDR, and Viet Nam, official transfers are excluded from the current account balance.

Table A15: Exchange rates to the US dollar (annual average). Annual average exchange rates are quoted as the local currencies per US dollar.

Table A16: Gross international reserves ($ million). Gross international reserves are defined as the US dollar value of holdings of foreign exchange, special drawing rights, reserve position in the IMF, and gold at the end of a given period. For the Marshall Islands and Taipei,China, this heading refers to foreign exchange reserves only. In some economies, the rubric is foreign assets and reserves of national monetary authorities and national oil funds, i.e., foreign assets of the Maldives Monetary Authority, net foreign reserves of the State Bank of Pakistan, assets of the National Oil Fund of Azerbaijan, and official external assets of Kiribati. The data for India are as of 6 February 2015.

Table A17: External debt outstanding ($ million). For most economies, external debt outstanding, public and private, includes medium- and long-term debt, short-term debt, and IMF credit. For Cambodia, and the Lao PDR, only public external debt is reported. For Azerbaijan, India, Kazakhstan, the Kyrgyz Republic, Malaysia, the Philippines, Singapore, Sri Lanka and Thailand, the figures for 2015 are as of the end of September.

Table A18: Debt service ratio (% of exports of goods and services). This table generally presents the total debt service payments of each economy, which comprise principal repayments (excluding on short-term debt) and interest payments on outstanding external debt, as a percentage of exports of goods and services. For Cambodia and the Lao PDR, debt service refers to external public debt only. For Papua New Guinea, Samoa, and Viet Nam, exports of goods are used as the denominator in the calculation of the ratio; for the Philippines, exports of goods, services, and income are used as the denominator. For Bangladesh, the ratio represents debt service payments on medium- and long-term loans as a percentage of exports of goods, nonfactor services, and workers' remittances; and for Azerbaijan, the ratio represents public and publicly guaranteed external debt service payments as a percentage of exports of goods and nonfactor services.

Table A1 Growth rate of GDP (% per year)

	2011	2012	2013	2014	2015	2016	2017
Central Asia	6.8	5.6	6.6	5.3	2.9	2.1	2.8
Armenia	4.7	7.2	3.3	3.5	3.0	2.0	2.3
Azerbaijan	0.1	2.2	5.8	2.8	1.1	–1.0	1.0
Georgia	7.2	6.4	3.3	4.6	2.8	2.5	3.5
Kazakhstan	7.5	5.0	6.0	4.3	1.0	0.7	1.0
Kyrgyz Republic	6.0	–0.1	10.9	4.0	3.5	1.0	2.0
Tajikistan	7.4	7.5	7.4	6.7	6.0	3.8	4.0
Turkmenistan	14.7	11.1	10.2	10.3	6.5	6.5	7.0
Uzbekistan	8.3	8.2	8.0	8.1	8.0	6.9	7.3
East Asia	8.3	6.6	6.8	6.6	6.0	5.7	5.6
China, People's Rep. of	9.5	7.7	7.7	7.3	6.9	6.5	6.3
Hong Kong, China	4.8	1.7	3.1	2.6	2.4	2.1	2.2
Korea, Rep. of	3.7	2.3	2.9	3.3	2.6	2.6	2.8
Mongolia	17.3	12.3	11.6	7.9	2.3	0.1	0.5
Taipei,China	3.8	2.1	2.2	3.9	0.7	1.6	1.8
South Asia	6.3	5.6	6.2	6.7	7.0	6.9	7.3
Afghanistan	7.2	11.9	3.7	1.3	1.5	2.0	3.0
Bangladesh	6.5	6.5	6.0	6.1	6.6	6.7	6.9
Bhutan	9.7	6.4	3.6	3.8	5.9	6.4	6.1
India	6.6	5.6	6.6	7.2	7.6	7.4	7.8
Maldives	8.7	2.5	4.7	6.5	1.5	3.5	3.9
Nepal	3.8	4.6	3.8	5.1	3.0	1.5	4.8
Pakistan	3.6	3.8	3.7	4.0	4.2	4.5	4.8
Sri Lanka	8.4	9.1	3.4	4.9	4.8	5.3	5.8
Southeast Asia	4.8	5.9	5.0	4.5	4.4	4.5	4.8
Brunei Darussalam	3.7	0.9	–2.1	–2.3	–1.1	1.0	2.5
Cambodia	7.1	7.3	7.4	7.1	7.0	7.0	7.1
Indonesia	6.2	6.0	5.6	5.0	4.8	5.2	5.5
Lao People's Dem. Rep.	7.8	7.9	7.8	7.5	6.7	6.8	7.0
Malaysia	5.3	5.5	4.7	6.0	5.0	4.2	4.4
Myanmar	5.6	7.3	8.4	8.7	7.2	8.4	8.3
Philippines	3.7	6.7	7.1	6.1	5.8	6.0	6.1
Singapore	6.2	3.7	4.7	3.3	2.0	2.0	2.2
Thailand	0.8	7.2	2.7	0.8	2.8	3.0	3.5
Viet Nam	6.2	5.2	5.4	6.0	6.7	6.7	6.5
The Pacific	8.1	5.8	3.8	9.4	7.0	3.8	3.1
Cook Islands	–2.6	4.1	–1.7	–1.2	–0.5	0.0	0.2
Fiji	2.7	1.4	4.7	5.3	4.0	2.7	4.5
Kiribati	2.7	3.4	2.4	3.8	3.0	1.8	2.0
Marshall Islands	1.3	4.0	1.9	–1.0	–0.5	1.5	2.0
Micronesia, Fed. States of	1.8	–0.5	–3.6	–3.4	–1.5	2.5	3.5
Nauru	46.9	25.7	15.4	17.5	–10.0	3.0	15.0
Palau	4.4	3.1	–1.7	4.7	6.7	3.0	7.0
Papua New Guinea	10.7	8.1	5.0	13.3	9.9	4.3	2.4
Samoa	5.6	0.4	–1.9	1.2	1.4	2.0	0.5
Solomon Islands	7.4	2.3	2.8	2.0	3.2	3.0	2.8
Timor–Leste	9.5	6.4	2.8	6.0	4.1	4.5	5.5
Tonga	2.9	0.8	–3.1	2.0	3.4	2.8	2.7
Tuvalu	8.5	0.2	1.3	2.0	2.0	3.5	3.0
Vanuatu	1.2	1.8	2.0	2.3	–1.0	2.5	3.8
Average	7.4	6.3	6.4	6.3	5.9	5.7	5.7

Table A2 Growth rate of per capita GDP (% per year)

	2011	2012	2013	2014	2015	2016	2017	Per capita GNI ($) 2014
Central Asia	5.2	4.1	5.1	3.8	1.2	0.6	1.2	
Armenia	5.3	7.6	3.1	3.9	3.2	2.4	−0.7	4,020
Azerbaijan	−1.1	0.9	4.5	1.5	−0.1	−2.2	−0.1	7,590
Georgia	6.4	5.7	3.7	4.5	2.6	2.5	3.5	3,720
Kazakhstan	5.9	3.6	4.5	2.8	−1.2	−1.1	−0.6	11,850
Kyrgyz Republic	4.8	−1.4	8.7	2.0	−0.5	−0.6	1.0	1,250
Tajikistan	6.9	6.1	3.4	2.8	4.2	2.2	1.8	1,080
Turkmenistan	13.1	9.5	8.6	8.7	4.9	4.9	5.4	8,020
Uzbekistan	5.3	5.6	6.3	6.3	7.0	5.2	5.6	2,090
East Asia	7.7	6.1	6.3	6.1	5.5	5.3	5.1	
China, People's Rep. of	9.0	7.2	7.2	6.7	6.3	6.0	5.7	7,400
Hong Kong, China	4.1	0.5	2.6	1.9	1.5	1.4	1.4	40,320
Korea, Rep. of	2.9	1.8	2.5	2.9	2.2	2.2	2.4	27,090
Mongolia	15.3	10.2	9.4	5.6	0.1	−1.9	−1.5	4,280
Taipei,China	3.5	1.7	1.9	3.8	0.6	1.5	1.7	22,610
South Asia	5.0	4.3	4.7	5.3	5.6	5.7	6.1	
Afghanistan	5.2	9.7	1.2	−0.6	−0.4	0.0	1.0	680
Bangladesh	5.1	5.2	4.6	4.6	5.1	5.3	5.5	1,080
Bhutan	7.8	4.6	1.8	2.1	4.2	4.8	4.6	2,370
India	5.3	4.3	5.3	5.9	6.2	6.1	6.5	1,570
Maldives	5.8	0.4	2.6	4.1	−0.7	1.2	1.7	6,410
Nepal	3.1	3.1	2.3	3.6	1.6	0.1	3.4	730
Pakistan	1.5	1.8	1.6	2.0	2.2	4.5	4.6	1,400
Sri Lanka	7.4	11.5	2.6	3.9	3.8	5.1	3.3	3,460
Southeast Asia	3.4	4.4	3.6	3.1	3.1	3.4	3.3	
Brunei Darussalam	2.0	−0.7	−3.7	−3.7	−3.7	−0.3	1.2	34,210
Cambodia	5.5	5.6	6.2	5.8	5.7	5.5	5.7	1,020
Indonesia	4.3	4.5	4.1	3.6	3.4	3.9	3.6	3,630
Lao People's Dem. Rep.	5.7	6.5	5.7	5.4	2.5	3.8	4.4	1,660
Malaysia	3.9	4.1	2.7	3.6	3.6	2.9	2.8	11,120
Myanmar	4.5	6.2	7.3	8.0	6.3	7.6	7.5	1,270
Philippines	2.8	4.8	5.2	4.3	4.1	5.3	4.5	3,500
Singapore	4.0	1.2	3.0	1.9	0.8	0.8	1.0	55,150
Thailand	0.4	6.7	2.2	0.3	2.3	2.5	3.0	5,780
Viet Nam	5.1	4.1	4.3	4.9	5.5	5.7	5.5	1,890
The Pacific	7.8	3.4	1.5	6.8	4.6	1.2	0.7	
Cook Islands	−21.1	7.0	−0.3	2.5	3.3	−14.7	−0.2	21,864
Fiji	18.9	0.9	4.4	4.8	3.5	2.2	4.0	4,870
Kiribati	0.6	1.3	0.3	1.7	0.9	−0.3	−0.1	2,950
Marshall Islands	0.8	3.6	1.5	−1.4	−2.5	1.0	1.5	4,390
Micronesia, Fed. States of	2.4	−1.1	−3.6	−3.4	−1.4	2.7	3.7	3,200
Nauru	45.3	22.2	12.1	16.0	−12.5	0.1	11.8	...
Palau	6.4	5.1	−1.3	3.7	5.7	1.9	6.0	11,110
Papua New Guinea	7.1	4.8	1.8	9.9	6.6	1.2	−0.7	2,240
Samoa	4.8	−0.3	−2.7	0.5	0.6	1.3	−0.2	4,060
Solomon Islands	4.9	0.0	0.5	−0.3	1.7	0.5	0.3	1,830
Timor-Leste	6.7	3.6	0.0	3.2	1.3	1.7	3.0	2,680
Tonga	3.2	0.7	−3.2	2.0	3.4	2.9	2.8	4,260
Tuvalu	7.1	−1.0	0.0	−0.4	0.2	1.7	3.9	5,720
Vanuatu	−1.4	−0.8	−0.5	−0.1	−3.3	0.2	1.5	3,160
Average	6.6	5.5	5.6	5.5	5.1	5.0	4.9	

... = data not available, GNI = gross national income.

Table A3 Growth rate of value added in agriculture (% per year)

	2011	2012	2013	2014	2015	Sector share (%), 2014
Central Asia						
Armenia	14.0	9.5	7.6	7.8	11.4	20.3
Azerbaijan	−8.0	5.8	4.9	−2.6	6.6	5.7
Georgia	8.5	−3.8	11.3	1.6	2.8	9.3
Kazakhstan	23.0	−17.6	10.9	0.7	...	4.7
Kyrgyz Republic	1.9	1.2	2.6	−0.5	6.2	17.1
Tajikistan	7.9	10.4	7.6	4.5	3.2	30.7
Turkmenistan	0.1	8.1	10.0	4.2	7.9	8.5
Uzbekistan	6.6	7.0	6.8	6.9	6.8	18.8
East Asia						
China, People's Rep. of	4.2	4.5	3.8	4.1	3.9	9.2
Hong Kong, China	0.8	−3.2	4.9	−6.0	−3.2	0.1
Korea, Rep. of	−2.0	−0.9	3.1	2.6	−1.6	2.3
Mongolia	−0.3	21.1	19.2	13.7	10.7	13.3
Taipei,China	4.5	−3.2	1.3	0.5	−3.1	1.9
South Asia						
Afghanistan	−7.9	31.5	0.0	−0.1	−2.0	23.5
Bangladesh	4.5	3.0	2.5	4.4	3.3	16.1
Bhutan	1.6	2.3	2.3	2.4	2.4	17.4
India	0.0	1.5	4.2	−0.2	1.1	17.4
Maldives	1.1	0.0	5.1	0.2	−1.4	3.4
Nepal	4.5	4.6	1.1	2.9	1.9	32.5
Pakistan	2.0	3.6	2.7	2.7	2.9	25.0
Sri Lanka	4.6	3.9	3.2	4.9	5.5	8.0
Southeast Asia						
Brunei Darussalam	−2.6	8.1	−1.2	4.8	...	0.8
Cambodia	3.1	4.3	1.6	0.3	0.2	29.0
Indonesia	3.9	4.6	4.2	4.2	4.0	13.7
Lao People's Dem. Rep.	1.8	2.5	3.5	2.9	2.0	24.3
Malaysia	6.8	1.0	1.9	2.1	1.0	9.0
Myanmar	−0.7	1.7	3.6	3.3	...	27.9
Philippines	2.6	2.8	1.1	1.6	0.2	11.3
Singapore	2.1	3.6	14.5	1.9	−3.6	0.0
Thailand	6.3	2.7	0.8	0.7	−4.2	10.2
Viet Nam	4.2	2.9	2.6	3.4	2.4	18.9
The Pacific						
Cook Islands	−7.3	7.7	2.3	18.0	3.6	8.5
Fiji	16.1	−2.0	6.8	−0.4	...	11.5
Kiribati	5.7	...	...	...	...	...
Marshall Islands	6.2	12.4	−0.8	−2.4	1.6	19.6
Micronesia, Fed. States of	3.2	4.3	−4.8	0.7	−2.3	26.5
Nauru	12.9	8.4	−2.8	2.9	...	4.4
Palau	9.5	1.5	−8.0	−1.7	6.2	4.1
Papua New Guinea	6.9	−1.6	1.8	3.3	2.1	23.9
Samoa	2.4	−7.2	−2.4	9.6	−1.8	9.3
Solomon Islands	2.3	−0.5	−0.8	7.1	2.1	28.0
Timor-Leste	−19.9	23.5	0.5	...	...	...
Tonga	2.0	0.5	3.7	3.1	−2.4	...
Tuvalu	...	...	...	...	...	...
Vanuatu	6.1	2.2	4.8	4.2	...	26.8

... = data not available.

Table A4 Growth rate of value added in industry (% per year)

	2011	2012	2013	2014	2015	Sector share (%), 2014
Central Asia						
Armenia	0.0	5.7	0.5	−2.3	2.5	28.0
Azerbaijan	3.4	−0.6	4.9	0.5	−1.9	57.9
Georgia	9.2	9.6	2.4	4.6	3.3	24.0
Kazakhstan	0.7	1.7	2.9	1.2	...	35.9
Kyrgyz Republic	7.0	−11.7	30.5	5.7	1.4	27.8
Tajikistan	5.7	10.4	3.9	13.3	11.2	15.7
Turkmenistan	26.5	8.6	7.3	11.4	3.1	47.3
Uzbekistan	7.5	8.0	9.0	8.6	8.0	33.7
East Asia						
China, People's Rep. of	10.6	8.2	7.9	7.3	6.0	42.7
Hong Kong, China	9.3	4.6	1.6	7.4	0.8	7.2
Korea, Rep. of	4.5	1.9	3.3	3.5	1.8	38.2
Mongolia	8.8	14.8	14.6	12.7	8.8	31.5
Taipei,China	6.0	3.3	1.7	7.0	−0.8	35.6
South Asia						
Afghanistan	9.8	7.2	3.1	2.4	1.4	22.3
Bangladesh	9.0	9.4	9.6	8.2	9.7	27.6
Bhutan	8.0	5.4	5.3	3.5	4.8	43.7
India	0.0	3.6	5.0	5.9	7.3	30.0
Maldives	12.1	0.8	−7.6	12.9	27.3	18.5
Nepal	4.3	3.0	2.7	6.2	2.6	15.1
Pakistan	4.5	2.5	0.6	4.5	3.6	20.9
Sri Lanka	9.3	9.0	4.1	3.5	3.0	28.6
Southeast Asia						
Brunei Darussalam	3.2	−1.4	−5.6	−4.4	...	66.8
Cambodia	14.5	9.3	10.7	10.1	11.7	27.2
Indonesia	6.3	5.3	4.3	4.3	2.7	43.0
Lao People's Dem. Rep.	14.2	13.7	9.7	8.5	8.0	32.4
Malaysia	2.4	4.9	3.6	6.1	5.2	37.6
Myanmar	10.2	8.0	11.4	12.4	...	34.4
Philippines	1.9	7.3	9.2	7.9	6.0	31.4
Singapore	7.1	2.1	2.5	2.8	−3.4	25.5
Thailand	−4.1	7.3	1.4	−0.3	2.2	36.8
Viet Nam	7.6	7.4	5.1	6.4	9.6	37.6
The Pacific						
Cook Islands	−8.1	21.8	−16.4	−14.8	−3.1	6.4
Fiji	21.2	−2.2	4.4	2.7	...	18.7
Kiribati	11.8	...	...	...	...	...
Marshall Islands	−2.5	2.4	3.7	−12.0	−6.6	10.1
Micronesia, Fed. States of	11.9	−1.6	−20.5	−28.5	−8.8	6.1
Nauru	85.6	79.2	−22.1	−22.9	...	24.2
Palau	5.3	−5.4	−15.5	1.7	16.4	7.5
Papua New Guinea	13.0	14.6	9.3	28.6	19.2	52.4
Samoa	8.0	0.2	−3.2	3.8	−6.2	26.2
Solomon Islands	38.2	−1.4	−2.0	−13.2	1.3	15.0
Timor−Leste	49.4	−4.0	−8.0	...	...	...
Tonga	5.5	1.2	−14.5	1.3	5.2	...
Tuvalu	...	...	...	...	...	...
Vanuatu	−19.4	−22.2	9.8	3.2	...	8.7

... = data not available.

Table A5 Growth rate of value added in services (% per year)

	2011	2012	2013	2014	2015	Sector share (%), 2014
Central Asia						
Armenia	6.1	6.9	2.8	5.8	1.1	51.7
Azerbaijan	–2.1	6.9	7.2	7.4	4.5	36.3
Georgia	5.6	6.2	3.5	4.7	3.1	66.7
Kazakhstan	6.0	10.6	7.0	6.0	...	59.4
Kyrgyz Republic	6.9	6.5	4.7	4.6	3.7	55.1
Tajikistan	11.0	14.5	19.3	1.0	–7.0	53.6
Turkmenistan	8.3	14.7	12.7	10.6	10.0	44.2
Uzbekistan	11.8	10.4	8.8	9.4	9.8	47.5
East Asia						
China, People's Rep. of	9.5	8.0	8.3	7.8	8.3	48.1
Hong Kong, China	5.2	1.8	2.7	2.4	1.9	92.7
Korea, Rep. of	3.1	2.8	2.9	3.1	2.8	59.4
Mongolia	17.8	10.3	7.8	7.8	1.1	55.2
Taipei,China	3.1	1.5	2.1	2.8	0.5	62.5
South Asia						
Afghanistan	12.7	7.3	5.3	2.2	2.8	54.2
Bangladesh	6.2	6.6	5.5	5.6	5.8	56.3
Bhutan	12.7	6.6	1.1	5.0	8.5	38.9
India	0.0	8.1	7.8	10.3	9.2	52.6
Maldives	5.8	1.5	6.4	5.0	–1.0	78.1
Nepal	3.4	5.0	5.7	6.3	3.9	52.4
Pakistan	3.9	4.4	5.1	4.4	5.0	54.1
Sri Lanka	8.9	11.2	3.8	5.2	5.3	56.7
Southeast Asia						
Brunei Darussalam	4.9	5.5	4.7	1.1	...	32.4
Cambodia	5.0	8.1	8.7	8.7	7.1	41.6
Indonesia	8.4	6.8	6.4	6.0	5.5	43.3
Lao People's Dem. Rep.	8.5	8.0	9.7	9.0	8.5	43.3
Malaysia	7.0	6.5	6.0	6.5	5.1	53.5
Myanmar	8.5	12.0	10.3	10.4	...	37.7
Philippines	4.9	7.1	7.0	5.9	6.7	57.3
Singapore	6.6	4.3	6.3	3.7	3.5	74.5
Thailand	3.8	8.4	4.1	1.7	5.0	53.0
Viet Nam	7.5	6.7	6.7	6.2	6.3	43.5
The Pacific						
Cook Islands	–1.7	1.6	–0.3	–2.4	–0.6	85.1
Fiji	19.5	3.0	4.5	6.9	...	69.9
Kiribati	–1.2	...	...	...	...	...
Marshall Islands	1.3	2.0	2.0	1.8	0.1	70.3
Micronesia, Fed. States of	0.1	–1.7	–0.7	–1.3	–0.2	67.3
Nauru	50.2	–10.6	50.9	35.9	...	71.4
Palau	4.3	2.8	–0.4	6.0	6.0	88.5
Papua New Guinea	12.9	11.2	4.7	4.2	3.2	23.7
Samoa	4.8	1.6	–1.1	–1.1	5.0	64.5
Solomon Islands	2.5	5.3	7.2	3.6	4.3	57.0
Timor-Leste	10.6	8.5	1.4	...	...	...
Tonga	1.8	0.5	–0.4	1.6	3.0	...
Tuvalu	...	...	...	...	...	...
Vanuatu	3.2	4.4	0.1	2.4	...	64.5

... = data not available.

Table A6 Inflation (% per year)

	2011	2012	2013	2014	2015	2016	2017
Central Asia	8.9	5.1	5.8	5.7	6.2	10.8	5.9
Armenia	7.7	2.6	5.8	3.0	3.7	3.8	4.0
Azerbaijan	7.9	1.1	2.4	1.4	4.0	12.0	5.2
Georgia	8.6	−0.9	−0.5	3.1	4.0	5.0	4.0
Kazakhstan	8.3	5.1	5.8	6.7	6.6	12.6	4.6
Kyrgyz Republic	16.6	2.8	6.6	7.5	6.5	10.0	8.0
Tajikistan	12.5	5.8	5.0	6.1	5.1	8.5	7.5
Turkmenistan	5.3	5.3	6.8	6.0	6.0	6.6	6.0
Uzbekistan	12.8	12.1	11.2	8.4	9.0	10.0	11.0
East Asia	5.0	2.6	2.4	1.9	1.3	1.6	2.0
China, People's Rep. of	5.4	2.6	2.6	2.0	1.4	1.7	2.0
Hong Kong, China	5.3	4.1	4.4	4.4	3.0	2.5	2.7
Korea, Rep. of	4.0	2.2	1.3	1.3	0.7	1.4	2.0
Mongolia	9.2	14.3	9.9	12.8	6.6	3.0	7.0
Taipei,China	1.4	1.9	0.8	1.2	−0.3	0.7	1.2
South Asia	9.4	9.3	9.3	6.8	5.0	5.2	5.7
Afghanistan	11.8	6.2	7.4	4.6	−1.5	3.0	3.5
Bangladesh	10.9	8.7	6.8	7.3	6.4	6.2	6.5
Bhutan	8.6	10.2	8.8	9.6	6.6	4.0	5.0
India	8.9	9.3	9.8	6.7	5.0	5.4	5.8
Maldives	11.3	10.9	2.3	2.1	1.0	1.2	1.4
Nepal	9.6	8.3	9.8	9.1	7.2	10.5	8.2
Pakistan	13.7	11.0	7.4	8.6	4.5	3.2	4.5
Sri Lanka	6.8	7.5	6.9	3.2	3.8	4.5	5.0
Southeast Asia	5.5	3.8	4.2	4.1	2.7	2.6	2.9
Brunei Darussalam	0.1	0.1	0.4	−0.2	−0.4	0.2	0.4
Cambodia	5.5	2.9	3.0	3.9	1.2	2.5	3.0
Indonesia	5.3	4.0	6.4	6.4	6.4	4.5	4.2
Lao People's Dem. Rep.	7.6	4.3	6.4	4.2	1.3	1.8	2.5
Malaysia	3.2	1.7	2.1	3.1	2.1	2.7	2.5
Myanmar	2.8	2.8	5.7	5.9	11.0	9.5	8.5
Philippines	4.6	3.2	3.0	4.1	1.4	2.3	2.7
Singapore	5.2	4.6	2.4	1.0	−0.5	−0.6	0.4
Thailand	3.8	3.0	2.2	1.9	−0.9	0.6	2.0
Viet Nam	18.7	9.1	6.6	4.1	0.6	3.0	4.0
The Pacific	6.4	5.5	4.9	3.5	3.4	4.5	4.7
Cook Islands	0.6	2.8	2.6	1.6	3.0	1.8	2.0
Fiji	7.3	3.4	2.9	0.6	1.4	3.0	3.0
Kiribati	1.5	−3.0	−1.5	2.1	1.4	0.3	0.8
Marshall Islands	5.4	4.3	1.9	1.1	0.5	2.0	2.5
Micronesia, Fed. States of	4.0	6.3	2.2	0.7	−1.1	−0.3	0.3
Nauru	0.7	−0.1	0.5	3.0	11.4	6.6	1.7
Palau	2.6	5.4	2.8	4.0	2.2	1.5	2.5
Papua New Guinea	4.4	4.6	5.0	5.2	5.1	6.0	6.0
Samoa	2.9	6.2	−0.2	−1.2	1.9	2.0	2.0
Solomon Islands	7.4	5.9	5.4	5.2	−0.3	4.4	5.7
Timor–Leste	13.2	10.9	9.5	0.7	0.6	2.0	3.0
Tonga	6.0	3.3	0.8	2.1	−0.7	−0.3	0.5
Tuvalu	0.5	1.4	2.0	1.1	2.0	3.5	2.0
Vanuatu	1.0	1.4	1.4	1.0	2.5	1.9	2.4
Average	5.9	3.9	3.8	3.0	2.2	2.5	2.7

Table A7 Change in money supply (% per year)

	2011	2012	2013	2014	2015
Central Asia					
Armenia	23.7	19.5	14.8	8.3	10.8
Azerbaijan	32.1	20.7	15.4	11.1	-0.9
Georgia	14.5	11.4	24.5	13.8	19.3
Kazakhstan	15.0	7.9	10.2	10.5	34.3
Kyrgyz Republic	14.9	23.8	22.8	3.0	14.9
Tajikistan	33.1	19.6	19.7	7.1	18.7
Turkmenistan	36.3	35.6	31.2	11.4	8.4
Uzbekistan	32.3	27.5	22.4	18.0	20.7
East Asia					
China, People's Rep. of	17.3	14.4	13.6	11.0	13.3
Hong Kong, China	12.9	11.1	12.4	9.5	5.5
Korea, Rep. of	5.5	4.8	4.6	8.1	8.2
Mongolia	37.0	18.7	24.2	12.5	-5.5
Taipei,China	4.8	3.5	5.8	6.1	5.8
South Asia					
Afghanistan	21.3	8.8	9.4	8.3	5.7
Bangladesh	21.3	17.4	16.7	16.1	12.4
Bhutan	21.2	-1.0	18.6	6.6	7.8
India	13.5	13.6	13.4	10.8	9.8
Maldives	20.0	5.0	18.4	14.7	13.6
Nepal	12.3	22.6	16.4	19.1	19.9
Pakistan	15.9	14.1	15.9	12.5	13.2
Sri Lanka	19.1	17.6	16.7	6.2	0.0
Southeast Asia					
Brunei Darussalam	10.1	0.9	1.5	3.2	-1.8
Cambodia	21.4	20.9	14.6	29.9	14.7
Indonesia	16.4	15.0	12.8	11.9	8.9
Lao People's Dem. Rep.	28.7	31.0	18.6	23.5	14.7
Malaysia	14.3	9.0	7.3	7.0	2.7
Myanmar	26.3	46.6	32.7	21.7	31.7
Philippines	7.1	9.4	31.8	11.2	9.4
Singapore	10.0	7.2	4.3	3.3	1.5
Thailand	15.1	10.4	7.3	4.7	4.4
Viet Nam	12.1	18.5	18.8	17.7	14.0
The Pacific					
Cook Islands	-13.4	19.3	-25.6	3.0	9.6
Fiji	14.8	6.3	21.2	10.6	11.2
Kiribati	...	...	...	...	...
Marshall Islands	...	...	...	...	...
Micronesia, Fed. States of	7.1	24.1	-4.9	5.1	-5.1
Nauru	...	...	...	...	...
Palau	9.0	22.7	4.5	24.7	2.6
Papua New Guinea	16.2	11.0	6.7	3.4	-3.3
Samoa	-0.8	-4.0	-0.8	18.7	...
Solomon Islands	25.8	17.4	12.5	5.5	15.0
Timor-Leste	9.3	26.2	22.9	19.9	7.1
Tonga	2.7	-1.6	7.0	7.9	2.4
Tuvalu	...	...	...	...	...
Vanuatu	1.3	-0.6	-5.5	8.6	...

... = data not available.

Table A8 Central government revenues (% of GDP)

	2011	2012	2013	2014	2015
Central Asia					
Armenia	23.3	22.2	23.5	23.6	22.7
Azerbaijan	30.1	31.6	33.5	31.2	31.5
Georgia	28.2	28.9	27.7	27.9	28.4
Kazakhstan	18.3	18.1	17.2	18.0	18.4
Kyrgyz Republic	31.8	34.9	34.4	35.9	37.4
Tajikistan	24.9	25.2	26.9	28.4	30.1
Turkmenistan	18.3	21.0	17.4	16.3	13.8
Uzbekistan	32.0	32.8	32.8	33.1	33.3
East Asia					
China, People's Rep. of	21.5	22.0	22.0	22.1	22.5
Hong Kong, China	22.6	21.7	21.3	21.2	19.0
Korea, Rep. of	19.0	19.4	18.8	18.3	21.5
Mongolia	28.5	26.2	27.8	25.8	23.9
Taipei,China	11.7	11.4	11.4	10.7	10.6
South Asia					
Afghanistan	21.4	25.4	26.6	24.5	29.2
Bangladesh	10.2	10.9	10.7	10.4	9.6
Bhutan	35.8	35.8	30.2	33.6	28.4
India	19.9	20.1	21.1	21.2	20.5
Maldives	27.7	26.2	27.7	32.2	36.3
Nepal	17.9	18.6	19.5	20.8	20.2
Pakistan	12.4	12.8	13.3	14.5	14.4
Sri Lanka	13.6	12.2	12.0	11.5	14.5
Southeast Asia					
Brunei Darussalam	55.5	49.4	41.8	32.8	16.5
Cambodia	12.4	14.4	13.5	17.4	17.1
Indonesia	15.5	15.5	15.1	14.7	13.0
Lao People's Dem. Rep.	16.4	17.7	18.1	17.2	19.3
Malaysia	20.3	21.4	20.9	19.9	18.9
Myanmar	11.3	21.8	22.0	25.3	20.9
Philippines	14.0	14.5	14.9	15.1	15.9
Singapore	14.7	15.4	15.2	15.8	16.0
Thailand	16.7	16.0	16.8	15.8	16.3
Viet Nam	26.1	22.7	23.1	21.5	22.1
The Pacific					
Cook Islands	32.4	33.9	34.4	41.8	42.7
Fiji	26.7	27.2	27.2	27.0	36.0
Kiribati	59.7	84.2	94.4	128.7	105.4
Marshall Islands	57.0	50.7	53.3	52.0	55.6
Micronesia, Fed. States of	63.1	64.3	60.4	55.9	63.1
Nauru	58.5	67.6	82.9	95.3	...
Palau	43.7	44.4	40.7	43.2	43.0
Papua New Guinea	15.3	29.4	28.8	27.4	23.1
Samoa	32.2	30.2	33.8	38.1	35.1
Solomon Islands	59.0	54.4	54.3	46.2	...
Timor-Leste	356.7	336.0	327.4	195.8	86.3
Tonga	26.1	27.4	25.2	37.5	40.7
Tuvalu	69.1	85.2	109.8	122.7	118.5
Vanuatu	22.3	21.8	21.4	23.2	23.6

... = data not available.

Table A9 Central government expenditures (% of GDP)

	2011	2012	2013	2014	2015
Central Asia					
Armenia	26.1	23.6	25.1	25.5	27.3
Azerbaijan	29.6	31.8	32.8	31.7	32.7
Georgia	31.8	31.7	30.3	30.7	32.1
Kazakhstan	20.2	20.8	19.1	20.7	20.6
Kyrgyz Republic	36.3	39.8	38.2	39.8	40.4
Tajikistan	27.0	25.1	28.2	29.0	32.4
Turkmenistan	14.6	14.7	16.1	15.4	14.8
Uzbekistan	31.9	32.3	32.8	32.6	34.2
East Asia					
China, People's Rep. of	22.6	23.6	23.8	23.9	26.0
Hong Kong, China	18.8	18.5	20.3	18.0	17.8
Korea, Rep. of	20.1	20.7	20.3	20.3	24.5
Mongolia	33.7	32.3	28.9	28.9	28.5
Taipei,China	13.4	12.9	12.2	11.5	11.6
South Asia					
Afghanistan	22.0	24.3	24.5	26.4	28.6
Bangladesh	14.0	14.4	14.5	14.0	13.9
Bhutan	37.9	36.9	34.4	29.8	30.6
India	27.7	27.0	28.2	28.3	27.8
Maldives	34.3	33.9	31.5	34.8	43.7
Nepal	20.2	20.9	18.8	20.2	21.5
Pakistan	18.9	21.6	21.5	20.0	19.7
Sri Lanka	19.9	17.8	17.4	17.2	19.0
Southeast Asia					
Brunei Darussalam	30.8	31.4	34.1	33.5	30.5
Cambodia	20.2	21.0	20.4	20.7	19.5
Indonesia	16.5	17.3	17.3	16.8	15.6
Lao People's Dem. Rep.	24.4	24.6	29.4	27.6	26.9
Malaysia	25.0	25.7	24.7	23.3	22.2
Myanmar	15.6	23.3	23.7	28.1	25.7
Philippines	16.0	16.8	16.3	15.7	16.8
Singapore	13.4	13.6	13.8	14.7	17.0
Thailand	15.9	16.0	16.3	16.4	16.0
Viet Nam	25.4	28.2	26.0	25.9	27.7
The Pacific					
Cook Islands	37.1	36.9	34.2	41.9	44.4
Fiji	28.0	28.3	27.6	31.2	38.5
Kiribati	81.8	80.8	84.9	107.7	106.5
Marshall Islands	54.9	51.4	52.6	47.7	53.5
Micronesia, Fed. States of	64.4	64.2	59.0	53.6	58.0
Nauru	57.9	68.5	82.5	95.3	...
Palau	42.5	43.4	40.0	39.8	38.1
Papua New Guinea	15.6	31.0	38.4	35.7	26.2
Samoa	36.7	37.3	37.6	43.3	39.0
Solomon Islands	50.2	50.6	49.9	44.2	...
Timor-Leste	121.4	112.1	101.7	115.9	100.5
Tonga	32.0	29.1	26.4	34.8	40.6
Tuvalu	78.0	84.5	86.6	104.7	112.8
Vanuatu	24.5	23.3	21.6	22.0	30.7

... = data not available.

Table A10 Fiscal balance of central government (% of GDP)

	2011	2012	2013	2014	2015
Central Asia					
Armenia	-2.8	-1.4	-1.6	-1.9	-4.6
Azerbaijan	0.6	-0.2	0.7	-0.5	-1.1
Georgia	-3.6	-2.8	-2.6	-2.9	-3.7
Kazakhstan	-1.9	-2.8	-1.9	-2.7	-2.2
Kyrgyz Republic	-4.5	-4.9	-3.8	-3.9	-3.0
Tajikistan	-2.5	0.1	-1.3	-0.6	-2.3
Turkmenistan	3.2	6.3	1.3	0.8	-1.0
Uzbekistan	0.1	0.5	0.0	0.5	-0.9
East Asia					
China, People's Rep. of	-1.1	-1.6	-1.9	-1.8	-3.5
Hong Kong, China	3.8	3.2	1.0	3.2	1.3
Korea, Rep. of	-1.1	-1.3	-1.5	-2.0	-3.0
Mongolia	-3.6	-5.6	-0.9	-3.2	-3.1
Taipei,China	-1.7	-1.6	-0.9	-0.8	-1.0
South Asia					
Afghanistan	-0.6	1.1	2.1	-1.9	0.7
Bangladesh	-3.9	-3.6	-3.8	-3.6	-4.3
Bhutan	-2.1	-1.1	-4.2	3.8	-2.2
India	-7.6	-6.6	-6.9	-4.1	-3.9
Maldives	-6.6	-7.7	-3.8	-2.7	-7.4
Nepal	-2.4	-2.2	0.7	0.6	-1.3
Pakistan	-6.5	-8.8	-8.2	-5.5	-5.3
Sri Lanka	-6.2	-5.6	-5.4	-5.7	-4.5
Southeast Asia					
Brunei Darussalam	24.7	18.0	7.7	-0.7	-14.0
Cambodia	-7.8	-6.6	-6.9	-3.6	-2.4
Indonesia	-1.1	-1.8	-2.2	-2.1	-2.5
Lao People's Dem. Rep.	-7.9	-6.9	-5.6	-4.2	-4.7
Malaysia	-4.7	-4.3	-3.8	-3.4	-3.2
Myanmar	-4.3	-1.6	-1.7	-2.9	-4.8
Philippines	-2.0	-2.3	-1.4	-0.6	-0.9
Singapore	1.2	1.6	1.3	0.0	-1.7
Thailand	-1.4	-2.3	-1.6	-2.5	-2.5
Viet Nam	-4.0	-4.6	-6.0	-5.7	-5.4
The Pacific					
Cook Islands	-4.8	-3.0	0.2	-0.1	-1.7
Fiji	-1.4	-1.1	-0.5	-4.1	-2.5
Kiribati	-22.1	3.5	9.5	21.0	-1.1
Marshall Islands	2.1	-0.7	0.7	4.3	2.1
Micronesia, Fed. States of	-1.2	0.1	1.4	2.3	5.1
Nauru	0.6	-0.9	0.3	0.0	-5.7
Palau	1.2	1.0	0.7	3.5	4.9
Papua New Guinea	-0.3	-1.6	-9.6	-8.3	-3.2
Samoa	-4.5	-7.2	-3.8	-5.3	-3.9
Solomon Islands	8.8	3.8	4.4	2.0	-2.2
Timor–Leste	235.3	223.9	225.6	79.9	-14.2
Tonga	-5.9	-1.6	-1.3	2.7	-0.2
Tuvalu	-8.9	0.6	23.1	17.9	5.7
Vanuatu	-2.2	-1.5	-0.2	1.2	-7.1

Table A11 Growth rate of merchandise exports (% per year)

	2011	2012	2013	2014	2015	2016	2017
Central Asia	35.4	1.6	0.6	−6.9	−33.7	−14.9	9.3
Armenia	19.5	5.9	7.9	3.8	−0.2	0.2	1.0
Azerbaijan	30.3	−5.4	−2.6	−11.1	−41.9	−12.2	7
Georgia	32.2	7.6	21.2	−4.1	−20.9	7.7	16.6
Kazakhstan	38.8	2.0	−1.5	−6.2	−42.4	−24.5	10.4
Kyrgyz Republic	27.7	−13.1	16.3	−13.5	−11.0	5.0	9.0
Tajikistan	5.2	41.0	−3.1	10.6	−8.9	5.0	7.0
Turkmenistan	73.0	18.9	−4.7	2.0	−33.9	−19.8	15.9
Uzbekistan	20.3	−7.6	6.5	−14.8	−12.3	2.0	4.0
East Asia	21.5	7.8	7.8	3.7	−5.3	0.0	1.9
China, People's Rep. of	21.6	9.2	8.9	4.4	−4.4	0.0	2.0
Hong Kong, China	12.5	7.0	8.1	1.9	−1.9	0.9	2.1
Korea, Rep. of	26.6	2.8	2.4	−0.8	−10.5	2.0	4.0
Mongolia	65.6	−9.0	−2.6	35.3	−19.1	−10.0	−15.0
Taipei,China	11.7	−0.6	1.6	2.8	−10.4	−5.0	−4.2
South Asia	24.8	−0.8	3.3	0.7	−14.5	0.3	6.0
Afghanistan	−5.1	2.7	−74.1	8.5	4.6	26.9	23.9
Bangladesh	39.2	6.2	10.7	12.1	3.3	8.0	9.0
Bhutan	26.8	−7.3	−11.5	−2.0	8.2	7.0	5.0
India	23.6	−1.1	3.9	−0.6	−18.0	−1.5	5.0
Maldives	75.4	−9.2	5.3	−9.1	−19.6	5.3	5.0
Nepal	11.7	5.7	−2.9	5.1	−3.9	−15.0	15.0
Pakistan	28.9	−2.5	0.3	1.1	−4.0	9.0	8.5
Sri Lanka	23.2	−7.4	6.3	7.1	−5.6	−2.0	10.0
Southeast Asia	20.0	3.3	−1.0	1.6	−11.7	−3.0	2.7
Brunei Darussalam	40.6	4.1	−8.1	−6.1	−42.9	−23.8	16.3
Cambodia	28.9	11.9	15.9	13.4	14.1	10.5	13.0
Indonesia	27.4	−2.0	−2.8	−3.7	−15.4	−7.0	−2.5
Lao People's Dem. Rep.	43.2	6.1	9.5	10.0	7.1	...	...
Malaysia	15.0	−3.0	−3.1	2.6	−15.5	−0.4	7.9
Myanmar	15.9	1.1	8.9	9.9	0.4	16.9	18.8
Philippines	4.1	21.2	−4.0	11.9	−13.1	−2.3	7.5
Singapore	17.7	0.4	0.0	0.1	−13.9	−3.5	2.0
Thailand	14.3	3.0	−0.1	−0.3	−5.6	−1.0	1.0
Viet Nam	34.2	18.2	15.3	13.8	7.9	10.0	14.0
The Pacific	20.4	1.3	−14.8	23.6	34.4	−2.8	5.8
Cook Islands	−3.5	−21.6	138.7	142.6	−7.7	−13.7	0.0
Fiji	29.9	12.6	−5.5	5.9	−9.1	−11.2	13.6
Kiribati	70.7	−11.4	1.1	−1.7	−21.0	2.2	15.1
Marshall Islands	58.6	14.8	−8.1	−11.3	−12.2	−15.7	5.3
Micronesia, Fed. States of	27.7	42.9	−13.2	−20.4	0.8	3.9	4.2
Nauru	52.8	80.8	−13.7	−12.8	...	...	...
Palau	10.2	17.0	−4.2	32.7	−46.8	−2.7	16.0
Papua New Guinea	17.9	−9.3	−13.1	35.6	24.3	8.6	1.7
Samoa	33.1	25.8	−6.3	−9.5	10.9	−16.1	−4.1
Solomon Islands	86.1	19.9	−10.3	1.6	−10.2	−7.4	−4.5
Timor-Leste	5.9	16.0	−46.9	−12.4	193.5	−45.0	20.0
Tonga	2.7	−15.0	38.4	22.4	−7.8	...	...
Tuvalu	5.2	95.1	−3.0	−4.5	−13.4	1.7	39.8
Vanuatu	24.9	−13.9	−31.2	68.6	...	...	...
Average	22.1	5.6	5.6	2.8	−8.1	−0.7	2.8

... = data not available.

Table A12 Growth rate of merchandise imports (% per year)

	2011	2012	2013	2014	2015	2016	2017
Central Asia	29.3	15.5	6.1	−7.4	−16.7	−16.5	3.9
Armenia	8.5	2.4	2.8	0.7	−15.5	−1.5	2.0
Azerbaijan	50.7	2.5	7.1	−16.3	0.3	−21.0	−1.5
Georgia	33.6	14.4	0.3	8.0	−15.2	3.8	12.5
Kazakhstan	22.7	20.9	4.1	−14.2	−22.9	−23.3	3.5
Kyrgyz Republic	32.0	26.2	9.2	−3.0	−29.0	5.0	5.0
Tajikistan	19.9	16.8	12.0	0.1	−20.1	−7.0	5.0
Turkmenistan	40.6	27.6	11.7	1.8	−22.4	−22.2	13.5
Uzbekistan	23.4	8.2	9.0	11.0	−11.0	2.0	2.5
East Asia	27.2	4.3	6.1	0.7	−13.8	−3.9	3.3
China, People's Rep. of	27.3	5.2	7.7	1.1	−13.4	−4.9	3.5
Hong Kong, China	15.4	9.5	9.6	2.6	−3.5	1.1	2.4
Korea, Rep. of	34.2	−0.7	−3.4	−2.1	−18.2	4.0	6.0
Mongolia	88.1	2.2	−5.9	−14.4	−27.5	−15.0	10.0
Taipei,China	13.0	−1.2	0.0	0.7	−16.6	−7.0	−7.7
South Asia	31.0	1.8	−5.9	0.5	−11.5	4.3	9.2
Afghanistan	3.3	11.2	−18.7	−3.9	−1.5	5.5	7.5
Bangladesh	52.1	2.4	0.8	8.9	11.2	9.0	11.0
Bhutan	41.7	−10.0	−8.8	0.5	7.5	8.0	7.0
India	31.1	0.5	−7.2	−1.0	−15.5	3.5	9.0
Maldives	36.6	−8.2	8.1	15.1	9.1	10.1	8.0
Nepal	8.9	4.7	10.9	13.9	8.0	−8.0	18.0
Pakistan	14.9	12.5	−0.5	3.8	−0.9	10.2	9.7
Sri Lanka	50.7	−5.3	−6.2	7.9	−2.5	−1.0	7.0
Southeast Asia	23.7	9.2	0.0	−1.2	−12.5	0.2	2.4
Brunei Darussalam	46.3	9.6	19.3	−25.3	−17.1	2.6	10.1
Cambodia	24.7	13.4	19.7	8.9	11.9	9.5	10.5
Indonesia	32.2	13.6	−1.3	−4.5	−19.8	−3.0	−2.1
Lao People's Dem. Rep.	31.7	34.5	17.4	5.0	5.8	...	...
Malaysia	13.9	1.7	−0.3	0.8	−14.7	2.5	6.3
Myanmar	27.2	19.5	11.5	26.7	14.4	11.8	12.1
Philippines	9.5	11.3	−4.8	8.0	−3.2	2.4	4.3
Singapore	18.4	0.8	−1.5	−1.0	−17.8	−5.0	1.5
Thailand	24.9	8.4	−0.1	−8.5	−11.3	0.8	4.0
Viet Nam	25.8	8.7	16.5	12.0	15.1	15.0	12.0
The Pacific	34.0	25.7	−12.0	−12.4	−3.4	5.6	3.5
Cook Islands	17.2	−0.5	−3.2	7.4	−6.4	−11.6	−2.6
Fiji	23.1	3.1	16.8	−3.2	−13.6	1.8	3.1
Kiribati	23.1	14.9	−7.5	10.5	−14.4	−3.3	3.2
Marshall Islands	−11.2	3.7	9.7	−7.4	−16.5	−10.8	4.6
Micronesia, Fed. States of	9.0	5.0	−2.3	−13.7	−22.4	−1.0	10.4
Nauru	61.8	17.5	59.3	59.1	...	...	...
Palau	21.7	11.1	5.5	21.3	−14.5	4.6	8.4
Papua New Guinea	46.2	22.7	−28.4	−20.3	2.6	6.9	2.8
Samoa	10.3	19.0	−8.0	8.1	−3.2	−13.5	−1.7
Solomon Islands	16.9	3.0	7.0	−1.0	−3.6	−3.0	5.4
Timor-Leste	30.7	67.1	3.7	10.9	−18.4	15.9	6.8
Tonga	15.3	18.2	3.0	−4.4	10.7	...	...
Tuvalu	14.3	−5.1	7.7	8.3	34.0	−23.6	22.1
Vanuatu	1.7	2.8	3.8	−57.5	...	...	...
Average	27.3	4.9	3.4	0.2	−13.4	−2.4	4.0

... = data not available.

Table A13 Trade balance ($ million)

	2011	2012	2013	2014	2015	2016	2017
Central Asia	68,778	56,710	49,393	45,342	8,717	5,200	8,874
Armenia	–2,110	–2,112	–2,092	–2,055	–1,477	–1,426	–1,471
Azerbaijan	24,328	22,217	20,621	18,928	7,070	7,038	8,156
Georgia	–3,494	–4,216	–3,493	–4,280	–3,862	–3,881	–4,219
Kazakhstan	44,844	38,145	34,792	36,699	12,633	9,113	11,828
Kyrgyz Republic	–1,665	–2,993	–2,909	–2,935	–2,357	–2,692	–2,873
Tajikistan	–2,765	–2,420	–2,958	–3,361	–2,544	–2,259	–2,354
Turkmenistan	6,272	6,527	4,032	4,143	996	1,084	1,479
Uzbekistan	3,367	1,561	1,400	–1,795	–1,742	–1,777	–1,673
East Asia	275,866	368,800	445,840	532,651	730,087	801,223	789,432
China, People's Rep. of	228,701	311,570	358,981	435,042	578,100	654,647	645,025
Hong Kong, China	–7,477	–18,918	–27,926	–32,373	–22,850	–24,113	–26,223
Korea, Rep. of	29,090	49,406	82,781	88,885	120,290	114,125	109,776
Mongolia	–993	–1,553	–1,321	994	1,206	1,259	333
Taipei,China	26,545	28,296	33,324	40,103	53,341	55,306	60,521
South Asia	–233,643	–244,932	–193,122	–192,848	–182,897	–203,746	–233,448
Afghanistan	–7,539	–8,609	–8,528	–8,106	–7,935	–8,195	–8,637
Bangladesh	–9,935	–9,320	–7,009	–6,794	–9,917	–11,117	–13,005
Bhutan	–460	–395	–377	–393	–419	–459	–503
India	–189,690	–195,656	–147,609	–144,940	–130,388	–147,930	–171,470
Maldives	–1,370	–1,261	–1,372	–1,660	–1,897	–2,099	–2,275
Nepal	–4,422	–4,623	–5,263	–6,079	–6,689	–6,223	–7,369
Pakistan	–10,516	–15,652	–15,355	–16,590	–17,222	–19,272	–21,456
Sri Lanka	–9,710	–9,416	–7,609	–8,287	–8,430	–8,450	–8,733
Southeast Asia	152,728	115,828	110,263	141,615	140,863	119,718	125,679
Brunei Darussalam	8,620	8,766	6,924	7,443	3,299	1,710	2,181
Cambodia	–2,145	–2,506	–3,214	–3,208	–3,426	–3,667	–3,819
Indonesia	33,825	8,680	5,833	6,983	13,281	6,949	6,251
Lao People's Dem. Rep.	–1,185	–2,567	–3,299	–3,265	–3,002	...	...
Malaysia	45,924	36,593	30,642	34,653	27,881	23,455	27,846
Myanmar	–175	–2,095	–2,596	–5,174	–7,652	–7,917	–7,902
Philippines	–20,429	–18,926	–17,662	–17,330	–21,698	–24,248	–23,938
Singapore	71,580	70,404	75,665	79,630	82,538	84,068	87,148
Thailand	16,989	6,670	6,661	24,583	34,593	31,052	25,994
Viet Nam	–450	8,714	8,713	12,126	7,396	400	4,014
The Pacific	–1,648	–3,925	–3,095	180	2,312	2,703	2,704
Cook Islands	–99	–99	–91	–88	–83	–73	–71
Fiji	–845	–770	–1,168	–1,027	–832	–989	–917
Kiribati	–75	–89	–82	–91	–79	–76	–77
Marshall Islands	–66	–63	–79	–76	–61	–57	–59
Micronesia, Fed. States of	–134	–125	–129	–115	–80	–77	–87
Nauru	7	26	4	–27	...	...	...
Palau	–112	–124	–132	–159	–142	–149	–161
Papua New Guinea	628	–1,439	–70	2,990	4,665	5,141	5,173
Samoa	–259	–307	–281	–309	–296	–256	–252
Solomon Islands	–5	66	–16	–5	–35	–52	–92
Timor-Leste	–373	–638	–679	–756	–585	–705	–750
Tonga	–118	–141	–144	–135	–151	...	...
Tuvalu	–8	3	1	–1	–10	–4	–2
Vanuatu	–183	–198	–225	–48	...	...	...
Total	262,080	292,481	409,279	526,940	699,081	725,098	693,240

... = data not available.

Table A14 Current account balance (% of GDP)

	2011	2012	2013	2014	2015	2016	2017
Central Asia	6.8	3.2	1.8	2.1	−3.4	−3.9	−3.0
Armenia	−10.4	−10.0	−7.6	−7.3	−4.6	−5.2	−5.0
Azerbaijan	26.0	21.4	16.6	13.9	0.4	−0.6	1.5
Georgia	−12.8	−11.7	−5.8	−10.6	−10.5	−9.5	−9.2
Kazakhstan	5.1	0.5	0.4	2.6	−2.8	−3.5	−3.1
Kyrgyz Republic	−9.6	−15.6	−15.0	−16.8	−17.0	−17.0	−15.0
Tajikistan	−4.8	−2.5	−2.9	−9.1	−5.9	−4.8	−5.5
Turkmenistan	2.0	0.0	−7.3	−5.8	−11.8	−12.3	−10.0
Uzbekistan	5.8	1.2	1.6	1.4	0.3	0.2	0.8
East Asia	2.2	3.0	2.5	2.9	3.8	3.6	3.3
China, People's Rep. of	1.8	2.5	1.6	2.1	2.7	2.7	2.5
Hong Kong, China	5.6	1.6	1.5	1.3	3.1	2.0	1.8
Korea, Rep. of	1.6	4.2	6.2	6.0	7.8	6.5	5.5
Mongolia	−26.5	−27.4	−25.4	−11.5	−4.8	−8.0	−15.0
Taipei,China	8.2	9.5	10.4	12.0	14.5	14.8	15.3
South Asia	−3.7	−4.2	−1.4	−1.3	−1.2	−1.4	−1.6
Afghanistan	3.2	3.9	7.3	6.4	4.5	2.0	−0.7
Bangladesh	−1.3	−0.3	1.6	0.8	−0.8	−0.5	−1.0
Bhutan	−30.0	−21.5	−25.4	−26.4	−28.2	−28.8	−27.0
India	−4.3	−4.8	−1.7	−1.5	−1.3	−1.6	−1.8
Maldives	−15.6	−7.3	−4.6	−4.1	−12.6	−12.6	−10.5
Nepal	−0.9	5.0	3.4	4.6	5.1	10.3	6.4
Pakistan	0.1	−2.1	−1.1	−1.3	−1.0	−1.0	−1.2
Sri Lanka	−7.1	−5.8	−3.4	−2.5	−2.0	−2.0	−1.8
Southeast Asia	5.2	2.5	1.9	3.0	3.7	2.8	2.7
Brunei Darussalam	34.7	29.8	20.9	27.8	6.5	−1.3	2.0
Cambodia	−9.0	−10.2	−14.9	−11.7	−11.1	−11.1	−10.0
Indonesia	0.2	−2.7	−3.2	−3.1	−2.1	−2.6	−2.8
Lao People's Dem. Rep.	−15.8	−28.5	−30.6	−25.0	−20.3	−17.0	−20.0
Malaysia	10.9	5.2	3.5	4.3	2.9	1.2	2.3
Myanmar	−1.9	−3.9	−4.9	−5.9	−8.9	−8.3	−7.7
Philippines	2.5	2.8	4.2	3.8	2.9	2.7	2.8
Singapore	22.0	17.9	17.6	17.4	19.7	18.8	19.5
Thailand	2.4	−0.4	−1.2	3.8	8.8	7.5	4.0
Viet Nam	0.2	5.9	4.5	4.9	0.3	−0.2	0.0
The Pacific	25.4	9.4	9.1	5.3	3.8	4.1	4.8
Cook Islands	26.8	30.3	34.7	38.6	33.1	37.3	41.3
Fiji	−4.9	−1.3	−9.8	−7.2	−4.0	−7.0	−4.4
Kiribati	−11.9	0.5	15.7	17.9	25.0	15.0	−10.0
Marshall Islands	−5.5	−9.1	−14.5	−7.2	6.9	11.1	8.9
Micronesia, Fed. States of	−18.1	−12.8	−9.7	6.7	17.2	19.5	30.1
Nauru	20.0	30.3	15.7	−7.3	...	...	...
Palau	−10.4	−16.8	−10.2	−12.6	2.1	−2.3	−1.3
Papua New Guinea	−23.3	−54.1	−32.9	−5.1	4.6	3.8	7.2
Samoa	−3.1	−7.7	−2.5	−7.0	−4.8	−4.3	−5.1
Solomon Islands	−9.7	1.5	−4.3	−5.4	−4.5	−5.9	−7.2
Timor−Leste	204.0	211.3	181.3	75.9	14.3	26.1	11.8
Tonga	−11.7	−6.9	−8.5	−5.0	−8.3	−1.9	−3.2
Tuvalu	−36.5	24.9	26.4	27.3	−37.4	−21.4	−18.7
Vanuatu	−7.5	−6.1	−0.8	22.7	−10.4	−15.0	−11.0
Average	1.8	1.8	1.8	2.3	2.9	2.6	2.4

... = data not available.

Table A15 Exchange rates to the United States dollar (annual average)

	Currency	Symbol	2011	2012	2013	2014	2015
Central Asia							
Armenia	dram	AMD	372.5	401.8	409.6	415.9	477.9
Azerbaijan	Azerbaijan new manat	AZN	0.8	0.8	0.8	0.8	1.0
Georgia	lari	GEL	1.7	1.7	1.7	1.8	2.3
Kazakhstan	tenge	T	146.6	149.1	152.1	179.2	221.7
Kyrgyz Republic	som	Som	46.1	47.0	48.4	53.7	64.5
Tajikistan	somoni	TJS	4.6	4.8	4.8	4.9	6.2
Turkmenistan	Turkmen manat	TMM	2.9	2.9	2.9	2.9	3.5
Uzbekistan	sum	SUM	1,710.9	1,885.4	2,095.0	2,311.2	2,573.5
East Asia							
China, People's Rep. of	yuan	CNY	6.5	6.3	6.2	6.1	6.2
Hong Kong, China	Hong Kong dollar	HK$	7.8	7.8	7.8	7.8	7.8
Korea, Rep. of	won	W	1,107.4	1,125.7	1,094.2	1,053.1	1,130.7
Mongolia	togrog	MNT	1,265.5	1,359.2	1,523.9	1,817.9	1,970.3
Taipei,China	NT dollar	NT$	29.5	29.6	29.8	30.4	31.9
South Asia							
Afghanistan	afghani	AF	47.7	51.0	55.3	57.6	61.4
Bangladesh	taka	Tk	71.2	79.1	79.9	77.7	77.7
Bhutan	ngultrum	Nu	45.3	50.3	54.9	61.5	62.1
India	Indian rupee/s	Re/Rs	47.9	54.4	60.5	61.0	64.2
Maldives	rufiyaa	Rf	14.6	15.4	15.4	15.4	15.4
Nepal	Nepalese rupee/s	NRe/NRs	72.1	80.7	87.7	98.0	99.2
Pakistan	Pakistan rupee/s	PRe/PRs	85.5	89.2	96.7	102.9	101.3
Sri Lanka	Sri Lanka rupee/s	SLRe/SLRs	110.6	127.6	129.1	130.6	136.0
Southeast Asia							
Brunei Darussalam	Brunei dollar	B$	1.3	1.2	1.3	1.3	1.4
Cambodia	riel	KR	4,016.0	4,033.0	4,027.0	4,030.0	4,030.0
Indonesia	rupiah	Rp	8,770.4	9,386.6	10,461.2	11,865.2	13,389.4
Lao People's Dem. Rep.	kip	KN	8,011.4	7,994.0	7,818.0	8,150.0	8,147.9
Malaysia	ringgit	RM	3.1	3.1	3.2	3.3	3.9
Myanmar	kyat	MK	5.4	856.9	964.4	995.0	1,165.1
Philippines	peso	P	43.3	42.2	42.4	44.4	45.5
Singapore	Singapore dollar	S$	1.3	1.2	1.3	1.3	1.4
Thailand	baht	B	30.5	31.1	30.7	32.5	34.3
Viet Nam	dong	D	20,489.6	20,828.0	20,934.6	21,148.8	21,675.6
The Pacific							
Cook Islands	New Zealand dollar	NZ$	1.3	1.2	1.2	1.2	1.3
Fiji	Fiji dollar	F$	1.8	1.8	1.8	1.9	2.1
Kiribati	Australian dollar	A$	1.0	1.0	1.0	1.1	1.3
Marshall Islands	US dollar	$	1.0	1.0	1.0	1.0	1.0
Micronesia, Fed. States of	US dollar	$	1.0	1.0	1.0	1.0	1.0
Nauru	Australian dollar	A$	1.0	1.0	1.0	1.1	1.3
Palau	US dollar	$	1.0	1.0	1.0	1.0	1.0
Papua New Guinea	kina	K	2.3	2.1	2.2	2.4	2.8
Samoa	tala	ST	2.4	2.3	2.3	2.3	2.4
Solomon Islands	Sol. Islands dollar	SI$	7.6	7.4	7.3	7.4	7.9
Timor-Leste	US dollar	$	1.0	1.0	1.0	1.0	1.0
Tonga	pa'anga	T$	1.9	1.7	1.7	1.8	1.9
Tuvalu	Australian dollar	A$	1.0	1.0	1.0	1.1	1.3
Vanuatu	vatu	Vt	94.6	92.6	96.9	102.4	108.6

Table A16 Gross international reserves ($ million)

	2011	2012	2013	2014	2015
Central Asia					
Armenia	1,933	1,799	2,252	1,489	1,771
Azerbaijan	10,274	11,277	15,014	15,549	7910
Georgia	2,818	2,873	2,823	2,699	2,521
Kazakhstan	29,328	28,269	24,715	29,209	27,876
Kyrgyz Republic	1,835	2,067	2,238	1,958	1,778
Tajikistan	572	650	636	511	494
Turkmenistan	22,400	26,400	29,300	32,400	...
Uzbekistan	18,049	22,133	22,515	24,140	24,400
East Asia					
China, People's Rep. of	3,255,786	3,387,863	3,880,383	3,899,285	3,386,629
Hong Kong, China	285,402	317,362	311,209	328,516	358,823
Korea, Rep. of	306,402	326,968	346,460	363,593	367,962
Mongolia	2,258	3,630	1,193	1,627	1,300
Taipei,China	385,547	403,169	416,811	418,980	426,031
South Asia					
Afghanistan	6,208	6,867	6,886	7,248	7,000
Bangladesh	10,912	10,364	15,315	21,508	25,020
Bhutan	796	674	917	998	959
India	294,397	292,046	304,223	330,213	346,788
Maldives	335	305	368	615	564
Nepal	3,836	4,960	5,614	6,939	8,146
Pakistan	14,784	10,803	6,008	9,098	13,526
Sri Lanka	5,958	6,877	7,495	8,208	6,480
Southeast Asia					
Brunei Darussalam	2,490	3,291	3,406	3,479	2,892
Cambodia	3,032	3,397	3,643	4,391	5,093
Indonesia	110,123	112,781	99,387	111,862	105,931
Lao People's Dem. Rep.	679	740	666	816	987
Malaysia	133,642	139,724	134,911	115,937	95,290
Myanmar	922	3,062	4,546	5,070	5,075
Philippines	75,302	83,831	83,187	79,541	80,667
Singapore	237,737	259,307	273,065	256,860	247,747
Thailand	175,124	181,608	167,289	157,108	156,514
Viet Nam	13,531	25,399	25,745	34,120	28,000
The Pacific					
Cook Islands	...	...	...	...	...
Fiji	831	915	755	750	764
Kiribati	...	...	...	...	...
Marshall Islands	...	...	...	...	...
Micronesia, Fed. States of	...	...	...	...	...
Nauru	...	...	...	...	...
Palau	...	...	...	...	...
Papua New Guinea	4,323	4,001	2,826	2,305	2,105
Samoa	...	157	137	155	167
Solomon Islands	412	499	532	507	527
Timor–Leste	...	...	...	...	...
Tonga	110	145	152	151	151
Tuvalu	...	...	...	...	...
Vanuatu	172	180	180	185	...

... = data not available.

Table A17 External debt outstanding ($ million)

	2011	2012	2013	2014	2015
Central Asia					
Armenia	3,568	3,739	3,899	3,785	4,310
Azerbaijan	4,841	5,470	6,059	6,478	6,894
Georgia	8,706	10,057	10,542	10,718	11,386
Kazakhstan	125,321	136,918	150,033	157,423	155,577
Kyrgyz Republic	4,754	5,190	5,929	6,359	6,167
Tajikistan	2,159	2,173	2,149	2,100	2,183
Turkmenistan	2,923	6,365	8,654	8,053	8,296
Uzbekistan	6,090	6,660	7,500	8,399	10,521
East Asia					
China, People's Rep. of	694,997	736,986	863,167	895,460	...
Hong Kong, China	982,701	1,029,853	1,160,364	1,301,233	1,303,869
Korea, Rep. of	400,034	408,928	423,505	424,391	396,559
Mongolia	9,628	15,386	19,022	20,942	21,603
Taipei,China	122,528	130,821	170,134	177,945	158,954
South Asia					
Afghanistan	1,242	1,320	1,230	1,360	1,360
Bangladesh	22,086	22,095	22,381	24,388	23,489
Bhutan	1,289	1,334	1,607	1,759	1,855
India	360,766	409,484	446,300	474,400	482,900
Maldives	900	811	792	742	688
Nepal	3,658	3,491	3,510	3,617	3,391
Pakistan	66,366	65,478	60,899	65,365	65,103
Sri Lanka	32,748	37,098	39,905	43,035	43,747
Southeast Asia					
Brunei Darussalam	...	...	...	...	...
Cambodia	3,645	4,274	4,828	5,264	5,674
Indonesia	225,375	252,364	266,109	293,770	310,722
Lao People's Dem. Rep.	2,990	3,037	4,611	...	...
Malaysia	169,171	196,861	212,279	213,873	194,256
Myanmar	15,300	13,700	10,200	8,800	9,700
Philippines	75,569	79,949	78,489	77,674	77,474
Singapore	1,415,335	1,437,268	1,527,241	1,708,393	1,855,549
Thailand	104,334	130,747	141,933	140,135	133,745
Viet Nam	37,644	42,158	45,243	...	...
The Pacific					
Cook Islands	26	38	59	61	67
Fiji	465	523	595	664	642
Kiribati	14	14	14	14	21
Marshall Islands	100	97	98	93	103
Micronesia, Fed. States of	91	91	91	95	...
Nauru	...	...	...	...	...
Palau	63	69	65	71	64
Papua New Guinea	1,068	1,126	1,252	1,465	2,293
Samoa	311	376	415	415	442
Solomon Islands	258	228	204	...	...
Timor-Leste	...	...	6	22	46
Tonga	148	190	198	185	198
Tuvalu	10	10	9	8	...
Vanuatu	63	69	65	71	64

... = data not available.

Table A18 Debt service ratio (% of exports of goods and services)

	2011	2012	2013	2014	2015
Central Asia					
Armenia	3.7	8.2	27.3	6.8	4.2
Azerbaijan	...	...	...	...	...
Georgia	9.1	22.5	18.1	13.5	15.6
Kazakhstan	33.1	34.8	35.1	36.6	...
Kyrgyz Republic	10.7	18.9	20.8	27.2	26.1
Tajikistan	4.3	7.6	10.6	14.3	...
Turkmenistan	1.6	1.8	2.3	...	...
Uzbekistan	3.6	6.4	3.5	5.1	7.0
East Asia					
China, People's Rep. of	1.7	1.6	1.6	1.9	...
Hong Kong, China	50.5	49.1	48.9	59.9	65.5
Korea, Rep. of	7.9	7.5	7.1	7.3	...
Mongolia	31.7	33.0	46.4	44.6	45.9
Taipei,China	2.1	1.2	2.0	1.7	1.8
South Asia					
Afghanistan	1.3	1.0	6.8	...	...
Bangladesh	2.5	2.4	2.5	2.7	2.3
Bhutan	51.7	127.1	229.2	27.1	19.9
India	6.0	5.9	5.9	7.5	7.5
Maldives	2.6	2.9	2.1	2.3	2.2
Nepal	11.1	10.6	9.5	8.9	8.1
Pakistan	12.7	15.2	20.6	23.0	18.1
Sri Lanka	12.7	19.7	23.5	20.2	...
Southeast Asia					
Brunei Darussalam	...	...	...	...	...
Cambodia	...	...	...	...	...
Indonesia	12.5	17.3	20.7	23.1	29.1
Lao People's Dem. Rep.	4.4	4.3	5.0	...	...
Malaysia	10.4	10.3	9.6	11.3	15.6
Myanmar	10.5	2.2	3.3	2.9	4.1
Philippines	9.9	7.3	8.2	6.3	5.3
Singapore	...	...	...	...	...
Thailand	3.5	4.2	4.0	4.9	4.6
Viet Nam	3.5	4.3	...	...	...
The Pacific					
Cook Islands	...	7.5	6.6	5.6	5.5
Fiji	8.3	1.5	1.6	1.7	1.9
Kiribati	3.1	3.9	3.8	2.4	2.9
Marshall Islands	23.2	9.6	8.9	9.5	11.8
Micronesia, Fed. States of	7.5	6.0	7.2	11.2	...
Nauru	...	...	...	...	...
Palau	4.9	5.1	4.2	4.2	5.3
Papua New Guinea	1.3	1.4	1.4	1.4	0.9
Samoa	0.1	...	...	...	...
Solomon Islands	2.4	3.5	6.8	2.8	...
Timor–Leste	...	...	...	...	...
Tonga	9.3	6.9	8.7	13.0	12.0
Tuvalu	3.5	0.8	2.4	2.3	...
Vanuatu	1.7	1.6	1.6	1.8	...

... = data not available.

www.ingramcontent.com/pod-product-compliance
Lightning Source LLC
Chambersburg PA
CBHW061234270326
41929CB00031B/3482